The Query Design Screen

(CHAPTER 6)

You use the query design screen to create queries that isolate selected recorc The query shown e searches the CUSTLIST da d Smith.

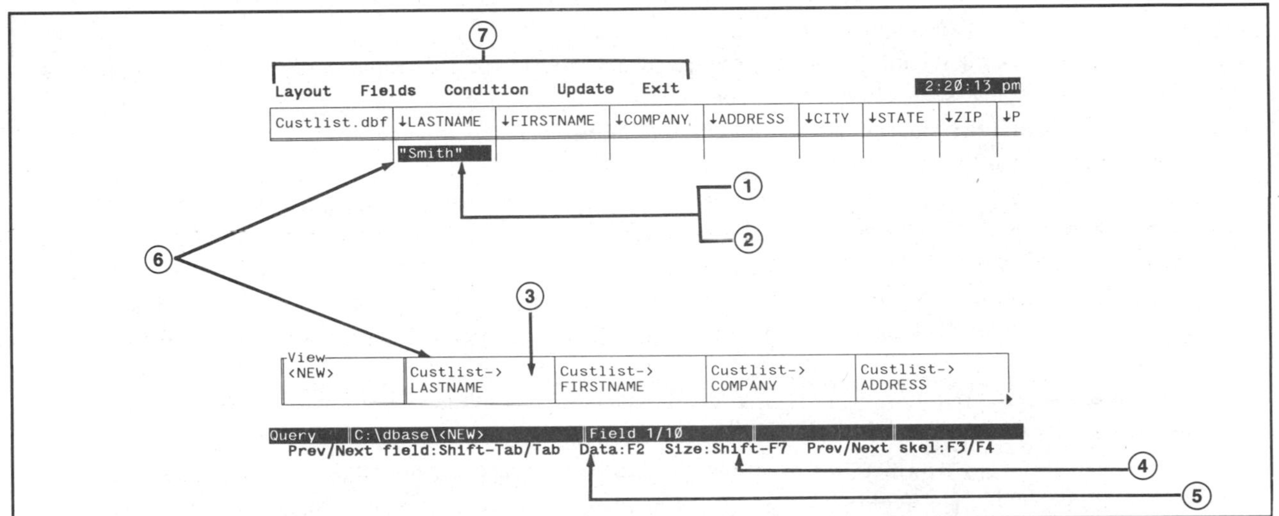

If you want to:	Here's how:
① Move the highlight left and right	Press Tab and Shift-Tab, or click the mouse.
② Extend the box downward for an OR query	Press ↓.
③ Add or remove a field from a view	Press Add Field (F5), or click the mouse on the field name in the file skeleton.
④ Narrow or widen a field in the file skeleton	Press or click Size (Shift-F7).
⑤ See the results of a query	Press or click Data (F2).
⑥ Switch between the file/view skeletons	Press or click Previous (F3) or Next (F4); or click the mouse on the skeleton you want.
⑦ Access pull-down menus	Press Menus (F10) and use ← and →; press Alt, plus the first letter of a menu bar option; or click on a menu bar option.

Computer users are not all alike.
Neither are SYBEX books.

We know our customers have a variety of needs. They've told us so. And because we've listened, we've developed several distinct types of books to meet the needs of each of our customers. What are you looking for in computer help?

If you're looking for the basics, try the **ABC's** series. You'll find short, unintimidating tutorials and helpful illustrations. For a more visual approach, select **Teach Yourself**, featuring screen-by-screen illustrations of how to use your latest software purchase.

Mastering and **Understanding** titles offer you a step-by-step introduction, plus an in-depth examination of intermediate-level features, to use as you progress.

Our **Up & Running** series is designed for computer-literate consumers who want a no-nonsense overview of new programs. Just 20 basic lessons, and you're on your way.

We also publish two types of reference books. Our **Instant References** provide quick access to each of a program's commands and functions. SYBEX **Encyclopedias** and **Desktop References** provide a *comprehensive reference* and explanation of all of the commands, features and functions of the subject software.

Sometimes a subject requires a special treatment that our standard series don't provide. So you'll find we have titles like **Advanced Techniques, Handbooks, Tips & Tricks**, and others that are specifically tailored to satisfy a unique need.

We carefully select our authors for their in-depth understanding of the software they're writing about, as well as their ability to write clearly and communicate effectively. Each manuscript is thoroughly reviewed by our technical staff to ensure its complete accuracy. Our production department makes sure it's easy to use. All of this adds up to the highest quality books available, consistently appearing on best-seller charts worldwide.

You'll find SYBEX publishes a variety of books on every popular software package. Looking for computer help? Help Yourself to SYBEX.

For a complete catalog of our publications:

SYBEX Inc.
2021 Challenger Drive, Alameda, CA 94501
Tel: (510) 523-8233/(800) 227-2346 Telex: 336311
Fax: (510) 523-2373

Understanding

dBASE IV 1.5

for DOS

Understanding dBASE IV® 1.5 for DOS®

Third Edition

Alan Simpson

SYBEX® San Francisco • Paris • Düsseldorf • Soest

Acquisitions Editor: Dianne King
Editor: Savitha Varadan
Technical Editor: Sheldon M. Dunn
Word Processors: Susan Trybull, Ann Dunn
Book Designer: Suzanne Albertson
Screen Graphics: Cuong Le
Typesetter: Stephanie Hollier
Proofreader: Lisa Haden
Indexer: Nancy Guenther
Cover Designer: Thomas Ingalls + Associates
Cover Photographer: Mark Johann

Library of Congress Card Number: 92-81035

ISBN: 0-7821-1107-6

Manufactured in the United States of America
10 9 8 7 6 5 4 3 2

To Susan, Ashley, and Alec

A.C.S.

To my husband and parents—Keith, Mom, and Dad

E.A.O.

ACKNOWLEDGMENTS

From Alan—Like all books, this one was a team effort. Many thanks and much credit go to the many people who helped nurse this book from the idea stage to the finished product in your hands, including:

Elizabeth Olson, who revised virtually the entire book from its previous edition, with contributions from Steve Davis.

All of the people at SYBEX involved in producing this edition of the book, including Savitha Varadan, editor; Mac Dunn, technical editor; Susan Trybull and Ann Dunn, word processors; Suzanne Albertson, book designer; Cuong Le, screen graphics technician; Stephanie Hollier, typesetter; and Lisa Haden, proofreader.

Martha Mellor and David Burby at Alan Simpson Computing, who also contributed time and effort, and helped handle the countless administrative tasks involved in getting the job done.

Bill Gladstone and the gang at Waterside Productions, who served as literary agents, as they do for all my books.

Many thanks to Susan and Ashley for their patience, love, and support; and to all of you who have read my earlier dBASE books and have taken the time to drop me a line. Your suggestions help make each new book better than the last.

From Elizabeth Olson, Revisor—Many thanks to Keith Olson for encouraging me to "go for it" and supporting me at every step; and to my parents, Al and Emily Gotkin, for the love and education that made everything possible.

CONTENTS AT A GLANCE

TABLE OF CONTENTS

CHAPTER 3

Creating a Database File

CHAPTER 4

Adding and Changing Information

CHAPTER 5

Sorting the Database

CHAPTER 6

Searching the Database

CHAPTER 7

Printing Formatted Reports

CHAPTER 8

Creating Custom Forms

CHAPTER 9

Performing Calculations

CHAPTER 10

Using Memo Fields to Store Documents

CHAPTER 11

Managing Groups of Records

CHAPTER 12

Using Functions to Control Your Data

CHAPTER 13

Managing Related Database Files

CHAPTER 14

Techniques for Managing Your Workspace

CHAPTER 15

Introducing Applications

CHAPTER 16

A Membership Management Application

CHAPTER 17

Adding Power with dBASE IV Commands

CHAPTER 18

Programming Techniques

CHAPTER 19

Business Data Processing

CHAPTER 20

Intelligent Custom Forms for Business Applications

CHAPTER 21

The Business Management Application

APPENDIX A

A DOS Primer

APPENDIX B

Installing dBASE IV

APPENDIX C

Summary of Changes in dBASE

APPENDIX D

Interfacing with Other Programs

APPENDIX E

dBASE IV Functions

APPENDIX F

dBASE IV Commands

APPENDIX G

INTRODUCTION

dBASE IV is the fourth major revision of the now classic dBASE database management system. And version 1.5 of dBASE IV is the first release offered by Borland International, the company that took the reins of this product in 1991. Borland has added a host of new features for users at all levels. We'll introduce those changes and improvements a little later in this Introduction.

If by any chance you've already seen the documentation that accompanies dBASE IV, you know one thing—dBASE IV is a large (and extremely powerful, I might add) product. I know that just sifting through the myriad of tools and options that dBASE IV offers can be frustrating and confusing, especially for beginners. Therefore, the main purpose of this book is to do some of that sifting for you, to simplify, to explain, and to help you start putting dBASE IV to work productively now.

WHO CAN USE THIS BOOK

This book is written as a tutorial for beginners, but because it focuses on the most practical and efficient techniques for "getting the job done" with dBASE IV version 1.5, experienced dBASE users will also benefit from reading it. The purpose of this book is two-fold. First, it helps you to develop specific skills in using dBASE IV by providing hands-on, step-by-step instructions for managing your data. Second, it attempts to provide a broad understanding of the vast potential and capabilities of dBASE IV through general examples and suggested applications.

Experienced dBASE users who take the time to learn the new features in dBASE IV version 1.5 will find that they can manage their data more easily and effectively and build custom applications with a fraction of the effort required by earlier versions of dBASE.

THE STRUCTURE OF THIS BOOK

This book is designed as a tutorial, not as a technical reference guide. Therefore, you are encouraged to read the chapters in the order that they are presented. Exactly how far into this book you read depends on the complexity of the work you want dBASE to handle. The book is organized as follows:

Chapters 1 through 7: Virtually all readers will want to be familiar with the material presented in Chapters 1 through 7, as these present the most fundamental techniques for storing, retrieving, sorting, searching, and printing information.

Chapters 8 through 14: These chapters describe more advanced techniques for managing information in a database, such as designing custom screens, performing calculations, and managing multiple related database files. Readers whose work requires more than the basics presented in earlier chapters will want to read these chapters.

Chapters 15 through 21: Here you'll find more advanced information for creating custom dBASE IV applications. Experienced dBASE users will especially want to read these chapters, because they demonstrate the new dBASE IV features for building powerful applications with minimal effort.

Appendix A: This optional appendix is provided for readers who have no prior computer experience whatsoever. If you have never used a computer before, you are encouraged to read Appendix A, "A DOS Primer," to become familiar with basic computer terminology and operations that apply to your use of dBASE IV.

Appendix B: This appendix provides instructions for installing dBASE IV on your microcomputer.

Appendix C: This appendix summarizes new features in dBASE IV for experienced dBASE users.

Appendix D: This appendix presents techniques for sharing data with other programs, such as word processors and spreadsheets.

Appendices E through H: These appendices present a categorized summary of all dBASE IV commands and functions, a list of the ASCII character codes, and dBASE file name extensions.

SPECIAL FEATURES

This book offers several unique features to make your learning easier and more enjoyable.

The Fast Track at the beginning of each chapter summarizes specific skills and techniques discussed within the chapter. Experienced dBASE users can use the Fast Track to locate specific information in the chapter. Beginners may want to refer to the Fast Track after reading the chapter for reminders about how to perform specific tasks.

Three special visual icons are used in the book to identify margin notes:

Identifies a practical tip or hint.

Identifies a special note that augments information in the text or presents reminders about previous techniques.

Identifies a warning about a potential problem.

On the end papers inside the front and back covers of this book, you'll find visual reminders of keys and techniques used in a variety of dBASE IV design screens. You can use these as quick reminders of specific techniques when working with dBASE IV on your own.

WHAT'S NEW IN VERSION 1.5?

NOTE

Appendix C also summarizes changes in dBASE IV since dBASE III PLUS.

Those of you with previous dBASE IV experience may be wondering just what's new in version 1.5. We'll summarize what's new here, and tell you where you can get more information about each new feature.

MOUSE SUPPORT

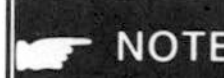

If you can't get your mouse to work in dBASE IV, see Appendix B, "Installing dBASE IV," for information on installing the mouse.

You can now use a mouse with dBASE IV, which can save a lot of time that you might otherwise spend "scrolling around" with the arrow keys. For the most part, mouse usage is intuitive in that you use a mouse in dBASE IV as you would in any product: to choose menu options, select text, and so forth.

The exact mouse techniques you use depend largely on what you happen to be doing at the moment in dBASE IV. So we'll discuss specific mouse techniques, as relevant, within the chapters that follow.

OTHER CHANGES AND IMPROVEMENTS

If you're an experienced dBASE IV user, and want additional information about other new and improved features, refer to "Summary of Changes in Version 1.5" in Appendix C. If you're an experienced dBASE III (or III PLUS) user, and are just now upgrading to dBASE IV, you can also refer to Appendix C for information on changes since dBASE III PLUS.

A SAMPLE DISK

This book presents many examples of databases, reports, custom screens, and applications. If you would like to use some of these examples without taking the time to type them yourself, you can purchase a disk with all the files (excluding dBASE IV itself, of course) described in this book. The disk includes the membership and business management applications presented in the later chapters. See the coupon near the last page for an order form.

CHAPTER 1

Understanding Database Management

dBASE IV IS A *DATABASE MANAGEMENT SYSTEM*. Although that may sound like something quite complicated, it is not.

A *database* is simply an organized collection of information, such as a list of names and addresses, sales transactions, stock prices, or baseball scores. Even if you've never touched a computer in your life, chances are you've already used quite a few databases. For example, think of a shoe box filled with index cards. On each card, you've written somebody's name and address, as shown in Figure 1.1. The shoebox full of index cards is a *database*, because it contains information. Rolodexes, file cabinets, and library card catalogs are other examples of common databases that you may have used.

A database *management system* is a set of tools to help you manage a database. For example, when you add new cards to your shoebox, arrange the cards into alphabetical order, look up an address, or throw away a card, you are *managing* the shoebox database.

A database management system such as dBASE IV lets you perform these same managerial tasks: adding, changing, deleting, sorting, printing, and looking up information in a database.

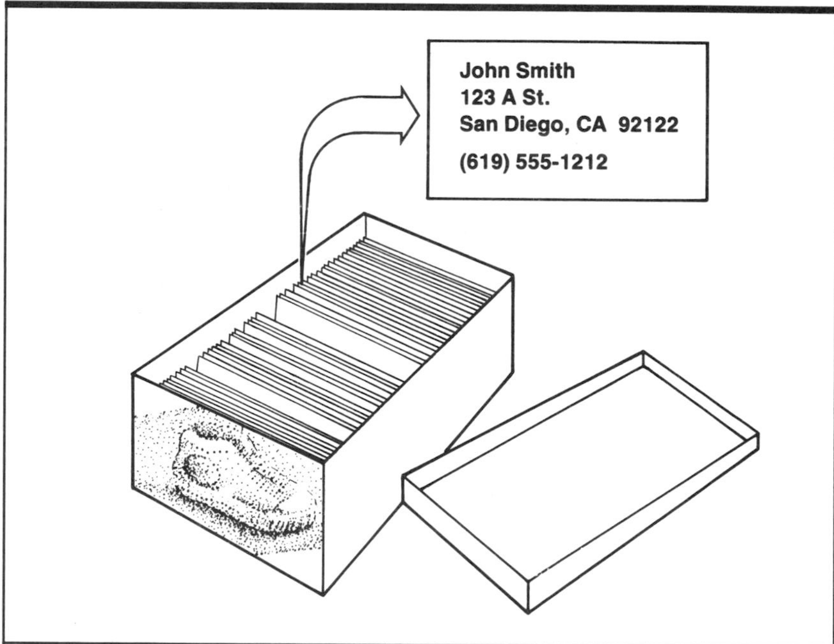

Figure 1.1: A "shoebox" database with names and addresses

UNDERSTANDING DATABASE FILES

Of course, dBASE doesn't store information on index cards in shoeboxes. Instead, it stores information in *database files* on a computer disk. Each database file consists of *records* (or *rows*) of information. Each record is divided into separate *fields* (or *columns*) of information. For example, Figure 1.2 shows a database file that contains names and addresses.

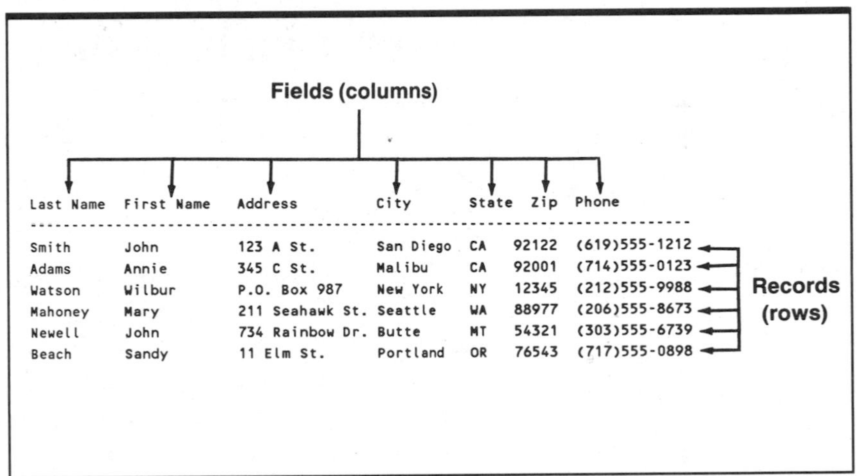

Last Name	First Name	Address	City	State	Zip	Phone
Smith	John	123 A St.	San Diego	CA	92122	(619)555-1212
Adams	Annie	345 C St.	Malibu	CA	92001	(714)555-0123
Watson	Wilbur	P.O. Box 987	New York	NY	12345	(212)555-9988
Mahoney	Mary	211 Seahawk St.	Seattle	WA	88977	(206)555-8673
Newell	John	734 Rainbow Dr.	Butte	MT	54321	(303)555-6739
Beach	Sandy	11 Elm St.	Portland	OR	76543	(717)555-0898

Figure 1.2: A dBASE IV database file of names and addresses

Notice that John Smith's name and address (from Figure 1.1) is the first record in the file. In all, the file consists of six records (rows) of information, equivalent to six index cards in the shoe box.

Notice also that the information in the database file shown in Figure 1.2 is divided into seven fields, or columns of information: Last Name, First Name, Address, City, State, Zip, and Phone. You need to break information into separate fields like this, because, unlike humans, computers don't understand the meaning of information based on its context.

For example, you and I can look at the index card in Figure 1.1 and figure out that (619)555-1212 is probably a phone number. We can figure this out based upon the context of the information (it "looks" like a phone number).

Computers, on the other hand, can't tell a phone number from an address from a potato pancake. (Computers may be fast, but they are definitely not too bright.) Therefore, it is up to you to divide the information on your index cards (or parts list, customer list, or whatever database you are storing) into meaningful fields of information. We'll discuss this topic in more detail in Chapter 2, when you create your first database file.

THE BIGGER PICTURE

Needless to say, most businesses do not store their information in a shoebox. Instead, they store information in such databases as Rolodex files, file cabinets, written lists, and tickler files. In most cases, the information in these databases can easily be stored in a few dBASE IV database files.

But business information is more than just data stored in files. Businesses usually have *forms*, such as credit applications, order forms, and other paper items that are used to gather information. Businesses also use *reports*: printed copies of information in a variety of formats, including invoices, form letters, mailing labels, organized lists, and packing lists, to name a few. Figure 1.3 shows an example of the "bigger picture" of a business database.

Notice in Figure 1.3 that the *forms* are used to provide the information to the database *files*, and the printed *reports* are derived from the information in the files. dBASE IV works on exactly the same principle as illustrated in Figure 1.3. Information is entered into forms on the computer screen and that information is stored in a file on the computer disk. Then, at any time in the future, you can print information from those files on the disk, in any format you wish, on your computer screen or printer.

In some cases, there is not a direct one-to-one relationship among forms, database files, and reports. For example, to print an invoice, you might need a name and address from the customer names and addresses file, order information from the order list, and part names and prices from the parts inventory. But this is no problem; dBASE IV can easily pull together information from separate database files into a single printed report.

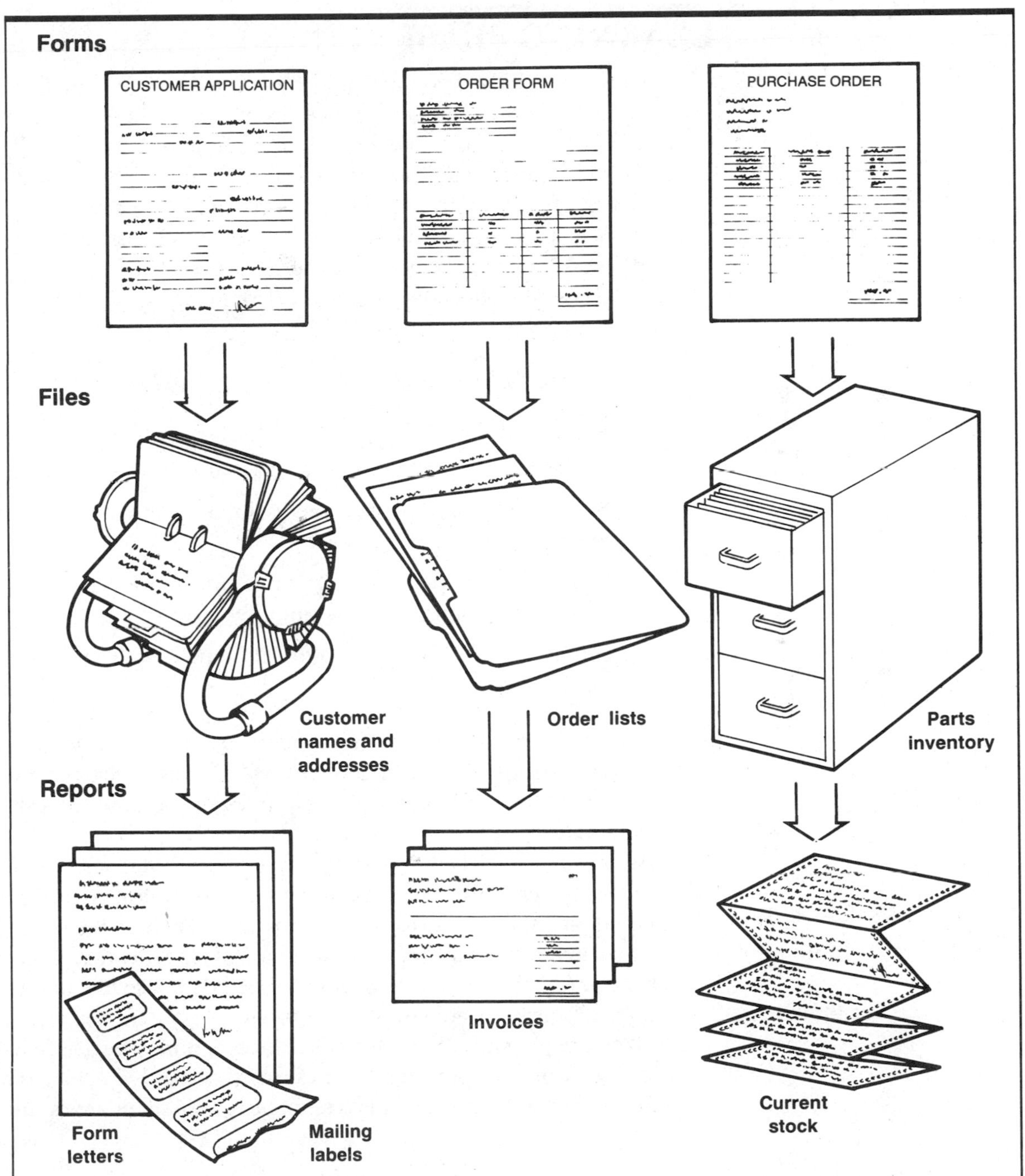

Figure 1.3: The larger view of a business database

LEARNING dBASE IV

Now, especially if you are new to computers, you may be wondering just how you are going to get from here to being able to tell dBASE to perform tasks like those shown in Figure 1.3. After all, *that* looks much more complicated than a shoebox full of index cards.

Using dBASE is not nearly as complicated as it might seem at first glance. Just think of the files in the center of Figure 1.3 as three shoeboxes full of information. All you need to do is learn to manage one database file (shoebox) effectively. In managing a database file, you execute a few basic tasks:

- ADD new information
- CHANGE information as necessary
- DELETE old information as necessary
- SORT information into some useful order (such as alphabetical or zip code order)
- SEARCH for particular types of information (such as an address or all past-due accounts)
- CALCULATE totals, subtotals, counts, averages, and so on, as needed

Once you know how to do these basic tasks, you can learn techniques for creating custom forms and reports, such as mailing labels and form letters. These techniques are easy to learn, because dBASE IV makes them easy.

After you've learned how to do all of these things for one database file, you can use the exact same techniques for creating and managing as many database files as you wish, such as the order list and parts inventory database files in Figure 1.3. So you see, all you really need to learn is to manage one shoebox database file, and in no time, you'll easily be able to manage many.

Of course, if you've never used one before, it may be a little scary to think of using a computer to do tasks that you've always done manually. But, rest assured, this is not nearly as difficult as you might think. There is no math or computer programming involved. You simply select options from *menus*, as you would in a restaurant. Believe me, you'll be a dBASE IV whiz before you know it.

WHAT YOU CAN DO WITH dBASE IV

Virtually any information that you manage without a computer can probably be managed much more quickly, accurately, and efficiently with dBASE IV. The kinds of information management that dBASE IV is especially good for include

- Mailing list management
- Inventory management
- Accounting and bookkeeping, including management of accounts receivable, accounts payable, the general ledger, and billing
- Project management
- Research management, including management of bibliographies, abstracts, and other reference material
- Scientific and statistical data recording and calculation

The main reasons for using dBASE rather than paper and pencil to manage information are speed and efficiency. For example, suppose you have a customer list of 10,000 names and addresses, and you want to send a form letter to all customers living in New York. Doing this by hand could take many hours; you would have to manually retrieve all New York names and addresses, enter them into perhaps a thousand or more letters, and sort them into zip code order for bulk mailing.

Having dBASE IV pull out the appropriate names and addresses and sort them into zip code order would probably take only a few seconds. Then you could tell dBASE to print all the form letters (and mailing labels) while you go out to lunch. The job may be complete before you get back.

How about a database with 15,000 records containing numbers for which you need totals, subtotals, or other calculations? Again, doing this math with a calculator or adding machine would take you a long time, but dBASE IV could do it in a few seconds or minutes.

So now do you think learning dBASE IV might be worth your time? If so, let's move on to the next chapter, where you'll get your first hands-on experience in using dBASE IV.

CHAPTER

2

A Guided Tour of dBASE IV

Before you can use dBASE IV, 14
it needs to be *installed* on your computer.

To interact with dBASE IV, 17
you can either click options with your mouse, or else use the keyboard.

To start dBASE IV 18
on most computers, you first switch to the dBASE directory by entering the command **CD\DBASE** at the DOS prompt. Then you enter the command **DBASE**.

To organize your work, 20
you can group objects that belong together (such as accounts receivable information, forms, and reports) in a *catalog*.

To get help 21
while using dBASE IV, press the Help key (F1), or click the Help:F1 option in the status bar near the bottom of the screen. To exit help, press the Escape key, or click outside the help window.

To access the pull-down menus, 25
click whatever option you want from the dBASE IV Control Center, or press Menus (F10), or hold down the Alt key and type the first letter of the option you want.

To escape from an undesirable situation, 26
press the Escape key until you are back in familiar territory.

Before turning off your computer, quit dBASE IV 31
by selecting Quit to DOS from the Exit pull-down menu in the Control Center or typing QUIT at the dot prompt.

NOW THAT YOU HAVE A BASIC IDEA OF WHAT DATA-base management is all about, it's time to get dBASE IV up and running on your computer and get a feel for the way it works. That's what this chapter is all about.

INSTALLING dBASE IV

Before you can use dBASE IV, it needs to be *installed* on your computer. The installation procedure need be performed only once, not each time you use dBASE. If you are sharing a computer with someone else, find out whether dBASE has already been installed. And while you're at it, ask that person how to start dBASE IV, because they may not have used the usual installation techniques.

If you are using a personal computer and are sure that dBASE IV is *not* already installed on it, then you will need to install the program. Both Appendix B in this book and the *Getting Started with dBASE IV* manual that came with your dBASE IV package provide instructions on how to install dBASE IV. If you do need to install dBASE, follow the instructions for your particular computer and then read the next section.

A QUICK TOUR OF THE KEYBOARD

If this is your first time using a computer, take a moment to locate some special keys on your keyboard that you will use regularly in your work with dBASE IV. Figure 2.1 (pages 15 and 16) shows these special keys on some common keyboards. Locate the keyboard that most closely matches your own and refer to this figure if you have trouble finding a particular key as you work the exercises later in the chapter.

ON ONES AND OH'S

An important point to keep in mind when using a computer is that you cannot use the letter "l" to stand for the number 1, as you can on a typewriter. Nor can you use the letter "o" to stand for zero.

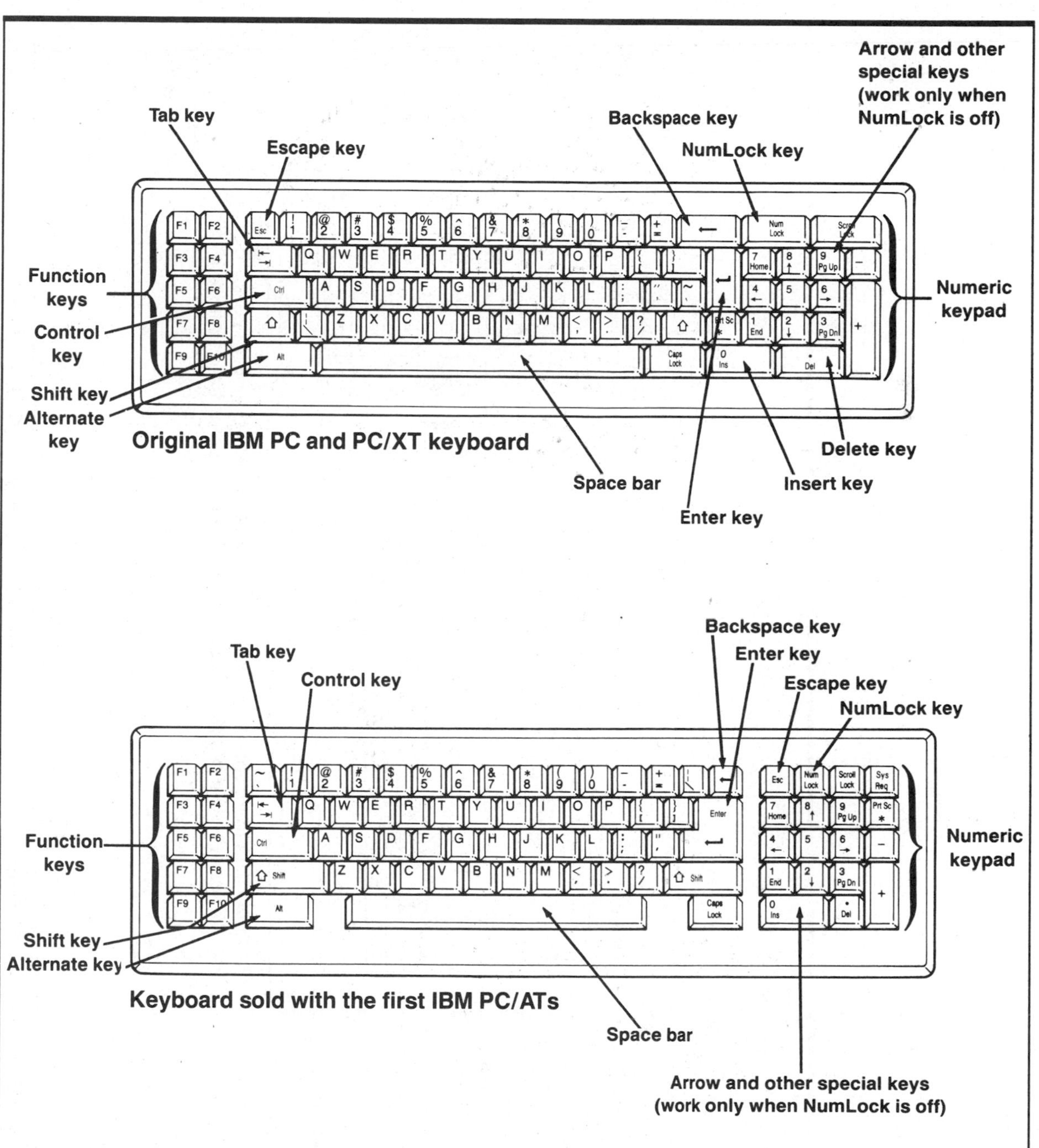

Figure 2.1: Some special keys on different types of keyboards

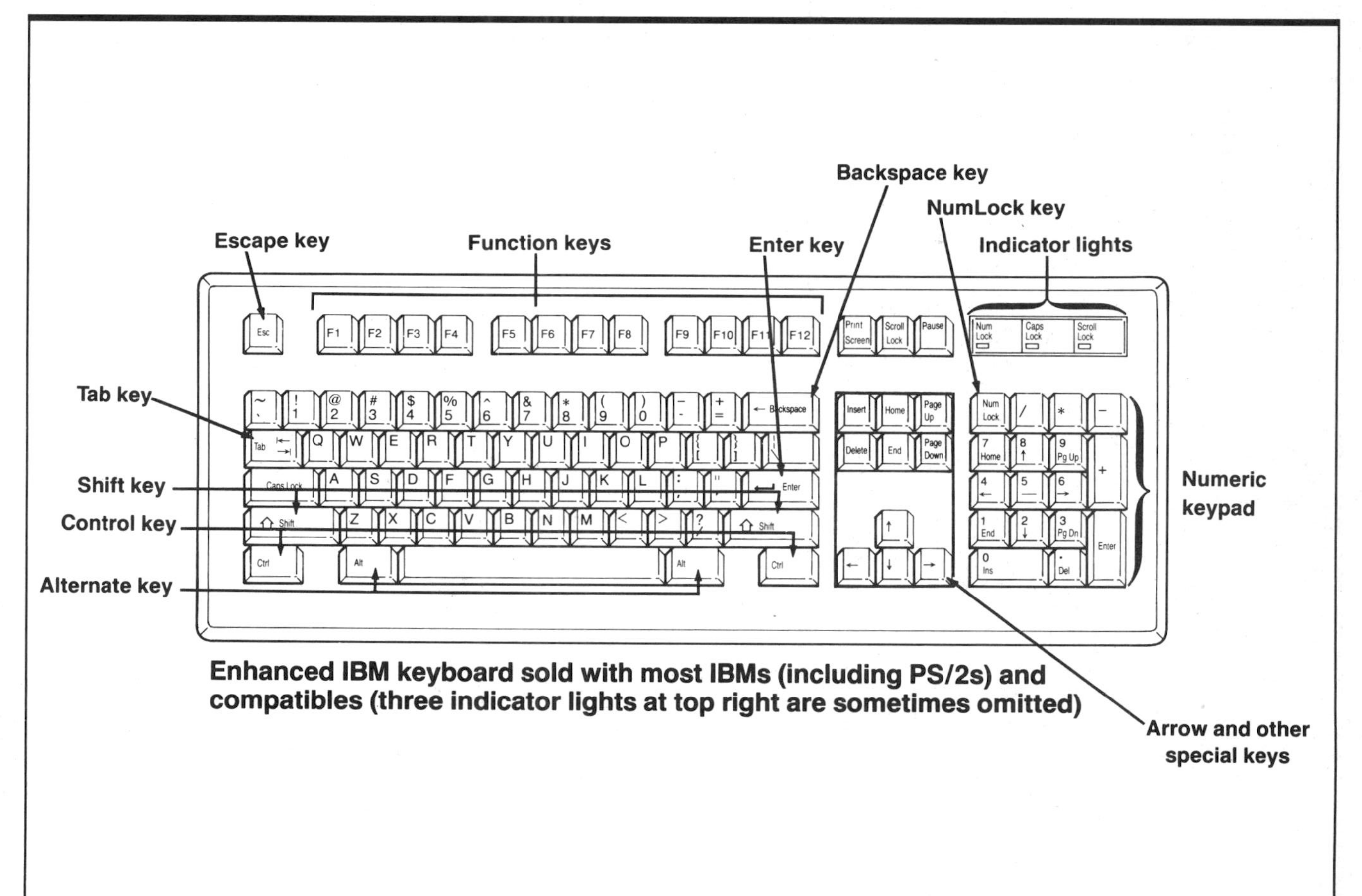

Figure 2.1: Some special keys on different types of keyboards (continued)

Both the 1 and the 0 must always be typed using the 1 and 0 keys, respectively, at the top of the keyboard, or the numeric keypad on the right side of the keyboard.

COMBINATION KEYSTROKES

During your work with dBASE, you'll often use combination keystrokes, such as Ctrl-N or Alt-F or Shift-F9. Such a combination keystroke means "hold down the first key and tap the second key." Here are some examples:

Ctrl-Y	Hold down the Ctrl key and tap the letter Y.
Alt-F1	Hold down the Alt key and tap the key labeled F1.
Shift-F2	Hold down the Shift key and tap the key labeled F2.

Incidentally, Ctrl stands for control and Alt stands for alternate. The keystroke combination Ctrl-N is pronounced Control N.

USING THE MOUSE

You can use a mouse instead of the keyboard to interact with dBASE IV. In this book, we'll use standard mouse terminology to describe mouse features and mouse actions:

Mouse pointer: A small square on the screen indicating where your next mouse action will take place. As you move the mouse, the mouse pointer moves in the same direction.

Mouse button: The "active" button on your mouse. This is typically the left button.

Click: Press the button, then release it (after positioning the mouse pointer to the option or text you want).

Double-click: Rapidly click the mouse button twice (after moving the mouse pointer to the option or text you want).

Drag: Hold down the mouse button, move the mouse pointer to a new area, then release the mouse button.

STARTING dBASE IV

When you turn on your computer, DOS (the computer's *Disk Operating System*) is in control. To use dBASE IV, you must tell DOS to locate and run the dBASE IV program. We'll lead you through this procedure in a moment.

Although you need not be familiar with DOS to learn dBASE IV, knowing a little about DOS can help you get along with your computer more easily. If you are an absolute beginner and are not familiar with DOS terms such as *drive* and *directory,* you might want to take some time to read Appendix A, "A DOS Primer."

For now, let's forge ahead and get dBASE IV up and running on your computer. Follow these steps (if you make a mistake, use the Backspace key to correct it):

TIP

If the name of the directory that you are logged onto does not appear on the screen, you can type the command **PROMPT PG** next to the DOS prompt (and then press ↵) to display the current disk drive and directory.

1. Turn on your computer so that the DOS prompt (usually C:\>) appears on the screen.
2. Switch to the dBASE directory (the area on the computer hard disk where dBASE IV is stored) by typing the command **CD\DBASE**. Be sure to use a backslash (\) rather than a forward slash (/). Press the Enter key (↵) after typing the command.
3. Type the command **DBASE** and press the ↵ key.

Depending on how you've installed dBASE IV, you may see a brief message about "cache testing" (described in Appendix C, but not of importance at the moment), followed by the dBASE IV copyright notice. You can press ↵ to proceed to the dBASE IV Control Center immediately, or wait a few moments, and you'll arrive there automatically.

If, instead, you see the message "Bad command or file name," then either dBASE is not installed on the computer at all, or dBASE is stored on another disk drive or directory. If someone else installed dBASE, you may need to ask to find out how to start dBASE. The person who installed dBASE may not have used the usual disk drive and directory.

EXPLORING THE dBASE IV CONTROL CENTER

After the copyright notice disappears, the dBASE IV *Control Center* will appear on your screen, as in Figure 2.2. On your computer, the names of various files may appear in the rectangular panels in the Control Center—particularly if you share a computer with others. Don't worry about that; it won't affect your work.

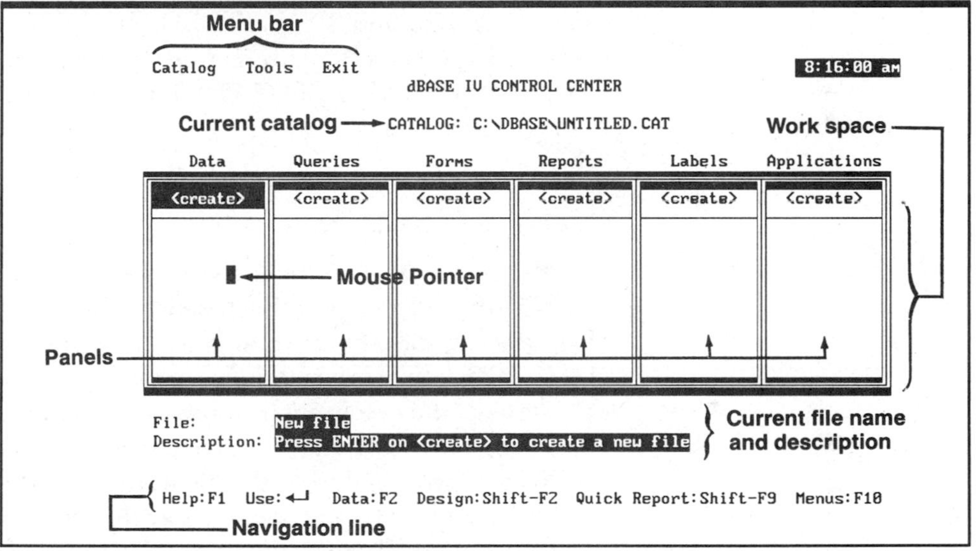

Figure 2.2: The dBASE IV Control Center

Let's take a moment to discuss the various parts of the Control Center. Use Figure 2.2 as a guide as you read.

THE MENU BAR

At the upper-left corner of the Control Center is the *menu bar*. On this screen, your menu bar options are Catalog, Tools, and Exit. Each option has a *pull-down* menu associated with it (which you cannot see at the moment). We'll discuss how to use the pull-down menus a little later in this chapter.

THE CURRENT CATALOG

Centered beneath the title of the Control Center screen is the name of the current catalog. A *catalog* is simply a tool for organizing related information in a database; it is like a department in a corporation. For example, you might store accounts receivable information in one catalog and inventory information in another.

The catalog name actually consists of several parts. In this example, "C:" is the name of the disk drive that contains the catalog, "\DBASE\" is the name of the directory on the hard disk where the catalog is stored, and "UNTITLED.CAT" is the name of the catalog. (Don't worry if your screen is showing something other than C:\DBASE\UNTITLED.CAT.) You'll learn more about catalogs in the next chapter.

THE WORK SPACE

The center of the screen shows the Control Center *work space*, which consists of six *panels*. Each panel will hold the names of various objects within the current catalog. An *object* is simply one piece of the overall collection of information. For example, in an accounts receivable system, the credit application for collecting data would be one object, the file of existing customers would be a second object, and the invoices produced from the file would be a third object.

There may not be any object names displayed on your screen at the moment. But usually, the leftmost panel, titled *Data*, holds the names of *database files* that store data. The panels labeled Forms, Reports, and Labels hold the names of *formats* used to display forms and to print reports and mailing labels. The panels labeled Queries and Applications hold the names of other objects, which you'll learn about in due time.

Each panel also includes the option <create>, which allows you to create your own database file, form, report, or whatever. You'll learn how to create these items later in this book.

THE CURRENT FILE NAME AND DESCRIPTION

The current file name and description section of the screen, beneath the work space, displays the name and description of the file that is currently highlighted in the panel. If <create> is highlighted instead of a file name, this area displays "New file" and "Press ENTER on <create> to create a new file." You'll learn how to create files and assign names and descriptions to them in the next chapter.

THE NAVIGATION LINE

The navigation line at the bottom of the screen lists some of the special keys that are currently available to you. For example, the notation Help:F1 tells you that you can get help by pressing the function key labeled F1.

THE MOUSE POINTER

If you have a mouse and it is properly installed, the mouse pointer appears as a small rectangle that moves in whatever direction you move the mouse. In general, you can move the mouse pointer to just about any option on the screen, then click the left mouse button to choose that option.

For example, as an alternative to pressing F1 to access help, you can move the mouse pointer to the Help:F1 option in the navigation line, then click the mouse button.

GETTING HELP

You can use the Help key at any time to get help with dBASE IV. The help screens are *context sensitive,* which means they provide help that is relevant to the operation you are currently performing.

The help screen for creating database files probably won't help you too much right now. You'll learn how to create a database file in the next chapter.

For example, right now the <create> option in the Data panel is probably highlighted. If you want to get some help with that option right now, you can do either one of the following:

- Move the mouse pointer to the Help:F1 option near the bottom of the screen, then click the active mouse button.
- Press the F1 key.

You'll see a help screen (also called a help *window*) titled Create Database Files on your screen, as in Figure 2.3.

Notice that the navigation line at the bottom of the screen has changed. Now it provides information about the keys that you can use while in the help system, such as ← and → to move the highlight bar, ↵ to select an option, F3 and F4 to scroll forward or backward through screens ("pages").

You can choose any option from the navigation line either by pressing the specified key, or by clicking the option with your mouse. For example, to scroll to the next screen, you could press the F4 key, or you could just click the Next Screen:F4 option on the navigation line with your mouse. To scroll back a screen, press F3 or click the Previous Screen:F3 option in the navigation line.

Notice too that there are several options at the bottom of the help window: CONTENTS, RELATED TOPICS, sometimes BACKUP, and PRINT. We'll talk about those options in the next section.

> **WARNING**
>
> If the arrow keys on your keyboard are combined with the numbers on the numeric keypad, the arrow keys will only work when the NumLock key is in the Off position. If you attempt to use an arrow key and nothing happens or a number appears on the screen, press the NumLock key once to set NumLock Off.

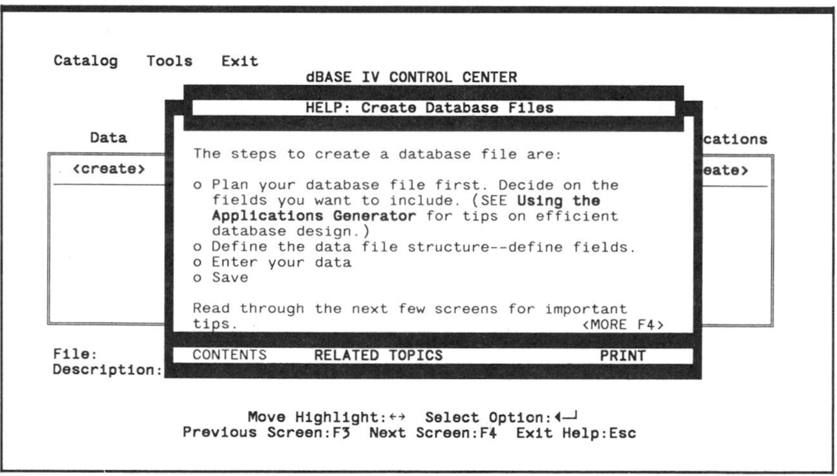

Figure 2.3: Help screen for creating database files

USING THE TABLE OF CONTENTS

Suppose you do not want help with creating database files. Instead, you want more general help with the Control Center. To locate the appropriate help area, you need to check the help system's table of contents. To do so, choose CONTENTS from the help window options, using either the keyboard or mouse:

- Click the CONTENTS option with your mouse.
- Or, use the ← and → keys to move the highlight to the CONTENTS option, then press ↵.

You'll see a list of topics concerning database files, but perhaps none that is broad enough for your needs. Notice in the navigation line at the bottom of the screen the two options More General:F3 and More Specific:F4. To see a more general table of contents:

- Click More General:F3 with your mouse.
- Or, press the F3 key.

The first entry of this more general table of contents offers information on using the Control Center. To see that help screen, choose the About the Control Center option. As usual, you can use either the mouse or keyboard:

- Click the About the Control Center option.
- Or, press ↑ or ↓ (or PgUp) as necessary to move the highlight to the About the Control Center option, then press ↵.

The help for the Control Center appears on the screen, as in Figure 2.4. Notice also that the Previous Screen:F3 and Next Screen:F4 options are still available in the navigation line, so you can scroll through pages within the help window.

HELP WINDOW OPTIONS

Here's a brief description of the options that appear at the bottom of the help window. To choose one of these options, either click the option you want with your mouse, or use the ← and → keys to move the highlight to the option you want, then press ↵:

CONTENTS	Displays a table of contents for the current topic. Whenever a table of

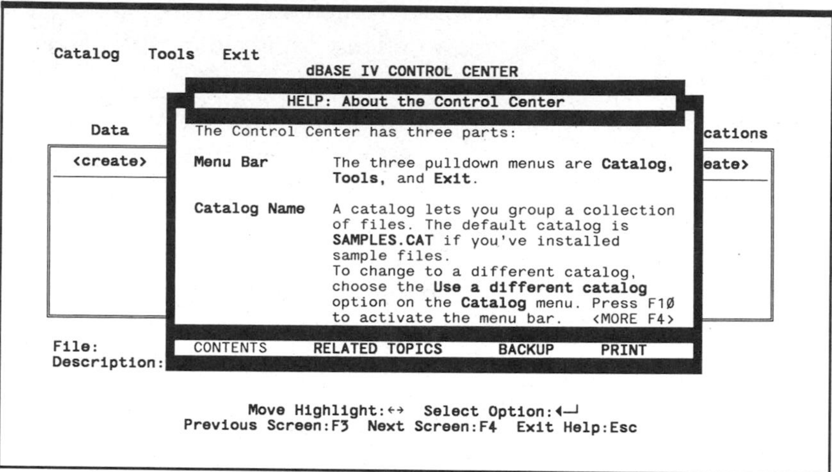

Figure 2.4: Help screen for the Control Center

	contents appears, you can use the More General:F3 and More Specific:F4 options in the navigation line at the bottom of the screen to change to a more general or more specific table of contents.
RELATED TOPICS	Displays a list of topics that are related to the current topic. (Press Esc if you change your mind.)
BACKUP	Scrolls back to the previous screen. (This option appears only if there is a previous screen.)
PRINT	Prints a copy of the current help window.

On a laser printer, you need to eject the page after printing a help screen. See your printer manual for instructions.

LEAVING THE HELP SYSTEM

Notice that the option for exiting help is provided in the navigation line, right at the bottom of the screen. Actually, however, there are three ways that you can exit the help system:

- Press the Escape key.
- Click the Exit Help:Esc option with your mouse.
- Or, move the mouse pointer to any "neutral" area *outside* the help window (so the mouse pointer is on some blank part of the screen), and click the left mouse button.

Undoubtedly you've noticed that help screens provide only limited information. Such brief instructions may not be very useful while you are learning dBASE IV. But later, when you are more familiar with basic dBASE operations, the help screens will serve as a quick reference to details that you may have forgotten.

USING THE PULL-DOWN MENUS

The pull-down menus attached to the menu bar at the top of the screen provide access to just about every feature that dBASE IV offers. There are several ways that you can choose options from these menus, and deciding which technique is best for you is simply a matter of personal preference:

- Click the option you want with your mouse.
- Press F10 to get to the menu bar, then use the ←, →, ↑, ↓, or other keys listed in Table 2.1 to move the highlight to the option you want. When the option you want is highlighted, press ↵ to select that option.
- Hold down the Alt key and type the first letter of the option you want on the menu bar. Once a pull-down menu is displayed, you can just type the first letter of the option you want in the menu.

If your Home, End, PgUp, and PgDn keys share numbers on the numeric keypad, these keys, like the arrow keys, will work *only* when the NumLock key is in the off position.

Table 2.1: Keys Used to Navigate the Pull-Down Menus

Key	**Effect**
→	Moves to the menu-bar option on the right, or exits submenu
←	Moves to the menu-bar option on the left, or exits submenu
↓	Moves down to the next available (unshaded) menu option on the current pull-down menu
↑	Moves up to the next available (unshaded) menu option on the current pull-down menu
PgUp	Moves to the first available option on the current pull-down menu
Home	Same as PgUp
PgDn	Moves to the last available option on the current pull-down menu
End	Same as PgDn
↵	Selects the currently highlighted option
First letter of any option	Selects that option
Esc	Backs up to the previous menu or to the Control Center

For example, to pull down the Catalog menu, you can just click the Catalog option in the menu bar with your mouse, press F10, or press Alt-C. The Catalog pull-down menu appears, as in Figure 2.5.

BACKING OUT OF MENUS

When you're first learning to use dBASE IV, you may often make mistakes while choosing menu options, which leads you to unfamiliar territory. You can "back out" of a menu selection until you get to more familiar territory using either of two techniques:

- Click anywhere outside of the menu to "back up" to the previous level (until you're in familiar territory).
- Press Escape until you're back in familiar territory.

For example, to leave the Catalog menu without making a selection from it, you can either move the mouse pointer to any "neutral" area outside the menu bar and menu and click the mouse button, or you can just press the Escape key.

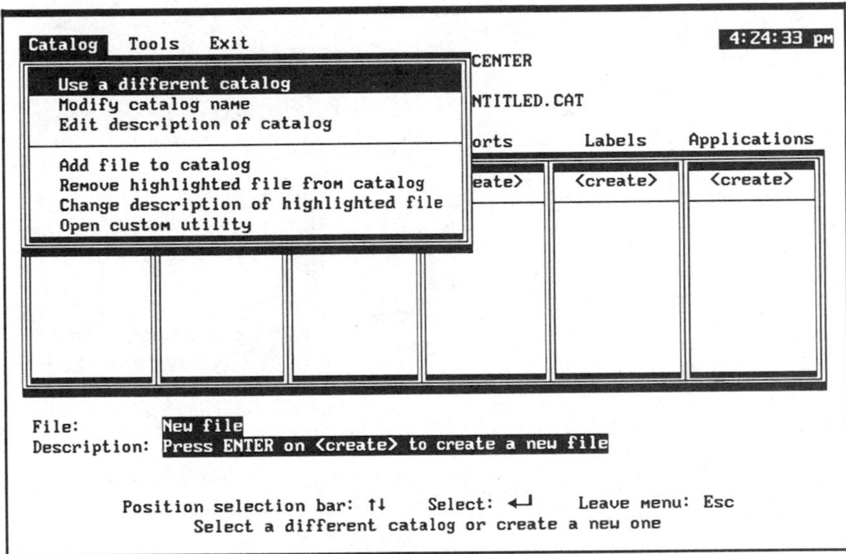

Figure 2.5: Pull-down menu for the Catalog option

SHADED OPTIONS

Whenever you access a pull-down menu, you may notice that some options on the menu are *shaded* (they appear darker than other items). The shaded options are not available at the moment, usually because they make no sense in the current situation. Even though you cannot use shaded options at a particular moment, they may be available later, in a different situation.

BULLETED OPTIONS

On some pull-down menus, you'll see an arrow (actually a right-pointing triangle) to the left of some options. This arrow means that a *submenu*, another menu containing more options, is available after you select the option.

For example, if you pull down the Tools menu, you'll see that the options Macros, Import, and Export each have an arrow to the left of them. If you choose Macros, for instance, a *submenu* of macro options will appear, as in Figure 2.6.

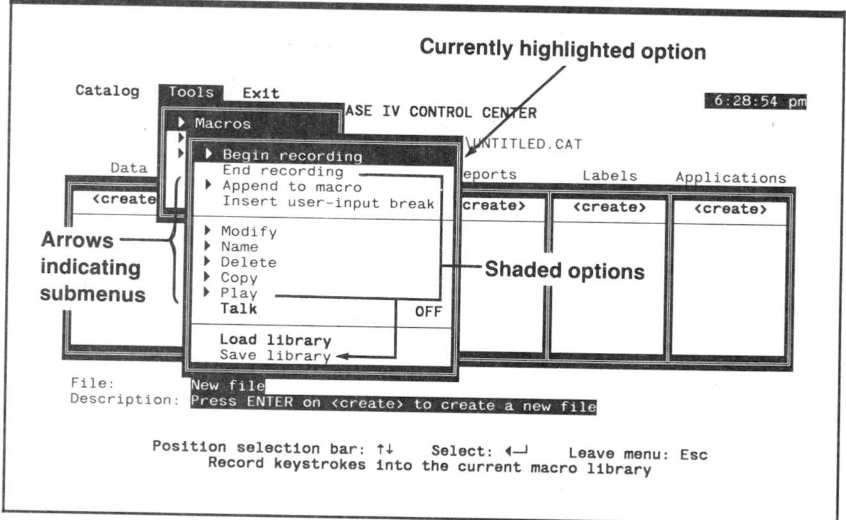

Figure 2.6: The Macros submenu

(If these menu options don't mean much to you at the moment, don't worry.) After you have viewed the submenu, press the Esc key twice to return to the Control Center.

MENU SEQUENCE CONVENTIONS USED IN THIS BOOK

Throughout the remainder of this book, we'll present a series of menu options in an abbreviated format, where the ► symbol points to the next option to choose. For example, you might see a step like this in future exercises:

- Choose Tools ► Settings.

This instruction means, "Pull down the Tools menu, then choose Settings from the menu that appears." You can use whatever method you want—mouse or keyboard. For example, you can click Tools, then click Settings with your mouse. Or you can press Alt-T to pull down the Tools menu, then type S to choose Settings (the first letter of the option is the key to press). Or, you can use the F10, arrow, and ↵ keys.

If you try this right now, you'll be taken to a screen for choosing settings, which we'll talk about later. For now, you can just "back out" of this screen, and return to the Control Center, by following this simple step:

- Press Escape, or click outside the menu that appears.

Soon you'll start actually using menu options to build a database. For now, this little exercise in *navigating* the pull-down menus is sufficient.

USING TYPEMATIC KEYSTROKES

Most computers offer a *typematic* feature, which allows you to hold down a key to repeat a keystroke. To try this feature, press F10 to pull down a menu. Then hold down the → key for a few seconds. You should see the pull-down menu move quickly from option to option. If the computer starts beeping, release the key that you are holding down. No harm done, but the highlight may take a few seconds to stop moving.

Remember that all the keys on the keyboard are typematic, so you can use this feature whenever you want.

ACCESSING THE DOT PROMPT

dBASE IV offers an optional *command-driven* technique for managing databases, where you type commands rather than select options from pull-down menus. For beginners, the dot prompt is virtually useless.

NOTE

As an alternative to entering the ASSIST command to leave the dot prompt and return to the Control Center, you can just press the F2 function key.

If you start experimenting on your own with menu options and find yourself inadvertently at the dot prompt, with no menus or work space on the screen, you need to return to the Control Center by entering the ASSIST command. Practice this now, so you know what to do if you reach the dot prompt accidentally. Here are the steps:

NOTE

The dot prompt also appears if you press Escape at the Control Center when no menus are displayed, and choose Yes when asked about abandoning the operation.

1. Choose Exit ► Exit to Dot Prompt.
2. The Control Center will disappear, and you'll see only a highlighted bar, a period (dot), and the blinking cursor (see Figure 2.7).
3. To return to the Control Center, type the command **ASSIST** (you can use upper- or lowercase letters).
4. Press the ↵ key and wait a few seconds.

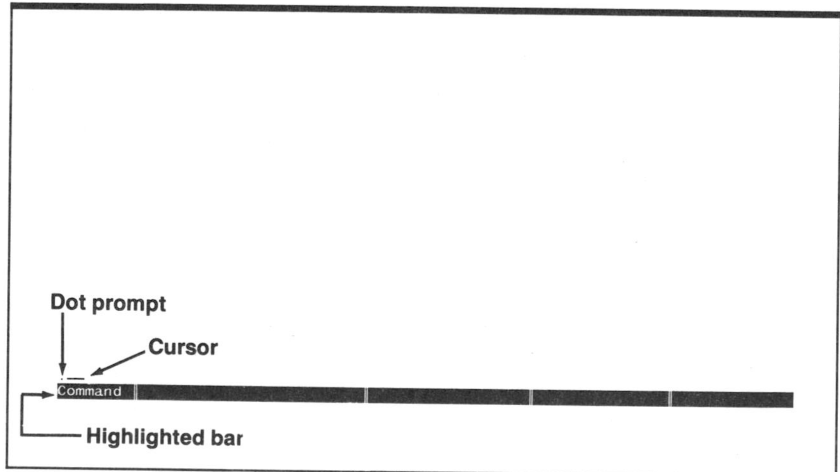

Figure 2.7: The dot prompt

The now-familiar Control Center will reappear on the screen. Keep this technique in mind, in case you should ever find yourself suddenly at the dot prompt, by accident, without the usual assistance you get from the Control Center.

SETTING INSTRUCTIONS ON

dBASE IV offers several modes of operation, which you control through the Settings menu. One setting, Instruct, tells dBASE to display prompt boxes and other aids which you'll see later, to help you learn dBASE. Many of the examples in this book assume that the Instruct setting is On. To make sure that this is indeed the case on your computer, follow these steps:

1. Choose Tools ► Settings.
2. Choose Instruct (by clicking that option, or by typing the letter **i**, or by using the ↑ and ↓ keys, as usual).
3. If the option next to Instruct is currently set to OFF, press ↵ or click the mouse button to change that setting to ON, as in Figure 2.8.
4. Choose Exit ► Exit to Control Center or click anywhere outside the Settings menu to return to the Control Center.

dBASE will "remember" this setting in the future, so unless you or somebody else changes that setting, you won't need to repeat these steps in the future.

EXITING DBASE IV

Whenever you finish a dBASE IV session, you should exit (or quit) dBASE IV before you turn off your computer. If you don't remember to do so, you may find that dBASE IV is not saving your work, and you'll have to reenter all your data.

To exit dBASE IV, follow this simple step:

- Choose Exit ► Quit to Dos.

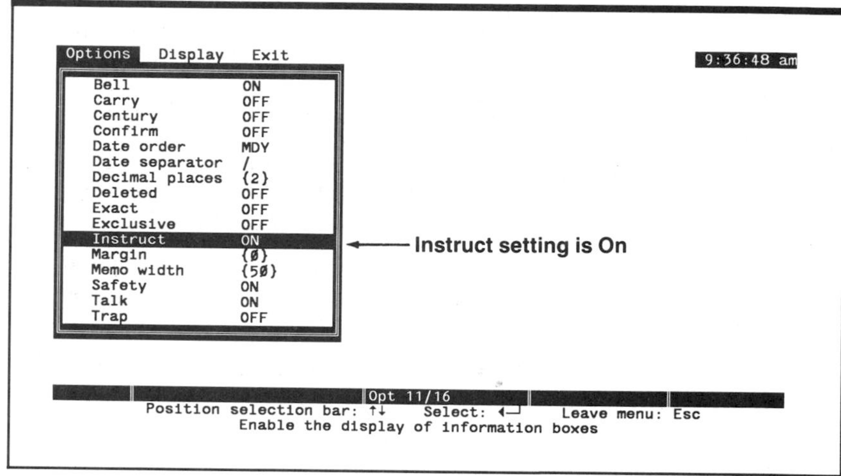

Figure 2.8: The Instruct setting

In the future, *always* quit dBASE IV to return to DOS before turning off your computer. Otherwise, you'll probably lose your work.

You'll see the message "*** END RUN dBASE IV" on your screen. Depending on how you installed dBASE IV, you might instead see the message "Uninstalled!" Don't be alarmed—the message simply means that the caching program has been removed from memory. dBASE IV is still safely installed on your computer for future use. Again, you need not be concerned about disk caching right now; it only affects the *speed* at which dBASE runs, not the *way* it runs. However, if and when you do want to look into disk caching, you can refer to Appendix C.

The last prompt to appear on your screen will be the DOS command prompt (usually C> or C:\DBASE>). When you see this prompt, dBASE has safely stored all of your information for future use (though in this case, you have not actually entered any specific information). You can now safely turn off your computer or use another program.

USING THE ON-DISK TUTORIAL

As an adjunct to the hands-on exercises that this book offers, you can use the dBASE IV on-disk tutorial, which came with your dBASE IV package. The tutorial program is currently stored on your hard disk if you opted to install the complete dBASE IV package. Here are the steps for using the dBASE IV on-disk tutorial:

1. Make sure you are at the DOS command prompt. If you are using dBASE IV, you must exit and return to DOS.
2. Switch to the directory that the tutorial is stored on (typically \DBASE\DBTUTOR, which you can access by typing the command **CD \DBASE\DBTUTOR** and pressing ↵).
3. Type **INTRO** and press ↵.
4. Follow the instructions as they appear on the screen.

From this point on, the tutorial is pretty self-explanatory. You can try all of the sessions that the tutorial offers, or only a few. As the instructions on the screen will indicate, you can leave the on-screen tutorial at any time by pressing the F5 key, then typing Q to quit at the Introduction to DBASE IV Main Menu.

If you want to pace yourself with the on-screen tutorial, I suggest that you just try the first two sessions—"1 What is a database" and "2 dBASE IV basics"—at this time. These will provide different examples of the concepts you've learned up to this point.

RETURNING TO dBASE IV AFTER THE TUTORIAL

To return to dBASE IV after taking a lesson and exiting back to the command prompt, follow these steps to return to the \DBASE directory and run dBASE IV:

1. Type **CD..** then press ↵.
2. Type **DBASE** then press ↵.

In the next chapter, you'll begin to put your new knowledge and skills to work by creating your first dBASE IV database file.

CHAPTER 3

Creating a Database File

To create a database catalog for organizing information, forms, and reports, select Catalog ► Use a Different Catalog ► <create>. Type the name of the new catalog (up to eight characters, no spaces or punctuation) and press ↵. 38

To use a previously created catalog, select Catalog ► Use a Different Catalog, then choose the name of the appropriate catalog from the list of catalog names that appears. 41

Every field in a database file must have a unique name, a data type (Character, Numeric, Float, Date, Logical, or Memo), an assigned width, an assigned number of decimal places (for Numeric and Float data types), and an Index setting. 41

To create a database file, select the <create> option from the Data panel in the Control Center. Then enter valid field names, data types, widths, decimal places, and index options for each field in the database design work area. 47

To enter a plain-English description of a database while defining the database structure, choose Layout ► Edit Database Description. Then type the description and press ↵. 51

To save a completed database structure, choose Exit ► Save Changes and Exit from the database design screen menus (or press Ctrl-End). Enter a valid file name for the database and press ↵. 52

IN THIS CHAPTER, YOU'LL START BUILDING YOUR first database. Of course, you'll need to have dBASE IV up and running on your computer. If you've forgotten the necessary steps, refer to the instructions in Chapter 2. When the dBASE IV Control Center appears on the screen, you're ready to forge ahead.

CREATING A DATABASE CATALOG

TIP

Additional information about managing catalogs, which may come in handy when you start managing many files, is presented in Chapter 14.

As mentioned in the previous chapter, a catalog is a tool for grouping together the various components of a database, such as the database files, forms, and report formats. To help you organize your first database, you'll create a catalog named LEARN. The general steps for creating a catalog are simple: You call up the Catalog menu, select Use a Different Catalog, select <create>, and enter a new name for the catalog. Let's create the catalog named LEARN now, following these steps:

1. Choose Catalog ► Use a Different Catalog.
2. Choose <create> from the submenu that appears (shown near the upper-right corner of Figure 3.1.)
3. You'll see this prompt:

   Enter name for new catalog: _

The name you enter for a catalog must follow these rules, which also apply to most of the names of the objects you'll create with dBASE IV:

- The name can be no more than eight characters long.
- The name can contain numbers (0 to 9), but *cannot* contain any blank spaces or punctuation marks, such as ? * . $: or ;. The underline character (_) and hyphen (-) are the only special characters allowed.
- You can use upper- or lowercase letters, but lowercase letters are automatically converted to uppercase.

Table 3.1 shows examples of valid and invalid file names.

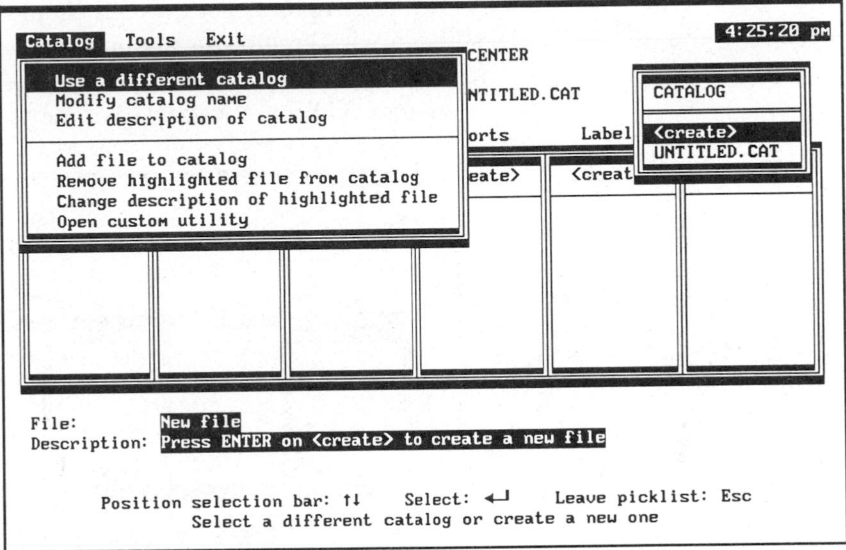

Figure 3.1: Submenu of catalog names

Table 3.1: Examples of Valid and Invalid File Names

File Name	Valid/Invalid
LEARN	Valid
MyData	Valid
June91	Valid
1991Qtr1	Valid
My_Data	Valid
My Data	Invalid; contains a space
Qtr1:91	Invalid; contains a colon
January1991	Invalid; too long
LEARN DBASE	Invalid; too long and contains a space

4. Type the new catalog name **LEARN** (if you make a mistake while typing the catalog name, press the Backspace key to back up and make corrections).
5. Press ↵.

At this point, your screen should look like Figure 3.2, with only the label <create> at the top of each panel. Note that the current catalog is named LEARN.CAT (dBASE IV automatically adds the *extension* .CAT to the catalog name you provide).

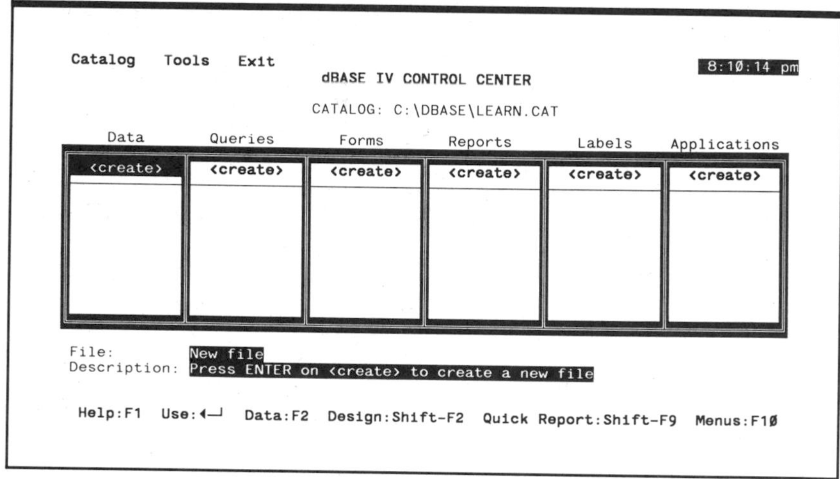

Figure 3.2: The LEARN catalog

> **NOTE**
> If somebody else has already created a catalog called LEARN on your computer, or if you've purchased and copied the sample disk described at the end of this book, then the panels will contain several file names. You can either continue to use the existing LEARN catalog or repeat steps 1 through 5 and use a name other than LEARN for your new catalog.

As you build the database and add forms, reports, and mailing labels, you'll see the catalog grow to remind you of the various objects you've created.

Now let's take a slight detour and discuss how you can quit dBASE at any time and get back to the LEARN catalog to resume your work. This will allow you to take a break at any time as you read along in this book.

TAKING BREAKS

Whenever you want to take a break from the exercises in this book and perhaps turn off the computer, you can exit dBASE using the same techniques discussed in Chapter 2: that is, choose Exit ► Quit to DOS from the menus. All of your work will be safely stored on disk for future use.

RETURNING TO THE LEARN CATALOG

To get back to dBASE to resume your work, run dBASE in the usual manner for your computer (as discussed in Chapter 2). When the Control Center appears, follow these steps to return to the LEARN catalog (if it is not already on the screen):

1. Choose Catalog ► Use a Different Catalog.
2. Choose LEARN.CAT (by double-clicking that name, or highlighting it and pressing ↵).

The screen displays LEARN.CAT above the work space as the current catalog name. At this point, you can pick up where you left off in the book.

DESIGNING A DATABASE FILE

Chapter 1 discussed the structure of database files, where information is stored in tabular records (rows) and fields (columns). Before you can store information in a database file, you need to *structure* an empty file that specifies the name and type of data that is stored in each field. There are a few basic rules of thumb to keep in mind when designing a database file, discussed in the following sections.

DEFINING FIELDS

The most important point to keep in mind in structuring a database is that each unique item of information should be stored in its own field. Try not to be influenced by how you want the information to look when it's printed later. The manner in which you *store* information in a database file in no way limits the manner in which you can print it later.

For example, in a file containing names and addresses, you might be tempted to store peoples' names in a single field called

Name, like this:

Name
John Smith
Annie Adams
Wilbur Watson
Mary Mahoney
John Newell
Sandy Beach

However, storing the names in this manner creates several problems. For example, you could not tell dBASE to sort the names into alphabetical order by last name because the last name and first name are within the same field. Similarly, you could not tell dBASE to search for the last name Mahoney, because dBASE has no way of isolating the last name as something to search for.

The simple solution to this problem is to store peoples' names in two fields, called LastName and FirstName, as shown here:

LastName	FirstName
Smith	John
Adams	Annie
Watson	Wilbur
Mahoney	Mary
Newell	John
Beach	Sandy

Because the last name and first name are separated, you can isolate the last name for both sorting and searching. If you want to include titles, such as Mr. and Ms., and middle initials, you should break the name into four different fields:

Title	LastName	FirstName	MI
Mr.	Smith	John	J.

Title	LastName	FirstName	MI
Ms.	Adams	Annie	T.
Dr.	Watson	Wilbur	H.
Mrs.	Mahoney	Mary	
Mr.	Newell	John	J.
Miss	Beach	Sandy	B.

The preceding structure gives you the most flexibility in using the names. For example, if you were printing form letters, you could join the four fields together to create an entire name, such as Mr. John J. Smith, and you could just as easily isolate the first name for the greeting in the letter: Dear John:. And of course you could still isolate the last name for sorting and searching.

A common mistakc that people make when structuring database files that contain names and addresses is grouping the city, state, and zip code into a single field, as follows:

CityStZip
San Diego, CA 92122
Malibu, CA 92001
New York, NY 12345
Seattle, WA 88977
Butte, MT 54321
Portland, OR 76543

Once again, grouping the data into a single field causes problems. For example, you could not sort the information into zip code order for bulk mailing, because dBASE cannot isolate the zip code. You could not isolate all of the records for a particular state, such as California (CA), or sort the data into state order.

To ensure maximum flexibility in managing your data, be sure to place the city, state, and zip codes in separate fields, as shown here. (Don't worry about the comma you may need between the city and state. You can add that to your printed reports without storing it in the database file.)

City	State	Zip
San Diego	CA	92122
Malibu	CA	92001
New York	NY	12345
Seattle	WA	88977
Butte	MT	54321
Portland	OR	76543

WHAT GOES IN A DATABASE FILE?

Basically, you can put anything that you want into a database file. But remember, dBASE can handle many database files simultaneously, so there is no need to put every bit of information that your business uses into a single file. Instead, use the same common sense that you do when storing information in Rolodex files or file drawers.

For example, you wouldn't mix your customer names and addresses with your parts inventory and accounts receivable in a single Rolodex file. Likewise, you wouldn't want to combine all of this information into a single database file either.

Occasionally, deciding how to divide information into separate database files is a little tricky, but we can save a discussion of these finer points for a later chapter.

ASSIGNING FIELD NAMES

Each field in the database file must have a unique name (that is, no two fields within a single file can have the same name). The name assigned to a field must conform to the following rules:

- The name can include no more than 10 characters.
- The first character must be a letter, but numbers can be used after the first letter.
- Blank spaces and punctuation marks are *not* allowed.
- The underscore character (_) is the only special symbol allowed.

You need not memorize all these rules; when you enter a field name, dBASE will make sure the name adheres to them.

SELECTING DATA TYPES

Each field in a database file must be categorized as a *data type* (or *field type*). dBASE offers six data types, listed in Table 3.2.

Table 3.2: The dBASE IV Data Types

Data Type	Description	Examples
Character	Any textual information that has no true numeric value and has maximum length of 254 characters	Jones Spark plug 123 Oak St.
Numeric	Any true numeric value on which you may want to perform arithmetic operations; usually used for quantities and prices	10 –123.45 100 1234.567
Float	Basically the same as Numeric, with some minor technical differences, as discussed in Chapter 9	10.0 –123.45 100.00 1234.567
Date	Any date stored in the format mm/dd/yy (for example, 12/31/93); always use this option to store dates	1/1/93 12/31/93 6/12/93
Logical	Contains either a true (.T. or T) or false (.F. or F) value and no other information; for example, you could create a field named *Paid* as the Logical data type, with .T. (or T) meaning the charge has been paid and .F. (or F) meaning it has not been paid	.T. or T .F. or F

Table 3.2: The dBASE IV Data Types (continued)

Data Type	Description	Examples
Memo	Very large volumes of text, perhaps including several paragraphs	abstracts, comments, lengthy descriptions

The correct data type for a particular field is usually obvious, though not always. For example, when storing phone numbers and zip codes, you might be tempted to use the Numeric data type. After all, we do say phone *number*, and the zip code 92122 certainly looks like a number. However, neither phone numbers nor zip codes are true numbers. Let's discuss why.

To dBASE, a true number is a quantity, such as the number of items purchased or a price or a test score. These numbers can contain only numeric digits (0 through 9) and, optionally, a decimal point (.) and a leading minus sign (–). Other characters, such as letters, parentheses, hyphens, and blank spaces, are not allowed in Numeric fields. A phone number, such as (619) 555-1212, contains parentheses and a hyphen. Some zip codes contain hyphens (such as 92038-2802), and some foreign postal codes contain letters (such as H3X 3T4).

If you give a zip code or phone number field the Numeric data type, you severely limit what you can enter into the field. Thus, before you assign the Numeric (or Float) data type to a field, ask yourself this question: "Is this an item for which I might want to calculate totals?" Certainly, you wouldn't need to total all the zip codes in a database or a group of phone numbers. In general, you should use the Numeric and Float data types only for fields on which you need to perform mathematical calculations.

One question that might occur to you is "How can I sort my mailing list into zip code order, if I don't make the zip codes numeric?" Don't worry about this; dBASE knows that the zip code 12345 comes before the zip code 12346 in a sort, regardless of whether the zip code is stored as a Character data type or a Numeric (or Float) data type.

Incidentally, the Numeric and Float (short for floating point) data types are basically the same, with a few minor technical differences. Chapter 9, which presents many aspects of managing numbers, including performing calculations, discusses these technical differences in detail.

You'll see the other data types—Character, Logical, Date, and Memo—in action as you read on.

CREATING A DATABASE FILE

Now let's get back to work and actually create some database files. We'll create a file called CUSTLIST (short for CUSTomer LIST) that stores customers' names and addresses and other useful information. To get started, select <create> from the Data panel using either one of these techniques:

- Use the arrow keys to move the highlight to <create> in the Data panel, as shown in Figure 3.3, then press ↵.
- Double-click the <create> option in the Data panel.

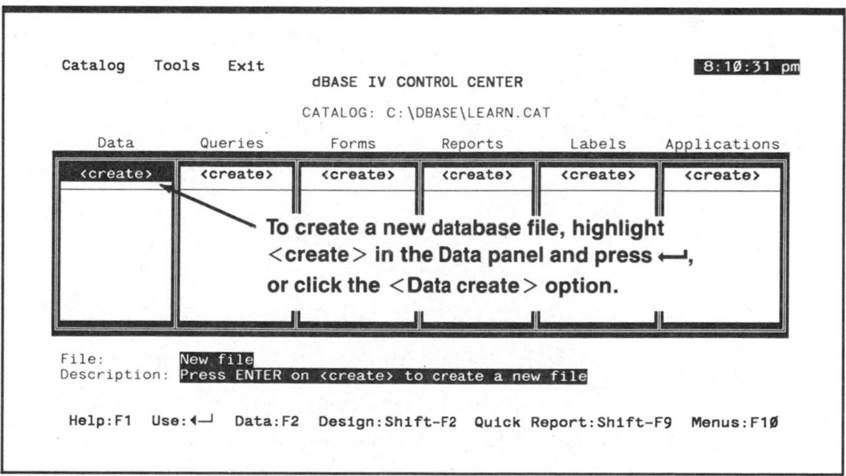

Figure 3.3: Creating a new database file

dBASE will take you to the *database design screen,* as shown in Figure 3.4. Note that the screen includes a table with seven columns labeled Num, Field Name, Field Type, Width, Dec (for decimal places), and Index. You'll define each field in your database structure within this table. Like the Control Center, the database design screen includes pull-down menu options at the top of the screen. The bottom two lines on the screen provide brief help and instructions. Pressing Help (F1) provides additional help.

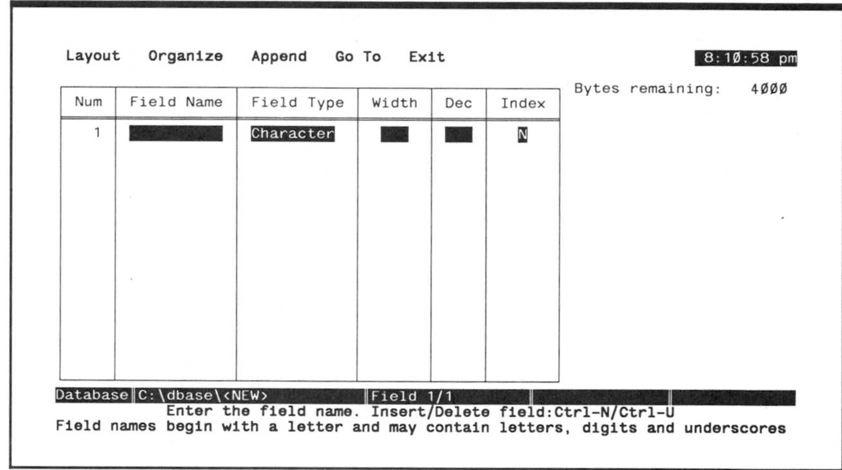

Figure 3.4: The database design screen

ENTERING FIELD NAMES

The first database file we'll create will contain the field names LASTNAME, FIRSTNAME, COMPANY, ADDRESS, CITY, STATE, ZIP, PHONE, STARTDATE, and PAID. You can think of CUSTLIST as a database of customers who subscribe to a newsletter. STARTDATE is the date that the subscription started and PAID is a field indicating whether the customer has paid for the subscription.

To enter a field name, first make sure that the blinking cursor is in the Field Name column on the screen. Type the field name and

As an alternative to pressing ↵ after typing a field name, you can just click the prompt in the Field Type or Width column next to the field name.

press ↵. In this example, follow these simple steps:

1. Type the field name **LASTNAME** (if you make a mistake as you type, you can use the Backspace key to make corrections).
2. Press ↵.

The cursor will jump to the Field Type column, where you need to select a data type for the LASTNAME field.

SELECTING A DATA TYPE

While the blinking cursor is in the Field Type column, you can click the mouse button or press the space bar to scroll through the various data types before making a selection. Each time you click or press the space bar, the name of a data type appears within the highlight, and a brief description of the data type appears at the bottom of the screen. To select the currently displayed data type, just press Enter or click the prompt in the Width column.

Follow these two steps to assign the Character data type to the LASTNAME field:

A shortcut for entering a data type is simply to type the first letter of its name; for example, type C for Character or D for Date.

1. If necessary, press the space bar or click the mouse button until the Character option appears.
2. Press ↵.

As soon as you press ↵, the cursor jumps to the Width column.

SPECIFYING A FIELD WIDTH

The next step in creating a database structure is to specify a maximum width for the field. The rule of thumb here is to select a reasonable maximum width, with just a touch of frugality. (The wider a field is, the more disk space it consumes.) For the LASTNAME field, a width of 15 should be sufficient. Follow these simple steps:

1. Type **15**.
2. Press ↵.

The cursor jumps to the Index column.

SPECIFYING DECIMAL PLACES

When you define a field as the Numeric or Float data type, the cursor jumps to the Dec column. In the Dec column, you specify the number of decimal places that the field requires. Chapter 9 discusses numeric data types and the various special features they offer.

INDEXING A FIELD

In the rightmost column, labeled Index, you can enter either Y (for yes), or N (for no) to indicate whether the field should be *indexed*. You'll learn more about indexing later. For now, just press ↵ to leave the Index option set to N.

At this point, the highlight jumps down to the next blank row, and you can enter the information for the next field. You can also move around the work area and make corrections or changes.

MAKING CHANGES AND CORRECTIONS

If you notice an error in your file structure or wish to make a change, you can use several keys to move the highlight and cursor around the database design work area. These are listed in Table 3.3.

Note that the keys won't always work if you attempt to leave a field that has incomplete or invalid data. You may have to experiment with several of the keys from Table 3.3 or type Ctrl-U to completely delete an incomplete or invalid field to get the cursor moving in the direction you want.

You can also move the blinking cursor into any available prompt simply by moving the mouse pointer to that prompt and clicking the left mouse button.

FINISHING THE CUSTLIST DATABASE

You can now enter the rest of the database file structure shown in Figure 3.5. Notice that ZIP and PHONE are both Character data types (as discussed earlier). When you enter the STARTDATE and PAID fields as the Date and Logical data types respectively, dBASE will automatically fill in the width as 8 and 1. You cannot (and need not) change the width of these fields.

Table 3.3: Keys Used to Change a Database File Structure

Key	Effect
↑	Moves highlight up one row
↓	Moves highlight down one row
←	Moves cursor one character to the left
→	Moves cursor one character to the right
Tab	Moves cursor one column to the right (only if valid information is already in the present column)
Shift-Tab	Moves cursor one column to the left (only if valid information is already in the present column)
Backspace	Moves cursor one space back, erasing along the way
Enter	Completes an entry and moves to the next column or row
Ctrl-N	Inserts a blank field between two existing fields
Ctrl-U	Deletes the current field definition
F3	Moves cursor left one column
F4	Moves cursor right one column
PgDn	Moves cursor to the last row on the screen
PgUp	Moves cursor to the first row on the screen
Home	Moves to Field Name column
End	Moves to Index column

NOTE

A single database file can contain a maximum of 255 fields, or can be a record size of 4,000 characters (bytes) of information, whichever comes first. However, Memo fields can contain much larger amounts, as discussed in Chapter 10.

You have not used the Numeric, Float, or Memo data type in this sample database file. These data types have some unique properties, which are discussed in Chapters 9 and 10.

ENTERING A DATABASE DESCRIPTION

As the finishing touch for the CUSTLIST database, we'll add a *description*, which is simply a sentence that describes, in plain English,

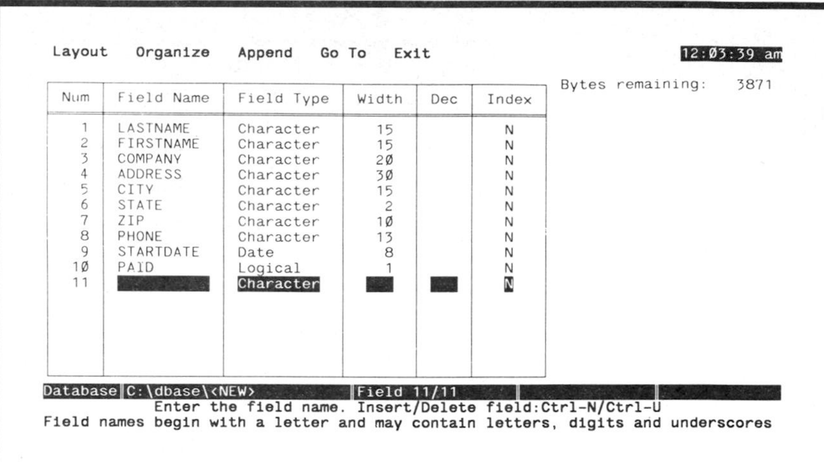

Figure 3.5: The completed CUSTLIST database file structure

what is stored in the database. To do so, follow these steps:

1. Choose Layout ► Edit Database Description from the menu bar at the top of the database design screen.
2. You'll see a prompt asking for the description of this .dbf file (i.e., database file). For this example, type in:

   Customer names and addresses

3. Press ↵ after typing your entry.

Later, you'll see that the database description appears in the Control Center when the name of the database is highlighted in the Data panel.

SAVING A DATABASE FILE STRUCTURE

To quickly move from one end of the menu bar to the other, press the arrow key pointing opposite to the direction that you want to go. The highlight will wrap around to the menu option at the opposite end.

Once you've finished entering the structure and description of a database file, you need to save your work. When your screen looks like Figure 3.5, follow these steps to save the new CUSTLIST database file structure:

1. Choose Exit ► Save Changes and Exit (or press Ctrl-End as a shortcut).

2. When you see the prompt "Save as:" type in the name **CUSTLIST** and press ↵.

WARNING

Selecting Overwrite in response to the "File already exists" prompt completely erases all data in the existing database file, replacing it with the empty database structure currently on the screen. Make sure you want to do this before you select the Overwrite option. Chapter 14 discusses file management in detail.

If you attempt to save a database file using a name that already exists, dBASE will beep and display the message "File already exists." You are also given two options: Overwrite, to replace the existing database with the new structure, and Cancel, to stop and use a different file name.

RETURNING TO THE CONTROL CENTER

After you've saved the database structure, you'll be returned to the Control Center. Here you can see the name of the new database file in the Data panel, as shown in Figure 3.6.

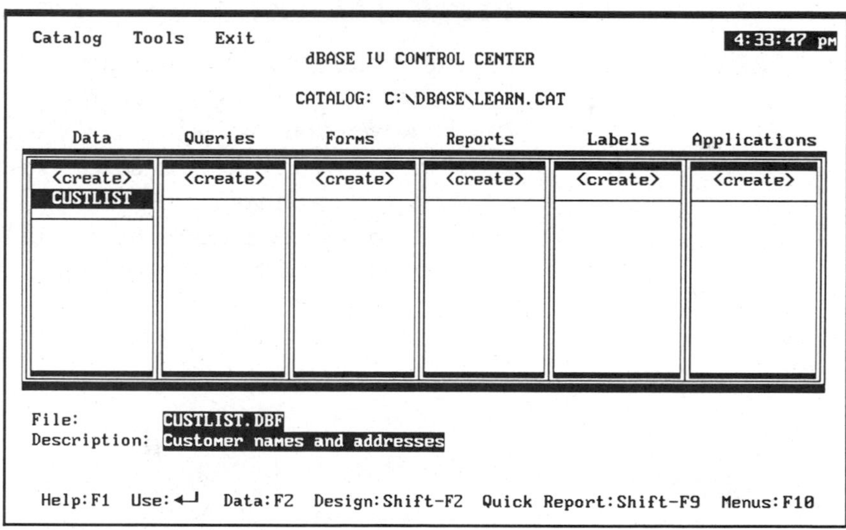

Figure 3.6: The CUSTLIST database file name in the Data panel

NOTE

Appendix A, "A DOS Primer," discusses basic DOS concepts such as *drive* and *directory*.

Let's take a moment to see what the Control Center now tells us:

- Centered near the top of the screen, **CATALOG C:\DBASE\LEARN.CAT** tells us that the current catalog is named LEARN.CAT, and that catalog is stored on the directory named DBASE on disk drive C.

- The current catalog contains one database file named CUSTLIST (you can see its name in the data panel).
- The **File:** and **Description:** prompts near the bottom of the screen tell you the complete location and name of the current file—C:\DBASE\CUSTLIST.DBF (dBASE automatically chose the current drive and directory as the place to store the file, and automatically added the .DBF extension). The description, "Customer names and addresses," you added yourself while designing the structure of the database.
- As usual, the keys available to you at this moment are listed at the bottom of the screen.

TIME TO RELAX

So far, so good. You've created a database file (at least, the *structure* of the file), and now you are ready to start storing information in it. However, you may want to take a break now to digest all of the information you've learned so far. To do so, quit dBASE IV now (*before* you turn off your computer, as discussed earlier). Remember, to quit dBASE, you access the Exit pull-down menu and select the option Quit to DOS, as described in Chapter 2.

CHAPTER

4

Adding and Changing Information

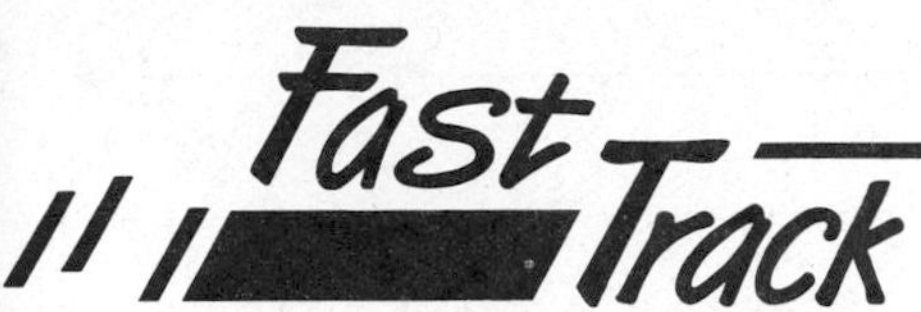

To use a specific catalog, 58

select Catalog ► Use a Different Catalog. Then select the appropriate catalog name from the submenu that appears.

To view the contents of a database file, 59

highlight or click on the name of the database file in the Data panel on the Control Center and press or click Data (F2).

To enter new data into a database file, 60

type the information on either the edit screen or the browse screen. Press ↵ after completing each field.

To switch from the edit screen to the browse screen, 62

press Data (F2).

To copy data from the previous record into a new record, 65

press the Ditto key (Shift-F8).

To save new data and return to the Control Center, 65

choose Exit ► Exit on either the browse or edit screen.

To change existing data, 66

use the editing keys, listed in Table 4.1, or the mouse on either the edit screen or the browse screen.

To undo changes to a record (before moving to a new record), 70

select Records ► Undo Change to Record.

To add records to a database that already contains information, 72

go to the edit or browse screen and select records ► Add New Records.

NOW THAT YOU'VE *STRUCTURED* A dBASE IV DATA-base file, the next step is to put some information into it. But before you can do *anything* to the CUSTLIST database, you need to open it (this is true of any and *all* databases you create with dBASE IV). If you are currently at the DOS command prompt, you have to do several things:

- Get to the proper directory and run dBASE.
- Get to the catalog (which you named LEARN.CAT) that the database is stored in.
- Open the database that you want to work with.

Though we've been through the steps for this procedure in preceding chapters, we'll take it step-by-step in the sections that follow to help reinforce what you've learned so far.

STARTING dBASE IV

Remember that whenever you exit dBASE IV, you need to switch back to its directory and run it again in order to gain access to your database. Assuming that you are currently at the DOS command prompt, and are using C:\DBASE as your dBASE IV drive and directory, follow these steps:

1. Type **CD \DBASE** and press ↵ to switch to your dBASE directory.
2. Type **DBASE** and press ↵.

Wait a few moments, and you'll get to the Control Center.

ACCESSING THE LEARN CATALOG

Remember that we put the CUSTLIST database in a catalog named LEARN. Now you need to make sure that LEARN.CAT is the current catalog. You can tell simply by looking at the name next to the CATALOG: prompt centered near the top of the screen. If the LEARN catalog is not the current catalog, here once again are the steps to open that catalog:

1. Choose Catalog ► Use a Different Catalog.
2. Choose LEARN.CAT by double-clicking on that name or by highlighting it and pressing ↵.

At this point, LEARN.CAT should appear as the current catalog name in the Control Center, with the CUSTLIST database name in the Data panel, as in Figure 4.1.

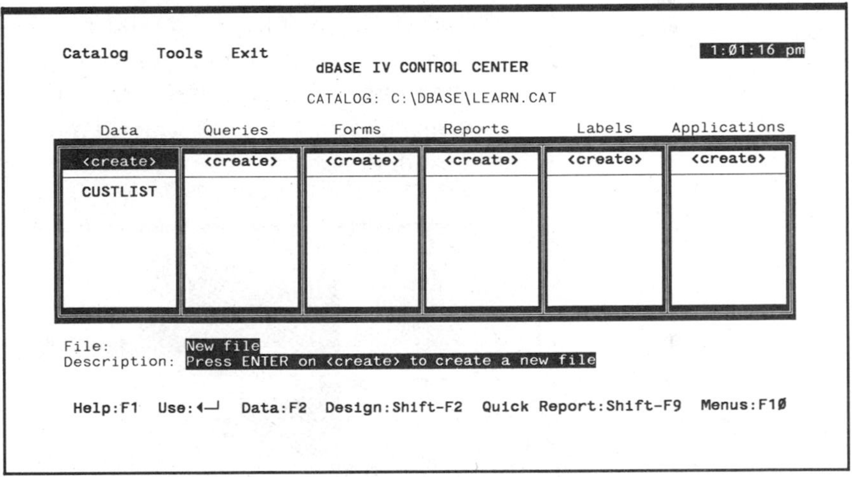

Figure 4.1: The LEARN catalog on the screen, ready for action

SELECTING A DATABASE FILE

Any single catalog may contain several database files. Therefore, before you start entering information into a database file, you need to tell dBASE IV which database file you want to use.

To select a database file and access its data (to add, view, or change information), highlight the database file name in the Data

NOTE

Throughout the remainder or this book we will use the convention "press or click" to indicate that you can either press a key or click the corresponding label on the navigation line near the bottom of the screen. For example, "press or click Data (F2)" means that you can either press the F2 key or click the Data: F2 label on the navigation line to display data in the currently highlighted database.

panel and then press the Data key (F2) , or click on the Data: F2 key label at the bottom of the screen. Suppose you want to add new information to the CUSTLIST database file. To do so, follow these steps:

1. Move the highlight to the CUSTLIST database file name in the Data panel using the arrow keys or by clicking on it with the mouse.
2. Press or click Data (F2) to view data in the CUSTLIST database file.

ADDING NEW DATA

At this point, you should see the *edit screen* for the CUSTLIST database, as shown in Figure 4.2. (If a different screen appears, press the F2 key.) As you can see, the edit screen looks like a blank form for a single record that you can fill out on the screen. (Later you'll learn how to create much fancier custom forms on the screen.)

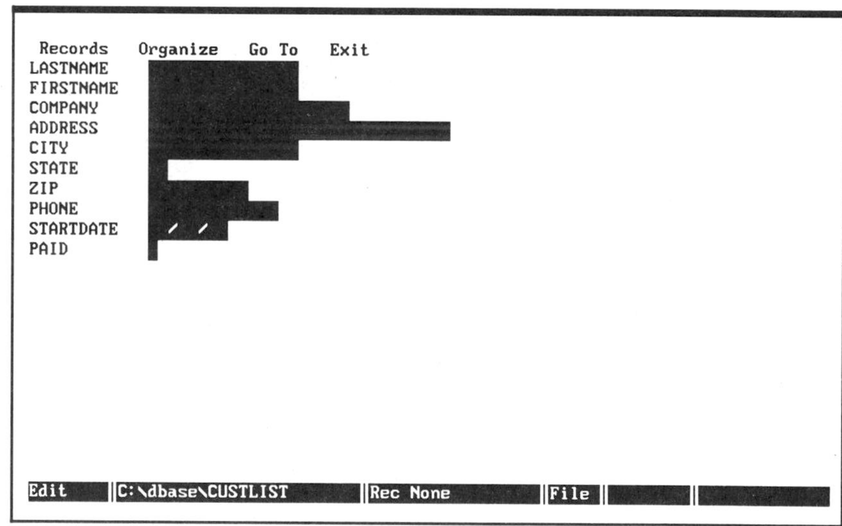

Figure 4.2: Edit screen for a record in the CUSTLIST database

Now suppose you want to enter information from the Rolodex card shown in Figure 4.3. To do so, follow the steps presented here. If you make a mistake while typing, just press Backspace to make corrections, or you can wait until we discuss more sophisticated editing techniques a little later in this chapter.

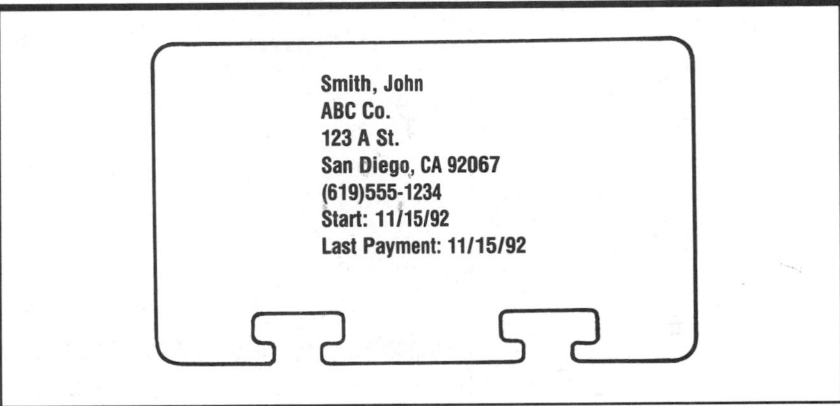

Figure 4.3: A Rolodex card to be entered as a database record

1. Type the last name **Smith** and press ↵.
2. Type the first name **John** and press ↵.
3. Type the company name **ABC Co.** and press ↵.
4. Type the address **123 A St.** and press ↵.
5. Type the city **San Diego** and press ↵.
6. Type the state **CA**.
7. Type the zip code **92067** and press ↵.
8. Type the phone number **(619)555-1234**.
9. Note that in the STARTDATE field, the slashes are already entered for you. To enter the date November 15, 1992, type **11**, then **15**, then **92**. At this point, your screen should look like Figure 4.4.
10. If you leave a Logical field, such as PAID, blank, dBASE interprets it as F (False). However, since John Smith has paid his dues (or membership fee, subscription, or whatever the PAID field holds), type the letter T now to change the entry to true.

NOTE

Notice that when your entry completely fills the field, you need not press ↵; dBASE will beep when you've filled the space provided and automatically move the cursor to the next field. (This assumes Set Confirm is Off.)

TIP

When entering data in a logical field, you can type T, t, Y, or y for true, or F, f, N, or n for false.

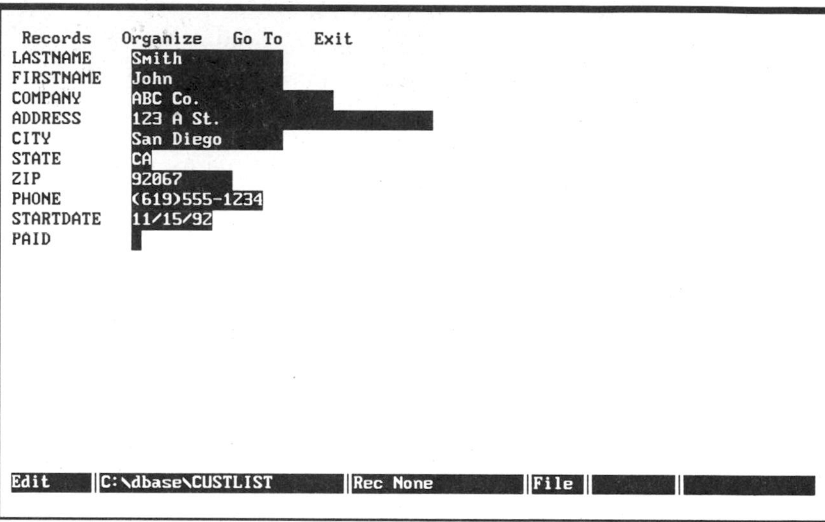

Figure 4.4: The first database record filled in on the screen

dBASE displays an edit screen for the next new record. At the bottom of the screen, EOF/1 means that you are at the end of the database file, and there is one record above this one.

BROWSING THROUGH THE DATABASE FILE

In the previous example, you entered new data on an edit screen. When using the edit screen, you can see only one database record at a time. You can also add and change data using the *browse screen*. On the browse screen, you can see several records, though usually not all the fields from each record.

To switch between the edit screen and the browse screen, you simply press the Data (F2) key. Do so now, and then press the ↑ key. You'll see part of the record that you just entered at the top of the database file, as shown in Figure 4.5.

You can scroll to the right to see the fields that are currently hidden by pressing the Tab or ↵ key. Each time you press Tab, the highlight moves one field to the right. To scroll all the way to the right (to the PAID field, which is not currently visible), you can either press the Tab key nine times or just press the End key. Figure 4.6 shows the browse screen with the highlight and cursor scrolled all the way to the right.

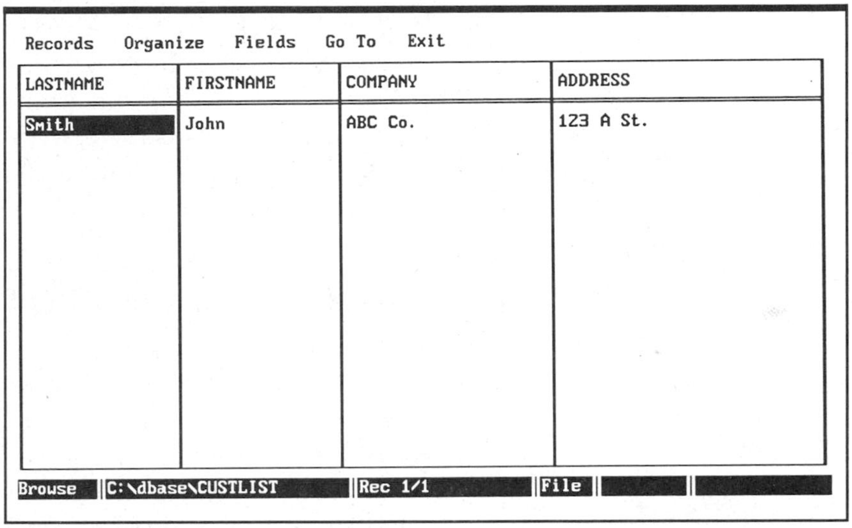

Records Organize Fields Go To Exit

LASTNAME	FIRSTNAME	COMPANY	ADDRESS
Smith	John	ABC Co.	123 A St.

Browse | C:\dbase\CUSTLIST | Rec 1/1 | File

Figure 4.5: The first database record, displayed on the browse screen

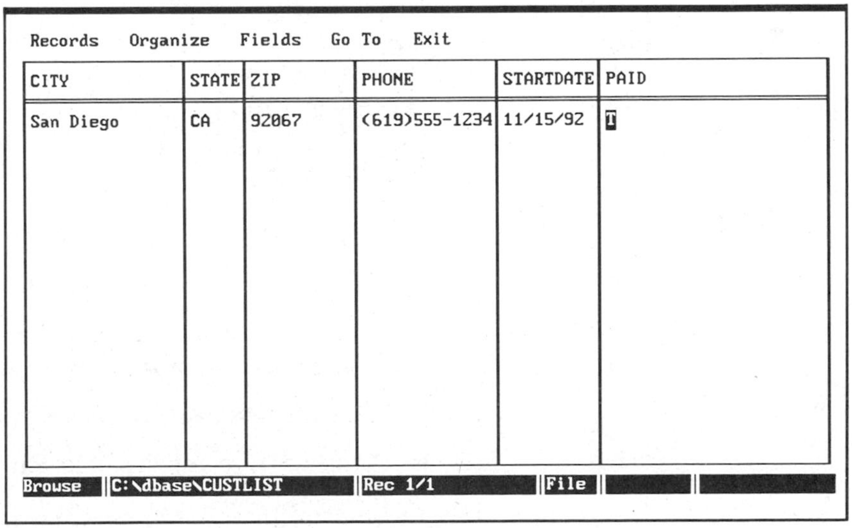

Records Organize Fields Go To Exit

CITY	STATE	ZIP	PHONE	STARTDATE	PAID
San Diego	CA	92067	(619)555-1234	11/15/92	T

Browse | C:\dbase\CUSTLIST | Rec 1/1 | File

Figure 4.6: Browse screen scrolled to the right

To scroll back to the left one column at a time, press the Shift-Tab key combination (hold down the Shift key while pressing the Tab key). To quickly scroll all the way back to the leftmost field, press the Home key.

If you are using the mouse, you can jump to a field simply by clicking on that field. You can move right or left one field by clicking on the rightmost and leftmost vertical borders of the browse screen. Similarly, you can scroll up and down by clicking on the top and bottom borders of the browse screen. (You will notice that the mouse pointer becomes an up or down arrow when it is located on the top and bottom border lines.)

ADDING NEW DATA IN BROWSE MODE

Suppose you want to add a new record while the current record is still displayed on the browse screen. This is simple enough: Just press the ↓ key to move down to the next row. Because there is currently no record there, dBASE will display a message box asking if you want to add new records. To add a record, select Yes.

Here is a sample name and address for another database record (but don't begin typing yet):

Annie Adams
345 C St.
Malibu, CA 92001
Tel: (714)555-0123
Start Date = 1/1/93
Paid Yet = No

Now, follow these steps to type the sample record, and you'll learn some new tricks along the way:

1. Make sure the highlight is in the LASTNAME field; then type the last name **Adams** and press ↵.
2. Type the first name **Annie** and press ↵.
3. Annie has no company affiliation, so press ↵ to leave the Company field blank.
4. Type the address **345 C St.** and press ↵.

5. Type the city **Malibu** and press ↵.
6. You can use the Ditto key (Shift-F8) to copy the State (CA) from the previous record to the current one. Press Shift-F8 now. You'll see CA entered as the state in the current record. Press ↵.
7. Type the zip code **92001** and press ↵.
8. Type the phone number **(714)555-0123**.
9. To enter the date January 1, 1991, you can type either **1/1/93** or **010193**; dBASE will automatically convert either entry to 01/01/93. Then press ↵.
10. When the cursor gets to the PAID field, type **F** to indicate "not paid."

At this point you've filled in the entire second record. Press ↑ twice and End to see the six rightmost fields, shown in Figure 4.7.

Records Organize Fields Go To Exit

CITY	STATE	ZIP	PHONE	STARTDATE	PAID
San Diego	CA	92067	(619)555-1234	11/15/92	T
Malibu	CA	92001	(714)555-0123	01/01/93	F

Browse | C:\dbase\CUSTLIST | Rec 1/2 | File

Figure 4.7: Part of the new record as seen on the browse screen

SAVING NEW RECORDS

You can add as many records as you want, using either the edit screen or the browse screen or by switching back and forth between them with the Data (F2) key. But for now, let's save the two new records and return to the Control Center.

From either the edit or the browse screen, choose Exit ► Exit.

The two new records are saved in the database file, and you are back at the Control Center.

VIEWING DATA

To view the contents of a database, highlight the database file names in the Data panel, and then press or click Data (F2). Do not use the pull down menus.

Let's return to the new records now and practice some editing techniques. To view the new data, use Data (F2) key exactly as before. That is, move the highlight to the name of the appropriate database file in the Data panel (CUSTLIST) and press the F2 key or click on the Data:F2 label. You'll be returned to the edit or browse screen, depending on which screen you were in when you saved the new data. Of course, you can press the Data key (F2) to switch from one screen to the other.

MAKING CHANGES

Suppose you want to change Annie Adams's address from 345 C St., Malibu, to 3456 Ocean St., Santa Monica. You can make changes whether you are at the edit screen or the browse screen. For this example, let's use the edit screen. Here are the steps to follow:

If you highlight a record in the browse screen and then press F2, that record will appear in the edit screen.

1. If the browse screen is showing, press F2 to display the edit screen.
2. If Annie Adams's record is not on the screen, press PgDn or PgUp until her data appears as in Figure 4.8.
3. To change the address, press ↓ three times to move the blinking cursor into the ADDRESS field, like this:

   345 C St.

4. Press → three times to move the cursor to the right of 345, like this:

   345_C St.

Don't forget that if your arrow, PgUp, PgDn, Ins, Del, and other keys share the numbers on the numeric keypad, these keys work only when NumLock is off.

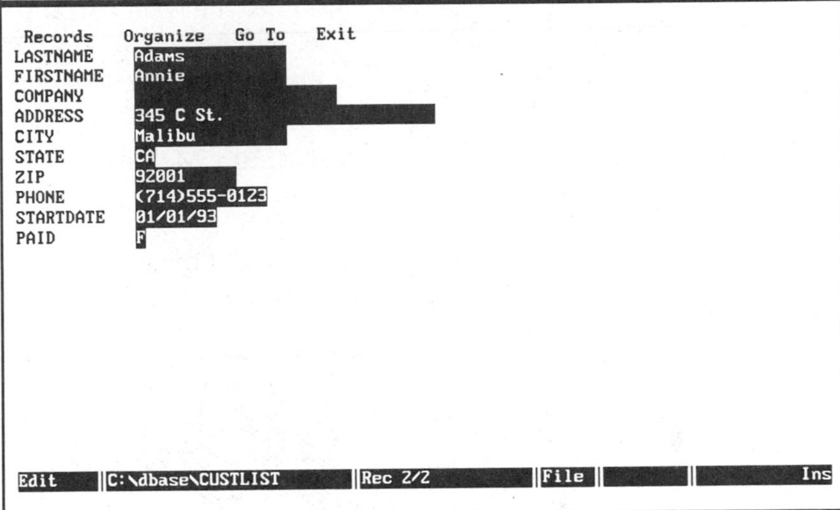

Figure 4.8: Annie Adams's record on the edit screen

Using the mouse, you can simply click on the space to the right of 345 in the ADDRESS field.

5. Look at the lower-right corner of your screen to see if the indicator "Ins" appears (as it does in Figure 4.8). If it does not, press the Ins (Insert) key until the "Ins" indicator appears. Now you are in Insert mode.
6. Type **6 Ocean**, so the entry looks like this:

   3456 Ocean_C St.

   Notice that the new text you typed was *inserted* into the existing text. That's because the Insert mode (controlled by the Ins key) is currently on.

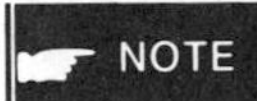

The Ins (Insert) key acts as a *toggle* for the Insert and Overwrite modes. Each time you press the key, dBASE switches from the current mode to the other mode.

7. Now press the Del (Delete) key twice to get rid of the unnecessary characters, so the address looks like this:

   3456 Ocean St.

8. To change the city, press ↵ to move down to the CITY field. You'll see the cursor at the start of the name *Malibu,* like this:

   Malibu

9. This time, you want to completely type over the existing city name, so press the Ins key once to turn off Insert mode. The Ins indicator at the bottom-right corner of the screen will disappear.
10. Type **Santa Monica**, which will completely overwrite Malibu.

Now you've changed the address and city for Annie's record. Your screen should look like Figure 4.9.

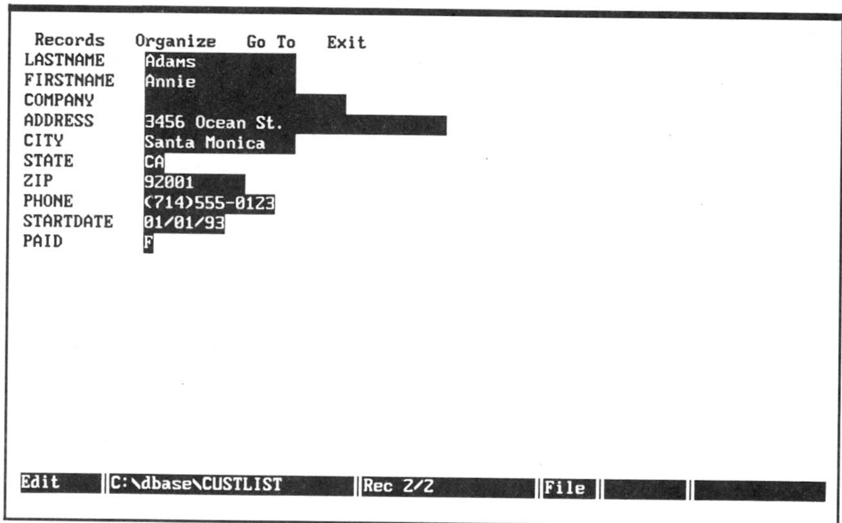

Figure 4.9: Annie Adams's record with the address and city changed

The changes you've made will not be saved until you either scroll to a new record using the PgUp or PgDn key or exit from the edit or browse screen. For now, save these changes in Annie's record by pressing PgUp to move up a record. When you do, the record for John Smith should appear on the edit screen.

You can use the same basic editing techniques you just learned, such as pressing the arrow keys to move the cursor, pressing Del (Delete) to delete a character, and pressing the Ins (Insert) key to switch between Insert and Overwrite modes, at almost any time while you are using dBASE IV. They work the same whether you are designing a database structure, creating forms, or creating report formats—and in many other situations as well. Table 4.1 lists these editing keys.

Table 4.1: Navigation and Editing Keys for the Browse and Edit Screens

Key	Effect
↓	Moves cursor down
↑	Moves cursor up
→	Moves cursor right one character
←	Moves cursor left one character
↵	Completes entry and moves to next field
PgDn	Moves down one record on edit screen or one screenful on browse screen
PgUp	Moves up one record on edit screen or one screenful on browse screen
Del	Deletes character over cursor
Backspace	Moves left one character, erasing along the way
Shift-F8	(Ditto) Carries data from same field in previous record to current record
Ctrl-Y	Deletes all characters to right of cursor
Ins	Switches between Insert and Overwrite modes
Home	Moves to first field on browse screen or first character in current field on edit screen
End	Moves to last field on browse screen or end of current field on edit screen
Tab	Moves to next field
Shift-Tab	Moves to previous field
Escape	Leaves current record without saving changes
F1	Displays help

Table 4.1: Navigation and Editing Keys for the Browse and Edit Screens (continued)

Key	Effect
F2	Toggles between browse and edit screens
F3	Same as Shift-Tab
F4	Same as Tab
F10	Accesses pull-down menus (the Exit option saves your work and returns you to Control Center)

If you are using the mouse, you can click on any field to relocate the highlight to that field. In the browse screen, you can click on the right or left borders to move the cursor one field to the left or right, or you can click on the top and bottom borders to move one field up or down. Of course, you can also use the mouse to access menu options by clicking on the menu name and the option.

UNDOING AN EDIT

Once in a while, you'll probably make the common mistake of changing or erasing a field's contents without paying enough attention to what you are doing. Suddenly, you realize that you've changed the wrong information and do not remember what the old information was. Fortunately, you can easily "undo" accidental changes to a record. To demonstrate, we'll change one field and delete the contents of another, and then reverse those changes:

NOTE

Selecting Undo Change to Record undoes *all* of the changes you've made in the current record, not just the last field you've changed. If you have not made any changes in the record currently on the screen, the Undo Change to Record option is shaded when you call up the Records menu, indicating that there are no changes to undo.

1. Press ↓ twice (or as many times as necessary) to move the cursor to the COMPANY field, or click on that field.
2. Type **HA HA HO HO** (or any other nonsense that suits your fancy).
3. Press ↵.
4. Press Ctrl-Y (hold down the Ctrl key and press Y) to erase everything to the right of the cursor (thereby emptying the ADDRESS field).

Suppose now you realize that you are making a mess of things. *Don't* move to another record. (Remember, your changes are not saved until you scroll to a new record or leave the edit or browse screen.) Instead, follow this step to undo your changes.

- Choose Records ► Undo Change to Record

You'll see John Smith's record back on the screen, exactly as it was before you made your erroneous changes.

USING THE STATUS BAR

Whether you are at the browse or edit screen, dBASE displays a highlighted *status bar* at the bottom of the screen to help you with your work. Figure 4.10 shows the location of the following information in the status bar:

- Type of screen in use (such as edit screen or browse screen).
- Location and name of the database file currently in use (C:\dbase\CUSTLIST in this example).
- Current record in the database and total number of records. For example, the message "Rec 1/2" means that you are currently viewing record number 1 in a database containing two records.
- Source of the data currently on the screen (a database file in this example).
- Settings of various toggle keys. For example, if "Num" appears, the NumLock key is on. If "Caps" appears, the CapsLock key is on. If "Ins" appears, you are in Insert mode, rather than Overwrite mode. Pressing the NumLock, CapsLock, or Ins key turns these settings (and the appropriate indicators) on and off.

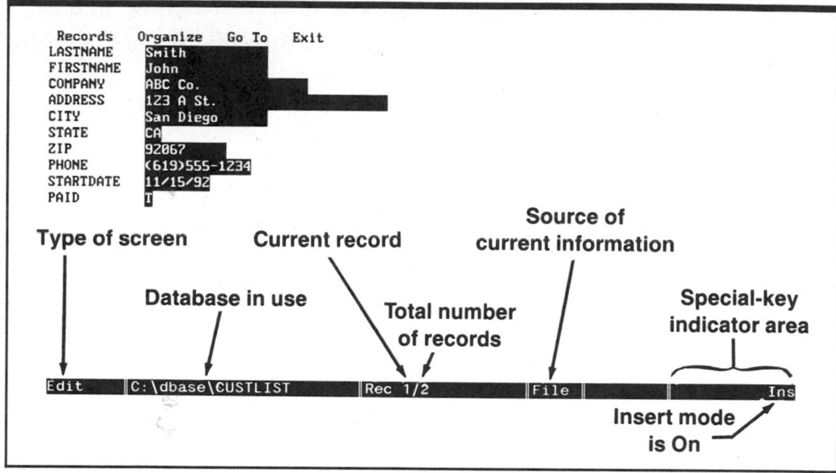

Figure 4.10: The status bar

ADDING MORE RECORDS

Now that you are armed with some basic editing techniques, go ahead and enter a few more sample records now (you'll use these in future exercises). To begin entering new records, follow this step:

- Choose Records ► Add New Records

Note that originally you did not select Add New Records to add new records to the database. You did not need to do so because the database was empty; dBASE assumed you'd be adding new data. Once you have added data to a database, however, you can add new records either by choosing Records ► Add New Records or by pressing PgDn (from the edit screen) or ↓ (from the browse screen) until you see the prompt box asking, "Add new records?" Select Yes.

Now type the sample data shown in Figure 4.11. You can use either browse or edit mode to enter these new records. Use the editing keys listed in Table 4.1 as necessary to help you position the cursor and make changes.

LastName	FirstName	Company	Address	City	State	Zip	Phone	StartDate	Paid
Watson	Wilbur	HiTech Co.	P.O. Box 987	New York	NY	12345	(212)555-9988	11/15/92	T
Mahoney	Mary		211 Seahawk St.	Seattle	WA	88977	(206)555-8673	12/01/92	T
Newell	John	LoTech Co.	734 Rainbow Dr.	Butte	MT	54321	(303)555-6739	12/15/92	T
Beach	Sandy	American Widget	11 Elm St.	Portland	OR	76543	(717)555-0898	12/15/92	T
Kenney	Ralph		1101 Rainbow Ct.	Los Angeles	CA	96607	(213)555-9988	12/30/92	F
Schumack	Susita	SMS Software	47 Broad St.	Philadelphia	PA	45543	(202)555-9720	12/30/92	T
Smith	Anita	Zeerocks, Inc.	2001 Engine Dr.	Hideaway	CA	92220	(415)555-9854	01/01/93	T

Figure 4.11: New records to add to the CUSTLIST database

SAVING YOUR WORK

After you have finished entering the records shown in Figure 4.11, save your work and return to the Control Center, using this step:

- Choose Exit ► Exit.

You'll be returned to the Control Center, where once again you'll see the CUSTLIST database name in the Data panel.

GETTING SOME PRACTICE

You might also want to try Session 3 from the on-screen tutorial (described at the end of Chapter 2) to review techniques from Chapters 3 and 4.

If you would like to make some more changes in the CUSTLIST database, use the same techniques discussed previously to return to the data. That is, make sure that the name CUSTLIST is highlighted in the Data panel; then click Data (F2).

You may want to practice with some of the editing keys described in Table 4.1 while the data is on the screen. (Remember that you can undo the changes made to a record by choosing Records ► Undo Change to Record.)

When you have finished experimenting, choose Exit ► Exit pull-down menu once again to return to the Control Center. Remember to exit dBASE before turning off your computer.

In Chapter 11 you'll learn more advanced editing techniques, including techniques for deleting records. Already, though, you've accomplished quite a bit. You know how to create a database, add records to it, view those records through the browse and edit screens, and make changes as needed.

HOW MANY RECORDS CAN dBASE IV HOLD?

So far, you've put nine records into the sample database. However, dBASE IV can handle many more. In fact, dBASE can handle approximately a billion (that's 1,000,000,000) records, or 2,000,000,000 characters, whichever comes first.

The CUSTLIST database contains 129 characters per record (the sum of the field widths). Hence, you could have about 15.5 million records in your CUSTLIST database, which should be adequate: After all, if it took you one minute to type each record, you would need about 29 years of nonstop typing to enter 15.5 million records!

CHAPTER

5

Sorting the Database

Fast Track

TYPICALLY, YOU ENTER INFORMATION INTO A DATAbase as it becomes available to you. Very often, you need to organize, or *sort*, that information into a more useful order, such as alphabetical order by name, or zip code order for bulk mailing. This chapter discusses techniques that you can use to sort your databases into any order you wish.

dBASE IV offers two ways to sort database files. Generally the fastest and most efficient method is *indexing*. A second, slower, and less efficient way to sort is by making a sorted copy of a database file. This chapter discusses both methods, focusing primarily on the preferred index method.

Once again, if you exited dBASE in the previous chapter, be sure to get it up and running on your computer again. If the LEARN catalog does not appear in the Control Center automatically, use the techniques discussed previously to access the LEARN catalog.

SORTING A DATABASE THROUGH AN INDEX

Sorting a database by index is an easy process, and can be accomplished using the Organize pull-down menu at the browse or edit screens (which you learned about in the previous chapter), or the database design screen which you used to initially create the CUSTLIST database in Chapter 3.

Let's take a moment to look at the general steps for creating a sort order (via an index), and then we'll try it out a little later. Here are the general steps:

- Go to the edit or browse screen (F2) or the database design screen (Shift-F2).
- Select Organize ► Create New Index.
- Select Name of Index, type in an index name (up to eight characters, no spaces or punctuation), and press ↵.
- Select Index Expression and type in an index expression, or build one using the Expression Builder (Shift-F1), as described in a moment.

- Select Order of Index, and choose between Ascending order (smallest-to-largest) or Descending order (largest-to-smallest) by pressing the space bar, or clicking the mouse.
- Press or click Ctrl-End when done.

You may have noticed that a couple of other options—"FOR clause" and "Order of index"—are listed on the menu for creating an index. You need not be concerned with those just yet; we'll stick with the basics for now. In the sections that follow, we'll create a couple of indexes to sort the CUSTLIST database you created in the preceding chapters.

SORTING BY LAST NAME

Suppose you want to put the customer names and addresses from the CUSTLIST database into ascending alphabetical order (A-Z) by last name. To do so, follow these steps:

1. In the Control Center's Data panel, move the highlight to CUSTLIST.
2. Press or click Data (F2) to view its contents.
3. If the edit screen appears (a single record only), press Data (F2) to switch to the browse screen.
4. Pull down the Organize menu, as in Figure 5.1.
5. Select Create New Index.
6. Select Name of Index.
7. You can assign any file name to the index you wish; for this example, type in LASTNAME and press ↵.
8. Select Index Expression.

Remember that even when an option is highlighted on a menu, you must still press ↵ to select it.

The Index Expression is the name of the field (or fields, as described later) that you want to sort by. You can either type in the field name or select it using the Expression Builder. For this exercise, we'll use the Expression Builder.

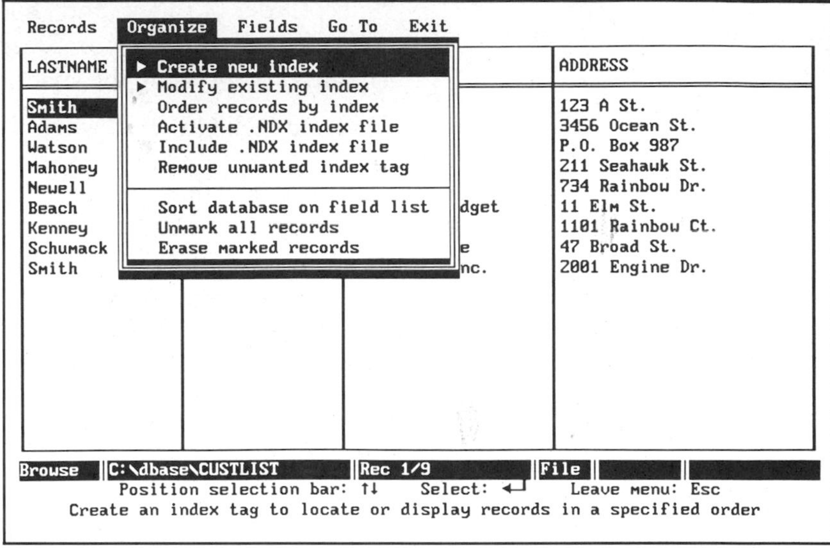

Figure 5.1: The Organize menu on the browse screen

You'll learn about the Operator and Function columns in the Expression Builder a little later; for now we'll just use the Fieldname column.

9. Press or click Shift-F1 to open the Expression Builder.
10. Highlight LASTNAME in the list of fields and press ↵, or double-click on LASTNAME.
11. To complete your entry, press ↵.
12. Select Order of Index and press the space bar or click the mouse until ASCENDING appears.
13. Select Display First Duplicate Key Only, and press the space bar or click the mouse until NO appears.

At this point, your screen should look like Figure 5.2. You can press or click Ctrl-End to complete your index definition and return to the browse screen. (If you hear a beep and see the message "Index TAG already exists: LASTNAME," don't worry about it; just select Overwrite.)

If you look at your browse screen now, you'll see that your customers are now listed in alphabetical order by last name, as shown in Figure 5.3.

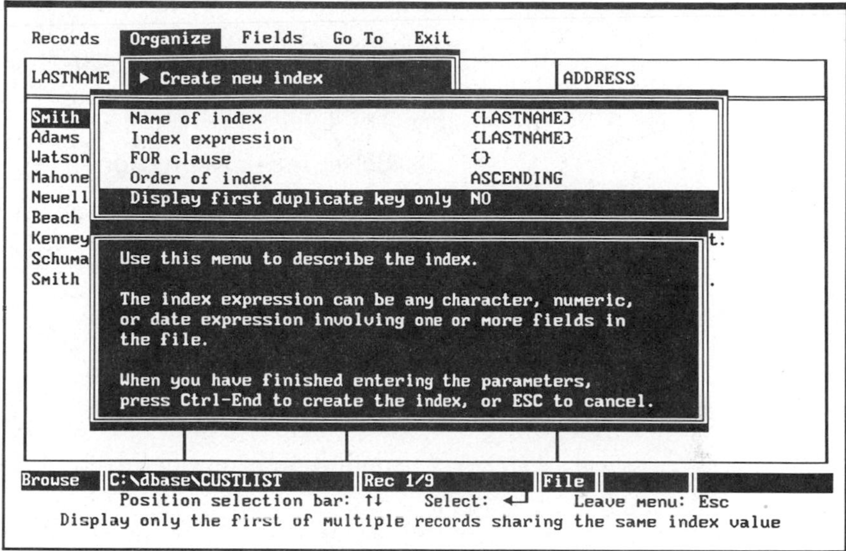

Figure 5.2: Index defined for the LASTNAME field

Records Organize Fields Go To Exit

LASTNAME	FIRSTNAME	COMPANY	ADDRESS
Adams	Annie		3456 Ocean St.
Beach	Sandy	American Widget	11 Elm St.
Kenney	Ralph		1101 Rainbow Ct.
Mahoney	Mary		211 Seahawk St.
Newell	John	LoTech Co.	734 Rainbow Dr.
Schumack	Susita	SMS Software	47 Broad St.
Smith	John	ABC Co.	123 A St.
Smith	Anita	Zeerocks, Inc.	2001 Engine Dr.
Watson	Wilbur	HiTech Co.	P.O. Box 987

Browse C:\dbase\CUSTLIST Rec 2/9 File

Figure 5.3: Records sorted into alphabetical order by last name

SORTING RECORDS BY ZIP CODE

Now let's suppose that you want to put your customer list into zip code order, perhaps for bulk mailing. To do so, you just need to create a second index by following the steps below:

1. Select Organize ► Create New Index ► Name of Index.
2. We'll name this index ZIP, so type ZIP and press ↵.
3. Select Index Expression.
4. Press or click Shift-F1 to access the Expression Builder.
5. Move the highlight to the ZIP field name and press ↵, or double-click on Zip.
6. Press ↵ to complete the selection.
7. The Order of Index and Display First... options should still be set at ASCENDING and NO respectively, so your index definition is now complete. Press or click Ctrl-End.

Again, if you hear a beep and see the "Index Tag already exists..." message, just select Overwrite to proceed. Your records will now be displayed in ascending zip code order (smallest to largest), as you can see by pressing the End key and looking at the ZIP field. Figure 5.4 also shows the records displayed in zip code order.

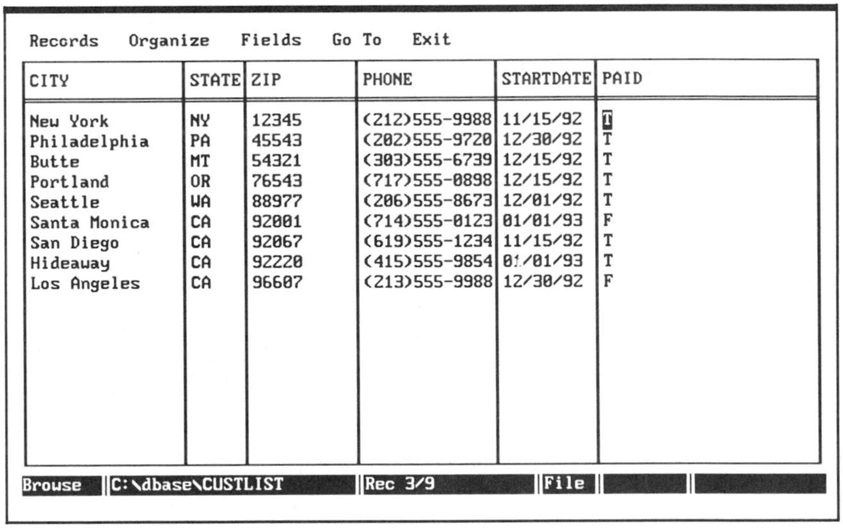

Records   Organize   Fields   Go To   Exit

CITY	STATE	ZIP	PHONE	STARTDATE	PAID
New York	NY	12345	(212)555-9988	11/15/92	T
Philadelphia	PA	45543	(202)555-9720	12/30/92	T
Butte	MT	54321	(303)555-6739	12/15/92	T
Portland	OR	76543	(717)555-0898	12/15/92	T
Seattle	WA	88977	(206)555-8673	12/01/92	T
Santa Monica	CA	92001	(714)555-0123	01/01/93	F
San Diego	CA	92067	(619)555-1234	11/15/92	T
Hideaway	CA	92220	(415)555-9854	01/01/93	T
Los Angeles	CA	96607	(213)555-9988	12/30/92	F

Browse | C:\dbase\CUSTLIST | Rec 3/9 | File

Figure 5.4: Records sorted into zip code order

ACTIVATING AN INDEX

Now you have created two indexes, one for displaying names in alphabetical order, the other for displaying them in zip code order. It only took dBASE IV a few seconds to create each one, mainly because this sample database is very small. Believe me, if there were hundreds, or thousands, of records in the CUSTLIST database, the time required to create each index would have been much longer.

However, one of the beauties of indexes is that once you create them, you need never re-create them in the future. Instead, you just select whichever index you want to use to instantly view your database records in a new sort order. The general steps for activating an existing index are quite simple, and they work whether you are at the browse screen, edit screen, or database design screen. Here are the general steps:

- Select Organize ► Order Records by Index.
- Select the name of the index you want to use or Natural Order if you want to view your records in their original (unsorted) order.

To try out these general steps now, let's first view the records in the CUSTLIST database in their original, unsorted order. Assuming that the database still appears on your browse screen, follow these steps:

1. Move the cursor back to the leftmost field.
2. Select Organize ► Order Records by Index ► Natural Order.

The records are now back to their original unsorted order. Now let's activate the LASTNAME index to quickly put them back into alphabetical order by last name. Follow the same basic steps, as listed below:

1. Select Organize ► Order Records by Index.
2. Select LASTNAME.

Instantly, the records are redisplayed in alphabetical order by name. (Admittedly, this may not be terribly impressive with this small database, but then again, your "real" databases will probably contain hundreds or thousands of records, and dBASE will reorganize those nearly as quickly as it reorganized the records in this small database.)

The real beauty of it all is that dBASE even takes care of the indexes for you at all times. That is, even if you add, change, or delete database records, dBASE will automatically keep all indexes up to date.

PERFORMING SORTS WITHIN SORTS

Sometimes sorting a database on a single field is not sufficient. For example, if you look back at Figure 5.3, you'll notice that John Smith is listed before Anita Smith. In the small CUSTLIST database, this does not create a problem, but if the database contained several hundred Smiths, you'd be hard pressed to find John Smith's records if all the Smiths were in random first-name order.

The ideal way to sort peoples' names is not simply by last name, but by first name within last name, as the telephone book does:

```
Smith   Anita
Smith   Barbara
Smith   Carla
Smith   Charles
Smith   John
Smith   Karen
```

To arrange a group of index cards in such an order, you might first sort all the cards into last-name order and then sort them into first-name order within identical last names—a sort within a sort. To sort database records into this kind of an order, you use an *index expression* that lists the fields to sort on, with the fields listed in priority order, with a plus sign between each field name.

For example, to sort records into alphabctical order by LASTNAME, with names alphabetized by FIRSTNAME within identical last names, you would use the index expression LASTNAME + FIRSTNAME. If this database included a field for middle initial, named MI, you could use the index expression LASTNAME + FIRSTNAME + MI to sort the database into last-name order, with names alphabetized by first-name and then middle initial within identical last names (for example, Smith, John A. would come before Smith, John B.).

In the next section, you'll learn how to modify an existing index, and in the process will see how to sort the CUSTLIST database into LASTNAME and FIRSTNAME order.

MODIFYING AN INDEX

The Organize menu, which you've already used to create and activate indexes, also lets you modify an existing index. Let's go ahead and modify the LASTNAME index now so that it displays customer names sorted by LASTNAME and by FIRSTNAME within common last names. Here are the steps:

1. Assuming you are still at the browse screen, select Organize ► Modify Existing Index.
2. Select LASTNAME as the index to modify.
3. Select Index Expression.
4. At this point, you *could* type + **FIRSTNAME** to change the index expression to LASTNAME + FIRSTNAME. However, we'll use the optional *Expression Builder* once again. Press or click Shift-F1 to call up the Expression Builder menu.
5. Highlight the + operator and press ↵, or double-click on the operator.
6. Use Shift-F1 again to bring back the Expression Builder.
7. Highlight FIRSTNAME and press ↵, or double-click on FIRSTNAME. The index expression now reads LASTNAME + FIRSTNAME as shown in Figure 5.5. Press ↵ to complete thc change.

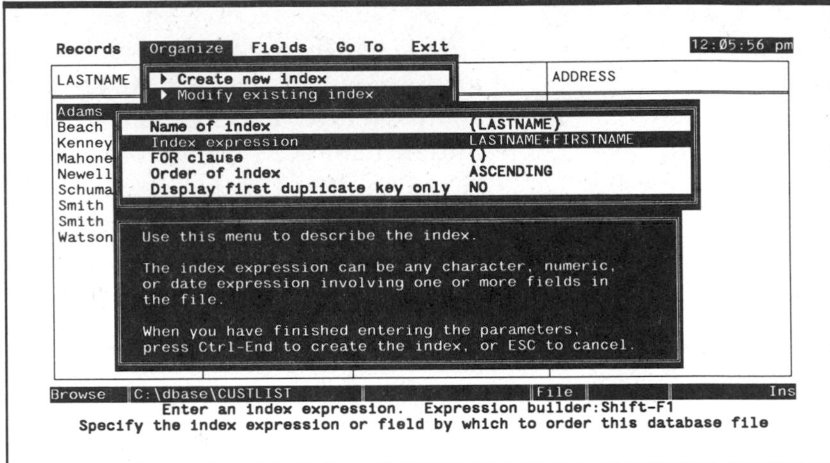

Figure 5.5: Modified index expression for the LASTNAME index

8. Press or click Ctrl-End to indicate that you've finished modifying the index.

The database appears in the new sort order, as in Figure 5.6. (Press PgUp and Home to scroll to the top of the browse screen, if necessary.) As you can see, Anita Smith is now properly listed before John Smith.

Records Organize Fields Go To Exit

LASTNAME	FIRSTNAME	COMPANY	ADDRESS
Adams	Annie		3456 Ocean St.
Beach	Sandy	American Widget	11 Elm St.
Kenney	Ralph		1101 Rainbow Ct.
Mahoney	Mary		211 Seahawk St.
Newell	John	LoTech Co.	734 Rainbow Dr.
Schumack	Susita	SMS Software	47 Broad St.
Smith	Anita	Zeerocks, Inc.	2001 Engine Dr.
Smith	John	ABC Co.	123 A St.
Watson	Wilbur	HiTech Co.	P.O. Box 987

Browse C:\dbase\CUSTLIST Rec 2/9 File

Figure 5.6: CUSTLIST database sorted by last and first names

EDITING WHEN AN INDEX IS ACTIVE

You may be wondering what would happen if dBASE were displaying records in sorted order on the browse screen and you changed somebody's last name. If you changed the name Adams to Zastrow, for example, when would dBASE re-sort the database to put Zastrow in its proper alphabetical position?

As you may recall from the previous chapter, whenever you change the contents of a database record, the change is not made permanent until you move to another record. (As you've seen, you can undo changes to a record as long as the cursor is still on that record.)

Re-sorting is based on a similar principle. dBASE does not re-sort until you move to a new record. To observe this for yourself, follow these steps:

1. Move the highlight to the last name Adams.
2. Type **Zastrow** in place of Adams and press ↵. The records are not in alphabetical order anymore, because Zastrow is still at the top. But remember: An edit is not complete until you move the highlight to a new record.
3. Press PgDn (or click on the bottom border) to move down.
4. Press PgUp (or click on the top border) to scroll back to the top of the database.

As you can see on your screen and in Figure 5.7, dBASE immediately re-sorted the display and Sandy Beach is now the top record.

Now scroll to the bottom of the browse screen and change Zastrow back to Adams. When you complete the edit (by pressing ↑ or clicking on a previous record), Annie Adams returns to her previous place in alphabetical order.

Suppose now that you change a zip code. How will this affect the index for the ZIP field? At the moment, the LASTNAME index controls the sort order of the records, so if you change a zip code, the browse screen will not be re-sorted. However, dBASE hasn't forgotten the ZIP index. dBASE will automatically update the ZIP index behind the scenes. When you later switch to the ZIP index to display

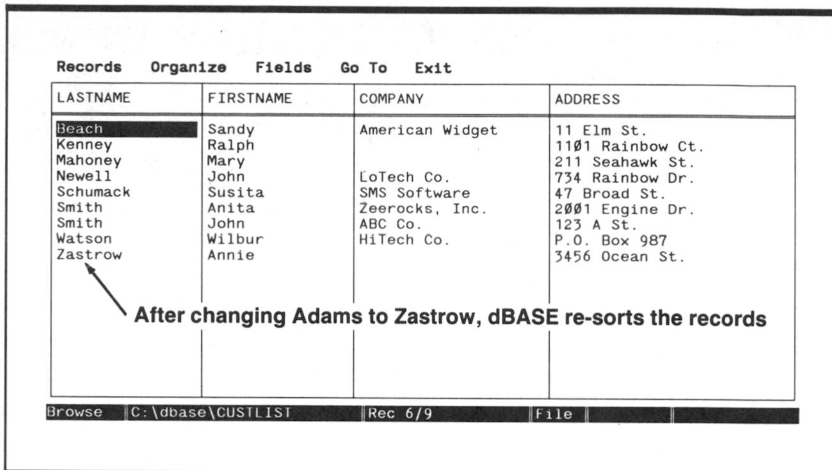

Records Organize Fields Go To Exit

LASTNAME	FIRSTNAME	COMPANY	ADDRESS
Beach	Sandy	American Widget	11 Elm St.
Kenney	Ralph		1101 Rainbow Ct.
Mahoney	Mary		211 Seahawk St.
Newell	John	LoTech Co.	734 Rainbow Dr.
Schumack	Susita	SMS Software	47 Broad St.
Smith	Anita	Zeerocks, Inc.	2001 Engine Dr.
Smith	John	ABC Co.	123 A St.
Watson	Wilbur	HiTech Co.	P.O. Box 987
Zastrow	Annie		3456 Ocean St.

Figure 5.7: dBASE re-sorted the browse screen after changing Adams to Zastrow

records in zip code order, the records will be displayed in correct zip code order.

Note that we've been using the browse screen in these examples because it allows you to see the effects of the re-sorting immediately. If you switch to the edit screen (by pressing F2), you'll only see one record at a time. But as you scroll up and down through records with the PgUp and PgDn keys, records will appear in the sort order determined by the current index.

WHAT IS AN INDEX?

Now that you've had some experience creating, activating, and modifying indexes, you might be wondering just what's happening "behind the scenes." Well, first of all, a dBASE index is much like the index at the back of this (or any other) book. In a book, the index lists topics in alphabetical order, followed by page numbers. So when you want to look up a topic, you flip through the index, find the appropriate page number, then turn to that page. This, obviously, is much faster than simply reading the book cover-to-cover until you happen upon the topic you are looking for.

A dBASE index works in a similar fashion. When you create an index, dBASE creates a sort of "mini database" that contains only the field (or fields) that you specified in the index expression, followed by the record number of the record. For example, you might envision the contents of the LASTNAME index as follows:

LASTNAME + FIRSTNAME		**Record Number**
Adams	Annie	2
Beach	Sandy	6
Kenney	Ralph	7
Mahoney	Mary	4
Newell	John	5
Schumack	Susita	8
Smith	Anita	9
Smith	John	1
Watson	Wilbur	3

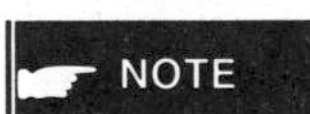

Actually, the "book index" analogy is a simplification—for those of you who are programmers, the index actually has a B + tree structure.

As you can see, the first record you entered into the database, John Smith, is in its proper alphabetical position in the index. The number 1 refers to the fact that John Smith is the first record in the database file.

When you activate an index, dBASE displays records in the order specified in the index. (As you'll learn in the next chapter, you can also use an index to locate information in the database very quickly.)

Even though you may create and activate indexes often, you will never actually see the contents of an index file directly. There is no need to, because once you create or activate an index, dBASE takes care of it for you automatically.

All the indexes that you create for a database file are stored in a file called the *production index file,* which has the same name as your database, but with the extension .MDX. (The .MDX is an abbreviation for "multiple index".) For example, the indexes that you created for your CUSTLIST database are stored in the production index file named CUSTLIST.MDX.

When you open your CUSTLIST database, dBASE automatically opens the CUSTLIST.MDX index file as well. All the indexes within the CUSTLIST.MDX index file are automatically updated as you add, change, or delete data. Whenever you activate one of the indexes in the CUSTLIST.MDX index file, that index then determines the sort order for displaying records.

The name you assign to an index, such as LASTNAME or ZIP in the previous examples, is called the index's *tag*. That is, the indexes that you created for the CUSTLIST.DBF database are stored in a file named CUSTLIST.MDX. CUSTLIST.MDX, in turn, contains two indexes, one tagged (named) LASTNAME, which is based on the expression LASTNAME + FIRSTNAME, and a second index tagged (named) ZIP, which is based on the ZIP field.

DELETING AN INDEX TAG

If for whatever reason you decide to get rid of an index, you can easily remove it from the multiple index file. Once again, you use the familiar Organize pull-down menu, which is available at the browse and edit screens as well as the database design screen. Here are the general steps for future reference (you need not delete an index just now):

- If you are at the Control Center, move the highlight to the database file and press or click Data (F2) to access the edit or browse screen.
- Select Organize ► Remove Unwanted Index Tag.
- Move the highlighter to the name of the index you want to remove.
- Press ↵, or click the mouse.

That's all there is to it. To leave the Organize menu, simply press the Escape key or click outside the menu.

LIMITATIONS ON INDEXES

There are a few limitations that you need to keep in mind when creating or using indexes, as summarized below:

- The maximum number of index tags that you can assign to a single database file is 47.
- You cannot use a Memo field in an index expression, nor can you use a Logical field unless you convert its data type (as described in Chapter 12).
- When combining fields in an index expression, such as LASTNAME + FIRSTNAME, all fields must be the Character data type; otherwise you'll simply receive the error message "Data type mismatch." If you do need to combine multiple data types in a single index expression, you must convert their data types (you'll learn how to do so in Chapter 12).

MANAGING INDEXES FROM THE DATABASE DESIGN SCREEN

As mentioned, you can also access the Organize pull-down menu in the database design screen. The Organize pull-down menu is available at that screen simply for convenience—it does not matter whether you use the Organize pull-down menus from the edit, browse, or database design screen.

The database design screen, however, does offer one alternative technique for creating an index. You can create an index of any single field simply by changing the N in the Index column of that screen to a Y. Using the Index column on the database design screen, however, only lets you define an index for a single field; you cannot use this technique to index on multiple fields as in the LASTNAME-+FIRSTNAME example.

When you've finished defining or modifying indexes in the database design screen, press Ctrl-End, or choose Exit ► Save Changes and Exit until you've returned to the Control Center. Don't forget that in order to see records in the sort order defined by the index, you must also activate the index on one of the data screens (for example, either the browse or edit screen).

PREVENTING DUPLICATES

You may have noticed the option Display First Duplicate Key Only on the Organize ► Create New Index and Organize ► Modify Existing Index menus. Here, again, is more technical jargon that serves to confuse an otherwise simple feature.

An index *key* is the field (or fields) that defines the sort order. In the indexes we've created thus far, the ZIP field is the key for the ZIP index, and the combined LASTNAME + FIRSTNAME field is the key for the LASTNAME index.

Normally dBASE displays all the records in the database in sorted order, whether or not you've activated an index. However, if you set the Display First Duplicate Key Only option to Yes for an index, dBASE will display only the first record of records with duplicate keys.

For example, suppose you had a database with 1,000 names and addresses in it, and created an index based on the STATE field. Furthermore, let's say you also set the Display First Duplicate Key Only option to Yes while creating this index.

Later, when you activate the index, you would not see 1,000 records. Instead, you'd only see one record for each state in your database. That is, once dBASE displayed one record with CA in the STATE field, it would not display any others.

What is the practical significance of this? Well, suppose you purchased mailing lists from several companies, and combined them into one database. You are not sure if some people's names and addresses appear on more than one list, nor do you want to take the time to find out by searching each and every list. However, you do not want to send more than one item to each address when you do your own mailing from these combined lists either.

What's the solution? Well, you could create an index using the expression ZIP + CITY + ADDRESS that displays only the first duplicate key, then use that index to print mailing labels. This would help to ensure that only one label was printed for each unique address, city, and zip code combination.

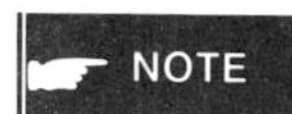

Upgrading from dBASE III PLUS to dBASE IV is described in Appendix D.

DBASE III PLUS COMPATIBILITY

You may have noticed two other options on the Organize pull-down menu—Activate .NDX index file and Include .NDX index file. These are included simply to provide some compatibility between dBASE IV and its predecessor, dBASE III PLUS.

While dBASE IV combines all indexes in a single file with the .MDX expression, earlier versions of dBASE stored each index in its own file, each with the extension .NDX. With this earlier method, it was very difficult to keep track of which index files belonged to which database, and also hard to make sure all of the indexes were updated properly.

The new method used in dBASE IV, where all indexes are stored in a single .MDX file, is much more convenient and reliable. Therefore, if you are upgrading from dBASE III PLUS to dBASE IV, you might want to re-create all your index files so that they will all be stored in a single .MDX file. (You can save a little time by copying your old dBASE III PLUS .NDX index files using the COPY INDEXES command described in Appendix D.)

One other alternative to re-creating or copying your old .NDX index files to the new dBASE IV format is to keep them in their original format, and use dBASE IV to manage them. The only advantage to this, of course, would be the "downward compatibility" it offers between dBASE IV and dBASE III PLUS. If that compatibility is important in your work, the two options on the Organize pull-down menu (summarized below) will let you keep your old .NDX index files up to date:

- **Activate .NDX index file**: Causes dBASE to search the current directory for a dBASE III PLUS index file with the name you select, then makes that the active (master) index file.
- **Include .NDX index file**: Opens a specified dBASE III PLUS .NDX file for automatic updating (as records are added, changed, or deleted), but does not make it the controlling (master) index.

Again, if you are not concerned about maintaining "old" dBASE III (and III PLUS) indexes, you need not be concerned about these two options.

SORTING A DATABASE FILE

As mentioned earlier in this chapter, dBASE IV offers *sorting* as an alternative to indexing a database file to display data in sorted order. However, sorting is generally slower and less efficient than indexing. Nonetheless, some people prefer sorting simply because it seems like a less abstract, more familiar means of putting information into an organized order.

When sorting, dBASE makes a copy of the original database with the records in sorted order. The records remain in their original order in the original database. To access the sorted records, you need to open the sorted copy of the database.

The menu option for sorting a database is on the Organize pull-down menu, like the options for indexing. To try out the sorting feature, follow the steps below to sort the CUSTLIST database record into descending order by the STARTDATE field:

ASCII, pronounced *askey*, is an acronym for the American Standard Code for Information Interchange.

1. If you are currently at the Control Center, move the highlighter to CUSTLIST and press or click Data (F2) until you get to the browse screen.
2. Select Organize ► Sort Database on Field List.
3. To sort the database into STARTDATE order, first press or click Shift-F1 to see a list of valid field names.
4. Highlight STARTDATE.
5. Press ↵ or click to select STARTDATE and then press ↵ to complete the entry.
6. The cursor jumps to the Type of Sort column, where you can select from four different sorting techniques, listed in Table 5.1. Note that the basic difference between the Dictionary technique and the ASCII technique is that ASCII considers uppercase letters "smaller than" lowercase letters and hence will place Zeppo before aardvark in an ascending sort.

   Both ASCII and dictionary sorts consider numeric characters to be "smaller than" alphabetic characters. Hence, if you sort a list of addresses in ascending order, all addresses

Table 5.1: Options for Sorting a Database

Order	Example Sort
Ascending ASCII (0..9, A..Z, a...)	123 999 Albert Zeppo van der Pool
Descending ASCII (z..a, Z..A, 9..0)	van der Pool Zeppo Albert 999 123
Ascending Dictionary (0..9, Aa..Zz)	123 999 Albert van der Pool Zeppo
Descending Dictionary (Zz..Aa, 9..0)	Zeppo van der Pool Albert 999 123

beginning with numbers (for example, 123 A St. to 999 Z St.) will be listed before addresses beginning with letters (for example, P.O. Box 2802). If you are sorting a Character field that does not use consistent capitalization, you'll want to use the dictionary technique. If you are sorting any other data type, you can use the ASCII technique instead.

NOTE

Indexes use the ASCII technique to display sort orders. Hence, an index of names places names that begin with lowercase letters (for example, van der Pool) at the bottom of the list (for example, beneath Zeppo). You can alter this order, however, as discussed in Chapter 12.

7. For this example, press the space bar or click until Descending ASCII appears; then press ↵. The highlight moves down to let you put more fields into the sort order. These are sort-within-a-sort fields, as discussed under indexing. For example, selecting LASTNAME as the first sort field and FIRSTNAME as the second sort field sorts the records in the same way that

the expression LASTNAME + FIRSTNAME sorted the index.

8. Rather than adding more fields to the sort list, press Ctrl-End to finish your work.
9. When dBASE presents the prompt "Enter name of sorted file:" you can enter any valid file name (eight characters maximum length, with no spaces or punctuation). In this example, type the file name **DATEORD** and press ↵.
10. When the screen asks for a description of the file, just press ↵ to leave it blank. (We'll be deleting this file before long, so there's no need to add a description.)

If you scroll to the STARTDATE field, you'll see that the records are *not* sorted into date order. Why not? Because the sorted records are in the database file named DATEORD; CUSTLIST has not been sorted.

Let's look at the DATEORD database file. Choose Exit ► Exit. When you return to the Control Center, you'll see a new database file in the Data panel, as shown in Figure 5.8.

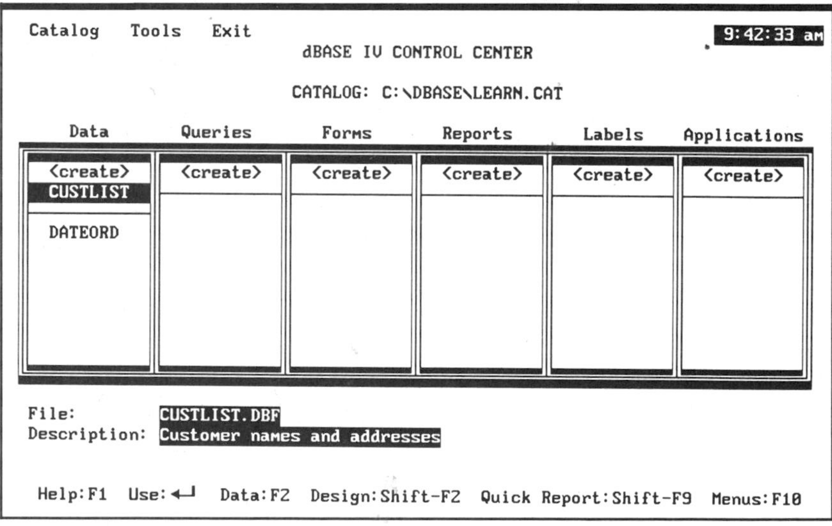

Figure 5.8: DATEORD database in the Control Center

To view the data in the DATEORD database, highlight DATEORD and then press or click Data (F2). When the browse screen appears, press End to scroll to the right. As you can see in Figure 5.9, the records are in descending date order (from January 1, 1993, to November 15, 1992).

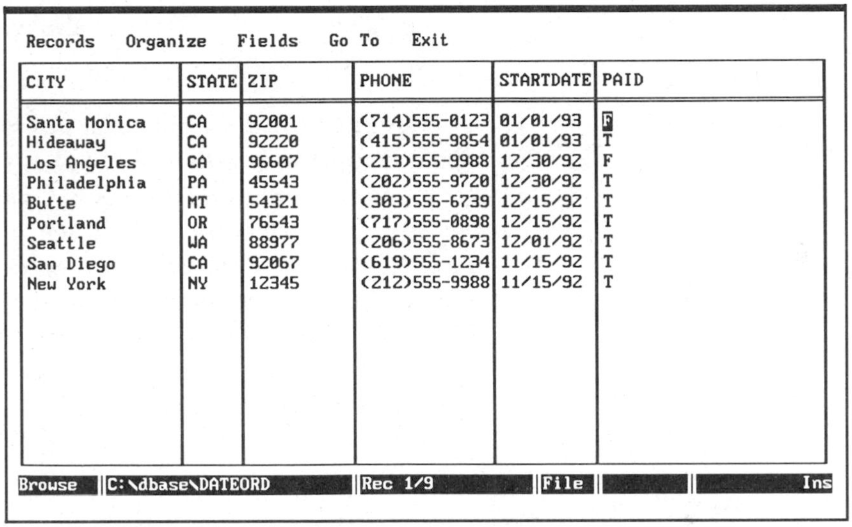

```
Records   Organize   Fields   Go To   Exit

CITY          STATE ZIP        PHONE          STARTDATE PAID
Santa Monica  CA    92001      (714)555-0123  01/01/93  F
Hideaway      CA    92220      (415)555-9854  01/01/93  T
Los Angeles   CA    96607      (213)555-9988  12/30/92  F
Philadelphia  PA    45543      (202)555-9720  12/30/92  T
Butte         MT    54321      (303)555-6739  12/15/92  T
Portland      OR    76543      (717)555-0898  12/15/92  T
Seattle       WA    88977      (206)555-8673  12/01/92  T
San Diego     CA    92067      (619)555-1234  11/15/92  T
New York      NY    12345      (212)555-9988  11/15/92  T

Browse  C:\dbase\DATEORD   Rec 1/9   File   Ins
```

Figure 5.9: Records sorted into descending order by date

When you are done viewing the data, choose Exit ► Exit to return to the Control Center.

As mentioned earlier, whenever you create an index, dBASE automatically manages it for you, updating it when you add, change, or delete information. This is *not* the case for sorted copies of files. Any changes you make to the CUSTLIST database have no effect on the DATEORD database (and vice versa).

Because of this, it is *not* a good idea to keep sorted copies of database files because you might accidentally use the wrong database file, and your work could quickly become confused. So let's get rid of the DATEORD database right now, using these steps:

NOTE

Providing Instruct is On (see Chapter 2), when you highlight a database file name and press ↵, a *prompt box* for making your next selection appears.

1. Make sure DATEORD is highlighted in the Control Center.
2. Press ↵ or click and select Close File.

3. Move the highlight to the DATEORD file name in the Data panel.
4. Choose Catalog ► Remove Highlighted File from Catalog.
5. The message "Are you sure you want to remove this file from the catalog?" appears. Select Yes.
6. The message "Do you also want to delete this file from the disk?" appears. Select Yes.

DATEORD does not exist anymore, so you need not worry about confusing it with CUSTLIST. (You'll learn more techniques for managing catalogs and files in Chapter 14.)

In the next chapter you'll learn how to *search* for particular records, such as those for all the customers who live in a particular state or all the customers who have not paid. But before we get to that, let's take a moment to recap some of the techniques you've learned so far, focusing particularly on those techniques that you will use consistently in the upcoming chapters.

A QUICK RECAP

One of the most confusing things for beginners is trying to learn new concepts (such as indexing), while at the same time simply trying to remember "what button to push when." Therefore, let's backtrack for a moment and take a look at some of the keys you've used consistently up to this point:

- **Data (F2)**: Always displays the *data* stored within a database. When data is already displayed, switches between the edit (one-record-at-a-time) screen and the browse screen.
- **Design (Shift-F2)**: Displays the underlying design, or structure of a file, for example, the name, type, width, and decimal of each field in the database. (The one exception—when you are at the browse or edit screen, where pressing Shift-F2 takes you to the Query Design screen.)

- **Menu (F10)**: Displays the pull-down menus regardless of whether you are at the Control Center, edit screen, browse screen, database design screen, or any of the other screens you'll encounter in upcoming chapters. The Exit option on the pull-down menus exits the current screen and goes back to the previous screen (unless you are already at the Control Center, in which case you can exit only to the dot prompt or back to DOS).

As Figure 5.10 points out, the bottom of the Control Center screen reminds you that these keys are available. If you are using a mouse, you can click on these keys' labels instead of pressing the keys. Unfortunately, not *all* screens offer this reminder, but then again you only need to remember that pressing Menu (F10) always displays your options.

In addition to the keys mentioned above, we've used a couple of "shortcut keystrokes," which you'll also find to behave consistently throughout future chapters:

- **Ctrl-End**: Saves any changes on the current screen and returns you to the previous screen (acts as a shortcut to choosing Exit ► Save Changes and Exit).

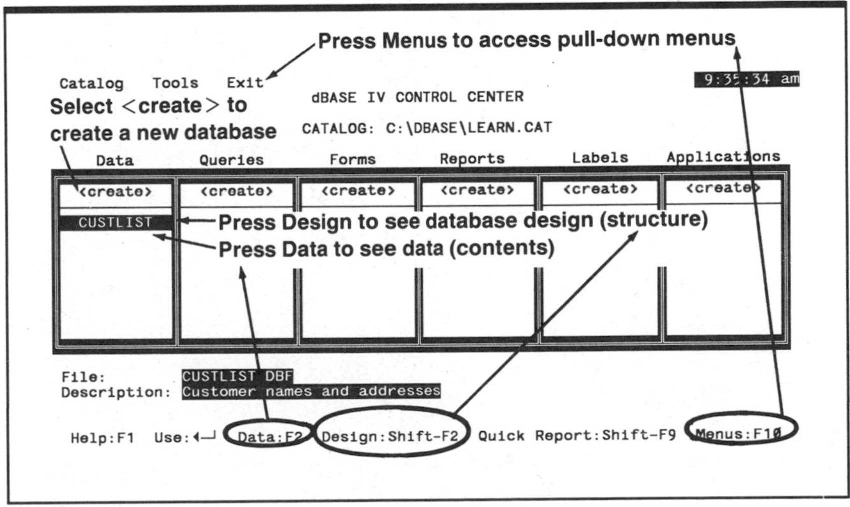

Figure 5.10: Summary of Control Center keystrokes

- **Escape**: Pressing Escape lets you leave a screen without saving any work. That is, it lets you "escape" from any place that you do not want to be (except for the dot prompt, as mentioned earlier).

If you can remember that these five keys are the ones you generally use to move from screen to screen, and if you first try to read the screen or pull down the menus for additional clues when you're feeling lost, you should find it pretty easy to move in and out of the various screens and capabilities that dBASE IV offers.

CHAPTER

6

Searching the Database

To position the browse highlight or edit screen 104
at a particular record, select an option from the Go To pull-down menu.

To locate a particular item of information in the database, 106
position the cursor or highlight to the field you want to search and select Go To ► Forward Search or Go To ► Backward Search.

To search an index quickly for specific information, 109
activate the appropriate index and select Go To ► Index Key Search.

To isolate records that meet some search criterion, 112
create a query by selecting <create> from the Queries panel on the Control Center.

To construct a query, 116
place *filter conditions* in the query screen and press or click Data (F2) to activate the query.

To refine your queries, 121
use the dBASE IV operators >, <, >=, <=, <>, #, $, like, and sounds like in your filter conditions.

To embed AND logic in a query, 128
place multiple filter conditions on the same row in the query.

To query for a range of values, 130
use the basic format >=<*low value*>,<=<*high value*> in the appropriate field of the query.

To embed OR logic in a query, 133
stagger filter conditions on two or more rows in the query.

To combine AND and OR logic in a query, **137**
you may need to repeat the AND condition in each row of the query.

To use a query to locate a record without filtering out any records, **141**
place the word Find beneath the file name in the file skeleton.

To sort the results of a query, **143**
highlight the field to sort on and select Fields ► Sort on This Field.

To use indexes in a query to speed query sorting, **148**
change the Include Indexes option on the Fields menu to Yes.

To select fields to display in the result of a query, **152**
use the Fields key (F5) or the mouse to add and remove fields from the view skeleton.

To save a query for future use, **158**
choose Exit ► Save Changes and Exit from the query design screen.

To activate a saved query, **161**
highlight its name in the Queries panel and press or click Data (F2).

To modify a saved query, **161**
highlight its name in the Queries panel and press or click Design (Shift-F2).

To deactivate a query and regain access to all database records, **162**
highlight a database name in the Data panel and press or click Data (F2).

REGARDLESS OF THE CONTENTS OR SIZE OF YOUR database, dBASE can always help you get to the information you need. In some cases, you may simply want to look up a piece of information, such as a person's address and phone number. In other cases, your searches might be more complex, such as for "all customers who live on the West Coast, subscribed before January 1, and still have not paid."

In this chapter, you'll learn techniques for searching your database. As you'll see, this is an area where dBASE IV shines. Before you begin, get dBASE IV up and running on your computer again and make sure the LEARN catalog appears in the Control Center.

THE BASIC SEARCHES

Both the browse screen and the edit screen include an option titled Go To in the menu bar, which provides options for simple, basic searches. To try some of these, move the highlight to the CUSTLIST database name in the Data panel on the Control Center and press or click Data (F2) to view its records. Pull down the Go To menu, as shown in Figure 6.1.

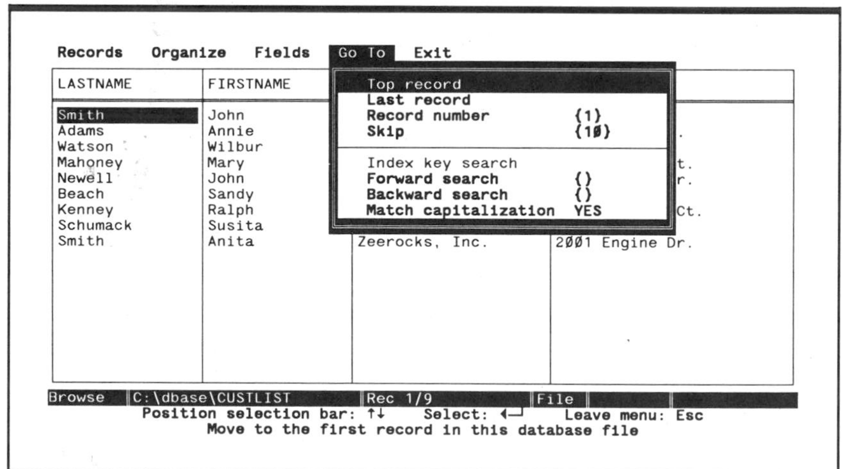

Figure 6.1: The Go To pull-down menu

POSITIONING THE HIGHLIGHT OR SCREEN

The first four Go To options let you position the browse highlight (or edit screen) on a particular record based on its position in the database file. Your options are as follows:

Top record	Moves the edit screen or browse highlight to the top record
Last record	Moves the edit screen or browse highlight to the bottom record
Record number	Moves the edit screen or browse highlight to a particular record based on its position in the database
Skip	Moves the edit screen or browse highlight a certain number of records from its current position

These options are simple to use and experiment with (though they are easier to understand if you first experiment while at the browse screen). For example, if you select Last Record, the highlight jumps to the last database record on the screen. If you select Top Record, the highlight jumps to the topmost record.

If you select Record Number, dBASE asks you to enter a record number. Type a number between 1 and the total number of records in your database and then press ↵. The highlight jumps to the appropriate record. (Note that the record number indicates the record's position in the database and not the index order if an index is in use.)

The Skip option moves the highlight a certain number of records up or down in the database. For example, if you select Skip, type the number 2, and press ↵, the highlight (or edit screen) skips forward two records (if possible). If you enter a negative number, such as −3, the highlight or screen jumps backward three records.

These simple searches are of limited value, because they assume you know the location of the record that you want to access. Furthermore, they do little more than mimic the action of the arrow, PgUp, PgDn, and other navigation keys. You'll probably use the lookup options, discussed next, more often.

SEARCHING FOR INFORMATION

Remember to move the highlight to the field you want to search before using Go To ► Search Forward or Search Backward. If the pull-down menu is already displayed, press Esc or click outside the menu to close it.

In most cases, you do not simply want to go to a particular position in a database. Instead, you want to find information, such as a person's address or phone number. The bottom half of the Go To menu displays options for locating information. To use the Forward Search and Backward Search options, you first move the highlight into the field that you want to search in the database. You then pull down the Go To menu and select either Forward Search, to search forward from the current record, or Backward Search, to search backward from the current record.

After dBASE finds the first record that matches the search requirement, you can use the Find Next key (Shift-F4) or Find Previous (Shift-F3) key to search forward or backward for other matching records. If no match is found, dBASE displays the message "Not Found" and waits for you to press any key to resume your work. Let's look at an example.

1. Use the Tab key to move the highlight to the STATE field in the browse screen.
2. Select Go To ► Top Record to start from the beginning of the database file.
3. To search for records with CA as the state, first bring back the Go To menu.
4. Select Forward Search.
5. When dBASE displays the prompt "Enter search string:" type **CA** (uppercase letters) and press ↵. The highlight moves to the first record that has CA in the STATE field. Suppose that this is not the specific record you were looking for, and you want to find the next record with CA in the STATE field.
6. Press Find Next (Shift-F4). The highlight moves to the next record with CA in the state field (record 7).

The word *string* is a computer term that simply means "a string of characters," which might be a single letter, a word, or several words, such as "X" or "ABC" or "Hello there" or "A-123" or "123 Oak St."

Each time you press Find Next (Shift-F4), dBASE will scroll forward to the next record in the database that has CA in the STATE field. Each time you press Find Previous (Shift-F3), the highlight will scroll back to the previous record with CA in the STATE field. You may want to experiment with these keys now.

The Backward Search option can be handy for making changes after entering a group of new records. For example, suppose you entered 100 new records and wanted to double-check the new record for Kenney. Rather than scrolling through the database, you could follow these steps:

1. Move the highlight to the LASTNAME field.
2. Select Go To ► Last Record to move to the last record in the database (new records are always appended to the end of a database file, so in this case you want to begin your search from the bottom).
3. Bring back the Go To menu.
4. Select Backward Search.
5. If the previous search value is still displayed next to the "Enter search string:" prompt, press Backspace a few times to erase it.
6. Enter the name to search for—in this example, **Kenney**—and press ↵.

As with forward searches, during backward searches you can use the Find Next and Find Previous keys to find other matching values.

EXPANDING SEARCH CAPABILITIES

When you search a database, dBASE looks for information that exactly matches your request. This can be inconvenient at times. For example, if you are looking for someone who lives on Rainbow St., a search for Rainbow in the ADDRESS field would not help, because the addresses contain the street number as well as the street name. If you were searching for a name but were not sure whether it was spelled Smith, Smyth, or Smythe, a search for Smith would not locate the other spellings.

Luckily, dBASE offers several techniques that you can use to add flexibility to your database search. These are discussed in the following sections.

MATCHING CAPITALIZATION At the bottom of the Go To pull-down menu, you'll see the option Match Capitalization. When you move the highlight to this option and press the space bar or click the mouse, the option setting changes from Yes to No. When the setting is Yes, a forward or backward search is case sensitive; the upper- and lowercase letters in the search string must match those in the database. When the setting is No, upper- and lowercase designations do not matter.

For example, if Match Capitalization is set to No, then a search for SMITH locates Smith, SMITH, or smith. However, if Match Capitalization is set to Yes, then a search for SMITH finds only SMITH, not Smith, smith, or SmItH, because the upper- and lowercase letters do not match.

WILDCARD SEARCHES You can use wildcard characters to locate items that match a pattern rather than an exact value. Use the wildcard character **?** to match a single character, and the wildcard character * to match any group of characters. For example, a search of the LASTNAME field for Sm* would find Smith, Smyth, Smythe, Smartalec, and any other name beginning with the letters *Sm*. A search for Sm?t* would locate Smith, Smyth, Smythe, and any other name that follows the pattern *Sm*, any other single letter, *t*, any other letters.

In the STARTDATE field, a search for 12/??/92 would locate any record with a date in December 1992. In the ZIP field, a search for either 92??? or 92* would locate a zip code beginning with the numbers 92 (that is, any zip code in the range 92000 to 92999). In the ADDRESS field, a search for *Rainbow* would locate any record with the word *Rainbow* in the address (such as 734 Rainbow Dr. and 1101 Rainbow Ct.). In the PHONE field, a search for (213)* would locate records with 213 as the area code.

The wildcard characters, ? and *, can be fun to experiment with. Also, because they can be used in several other contexts within dBASE (and outside of dBASE as well), you should at least be familiar with them.

INDEX SEARCHES

When you start working with larger databases, you may find the Forward Search and Backward Search options to be quite slow. As an alternative, you can use the Index Key Search option on the Go To pull-down menu. This option uses an index to search for data and can usually find information in any size database in less than a second.

To use the Index Key Search option, you need to activate the index that contains the field you want to search. For example, to search the LASTNAME field using an index, you need to activate an index that uses only LASTNAME as the key, or uses LASTNAME as the first field in the index expression (such as the LASTNAME+FIRSTNAME index).

ACTIVATING THE SEARCH INDEX

To use Index Key Search, you first need to activate the appropriate index. (If an appropriate index does not exist yet, you can create one using the technique discussed in the previous chapter.) Assume you want to use an index to search for records by people's last names. You activate the LASTNAME index in the CUSTLIST database by following these steps:

1. If you are at the Control Center, highlight CUSTLIST in the data panel, then press or click Data (F2) to get to the edit or browse screen.
2. Open the Organize pull-down menu.
3. Select Order Records by Index.
4. From the submenu, select the LASTNAME index.

Now that the index is activated, you can conduct your search.

You can use either the browse or edit screen for this search. For a change of pace, use the edit screen. If the browse screen is displayed, press F2 again to display the edit screen.

PERFORMING THE SEARCH

To search for a last name, follow these steps:

1. Select Go To ► Index Key Search; dBASE presents the prompt

   Enter search string for
   LASTNAME + FIRSTNAME:

   LASTNAME + FIRSTNAME is the expression for the current index; dBASE displays this to tell you what field you currently can search.

2. To find the record for Smith, type **Smith** (using the correct upper- and lowercase letters) and then press ↵.

dBASE will immediately locate and display the first record for Smith in the database, as shown in Figure 6.2. You cannot use the Find Next or Find Previous key with an index search to scroll through records for other Smiths. However, because the index groups all the Smiths together (because the records are presented in alphabetical order), you can use the PgDn and PgUp keys to scroll through nearby Smith records.

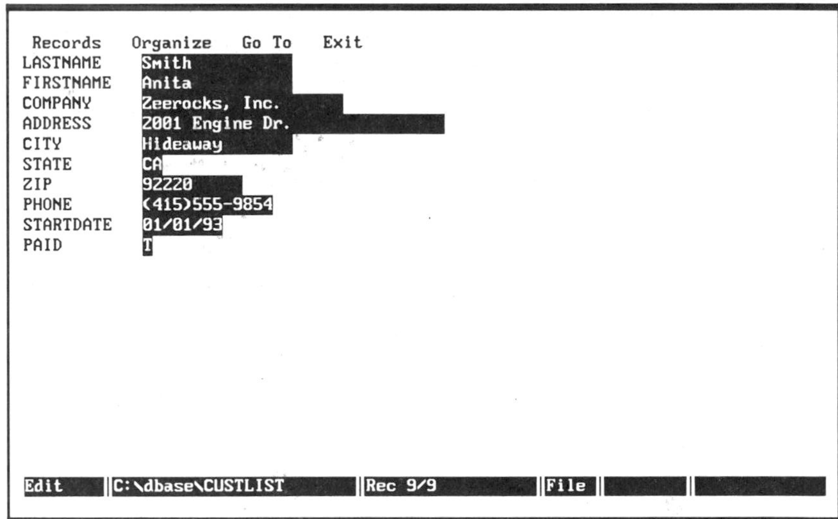

Figure 6.2: Index search locating the first Smith record in the database

INDEX SEARCH LIMITATIONS

Although index key searches are very fast, they are not as flexible as the forward and backward searches discussed previously. An index search works only when upper- and lowercase letters match exactly, even when the Match Capitalization option is off. A search for SMITH would not find Smith, for example.

Also, you cannot use wildcard characters with index searches. A search for Sm?th or Smi* will not find any matching database record. However, dBASE offers some flexibility in index searches. When dBASE searches an index, it looks for a match between the value you are searching for and the leftmost characters in the database field. For example, an index search for Sm would take you to the first record in the database that has *Sm* as the first two letters in the last name. You could then use PgDn (on the edit screen) or ↓ (on the browse screen) to scroll through other nearby records.

The fact that dBASE searches the leftmost characters of the index has a disadvantage as well. For example, even though the index expression for the current index is LASTNAME + FIRSTNAME, you could not use the index to search for the first name John or Anita.

If you do want to search for multiple fields, the following tidbit of information may help you avoid confusion in the future. An index field always has the same width as the field in the database structure. For example, when you created the CUSTLIST database, you assigned a width of 15 characters to the field. Therefore, the LASTNAME in the index has a fixed width of 15 characters. Hence, a search for

```
Smith Anita
```

would find no matching record in the database because Smith has only one blank space after it. However, a search for

```
Smith          Anita
```

would find Anita Smith's record, assuming that there are 10 spaces between Smith and Anita.

Ten blank spaces are required between Smith and Anita because Smith is five letters long, and the 10 blank spaces pad the last name to the width of the database field: 15 characters in this example. You may have little need of this approach, as there are many other ways to search multiple fields. However, knowing how dBASE works may help you avoid problems when trying to search an index such as LASTNAME +FIRSTNAME for a complete name such as Smith Anita.

To leave the edit screen and return to the Control Center, press Esc or select Exit ► Exit.

USING QUERIES

The searches discussed so far are all alike in one way: They help you *locate* a particular item of information in a database. In some situations, you may instead want to *isolate* or *filter* some type of information. For example, if you want to send a form letter to all California residents in your customer database, you will want to isolate records that have CA in the state field, filtering out all other records.

These kinds of searches are called *queries,* because you query (ask) dBASE for some information, and dBASE answers by displaying only records that meet your requirements. Queries are not handled through the Go To pull-down menu. Instead, they are handled via the *query design screen*.

The technique that you use to construct queries is called *query by example,* often abbreviated QBE. The name comes from the technique you use: dBASE presents a skeleton of the database file in use, and you give examples of the kinds of information that you want dBASE IV to display.

GENERAL STEPS FOR QUERIES

You'll have many hands-on opportunities to actually try some queries in this chapter. But first, let's take a moment to summarize the basic steps involved:

- Make sure the database that you want to query is open (above the line in the Data panel).
- Move the highlighter to the Queries panel.
- Select <create> (by highlighting it and pressing ↵ or clicking the mouse).

- Move the highlighter to the field you want to search.
- Type the value you want to search for, using proper *delimiters* (described under "Delimiters Used with Queries" later in this chapter).
- Press or click Data (F2) to perform the query and see the results, and press Data (F2) additionally to switch between the browse and edit screens as usual.
- Press Design (Shift-F2) or select Exit ► Transfer to Query Design when you've finished viewing your data.
- At this point you have several choices:
  - To change the current query, just make your changes, then press or click Data (F2) to see the results.
  - To get back to the Control Center without saving your query, press Esc or select Exit ► Abandon Changes and Exit, and select Yes when asked about abandoning the current query.
  - To save your query and return to the Control Center, press Ctrl-End, or select Exit ► Save Changes and Exit and enter a valid file name for the query (described in "Saving Queries for Future Use" near the end of this chapter).

Remember that if you start feeling lost or confused while switching among the various screens, there are these quick sources of help available to you:

- Look at the navigation line at the bottom of the screen to see what keys are available at the moment.
- If you are *not* at the Control Center, selecting an option from the Exit pull-down menu will usually get you back to the Control Center (as will pressing Esc).
- Figures inside the front cover of this book will also help you navigate the Control Center and Query Design screens.

Let's go ahead and actually perform a query now, discussing each step in more detail.

SELECTING A DATABASE TO QUERY

Before you can query a database, you must make sure that the database is *open* (in use) at the moment. You can easily see if a database file is open by looking at its position in the Data panel of the Control Center. If the name of the database file appears *above* the line the database is open and ready for action. If the database name is below the line, the file is not open and cannot be queried. Figure 6.3 indicates that the CUSTLIST database is in use at the moment.

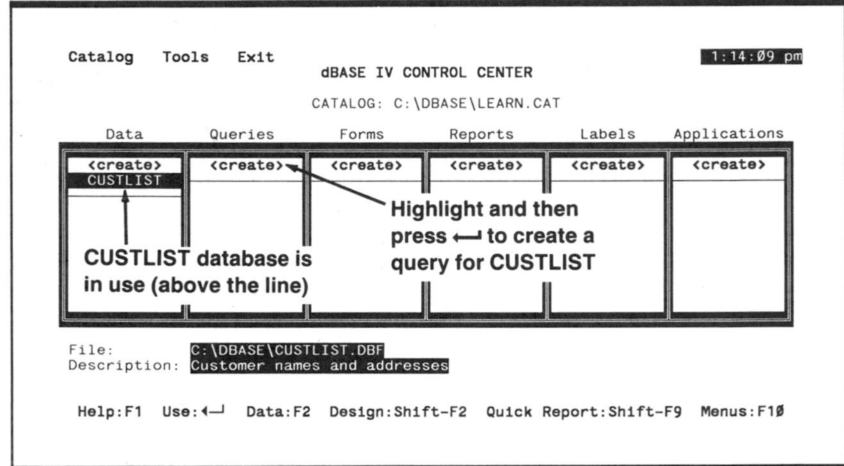

Figure 6.3: The CUSTLIST database is open and ready for use

Remember, prompt boxes are only available if the Instruct setting, discussed in Chapter 2, is On.

Once you highlight a database file name and press or click either Design or Data, dBASE opens that database file and keeps it open. You can also open (or close) a database file at any time by highlighting its name in the Data panel and pressing ↵ or by double-clicking the mouse. A prompt box will present your options. If the database file is not open, you'll be given the option "Use File" to open the database. If the database is open, you'll be given the option "Close File" to close it. You'll also have the option to "Modify Structure/Order" (which takes you to the database design screen), or to "Display Data" (which transfers you to the browse/edit screen). Note that these two options can be used as alternatives to pressing or clicking Design (Shift-F2) and Data (F2).

If you want to try this procedure now, make sure the highlight is on the CUSTLIST database name in the Data panel and then press ↵ or double-click the mouse on CUSTLIST. You'll see the three options that we just described. Use the usual technique to select an option. When you return to the Control Center, make sure that the CUSTLIST database is still open before you proceed to the next section.

THE QUERY DESIGN SCREEN

To design a query for the currently open database file you need to get to the query design screen. To do so, follow these steps:

- Highlight <create> in the Queries panel and press ↵.
- Or double-click the mouse on <create> in the Queries panel.

You'll find yourself at the query design screen (or *surface*, as it is sometimes called), shown in Figure 6.4. Like other dBASE work areas, the query design screen includes a menu bar at the top of the screen and a status bar and navigation line at the bottom of the screen. The query screen also includes a *file skeleton* and a *view skeleton*.

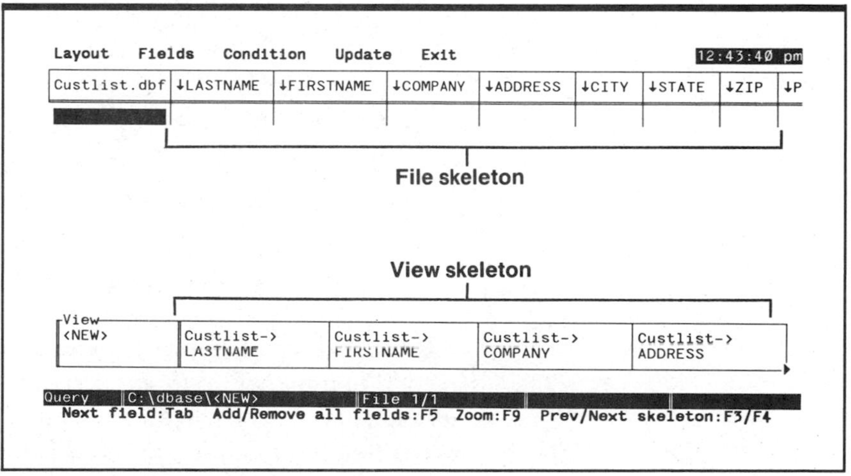

Figure 6.4: The query design screen

THE FILE SKELETON The file skeleton is near the top of the screen. In the leftmost column is the name of the database file that the skeleton represents: CUSTLIST.DBF, in this example. Each field name in the database is listed in boxes to the right of the database name. You can use the Home, End, Tab, and Shift-Tab keys to scroll left and right through these field names and to view those that are off the right edge of the screen. Or, you can simply click in the box below each field name to move the highlight to that field. You'll use the file skeleton in a moment, to specify search criteria.

THE VIEW SKELETON The view skeleton, near the bottom of the screen, shows the names of the fields that will be displayed by the query. Initially, the query feature assumes that you want to display all fields, so all fields are included. You'll learn more about how to use the view skeleton later.

DEFINING RECORDS TO DISPLAY

To specify which records you want a query to display, you enter *filter conditions* in the file skeleton near the top of the screen. You put the filter condition under the appropriate box and then press or click Data (F2) to see the results. Let's create a filter condition to display only records from the CUSTLIST database that have CA in the STATE field. Here are the steps:

1. Press the Tab key six times or use the mouse to move the highlight to the STATE field.
2. Type the condition **"CA"** (including the double quotation marks) and press ↵, so your screen looks like Figure 6.5.
3. Press or click Data (F2) to see the results of the query (dBASE might take a few seconds).

If the edit screen appears, press Data (F2) to switch to the browse screen. Then press End to scroll to the right to get a better view of the query results. As you can see on your screen (and in Figure 6.6), only records that have CA in the STATE field appear.

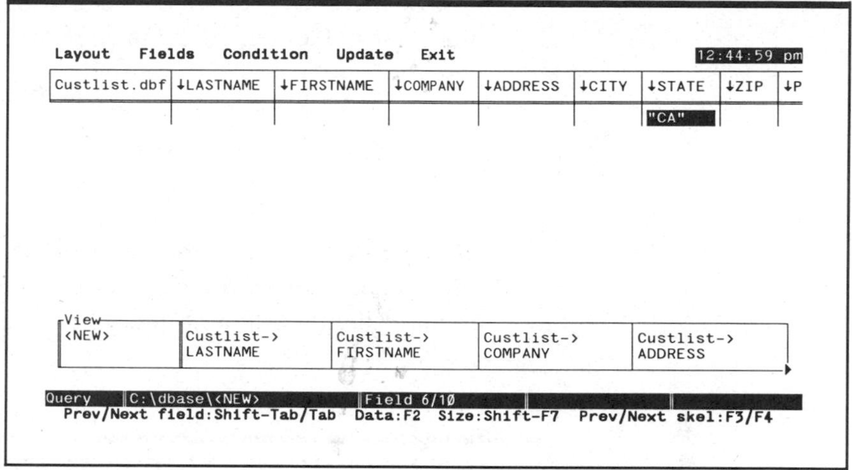

Figure 6.5: A query for records with CA in the STATE field

Records Organize Fields Go To Exit

CITY	STATE	ZIP	PHONE	STARTDATE	PAID
San Diego	CA	92067	(619)555-1234	11/15/92	T
Santa Monica	CA	92001	(714)555-0123	01/01/93	F
Los Angeles	CA	96607	(213)555-9988	12/30/92	F
Hideaway	CA	92220	(415)555-9854	01/01/93	T

Browse C:\dbase\<NEW> Rec 1/9 View

Figure 6.6: Results of the query for records with CA in the STATE field

As you'll see in coming chapters, you can use filtered databases to print mailing labels and form letters, perform calculations, make copies of database files, simplify editing, and facilitate other tasks. In fact, you'll probably find that you use queries more than any other feature of dBASE IV.

To leave the "queried" version of your database and return to the Control Center, follow these steps now:

1. Press Esc, or select Exit ► Exit.
2. A prompt will ask if you want to save the current query. In this case, we won't save the query, so select No.

Now you are back to the Control Center. Before we proceed with other examples of queries, let's discuss how different data types require slightly different querying techniques.

DELIMITERS USED WITH QUERIES

If you want to take a break during this chapter, select Exit ► Abandon Changes and Exit from the query design screen. When dBASE asks if you are sure you want to abandon, select Yes. You'll be returned to the Control Center, where you can exit dBASE IV gracefully before turning off your computer.

As you know, dBASE lets you store information as various data types, such as Character, Date, Logical, and so forth. Depending on the data type of the field you want to search at the moment, you'll need to use specific *delimiters* (punctuation marks around the information you are searching for). In summary, these delimiters are:

Data Type	Delimiter	Example
Character data	" "	"CA"
Date data	{ }	{12/31/91}
Logical data	. .	.T. or .F.
Numeric or Float	None	123.45

Let's take a look at some examples and get some hands-on practice with queries now.

If you forget to put quotation marks around the filter condition in a Character field search, dBASE will still accept the value and execute the query. However, the results of the query will probably not be what you had in mind.

QUERYING CHARACTER FIELDS

In your first sample query you isolated names and addresses of California residents by searching for "CA" in the STATE field of the CUSTLIST database. You used the quotation marks because STATE is a Character (data type) field. Let's try another example now, this time searching the LASTNAME field, which is also the

Character data type. Follow these steps:

1. Make sure the CUSTLIST database is open.
2. Highlight <create> in the Queries panel.
3. Select <create>.
4. Move the highlighter to the LASTNAME field.
5. Type **"Smith"** and press ↵.
6. Press or click Data (F2) to perform the query.

WARNING

If you forget to remove the previous filter condition from the query design screen before entering a new one, the old filter condition will affect the new query.

As you can see in Figure 6.7, only records that have Smith in the LASTNAME field are displayed.

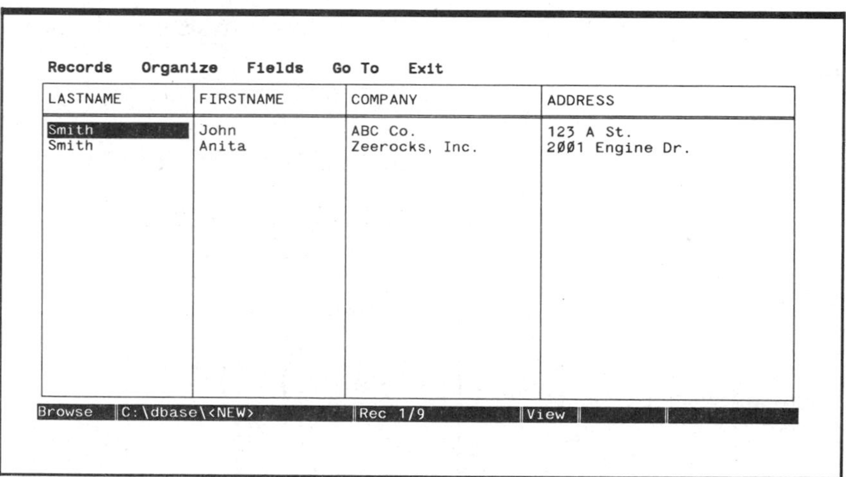

Figure 6.7: Results of query for records with Smith in the LASTNAME field

Note that the query is carried over to the edit screen if you press Data (F2) now. When the edit screen appears, the record for the first Smith is on the screen. When you press PgDn to move to the next record, the next Smith record appears. If you press PgDn again, dBASE displays the prompt box asking, "Add new records?", as though there were no other records in the database. For now, answer No. Then press F2 to return to the browse screen.

QUERYING DATE FIELDS

To isolate "blank" dates, use {} as the search value. To isolate non-blank dates, use {} = .F. as the search value.

When querying a field of the Date data type, such as START-DATE, you must enclose the date you are searching for in curly braces ({}). Let's construct a query to isolate records with START-DATE values of 12/15/92.

1. Press Design (Shift-F2), or select Exit ► Transfer to Query Design, to return to the query design screen.
2. With the highlight still in the LASTNAME field, press Ctrl-Y to remove "Smith."
3. Press End and then Shift-Tab or use the mouse to move to the STARTDATE field.
4. Type **{12/15/92}** and press ↵.
5. To view the results of the query, press or click Data (F2).

If you scroll to the STARTDATE field in the browse screen, you'll see that only records with 12/15/92 in the STARTDATE field are displayed, as in Figure 6.8.

Records Organize Fields Go To Exit

CITY	STATE	ZIP	PHONE	STARTDATE	PAID
Butte	MT	54321	(303)555-6739	12/15/92	T
Portland	OR	76543	(717)555-0898	12/15/92	T

Browse | C:\dbase\<NEW> | Rec 5/9 | View

Figure 6.8: Results of query for records with STARTDATE {12/15/92}

After viewing the results of the query, press Design (Shift-F2) to get back to the query design screen.

QUERYING LOGICAL FIELDS

In Logical fields you can use .T., .t., .Y., or .y. for true; and .F., .f., .N., or .n. for false—where Y and N stand for yes and no. The periods are required by dBASE to distinguish these entries from regular characters.

When you query a field that is the Logical data type, such as PAID in the CUSTLIST database, you can enter either .T. or .F. as the value to search for.

To try this, you'll isolate records in the PAID field that are marked true (that is, they contain T). Follow these steps:

1. At the query design screen, move to the STARTDATE field and press Ctrl-Y to remove **{12/15/92}**.
2. Press Tab to move to the PAID field.
3. Type **.T.** and press ↵.
4. Press or click Data (F2) to execute the query.

When the browse screen appears, press the End key to scroll to the PAID field. Notice that only records marked true (T) are displayed.

After viewing the records, press Design (Shift-F2) or select Exit ► Transfer to Query Design, to return to the query design screen.

USING OPERATORS IN QUERIES

If you don't use an operator in a query, then equals (=) is assumed. That is, putting "CA" in the STATE field tells dBASE that you want to see records where STATE equals "CA".

dBASE IV includes many *relational operators* that you can use to refine your queries. Table 6.1 lists these operators and their meanings.

Table 6.1: The dBASE IV Relational Operators

Operator	Meaning
=	Equals
>	Greater than
<	Less than
>=	Greater than or equal to
<=	Less than or equal to

Table 6.1: The dBASE IV Relational Operators (continued)

Operator	Meaning
<> or #	Not equal to
$	Contains
Like	Pattern match using wildcard characters
Sounds like	Soundex search for words that sound alike

While building a query, you can select operators from the Expression Builder by pressing Shift-F1. Move the highlight to the Operator panel in the Expression Builder and use PgDn and PgUp to scroll through the operators. To select an operator, highlight it using the arrow keys and then press ↵, or double-click on the operator with the mouse.

You can edit information on the query design screen using the same techniques that you use to edit information in a database. Use the mouse or the arrow keys to position the cursor, the Ins key to switch between Insert and Overwrite modes, the Backspace or Del key to delete characters, and so forth.

These operators can be interesting to play with, and after you learn the basics in this section, you may want to try a few queries on your own.

To use an operator in a query, precede the value that you are searching for with the appropriate operator. To see how this works, create a query that displays records for people whose last names begin with the letters A through M. Here are the steps:

1. At the query design screen, remove the .T. in the PAID field by highlighting that field and pressing Ctrl-Y.
2. Move the highlight to the LASTNAME field.
3. Type the filter condition **<"N"**, including the quotation marks. Press ↵.
4. To see the results of the query, press or click Data (F2).

The browse screen, as Figure 6.9 shows, displays only records with the appropriate last names. The filter condition <"N" told dBASE to display only records with last names that are less than N, so only records that have last names beginning with the letters A through M are displayed.

If you use Design (Shift-F2) to return to the query design screen, change the filter condition in the LASTNAME field to > = "N" (greater than or equal to N), and then press or click Data (F2), dBASE will display records that have last names beginning with the letters N through Z.

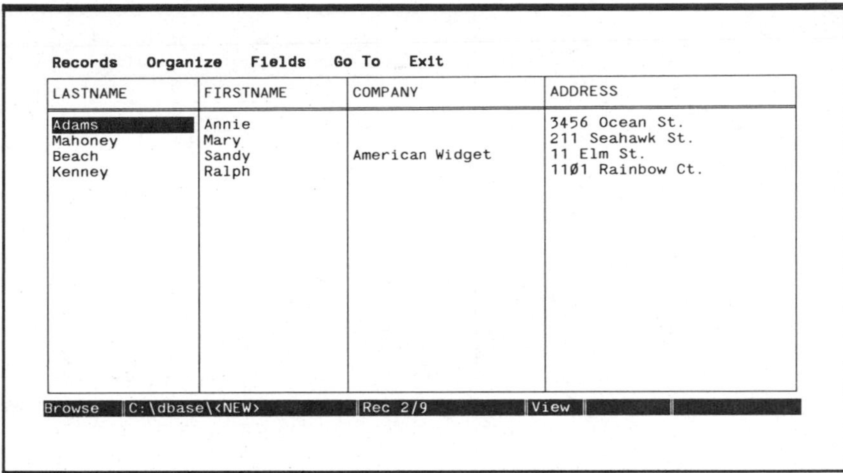

Figure 6.9: Results of query for records with last names <“N”

SEARCHING FOR CLOSE SPELLINGS

Suppose you want to look up Ralph Kenney's address, but you misspell the last name as Kinny. When you perform the lookup operation, dBASE informs you that there is no Kinny. This is a good opportunity to use the *sounds-like* operator, which uses a technique called *soundex* to locate words that sound alike, regardless of their spelling. Follow these steps:

1. If the browse or edit screen is displayed, press Shift-F2 or select Exit ▶ Transfer to Query Design to return to the query design screen.
2. Move the highlight to the LASTNAME field and press Ctrl-Y to empty that field.
3. Enter the filter condition **Sounds like “Kinny”** (you must use the quotation marks, as in Figure 6.10) and then press ↵.
4. Press or click Data (F2) to execute the query.

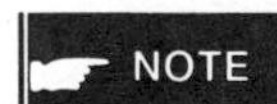

When entering lengthy conditions on the query design screen, the column widens automatically to make room.

As Figure 6.11 shows, the query located the record for Kenney.

Layout Fields Condition Update Exit
12:58:22 pm
Custlist.dbf
↓LASTNAME
↓FIRSTNAME
↓COMPANY
↓ADDRESS
↓CITY
↓STATE
Sounds like "Kinny"
View
<NEW>
Custlist-> LASTNAME
Custlist-> FIRSTNAME
Custlist-> COMPANY
Custlist-> ADDRESS
Query
C:\dbase\<NEW>
Field 1/10
Prev/Next field:Shift-Tab/Tab Data:F2 Size:Shift-F7 Prev/Next skel:F3/F4

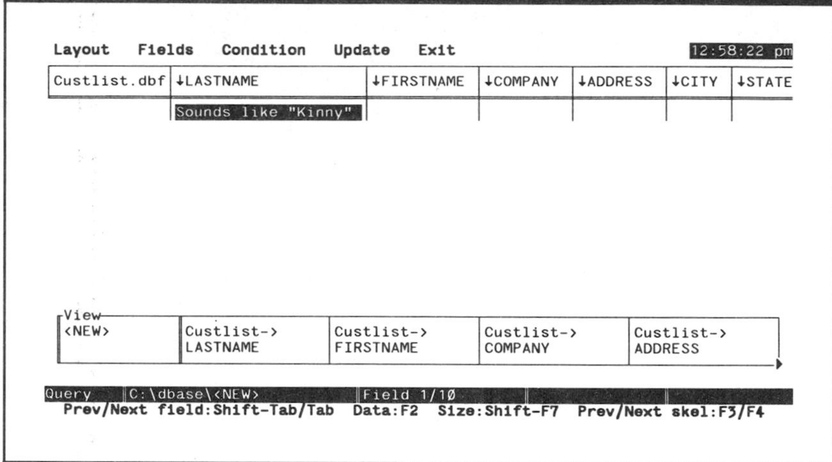

Figure 6.10: Search for records with names that sound like Kinny

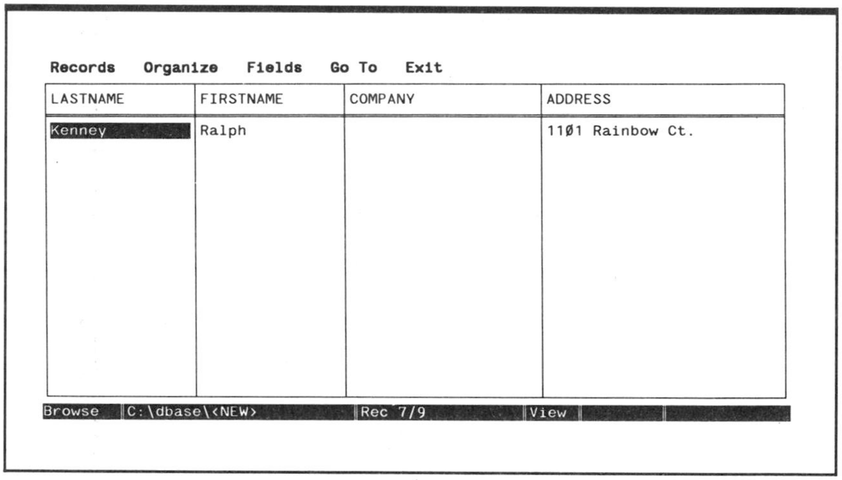

Records Organize Fields Go To Exit
LASTNAME
FIRSTNAME
COMPANY
ADDRESS
Kenney
Ralph
1101 Rainbow Ct.
Browse
C:\dbase\<NEW>
Rec 7/9
View

Figure 6.11: Results of query for Sounds like "Kinny"

PATTERN-MATCHING SEARCHES

Remember the pattern-matching searches discussed previously, where you used the wildcard characters ? to stand for any single character and * to stand for any group of characters? You can use these same wildcards with queries, provided you use the *Like* operator first.

Suppose you want to search for zip codes that begin with 92. Here are the basic steps:

1. If necessary, press Design (Shift-F2) or select Exit ► Transfer to Query Design to return to the query design screen.
2. Erase the current filter condition from the LASTNAME field in the query design screen (using Ctrl-Y).
3. Place the filter condition **Like "92*"** in the ZIP field, as shown in Figure 6.12.

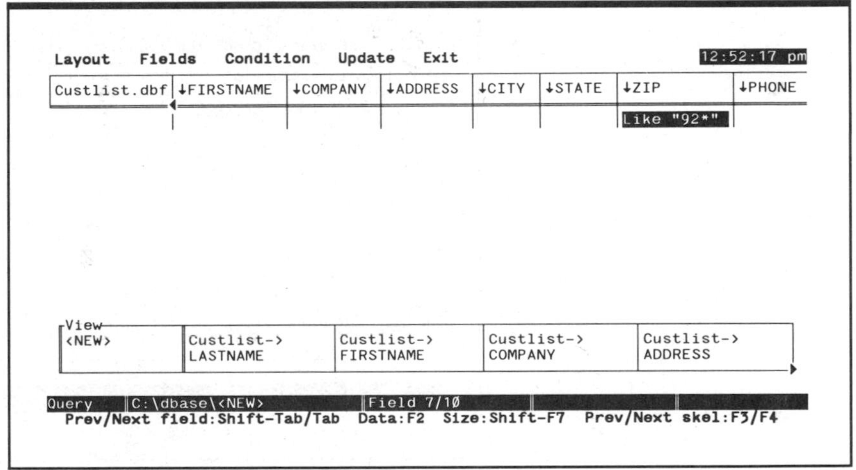

Figure 6.12: Query for records with zip codes beginning with 92

When you use Data (F2) to see the results of the query, you'll find that only records with zip codes that start with 92 appear on the browse screen. (Press the End key to scroll to the right edge of the browse screen to see the zip codes.) Press Design (Shift-F2), or select Exit ► Transfer to Query Design, as usual after viewing the data to return to the query design screen. Use Ctrl-Y to erase the filter condition.

EMBEDDED SEARCHES

You can use the *contains* operator, $, to search for text embedded within a Character field. For example, suppose, again, that you want to view records with Rainbow in the street address. Here are the steps:

1. First delete any previous filter conditions from the query design screen.
2. Move the highlight to the ADDRESS field.
3. Enter the filter condition **$ "Rainbow"** (again, the quotation marks are mandatory).

Figure 6.13 shows how the query design screen should look.

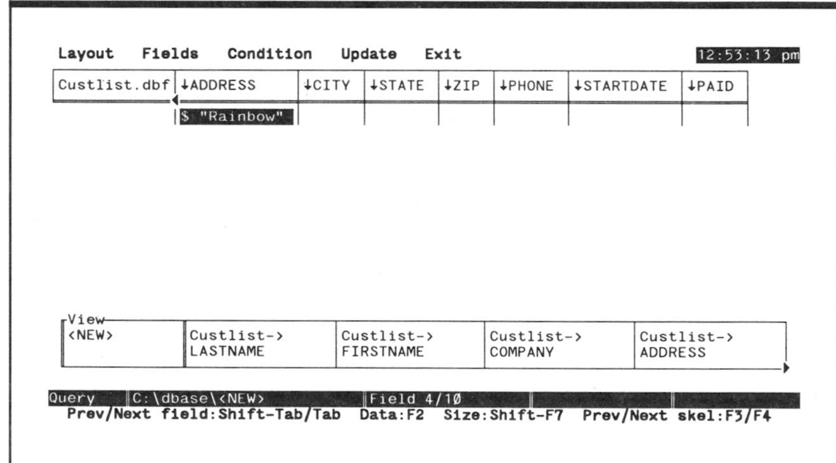

Figure 6.13: Query for records with addresses with Rainbow embedded

When you press or click Data (F2) to view the results, you'll see that only records with Rainbow in the ADDRESS field are displayed, as in Figure 6.14.

EXCEPT SEARCHES

You can use the not-equal-to operator, # or < >, to execute a query that shows all records *except* those that meet some condition. For example, suppose you want to view all the records in CUSTLIST except those with CA in the STATE field. To do so, return to the query design screen and remove the filter condition currently in the ADDRESS field.

Then move the highlight to the STATE field and enter the filter condition # **"CA"**, as in Figure 6.15. When you press or click F2 to execute the query and then scroll to the STATE field in the browse screen, you'll see that none of the records displayed has CA in the STATE field (see Figure 6.16).

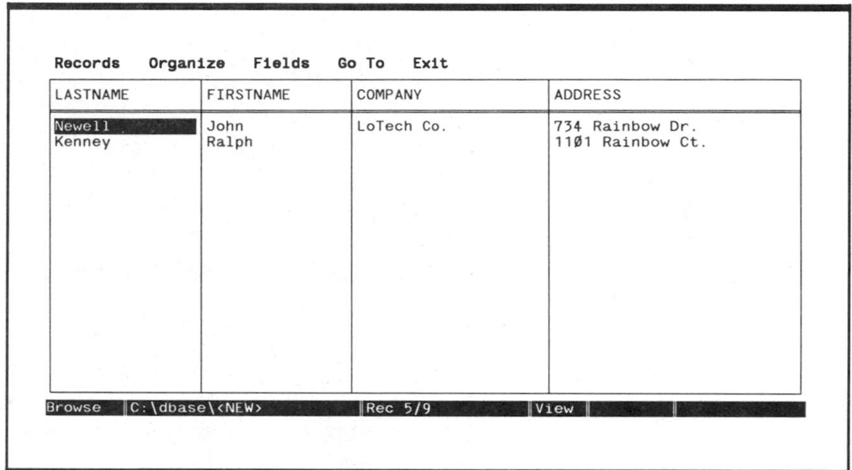

Figure 6.14: Results of $ "Rainbow" query of ADDRESS field

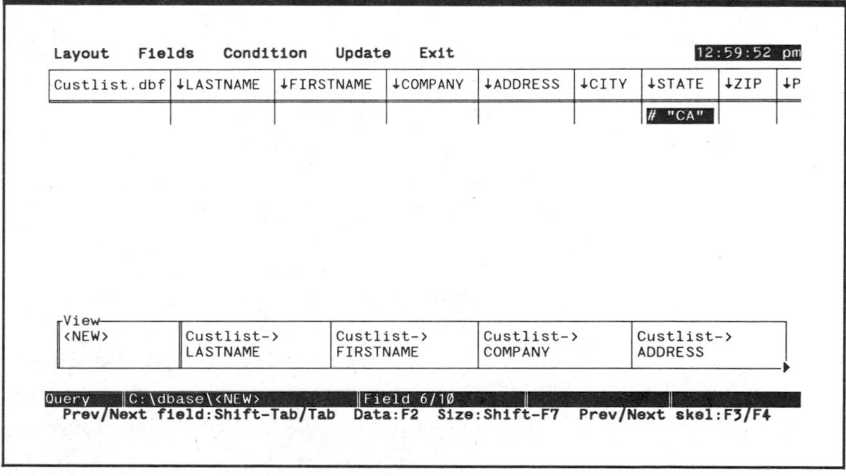

Figure 6.15: Query for records that do not have CA in the STATE field

CITY	STATE	ZIP	PHONE	STARTDATE	PAID
New York	NY	12345	(212)555-9988	11/15/92	T
Seattle	WA	88977	(206)555-8673	12/01/92	T
Butte	MT	54321	(303)555-6739	12/15/92	T
Portland	OR	76543	(717)555-0898	12/15/92	T
Philadelphia	PA	45543	(202)555-9720	12/30/92	T

Records Organize Fields Go To Exit

Browse C:\dbase\<NEW> Rec 3/9 View

Figure 6.16: Results of query for STATE # "CA"

By now, you should be feeling that dBASE IV can help you isolate just about any information in your database that you want. You might want to experiment with some queries of your own for a while.

Remember when experimenting on your own: If your query does not produce the results you expected when you press or click Data (F2), press Design (Shift-F2) or select Exit ► Transfer to Query Design to return to the query design screen. Then scroll through the fields to see if you forgot to erase any filter conditions from the previous query. If you find an old filter condition, remove it (using Ctrl-Y or Del) and try the query operation again.

DESIGNING QUERIES WITH AND

As you develop larger databases, you may want to use more sophisticated queries. For example, you might want to ask dBASE to display records for customers who live in California *and* began subscribing in 1992 *and* have not paid yet. To ask such questions of dBASE, you create queries that use AND logic.

There is a simple rule of thumb for creating AND queries: You put all of the filter conditions for the query on the same row in the query design screen.

Suppose you specifically want to isolate a record (or records) for a customer named Anita Smith. To do so, you need to put **"Smith"** in the LASTNAME field and **"Anita"** in the FIRSTNAME field on the same row in the query design screen, as shown in Figure 6.17. (To speed along the rest of this chapter, instructions assume that you know how to use the Design (Shift-F2) and Data (F2) keys to switch back and forth between the query design and browse screens. We'll also assume that you know how to erase old filter conditions from the query design screen and enter new ones.)

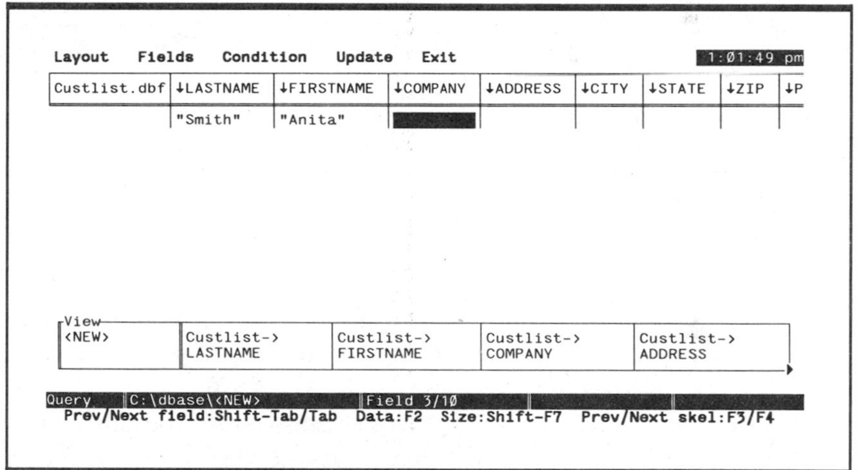

Figure 6.17: A query for records containing Anita Smith

When you execute the query, only Anita Smith's record will appear on the browse screen. (Press Shift-F2 or select Exit ► Transfer to Query Design to return to the query design screen.)

Suppose you want to list all customers who live on Broad St. in Philadelphia. That is, you want to display all records with Broad St. *embedded* in the ADDRESS field *and* Philadelphia in the CITY field. You need to set up your query as in Figure 6.18.

Once again, notice that the two filter conditions are on the same row within the query. Pressing or clicking Data (F2) will display

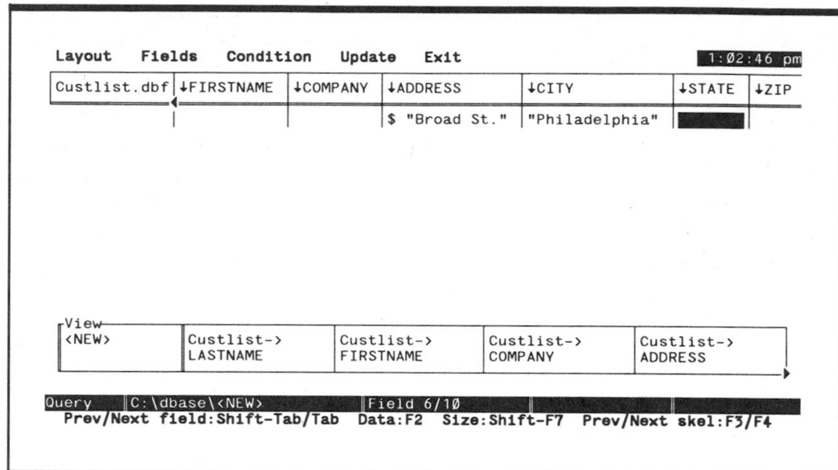

Figure 6.18: A query for records of customers living on Broad St. in Philadelphia

Susita Schumack's record in the CUSTLIST database, the only customer in this database who lives on Broad St. in Philadelphia.

So now, how would you list all customers who have not paid yet, and who began subscribing prior to January 1, 1993—that is, customers with F in the PAID field and dates less than 1/1/93 in the STARTDATE field? Figure 6.19 shows how to set up the query.

Press Data (F2) to execute the query. Press End to scroll to the right edge of the browse screen to view the STARTDATE and PAID fields.

If you want to limit the preceding query to California residents who have not paid yet and who began subscribing prior to January 1, 1992, you would just need to add **"CA"** (with quotation marks) to the STATE field in the query design screen. Make sure that "CA" is in the top row of the query screen (the same row as the other filter conditions). Then press F2 to execute the query.

SEARCHING FOR RANGES

Often you need to search for data that falls within some range of values, such as zip codes in the range 92000 to 92555 or names in the alphabetical range A through J. You might want to search for records that fall within a particular range of dates, such as November 15,

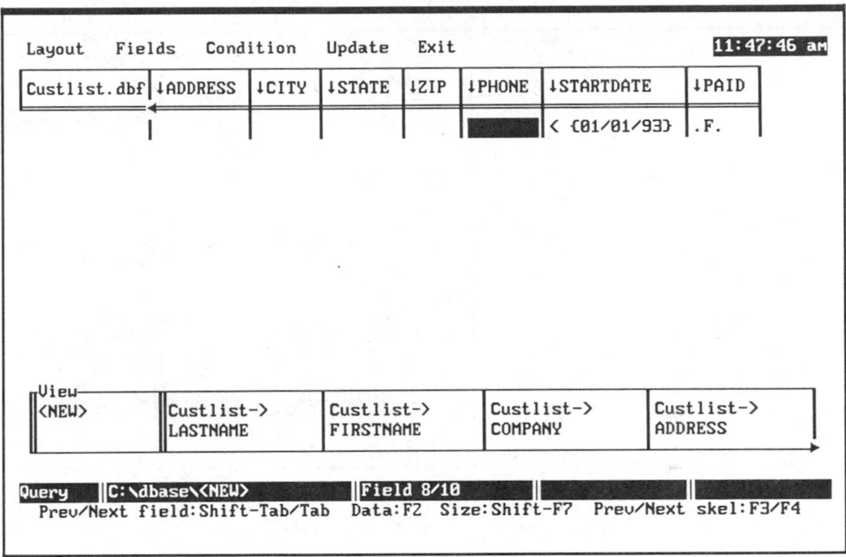

Figure 6.19: Query for records of customers who began subscribing before 1/1/93 and have not paid

1992, to December 15, 1992. Range searches can be particularly useful in Numeric fields: for example, "Display all employees with salaries in the range of $20,000 to $30,000." (Chapter 9 discusses Numeric fields.)

To perform a range search, use an AND query within a single field. Use the > = operator before the low end of the range, and the < or < = operator before the high end of the range; separate the two with a comma.

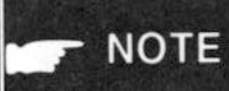
NOTE

To dBASE, "Ja" is *not* less than or equal to "J" alone; "Ja" is greater than "J" alone. Therefore, to search for names beginning with the letters A through J, you could use either > = "A", < = "Jz", or simply > = "A",<"K".

Suppose, for example, that you wanted to pull out records of people whose last names begin with the letters A through J. The filter condition > = "A",<"K" would do the trick, because it isolates names that begin with any letter that's greater than or equal to "A", but less than "K".

Suppose you want to view customers in the zip code range 80000 to 97000: that is, records with zip codes that are greater than or equal to 80000 *and* are also less than or equal to 97000. To do so, you place the filter condition > = "80000",< = "97000" in the ZIP field, as shown in Figure 6.20. Figure 6.21 shows the results of this query.

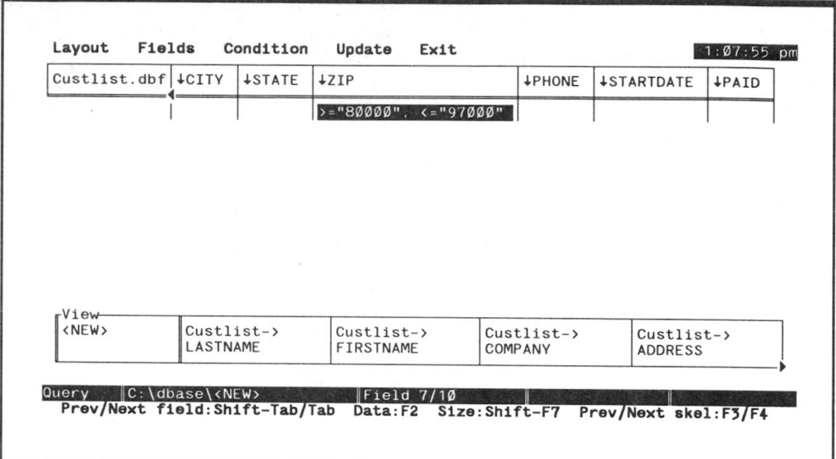

Figure 6.20: Query for records of customers in the 80000 to 97000 zip code range

Records Organize Fields Go To Exit

CITY	STATE	ZIP	PHONE	STARTDATE	PAID
Seattle	WA	88977	(206)555-8673	12/01/92	T
Santa Monica	CA	92001	(714)555-0123	01/01/93	F
San Diego	CA	92067	(619)555-1234	11/15/92	T
Hideaway	CA	92220	(415)555-9854	01/01/93	T
Los Angeles	CA	96607	(213)555-9988	12/30/92	F

Browse C:\dbase\<NEW> Rec 4/9 View

Figure 6.21: Results of the zip code range query

Suppose you want to view customers who began subscribing on dates between 11/15/92 and 12/15/92. You use exactly the same kind of filter condition as in the previous examples, including the curly braces for the Date data type. Figure 6.22 shows the appropriate filter condition > = {11/15/92},< = {12/15/92}, in the STARTDATE field of the query form.

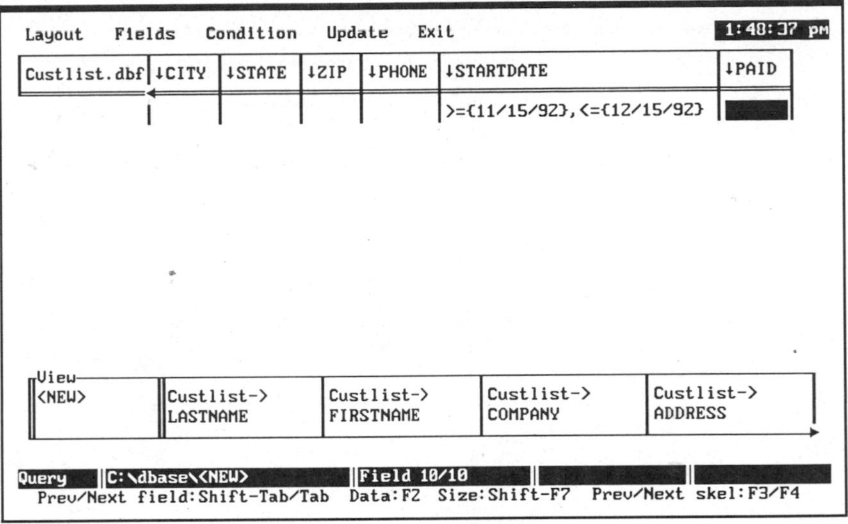

Figure 6.22: A query for records with STARTDATE values between 11/15/92 and 12/15/92

DESIGNING QUERIES WITH OR

Now that you've seen how to construct an AND query, you may be wondering how to create a query that says "Show me all the customers who live in Washington *or* Oregon *or* California." The answer to this question is that you design an OR query.

To design an OR query, you need to stagger the values that you are searching for on separate rows within the query design screen. Initially, dBASE IV displays only a single row for entering information into a query form. But you can easily create more rows by pressing ↓. To see how this works, create a query that displays customers who live in either California or Washington:

1. Start with an empty query design screen (use the Tab and Shift-Tab keys or the mouse to scroll from field to field and use Ctrl-Y to delete any existing filter conditions).
2. Move the highlight to the STATE field in the query design screen.

3. Type "**CA**" to specify California as a state to search for.
4. Press ↓ to add a new row.
5. Type "**WA**" to specify Washington as a state to search for.
6. Press ↵. Your query screen should look like Figure 6.23.

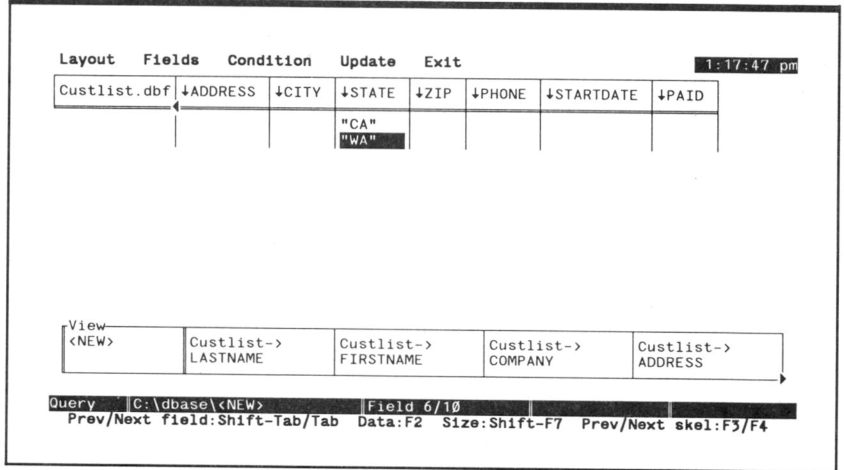

Figure 6.23: A query for records of customers who live in California or Washington

Staggering the filter conditions onto two separate rows tells dBASE that you want records that have *either* CA or WA in the STATE field. Press or click Data (F2) to verify this. After you press the End key to scroll to the right of the browse screen, your screen should look like Figure 6.24.

After viewing the results of the query, return to the query screen. To erase both filter conditions, follow these steps:

1. Press Ctrl-Y to erase the bottom filter condition.
2. Press ↑ to move up to the top filter condition (the second row will disappear, because it is now empty).
3. Press Ctrl-Y to erase the top filter condition.

Incidentally, you are not limited to two rows in OR queries. You can use the ↓ key to create up to 12 rows. For example, the query in

Records Organize Fields Go To Exit

CITY	STATE	ZIP	PHONE	STARTDATE	PAID
San Diego	CA	92067	(619)555-1234	11/15/92	T
Santa Monica	CA	92001	(714)555-0123	01/01/93	F
Seattle	WA	88977	(206)555-8673	12/01/92	T
Los Angeles	CA	96607	(213)555-9988	12/30/92	F
Hideaway	CA	92220	(415)555-9854	01/01/93	T

Browse C:\dbase\<NEW> Rec 1/9 View

Figure 6.24: Results of the OR query

Figure 6.25 uses 4 rows to display records for residents of PA, NY, MT, or WA (that is, for people who live in PA *or* NY *or* MT *or* WA).

USING OR QUERIES WITH MULTIPLE FIELDS

Suppose you want to view records that have a value in one field *or* some other value in another field? For example, suppose you are a

Layout Fields Condition Update Exit 1:21:49 pm

Custlist.dbf	↓ADDRESS	↓CITY	↓STATE	↓ZIP	↓PHONE	↓STARTDATE	↓PAID
			"PA"				
			"NY"				
			"MT"				
			"WA"				

View <NEW>	Custlist-> LASTNAME	Custlist-> FIRSTNAME	Custlist-> COMPANY	Custlist-> ADDRESS

Query C:\dbase\<NEW> Field 6/10
Prev/Next field:Shift-Tab/Tab Data:F2 Size:Shift-F7 Prev/Next skel:F3/F4

Figure 6.25: Query to view records of Pennsylvania, New York, Montana, or Washington residents

salesperson who works primarily on the phone, and you have been assigned a territory that includes the entire state of California, plus the entire 717 telephone area code (which, for this example, includes, but extends outside of, the state of California).

You cannot find the appropriate records for your customers by executing a query that asks for records that have CA in the STATE field *and* (717) in the PHONE field, because that query would limit the display to records with the 717 area code within the state of California. Instead, you want to display records that have CA in the STATE field (regardless of area code) *or* 717 in the PHONE field (regardless of the state).

To execute such a query, you need to stagger the STATE and PHONE filter conditions onto two separate rows, to tell dBASE that you want records meeting one condition *or* the other. Figure 6.26 shows how to design such a query. (Remember to use the ↓ key to create a second row in the query design screen before entering **$ "(717)"** into the PHONE field.)

Even though you are searching two different fields in the query shown in Figure 6.26, because the two fields are on two different rows in the query design screen dBASE will understand that you are requesting OR logic in the query. When you press or click Data (F2), the browse screen will display records that have either CA in the STATE field or (717) embedded ($) in the PHONE field, as shown in Figure 6.27.

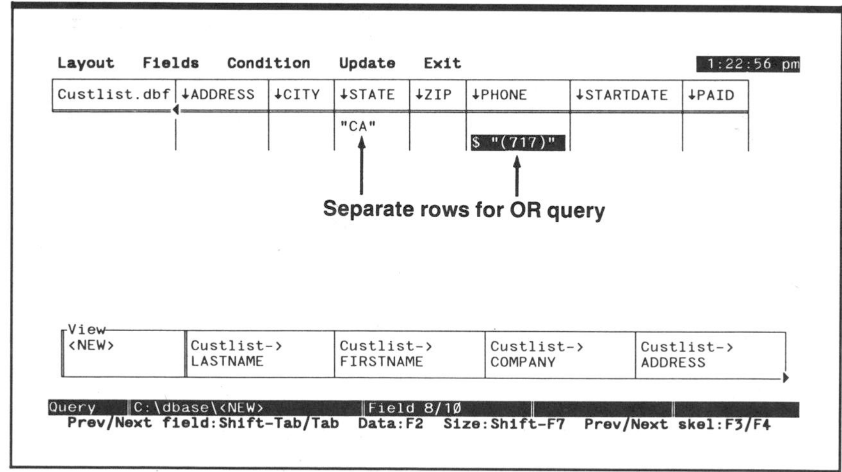

Figure 6.26: A query for records with either CA in the STATE field or (717) in the PHONE field

Records Organize Fields Go To Exit

CITY	STATE	ZIP	PHONE	STARTDATE	PAID
San Diego	CA	92067	(619)555-1234	11/15/92	T
Santa Monica	CA	92001	(714)555-0123	01/01/93	F
Portland	OR	76543	(717)555-0898	12/15/92	T
Los Angeles	CA	96607	(213)555-9988	12/30/92	F
Hideaway	CA	92220	(415)555-9854	01/01/93	T

Browse ‖C:\dbase\<NEW> ‖Rec 1/9 ‖View ‖

Figure 6.27: Results of the query for either CA in the STATE field or (717) in the PHONE field

COMBINING AND AND OR QUERIES

There is still another type of query that you may need to pose to dBASE IV—a query that combines AND and OR logic. For example, suppose you want to see records for all the people in the states of California, New York, and Washington who have paid. At first you might think that the logic for this requires the query "Locate customers who have paid AND live in Washington or California or New York." If so, you might set up the query incorrectly, as in Figure 6.28.

When you execute the query shown in Figure 6.28, the results will look like Figure 6.29. The query in Figure 6.28 intended to display only CA, NY, and WA records with T in the PAID field, but as you can see in Figure 6.29, some records with F in the PAID field are displayed. Why?

Actually, dBASE did exactly what you asked. As it considered each record, it asked, "Does this record have WA in the STATE field *and* T in the PAID field, *or* does this record have CA in the STATE field, *or* does this record have NY in the STATE field?" The plain-English translation of the query in Figure 6.28 is "Display records that have WA in the STATE field and T in the PAID field, or CA in

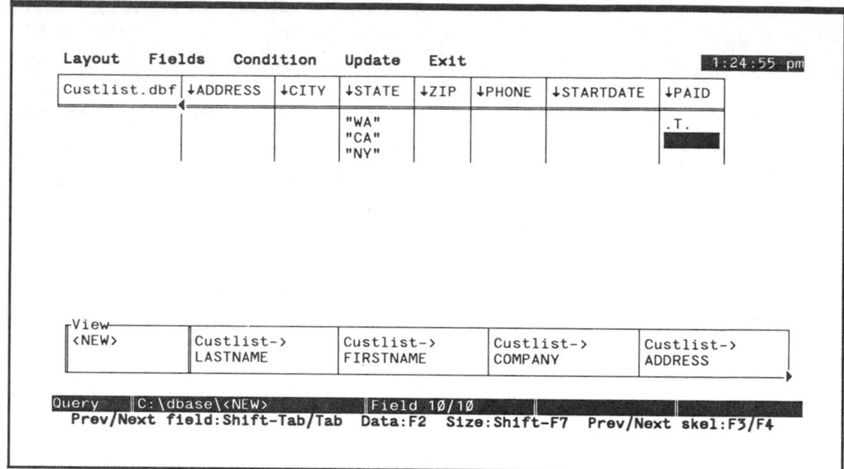

Figure 6.28: *Not* the way to set up the query to display records for all people in California, New York, and Washington who have paid

Records Organize Fields Go To Exit

CITY	STATE	ZIP	PHONE	STARTDATE	PAID
San Diego	CA	92067	(619)555-1234	11/15/92	T
Santa Monica	CA	92001	(714)555-0123	01/01/93	F
New York	NY	12345	(212)555-9988	11/15/92	T
Seattle	WA	88977	(206)555-8673	12/01/92	T
Los Angeles	CA	96607	(213)555-9988	12/30/92	F
Hideaway	CA	92220	(415)555-9854	01/01/93	T

Browse C:\dbase\<NEW> Rec 1/9 View

Figure 6.29: Results of incorrect query

the STATE field (regardless of what's in the PAID field), or NY in the STATE field (regardless of what's in the PAID field)."

However, this is not what you *meant* when you created the query. To see records for all WA, CA, and NY residents who have paid, you need to set up the query as shown in Figure 6.30.

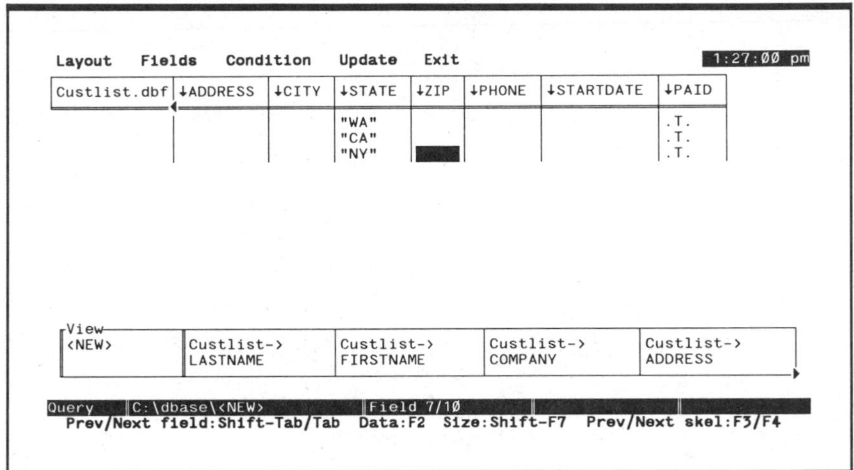

Figure 6.30: A query that combines AND and OR logic

The query in Figure 6.30 meets your needs exactly, because when dBASE uses the query, it asks, "Does this record have WA in STATE and T in PAID, or CA in STATE and T in PAID, or NY in STATE and T in PAID?" It then displays only records that meet all these criteria, as Figure 6.31 shows.

If you find AND and OR combinations confusing, think of them this way. dBASE considers each row in the query to be a single

Records Organize Fields Go To Exit

CITY	STATE	ZIP	PHONE	STARTDATE	PAID
San Diego	CA	92067	(619)555-1234	11/15/92	T
New York	NY	12345	(212)555-9988	11/15/92	T
Seattle	WA	88977	(206)555-8673	12/01/92	T
Hideaway	CA	92220	(415)555-9854	01/01/93	T

Browse C:\dbase\<NEW> Rec 1/9 View

Figure 6.31: Results of query combining AND and OR logic

question. For example, the query in Figure 6.30 can be viewed as three separate questions:

> Does this record have WA in STATE and T in PAID?
>
> Does this record have CA in STATE and T in PAID?
>
> Does this record have NY in STATE and T in PAID?

While executing the query, dBASE poses all three questions to every record in the database. If a particular record answers yes to any one question, that record is immediately displayed on the screen. A record that answers no to all three questions is not displayed.

The incorrect query in Figure 6.28 asked each record these questions:

> Does this record have WA in STATE, and T in PAID?
>
> Does this record have CA in STATE?
>
> Does this record have NY in STATE?

Although they weren't what we wanted, the results displayed by the query were accurate for these questions.

HOW COMPLEX CAN A QUERY BE?

You may be wondering how complex a query you can create. For example, can you design a single query with 12 rows of AND and OR logic, with many sounds-like operators, range searches, and Like pattern matches? The answer is yes—dBASE imposes no limitations on your queries, as long as the query makes sense.

The most common error people make is entering filter conditions into a query that do not make sense. For example, entering **"CA","WA"** in the STATE field of the CUSTLIST query screen would not display any records because the query asks for records that have both CA *and* WA in the STATE field. But a single person can (presumably) live in only one state. That is, no single record could possibly have both CA and WA in the STATE field at the same time.

(Perhaps the creator of the query meant to display records with *either* CA *or* WA in the STATE field, in which case the two filter conditions would have to be staggered onto two separate rows.)

USING QUERIES TO LOCATE A RECORD

All of the examples presented so far have demonstrated a technique for using queries to *isolate* records that meet some query condition. You can also use queries simply to *find* a particular record in the database. This is a handy technique for locating a specific record in a database, without filtering out any other records. It's also a valuable alternative to the Forward Search option on the Go To menu, because it allows you to search multiple fields, using all of the capabilities of the query design screen.

To use a query to locate a particular record, you enter the filter conditions in the query as usual. Then you enter the word **Find** beneath the database file name in the file skeleton. Figure 6.32 shows an example in which the query will locate the first record with Mahoney in the LASTNAME field and Mary in the FIRSTNAME field.

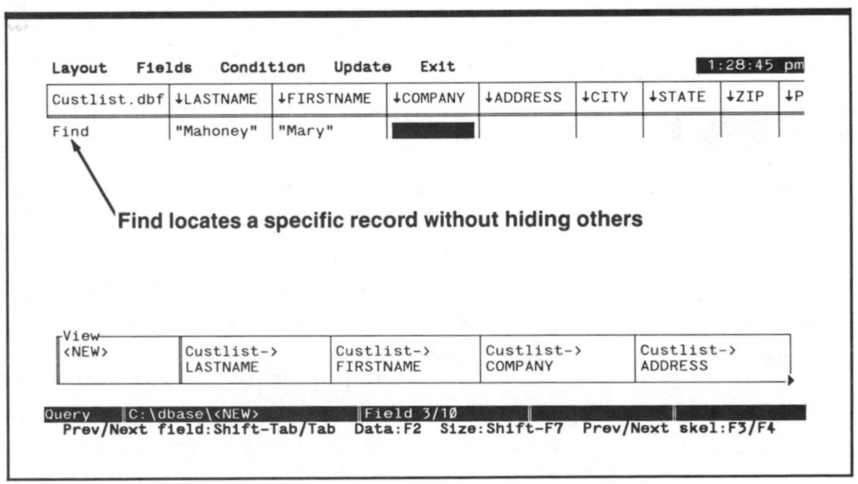

Figure 6.32: Query to locate Mary Mahoney's record

When you press or click Data (F2) to execute the query, the highlight will be positioned on Mary Mahoney's record. All other database records are still accessible, with the usual arrow, PgUp and PgDn keys.

USING THE EXPRESSION BUILDER IN QUERIES

The Expression Builder provides a handy alternative to manually typing text into your queries. Figure 6.33 shows the same filter conditions that we used in Figure 6.32 to create a query for the CUSTLIST database. But here, instead of typing FIND into the file skeleton (beneath the database file name), we opened the Expression Builder to display all the possible choices for field names, operators (such as .AND. and .OR.), functions (which you'll learn about in Chapter 12), and QBE operators (such as FIND); then we moved the cursor to FIND in the QBE Operator column of the Expression Builder. When we select this FIND operator, the word FIND will be inserted automatically into the file skeleton, without our having to type it in. Thus, the Expression Builder not only serves as a reminder of the available fields, operators, functions, and QBE operators, but also inserts them into the query.

To use the Expression Builder, follow these general steps:

As with other features in dBASE IV, if you change your mind about using the Expression Builder, you can cancel the operation by pressing Esc or clicking the mouse outside the Expression Builder.

1. Move the cursor to the appropriate field, the skeleton, or condition box on the queries design screen.
2. Press Shift-F1 to display the Expression Builder, as shown in Figure 6.33.
3. If necessary, move the highlight to the Expression Builder column that contains the field name, operator, function, or QBE operator that you want to use. For example, move the highlight to the QBE Operator column if you want to insert the FIND operator.
4. Highlight the choice you want by pressing the arrow keys, clicking the choice with your mouse, or by typing the first letter (or the first few letters) of your choice.

5. Press ↵ or click the mouse to select the item you want. Alternatively, you can combine steps 4 and 5 by double-clicking on the item you want.

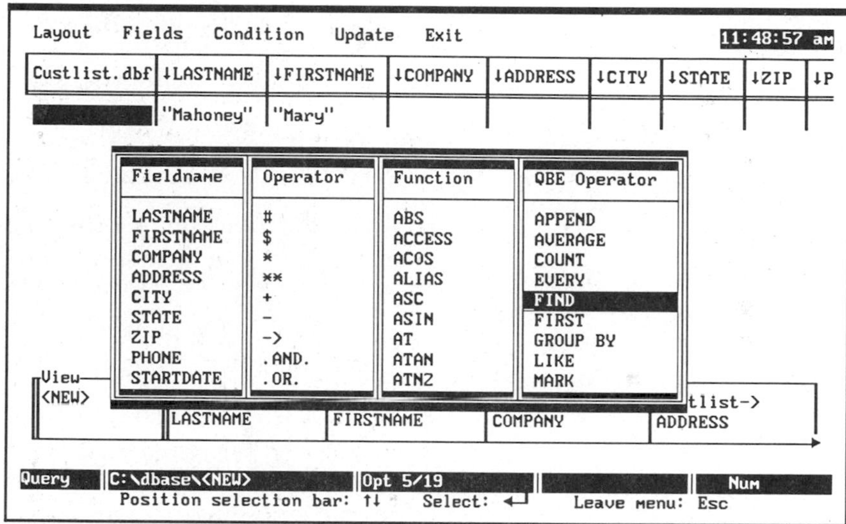

Figure 6.33: Press Shift-F1 in the queries design screen to display the Expression Builder.

SORTING QUERY DISPLAYS

So far, the results of all your queries have displayed records in the order that you originally entered them. But there may be times when you want the results of your queries to be sorted. For example, you might want to send form letters to California residents and to print them in zip code order for bulk mailing. Hence, you need a *query* to isolate records with CA in the STATE field and a *sort order* to arrange the records into zip code order.

To sort the results of a query, select Fields ► Sort on This Field on the query design screen (perhaps after you've already entered your filter conditions). Then execute your query as usual with the Data (F2) key. To see how this works, isolate records that have CA in the STATE field and sort those records into alphabetical order by city. Here are the steps:

1. As usual, work your way to the query design screen and erase any old filter conditions.
2. Move the highlight to the STATE field.
3. Enter the filter condition **"CA"** and press ↵.
4. Move to the CITY field.
5. Select Fields ► Sort on This Field.
6. From the submenu of sorting options, select Ascending Dictionary. (Note that these sorting options are the same as those presented in Table 5.1.) The CITY field now contains the sort condition *AscDict1,* which stands for "ascending dictionary order—first field." Figure 6.34 shows the completed query.
7. Press or click Data (F2) to execute the query.

If you scroll to the CITY and STATE fields in the browse screen, you'll see that only records with CA in the STATE field are displayed, and the cities are in alphabetical order, as Figure 6.35 shows.

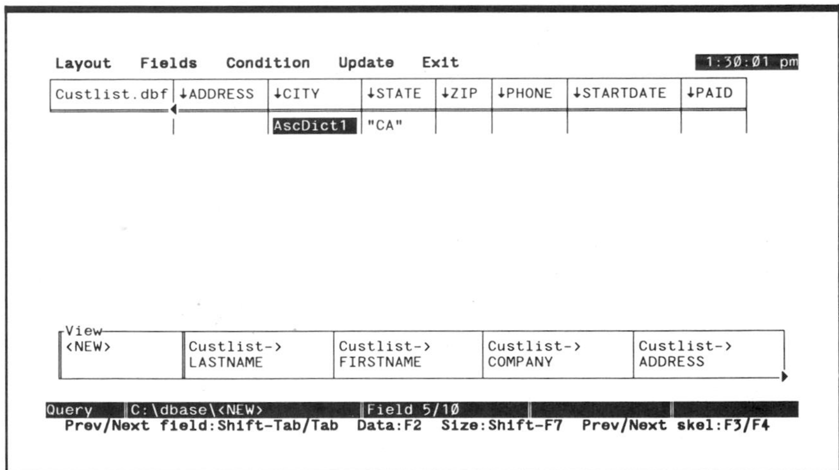

Figure 6.34: Query for records of California residents, sorted alphabetically by city

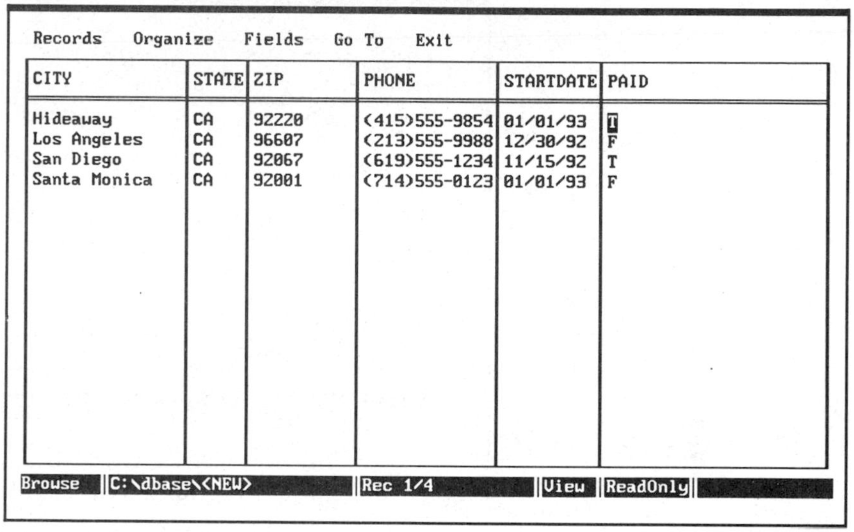

Records   Organize   Fields   Go To   Exit

CITY	STATE	ZIP	PHONE	STARTDATE	PAID
Hideaway	CA	92220	(415)555-9854	01/01/93	T
Los Angeles	CA	96607	(213)555-9988	12/30/92	F
San Diego	CA	92067	(619)555-1234	11/15/92	T
Santa Monica	CA	92001	(714)555-0123	01/01/93	F

Browse | C:\dbase\<NEW> | Rec 1/4 | View | ReadOnly

Figure 6.35: Results of query for records of California residents, sorted alphabetically by city

SORTING MULTIPLE FIELDS You can perform sorts within sorts in a query form, simply by selecting fields to sort on in most-important to least-important order. For example, if you want to sort the results of a query alphabetically by last name and then alphabetically by first name within last names, you move the highlight to the LASTNAME field, select Field ► Sort on This Field, move the highlight to the FIRSTNAME field, and select Fields ► Sort on This Field again.

dBASE includes a number in the sort condition so that you can see the field's position in the sort order. For example, in Figure 6.36 *AscDict1* indicates that LASTNAME is the first (primary) sort field, and *AscDict2* indicates that FIRSTNAME is the secondary sort field. (The sorted result is the same as when you use LASTNAME + FIRSTNAME in an index.)

Note that dBASE continues to add 1 to the AscDict symbol each time you select Sort on This Field from the Fields menu, as long as you are still in the same querying session. (A query session ends when you exit the query design screen and return to the Control Center.) Therefore, your queries might show symbols like *AscDist3,*

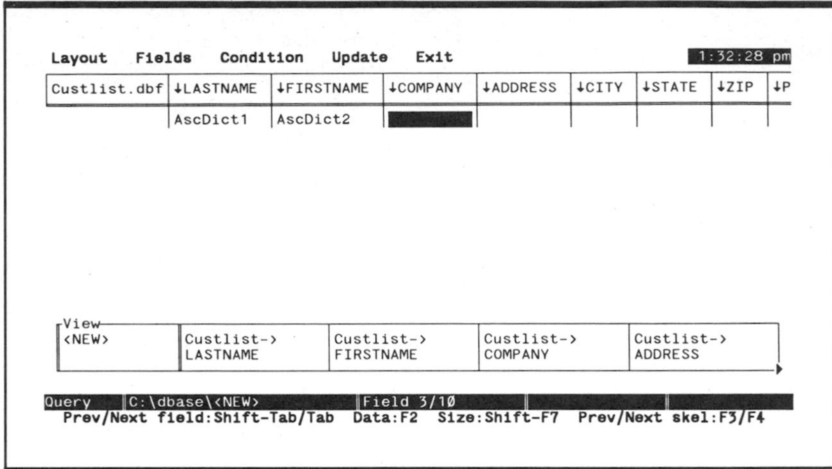

Figure 6.36: Query for sorting alphabetically by name

AscDict4, and so on. Don't worry about this—the sorting precedence remains the same.

AscDict stands for Ascending Dictionary order. Other abbreviations for sort order options are *DscDict* for Descending Dictionary, *Asc* for Ascending ASCII, and *Dsc* for Descending ASCII order.

For instance, if LASTNAME contains *AscDict1,* and if FIRSTNAME contains *AscDict2,* the data are sorted by first name within common last names. If LASTNAME contains *AscDict3* and FIRSTNAME contains *AscDict4,* you get the same results; first names are still sorted within common last names.

COMBINING FILTER AND SORT CONDITIONS Any field on the query design screen can contain both a filter condition and a sort condition. First put in all of your filter conditions, and then select fields to sort on. dBASE will automatically place the sort condition, preceded by a comma, after the filter condition.

Figure 6.37 shows an example where the query will display only records that begin with the letters "A" through "N." The resulting records will be displayed in alphabetical order by STATE (that is, CA will precede MT, which will precede NY). Within each state, cities will be in alphabetical order (that is, within California, Hideaway will precede Los Angeles, which will precede Malibu, which will precede San Diego).

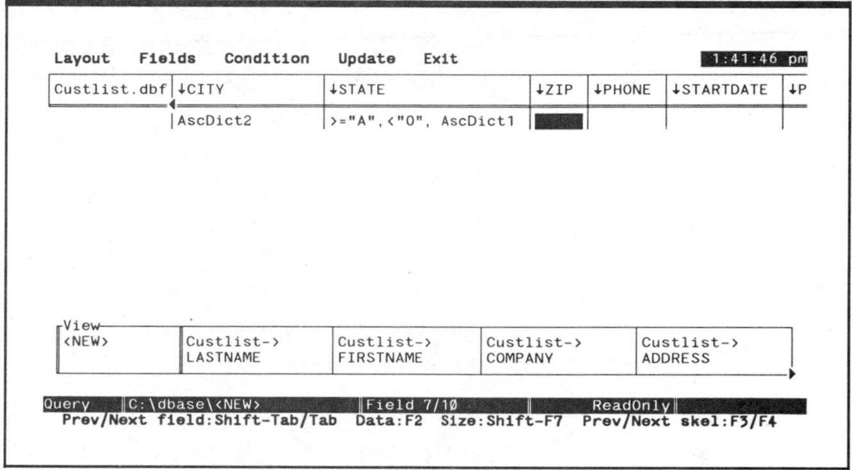

Figure 6.37: A filter and sort condition combined in the LASTNAME field

HOW QUERIES SORT RECORDS

In Chapter 5, we discussed the difference between using an index to display data in sorted order and using the Organize ► Sort Database on Field List option on the browse or edit screen to create a separate, sorted database file. All of the sorts that we've performed so far in this chapter have actually used the latter technique, sorting to a separate database file. The resulting browse screen displayed the data from the separate, sorted file (not from the original CUSTLIST file).

Whenever dBASE uses a separate file to display the results of a sorted query, the message ReadOnly appears in the status bar of the resulting browse or edit screen (Figure 6.35 shows an example). This message reminds you that the data on this screen can only be read; you cannot enter new data or make changes.

If you attempt to make changes to data on the ReadOnly browse or edit screen, dBASE will beep and reject your keystrokes. This protects you from inadvertently making changes on the sorted copy of the database, rather than on the original database.

As you begin to work with larger databases, you will notice that dBASE takes quite a while to display the results of a sorted query. That's because the query uses the inefficient "sort" method, rather than the quicker and more efficient index method, to organize the records. Again, the delay may not seem significant when you are working with the small CustList database. But when you begin managing databases with hundreds or thousands of records, such sorts can be very time consuming.

You may be wondering if there is some way around these slow, uneditable query results. The answer is yes, there is. And perhaps you will not be too surprised to learn that the answer involves indexes. If you use an index to sort the results of the query, you'll get your results more quickly and you'll be able to make changes in the resulting browse screen.

USING INDEXES TO SORT QUERY RESULTS

Let's start this section with an entirely new query session. (It's not absolutely necessary to do so, but it will be easier to follow step-by-step instructions if you start with a clean slate.) Follow these steps:

1. If the browse screen is showing, press Design (Shift-F2) or select Exit ► Transfer to Query Design to return to the query design screen.
2. Select Exit ► Abandon Changes and Exit.
3. If asked about Abandoning, select Yes. You'll be returned to the Control Center.

The CUSTLIST database name should still be above the line in the Data panel, indicating that it is still open and ready for use. To get back to the query design screen, follow these simple steps:

1. Make sure the highlight is on <create> in the Queries panel.
2. Press ↵ or click the mouse.

Now you are back in the query design screen, and can be certain that there are no old filter conditions or sort operators lying around. Let's use the ZIP index that you created in Chapter 5 to sort the results of a query. We'll ask dBASE to display only California residents, and to display them in zip code order. Here are the steps:

1. To include indexes in your query, select Fields ► Include Indexes.
2. To isolate records for California residents, press the Tab key until you get to the STATE field, enter the filter condition **"CA"** (including the quotation marks), and press ↵.
3. Press the Tab key to move to the ZIP field. Notice that a triangle (▲) appears next to the ZIP field name. This ▲ sign tells you that ZIP is an index field.
4. Select Fields ► Sort on This Field.
5. From the submenu, select Ascending ASCII. Notice in Figure 6.38 that the ZIP field now contains the sort operator Asc1, the same sort operator you would use if no index file were involved. However, dBASE automatically uses the ZIP index to speed the sort because it now "knows" that ZIP is an index field.

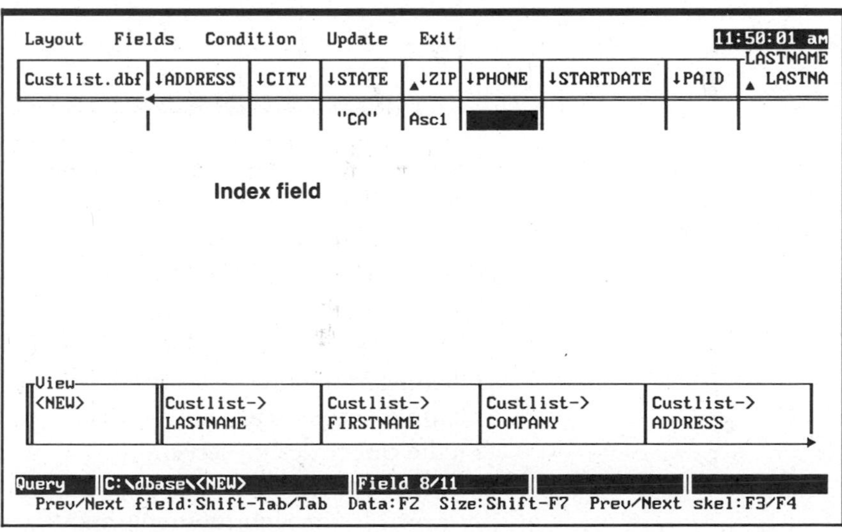

Figure 6.38: Query to display records for California residents, sorted by zip code

6. To execute the query, press or click Data (F2). As you can see in Figure 6.39, the browse screen displays CA residents only, sorted into zip code order. Notice that the ReadOnly message does not appear in the status bar. You can, therefore, change any data in the current browse screen, but there is no need to do so now.
7. Press Design (Shift-F2) or select Exit ► Transfer to Query Design to return to the query design screen.

```
Records   Organize   Fields   Go To   Exit

CITY         | STATE | ZIP    | PHONE         | STARTDATE | PAID
Santa Monica | CA    | 92001  | (714)555-0123 | 01/01/93  | F
San Diego    | CA    | 92067  | (619)555-1234 | 11/15/92  | T
Hideaway     | CA    | 92220  | (415)555-9854 | 01/01/93  | T
Los Angeles  | CA    | 96607  | (213)555-9988 | 12/30/92  | F

Browse  | C:\dbase\<NEW>  | Rec 2/9  | View |
```

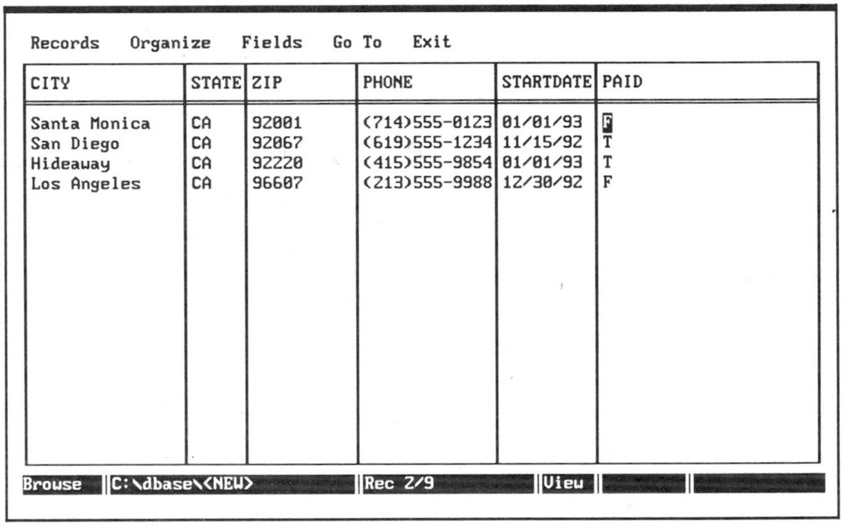

Figure 6.39: Results of query to display records for California residents, sorted by zip code

USING COMPLEX INDEXES In the preceding example, the ZIP field was marked with a ▲ to indicate that it was an index field. What about the LASTNAME + FIRSTNAME index you created in Chapter 5? That's a *complex index* because it uses more than one field. Complex indexes are always displayed to the right of database fields on the query design screen.

To verify this, you can press the End key to move to the rightmost column. In the rightmost column you will find the additional field ▲ LASTNAME + FIRSTNAME, with the ▲ symbol again indicating that this is an index field. You can use this field just as you would use any other field in the query design screen, both for sorting and for querying.

Suppose you again want to display records for California residents only, but this time in alphabetical order by last and first name. Here are the steps to do so:

1. Remove the Asc1 operator from the ZIP field.
2. Move to the ▲ LASTNAME + FIRSTNAME query field.
3. Select Field ► Sort on This Field.
4. Select Ascending ASCII. Now you've specified that you want both to search for California residents and to use the index to control the sort order of the display. Figure 6.40 shows how the query form looks.

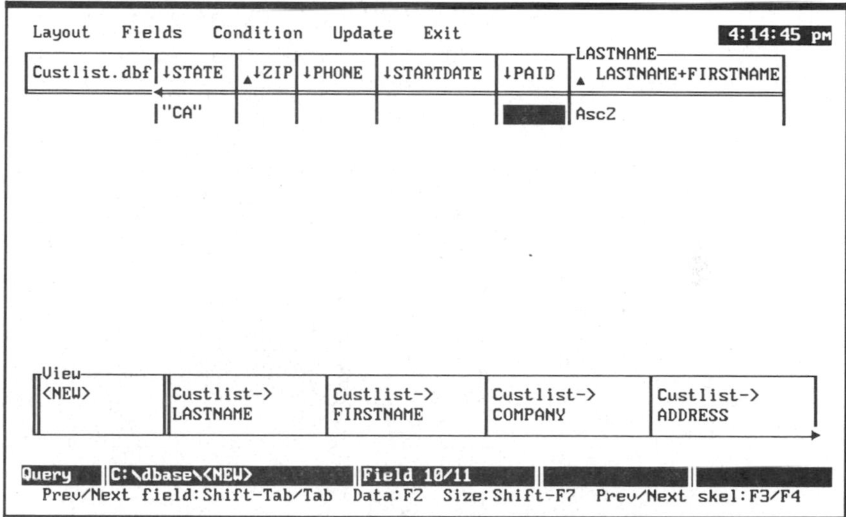

Figure 6.40: Search for CA records, with LASTNAME + FIRSTNAME sort specified

5. Press or click Data (F2) to execute the query. The browse screen displays only CA records, listed in alphabetical order by last and first name.
6. After viewing the results of the query, press Design (Shift-F2) or select Exit ► Transfer to Query Design to return to the query design screen.

By now you've come a long way in gaining access to the data in a database. You've learned how to sort your database records and how to search for records that contain a particular value. In addition, you've seen how to combine sorting and searching. Because you've used indexes to handle your sorting, you've learned the fastest, most efficient techniques for performing these tasks.

Perhaps this would be a good time to take a break. Follow these steps to leave the query design screen and return to the Control Center:

1. Select Exit ► Abandon Changes and Exit.
2. When prompted, select Yes to abandon the query design screen.

You'll be returned to the Control Center. From there, you can quit dBASE IV if you wish. To resume with the next section later, get dBASE IV up and running again and open the LEARN catalog using the steps discussed earlier in this chapter.

SELECTING FIELDS TO DISPLAY IN A QUERY

Previously in this chapter, you've used the query design screen to tell dBASE which *records* you want to display in the results of a query. For example, you've designed queries to display records that have "CA" in the STATE field. You can also use the query design screen to display only certain *fields* in the results of a query. To create a personal phone list, for example, you might want dBASE to display only the LASTNAME, FIRSTNAME, and PHONE fields. To determine which fields are displayed in the results of a query, use the view skeleton at the bottom of the query design screen.

We'll go through the steps involved in deciding which fields to display in a moment. But you'll want to start with a new query design screen. If you did not follow steps 1 and 2 to take a break at the end of the preceding section, do so now. We'll start the next steps from the Control Center. First, we need to get to the query design screen:

1. If the CUSTLIST database name is not above the line in the Data panel of the Control Center, move the highlight to it, click or press ↵, and select Use File.
2. Move the highlight to <create> in the Queries panel and click or press ↵ (or double-click on <create>) to create a new query.

Now you are in the query design screen, where we can start to experiment with the view skeleton. There are several techniques you can use to move field names into and out of the view skeleton. By default, dBASE includes all field names in the view skeleton. You can remove all the field names and put them back in by positioning the highlight beneath the file name in the File Skeleton and pressing F5 (see Figure 6.41).

To try this, first press Home to ensure that the highlight is beneath the file name Custlist.dbf. Then press F5 a few times, and notice that each time you do so, the field names in the view skeleton disappear or reappear.

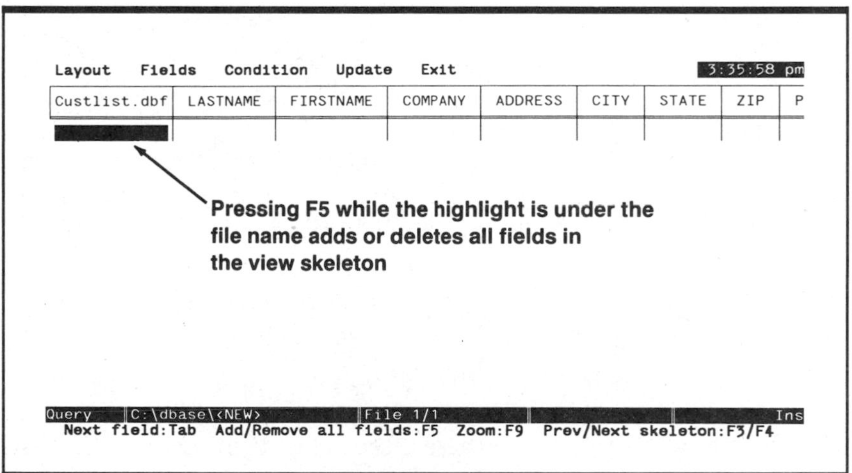

Figure 6.41: All fields are removed from the view skeleton

Now let's try a practical example by creating a personal phone list from the CustList database. Follow these steps:

1. Make sure the highlight is beneath Custlist.dbf in the file skeleton.
2. Press F5 until the view skeleton is empty (no field names appear at the bottom of the screen).
3. Press the End key and then press the Shift-Tab key twice to move the highlight to the PHONE field (or just click in that field).
4. Press Field (F5) or double-click on the field name to copy this field into the view skeleton. You'll notice two things: first, the Custlist->PHONE field now appears in the view skeleton, and, additionally, the ↓ symbol appears to the left of the field name PHONE in the file skeleton. Both changes serve as reminders that the field will be displayed in the results of the query.
5. Move the highlight to the FIRSTNAME field.
6. Press Field (F5) or double-click on the field name to copy the field to the view skeleton.
7. Move the highlight to the LASTNAME field.
8. Press Field (F5) or double-click on the field name to copy the LASTNAME field to the view skeleton.

As Figure 6.42 shows, the view skeleton now displays the three fields that will be displayed as a result of the query: PHONE, FIRSTNAME, and LASTNAME.

Now you can press or click Data (F2) to see the results. You'll see that the browse screen displays the PHONE, FIRSTNAME, and LASTNAME fields of all the records in the database, as shown in Figure 6.43.

If you press F2 to switch to the edit screen, it too will display only these three fields. Press Design (Shift-F2) or select Exit ► Transfer to Query Design to return to the query design screen after viewing the results of the query.

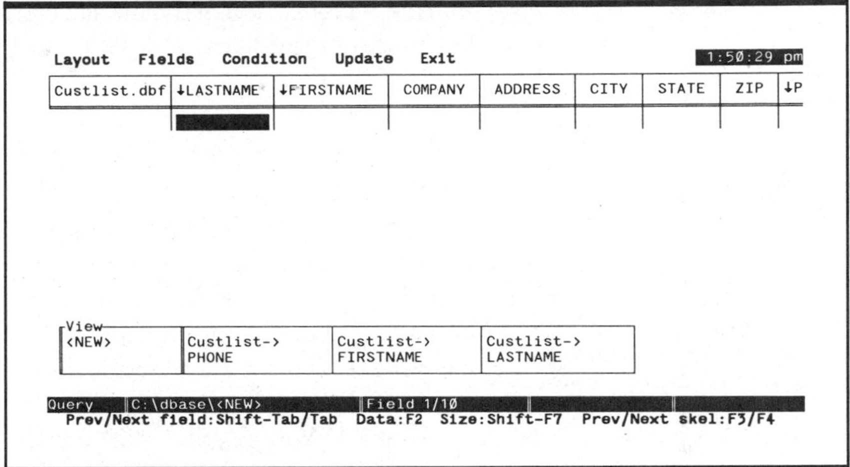

Figure 6.42: PHONE, FIRSTNAME, and LASTNAME fields displayed

Records Organize Fields Go To Exit

PHONE	FIRSTNAME	LASTNAME
(619)555-1234	John	Smith
(714)555-Ø123	Annie	Adams
(212)555-9988	Wilbur	Watson
(2Ø6)555-8673	Mary	Mahoney
(3Ø3)555-6739	John	Newell
(717)555-Ø898	Sandy	Beach
(213)555-9988	Ralph	Kenney
(2Ø2)555-972Ø	Susita	Schumack
(415)555-9854	Anita	Smith

Browse C:\dbase\<NEW> Rec 1/9 View

Figure 6.43: Results of view skeleton displaying the fields PHONE, FIRSTNAME, and LASTNAME

The file skeleton and view skeleton in the query design screen work somewhat independently of one another in that you can place a filter condition in any field in the file skeleton, regardless of whether the view skeleton includes that field. For example, even though the view skeleton you created tells dBASE to *display* only the PHONE, FIRSTNAME, and LASTNAME fields, you could still enter **"CA"** into the STATE field of the file skeleton to limit the phone number list to California residents.

MANAGING THE VIEW SKELETON

NOTE

You can also switch to the file skeleton by clicking in the empty space just below the database name or any field name in that skeleton; to switch to the view skeleton, click the horizontal line just above any field name in that skeleton.

You've seen that you can use the F5 key or the mouse to move fields into the view skeleton. You can also work directly with the view skeleton by pressing the Next key (F4). When you do so, the highlight moves to the view skeleton and a new set of navigation key options appears at the bottom of the screen. (One of the options, Prev/Next Skel:F3/F4 reminds you that you can move back to the previous skeleton by pressing F3, and forward to the next skeleton by pressing F4. You can also click on one of these key labels at the bottom of the screen with the mouse instead of pressing the keys.)

MOVING FIELDS IN THE VIEW SKELETON To move a field in the view skeleton, thereby rearranging the order in which fields are displayed, first make sure that the highlight is in the view skeleton. Then use the Tab or Shift-Tab key, or the mouse, to highlight the field that you want to move. Finally, press or click Move (F7). dBASE will highlight the frame around the field and present the instructions "TAB or BACKTAB to move fields. <Return> to end." This means that dBASE wants you to use the Tab or Shift-Tab key or to click on one of the labels in the instruction line to move the highlighted box to the new location for the field. You can also use → or ← to move the box. When the field is in its new location, press ↵ or click on <Return>. Go ahead and experiment on your own if you like.

SELECTING GROUPS OF FIELDS While at the view skeleton, you can press or click Select (F6) to highlight a group of adjacent fields to work with. To use Select, move the highlight to the leftmost or rightmost field in the group you want to select. Press or click Select (F6) and use the Tab or Shift-Tab key (or → or ←) to extend the highlight to the left or right, as instructed on the screen (but don't highlight *all* the fields, or you won't be able to move them). Press ↵ or click on <Return> after highlighting a group of fields.

Once you have highlighted a group of fields, pressing or clicking F5 removes all those fields from the view. Pressing or clicking F7 allows you to move that entire group of fields to a new location. After you complete your job, the highlighting disappears. You may want to try some of these features of the view skeleton on your own.

CONTROLLING THE FILE SKELETON COLUMN WIDTHS

As you've undoubtedly noticed by now, whenever you type a query condition into the file skeleton (at the top of the query design screen), the column automatically widens to accommodate your entry. If you enter many wide conditions, you may find it difficult to read your query design screen.

If, for whatever reason, you want to narrow or widen fields in the file skeleton, follow these simple general steps:

- Move the highlighter to the field you want to widen or narrow.
- Press or click Size (Shift-F7).
- Press ← and/or → or move the mouse pointer to narrow or widen the column to your liking.
- Press ↵ or click the mouse.

Even if the filter condition within the column is wider than the width you've allotted for it, the query will still work. And, you can still edit the filter condition by scrolling through it with the ← and → keys.

Once you set the column width using this technique, it remains fixed and will not change, even if you change the query within it. If you want to return the column to the normal "elastic" mode, where it adjusts to accommodate its contents, move the highlighter back to the column and press or click Size (Shift-F7) twice.

Note that changing the width of a column in the file skeleton of the query design screen does not affect the actual width of the field in the database, nor the width of the field as displayed on the browse and edit screens.

SAVING QUERIES FOR FUTURE USE

You can save any query that you create as a file using a valid DOS file name (eight letters maximum, no spaces or punctuation; dBASE will automatically add the extension .QBE to the file name you provide). Then you can reuse that query at any time in the future, without reentering all the keystrokes for filter conditions and so forth.

Figure 6.44 shows a sample query that displays California residents' phone numbers, sorted in alphabetical order by name. The query combines many of the techniques we've discussed in this chapter. You should be able to create it on your own without step-by-step instructions, but I'll give you some hints to help out:

- First, limit the view skeleton to the LASTNAME, FIRSTNAME, and PHONE fields (in that order) using Field (F5), Previous/Next skeleton (F3 and F4), and other keys or mouse clicks described in the navigation line.
- Enter the "CA" filter condition under the STATE field of the file skeleton.
- Include indexes in the file skeleton query to speed up the search. Select Fields ► Include Indexes.
- Specify LASTNAME + FIRSTNAME index as the index for controlling the sort order (by positioning the highlight and selecting Fields ► Sort on This Field ►).

When you are done, your query should look like Figure 6.44. To verify that you got it right, execute the query with the Data (F2) key. The browse screen should show the four California residents and their phone numbers:

LASTNAME	FIRSTNAME	PHONE
Adams	Annie	(714) 555-0123
Kenney	Ralph	(213) 555-9988
Smith	Anita	(415) 555-9854
Smith	John	(619) 555-1234

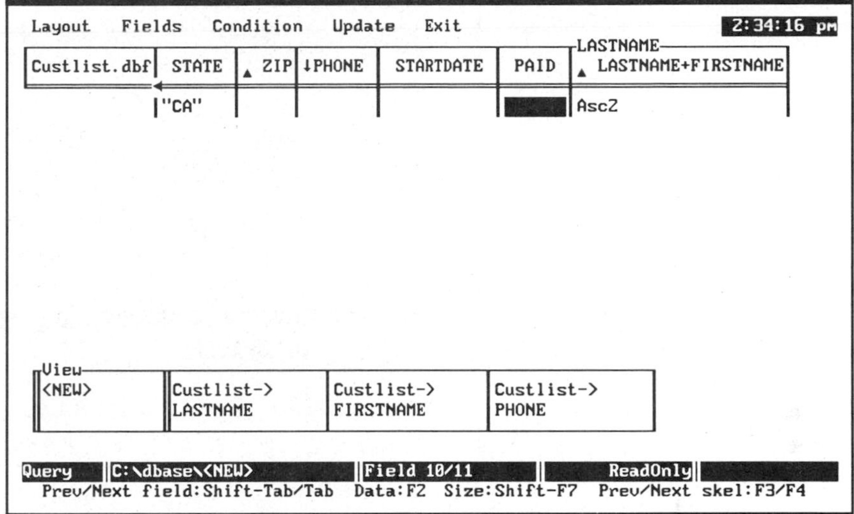

Figure 6.44: Query to display California customers' phone numbers

Suppose you want to save this query for future use so that you can always print current phone numbers for California residents without rebuilding the query. First assign a description to the query by following these steps:

1. Press Design (Shift-F2) or select Exit ► Transfer to Query Design to return to the query design screen.
2. Select Layout ► Edit Description of Query.
3. Type a description, such as **California phone numbers**, in this example. Press ↵.

To save the query and its description, follow these steps:

1. Select Exit ► Save Changes and Exit.
2. When dBASE displays the prompt "Save as:" enter a valid DOS file name. In this example, type **PHONELST** and press ↵.

You'll be returned to the Control Center where the new PHONELST query will be listed in the Queries panel. When you highlight the PHONELST query, you'll also see its description, as in Figure 6.45.

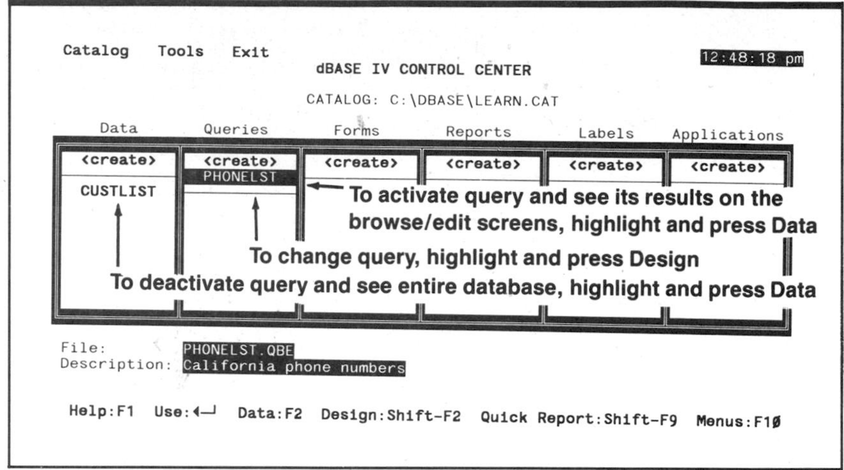

Figure 6.45: PHONELST query listed in the Queries panel

Figure 6.45 also summarizes three basic techniques that you can use with a saved query. Later examples in this book will give you more experience with these techniques. Here we'll discuss them in some detail, but before we do, you'll need some additional background.

In dBASE IV a saved query is also referred to as a *view*. This is because a query provides a particular way of viewing the data in a database. For example, the PHONELST query you just created shows you a particular slice of the CUSTLIST database, the LASTNAME, FIRSTNAME, and PHONE fields with only California residents displayed in alphabetical order by name.

Unlike a database file, a query (view) does not actually contain data. Instead, it contains instructions that dBASE IV reads to see how you want to view the data in a database. Therefore, any changes you make to the original database (CUSTLIST in this example) will indeed be reflected in the view the next time you use it. For example, if you were to change a California resident's phone number in the CUSTLIST database, the next time you used the PHONELST query, the new phone number would be displayed.

Views are a two-way street; because PHONELST shows data that is actually from the CUSTLIST database, if you change any data displayed by the PHONELST view, that change occurs in the CUSTLIST database.

As you'll discover in the following sections, the techniques that you use to manage a view from the Control Center are no different from those you use to manage a database file.

ACTIVATING A SAVED QUERY

To view database data through a saved query, highlight the name of the query in the Queries panel and press or click Data (F2). (This is similar to viewing the contents of the entire database, where you highlight the name of the database in the Data panel and press or click F2). If you highlight the PHONELST view and press or click F2, you'll be taken to the edit or browse screen where you'll see entries from the LASTNAME, FIRSTNAME, and PHONE fields of the CUSTLIST database. From there, you can use the usual F2 key to switch between the edit and browse screens at your convenience.

When you've finished looking at (or editing) the data through the view, select Exit ► Exit or press Esc or Ctrl-End, to return to the Control Center. At the Control Center, you'll notice that the PHONELST name is above the line in the Queries panel, indicating that it is still in use. If you want to view the entire CUSTLIST database again, open it by highlighting its name in the Data panel and pressing or clicking F2.

CHANGING A QUERY

If you want to change the query, highlight its name in the Queries panel and press or click Design (Shift-F2). You'll be taken to the query design screen where you can make any changes you wish to the query.

While you are in the query design screen, you can modify the query in any way you wish using the same techniques that you used to create queries in this chapter. You can also see the results of the query using Data (F2), as you did in previous examples. To return to the query design screen, use Design (Shift-F2), just as you did before.

When you have finished making changes to the query, select Exit ► Save Changes and Exit, or press Ctrl-End, to return to the Control Center. The name of the query will still be accessible in the Control Center, and any changes you've made will be included the next time you activate the query.

DEACTIVATING A QUERY

When you want to stop using a query and regain access to all the records and fields in your database file, simply opening the database file deactivates the query. For example, to deactivate the PHONELST query and regain access to all the records and fields in the CUSTLIST database, highlight CUSTLIST in the Data panel and press or click Data (F2). You'll be sent to the browse (or edit) screen, where you will see the entire CUSTLIST database.

To leave the edit or browse screen and return to the Control Center, select Exit ► Exit. When you get back to the Control Center, the CUSTLIST database name will be above the line in the Data panel, indicating that the CUSTLIST database is open and ready for use. The PHONELST query name will be below the line, indicating that it is no longer active (that is, no longer affecting your view of the CUSTLIST database).

ALTERNATIVE TECHNIQUES

Just as the Data panel offers alternatives to the Data and Design keys, so does the Queries panel. If you highlight the name of a saved query in the Queries panel and click on it or press ↵ (or double-click on that name), you'll see three options in a prompt box (available only if the Instruct setting, discussed in Chapter 2, is on). If the query is not already active, the three options will be

Use View   Modify Query   Display Data

If the highlighted query is active when you press ↵, the three options will be

Close View   Modify Query   Display Data

Selecting Use View puts the view name above the line in the queries panel. Selecting Close View deactivates the query, putting its name below the line. Selecting Modify Query takes you to the queries design screen (exactly as though you had pressed the Design key) and lets you make changes to the query. Selecting Display Data activates the view and takes you to the edit or browse screen (as though you had pressed the Data key).

Starting in the next chapter, you'll see how to use saved queries (views) to isolate records for printing information such as mailing labels and form letters. This is where the saved query really comes in handy. It allows you to isolate targeted records (those of New York residents, for example), and then print letters and labels in zip code order to take advantage of cheaper bulk mailing rates.

CHAPTER

7

Printing Formatted Reports

To print an instant report of all the records in a database or query, **168**
highlight the name of the database or query in the Control Center, press or click Quick Report (Shift-F9), and select Begin Printing.

To design a format for printing labels, **174**
open the database that contains the data you want to print and then select <create> from the Labels panel in the Control Center.

To add fields to a label or report format, **178**
press or click Add Field (F5), or choose Fields ► Add Field from the menu, or double-click the mouse.

To print labels **182**
after designing a format, select the name of the label format from the Labels panel in the Control Center and select Print Label from the submenu.

To design a report format, **194**
open the database that contains the data you want to print and then select <create> from the Reports panel in the Control Center.

To quickly develop an initial report design, **197**
choose Layout ► Quick Layouts from the menu on the reports design screen, then select a general format.

To change or rearrange a report or label format, **200**
use editing keys, or press or click Select (F6), followed by Move (F7) and Copy (F8).

To print a report 206

using a completed format, select the name of the format from the Reports panel in the Control Center and select Print Report and Begin Printing from the menus that follow.

To print labels or reports in sorted order, 216

activate (or create) the appropriate index on the database design screen. Then print the report or labels as you would normally.

To print labels or reports from the results of a query, 217

first activate the query by selecting it from the Queries panel in the Control Center and selecting Use View from the submenu that appears. Then print the labels or report as you would normally.

To modify an existing label or report format, 218

open the associated database or query, highlight the name of the format in the Control Center, and then press or click Design (Shift-F2).

To control printer operations, 225

use options from the Print pull-down menu that appears whenever you print labels or a report.

THIS CHAPTER PRESENTS TECHNIQUES FOR USING your printer and formatting your dBASE IV information into a variety of useful reports, such as customer lists, mailing labels, and form letters. As usual, if you exited dBASE IV at the end of the previous chapter, be sure to get it up and running again and bring the LEARN catalog into the Control Center.

USING QUICK REPORT

The quickest and easiest way to get a printed copy of your information is to use the Quick Report option (Shift-F9) from the Control Center. This technique simply dumps data from your database onto the printer, without much regard for formatting. To use Quick Report, you highlight the name of the database file or query that you want to print from, then press or click Quick Report (Shift-F9) and select Begin Printing from the menu that appears. Let's work through an example, printing the results of the PHONELST query that you created at the end of the previous chapter. Here are the steps:

1. Move the highlight to the PHONELST query in the Queries panel.
2. Press or click Quick Report (Shift-F9).
3. If dBASE asks whether you want to use the current view or PHONELST.qbe, select PHONELST.qbe (you'll learn more about this in a moment).
4. From the submenu that appears, press ↵ to select Begin Printing.
5. Before printing starts, dBASE IV generates a *program* that it uses to print the report. This task may take a few seconds.
6. As dBASE prints the report, you'll see another submenu that allows you to cancel or pause printing. Don't do anything; the submenu will disappear when printing is complete.

Figure 7.1 shows the printed report. As you may recall, the PHONELST query included only the LASTNAME,

FIRSTNAME, and PHONE fields for California residents, so the Quick Report displays only this information. (If you repeat the preceding steps, highlighting CUSTLIST rather than PHONELST in step 1, the report will display all the information in the CUSTLIST database file, probably spread across a few pages.)

```
Page No.    1
01/15/93

LASTNAME         FIRSTNAME        PHONE

Adams            Annie            (714)555-0123
Kenney           Ralph            (213)555-9988
Smith            Anita            (415)555-9854
Smith            John             (619)555-1234
```

Figure 7.1: Printed output from the PHONELST query

SELECTING DATA TO PRINT

Before we go on, let's backtrack for a moment and discuss the choice between the current view and CUSTLIST.DBF that you may have made to print the data in the CUSTLIST file. Understanding that choice will tell you a lot about how to select data for printing in dBASE IV.

In some situations, dBASE IV may not be sure if you want to print data directly from a database file or from a query (for example, if a database file is in use, but a query is highlighted in the Control Center). If dBASE IV is not sure where you want to print from, it displays options that let you clarify the source of the report, as in Figure 7.2.

In Figure 7.2, dBASE asks whether you want to use the current view (or query) or the original CUSTLIST.DBF database file. You can select either option using the usual technique of highlighting and pressing ↵, or by clicking on the option. Keep in mind that database files always have the extension .DBF, and queries (views) always have the extension .QBE. Selecting a .DBF file always prints the

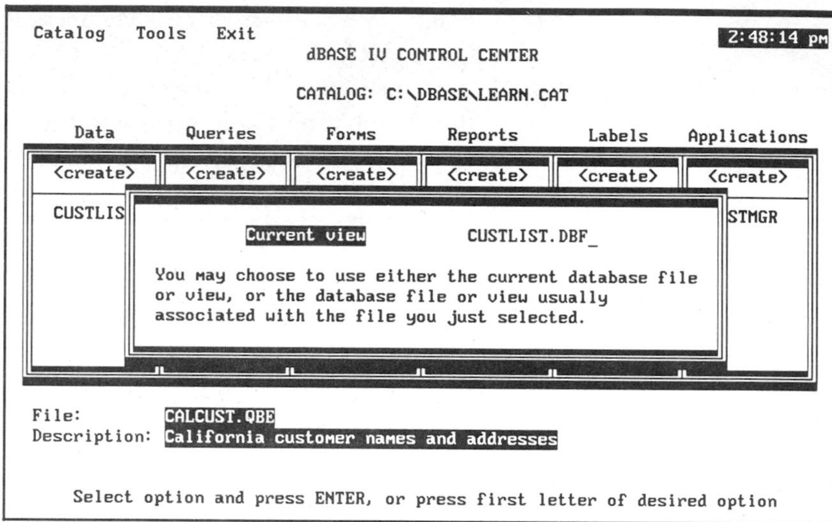

Figure 7.2: dBASE IV prompt for the source of data for the report

entire contents of the database file. Selecting a .QBE query, or view, prints only the fields and records that are specified in the query.

After you've made your selection, you'll see the submenu of printing options, which we'll discuss in more detail later. (As usual, you can press Esc or click the mouse any place outside the submenu to back out of the submenu and return to the Control Center.)

GENERAL TECHNIQUES FOR DESIGNING AND PRINTING REPORTS

As a shortcut for the second and third steps, you can double-click your mouse on <create> in either the Labels or the Reports panel.

The Quick Report option provides a quick and easy method for printing data in a somewhat formatted manner. When you want more control over the format of your output, such as when printing business reports, mailing labels, form letters, or whatever, you'll want to use the *labels design screen* and *reports design screen* discussed in this chapter.

You'll have an opportunity to create several reports in this chapter. But before proceeding, let's take a moment to summarize the general steps for creating custom report formats, be they mailing labels, form letters, or business reports:

- Make sure the database that you want to print the data from is already open (above the line in the Data panel).
- If you want to print labels, highlight <create> in the Labels panel; for any other type of formatted report, highlight <create> in the Reports panel.
- Press ↵ or click the mouse button.
- If you are designing a report rather than labels:
    - Choose Layout ► Quick Layouts and select one of the quick layouts.
    - Choose Words ► Modify Ruler, then set your margins.
- If you are designing labels rather than a report:
    - Define a label size by selecting an option (or options) from the Dimensions pull-down menu.
- Use the techniques described in this chapter (and summarized in Tables 7.1 and 7.2 and the inside of the back cover of this book) to design the report format to your liking.
- Press Ctrl-End, or choose Exit ► Save Changes and Exit to save the format.
- When prompted, type a valid DOS file name (no extension) and press ↵.

NOTE

All techniques for changing and refining formats can be used at any time, regardless of whether you are creating a new format or changing an existing one.

Table 7.1: Keys for Editing Label and Report Formats

Key	Effect
↓	Moves down one row
↑	Moves up one row
→	Moves right one character or to end of field template
←	Moves left one character or to beginning of field template
Ctrl-→	Moves one word to the right

Table 7.1: Keys for Editing Label and Report Formats (continued)

Key	Effect
Ctrl-←	Moves one word to the left
PgUp	Moves to top of screen
PgDn	Moves to bottom of screen
End	Moves to end of line
Home	Moves to beginning of line
Ins	Toggles Insert mode on/off
↵	If Insert mode is off, moves down one row; if Insert mode is on, inserts a new line; on reports design, opens and closes bands when cursor is on a border
F1	Provides help
F5	Adds a new field template or changes the currently highlighted one
F6	Selects field template or block
F7	Moves field or block selected with F6
F8	Copies field or block selected with F6
Shift-F7	Changes size of currently selected field template
Ctrl-N	Inserts a new line
Backspace	Erases character to the left
Del	Deletes character, field template, or block selected with F6
Ctrl-T	Removes word or field to right
Ctrl-Y	Removes entire line
Tab	Moves to next tab setting (reformats paragraph in word-wrap editor)
Shift-Tab	Moves to previous tab setting (reformats paragraph in word-wrap editor)
Esc	Abandons current format without saving changes, or unselects currently selected block or template

Table 7.2: Mouse Operations for Editing Label and Report Formats

Operation	**Action**
Add a field	Position the mouse pointer and double-click, or position the mouse pointer and click once, then click Add field:F5 on the navigation line. Choose a field from the fields list.
Modify a field	Double-click the field.
Highlight or unhighlight an item	Click the item to highlight it, or click outside the item to unhighlight it.
Select a field template or block	Click the beginning of the template or block, then click Select:F6 on the navigation line. Move the mouse to highlight the end of the template or block, then press ↵ or click the mouse. Alternatively, you can move the mouse pointer to the beginning of the template or block, press the mouse button and drag to highlight the end of the template or block, then release the mouse button.
Move or copy a selected field or block	Select the field or block, click Move:F7 or Copy:F8 on the navigation line, move the mouse to the new position, then press ↵ or click the mouse.
Change the size of a field template	Click the field template, then click Size:Shift-F7 on the navigation line. Move the mouse pointer to the desired size, then click.

It may take a few minutes for dBASE to prepare your complete report format, but eventually you'll be returned to the Control Center. At any time in the future, you can print the data in your database using the format you designed by following these general steps:

- Highlight the name of the format in the Reports or Labels column and press ↵ or double-click that format.
- Select Print Label or Print Report (depending on which you are printing at the moment).
- Press ↵ to select Begin Printing.

You'll be returned to the Control Center when printing is done.

As you will see, there are many features available to you, all designed to give you as much control over the appearance of your printed report as possible. To get some hands-on experience with these features, we'll start by designing the easiest type of format, mailing labels.

DESIGNING A LABEL FORMAT

To print labels, you first design the appearance, or *format,* of the label using the labels design screen (or *labels design work surface*). Note that dBASE IV uses the term *labels* rather loosely. Not only can you use the labels design screen to print any type of mailing label, but you can also use it to print envelopes, Rolodex-like cards, and general-purpose labels such as identification stickers.

SELECTING A DATABASE

Before you begin to design a label format, you need to make sure the appropriate database file (or query) is open. In this example, you'll design labels for the CUSTLIST database. Recall that if a database or query is currently in use (open), its name appears above the line in the Data panel. If you need to open the CUSTLIST database now, follow these steps:

1. Highlight the name CUSTLIST in the Data panel and press ↵ or double-click it with your mouse.
2. If the Use File option appears, select it. (Otherwise, press Esc to cancel the selection, because CUSTLIST is already open.)

USING THE LABELS DESIGN SCREEN

After you've specified the database file that you want to print labels from, you need to move to the labels design screen. To do so, move the highlight to the <create> option in the Labels panel and press ↵, or double-click that option with your mouse (as shown in Figure 7.3). You'll see the labels design screen.

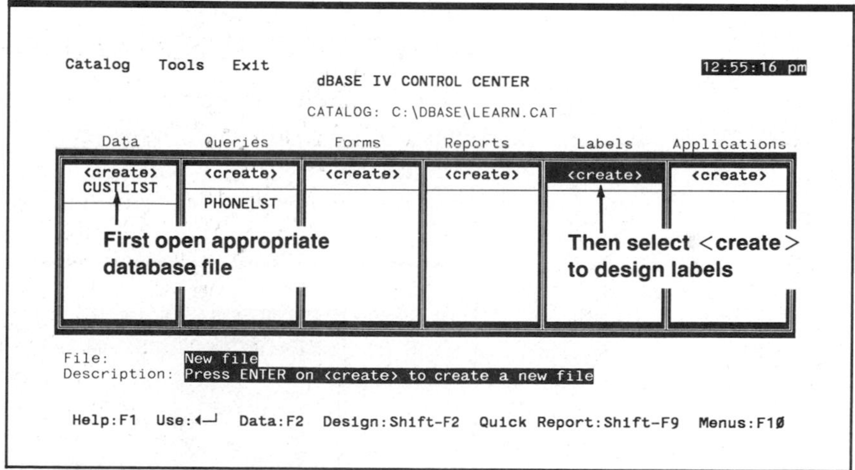

Figure 7.3: Steps for designing labels

As you can see in Figure 7.4, the labels design screen has the same familiar components as most other dBASE screens: a menu bar at the top and a status bar and navigation line at the bottom. The box in the center of the screen represents a blank label, and this is where you design your label format. The ruler above the box shows you the width of the label (in inches). In this example, the printed label will be 3½ inches wide.

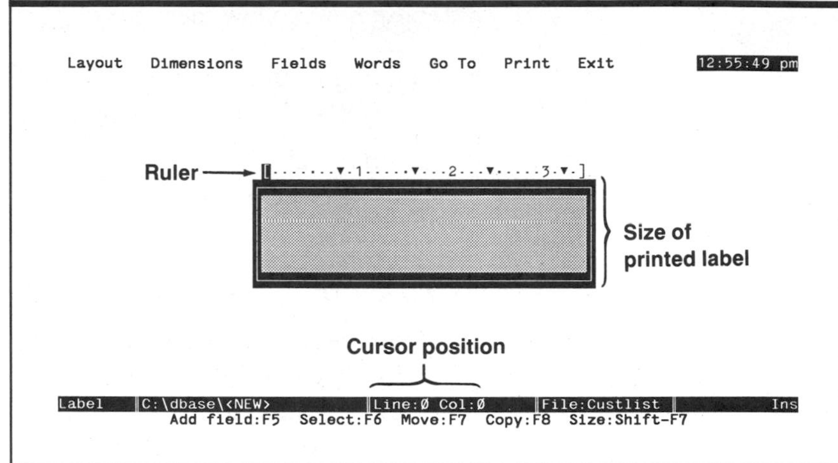

Figure 7.4: The labels design screen

SELECTING A GENERAL LABEL FORMAT

The window at the center of the screen is sized to show the space available on the printed label. Before you actually design the label format, you select your label size. To do so, pull down the Dimensions menu. You'll see the submenu shown in Figure 7.5.

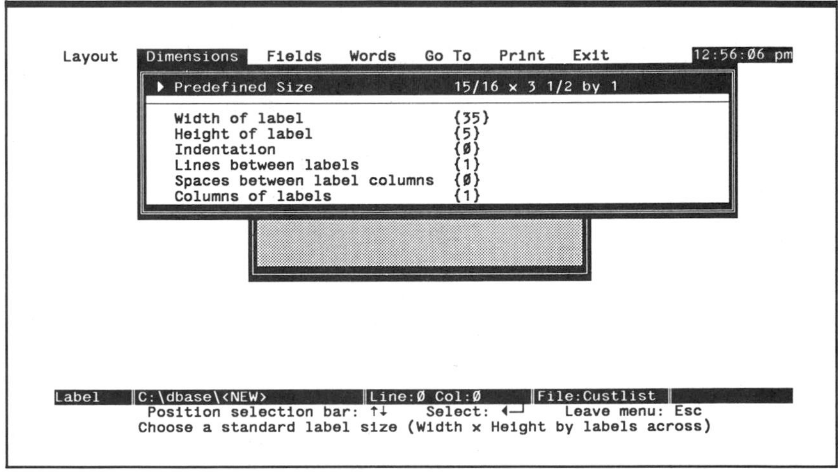

Figure 7.5: Label Dimensions submenu

On this submenu, you can select one of dBASE IV's predefined label sizes, or you can individually select options from the bottom half of the menu to specify your own label size. If you select Predefined Size, you'll see a submenu of common label sizes, as in Figure 7.6.

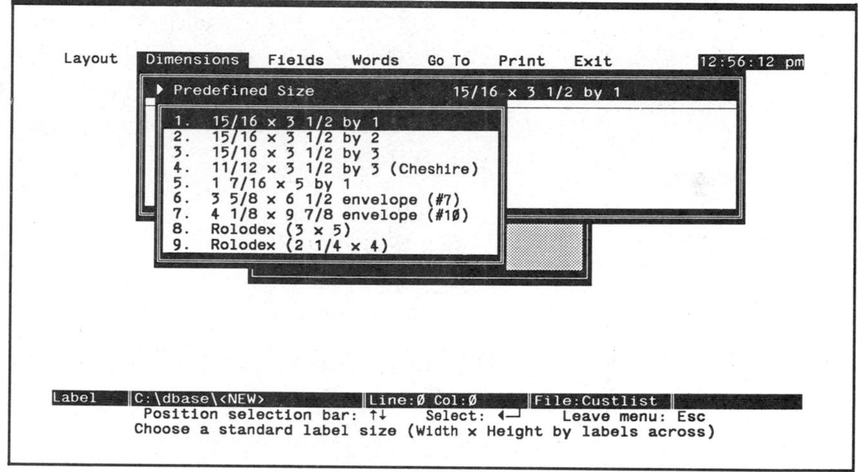

Figure 7.6: Predefined label sizes

The label sizes are described using the height and width in inches and the number of labels printed across each page. For example, the option $\frac{15}{16} \times 3\frac{1}{2}$ by 3 prints labels that are $\frac{15}{16}$ (or about 1) inch tall, $3\frac{1}{2}$ inches wide, and printed three across a page (like many photocopy-machine labels). Select any option you wish by highlighting it and then pressing ←┘, or by clicking it with your mouse. (In this example, we'll use option 2, for two labels across.)

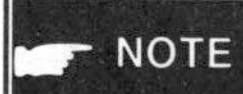

If you do need to create a custom label format, use the Help key (F1) while selecting label dimensions for explanations of the various settings.

If the label size that you want is not available from the predefined sizes, select individual options for the label format from the bottom half of the Dimensions pull-down menu. Note that the Width of Label option assumes that your printer is using the standard print size of 10 characters per inch (*pica* type). Similarly, the Height of Label option assumes the common print size of 6 lines per inch. If your printer uses different print sizes, you may have to adjust these settings accordingly, which might require a little experimentation.

PLACING FIELDS ON A LABEL

After you've selected a label size, you need to tell dBASE how to print each label. You do this by placing *field templates* that show where information from the database is to be printed on the empty label on the screen. To place a field template, you first move the cursor to where you want the data to be printed on the label. Then either press or click Add Field (F5), or choose Fields ► Add Field from the menu.

Alternatively, you can place a field template by double-clicking the mouse where you want the data to be printed.

To see how this works, let's create a mailing label format to print labels that look like this:

John Smith
ABC Co.
123 A St.
San Diego, CA 92067

First, notice that the message "Line:0 Col:0" appears centered in the status line near the bottom of the screen. This line tells you the line and column position of the cursor at any given moment. Use this message to help you follow these steps:

1. With the cursor at line 0, column 0, press or click Add Field (F5) or double-click the mouse to add a new field. You'll see a submenu of items that you can place on the label, as in Figure 7.7.
2. Use ↓ to highlight FIRSTNAME, then press ↵; or double-click on FIRSTNAME with your mouse. You'll see information about the field you've selected, with options to change the Template and Picture Functions. These options are irrelevant at the moment, but we'll discuss them later.
3. As instructed in the lower window on the screen, press or click Accept (Ctrl-End) to proceed. You'll notice that a series of X's fills in a portion of the screen, as in Figure 7.8. These X's are the field template. They show the maximum amount of space that the information in the FIRSTNAME field from the database will occupy on the printed label. Now you can add the LASTNAME field to the label format.

NOTE

For brevity in this exercise, we show both the keyboard and mouse techniques the first time you use them, then just list the keyboard techniques. Of course, you should use whichever technique you prefer.

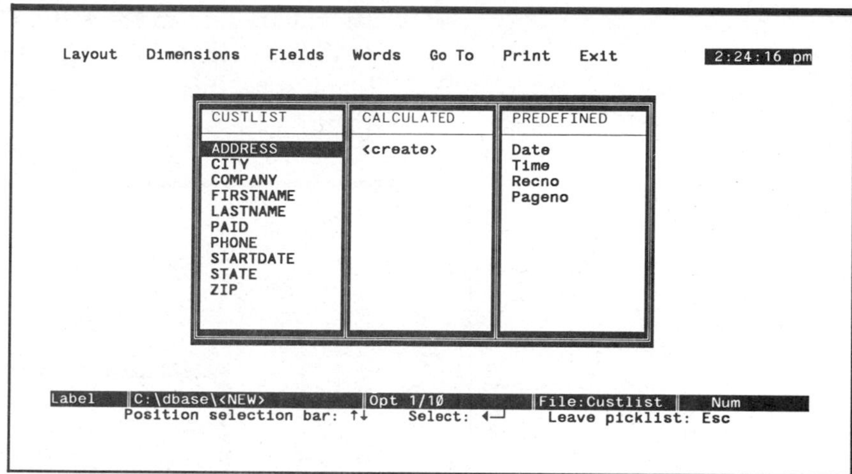

Figure 7.7: Submenu of items that can be placed on the label

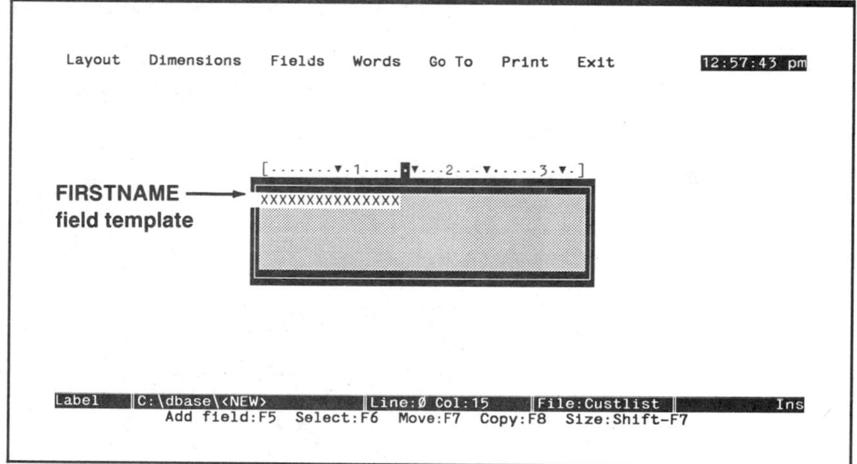

Figure 7.8: FIRSTNAME field added to the sample label

To guarantee that a space separates two fields on a printed label or report, press the space bar when the cursor is at the place where you want the space to appear.

4. Press the space bar to insert a space between the FIRSTNAME and LASTNAME fields (it will appear as a solid box).
5. Press Add Field (F5) again and select LASTNAME.

6. Press Ctrl-End to leave the Display Attributes menu. The LASTNAME field is added to the sample label. Note the blank space between the first and last names, as shown in Figure 7.9.

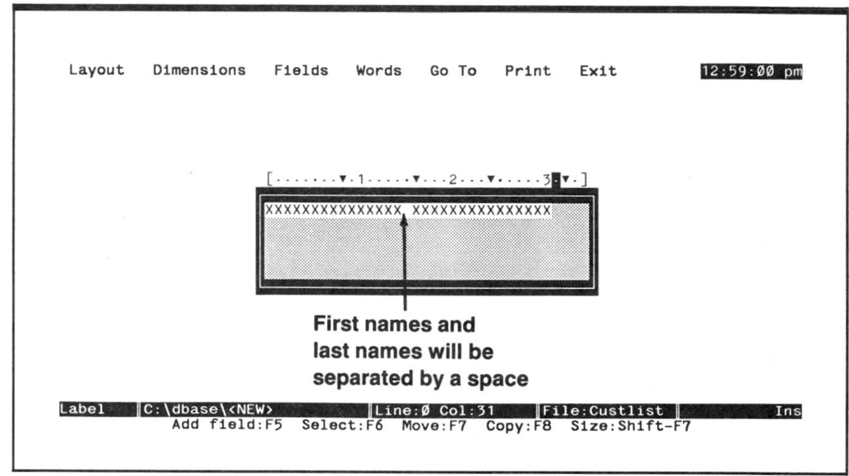

Figure 7.9: FIRSTNAME and LASTNAME fields separated by a space

7. Press ↵ to move the cursor down to the next row (line 1, column 0).
8. To place the COMPANY field, press F5 and select COMPANY.
9. Press Ctrl-End to leave the Display Attributes menu.
10. Press ↵ to move the cursor to line 2, column 0.
11. Press F5 and select ADDRESS.
12. Press Ctrl-End.
13. Press ↵ to move the cursor to line 3, column 0.
14. To place the CITY field, press F5 and select CITY.
15. Press Ctrl-End.
16. To place a comma and a space after the city name, type a comma and then press the space bar.
17. To place the STATE field, press F5 and select STATE.

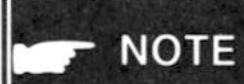
NOTE

The comma and space in the format are *text* that will appear on each label. You can actually add *any* text to a label format simply by typing it at the place where you want it to appear on each label.

18. Press Ctrl-End.
19. To put two spaces between the STATE and ZIP code fields, press the space bar twice.
20. To place the ZIP field, press F5 and select ZIP.
21. Press Ctrl-End.

Your label format should now look like Figure 7.10.

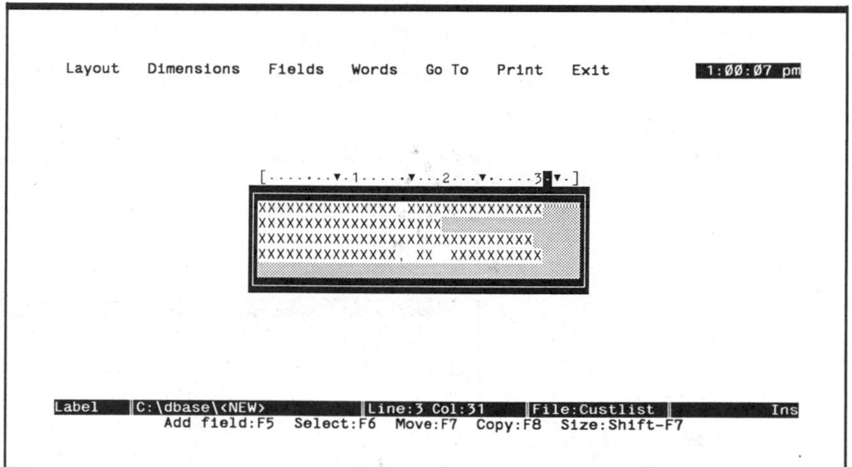

Figure 7.10: Completed mailing label

If you made some mistakes along the way, you can use several techniques to correct them. You can use the usual arrow, Ins, Del, and other editing keys to make changes, or you can use some of the techniques discussed in the section "Changing Report and Label Formats" later in this chapter. If you prefer to just start over, you can select Exit ► Abandon Changes and Exit, then Yes from the next window to appear.

SAVING A LABEL FORMAT

To add a description to the label format and save it for future use, follow these steps:

1. Choose Layout ► Edit Description of Label Design from the menu.

2. Type **2-across mailing labels** (or any other description you like). Then press ↵.
3. Choose Exit ► Save Changes and Exit from the menu.
4. When dBASE presents the prompt "Save as:" type a valid file name (maximum eight characters, with no spaces or punctuation). In this example, type **Mailing** and press ↵.

There will be a delay while dBASE IV writes a program to print labels in the format you wish. When this is done, you'll be returned to the Control Center. When you return to the Control Center, you'll see the MAILING label format file name in the Labels panel, as in Figure 7.11.

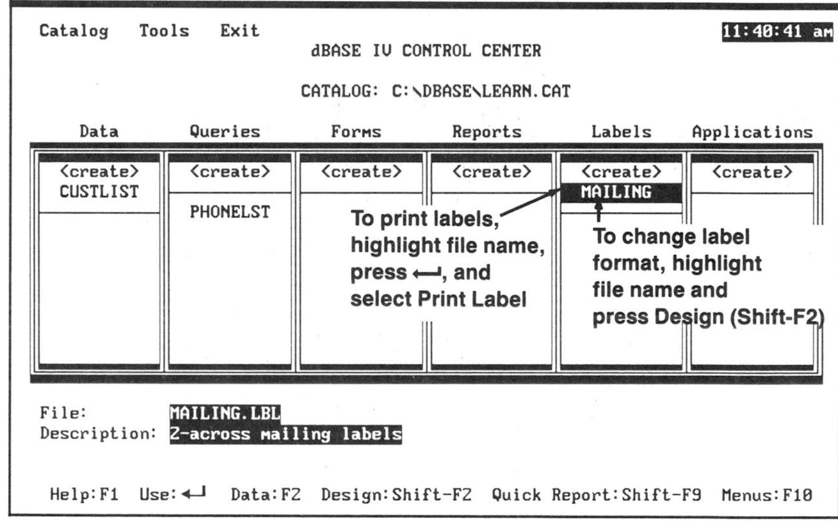

Figure 7.11: The MAILING label format in the Labels panel

NOTE

You can also preview or print labels while designing them, by selecting either Begin Printing or View Labels on Screen from the Print pull-down menu on the labels design screen.

PRINTING LABELS

Now that you have designed the format of the labels, you can use that format to print the names and addresses from the CUSTLIST database. Follow these steps:

1. Make sure the label format name MAILING is highlighted in the Labels panel and press ↵ or double-click that format name.

2. From the options that appear, select Print Label.
3. From the Print Menu that appears next, select either Begin Printing (to actually print the labels) or View Labels on Screen (to see the labels on the screen only).

If you selected View Labels on Screen, you'll see the labels on your screen. dBASE will pause after each screenful and display a prompt at the bottom of the screen indicating that you should press the space bar to scroll to the next screenful. Do so at your leisure until you get back to the Control Center.

If you selected Begin Printing, your printer is probably printing the mailing labels right now. If you have a laser printer, you may need to eject the page to see the printed labels. To do so, repeat steps 1 and 2. Then select Eject Page Now from the Print menu and press Esc to leave the Print menu. Figure 7.12 shows the printed labels.

This exercise assumes that you are printing these sample labels on plain paper. When you print on real mailing labels, you may need to experiment a bit to get the data properly aligned on the labels. See the section "Controlling the Printer" near the end of this chapter for help with label alignment.

MODIFYING THE LABEL FORMAT

You can change the format of labels at any time by returning to the labels design screen. To do so, follow these basic steps:

1. Highlight the name of the mailing label format in the Labels panel (MAILING, in this case).
2. Press or click Design (Shift-F2), or press ↵ and select Modify Layout from the options that appear.

When you get to the labels design screen, you can use editing keys (listed in Table 7.1 earlier in this chapter) and techniques to make changes and corrections (you'll learn more about editing techniques soon). Notice that even though the labels design screen shows only templates (X's) of where data will be printed on the label, you can easily determine which database field is associated with each template. Just use the usual arrow keys to move the cursor into the

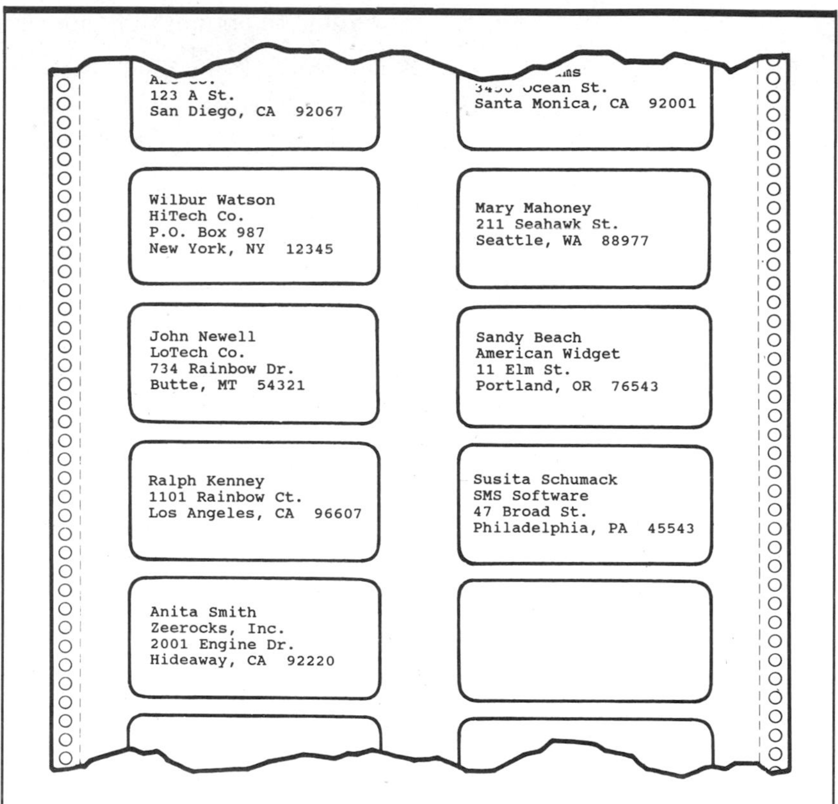

Figure 7.12: Mailing Labels printed from the CUSTLIST database

template of interest, or click the mouse on that template, then look at the bottom of the screen.

For example, when the cursor is in the FIRSTNAME field template, the bottom of the screen displays

CUSTLIST->FIRSTNAME Type:Character Width:15 Decimal: 0

This line informs you that the current template will display the contents of the FIRSTNAME field from the CUSTLIST database. The line also indicates the data type, width, and number of decimal places, as defined in the database structure.

When you have finished viewing or editing your label format, choose Exit ► Save Changes and Exit from the menu. You'll be returned to the Control Center.

Rather than go into any more detail on creating mailing label formats right now, let's discuss how you can use similar techniques to design and create *reports*. As you'll see later, many of the techniques that you use to design reports and labels are identical.

DESIGNING PRINTED REPORTS

Just as the labels design screen lets you specify how data from the database should be displayed on a label, the reports design screen lets you specify how data should be printed on a full page. Unlike labels, full printed pages might consist of many different sections of text, such as page headings, page numbers, totals sections, subtotals sections, and other types of information.

DESIGNING REPORT SECTIONS

Part of designing a report involves deciding what goes into each section of the printed report. Figure 7.13 shows two pages of a somewhat typical report and the various sections displayed in the report. These sections are as follows:

Page header	The page header is printed once at the top of each page.
Report intro	The report introduction is printed once at the beginning of the report.
Detail	The detail section is the body of the report. Typically, this section displays records from a database file.
Report summary	The report summary is printed once at the end of the report and can be used to display totals or closing information about the report.
Page footer	The page footer is printed once at the bottom of each page and can be used to display page numbers or other useful information.

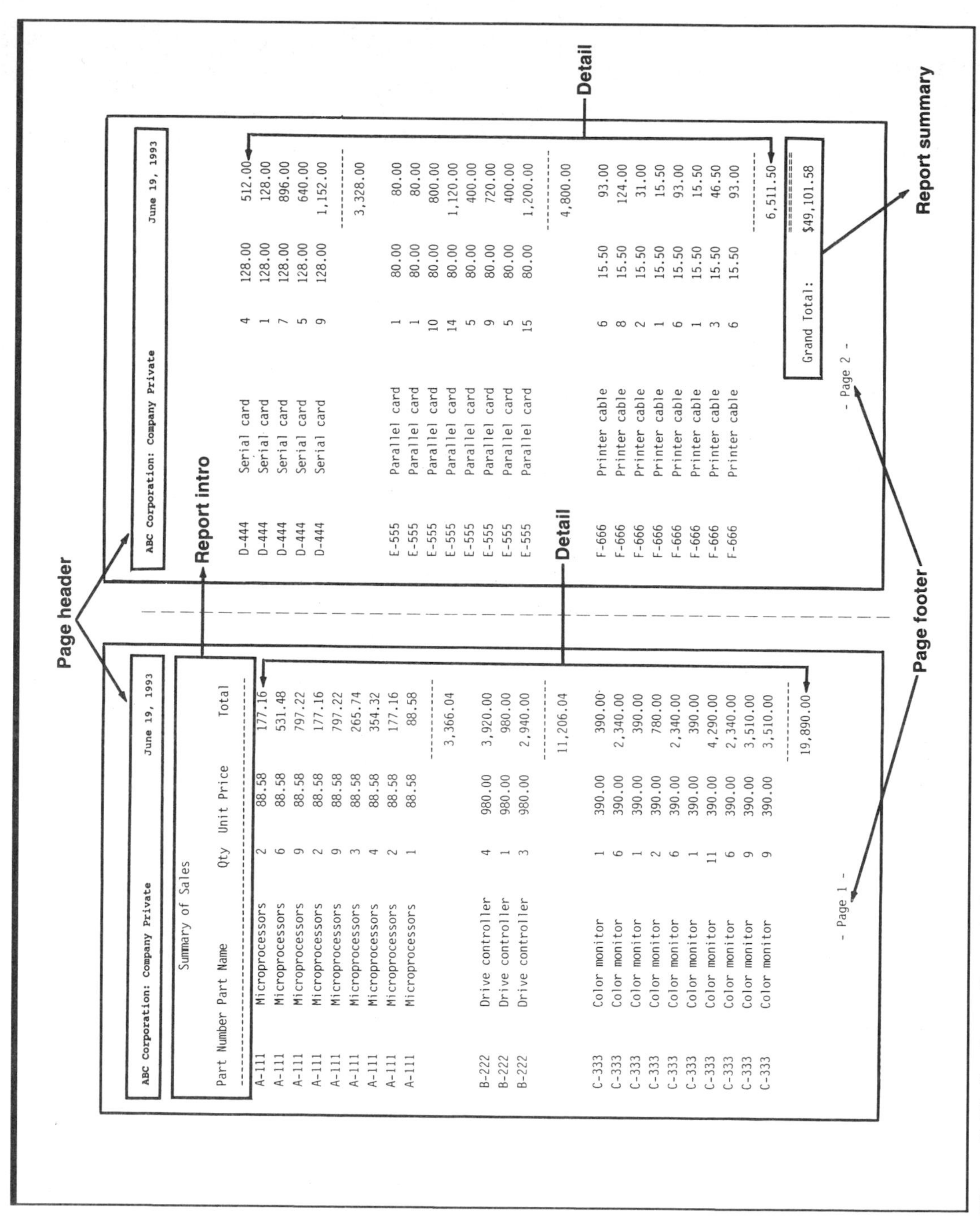

ABC Corporation: Company Private June 19, 1993

Summary of Sales

Part Number	Part Name	Qty	Unit Price	Total
A-111	Microprocessors	2	88.58	177.16
A-111	Microprocessors	6	88.58	531.48
A-111	Microprocessors	9	88.58	797.22
A-111	Microprocessors	2	88.58	177.16
A-111	Microprocessors	9	88.58	797.22
A-111	Microprocessors	3	88.58	265.74
A-111	Microprocessors	4	88.58	354.32
A-111	Microprocessors	2	88.58	177.16
A-111	Microprocessors	1	88.58	88.58
				3,366.04
B-222	Drive controller	4	980.00	3,920.00
B-222	Drive controller	1	980.00	980.00
B-222	Drive controller	3	980.00	2,940.00
				11,206.04
C-333	Color monitor	1	390.00	390.00
C-333	Color monitor	6	390.00	2,340.00
C-333	Color monitor	1	390.00	390.00
C-333	Color monitor	2	390.00	780.00
C-333	Color monitor	6	390.00	2,340.00
C-333	Color monitor	1	390.00	390.00
C-333	Color monitor	11	390.00	4,290.00
C-333	Color monitor	6	390.00	2,340.00
C-333	Color monitor	9	390.00	3,510.00
C-333	Color monitor	9	390.00	3,510.00
				19,890.00

- Page 1 -

ABC Corporation: Company Private June 19, 1993

D-444	Serial card	4	128.00	512.00
D-444	Serial card	1	128.00	128.00
D-444	Serial card	7	128.00	896.00
D-444	Serial card	5	128.00	640.00
D-444	Serial card	9	128.00	1,152.00
				3,328.00
E-555	Parallel card	1	80.00	80.00
E-555	Parallel card	1	80.00	80.00
E-555	Parallel card	10	80.00	800.00
E-555	Parallel card	14	80.00	1,120.00
E-555	Parallel card	5	80.00	400.00
E-555	Parallel card	9	80.00	720.00
E-555	Parallel card	5	80.00	400.00
E-555	Parallel card	15	80.00	1,200.00
				4,800.00
F-666	Printer cable	6	15.50	93.00
F-666	Printer cable	8	15.50	124.00
F-666	Printer cable	2	15.50	31.00
F-666	Printer cable	1	15.50	15.50
F-666	Printer cable	6	15.50	93.00
F-666	Printer cable	1	15.50	15.50
F-666	Printer cable	3	15.50	46.50
F-666	Printer cable	6	15.50	93.00
				6,511.50

Grand Total: $49,101.58

- Page 2 -

Figure 7.13: Sections of a typical report

When you begin developing a sample report a little later in this chapter, you'll see how to control exactly what is printed in each section of the report.

GENERAL REPORT FORMATS

To help you design your reports, dBASE offers three general report layouts: the column layout, the form layout, and the mailmerge layout. You can use any of the general layouts as the starting point for designing your report. These general formats are summarized here.

Column layout	Data is printed in even-sized columns. A report that presents data as a list or that includes totals or subtotals would likely use a column layout. The sample report in Figure 7.13 uses a column layout to print sales information.
Form layout	Data is not presented in even columns, but is instead stacked or arranged in some other free-form format. (The customer list report shown in Figure 7.14 later in this chapter uses the form layout. Note that there are no evenly spaced columns of information on the screen.)
Mailmerge layout	This layout is usually used to combine a large body of text with information from a database. This is the layout you use to create form letters. (*Mailmerge* is a computer term derived from the fact that you *merge* the text of a typewritten letter with names and addresses from a database to create form letters, or *mail*.)

In this book, you'll have opportunities to work with all of these different layouts. However, this chapter focuses on only the Form and Mailmerge layouts.

GENERAL TECHNIQUES FOR THE REPORTS AND LABELS DESIGN SCREENS

Before you actually begin designing fancy reports, let's take a moment to cover some of the most important techniques that you'll be using. Remember, these techniques work with *any* report, including labels, the Column layout, the Form layout, and the Mailmerge layout.

Remember too that throughout these sections *text* refers to normal typed text on the screen, like field names, blank spaces, and punctuation. *Field templates* refer to the templates (like XXXX and MM/DD/YY) that represent fields from the database.

ADDING AND DELETING TEXT

You can place text, such as words, punctuation marks, and blank spaces, anywhere in a report or label format. You've seen examples of this already, when you placed a comma and a space between the CITY and STATE fields on the label format so the contents of those fields would be printed in the format *San Diego, CA*. Here are the general techniques to follow:

NOTE

When moving the cursor, you can use any of the cursor positioning keys listed in Table 7.1, or you can click the mouse on the new position where you want the cursor to appear.

INSERTING NEW TEXT To insert new text into a report or label format:

- Move the cursor to where you want the start of the new text to appear.
- Make sure you are in Insert Mode (press the Ins or Insert key until the Ins indicator appears in the status bar, near the lower-right corner of the screen).
- Type your new text (you can also press the space bar to insert blank spaces).

CHANGING EXISTING TEXT If you simply want to change existing text (not insert new text), use the same basic steps above, but without the insert mode on (pressing the Ins or Insert key turns the insert mode on and off). The new text that you type will overwrite existing text. However, any field templates to the immediate right of the cursor will still scroll to the right to make room for new text.

DELETING A SMALL AMOUNT OF TEXT If you want to delete a small amount of text on a single line (such as a few words or characters), just follow these simple steps:

- Move the cursor to the leftmost character that you want to delete.
- Press the Del (or Delete) key until all the text is deleted.

Be careful not to delete any field templates, or you'll have to figure out which ones you've deleted, then put them back onto the screen using the techniques for adding fields described later in this section.

ADDING AND DELETING LINES

Any blank lines on a report (or mailing label) format also show up as blank lines on the final printed report and labels. Therefore, you may occasionally want to insert or delete blank lines to gain more control over the spacing between lines in your printed report. You might also need to insert new blank lines into a report or mailing label format in order to insert more fields or text. To insert or delete a line on a report format, the sections that follow will give you the techniques you need.

INSERTING NEW BLANK LINES To insert a new blank line in a label format or a report band, follow these basic steps:

When designing a label format, you can only insert a new row if there is enough room on the label format to fit in another row.

- Move the cursor to the appropriate position:
    - If you want to place a new blank line above all other lines in the band (or on the label), move the cursor to the beginning of the first line (Line: 0 Column: 0) of the report band.
    - If you want to insert a new blank row between two existing rows, move the cursor to the left edge (Column 0) of the bottom of those two rows.

- If you want to insert a blank row at the bottom of the report band (below all current rows), move the cursor to the end of the last line in the report band.
- Make sure the Insert mode is on (press the Ins or Insert key until the Ins indicator appears at the right side of the status bar near the bottom of the screen).
- Press ↵ or choose Words ► Add Line from the menu.

The blank row is inserted immediately.

DELETING A LINE To delete an entire line (including the space it occupies), you can usually follow this simple procedure:

- Move the cursor to the start of the line you want to delete.
- Press Ctrl-Y or choose Words ► Remove Line from the menu.

Note that this does not always let you remove the last line near the bottom of a report band, mainly because dBASE often keeps a blank line between bands so that they will appear on the final report, producing a more neatly formatted report. However, you can delete the last line from a report band by moving text into it, and then perhaps deleting any blank lines above the moved text. See "Moving, Copying, and Deleting Blocks" later in this chapter.

ADDING AND DELETING FIELD TEMPLATES

As you know, a field template indicates the place where the contents of a field will be displayed in the final printed report. You can easily add and delete field templates from any report or label format using the procedures described in the sections that follow.

ADDING FIELD TEMPLATES FROM THE DATABASE If you want to display a field from the database on your printed label or report,

You can also highlight a field name by starting to type the name; juse type as many letters as necessary to move the highlight to the field you want. For example, to highlight the STATE field in the CUSTLIST database, type STAT.

follow these general steps:

- Move the cursor to where you want the field to start on your printed labels or report, then press or click Add Field (F5), or choose Fields ► Add Field from the menu. Alternatively, you can double-click the mouse where you want the field to start.
- Select the name of the field that you want displayed from the leftmost column of the window that appears. To select the field name, move the highlight to the name and press ↵, or double-click the field name.
- Press or click Accept (Ctrl-End) to leave the next window that appears.

You'll see the new field template on the screen immediately.

DELETING A FIELD TEMPLATE To delete a field from the format, follow this simple procedure:

- Move the cursor into the field template that you want to delete, or click on the field with your mouse.
- Press the Del (or Delete) key.

That's all there is to it.

MOVING, COPYING, AND DELETING BLOCKS

You can easily move, copy, and/or delete *blocks* of text on the reports or labels design screen. A block is simply any section within a report band—be it text, a field template, or any combination of text and field templates.

The basic procedure is fairly simple, but there is always the slight chance that you might inadvertently overwrite or delete some existing text or field templates, and therefore lose some of your work. To avoid this, it's a good idea to first do a "quick save" of your work so far without leaving the reports or labels design screen. The next section describes how.

QUICK SAVE OF A FORMAT To perform a quick save of a format without leaving the design screen, follow these steps:

- Choose Layout ► Save This Report (if you're designing a report) or Layout ► Save This Label Design (if you're designing labels).
- If you've previously saved the file, just press ↵ to accept the previous name. Otherwise, type in a valid DOS file name (eight letters, no spaces or punctuation, and no extension), then press ↵.

When dBASE finishes saving the file (and the pull-down menu disappears) you can proceed with your move, copy, or delete operation.

When highlighting a large block, any partially highlighted field templates will be ignored when you copy, move, or delete the block. So if you want to include a template in an operation, be sure the entire template is highlighted.

HIGHLIGHTING A BLOCK To highlight a block on the labels or reports design screen, follow these steps:

- If you are moving a field template, move the cursor into that template, or click the template with your mouse. If you are moving a larger block, move the cursor to a corner of that block, or click that corner with your mouse.
- Press or click Select (F6).
- If you are moving only a single field template, skip to the next step now. Otherwise, use the →, ←, ↓, and ↑ keys or move your mouse to extend the highlight over the entire block you wish to move, copy, or delete.
- Press ↵ to complete the selection, or click the mouse button.
- Here's a "mouse-only" method for highlighting a block: Move the mouse pointer to one corner of the block, then press and hold the mouse while you drag the mouse to highlight the opposite corner of the block. Release the mouse button when highlighting is complete.
- If you want to delete the highlighted field template or block, press the Del (or Delete) key, then skip the remaining steps.

- To move the highlighted block, press or click Move (F7); to copy the block, press or click Copy (F8).
- Use the ↑, ↓, →, and ← keys or move the mouse to move the "ghost image" of the block to where you want the highlighted area moved or copied.
- Press ↵ or click the mouse button to complete the move/copy.

It's a good idea to press Esc once after pressing ↵ to complete the move/copy, as this immediately "unselects" the current block or template and prevents you from inadvertently deleting the whole thing when you press the Del or Delete key.

If you have moved the "ghost image" so that it is overlapping existing text and field templates, you'll see the message "Delete covered text and fields? (Y/N)." You will need to determine on your own whether it's okay to delete the text and field templates that are currently covered by the ghost image.

If you are moving the entire format (that is, all the text and field templates), then you can simply answer Yes (by typing Y or clicking Yes), because everything that is being deleted will immediately be replaced as soon as the move/copy is complete.

However, if you are moving or copying a small area, you might want to double-check before answering Yes. Answer No (by typing N or clicking No) to see what exactly is being covered by the ghost image. Then,

- If it's okay to delete the text and field templates that are covered by that image, press ↵ or click the mouse button and answer Yes when asked again about deleting that covered area.
- If it's not okay to delete the covered text and field templates, reposition the ghost image to a new location (using the arrow keys or your mouse), then press ↵ or click the mouse button to complete the move/copy.
- If you cannot find a satisfactory location for the ghost image, press Esc three times in response to the "Delete covered text and fields?" prompt to cancel the operation and "unselect" the currently selected area.

RECALLING THE QUICK SAVE If during the course of your move/copy/delete operations you manage to make more of a mess than an improvement, but remembered to do your "quick save" before you got started, you can simply abandon the current version of the format and retrieve the copy you previously saved. Here's how:

- Press Esc and answer "Yes" to the prompts about abandoning the current format until you get back to the Control Center.
- At the Control Center, highlight the name of the format you were just working on (chances are, it is already highlighted).
- Press or click Design (Shift-F2).

A copy of the format as it was when you last saved it is now on the design screen, ready for editing. Any mistakes you made since the last time you saved the format, of course, are not included because they were never saved.

THE CUSTOMER LIST REPORT

To give you some experience with the reports design screen, we'll develop a sample customer list report that displays some CUSTLIST data in the format shown in Figure 7.14. This format is relatively simple. The page header contains only the current date—6/30/93 in the example. The report intro is Customer List. The detail lists the name, address, and other information about each person. The page footer displays the word *Page* and the page number.

To start developing the report, you need to get to the reports design screen. Let's get started.

USING THE REPORTS DESIGN SCREEN

To access the reports design screen, open the database file that contains the data that you want to print and then select <create> from the Reports panel. Here are the steps to begin creating the sample customer list report for this chapter:

1. If CUSTLIST is not currently in use, highlight CUSTLIST in the Data panel and press ↵, or double-click on CUSTLIST in that panel. Then select Use File.

```
06/15/93


                              Customer List

Smith, John   ABC Co.
     123 A St.
     San Diego, CA   92067
     Phone: (619)555-1234
     Starting date: 11/15/92  Paid: Y

Adams, Annie
     3456 Ocean St.
     Santa Monica, CA   92001
     Phone: (714)555-0123
     Starting date: 01/01/93  Paid: N

Watson, Wilbur   HiTech Co.
     P.O. Box 987
     New York, NY   12345
     Phone: (212)555-9988
     Starting date: 11/15/92  Paid: Y

Mahoney, Mary
     211 Seahawk St.
     Seattle, WA   88977
     Phone: (206)555-8673
     Starting date: 12/01/92  Paid: Y

Newell, John   LoTech Co.
     734 Rainbow Dr.
     Butte, MT   54321
     Phone: (303)555-6739
     Starting date: 12/15/92  Paid: Y

Beach, Sandy   American Widget
     11 Elm St.
     Portland, OR   76543
     Phone: (717)555-0898
     Starting date: 12/15/92  Paid: Y

Kenney, Ralph
     1101 Rainbow Ct.
     Los Angeles, CA   96607
     Phone: (213)555-9988
     Starting date: 12/30/92  Paid: N

Schumack, Susita   SMS Software
     47 Broad St.
     Philadelphia, PA   45543
     Phone: (202)555-9720
     Starting date: 12/30/92  Paid: Y




                              Page:    1
```

Figure 7.14: The Customer List report

2. Highlight <create> in the Reports panel and press ↵, or double-click <create> in that panel. You'll see the reports design screen, partially obscured by the Layout menu. For now, press Esc to remove the Layout menu. Your screen should look like Figure 7.15.

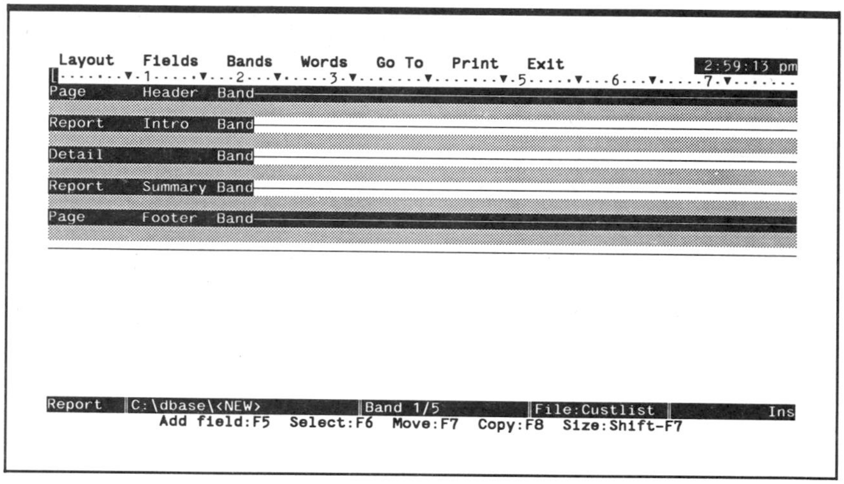

```
Layout   Fields   Bands   Words   Go To   Print   Exit                2:59:13 pm
[·······▼·1·····▼···2···▼·····3·▼·······▼·······▼·5·····▼···6···▼·····7·▼·······
Page     Header  Band
Report   Intro   Band
Detail           Band
Report   Summary Band
Page     Footer  Band

Report  C:\dbase\<NEW>          Band 1/5          File:Custlist            Ins
        Add field:F5  Select:F6  Move:F7  Copy:F8  Size:Shift-F7
```

Figure 7.15: The reports design screen

As you can see, the reports design screen has many of the same characteristics as other design screens. The menu bar at the top of the screen has pull-down menus associated with it, which you open, as usual, by pressing F10, by clicking the menu bar with your mouse, or by pressing the Alt key and typing the first letter of the option you want. The ruler just beneath the menu bar shows margins and tab stops. At the bottom of the screen, the navigation line displays special keys that you can use to format your report.

The center of the screen, where you design the format of the report, is currently divided into five *bands*. Each band corresponds to a section of the printed report. Anything that you place within a band is printed only in the corresponding section of the report. For example, any text that you place in the Page Header band is printed at the top of each printed page.

SELECTING A GENERAL FORMAT

As mentioned earlier, dBASE IV lets you select from three general layouts for printing your report: column layout, form layout, and mailmerge layout. You can use a general layout as the starting point for designing your own report. For this particular example, we'll use the form layout as the starting point. Follow these steps:

1. Choose Layout ► Quick Layouts.
2. Choose Form Layout.

dBASE creates a general report format with the page number and date in the Page Header band. The Detail band contains the name of each field in the CUSTLIST database and a template for each field. Figure 7.16 shows this initial report format.

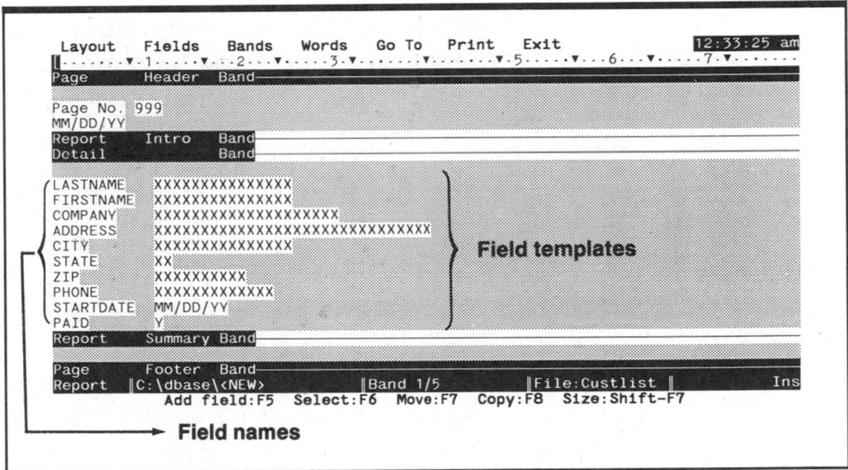

Figure 7.16: Initial form layout suggested by dBASE IV

SETTING THE RIGHT MARGIN

After you have selected a general format for your report, it's a good idea to then select margins. Selecting margins now will let you more easily center titles or other information in your report. When printing on 8 1/2 by 11-inch paper, a right margin setting of about 64 will provide adequate left and right margins on the printed page. To set the margins for the customer list report now, follow these steps:

1. Choose Words ► Modify Ruler from the menu (the cursor will move to the ruler).
2. Press Tab eight times to move to column 64.
3. Type] to mark the right margin (the] key is near the ↵ key on most keyboards).
4. Press Ctrl-End or ↵ to finish modifying the ruler, or click the mouse button.

Most tractor-feed printers allow you to slide the paper to the left or right to set the left margin.

Notice that you adjusted only the position of the right margin in the preceding steps. There is usually no need to adjust the left margin, because dBASE automatically prints a left margin on the printed page. That is, even if you leave the left margin at column zero (where it is now, as you can see by the [symbol in the ruler), your printed report will still have about a 1-inch margin on the left. (See "Controlling Page Length and Margins" under "Controlling the Printer" later in this chapter if you need to adjust the left margin.)

REARRANGING THE INITIAL FORMAT

Now you can rearrange the field templates and text on the initial format into any format that you wish. We'll do so in the sections that follow and make use of many of the reports design screen editing keys and mouse operations (listed in Tables 7.1 and 7.2 earlier in this chapter). Figure 7.17 at the end of this section shows the report format that we want for the customer list report as it appears on the reports design screen when completed. You can use that figure as a guide as you rearrange the format in the sections that follow.

The cursor's line and column positions do not appear on your screen until the cursor is inside a band.

Notice that, as with labels, the current position of the cursor is indicated in the status line. Use this indicator to help you position the cursor as you follow the steps below. But be sure that the cursor is in the correct band, because lines are numbered starting at zero within each band.

CHANGING THE PAGE HEADER BAND

First let's delete the page number from the Page Header band. Later, we'll put the page number at the bottom of each page. Here are the steps:

1. Press ↓ to move the cursor to line 0, column 0 in the Page Header band, or click the mouse on that location.
2. Press Ctrl-Y twice to delete the next two lines.
3. Press End to move the cursor to the end of the date template (MM/DD/YY), or click the mouse on that location.
4. Press Ctrl-N twice to insert two blank lines.

The page header now consists of the current date and two blank lines. dBASE will print this page header at the top of every page.

NOTE

For all steps that position the cursor on the report design screen, you can either use the cursor positioning keys given in the steps, or you can click the mouse button at the appropriate location on the screen. Choose whichever method is most convenient for you. Regardless of which method you choose, be sure to double-check the report band, and the line and column number in the status line before updating your report format.

ADDING A REPORT INTRODUCTION

Now let's add a report introduction, which will appear on the first printed page. Here are the steps:

1. Press ↓ three times to move the cursor to the Report Intro band border. (The line position at the bottom of the screen shows Band 2/5.)
2. Press ↵ to open the band.
3. Press ↓ to move the cursor into the band, or click the mouse at that location (the cursor position states that you are at line 0, column 8).
4. Make sure insert mode is on. (If the Ins indicator does not appear in the lower-right corner in the status bar, press the Ins key until it does.)
5. Press ↵. Notice that this adds a new blank line in the Report Intro header, which will in turn print a blank line on the printed report.
6. Type the report heading **Customer List**.

NOTE

Pressing ↵ adds new blank lines *only* when Insert mode is on. Pressing Ctrl-N adds a new blank line regardless of whether Insert mode is on.

7. To center the heading, choose Words ► Position. Then select Center from the submenu.
8. Press End and ↵ to add another blank line.

This takes care of the page header and report introduction. Let's get to work on the Detail band now.

MODIFYING THE DETAIL BAND

Before we start modifying the Detail band, let's look at what it contains. The field names at the left (such as LASTNAME and FIRSTNAME) are text that will appear on the report exactly as they do on the screen (unless you remove them). The field templates (such as X's, MM/DD/YY, and Y) show where the data from the database will appear (just as in the labels design screen). For example, the name Smith will appear in place of the X's to the right of LASTNAME, and the start date will appear in place of MM/DD/YY to the right of STARTDATE.

Our printed report will not use any of the field names, but will use all of the field templates. Reformatting the field templates into the format we want will require many steps, but these steps will give you some good hands-on experience in using the reports design screen, which you will use to develop your own formatted reports in the future. Also, remember that you have to design a report format only once. You can then use this format over and over again to print data. Therefore, time spent designing a report is time well spent.

Keep in mind that in addition to using cursor positioning keys and function keys when designing a report, you can also use your mouse to move the cursor, to select actions from the navigation line, to choose field templates, and to rearrange items on the report design, as discussed earlier under "General Techniques for the Reports and Labels Design Screens." The steps below list both the keyboard and the mouse techniques the first time they are used to accomplish a given task (such as positioning the cursor or moving a field template), then switch to just the keyboard technique to keep things a bit simpler. Of course, you can use whichever technique you find most convenient.

1. Press ↓ three times to move the cursor to the *L* in the LASTNAME field name, or click the mouse on that letter in the field name.
2. Press End to move the cursor to line 1, column 26, or click the mouse at that location.
3. Type a comma and then press the space bar. This will ensure that a comma and blank space appear after the last name on the printed report.

NOTE

Remember that whenever the cursor is in a field template, the name of the field appears at the bottom of the screen.

4. Use the ↓ and ← keys to move the cursor to the FIRSTNAME template (line 2, column 1), or click the mouse at that location.
5. Press or click Select (F6), then press ↵ or click the mouse button to select that template (it will be highlighted on your screen).
6. Press or click Move (F7).

When you press Select (F6) or Move (F7), the navigation line provides instructions regarding what to do next.

7. Use the ↑ and → keys, or move the mouse, to move the ghost image of the template to line 1, column 28.
8. Press ↵ or click the mouse button to complete the move.
9. Press End to move to the end of the template.
10. Press the space bar three times to insert three blank spaces.
11. Use the ↓ and ← keys to move the cursor to the COMPANY field template (line 3, column 11).
12. Press Select (F6) and ↵ to select the template.
13. Press Move (F7) and use the arrow keys to move the ghost image to line 1, column 46.
14. Press ↵ to complete the move.

Ignore the field names to the left of the templates during these steps—you'll be removing them soon anyway.

15. Use the arrow keys to move the cursor to the ADDRESS field template (line 4, column 11).
16. Press Select (F6), End, ↓, and then ↵ to select the ADDRESS and CITY field templates.
17. Press Move (F7) and use the arrow keys to move the ghost image to line 2, column 16.

18. Press ↵ to complete the move.
19. Use the arrow keys to move to the end of the CITY field template (line 3, column 31).
20. Type a comma and then press the space bar (so that the printed report will show a comma and blank space).
21. Use the arrow keys to move the cursor to the STATE field template (line 6, column 11).
22. Press Select (F6) and then ↵ to select the template.
23. Press Move (F7) and use the arrow keys to move the ghost image to the right of the comma and space (line 3, column 33).
24. Press ↵ to complete the move.
25. Press End to move to the end of the STATE template (line 3, column 35).
26. Press the space bar three times to insert three blank spaces.
27. Use the arrow keys to move the cursor to the ZIP template (line 7, column 11).
28. Press Select (F6) and then ↵ to select the template.
29. Press Move (F7), move the ghost image to line 3, column 38, and then press ↵ to complete the move.
30. Move the cursor to line 4, column 16.
31. Type the word **Phone:** and then press the space bar.
32. Move the cursor into the PHONE field template (line 8, column 11).
33. Press Select (F6) and then ↵ to select the template.
34. Press Move (F7), use the arrow keys to move the ghost image to line 4, column 23, and then press ↵ to complete the move.
35. Move the cursor to line 5, column 16.
36. Type the words **Starting date:** and press the space bar.
37. Move the cursor to the STARTDATE field template (MM/DD/YY in line 9, column 11).

Selected (highlighted) text or fields remain selected after moving or copying. You can press Esc once to "unselect" text or fields.

38. Press Select (F6) and then ↵ to select the template.
39. Press Move (F7), move the ghost image to line 5, column 31, and press ↵.
40. Press End and then press the space bar twice to move the cursor to line 5, column 41.
41. Type the word **Paid:** and then press the space bar.
42. Move the cursor into the PAID field template (the Y in line 10, column 11).
43. Press Select (F6) and then press ↵.
44. Press Move (F7), move the ghost image to line 5, column 47, and then press ↵.
45. Press Home, and ↑ several times until the cursor gets to the *L* in the LASTNAME field name (line 1, column 0).
46. Press Select (F6), press the → key eight times, and press the ↓ key nine times to highlight all the field names (but *not* any of the field templates).
47. Press ↵ to finish highlighting the field names.
48. Press the Del key to delete all the field names.
49. To move all the field templates up and to the left, first move the cursor to line 1, column 11 (to the first X in the LASTNAME field template).
50. Press Select (F6), press End, and press ↓ four times to highlight all the field templates and text. Then press ↵.
51. Press Move (F7), press Home, and press PgUp to move the upper-left corner of the ghost image to line 0, column 0.
52. Press ↵ to complete the move.
53. dBASE displays the message "Delete all covered text and fields? (Y/N)" because the ghost image is overlapping other text and fields. Type **Y** or click Yes to answer Yes.
54. Press ↓ until the cursor gets to line 5, column 0.

55. Press Ctrl-Y five times to delete blank lines beneath the cursor position, leaving a single blank line at the bottom of the Detail band.

If you are new to computers (and a terrible typist to boot), it may have taken you a while to complete all those steps. But after you get a little practice with the reports design screen, you'll be able to perform these many steps in just a few minutes.

REARRANGING THE PAGE FOOTER BAND

The Customer List report just needs to print page numbers centered at the bottom of each page now, and you'll be done. Here are the steps to follow:

1. Press ↓ to move to the Report Summary band border (the center of the status bar shows "Band 4/5" when you get there).
2. Press ↵ to close the band (as we will not include a report summary in the customer list).
3. Press ↓ twice to move to the Page Footer band (the status bar now shows that you are at line 0, column 0).
4. Press Ctrl-N to insert a blank line.
5. Press ↓ once to move to line 1, column 0 in the Page Footer band.
6. Type the word **Page:** and then press the space bar.
7. Press or click Add Field (F5), or double-click at the cursor location to add a field template.
8. A menu appears showing all of the fields that can be placed in the current report format. Select Pageno from the column labeled PREDEFINED.
9. Press or click Accept (Ctrl-End) to leave the display attributes window.
10. To center the page number, choose Words ► Position.
11. Select Center from the submenu.

Note that the page number template appears as 999 on the report format, which indicates that dBASE is saving space for three digits in the page number. We'll discuss the other options that appeared on the screen when you pressed F5 a little later.

You are now finished designing the report. Your screen should look like Figure 7.17.

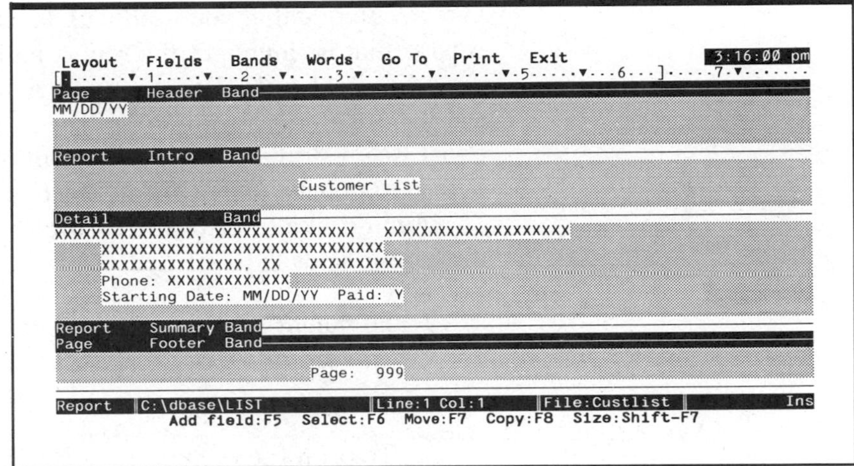

Figure 7.17: The completed format for the Customer List report

SAVING A REPORT FORMAT

Now let's save all this hard work and then use this format to print a customer list. First, as we've done before, we'll add a description to the format.

1. Choose Layout ► Edit Description of Report.
2. Type the description **List of customer names and addresses** and then press ←┘.
3. To actually save the report format and description, choose Exit ► Save Changes and Exit.
4. When dBASE presents the prompt "Save as:" type a valid file name—**LIST**, in this example—and press ←┘.

dBASE will take some time to write a program for itself to print the report later. When that's all done, it will return you to the Control Center. You'll see the LIST report name in the Reports panel.

PRINTING THE CUSTOMER LIST

When you get back to the Control Center, you can use the same basic technique that you used with labels to print the Customer List report; that is, highlight the report name in the Reports panel and press ↵, or double-click the report name. Select Print Report from the options that appear. When the print submenu appears, select either Begin Printing to actually print the report or View Report on Screen to preview the printed report on your screen.

If you'd like to print the customer list report right now, follow these basic steps:

1. Highlight LIST in the Reports panel of the Control Center and press ↵, or double-click that report.
2. Select Print Report.
3. To print the report, select Begin Printing. Optionally, to see the report on the screen only, select View Report on Screen.

NOTE

In the section titled "Controlling the Printer" later in this chapter, we'll solve any formatting problems you may have encountered while printing.

The results should look like the original example of the report shown in Figure 7.14. If you are using a laser printer, you may need to eject the page from the printer. Follow steps 1 and 2 and select Eject Page Now from the Print menu. Then press Esc to return to the Control Center. If you opted to view the report on the screen only, follow the instructions at the bottom of the screen until you are returned to the Control Center.

In the next section, you will create yet another printed report: a form letter. If you are ready to take a break now, go ahead and exit dBASE IV in the usual manner (choose Exit ► Quit to DOS). When you are ready to proceed with the next section in this chapter, get dBASE up and running again on your computer and make sure the LEARN catalog is in the Control Center.

CREATING FORM LETTERS

To create form letters with dBASE IV, you can take advantage of a special feature called the *word-wrap editor*, so called because it automatically wraps paragraphs inside of any margins, always breaking lines between words rather than within words. This capability gives you much of the power and flexibility of a word processor—you can easily create, change, delete, and add text to perfect your letter, and the word-wrap editor takes care of the formatting automatically.

Even though the word-wrap editor offers special features, keep in mind that a form letter is like any other report in dBASE. You create the form letter through the reports design screen. After you have saved it, its name appears in the Reports panel of the Control Center, and you can print it at any time using the same techniques you use to print mailing labels and other reports.

As in the previous section, called "Modifying the Detail Band," we'll start out by listing both the keyboard and mouse steps for accomplishing a given task, then switch to showing just the keyboard steps. As always, you can choose whichever method you prefer.

Let's create a sample form letter now, so you can gain some experience with the word-wrap editor. Figure 7.18 shows a copy of the letter you will eventually create. Note that the name and address on the letter come directly from the database. dBASE will print a letter for every record in the database or for records you specify in a query (for example, for New York residents only or for people who are late in paying). Follow these steps to get started:

1. If the CUSTLIST database name is not above the line in the Data panel, highlight CUSTLIST and press ↵, or double-click CUSTLIST. Then select Use File to open that database.
2. Highlight <create> in the Reports panel and press ↵, or double-click <create> in that panel with your mouse.
3. When you get to the reports design screen, choose Layout ► Quick Layouts.
4. Select Mailmerge Layout to start creating your form letter.

dBASE automatically closes all report bands except for the Detail band. The Detail band lengthens to accommodate a large body of text. But you are not limited to the space initially displayed in the Detail band; the Detail band will lengthen to accommodate as much text as you enter.

```
01/15/93

Anita Smith
2001 Engine Dr.
Hideaway, CA  92220

Dear Anita:

Believe it or not, this is a form letter!  My new dBASE IV
program lets me add text, delete it, and make changes and
corrections.

Not only can I type up a storm, but I can also use dBASE IV's
many other capabilities with my form letters, including:

        Sorting form letters and matching mailing labels into zip
        code order for bulk mailing.

        Selecting particular people to print letters and mailing
        labels for, such as yourself, Anita.

Sincerely,

Alfred Winstein
```

Figure 7.18: Sample form letter

SETTING MARGINS

It's especially important to set your right margin immediately *after* selecting the Mailmerge Layout option from the Quick Layouts menu, but *before* you start typing your text. Otherwise, you will have to reset the right margin for each paragraph you type. So let's go ahead and set the right margin for this form letter now, before typing any text. Follow these steps:

1. Choose Words ► Modify Ruler.
2. Press Tab eight times to move the cursor to column 64 on the ruler.
3. Type] to mark the right margin.
4. Press Ctrl-End, press ↵, or click the mouse to finish the operation.

Now that the margins are set, you can start typing the text of your letter.

WRITING THE TEXT OF THE LETTER

Because you selected mailmerge layout as the general format for the report, the Detail band is already in word-wrap mode, which means that you can take advantage of the word-wrap editor right now.

When using the word-wrap editor, there is just one important point to keep in mind: *Do not press the ↵ key until you get to the end of a paragraph*. If you are accustomed to typing on a conventional typewriter, you'll be tempted to press ↵ as soon as you get to the end of a line. Or you might be tempted to press ↵ as soon as you get to the end of a sentence. But you'll need to break these habits right now and let dBASE take care of formatting lines and sentences within paragraphs.

Type the first paragraph of the letter now, as shown here. Don't worry about matching the spacing or margins on your screen to those here—just type the paragraph without ever pressing ↵. (You can still use the Backspace and other editing keys to make corrections as necessary.)

> Believe it or not, this is a form letter! My new dBASE IV program lets me type up a storm. I can add text, delete it, and make changes and corrections.

After you type the paragraph, you'll no doubt notice that dBASE has automatically word-wrapped the entire paragraph to the margins you've specified. The paragraph is a single *block* of text now. As you'll see, you can do quite a few things with a block of text. But for now, let's proceed with the letter.

Press ↵ twice to start a new paragraph (block). Then type the next block of text (again, without pressing ↵).

> Not only can I type up a storm, but I can also use dBASE IV's many other capabilities with my form letters, including:

Now press ↵ twice and type the following sentence, again without pressing the ↵ key:

> Sorting form letters and matching mailing labels into zip code order for bulk mailing.

After typing the entire preceding sentence, press ↵ twice. Then type the following sentence (without pressing ↵):

> **Selecting particular people to print letters and mailing labels for, such as yourself,**

Now press ↵ twice and type the word **Sincerely,** (including the comma). Then press ↵ twice again and type the name **Alfred Winstein**.

At this point, the Detail band on your reports design screen should look something like Figure 7.19. Of course, this is only the body of the letter, and we still need to add the name and address. But before we do so, let's take a look at some of the interesting formatting features of the word-wrap editor.

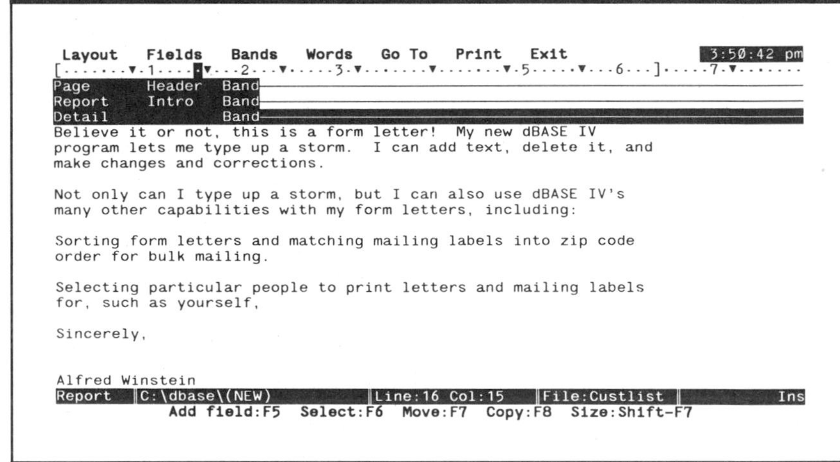

Figure 7.19: The text of the form letter

WORKING WITH BLOCKS OF TEXT

You can use all the usual editing keys to make changes and corrections to your form letter, including the arrow keys to position the cursor, the Del key to delete characters, the Backspace key, and the Ins key to switch between insert and overwrite modes. You can also use any special key listed in the navigation line. And, of course, you can use your mouse to position the cursor and choose options from the navigation line.

As in the customer list report you developed earlier in this chapter, you can mark blocks of text to copy, move, or delete. For example, suppose you want to remove the words "type up a storm. I can" from the first paragraph of the letter. Follow these steps to do so:

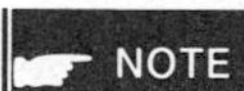

You can also select a block by dragging the mouse from one corner to the opposite corner of the block, as described earlier.

1. Press the ↑ and other arrow keys, as necessary, to move the cursor to the letter *t* in *type* (at line 1, close to column 16), or click your mouse at that location.
2. Press or click Select (F6).
3. Press → until the highlight covers the words *type up a storm. I can* or move the mouse to highlight that text (if you go too far, press ← to back up).
4. Press ↵ or click the mouse to complete the selection (or highlighting).
5. Press the Del key to delete the highlighted text.
6. The prompt "Perform the block deletion?" will appear on the screen to double-check your intentions.
7. Press Y for Yes, or click the Yes option.

Instantly, dBASE removes the highlighted text and automatically reformats the entire paragraph so that it still fits perfectly within the margins. Keep in mind that once you highlight a block of text by pressing or clicking Select (F6), you can also move or copy that text by pressing or clicking Move (F7) or Copy (F8). (The navigation line at the bottom of the screen reminds you that these features are available.) You may want to experiment with those features on your own at a later time.

REFORMATTING PARAGRAPHS

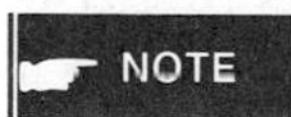

You can control the amount of indentation by changing the tab stops, as discussed later in this chapter.

Now suppose you want to indent the last two sentences (or blocks) in the letter. Indenting is a breeze in the word-wrap editor, as you'll see when you follow these steps:

1. Use the arrow and Home keys or your mouse to move the cursor to the letter *S* in the word *Sorting* (about line 7, column 0).

2. Press the Tab key.
3. Use the ↓ key or your mouse to move the cursor to the letter *S* in the word *Selecting* (about line 10, column 0).
4. Press the Tab key again.

Both blocks of text are now indented, and dBASE has reformatted each one accordingly, as shown in Figure 7.20. (If you feel like experimenting a bit, try pressing the Tab key three times to indent further and then press the Shift-Tab key three of times to delete the indent. Watch what happens on the screen each time you press Tab and Shift-Tab.)

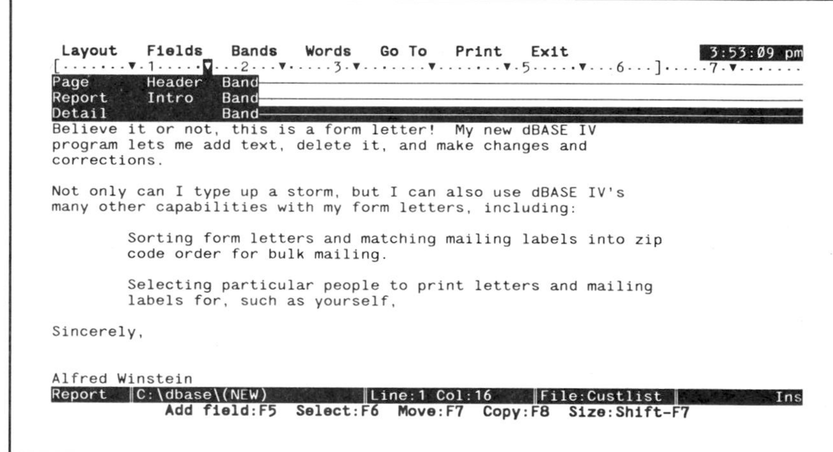

Figure 7.20: Two blocks of text indented using the Tab key

ADDING DATABASE FIELDS

Our form letter is not quite ready for printing yet because it is not addressed to anyone. Let's place some field templates from the CUSTLIST database on the form letter to show dBASE where it needs to place names and addresses when it prints the letter.

To place field templates on the letter, use the same techniques that you used when placing field templates on the mailing labels and customer list report. That is, position the cursor where you want the field to begin and press or click Add Field (F5), or choose Fields ►

Add Field from the menu. Alternatively, double-click the mouse where you want the field to begin. Then select the name of the field you want to display and press or click Accept (Ctrl-End). Let's go through this procedure step by step. Again, for brevity, we'll start out by giving you both the keyboard and mouse steps, then continue with just the keyboard steps.

1. Press the Home and ↑ keys until the cursor gets to the letter *B* in the word *Believe* (line 0, column 0 in the Detail band) or click the mouse at that location.
2. Press Ctrl-N eight times to make room.
3. To place the current date at the top of the form letter, press or click Add Field (F5), and select Date from the PREDEFINED column of the submenu that appears.
4. Press or click Accept (Ctrl-End) to leave the Display Attributes menu that appears.
5. Press ↓ twice to move to line 2, column 0.
6. Press Field (F5) and select FIRSTNAME from the CUSTLIST panel of the submenu that appears.
7. Press Ctrl-End to leave the Display Attributes menu.
8. Press the End key and then press the space bar to insert a blank space.
9. Press Field (F5), select LASTNAME, and press Ctrl-End.
10. Press ↓, press Field (F5), and select ADDRESS.
11. Press Ctrl-End to leave the Display Attributes submenu.
12. Press ↓, press Field (F5), and select CITY.
13. Press Ctrl-End to leave the Display Attributes menu.
14. Press the End key to move to the end of the CITY field template.
15. Type a comma (,) and then press the space bar.
16. Press Field (F5) and select STATE from the CUSTLIST panel of the submenu that appears.

17. Press Ctrl-End to leave the Display Attributes submenu.
18. Press the End key to move to the end of the STATE field template (line 4, column 19).
19. Press the space bar twice to insert two blank spaces.
20. Press Field (F5), select ZIP, and press Ctrl-End to leave the Display Attributes submenu.
21. Press the ↓ key twice to move to line 6, column 0.
22. Type the word **Dear** and press the space bar to insert a space.
23. Press Field (F5), select FIRSTNAME, and then press Ctrl-End to leave the Display Attributes submenu.
24. Press the End key to move to the end of the FIRSTNAME field template and then type a colon (:).

Steps 22 through 24 set up your form letter to present a greeting at the top of your letter, such as **Dear John:**. At this point, your letter should look like Figure 7.21. (Some of the text is scrolled off the bottom of the screen, but don't worry; it's still there.)

You're not quite finished yet, because the form letter prints the recipient's first name again near the bottom of the letter. Follow these

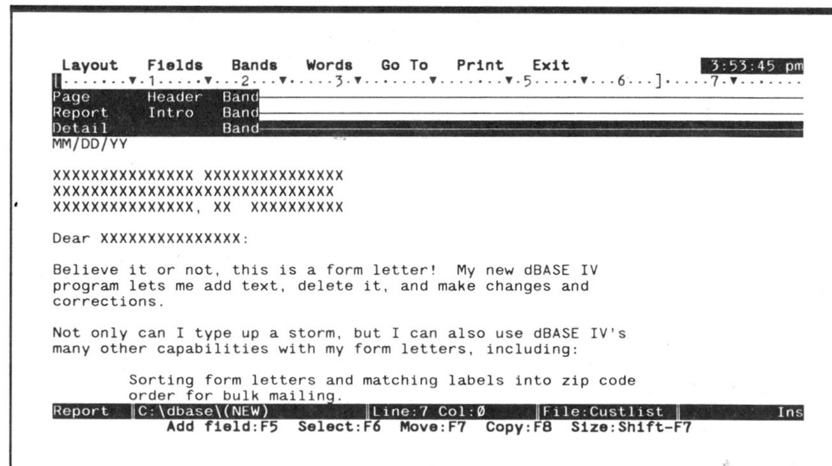
```
Layout  Fields  Bands  Words  Go To  Print  Exit                  3:53:45 pm
[·······▼·1·····▼···2···▼·····3·▼·······▼·······▼·5·····▼···6···]·····7·▼·······
Page      Header  Band
Report    Intro   Band
Detail            Band
MM/DD/YY

XXXXXXXXXXXXXXX XXXXXXXXXXXXXXX
XXXXXXXXXXXXXXXXXXXXXXXXXXXXXX
XXXXXXXXXXXXXXX, XX  XXXXXXXXXX

Dear XXXXXXXXXXXXXXX:

Believe it or not, this is a form letter!  My new dBASE IV
program lets me add text, delete it, and make changes and
corrections.

Not only can I type up a storm, but I can also use dBASE IV's
many other capabilities with my form letters, including:

        Sorting form letters and matching labels into zip code
        order for bulk mailing.
Report  ║C:\dbase\(NEW)      ║Line:7 Col:0    ║File:Custlist ║          Ins
          Add field:F5  Select:F6  Move:F7  Copy:F8  Size:Shift-F7
```

Figure 7.21: Form letter with field templates added

steps to place the FIRSTNAME template accordingly:

1. Press the ↓ key about 13 times and then press the End key to move the cursor to the right of the words "such as yourself," or click the mouse at that location;
2. Press the space bar to insert a blank space.
3. Press Add Field (F5) and select FIRSTNAME as the field to place.
4. Press Ctrl-End to leave the Display Attributes submenu.
5. Press the End key to move past the end of the FIRSTNAME field template (about line 19, column 53).
6. Type a period (.).

SAVING THE FORM LETTER

Now you have finished the sample form letter. Go ahead and add a description to the form letter and save it using the file name FORMLET, following these steps:

1. Choose Layout ► Exit Description of Report.
2. When prompted, type the description **Example form letter** and then press ↵.
3. Choose Exit ► Save Changes and Exit.
4. When prompted, type a file name such as **FORMLET** and then press ↵.

You'll need to wait a few seconds while dBASE prepares a program for printing the form letter. When dBASE is done with this task, it returns you to the Control Center. The name of the form letter, FORMLET, will appear in the Reports panel of the Control Center.

PRINTING THE FORM LETTER

To print the form letter, follow the same basic steps you used to print mailing labels and the customer list report. That is, highlight

FORMLET in the Reports panel and then press ↵, or double-click on FORMLET with your mouse. Select Print Report from the options that appear and then either Begin Printing or View Report on Screen from the Print menu. Then follow the instructions that appear on the screen.

Figure 7.18 earlier in this chapter presented an example of how the printed letter will appear on your screen or printer. Of course, dBASE will print many letters: one for each record in the CUST-LIST database. The general format of each letter will be the same, but each will be addressed to a single individual in the CUSTLIST database.

SORTING REPORTS AND LABELS FOR PRINTING

To print reports or mailing labels in sorted order, activate the appropriate index and then print the report or labels. The following example prints the Customer List in alphabetical order. Here are the steps:

1. From the Control Center, highlight or click on CUSTLIST in the Data panel, then press or click Data (F2) to get to the edit/browse screen.
2. Choose Organize ► Order Records by Index.
3. Select the LASTNAME index.
4. Press Ctrl-End or choose Exit ► Exit from the menu.
5. In the Reports panel, highlight LIST and press ↵, or double-click LIST with your mouse.
6. Select Print Report.
7. Select either Begin Printing or View Report on Screen, whichever you prefer.

The report will be sorted in the order you wanted. To print mailing labels and form letters in zip code order, you follow the same basic steps, but select ZIP as the index for organizing records in step 3.

USING QUERIES TO PRINT REPORTS AND LABELS

You can use any existing query to filter records that are printed in a report or as labels. The only requirement is that the view skeleton in the query must include all the fields that the form or report displays.

The PHONELST query created in Chapter 6 did not include all the fields from the CUSTLIST database, so let's create a new query now. Here are the steps to create a query called CALCUST to list all California customers in zip code order:

1. If necessary, open the CUSTLIST database by highlighting its name in the Data panel and pressing ↵, or by double-clicking its name. Then select Use File.
2. Highlight <create> in the Queries panel and press ↵, or double-click <create> in that panel.
3. Tab to the STATE field, or click on it, then enter the filter condition **"CA"** (including the quotation marks). Press ↵.
4. Choose Fields ► Include Indexes.
5. Tab to the ZIP field, or click on it, then choose Fields ► Sort on This Field from the menu.
6. Select Ascending ASCII. "AscDict1" should appear in the ZIP field.
7. Choose Layout ► Edit Description of Query.
8. Type the description **California customer names and addresses** and press ↵.
9. Choose Exit ► Save Changes and Exit.
10. Type the file name **CALCUST** and press ↵ when prompted for a file name.

When you return to the Control Center, you can use the query to print reports (including form letters) or mailing labels by activating the query and then printing the appropriate reports. Here are the exact steps:

1. If CALCUST is not already in use (if it does not appear above the thin line in the Queries panel), highlight CALCUST in the Queries panel and press ↵, or double-click it with your mouse. Then select Use View.
2. Highlight the name of a report or label format in the Reports or Labels panel (either LIST or MAILING in this example), then press ↵, or double-click that format with your mouse.
3. Select Print Label or Print Report.
4. If dBASE double-checks your intentions, select Current View.
5. Select Begin Printing or View Labels/Report on Screen, whichever you prefer.

NOTE

The remainder of this chapter discusses general options and techniques for printing reports and labels. You may just want to skim through all of this for now and refer to this chapter later if you need help with a particular problem.

The printed report will list only California residents, sorted into zip code order.

The query will stay in effect for any other reports that you print, until you deactivate it either by opening another query or database file, or by selecting the current query name from the Queries panel and choosing Close View.

MODIFYING AN EXISTING FORMAT

After you've printed your reports or labels, you may decide you want to make some changes to the format. Some changes, such as margins, page length, and page alignment, may be printer issues, in which case you may want to adjust your printer settings rather than the report format. See the section "Controlling the Printer" later in this chapter for more information.

In other cases you might want to change the size and or placement of text and fields in the report or labels. In that case, you want to return to the reports design (or labels design) screen, and make your changes. Here's how:

- Highlight the name of the report or label format that you want to change in the Reports or Labels panel of the Control Center, or click on that format with your mouse.
- Press or click Design (Shift-F2).

Here you can use all the techniques we described earlier to add, delete, move, or copy text and field templates. Some additional techniques that you can use to refine the appearance of reports and labels are discussed in the sections that follow.

As usual, whenever you've finished modifying your format, just choose Exit ► Save Changes and Exit (or just press Ctrl-End) to save your work and return to the Control Center.

CONTROLLING BLANK LINES

You may find that your report has too few or too many blank lines when printed. Blank lines are caused by two sources: blank lines in the report (or label) format, and the printer's line spacing setting.

Figure 7.22 shows blank lines in the CUSTLIST report format. Compare that figure to the printed report shown back in Figure 7.14 to see exactly how the blank lines on the format become blank lines on the printed report.

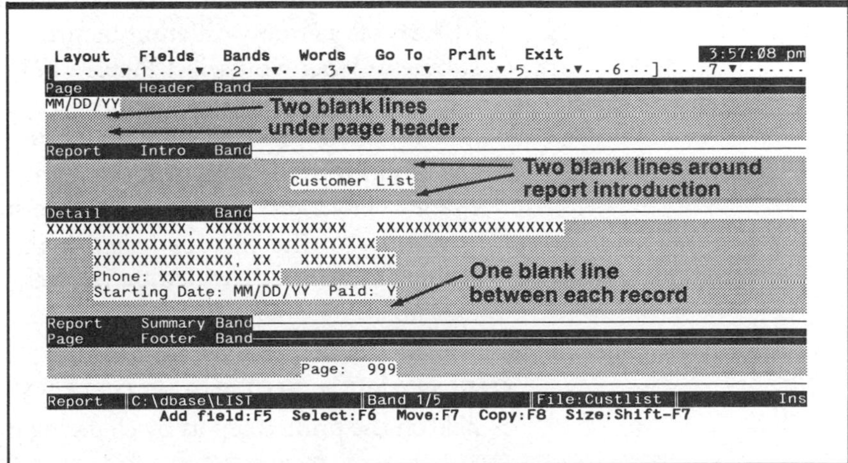

Figure 7.22: Blank lines in a report format

If the line spacing on your printed report or labels is too wide or narrow (for example, everything is double-spaced rather than single-spaced), and there are no blank lines in the report format to account for these blank lines, then most likely the printer line spacing is set incorrectly. See the section on line spacing in "Controlling the Printer" later in this chapter.

FORMATTING FIELDS

dBASE IV automatically assigns certain Display Attributes to field templates used in label and report formats. Sometimes these automatic attributes may not quite fit your needs, and you may want to change them. You can change the display attribute of a field template in a label or report format by following these steps:

As a shortcut, you can just double-click the field template with your mouse.

- Move the cursor into the field template that you want to change.
- Press or click Add Field (F5), or choose Fields ► Modify Field from the menu.

These steps display a submenu that describes the field and presents the Template and Picture Functions options.

CHANGING A FIELD'S PICTURE FUNCTIONS A *picture function* is a code that tells dBASE how to display a piece of information. dBASE offers many different picture functions, which are listed on a submenu when you select Picture Functions while adding or changing a field template, as shown in Figure 7.23. You can turn any available function on or off by highlighting that option and pressing the space bar or by clicking the option with your mouse. The options relevant to label and report formats are summarized in Table 7.3.

Many of the picture functions affect how data are displayed within the width provided by the field template, as the next section explains.

CHANGING A FIELD'S WIDTH You can control the width of a field on the printed report by changing the size of the field template. By

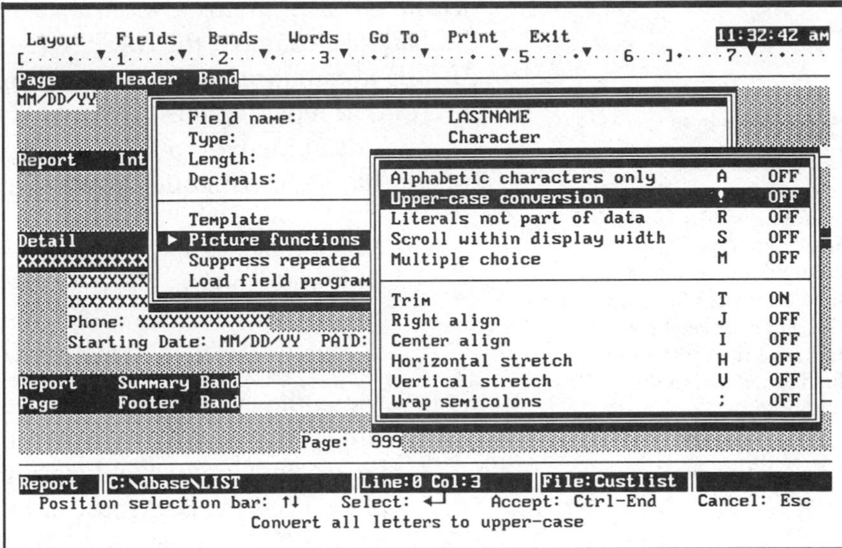

Figure 7.23: Picture Function options for Character fields

Table 7.3: Common Picture Functions for Reports and Labels

Picture function	Symbol	Effect
Uppercase conversion	!	Displays all letters (a–z) in uppercase (A–Z)
Trim	T	Removes leading and trailing blanks
Right Align	J	Right-aligns text within the space allotted for the field
Center Align	I	Centers text within the space provided
Horizontal Stretch	H	Adjusts template width to width of data
Vertical Stretch	V	Wraps text onto several lines within the allotted width

default, dBASE assigns a width that matches the field's width in the database. For example, the LASTNAME field is 15 characters wide, so dBASE automatically places the template XXXXXXXXXXXX-XXX in the report or label format to display data from that field.

To widen or narrow a field, you can use either of two techniques (notice that both techniques let you use the keyboard or the mouse):

NOTE

You cannot alter the template widths for the Date data type. Also, changing the width of a field template affects only the report or label format, not the width of the field as defined in the database.

- Move the cursor to the field template, or click the template with your mouse. Press or click Size (Shift-F7). Use the → and ← keys or move your mouse to the right or left to widen or narrow the field. Then press ↵ or click the mouse.
- Move the cursor to the field template, or click the template with your mouse. Press or click Add Field (F5), or choose Fields ► Modify Field from the menu. Then select Template. Press the Backspace or Del key to narrow the template, or type X's (or other characters from Table 7.3) to widen the template. Press or click Accept (↵), then press or click Accept (Ctrl-End) when done.

Note that if you use the latter technique, dBASE will display a submenu of *character input symbols*. These are more relevant to custom forms than they are to reports, so we'll discuss them in Chapter 8.

How dBASE fits data from the database into the space allotted by the field template on the report depends upon three picture functions: Trim, Horizontal Stretch, and Vertical Stretch. For example, suppose your database contains a field named Address that is 30 characters wide, but on your report, you narrow the template to 15 characters (that is, XXXXXXXXXXXXXXX). How would dBASE display the address 3456 Rancho Santa Fe Dr.?

If you assign the Trim picture function to the ADDRESS field, dBASE will *truncate* the data to fit within the template. That is, only the first 15 characters will be displayed, as follows:

```
3456 Rancho San
```

If you assign the Vertical Stretch picture function to the ADDRESS field, dBASE will word-wrap the address within the width allotted. Hence, if you print the example address using a template that is 15 characters wide and the Vertical Stretch picture function, the sample address will appear on the report as

3456 Rancho
Santa Fe Dr.

> NOTE
>
> The Horizontal Stretch option is available only in the Mailmerge layout. Vertical Stretch is available only in the Column and Form layouts.

If you assign the Horizontal Stretch picture function, dBASE will automatically adjust the size of the template to fit the data being displayed. Thus, it will not matter what size you make the template. (In fact, you cannot alter the size of a field template that has the Horizontal Stretch function assigned to it.) Hence, regardless of the size of the template, the Horizontal Stretch picture function always displays the full address, in this case

3456 Rancho Santa Fe Dr.

The Horizontal Stretch function also trims off any leading or trailing blanks when it prints data.

Note that when you assign the Vertical Stretch picture function to a field, the template appears as V's rather than X's. When either V's or X's appear, you can press or click Size (Shift-F7) to size the template. When you assign the Horizontal Stretch picture function to a field, the template appears as H's, and you cannot resize the field template.

The Center and Right Align picture functions also let you determine how data is displayed within the width provided by the field template. If you assign the Center picture function, text will be centered within the width, as in these examples:

```
123 Appleton Court
  34 Reposo Alto
     123 A St.
   P.O. Box 3384
```

If you assign the Right Align attribute to the field, text will be right-aligned within the width allotted by the field template, as follows:

```
123 Appleton Court
    34 Reposo Alto
         123 A St.
     P.O. Box 3384
```

After you've selected options from the Picture Functions pull-down menu, press or click Accept (Ctrl-End) to accept those changes and return to the Display Attributes submenu. You can then press or click Accept (Ctrl-End) a second time to return to the design screen.

DRAWING LINES AND BOXES

You can draw lines and boxes on a report format using the Box and Line options from the Layout pull-down menu. However, not all printers can print the lines and boxes. Chapter 8 discusses specific techniques for drawing lines and boxes.

SAVING YOUR CHANGES

After you've modified your label or report format, don't forget to save your work by choosing Exit ► Save Changes and Exit. If you do *not* want to save your changes, choose Exit ► Abandon Changes and Exit instead.

If you want to save your modified format as a new file (leaving the original, unmodified format intact), choose Layout ► Save This Report and provide a new file name. Then choose Exit ► Abandon Changes and Exit.

FINDING TEXT ON THE DESIGN SCREENS

The Go To pull-down menu provides search and replace options for specific text on the reports and labels design screens. (This menu is very similar to the Go To menu discussed in Chapter 6.) These options can be handy for making corrections in a report format. For example, suppose you inadvertently use the word *peace* in place of *piece* in a form letter and want to correct all the mistakes.

NOTE

Before you use the Replace option with a form letter, make sure that the cursor is in the Detail band.

You could choose Go To ► Replace to automatically search for and replace the mistakes. When prompted, enter **peace** as the search string. Then, when prompted, enter **piece** as the replacement text. dBASE will search for the first occurrence of the word *peace* in the letter, highlight that word, and display these options:

Replace: R Skip: S All: A Cancel: Esc

You can select any single option. Selecting Replace (by typing **R**) replaces the current word and moves on to the next occurrence of the word *peace*. Selecting Skip (by typing **S**) skips the current word without replacing it and moves on to the next occurrence of the word *peace*. Selecting All (by typing **A**) replaces all remaining occurrences of the word *peace* with *piece* without asking for permission. Pressing Esc cancels the search and replace operation.

CONTROLLING THE PRINTER

As you've seen in several of the preceding hands-on examples, all dBASE printing is handled by the Print pull-down menu, shown in Figure 7.24. This menu is available at the Control Center, and at the Reports and Labels Design screens as well.

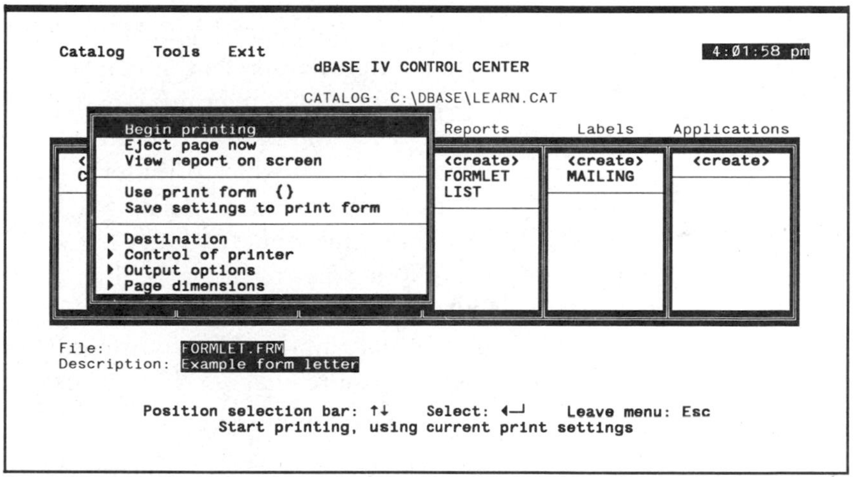

Figure 7.24: The Print pull-down menu

While trying some of the hands-on examples of reports and label formats, you used the Begin Printing option on the Print menu to actually start printing.

You may have also discovered that your printer seems "out of whack." Perhaps text is too far to the left or right, or there are too many or too few lines per page, or perhaps nothing at all printed!

Most of these options can be fixed with the other options on the Print pull-down menu. We'll discuss those other options in the sections that follow.

ABOUT PRINT FORMS

Before you start changing individual options on the Print menu, it's useful to get an understanding of *print forms*. A print form is simply a collection of printer settings, or *printer defaults,* that tell dBASE some general things about how to print your report or labels.

Print forms are stored on disk in files with the extension .PRF. One print form, named REPORT.PRF, contains the "global" defaults, that is, the defaults used by all report and label formats that you design.

Each time you create a new report or label format, dBASE automatically creates a print form for that particular format as well. For example, when you created the FORMLET report, dBASE also automatically created a file named FORMLET.PRF that contained printer information for the form letter. The FORMLET.PRF file settings affect only the printing of the FORMLET report.

Notice the option Use Print Form on the Print menu. This option tells you which print form is currently in use. However, if the "global" print form, REPORT.PRF, is in use, this option shows nothing other than two curly braces ({}).

Notice also the Save Settings to Print Form option on the Print menu. That option lets you save any printer settings that you choose from the Print menu for future use. Now, keep in mind the following facts as you read about the various options on the Print menu in the sections that follow:

- If you do not use the Save Settings to Print Form option on the Print menu to save your print settings, those settings affect only the next printing that you perform with the Begin Printing option. The settings are "forgotten" immediately after that printing is finished.
- If you use the Save Settings to Print Form option after making selections from the Print menu to save those settings to a particular print form file, such as FORMLET.PRF for the FORMLET report, then those settings will be used

whenever you print the FORMLET report in the future. However, no other report formats will be affected by the settings stored in FORMLET.PRF.

- If you use the Save Settings to Print Form option to save your current settings in a file named REPORT.PRF, then all future reports and labels that you design will use those settings, unless you change them while designing that particular report or label format.

The last option, saving your settings to the REPORT.PRF file, is a very useful one because it lets you determine general settings for your particular printer. Even when the Use Print Form option on the Print menu shows only {} rather than a print form file name, you can rest assured that it is using settings you've previously saved in the REPORT.PRF file.

Keep in mind, however, that saving settings to the REPORT.PRF file affects *only* report and label formats you design in the future. To alter print settings on existing report or label formats, you'll need to change the print settings for those formats individually.

The actual steps for saving printer settings to a print form are listed below:

- Choose Print ► Save Settings to Print Form.
- If a suggested print form file name is shown, and that selection is acceptable, just press ↵. Otherwise, type in a valid file name for the print form (for example, REPORT if you want to make the new settings "global defaults"), then press ↵.
- If dBASE asks if it's all right to overwrite the existing file, just press ↵ type O, or click Overwrite to overwrite the file.

Your printer settings are now saved for future use. To verify this, you can scroll through the other options on the Print menu to make sure the settings are as you want them.

USING MULTIPLE PRINTERS

If you have multiple printers attached to your computer, the first thing you should do before printing is make sure the proper printer is selected. Here's how:

- Get to the Print pull-down menu from either the Control Center or the reports or labels design screen.
- Choose Destination.
- Highlight the Write To option and press ↵ or the space bar until PRINTER appears. Alternatively, just click the mouse on Write To until PRINTER appears.
- Highlight the Printer Model option and press ↵ or the space bar until the printer model you are using appears. Alternatively, just click the mouse on Printer Model until your printer model appears.
- Press Ctrl-End.
- If you want to save that selection, use the Save Settings to Print Form option as described in the section "About Print Forms" earlier in this chapter.

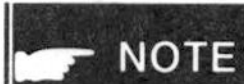

If you don't see your printer model, you may need to install it with the DBSETUP program, as described in Appendix B.

CONTROLLING VERTICAL ALIGNMENT

When printing reports or labels, you want to make sure that dBASE always starts printing at the top of the page, rather than near the middle or bottom. On tray-fed printers (like most laser printers) this is usually an easy thing to accomplish—basically you don't have to do anything to the paper and/or printer.

But on printers that use tractor-feed paper, you have to make sure that the paper is properly aligned before you start to print. If there is any doubt in your mind about whether the report will be vertically aligned correctly, follow these simple steps:

- Turn off the printer.
- Manually crank the paper in the printer so that there is a page perforation just above the print head (the thing that does the actual printing on your printer).
- Turn the printer back on.
- Begin printing.

Once you complete the steps above, you should never "manually" crank the paper through the printer, as doing so will throw the vertical alignment out of whack (and possibly even damage the printer). Instead, use the Eject Page Now option from the Print menu, or the Form Feed button on your printer, to eject any partially printed pages from your printer.

CONTROLLING EXTRA PAGES

You may find that dBASE prints a blank page before printing your report, and/or does not print the last page of your report (or prints nothing at all when printing a one-page report!). These situations can be handled using Control of Printer ► New Page from the Print Menu. Your options there are as follows.

BEFORE	Ejects the current page before printing the report or labels
BOTH	Ejects the current page before and after printing the report or labels
NONE	Does not eject any pages from the printer
AFTER	Ejects the current page after printing the report

The best all-around setting for this option is AFTER, since it wastes the least amount of paper and also helps keep pages aligned properly in the printer. It also prevents the problem of missing pages, which are generally caused by incomplete pages stored within the printer's buffer (memory), waiting to be ejected from the printer.

To change the page eject technique default (for future reports), follow these general steps:

- Highlight or click on any name in the Data panel of the Control Center (so that a particular report or label is not selected).
- Press or click Quick Report (Shift-F9) to get to the Print menu.
- Choose Control of Printer.

- Highlight New Page and press ↵ or the space bar until the option you want is selected (most likely, AFTER). Alternatively, just click the mouse on New Page until you see the option you want.
- Press Ctrl-End.
- Choose Save Settings to Print Form.
- Type **REPORT** and press ↵.
- Press ↵, type **O**, or click Overwrite if prompted.

Now the page eject technique you selected will be used in future reports that you design. Remember, existing report formats will continue to use whatever setting is currently in their print form (.PRF) files until you change those settings.

PAGE ADVANCE TECHNIQUE Another way to control how and when pages are broken while printing reports or labels is through Control of Printer ► Advanced Page Using on the Print menu. Two options are provided:

FORM FEED	Printer settings are used to determine where the top of the next page is
LINE FEEDS	dBASE counts how many lines are necessary to get to the top of the next page

Typically, you use the FORM FEED option when using a standard size paper, such as $8^1/_2 \times 11$ inches, or a size that your printer allows you to use through buttons or options on the printer itself (as described in your printer manual).

The Length of Page option is discussed under "Controlling Margins and Page Length" later in this chapter.

If your printer cannot handle an odd page length that you need to use, switch to the LINE FEEDS option (but only for reports or labels that require that odd page size). You will also need to be certain to set the Length of Page option on the Page Dimensions menu to the correct number of lines on each page so that dBASE can accurately count how many lines are needed to get to the top of the next page.

To change this setting, follow these general steps:

- In the Control Center, highlight the name of the report for which you want to change the page advance method, and press ↵ or double-click that report.
- Choose Print Report.
- Choose Control of Printer.
- Highlight Advance Page Using and press ↵ or the space bar until the option you want is shown. Or, just click the mouse on Advance Page Using until you see the option you want.
- Press Ctrl-End.
- Choose Save Settings to Print Form and press ↵ to save the selection to the print form file for the current report.
- Choose Overwrite if prompted.

FORCING PAGE BREAKS Another way to control page breaks is by inserting a page break character right into the report format. You do this using Words ► Insert Page Break in the Reports Design screen. See the section on "Creating a Cover Page" near the end of this chapter for an example.

CONTROLLING MARGINS AND PAGE LENGTH

Perhaps the trickiest things to control when printing with dBASE are the margins and page length. Let's take it one step at a time starting with the left margin.

CONTROLLING THE LEFT MARGIN We usually think of the white space between the left edge of a page and the start of text as the left margin. However, in dBASE terminology, that white space is actually called the *page offset.* The left margin that you set with the [symbol on the design screen tab ruler is actually added to the distance defined by the page offset.

Now, on dot-matrix printers, the offset is largely determined by how the paper is positioned in the printer. On laser printers (and other tray-fed printers), the offset is typically .25 to .30 inches, the width of the roller that feeds the paper through the printer.

Determining an accurate page offset is a matter of adjusting the offset accordingly. For example, suppose your printer's "normal" print size is 10 characters to the inch (which you can easily determine simply by measuring with a ruler any printout you've produced so far with dBASE). Furthermore, let's say dBASE normally prints a 1/2-inch left margin on your report.

Now, suppose you would prefer a 1-inch margin. Well, you need to add 1/2-inch to the existing margin. Given that your printer is printing 10 characters to the inch, 1/2-inch would be five characters. So to get your 1-inch margin, you would need to change the page offset to 5.

The general steps for changing the page offset are listed below (using the "global default" technique, since it is likely that you'll want to use the same margin in most printouts):

- Highlight or click on any name in the Data panel of the Control Center (so that a particular report or label format is not selected).
- Press or click Quick Report (Shift-F9) to get to the Print menu.
- Choose Page Dimensions.
- Choose Offset from Left.
- Type in the number of spaces required to achieve the offset you want (for instance, 5 from the example preceding these steps), then press ↵.
- Press Ctrl-End.
- Choose Save Settings to Print Form, then type **REPORT** and press ↵ to save the settings to the REPORT.PRF print form for future reports.
- Press ↵, type **O**, or click Overwrite if prompted.

Remember, saving the settings to the REPORT.PRF file affects future reports that you design. To change the page offset for an existing report format, you need to save the new offset to the print file for that report.

SETTING THE RIGHT MARGIN Setting the right margin is basically a matter of determining how many characters will fit across the page within the margins you specify. This, of course, is partly determined by how many characters to the inch your printer will print.

Controlling the print size is covered a little later in this chapter.

For example, suppose you want to print a particular report that uses condensed print on 8½- by 11-inch paper, and you want 1-inch margins on both the left and right side of the page. Furthermore, "condensed print" on your particular printer is about 15 cpi (characters per inch). In this case, you want to print lines that are 6.5 inches wide (the 8.5 inch page width minus the two inches for the margins). At 15 cpi, you can print about 98 characters across a 6.5 inch line (15 times 6.5 is about 98).

Now let's deal with the 1-inch margins. Let's say that when you leave the page offset at 0, your printer usually leaves about a ¼-inch left margin. But in this example you want a 1-inch margin. So, you need to change the page offset to 11 characters using Page Dimensions ► Offset from Left from the Print menu. Why 11 characters? Because your printer is already printing a ¼-inch margin, so you need another ¾-inch. At 15 cpi, ¾-inch is about 11 characters (0.75 times 15 is about 11).

Finally, you need to set the right margin to 98. You've already had some experience with setting the right margins (see "Creating Form Letters" earlier in this chapter). As you may recall, you do this in the Reports Design screen using Words ► Modify Ruler. In this particular example, you would leave the left margin ([) at zero (since 0 on the ruler is the spot at the right of the page offset), and then set the right margin (]) at 98.

Save the report format as a print form, and when you print the report, you'll have perfect 1-inch margins on both sides of the paper, with 98 characters of text between the margins. The same basic logic used to create this example can be used to control the page layout with any combination of print size, margin size, and paper width.

CONTROLLING THE PAGE LENGTH The length of the page you are printing on is determined by the number of *printable* lines on the page. Normally, dBASE assumes this to be 66 lines, because most printers print 6 lines to the inch and print on 8½- by 11-inch paper (6 lines per inch times 11 inches is 66 lines).

Many laser printers come factory preset to print only 60 lines per page. If you attempt to print 66 lines on such a printer, some lines from the bottom of page 1 will spill over onto the top of page 2, then page 2 will begin on the next page after that, and so forth.

NOTE

You need to count blank lines as well, which can be a little tricky. You may have to experiment to get exactly the right setting.

There is a fairly simple solution to determining the exact number of lines that you can print per page: Print one or more pages and count how many lines from page 1 spilled over onto page 2. Then subtract that amount from the number of lines printed per page. For example, if 6 lines spill over onto page 2 when the page length is set at 66, simply change the page length to 60. Here are the general steps for changing the page length:

- Get to the Print menu (either from the Control Center or the Reports/Labels design screen.
- Select Length of Page.
- Type in the correct page length (that is, 60 from the example described above).
- Press ↵.
- Press Ctrl-End.
- Save the change, either to the current format only, or to the general print form settings in REPORT.PRF (as described earlier).

When using nonstandard-sized paper, such as a preprinted form that is 7½ inches long, you may need to adjust both the page length and the page advance technique, and perhaps use a little trial-and-error experimentation as well. See the earlier section titled "Page Advance Technique" for information on this topic.

CONTROLLING THE TOP AND BOTTOM MARGINS There are no settings per se for the top and bottom margins of the page in a report printed via the report generator. The amount of white space at the top and bottom of each page is determined by the number of blank lines at the top and bottom of the Page Header and Page Footer bands (respectively), or at the top and bottom of the Report Intro and Report Summary bands (respectively) if the Page Header and Footer bands are closed.

If you change the amount of white space in any of the aforementioned bands, you need not change the page length to accommodate those changes. The blank lines at the top and bottom of each page are just counted as printed lines.

SETTING THE INDENTATION LEVEL AND TAB STOPS

For the most part, you really need only be concerned with indentation level and tab stops when you are working in a word-wrap band, that is, when you are creating form letters. The indentation level lets you determine how far in the first line of each paragraph will be indented. Changing the tab stops lets you determine how far in an entire paragraph will be indented. In addition, you can create "outdents" (such as numbered lists) by reversing the order of the tab stop and indentation level symbols.

To set the indentation level and tab stops, follow these general steps (after choosing Quick Layouts ► MailMerge Layout on the Reports Design screen):

- Choose Words ► Modify Ruler.
- Use the following keys to change the ruler:

→ ←	Moves cursor to the left and right without making changes
Tab, Shift-Tab	Moves the cursor to the left and right one tab stop
[	Marks the left margin
]	Marks the right margin
#	Sets the indentation level for the first line of a paragraph

!	Marks a tab stop (appears as a triangle)
=	Sets tab stops at even intervals
0	Resets margins and indentation back to zero
Del	Deletes current tab stop (Backspace also does this)
Esc	Abandons current changes and uses previous settings
Ctrl-End	Saves current settings

- Press Ctrl-End or click the mouse when you've finished modifying the ruler.

Remember that when you are in word-wrap mode, dBASE lets you reset the tab ruler for each paragraph. But to simplify matters, it's a good idea to set your margins, type in the entire body of the letter, then make changes and refinements. That way, you won't have to modify the tab ruler for each paragraph you type in.

CONTROLLING LINE SPACING

Normally dBASE prints everything single spaced. You can, however, switch to double or triple spacing if your printer can do so. To change spacing of the entire report (or all the labels), follow these general steps:

- Choose Print ► Page Dimensions.
- Highlight Spacing of Lines and press ↵ or the space bar until the spacing you want is shown. Or, just click the mouse on Spacing of Lines until you see the spacing you want.
- Press Ctrl-End (or ←).

As described earlier, you can save those settings to a print form if you wish.

You can also adjust the spacing in individual bands of a report. For example, you might want to single-space page headers and footers but double-space the body of the report. Here's how to change the spacing of an individual report band:

- Bring the report format to the Reports Design screen.
- Move the cursor to the band whose spacing you want to change, or click on that band.
- Choose Bands from the menu.
- Highlight Spacing of Lines for Band and press ↵ or press the space bar until the spacing you want is shown. Or, just click the mouse on Spacing of Lines for Band until you see the spacing you want.
- Press Ctrl-End (or ←).

Note that if you select DEFAULT as the spacing option, the report will use whatever setting is determined on the Print pull-down menu when you print the report.

PRINTING PART OF A REPORT

You can print any page or group of pages from a report. This is handy for making last minute corrections. For example, suppose you print a 20-page list of names and addresses, and notice an error on page 11. You could correct the error, then print only page 11 rather than the entire report.

To print a specific page or set of pages, follow these steps:

- Highlight the name of the report (or labels) that you want to print in the Reports panel of the Control Center, and press ↵ or double-click that report or label.
- Select Print Report.
- Select Output Options.
- Select Begin on Page.

- Type in the number of the first page you want to print, and press ↵.
- Select End after Page.
- Erase the old setting with the Delete (Del) key, then type the number of the last page you want printed (if this is the same as the Begin on Page selection, then only that page will be printed).
- Press Ctrl-End.
- Select Begin Printing when you are ready to start printing.

CONTROLLING PAGE NUMBERS

Normally dBASE starts numbering pages from page 1. However, if you are compiling a large report that is made of several smaller reports, you may want to number all the pages sequentially. Therefore, the first page of a report would not necessarily be 1. For example, if the first report constitutes pages 1–50 of a large document, and the second report constitutes pages 51–100, then the first printed page of the second report should be numbered page 51.

To have dBASE start numbering pages from some number other than 1, follow these steps:

- Highlight the name of the report (or labels) that you want to print in the Reports panel of the Control Center and press ↵, or double-click that report or label name.
- Select Print Report.
- Select Output Options.
- Select First Page Number.
- Type in the page number that you want printed on the first page, then press ↵.
- Press Ctrl-End.
- Select Begin Printing when you are ready to start printing.

PRINTING MULTIPLE COPIES

To print multiple copies of a report (or labels) follow these simple steps:

- Highlight the name of the report (or labels) that you want to print in the Reports panel of the Control Center and press ↵, or double-click that report or label name.
- Select Print Report.
- Select Output Options.
- Select Number of Copies.
- Type in the number of copies you want printed, then press ↵.
- Press Ctrl-End.
- Select Begin Printing when you are ready to start printing.

PRINTING INDIVIDUAL SHEETS

In some situations you might need to manually feed one page at a time into your printer, for example, if you normally use tractor-feed paper but want to print on letterhead which is not tractor-fed. In these situations, you need to have dBASE pause between each printed page so that you have time to remove the printed page and put in the next page to be printed.

To have dBASE pause between pages, follow these steps:

- Highlight Wait between Pages ↵ and press the space bar to change the setting to Yes. Or, just click the mouse on Wait between Pages until the setting changes to Yes.
- Select Print Report.
- Select Control of Printer.
- Highlight Wait between Pages and press ↵ and press space bar to change the setting to Yes. Or, just click the mouse on Wait between Pages until the setting changes to Yes.
- Press Ctrl-End (or ←).
- Choose Begin Printing when you are ready to start printing.

SENDING CUSTOM CODES

See Appendix B for special codes for PostScript printers.

If you want to activate a special printing feature that is not available from the dBASE menus, you can send a code directly to the printer to activate, and deactivate, that feature. The special codes that you need to send to your printer are generally listed in the manual that came with your printer.

For example, in the manual for the Hewlett Packard IID printer, I find that in order to print on manually loaded standard size envelopes, I need to send the code

    Esc&l81a2h1O

to the printer. To reset the printer to print on normal paper when the envelopes are done, I need to send the code

    EscE

Figure 7.25 shows a suggested label format designed to print on this type of envelope. The text in the upper-left corner is the return address; the *X*s represent fields from the CUSTLIST database in the same format used to print mailing labels in the earlier example in this chapter.

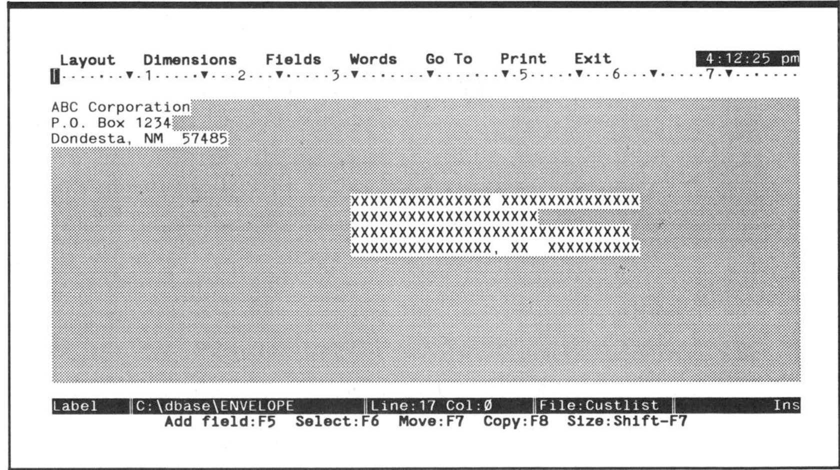

Figure 7.25: Label format for printing directly on envelopes

Rather than use the predefined envelope size on the Dimensions pull-down menu (in the labels design screen), I created the following (more accurate) size:

Width of label	95
Height of label	18
Indentation	0
Lines between labels	0
Spaces between label columns	0
Columns of labels	1

WARNING

Printer control codes are usually fussy about upper- and lowercase letters. The code {ESC}&L81A2H1o is not the same as {ESC}&l81a2h1O.

On the Print pull-down menu, we made these adjustments:

Destination	
Write to	PRINTER
Printer model	HP LJIID1 6
Control of Printer	
New Page	NONE
Starting Control Code	{ESC}&l81a2h1O
Ending Control Code	{ESC}E

The printer destination in this example, HP LJIID1 6, is the printer driver for "normal" LaserJet printing (single sided, 6 lines to the inch). However, the Starting Control Code immediately sends a message to the printer to prepare to print envelopes instead.

When you print this label format, the LaserJet blinks and asks you to feed an envelope. You can either feed one envelope at a time or, if you have an envelope feeder, press the printer's Continue button to feed envelopes from a tray.

As another example of codes, suppose you want to print in landscape mode (sideways on the page), using a very small print size. On the LaserJet IID you can send

```
{ESC}&l1o5.45C{ESC}(s16.66 H
```

as the starting control code, and

{ESC}E

as the ending control code. If you set the offset from left of page to 8, and set the right margin to about 155, you'll get a neatly formatted report with about 1/2-inch margins on both sides of the text.

Again, finding the correct code to send to your printer is a matter of locating the codes in your printer manual. Wherever your printer manual tells you to send an Escape, Esc, or ASCII 27 character to your printer, you want to express that as {Esc} when typing in the code at the Print pull-down menu.

Ctrl-key codes are numbers in the range of 1 to 26. For example, Ctrl-A would be expressed as {1}, Ctrl-B would be {2}, Ctrl-C as {3}, and so forth up to Ctrl-Z, expressed as {26}.

ALIGNING LABELS

Because labels are more expensive than paper, you might want to print your test labels on plain paper until you have the format just right. After printing, align the sheet of paper directly over the blank labels and hold both sheets together up to a light, so you can see how the text lines up with the label outlines.

Getting text to align properly on labels is one of those computer jobs that sometimes takes a lot of patience. There are several tricks to dealing with labels, and exactly which ones you use depends on whether you are using continuous (tractor-fed) labels, or sheet labels—individual sheets often used with all laser printers and other tray-fed papers. The sections below will discuss the differences between these types of labels, and provide some tips for dealing with alignment problems.

TRACTOR-FEED LABELS With tractor-feed labels you need to be able to align the labels in the printer properly before printing the first label. Therefore, when you put the finishing touches on your label format, you want to be sure the labels are in a position in the printer that will be easy to replicate in the future. Here's a tip on getting started:

- Design a label format, as described in the section titled "Designing a Label Format" earlier in this chapter.
- Turn off the printer (never change paper, or hand-crank paper through the printer, while the printer is turned on).

- If there is paper in the printer instead of labels, remove the paper and insert the labels without changing the position of the paper guide at the left so that you do not alter the left margin position (move the right-margin tractor into the left to align with the holes in the labels).
- Move the label to a position that will be easy to remember and repeat in the future—for example, near the upper-left corner at the print head.
- Turn on the printer (*after* aligning the labels).
- Print at least two labels.

Now, rather than messing with the labels' position in the printer, modify the label format to accommodate the printer, using the suggestions described in "Troubleshooting Label Alignment" later in this chapter.

SHEET LABELS If you want to print labels with a laser printer, first be sure to buy laser printer sheet labels. (Don't use labels designed for copy machines—they may melt inside your printer!) You can usually buy laser printer labels at any office supply or stationery store. (Avery Labels Corporation makes several sizes of laser printer labels.)

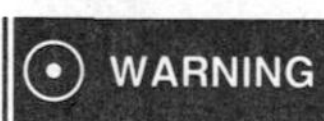

If the last command in your AUTOEXEC.BAT file starts a program or DOS shell, place the SETDTL_LBLOPT = ON command above that last command.

Laser printer labels require unique formatting because of the "dead zone" (an area that is never printed on) at the top and bottom of each label page. dBASE IV Version 1.5 offers a small add-in program that can handle the dead zone on laser printers, but you need to tweak things around a bit to use it. Specifically, you need to put the command DTL_LBLOPT = ON in the DOS environment. It's probably best to put the appropriate commands in your AUTOEXEC.BAT file so that they will be there whenever you start your computer. In case you are not a DOS whiz and programmer, here are the exact steps to do so:

- Starting from the Control Center, press Esc and answer Yes to get to the dBASE dot prompt.
- Type **MODIFY COMMAND C:\AUTOEXEC.BAT** (Be sure to use a backslash, \, rather than a slash, /.)

- Press ↵.
- Press Page Down (PgDn) until the cursor is at the bottom of the file (if the cursor ends up at the end of the last line, press ↵ to move down to the next blank line).

If you make any mistakes while changing your AUTOEXEC.BAT file, don't save those changes! Instead, press Esc and answer Yes when asked about abandoning.

- Carefully type **SET DTL_LBLOPT = ON** (notice that that's an underscore (_) not a hyphen (-) and the only blank space is after the word SET).
- Press ↵.
- Press Ctrl-End to save your changes.

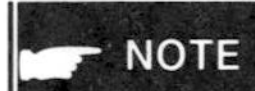

You can learn more about the AUTOEXEC.BAT file from your DOS manual or book. The dBASE MODIFY COMMAND editor is covered in Chapter 17 of this book.

Those steps will automatically place the proper command in the DOS environment each time you start your computer in the future. To make sure, follow the steps below to test your changes now:

- At the dot prompt, type **QUIT** and press ↵ to leave dBASE.
- Prepare your computer for a normal startup. (If your computer starts from the hard disk, drive A should be empty; otherwise, put your DOS startup disk in drive A.)
- Reboot your computer—hold down the Ctrl and Alt keys, then press the Delete (Del) key. Release all three keys.
- When your computer is restarted and you see the DOS prompt, type **SET** and press ↵.

Among the items already in the environment, you should see DTL_LBLOPT = ON. You need never repeat any of the steps above in the future, because the commands are automatically loaded when you start your computer. Now you can run dBASE IV in the usual manner on your computer.

In the future, whenever you change and save a label format, you will see an additional menu before dBASE creates the label format:

```
Top Margin        (0 to 99)
Bottom Margin     (0 to 99)
Advance By        Default/Line Feeds/Form Feed
Widow Checking    Yes/No
```

These options are described in the following list:

Top Margin	Specifies the number of blank lines from the top of the page to the top of the first label
Bottom Margin	Specifies the number of blank lines from the bottom of the last label to the bottom of the page
Advance By	The usual setting, DEFAULT, uses whatever is defined on the Print menu when labels are printed. Can be set to FORM FEED for normal 8½- x 11-inch label sheets, or LINE FEEDS for unusual sheet sizes.
Widow Checking	Prevents labels from being split across two sheets. Change to ON if the last labels on a page are split across two sheets; change to OFF if the last row of labels is not printed at all.

To change a margin setting on this menu, move the cursor to the option, press ↵, type in the number, and press ↵ again. To change the Advance By or Widow Checking option, move the cursor to the option and press ↵ or the space bar until the option you want is selected. When you've finished making your selections, press Ctrl-End.

Most laser printer labels already allot space for the dead zone at the top and bottom of each sheet, so you will want to make sure to set the Length of Page option to 60 lines in the label design's print form file, as described earlier in this chapter. Also, the top and bottom margins on most laser printer sheets are usually the same, so the settings on the menu should be equal. For example, if you set the Top Margin to 3, you should also set the Bottom Margin to 3. It might take a little trial-and-error to get the exact margins you want.

TROUBLESHOOTING LABEL ALIGNMENT Here are some tips to help you troubleshoot label alignment problems.

PROBLEM: Text prints too far to the left on the label.

SOLUTION: Increase the offset from the left side of the page using Page Dimensions on the Print menu. Save your change to the print form for the labels.

PROBLEM: Text prints too high on the label.

SOLUTION: If you are using continuous labels, go back to the label design screen by highlighting the name of the label format in the Labels panel and pressing or clicking Design (Shift-F2). With the cursor in the upper-left corner of the label design, press Ctrl-N to insert blank lines at the top of the form (as shown in Figure 7.26). This will cause blanks to be printed at the top, rather than at the bottom of each label. Save the format, and reprint the labels.

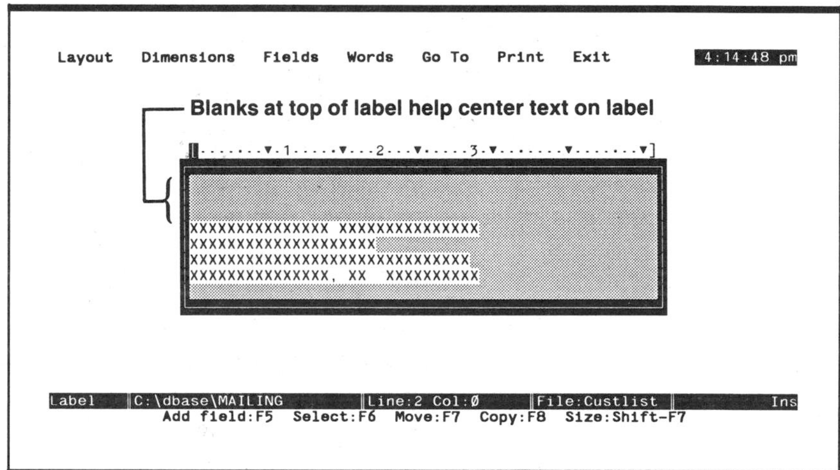

Figure 7.26: Padding the tops of labels with blank spaces

If you are using laser printer labels, you may need to adjust the top and bottom margins on the last menu that appears when you save the label format.

PROBLEM: Labels start out okay, but get progressively further out of alignment.

SOLUTION: The number of lines being printed per label is incorrect. For example, if the first label prints properly, but the text on the second label is too high, the number of lines being printed per label is incorrect. Return to the labels design screen and choose Dimensions ► Lines between Labels or Dimensions ► Height of Label to print more or fewer lines per label.

PROBLEM: Labels in the first column line up properly, but columns to the right are misaligned.

SOLUTION: Go back to the labels design screen and choose Dimensions ► Spaces between Label columns to put either more or less space between labels, or choose Dimensions ► width of Label to adjust the label width.

PROBLEM: Labels print perfectly sometimes, terribly at other times.

SOLUTION: This usually happens only with continuous labels, and is usually caused by the labels being misaligned when printing begins. Always remember to turn off the printer, properly align the labels, then turn the printer back on before printing the labels.

You can check the alignment before actually printing by choosing Generate Sample Labels from the Print menu. This option will fill a row of labels with *X*s so that you can see exactly how the labels are aligned in reference to how text will be printed. After printing a sample label, the screen asks "Do you want more samples? (Y/N)." You can keep typing Y (for Yes) and adjusting the labels until they are perfectly aligned in the printer. Then type N (for No), and dBASE will print the labels.

USING SPECIAL PRINTER FEATURES

Both the labels and reports design screens offer options for taking advantage of any special features that your printer offers, such as controlling the size of print, controlling printer features such as boldface and italic, and controlling the quality of print. In the reports design screen, you can control these features on a band-by-band manner using the Bands pull-down menu.

It's important to understand that dBASE can only *use* the features that are built into your printer; dBASE cannot force your printer to do something that it's not designed to do.

Unfortunately, dBASE doesn't "know" whether or not your printer has a particular feature either, and this can lead to some confusion. For example, if you tell dBASE to print a report heading in boldface italic in the reports design screen, it will accept your request without a problem. However, if your printer does not support boldface italic, the heading will appear as normal text when you print the report. In other words, dBASE doesn't warn you that you've selected an unavailable printer feature; it simply ignores your request when you print the report.

So, it's a good idea to check your printer manual and find out what features it offers before you try using them in your reports or labels. That way, you won't be confused when a requested feature does not appear in your printout.

CHANGING PRINT SIZE

If your printer has the ability to print in various sizes, you can change the size of print either for the entire report or just for specific bands within the report. For example, you might want to use a small print size so that you can fit more columns of data across a page.

As with some other features described in this chapter, whether or not this feature actually works depends on whether or not your printer has the capability to print in different sizes. dBASE can only *use* the features that your printer has available; it cannot force your printer to do something it's not designed to do.

dBASE offers four print sizes to choose from:

PICA	10 characters to the inch
ELITE	12 characters to the inch

CONDENSED	Varies, but usually about 16.6 characters per inch (cpi)
DEFAULT	The current setting at the printer

To take full advantage of a specific print size, you'll probably want to adjust the right margin to allow the maximum width, as described under "Setting the Margins and Page Length" earlier in this chapter.

CHANGING THE PRINT SIZE FOR THE ENTIRE REPORT To change the print size for the entire report, follow these general steps (assuming that you are still at the reports design screen):

- Choose Print ► Control Printer.
- Highlight Text Pitch and press ↵ or the space bar until the size you want is shown. Or, just click the mouse on Text Pitch until you see the size you want.
- Press Ctrl-End twice to leave the two menus.

CHANGING THE SIZE FOR A SINGLE BAND To change the print size for a particular band in the report (assuming that you are still in the reports design screen):

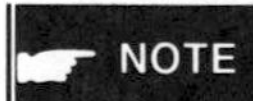

When you mix print sizes in a single report design, the text will not line up on the printed report as it does on the screen, because the screen shows all text at the same size. You will need some trial-and-error adjustments to get text to line up the way you want.

- Move the cursor to the band whose print size you want to change, or click on that band.
- Choose Bands from the menu.
- Highlight Text Pitch for Band and press ↵ or the space bar until the size you want is shown. Or, just click the mouse on Text Pitch for Band until you see the size you want.
- Press Ctrl-End.

You will not notice any change on the screen, but as long as your printer supports the size you chose, you will notice the change when you print the report.

CHANGING PRINT ATTRIBUTES

On laser printers, features like boldface and italic are supported only if the current font supports those features.

When you want text to align neatly into columns on a printed report, you should use a monospaced font such as Courier.

If you have several printers attached to your computer, and will be selecting fonts, be sure to select the correct printer before selecting fonts.

Many printers offer the capability to change the style, or *attribute,* of text and offer boldface, underline, italic, superscript, and subscript. dBASE lets you take advantage of these features in your printed reports and labels as well. You can assign these features from the reports or labels design screen either before or after you've entered text and field templates.

You can also select a font for any portion of your report or label, providing that you've set up dBASE IV to use the fonts that are available for your printer (as discussed in Appendix B). A font is basically a typeface, such as Courier, Times-Roman, or Helvetica. If your printer does offer a wide variety of fonts, you can probably see examples of them in your printer manual.

To assign special print features or fonts to existing text and/or field templates, follow these general steps:

- Move the cursor to where you want to start activating a print feature, or into the field template where you want to assign a print feature. You can also click your mouse on the start of the text or on the field template where you want the print feature to begin.
- Press or click Select (F6).
- If you are changing only a field template, skip to the next step. Otherwise, use the arrow keys or move the mouse to highlight the entire area that should use the new print feature.
- Press ↵ or click the mouse to complete your selection.
- Choose Words ► Style from the menu.
- Move the cursor to the print feature or font you want and press ↵ to turn it on, or click the mouse on that feature or font.

You can combine features (such as boldface and italic) simply by repeating the last four steps until all of the features you want activated have been turned on. You cannot, however, combine fonts (it would make no sense to do so, since each font is actually a unique typeface).

If you select more than one font while working with a single highlighted block, only the most recent selection will take effect.

If you would like to activate a print feature or font before typing new text, follow these general steps:

- Position the cursor to where you are going to start typing the text.
- Turn on the feature(s) and/or font that you want using the options on the Words pull-down menu.
- When you want to return to "normal" print, choose Words ► Style ► Normal (both the font and the style return to normal).

None of these options affects the way the report appears on the reports design screen. Also, when "printing" the report or labels to the screen, these print attributes may have an unpredictable effect on the screen. (For example, the screen might interpret "boldface" as "blinking".) The only way to check your work is to actually print a copy of the report or labels.

CONTROLLING PRINT QUALITY

Some dot-matrix printers offer two or more options for print quality: draft quality (for faster printing) and near letter quality (for neater, though slower, printing). If your printer supports these features, you have three options for controlling the print quality of a report or labels:

YES	Uses the slower, neater near letter-quality print
NO	Uses the faster draft-quality print
DEFAULT	Uses whatever the printer is set to at the moment

To change the print quality overall for report or labels, follow these general steps:

- At either the Control Center or the design screen, pull down the Print menu.

- Choose Control of Printer.
- Highlight Quality Print and press ←┘, until the quality you want is shown. Or, just click the mouse on Quality Print until you see the quality you want.
- Press Ctrl-End to return to the Print menu.

As with other printer features mentioned above, you can select a print quality for individual bands in a report design. Follow these general steps to do so:

- In the reports design screen, move the cursor to the band whose print quality you want to change, or click on that band.
- Choose Bands from the menu.
- Highlight Quality Print for Band and press ←┘ or the space bar until the quality you want is shown. Or, just click the mouse on Quality Print for Band until you see the quality you want.
- Press Ctrl-End to return to the design screen.

When defining a print quality for an individual band, the DEFAULT option uses the Text Pitch setting on the Print menu.

CREATING A COVER PAGE

Normally dBASE IV prints text from the page header and page footer bands in the report intro band, on the first page of the report. In some cases, however, you might want to use the Report Intro band as an independent cover sheet or cover letter. In this situation, you probably do not want a header and footer printed in the report intro band, and you probably want to eject a page between the cover page and the first printed page of the report. Here are the steps to follow to set up the first page of a report as a cover page, assuming that you are at the reports design screen already:

- Choose Bands ► Page Heading in Report Intro.
- Press ←┘ or click the mouse to change the option to No (the menu will also disappear from the screen).

- Move the cursor to the last line of text in the Report Intro band and press the End key to move to the end of that line, or click the mouse at that location.
- Press ↵.
- Choose Words ► Insert Page Break.

You will see a dotted line across the bottom of the Report Intro band, which indicates that when you print a report, dBASE will start printing remaining bands on the next page.

OPENING AND CLOSING REPORT BANDS

When you print a report, only open bands are printed; closed bands are ignored. Hence, if a band has a blank line in it, that blank line is printed on the report. To prevent that blank line from printing, close the band. The technique for opening or closing a band is the same:

- Move the cursor into the band border (both the title and the thin line of the band border will be highlighted), then press ↵. Alternatively, you can click the mouse on the band border.

If the band is already open, press ↵ or click the border to close it. If the band is closed, pressing ↵ or clicking the border will open it.

As a shortcut, you can open all the bands in the report format by choosing Bands ► Open All Bands from the menu.

PAUSING AND CANCELING PRINTING

While dBASE IV is actually printing, it displays the following instructions:

```
Cancel printing: ESC
Pause printing: CTRL-S
```

Resume printing with any key

Note that printing might not stop or
pause immediately if your printer has
a buffer

WARNING

If your printer has a *buffer* (a storage area for text that is waiting to be printed), pausing or canceling will not take effect until the buffer is empty.

You can cancel printing altogether by pressing the Esc key. To temporarily pause printing, press Ctrl-S and then press any key later to resume printing.

PRINTING A DATABASE STRUCTURE

Before we leave the topic of printing, note that you can also easily print a copy of your database structure. This can be handy to keep available as an instant reference to the fields in a particular database. To print a copy of a database structure, follow these simple steps:

1. Highlight or click on the database name in the Data panel (CUSTLIST in this example), then press or click Design (Shift-F2).
2. Choose Layout ► Print Database Structure.
3. Choose Begin Printing.
4. If you need to eject the page from the printer, choose Layout ► Print Database Structure ► Eject Page Now. Then press Esc twice.
5. Choose Exit ► Abandon Changes and Exit to return to the Control Center.

Figure 7.27 shows a printed copy of the structure of the CUSTLIST.DBF database file.

In the next chapter, we'll discuss how to create custom forms for entering and changing data. Many of the techniques that you learned while using the reports design and labels design screens in this chapter also apply to the forms design screen discussed in Chapter 8.

```
Page #      1

Structure for database: C:\DBASE\CUSTLIST.DBF
Number of data records:         9
Date of last update    : 01/15/93
Field  Field Name  Type        Width    Dec    Index
    1  LASTNAME    Character      15               N
    2  FIRSTNAME   Character      15               N
    3  COMPANY     Character      20               N
    4  ADDRESS     Character      30               N
    5  CITY        Character      15               N
    6  STATE       Character       2               N
    7  ZIP         Character      10               Y
    8  PHONE       Character      13               N
    9  STARTDATE   Date            8               N
   10  PAID        Logical         1               N
** Total **                      130
```

Figure 7.27: Printed copy of the CUSTLIST database structure

CHAPTER 8

Creating Custom Forms

To create a custom form, **260**

first open the database that the form is to provide access to. Then select <create> from the Forms panel of the Control Center.

To add and rearrange items on a custom form, **261**

use the same basic keys that you used to create label and report formats.

To add boxes, lines, and graphics characters to a form, **266**

choose Layout ► Box or Layout ► Line.

To control what information is entered into a field, **270**

move the cursor to the appropriate field template and press F5, or double-click the appropriate field template. Then change the field's template, picture functions, or edit options.

To save a completed form design, **279**

choose Exit ► Save Changes and Exit.

To use a custom form, **279**

make sure the appropriate database file is open. Highlight the form name in the Forms panel of the Control Center, then press ↵ or double-click that form name; then select Display Data. Alternatively, highlight or click on the form name, then press or click Data (F2).

To add new data through a custom form, **280**

perform the steps for using a custom form and then choose Records ► Add New Records.

To change a form's design, 281

make sure the appropriate database file is open. Highlight the form name in the Forms panel of the Control Center, then press ↵ or double-click that form name; then select Modify Layout. Alternatively, highlight or click on the form name, then press or click Design (Shift-F2).

THIS CHAPTER DISCUSSES TECHNIQUES FOR CREATing custom forms for entering and editing data. As you'll see, custom forms have several advantages over the simple edit screen that you've used previously for adding and changing records. Besides looking better, custom forms can actually do some of the work involved in entering data and can trap and correct errors before they are stored in the database.

Figure 8.1 shows an example custom form for the CUSTLIST database that you'll develop in this chapter. As you can see, the custom form is quite a bit more attractive than the standard form presented on the edit screen. For instance, field names (such as LASTNAME) are replaced with plain-English descriptions (such as Last Name). The box at the top of the screen provides information about the purpose of the form (for example, Enter/Edit Customer Information), and the box at the bottom of the screen lists important keys. The PAID field accepts the more natural Y and N (for yes and no), rather than T and F (for true and false).

As you'll see in this chapter, the dBASE IV forms design screen lets you be as creative as you wish when developing custom forms for your database files.

If you've exited dBASE IV, be sure to get it up and running and then bring the LEARN catalog into the Control Center so you can try the techniques discussed here.

USING THE FORMS DESIGN SCREEN

To create a custom form, you first open the database file for which you want to design the form and select <create> from the Forms panel of the Control Center. To do so, follow these steps:

1. If CUSTLIST is not already open, highlight CUSTLIST and press ↵, or double-click CUSTLIST. Then select Use File.
2. Highlight <create> in the Forms panel and press ↵ or double-click <create> in the Forms panel.

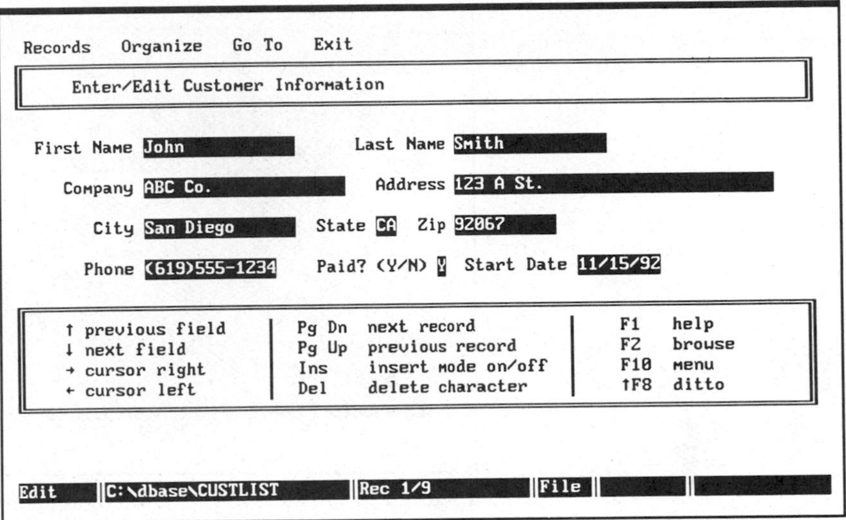
Records Organize Go To Exit
Enter/Edit Customer Information
First Name John   Last Name Smith
Company ABC Co.   Address 123 A St.
City San Diego   State CA Zip 92067
Phone (619)555-1234   Paid? (Y/N) Y Start Date 11/15/92
↑ previous field | Pg Dn next record | F1 help
↓ next field | Pg Up previous record | F2 browse
→ cursor right | Ins insert mode on/off | F10 menu
← cursor left | Del delete character | ↑F8 ditto
Edit | C:\dbase\CUSTLIST | Rec 1/9 | File

Figure 8.1: A custom form for the CUSTLIST database

You'll be taken to the forms design screen, with the Layout pull-down menu already displayed. You'll notice that the forms design screen is similar to the reports design screen except that the word "Form" appears in the lower-left corner of the screen, and there are no bands.

CREATING A QUICK LAYOUT

The easiest way to create a form is first to allow dBASE to create a simple form similar to the standard edit screen on the forms design screen. To do so, choose Layout ► Quick Layout. Your screen will look like Figure 8.2. You can use this initial form as the starting point for designing your own custom form.

Now let's rearrange the quick layout and add text and boxes to create the custom form shown in Figure 8.1.

PLANNING A FORM

Before you start actually moving items around on the form, keep in mind a few important points. First, note that the current row and

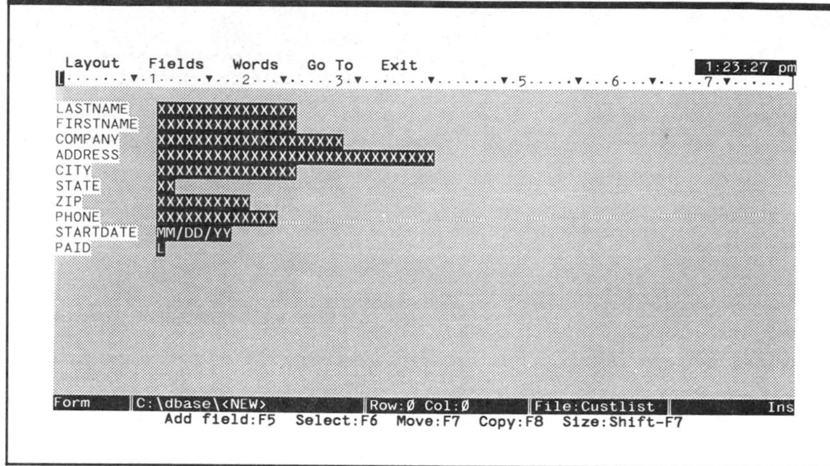

Figure 8.2: Quick layout of a form on the forms design screen

column position of the cursor is displayed in the center of the status bar near the bottom of the screen. A custom form can be as wide as the screen (from column 0 to column 79).

Second, when you use the form later to enter or change data, the top row of the screen (row 0 on the form) will display the menu bar and rows 22, 23, and 24 at the bottom of the screen will display the status bar and other messages. Therefore, when designing a form, try to use only rows 1 through 21.

MOVING TEXT AND FIELDS

If you need to take a break while developing this form, see the section "Saving Your Form" later in this chapter to save the work you've done so far. To resume your work later, see the section "Modifying an Existing Form."

The basic editing keys and mouse operations for rearranging and designing a custom form are the same as those used for report and label design. (See Tables 7.1 and 7.2 in Chapter 7 for quick reference.) If you are feeling creative and want to use those keys and mouse operations to design your own form, then by all means feel free to do so. However, if you want some help designing the exact form shown in Figure 8.1, follow these steps to get started. As in Chapter 7, we'll start out by showing both the keyboard and mouse methods of performing a given task, then just list the keyboard instructions to keep things simple. Use whichever method or combination of methods you prefer for this hands-on exercise.

1. Make sure Insert mode is on (press the Ins key until the "Ins" indicator appears in the status bar).
2. With the cursor at row 0, column 0, press ↵ six times to insert six blank lines at the top of the form.
3. Use the arrow keys to move the cursor to row 2, column 6 or click the mouse at that location, and then type **Enter/Edit Customer Information**.
4. Use the ↓ and ← keys to move the cursor to row 5, column 2 and then type **First Name**.
5. Press ↓ three times to move the cursor to the FIRSTNAME template (row 8, column 11).
6. Press or click Select (F6), and then press ↵ or click the mouse again.
7. Press or click Move (F7). Move the ghost image to row 5, column 13, then press ↵ or click the mouse.
8. Move the cursor to row 5, column 34 and type **Last Name**.
9. Move the cursor to inside the LASTNAME template (row 7, column 11).
10. Press the Select key (F6) and then the ↵ key.
11. Press Move (F7), move the cursor to row 5, column 44, and then press ↵.
12. Move the cursor to row 7, column 0 and press Ctrl-T to remove the LASTNAME field name.
13. Press ↓ to move to row 8, column 0 and then press Ctrl-T again to remove the FIRSTNAME field name.
14. Move the cursor to row 7, column 5 and type **Company**.
15. Move the cursor to the COMPANY template (row 9, column 11), press Select (F6), and press ↵.
16. Press Move (F7), move the cursor to row 7, column 13, and press ↵.

17. Move the cursor to row 7, column 36 and type **Address**.
18. Move the cursor to inside the ADDRESS template (row 10, column 11).
19. Press Select (F6) and then ↵.
20. Press Move (F7), move the ghost image to row 7, column 44, and press ↵.
21. Move the cursor to row 9, column 0 and press Ctrl-T.
22. Press ↓ to move the cursor to row 10, column 0 and press Ctrl-T to erase ADDRESS.
23. Use the arrow keys to move the cursor to row 9, column 8 and type **City**.
24. Press ↓ to move to the CITY template, press Select (F6), and press ↵.
25. Press Move (F7), move the ghost image to row 9, column 13, and press ↵.
26. Move the cursor to row 9, column 30 and type **State**.
27. Move the cursor to the STATE template (row 12, column 11), press Select (F6), and press ↵.
28. Press Move (F7), move the ghost image to row 9, column 36, and press ↵.
29. Move the cursor to row 9, column 40 and type **Zip**.
30. Move the cursor to the ZIP template (row 13, column 11), press Select (F6), and press ↵.
31. Press Move (F7), move the ghost image to row 9, column 44, and press Enter.
32. Move the cursor to row 11, column 0 (the "C" in CITY).
33. Press Select (F6), press ↓ five times, press → eight times so that all remaining field names are highlighted, and then press ↵.
34. Press the Del key to delete the highlighted block.
35. Move the cursor to row 11, column 7 and type **Phone**.

36. Move the cursor to the PHONE template (row 14, column 11), press Select (F6), and press ↵.
37. Press Move (F7), move the ghost image to row 11, column 13, and press ↵.
38. Move the cursor to row 11, column 30 and type **Paid? (Y/N)**.
39. Move the cursor to the PAID template (the "L" in row 16, column 11), press Select (F6), and press ↵.
40. Press Move (F7), move the ghost image to row 11, column 42, and press ↵.
41. Move the cursor to row 11, column 45 and type **Start Date**.
42. Move the cursor to the STARTDATE template (MM/DD/YY in row 15, column 11).
43. Press Select (F6) and then ↵.
44. Press Move (F7), move the ghost image to row 11, column 56, and press ↵.

At this point, your screen should look like Figure 8.3. (If you made a mistake, you should be able to rearrange things on your own by now to make your form look like the figure.)

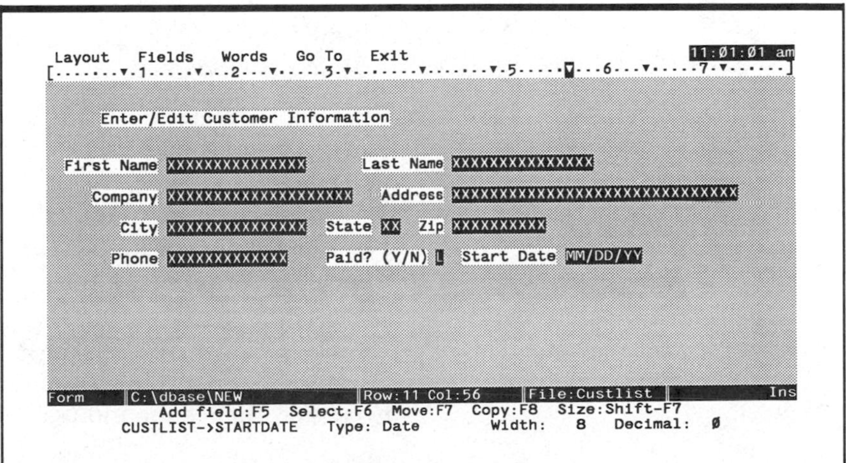

Figure 8.3: Fields rearranged on the form

ADDING BOXES AND LINES

You can draw boxes and lines on the reports design screen too, using the same techniques discussed here. However, not all printers can display the boxes or special graphics characters.

Now let's add some boxes and lines to our form to make it look a little better. Options for drawing boxes and lines are on the Layout pull-down menu. The technique is quite easy, as the following steps demonstrate:

1. Move the cursor to row 1, column 0, the upper-left corner of the first box you'll draw.
2. Choose Layout ► Box.
3. Select Double Line.
4. At the bottom of the screen, dBASE displays the instructions "Position upper left of box with cursor keys, complete with ENTER." The cursor is already positioned, so just press ↵ or click the mouse at row 1, column 0.
5. The instructions now read "Stretch box with cursor keys, complete with ENTER." Press ↓ twice, hold down the → key until the lower-right corner moves to row 3, column 78, and then press ↵. Or, move the mouse to row 3, column 78, then click the mouse button. You'll see a double-line box around the form title.

Now draw the box at the bottom of the form.

1. Move the cursor to row 13, column 0.
2. Choose Layout ► Box.
3. Select Double Line.
4. Press ↵ or click the mouse at row 13, column 0 to mark the upper-left corner of the box.
5. Use the ↓ and → keys or the mouse to extend the box to row 18, column 78.
6. Press ↵ or click the mouse.

Notice that while the cursor is on the box frame, the frame is highlighted. As long as the frame is highlighted, you can manipulate the box.

For example, you can press or click Select (F6) to select the box. Then you can use Move (F7) or Copy (F8) to move or copy the box. You can also press Del to delete a selected box, or you can press or click Size (Shift-F7) to resize a selected box, using the usual arrow keys or mouse movements. Keep these options in mind whenever you draw boxes.

Now let's add a line to the lower box. Here are the steps:

1. Move the cursor to row 14, column 25.
2. Choose Layout ► Line.
3. Select Single Line.
4. Press ↵ or click the mouse at row 14, column 25, to mark the current cursor position as the start of the line.
5. Press ↓ three times to move the cursor to row 17, column 25, then press ↵ or click the mouse to complete the line.
6. To copy the line to column 55, move the cursor to row 14, column 25.
7. Press or click Select (F6).
8. Press ↓ three times to highlight the entire line, then press ↵ or click the mouse button.
9. Press or click Copy (F8).
10. Move the ghost image to row 14, column 55 and press ↵ or click the mouse button.

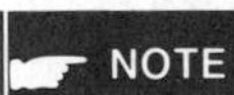

Because it's not easy to move the mouse in a perfectly straight line, we recommend that you use the arrow keys in steps 5 and 8.

As you've seen in the preceding steps, box drawing and line drawing use the same basic techniques. That is, you choose either Layout ► Box or Layout ► Line, and you select a style, either single line or double line. Then you mark the starting point for the box or line by pressing ↵ or clicking the mouse. Draw the box or line using the arrow keys (or the mouse, if you're drawing boxes), and complete the box or line by pressing ↵ or clicking the mouse again. The bottom of the screen provides instructions to help you as you work (though it doesn't include mouse instructions).

The only difference between drawing boxes and lines is that the Box option always draws an even, rectangular box. The Line option is generally used to draw straight lines, but it can actually be used to draw any shape or even a single special graphics character, as you'll see in the next section.

ADDING GRAPHICS CHARACTERS

While you were drawing boxes and lines, you may have noticed the option Using Specified Character on the submenu. This option allows you to use characters other than the single- and double-line characters to draw boxes. This option can also be used to individually place special graphics characters on the screen. When you select this option, you'll see a submenu of graphics characters and ASCII numbers assigned to those characters. Use the PgDn and PgUp keys to scroll through the menu. When the character you want is highlighted, press ↵ or click the mouse to select it.

To demonstrate, let's add some cursor arrows to the current form.

1. Move the cursor to row 14, column 5.
2. Choose Layout ► Line.
3. Select Using Specified Character.
4. Press PgDn and then ↓ seven times until you get to the ↑ symbol (number 24 in the leftmost column of the submenu).
5. Press ↵ or click the mouse to select the ↑ symbol.
6. You now need to draw a line that is one character long. To do so, press ↵ or click the mouse to mark the start of the line, press → once to draw the short line, and then press ↵ or click the mouse again to complete the line. The arrow now appears on the screen.
7. Move the cursor to row 15, column 5.
8. Choose Layout ► Using Specified Character.
9. Use ↓ to highlight character 25 on the submenu and ↵ to select it.
10. Press ↵, then →, and then ↵ again to place the arrow on the screen.

11. Move the cursor to row 16, column 5.
12. Choose Layout ► Line ► Using Specified Character.
13. Use ↓ to highlight character number 26 on the submenu and ↵ to select it.
14. Press ↵, then →, and then ↵ again to place the character on the screen.
15. Move the cursor to row 17, column 5.
16. Choose Layout ► Line ► Using Specified Character.
17. Use ↓ to highlight character number 27 on the submenu and ↵ to select it.
18. Press ↵, then →, and then ↵ again to place the character on the screen.

TIP

To draw the ↵ symbol on a form, you can place the ASCII characters numbered 17, 196, and 217 next to each other on the forms design screen.

In the form, we will use ↑ to stand for the Shift key next to F8 (because there is not enough room to spell out Shift). You can copy the ↑ arrow to the appropriate place by following these steps:

1. Move the cursor to row 14, column 5 (the ↑ symbol).
2. Press or click Select (F6), then press ↵ or click the mouse.
3. Press or click Copy (F8), move the cursor to row 17, column 60, and press ↵ or click the mouse.

The form is nearly complete now. You just need to add some helpful text inside the box at the bottom of the screen. You should be able to do this on your own by now, without step-by-step instructions. However, before you begin typing the text, you should be sure to turn insert mode off (press Ins until the Ins indicator disappears from the lower-right corner of the screen).

To type the text, just position the cursor, using the arrow keys or the mouse, to where you want the text to begin. Then type the text. Use the completed form shown in Figure 8.4 as a guide to help you position the cursor and enter the text. If you make a mistake, remember that all of the standard editing keys are available to you at all times (including Backspace, Del, the arrow keys, and the special keys listed in the navigation line at the bottom of your screen).

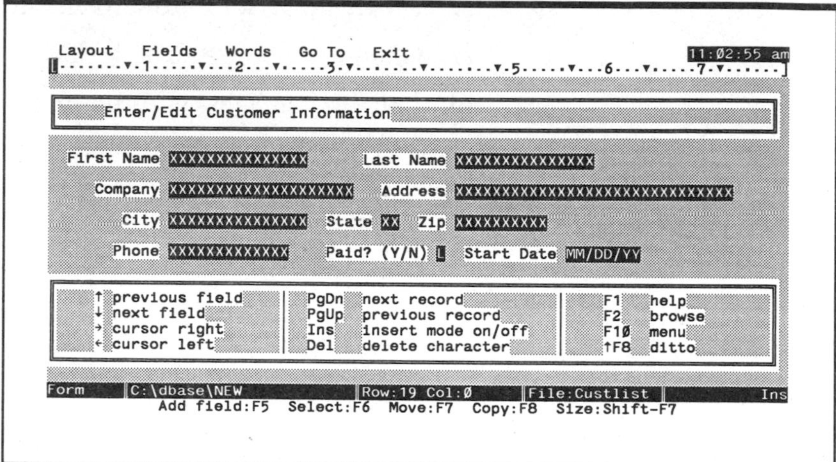

Figure 8.4: The custom form so far

After you've added the remaining text to the bottom of the form, the basic appearance of the form is complete. But before you save the form and test it, let's take a look at some additional features that you can use to enhance your form. Specifically, we'll focus on techniques that make it easier to enter and edit data using the completed form and techniques that allow the form to trap errors before they get into the database. (You'll see these features in action later, after you finish designing and saving the form.)

CONTROLLING INPUT

There are three ways that you can control what is actually entered into a field on the form so you can trap errors as they occur, before they are actually stored in the database. The same techniques can also ensure that data in a field is consistent: for example, that all phone numbers are entered with an area code, in the format (999)999-9999. You can control input using template characters, picture functions, and edit options. The following sections discuss these methods.

MODIFYING FIELD TEMPLATES

As you know from experience in the labels and reports design screens, a field template marks the place where actual database data will appear. Initially, Character fields use templates such as XXXX-XXXXXXXX, Date fields use the template MM/DD/YY, and Logical fields use the template L. You can also use other template characters, as summarized in Table 8.1.

Table 8.1: Characters Used in Field Templates

Symbol	Description
A	Accepts only alphabetic characters A-Z and a-z and no numbers, spaces, or punctuation
N	Accepts alphabetic and numeric characters, A-Z, a-z, and 0-9, but no spaces or punctuation
Y	Accepts either Y or N
#	Accepts numeric digits 0-9, spaces, periods (.), and plus (+) and minus (-) signs
L	Accepts T, F, Y, and N
X	Accepts any character
!	Accepts any character and converts letters to uppercase
9	Accepts real numbers only, including plus and minus signs
Other	Any other characters are *literal* characters and are actually stored in the database

Here are some examples of templates and template characters:

!XXXXXXXXXXXXXX	Accepts any characters, but capitalizes the first character; for example, entering **smith** produces Smith

AAAAAAAAAAAAAAA	Accepts only letters, such as Smith or SMITH, but would not accept 123 A St. (because of the numbers) or Tom Jones (because of the space)
(999)999-9999	Accepts any numbers, 0-9, and automatically adds parentheses and hyphens; hence, entering **2139876543** produces (213)987-6543
999-99-9999	Accepts any number and inserts hyphens; for example, entering **123456789** produces 123-45-6789
!-!!!	Accepts any characters, but converts letters to uppercase and inserts a hyphen; for example, entering **a1j3** produces A-1J3
!-999	Accepts a character followed by any three numbers, converting the character to uppercase; hence, entering **x555** produces X-555 (you could not enter a1j3 into this field, because the "j" appears where a number is required)

WARNING

When changing template characters, make sure that Insert mode is off so you don't change the size of the template.

To try some of these template characters, we'll make some changes to the current form. Remember, you cannot actually see the effects of these changes until after you've completed and saved the form (you're still designing it right now). The general technique that you use to change field templates includes these steps:

- Highlight the field template you want to change and press or click Add Field (F5), or choose Fields ► Modify Field from the menu. Alternatively, you can double-click the field template with your mouse.

- Make your changes.
- Press or click Accept (Ctrl-End) when you are done.

The exact steps we'll use in this sample form are as follows:

1. Make sure Insert mode is off.
2. Move the cursor to the FIRSTNAME field template (row 5, column 13) and press F5. Or just double-click that field template with your mouse.
3. Select Template from the submenu of options. A list of template characters appears and the cursor is readied to make changes, as shown in Figure 8.5.
4. Press Home to move to the first character in the template, or click the mouse on the first character.
5. Type ! and then press ↵.
6. Press or click Accept (↵) to save the change.

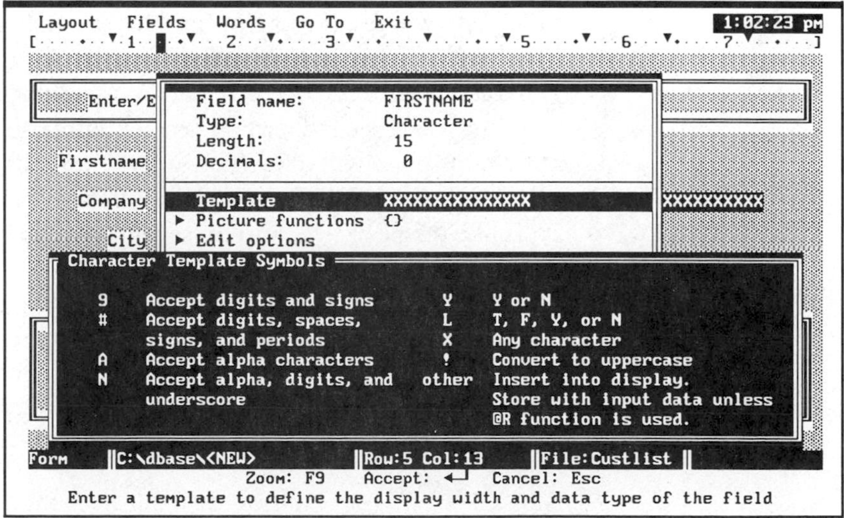

Figure 8.5: Template characters displayed on the screen.

The template for the First Name field now looks like this:

!XXXXXXXXXXXXXX

To change the template for the LASTNAME field, repeat steps 2 through 6 for the LASTNAME field template (row 5, column 44).

Since you've already seen how to use the mouse to modify field templates, we'll just list the keyboard steps for the remainder of this section. As always, you should use whichever method works best for you. Now, here are the steps for adding a template that will insert parentheses and hyphens to the PHONE field:

1. Move the cursor to the PHONE field template (row 11, column 13).
2. Press F5.
3. Select Template.
4. Press Home.
5. Type the new template **(999)999-9999** and press ↵.
6. Press Ctrl-End.

Note that the Phone field template includes parentheses and a hyphen, which are not special characters listed in Table 8.1. These "other" characters are called *literal characters*, or just *literals*. Literal characters actually become part of the data stored in the field.

As you'll see later when you actually use the form, the (999)999-9999 template will allow you to type any 10 numeric digits into the PHONE field. The form will automatically display the literal characters like this: ( ) - , and these will actually be stored in the database after you type a phone number.

Now let's change the PAID field template so that it accepts only a Y (yes) or N (no) entry by following these steps:

1. Move the cursor to the PAID field template (row 11, column 42).
2. Press F5.
3. Select Template (note your options on the screen).

4. Press ← and then type the letter **Y**.
5. Press ↵ and then Ctrl-End.

You can now see the new template characters in their fields, as shown in Figure 8.6. Before we test these, let's look at another technique for controlling data entered onto the screen: using picture functions.

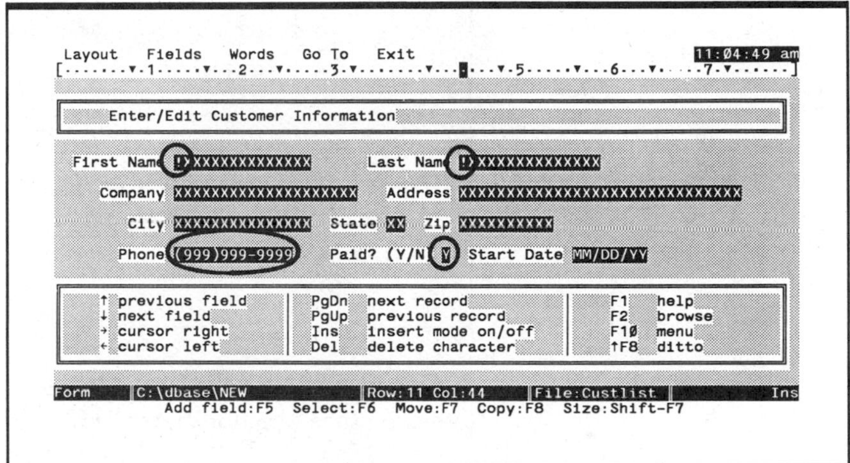

Figure 8.6: New template characters on the form

USING PICTURE FUNCTIONS

Whereas template characters control the individual characters that are typed into a field, picture functions affect the entire field. Table 8.2 summarizes the picture functions. (They are discussed in more detail later in the chapter.)

The basic technique for assigning a picture function to a field is to highlight the field and press or click Add Field (F5), (or to double-click the field), select Picture Functions, and then select the functions you want. To see how this works, we'll assign the ! (uppercase)

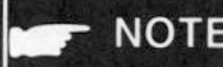

NOTE

Although the picture functions H, V, and semicolon (;) also appear on the Picture Functions submenu, they are unavailable when you're designing a form.

Table 8.2: Picture Functions for Custom Forms

Function	Effect
A	Accepts alphabetical characters only (entire field)
!	Accepts any data, but converts all letters to uppercase
R	Removes literal characters from entry before storing them on the database
S	Allows long text to be entered into short field displays
M	Allows multiple-choice options to be displayed in a form and selected by pressing ↵
T	Removes leading and trailing blank spaces
J	Right-aligns data in field template
I	Centers data in field template

function to the STATE field in the current form. (You'll use some other picture functions later.) Here are the steps:

1. Move the cursor to the STATE template (row 9, column 36).
2. Press F5.
3. Select Picture Functions.
4. Highlight Upper-case Conversion and press the space bar to turn the option on, or just click Upper-case Conversion.
5. Press Ctrl-End to leave the submenu. You'll now see the picture function displayed as {!}.
6. Press Ctrl-End to save the change.

You won't notice any change on the design screen, because picture functions do not appear in the field template. (Of course, you can see what picture functions are assigned to a field template at any time by moving the cursor into the template and pressing F5 or by double-clicking the template.)

CONTROLLING EDIT OPTIONS

Another way that you can control what is entered into a field is through edit options. These options are summarized in Table 8.3 and discussed in more detail later in this chapter.

Table 8.3: Edit Options for Custom Forms

Edit option	Effect
Editing Allowed	If Yes, field contents can be changed; if No, field contents can be viewed, but not changed
Permit Edit If	Allows you to enter a logical formula to determine when a field can be changed
Message	Lets you enter a message that is displayed at the bottom of the screen when the field is highlighted
Carry Forward	If Yes, data entered into one record is automatically carried over to the next record when you add new records (data for only the current field is carried forward)
Default Value	Lets you automatically place a suggested value into a field, which can be accepted, or changed, when you actually enter data
Smallest Allowed Value	Specifies the smallest allowable value for the field
Largest Allowed Value	Specifies the largest allowable value for the field
Range Must Always Be Met	If Yes, data must be entered into the field, and it must fall within the specified smallest and largest allowed value range. If No, the field can be left blank by pressing ↵ during data entry; however, any data entered into the field must fall within the specified value range.

Table 8.3: Edit Options for Custom Forms (continued)

Edit option	Effect
Accept Value When	Lets you define a logical formula that determines whether a value can be entered into a field
Value Must Always Be Valid	If Yes, data must be entered into the field, and it must meet the Accept Value When requirements. If No, the field can be left blank by pressing ↵ during data entry; however, any data entered into the field must meet the Accept Value When requirements.
Unaccepted Message	Lets you define a message that is displayed on the screen if an unacceptable value is entered into a field

Let's use some edit options on the current form. We'll use the Default Value option to display the current date in the STARTDATE field and the Message option to display a message when a field is highlighted.

1. Move the cursor to the STARTDATE template (row 11, column 56).
2. Press F5 and select Edit Options.
3. Select Message and type **Press Enter to accept suggested date, or type in a new date**.
4. Press ↵ after typing the entire message.
5. Select Default Value.
6. Type **DATE( )** (a special dBASE function, discussed in Chapter 12, that displays the current date) and press ↵.
7. Press Ctrl-End to leave the submenu.
8. Press Ctrl-End to save your selections.

Note that you will not see any immediate effects on the form that you are designing. However, you'll see these edit options in action when you use the completed form.

SAVING YOUR FORM

At this point, you can add a description to the form and then save it. Here are the steps:

1. Choose Layout ► Edit Description of Form.
2. Type the description **Form for entering/editing customer information** and press ↵.
3. Choose Exit ► Save Changes and Exit.
4. When prompted, type the file name **CUSTFORM** and press ↵.

After dBASE creates the appropriate form (in its own language), you'll be returned to the Control Center. You'll see the name of the new form, CUSTFORM, in the Forms panel of the Control Center.

USING A FORM

To use any custom form, you simply highlight its name on the Forms panel of the Control Center and press or click Data (F2). To use the CUSTFORM form that you just created, follow these simple steps:

1. If necessary, use the arrow keys or click the mouse to highlight CUSTFORM in the Forms panel.
2. Press or click Data (F2).

The form will appear, looking just like Figure 8.1 at the beginning of this chapter. You can use the usual keys, including PgDn and PgUp to scroll through records and to enter and change information.

Also, you can still use the Data key (F2) to switch back and forth between the custom form and the browse screen.

USING A FORM TO ADD NEW DATA

Let's use the custom form to add a new record to the CUSTLIST database and test some of the features we put into the form. Here are the basic steps:

1. If the browse screen is displayed, press F2 to get back to the custom form.
2. Choose Records ► Add New Records.

You'll see the custom form on the screen with most of its fields empty, as in Figure 8.7. Notice that Start Date already displays the current date.

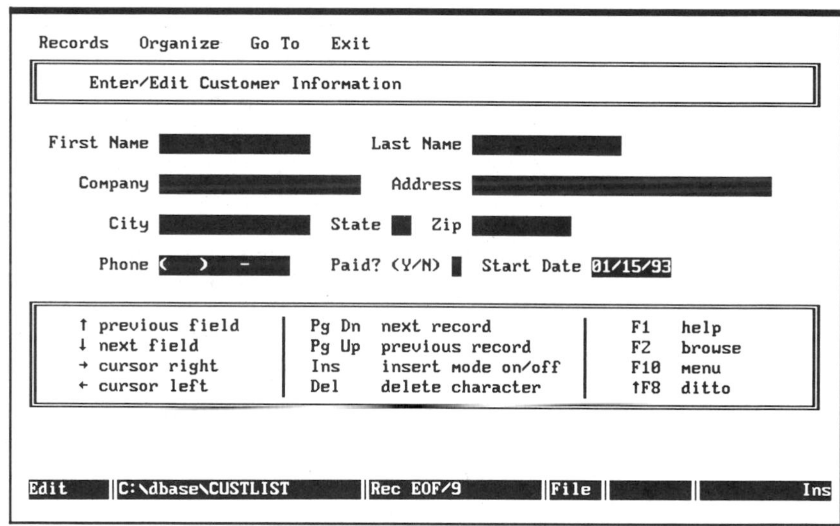

Figure 8.7: Blank custom form, ready to accept a new record

Now, type **fred** as the First Name entry. Notice that your entry is immediately converted to Fred. Press ↵ and type **jones** as the Last Name entry. Your entry is converted to Jones. Both of these instant conversions are caused by the !XXXXXXXXXXXXX templates that you specified for these fields in the form design.

You did not customize the COMPANY, ADDRESS, or CITY field templates, so it is important to enter data correctly in these fields. For Company, enter **American Sneaker**. For Address, enter **P.O. Box 3381**. For City, enter **Newark**. When you get to State, type **nj**. You'll see the entry immediately converted to **NJ**, because of the ! picture function that you assigned to the STATE field. For Zip, enter **01234**.

When you get to the Phone entry line, first try typing **ABC**. dBASE will beep and reject the letters, because you specified the field template (999)999-9999, and the 9 template character does not accept letters. Now type **2025550987**. dBASE already displays the parentheses and hyphen, so the phone number reads (202)555-0987.

For Paid, try entering a letter such as **J** or **Q**. Once again, dBASE beeps and rejects the entry, because you used the Y template, which accepts only Y or N for the PAID field. Type **Y** now.

When you get to Start Date, you'll see the message "Press Enter to accept suggested date, or type in a new date" at the bottom of the screen. (This is the custom message that you entered during forms design.) The Start Date line will already display the current (system) date. You can either type a new date or just press ↵ to accept the current date.

After you press ↵, dBASE scrolls down to a new blank record. (To change the previous record, you can press PgUp.) You could add more new records now. But for the time being, return to the Control Center by choosing Exit ► Exit (or by pressing ↵ while a blank record is displayed).

NOTE

The rest of this chapter discusses general features for designing custom forms. If you wish, you can refer to these sections as you need them, rather than reading them now.

MODIFYING A FORM

To change an existing form design, first make sure the appropriate database file is open (in this example, the CUSTLIST file name must be above the line in the Data panel). Then highlight the name of the form that you want to edit and press ↵ or double-click that form. Select Modify Layout from the menu that appears.

You can use the same techniques used to create the form to make changes in the form. When you are done making changes, choose

Exit ► Save Changes and Exit. (If you prefer *not* to save your changes, choose Exit ► Abandon Changes and Exit instead.) You'll be returned to the Control Center.

MORE OPTIONS FOR CUSTOM FORMS

The CUSTFORM custom form that you just created provided some hands-on exercises for creating custom forms and demonstrated the effects of customizing field templates and assigning picture functions and edit options to fields in the form. The CUSTFORM form used only a few of the many options that the forms design screen offers. For the remainder of this chapter, we'll discuss additional options and features of the forms design screen. You may want to use some of these in the future when you begin creating your own custom forms.

PICTURE FUNCTIONS

You cannot assign picture functions to field templates for the Date or Logical data types.

Picture functions operate on data as it is entered into or changed in a custom form. To assign picture functions to a field template in the forms design screen, you move the cursor to the appropriate field template and press or click Add Field (F5) (or just double-click the field template). The Picture Functions option on the menu that appears will display the currently assigned picture functions (if any) between curly braces. To add or change picture functions, highlight the Picture Functions option and press ↵ or click that option with your mouse.

You will see a menu of picture function options that are available for the current data type. Each option can be turned on or off by highlighting the option and pressing the space bar. The picture functions available for the Character data type are discussed in the following sections. (Picture functions for the Numeric data type are discussed in Chapter 9.)

ALPHABETIC CHARACTERS ONLY If you assign the Alphabetic Characters Only picture function to a field template, the field will only accept letters (A to Z and a to z) later when you use the completed form. Note that the field will not even accept blank spaces. Thus, a field template that has this picture function turned on could not accept "123 Appleton Way" or "Pulver-Smith" as an entry.

UPPERCASE CONVERSION The Uppercase Conversion picture function, when turned on, converts all lowercase letters entered in the field to uppercase. For example, suppose you assign this picture function to a database field named PARTCODE. Later when you use the form to add or edit data, dBASE will convert an entry such as Ak7-7jl to AK7-7JL.

LITERALS NOT PART OF DATA The Literals Not Part of Data picture function, when turned on, removes all literals from data typed in a form before storing the data in the database. Normally this option is turned off. For example, suppose you specify the field template (999)999-9999 for entering data into a field named PHONE. When you type a phone number into the field, dBASE will fill in the literals (the parentheses and hyphen) and store your entry in the database with these characters included. But if you turn on the Literals Not Part of Data picture function for the PHONE field, dBASE will remove the literals after you enter a phone number. That is, the form will still *display* the phone number with the parentheses and hyphen inserted, but dBASE will *store* only the numbers in the database. Hence, if you enter (213)555-1212 as the phone number, the actual database record will contain 2135551212.

The only advantage of using the Literals Not Part of Data picture function is that it saves a little bit of disk space by not storing the repetitive parentheses and hyphen. However, when designing report formats, you would always need to be certain to include the (999)999-9999 template to display data from the PHONE field; otherwise, phone numbers would be printed without the parentheses and hyphen.

SCROLL WITHIN DISPLAY WIDTH You can define a width of up to 254 characters for the Character data type when you create a database. However, a standard screen is only 80 characters wide. Now suppose you created a database with a Character field named

REMARKS and a width of 100 characters. (Perhaps you use this field to enter general comments about customers or whatever other information is stored in the database.) How would you place such a field in a custom form?

Your best bet is to modify the field template to whatever size best fits on your custom form. You could use the full 80-character width of the screen or any smaller width.

Let's assume that you use a field template that consists of 40 X's to display the REMARKS field on your custom form. To ensure access to the full 100 characters that the REMARKS field offers, you would need to turn on the Scroll within Display Width picture function. Later, when you use the completed custom form, the form will display a highlight that is 40 characters wide for entering data into the REMARKS field. But when the cursor gets to that field in the form, you can still type up to 100 characters into the field. As you type beyond the fortieth character, the text in the field will scroll to the left to make more room.

When viewing existing data through the completed form, the form will initially display only the first 40 characters stored in the REMARKS field. But once the cursor gets to the REMARKS field, you'll be able to use the ← and → keys to scroll to the left and right within the field and thereby view all 100 characters.

MULTIPLE CHOICE The Multiple Choice picture function allows you to create a multiple-choice field on your custom form. A multiple-choice field is one that allows only certain entries. For example, suppose you create a database of members in a club, and that database includes a Character field named STATUS. Any given member can have the status REGULAR, OFFICER, HONORARY, or EXPIRED. Because only these four options are acceptable entries for the field, there is no need to even allow the field to accept other data.

When you use a completed custom form that has a multiple-choice field in it, the form initially displays one of the acceptable values in the field. When the cursor gets to that field on the form, you can press ↵ to use the displayed value, or press the space bar or click the mouse to view other possible options. You can also type the first character to see the next option that begins with that letter. When the option that you want to enter in the field is displayed on the form, you press the ↵ key to accept it.

Actually, the STATE field in the CUSTLIST custom form could be defined as a multiple-choice field, because it allows only two-letter state abbreviations (which implies that all customers in the CUST-LIST database live in the United States). To see a multiple-choice field in action, follow these steps to modify the CUSTLIST form:

1. If the CUSTLIST database is not in use (that is, if its name is not above the line in the Data panel of the Control Center), highlight CUSTLIST and press ↵, or double-click CUST-LIST. Then select Use File.
2. To modify the CUSTFORM form, highlight CUSTFORM in the Forms panel and press or click Design (Shift-F2).
3. Use the arrow keys to move the cursor to the STATE field template (row 9, column 36), or click that field with your mouse, then press or click Add Field (F5). Alternatively, simply double-click the mouse on the STATE field template.
4. Select Picture Functions.
5. Highlight Multiple Choice and press ↵, or click that option. The screen displays the prompt "Enter multiple choices:".
6. Type all the possible entries for the field, separating entries with a comma. (It's best to enter them in alphabetical order.) For this example, type the two-letter state abbreviations shown here. Do not include any blank spaces and do not press ↵ until you've typed all the two-letter abbreviations. Use the Backspace key to make corrections.

   AK,AL,AR,AZ,CA,CO,CT,DC,DE,FL,GA,GU,HI,IA,ID,IL,
   IN,KS,KY,LA,MA,MD,ME,MI,MN,MO,MS,MT,NC,ND,NE,
   NH,NJ,NM,NV,NY,OH,OK,OR,PA,RI,SC,SD,TN,TX,UT,VA,
   VI,VT,WA,WI,WV,WY

7. Press ↵ after typing all the abbreviations.
8. Press or click Accept (Ctrl-End) twice to leave the menus.
9. Choose Exit ► Save Changes and Exit.

Never use double quotation marks ("") when listing options for a multiple-choice field.

Now you can try the new multiple-choice field. To use the CUSTFORM form, make sure its name is highlighted in the Forms panel and press or click Data (F2). Then press the ↓ key until the cursor reaches the State highlight on the form or click that field with your mouse. While the cursor is in the State highlight, you can experiment with the following techniques to select a state:

- Type the first letter of a state abbreviation (such as *M*) to see the first option that begins with that letter.
- Type the first letter of a state abbreviation repeatedly to see all state abbreviations that start with that letter.
- Press the space bar or click the mouse to scroll through state abbreviations without regard to the first letter in the abbreviation.

Feel free to experiment with the multiple-choice field for as long as you want. When you are finished, you can just press the Esc key to quickly return to the Control Center. (Any changes you made will not be saved.)

When you are creating a multiple choice field and defining the list of acceptable options, remember to type those options in alphabetical order and separate each with a comma. If you want an empty Character field to be an acceptable entry, start the list of acceptable options with a comma. dBASE will consider the "nothing" in front of the first comma to mean "a blank entry is acceptable." In a Numeric or Float field, use 0 rather than a blank entry.

Normally, the first item in the list of acceptable choices is the one that is displayed on the screen later when you are adding new records. You can, however, have the field display any other value from the list of acceptable entries by using that value as the Default Value on the Edit Options menu.

TRIM, RIGHT ALIGN, AND CENTER ALIGN The Trim, Right Align, and Center Align picture functions determine how data is displayed within the field template. Normally, character data is left-aligned within the width provided by the field template. If you turn on the Trim option along with the Right Align or Center align picture function, you can align character strings in different ways. Some examples follow (where the | characters mark the width of the field highlight on the form):

```
| Smith                        |   Left-Aligned (default)
|           Smith              |   Centered
|                        Smith |   Right-aligned
```

EDIT OPTIONS

In the CUSTLIST custom form, you used the Default Value edit option to display the current date in the STARTDATE field highlight as the default date. You also used the Message edit option to define a custom message at the bottom of the screen whenever the cursor landed in the STARTDATE field highlight on the custom form. This section discusses all of the edit options available for custom forms.

The general technique you use to assign or change an edit option for a field is similar to the technique you use to change templates and picture functions. You need to get to the forms design screen. Then move the cursor inside the appropriate field template and press or click Add Field (F5), or simply double-click the field template you want to change. Select Edit Options, then select any of the options from that submenu using the usual methods: Highlight the option you want and press ↵; type the first letter of that option; or click that option with your mouse.

EDITING ALLOWED The Editing Allowed edit option lets you determine whether a particular field can be edited. By default, all fields on a custom form can be changed when the completed form is used. If you change the Editing Allowed option to No, the form will display the contents of a field, but you will not be able to change those contents.

PERMIT EDIT IF The Permit Edit If option lets you enter an expression that defines when a field can be edited. The expression you enter can take the form of any filter condition that you would use in a query, except that it must be a *complete expression*. For example, in the query design screen, you can place the *incomplete expression* "CA" in the STATE box to limit the display to California residents. But when creating an expression for the Permit Edit If edit option, you need to use the complete expression, STATE = "CA".

Use the Permit Edit If option when you want your custom form to permit a field to be edited only when some other field's contents meet a particular condition. For example, suppose you have a database with two Character fields, one named PARTCODE and the other PARTNAME. To ensure that a part is assigned a part code before the part name is entered onto the custom form, you could use the Permit Edit If expression PARTCODE <> " " (part code does not equal blank) in the PARTNAME field.

Table 8.4 shows examples of expressions that you could use in the Permit Edit If edit option (though, as mentioned, you can use any valid expression, and dBASE poses virtually no limitations). You'll see further examples of valid expressions as you read through this book. In addition, Chapter 12 discusses dBASE IV functions, such as DATE( ), that can be useful in custom form edit options.

Table 8.4: Examples of Valid Expressions

Expression	Meaning
LASTNAME <> " "	True when the first character in a Character field named LASTNAME is not a blank space
STARTDATE < = DATE( ) + 30	True when the Date field named STARTDATE contains a date that is no more than 30 days beyond the current date
"-" $ PARTCODE	True when the Character field named PARTCODE has a hyphen (-) embedded in it
PAID	True when the Logical field named PAID contains T
.NOT. PAID	True when the Logical field named PAID contains F

Remember that when you use your custom form in the future, dBASE will always move the cursor from field to field from left to right and from top to bottom. Therefore, when placing a field on your custom form, place any field that depends on the contents of another field below (or to the right of, if the fields are on the same line) the field that it depends on. This placement allows the independent field to be filled before the dependent field decides whether to permit editing.

For example, when you use the PARTCODE and PARTNAME fields discussed previously, make certain that the field template for the PARTNAME field, which depends on the PARTCODE field, is either to the right (on the same row) or below the PARTCODE field template when you design your form. That way, when you use the form later to enter data, the cursor will first land in the PARTCODE field, letting you fill in a part code before you fill in a part name. Figure 8.8 illustrates this placement.

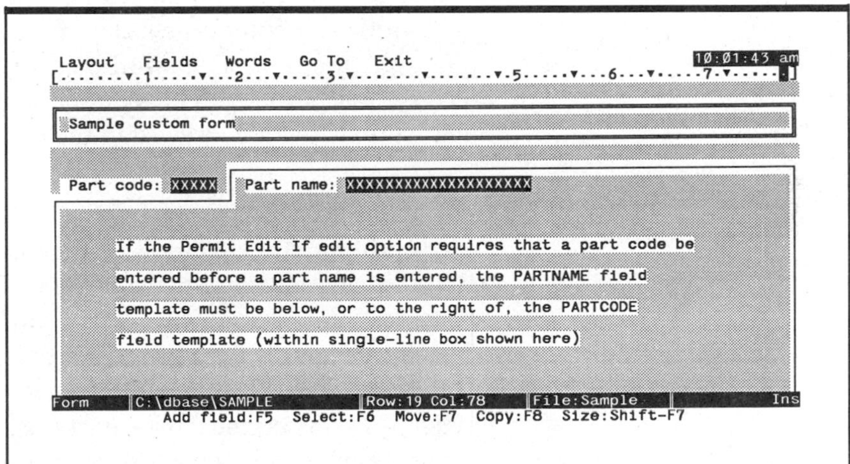

Figure 8.8: Placement of dependent fields on a custom form

MESSAGE As you saw in the sample CUSTFORM form that you developed earlier in this chapter, the Message edit option lets you create a custom message that appears centered at the bottom of the screen when the cursor is in the appropriate field. You can create a separate and unique message for each field in your custom form.

The message can be no more than 79 characters wide and cannot contain double quotation marks (").

CARRY FORWARD Normally when you enter new records into a database, each new record is displayed with empty fields (except those that use a default value, as discussed later). Alternatively, you can tell dBASE to carry the value entered into a particular field in a new record to the next new record. In the next new record, you can accept the value carried forward by pressing ↵ when the cursor gets to that field, or you can type a new value.

For example, suppose that you set the Carry Forward option to Yes for the STATE field in the CUSTLIST database. Then when you use the form to enter new records, you specify CA as the state for the first new record. When you finish entering all the data for that record and dBASE scrolls to the next new record, you'll see CA in the STATE field, because the previous entry was carried forward.

Each new record that you add will display CA in the STATE field, until you enter a new state for a particular record. From that point on, the new state will be carried forward to additional new records. Each time you change the state in a particular record, that new value is carried forward to the ensuing new records.

DEFAULT VALUE The CUSTFORM custom form that you developed earlier in this chapter used the dBASE DATE( ) function to display the current date in the STARTDATE field highlight on the custom form. As you saw when you used the completed form, the default value is displayed as a suggestion when you add new records to the database. You can either accept the suggested value as is (by pressing ↵ when the cursor is in the field) or type a new value.

You can enter any value as a default value, as long as you use the correct data type. For example, if most of the records in the CUSTLIST database will have Los Angeles as the city, then you can assign "Los Angeles" as the default value for that field. (The quotation marks are required, because the CITY field is the Character data type.) To use a specific date as the default value for a Date field, enclose the date in curly braces: {01/01/93}. You can also specify .T. or .F. as the default value for a Logical field.

SMALLEST AND LARGEST ALLOWED VALUE You can use the Smallest Allowed Value and Largest Allowed Value edit options independently or together to define ranges of acceptable values for a specific field in a database. Remember to use the proper delimiters for the data type of the field (for example, quotation marks for Character fields and curly braces for dates).

For example, suppose the current year is 1993 and you want the CUSTLIST custom form to accept only STARTDATE values in the range January 1, 1993, to December 31, 1993. To restrict the data entered in this way, you specify {01/01/93} as the lowest acceptable value for the field and {12/31/93} as the highest acceptable value.

Or suppose you have a database of part codes, part names, and so forth. The field named PARTCODE on this database is the Character data type, and all codes in your business begin with a letter between *M* and *P* (for example, perhaps M-000 to P-999). To ensure that no part numbers outside this range are entered into the database, you could specify "M-000" (including the quotation marks) as the lowest acceptable value for the field and "P-999" as the highest acceptable value.

Later, when you use the custom form to enter data in the database, entering an invalid value will cause dBASE to beep and display the message

```
Range is 01/01/93 to 12/31/93 (press SPACE)
```

or the message

```
Range is M-000 to P-999 (press SPACE)
```

at the bottom of the screen. You must then press the space bar and enter a new, valid value before proceeding.

RANGE MUST ALWAYS BE MET The Range Must Always Be Met edit option specifies whether the range specified in the Smallest Allowed Value and Largest Allowed Value edit options must always be met.

If you set this option to Yes, you cannot leave this field blank when using the custom form for data entry, and the data must fall within the range set up in the Smallest Allowed Value and Largest Allowed Value options. That is, you won't be allowed to continue to the next field (or the next record), until you correctly enter data that falls within the specified range.

If you set this option to No, you will be allowed to press ↵ to leave this field blank during data entry. However, if you do enter any data into the field while using the custom form, it must fall within the specified range for the smallest and largest allowed value.

A word to the wise: Once you've typed in any data for a field where you've specified a required range, any changes you make to that field must always meet the range requirements when you use the custom form. Furthermore, even if you've set Range Must Always Be Met to No, you cannot erase an existing value for the field (by pressing Ctrl-Y at the beginning of that field) and leave the field blank; you must enter a value in the required range.

For example, suppose you specify a range "M-000" as the lowest acceptable value for the PARTCODE field and "P-999" as the highest acceptable value. If you set Range Must Always Be Met to No, you'll be allowed to leave the PARTCODE field blank (by pressing ↵) when you first enter data for parts. However, if you type in a value for the PARTCODE field, it has to fall within the range of M-000 through P-999, and once you enter a value for this field, you won't be able to blank out the field while you're using the custom form. Of course, you're not completely stuck: If you need to enter a value that doesn't meet the range requirements, or you need to blank out the field, you can just use any other form that doesn't specify a range, or highlight the database in the Data panel of the Control Center and press or click Data (F2) to edit the field.

ACCEPT VALUE WHEN The Accept Value When edit option is similar to the Smallest and Largest Allowed Value options discussed above, but provides a little more flexibility. You can use any valid expression (such as the expressions discussed in the section "Permit Edit If") to test the data as soon as it is entered in the field when the form is in use. Later, when you use the completed form to enter and edit data, the field will accept only entries that cause the expression to evaluate to true. Any other entry will be rejected and will need to be reentered.

For example, suppose you created a database for storing accounts receivable that included a field named DATEPAID. The DATEPAID field would be the Date data type. To ensure that no back-dated payments could be entered into the database, you would want the DATEPAID field to accept only dates greater than or equal to the current date.

To make dBASE do so, you enter **DATEPAID > = DATE( )** as the Accept Value When expression for the DATEPAID field. (Remember, DATE( ) is a dBASE IV *function* that always represents the current date.) Later, when you use the form to enter or edit data, any date that you enter into the DATEPAID field will have to be greater than (later than) or equal to the current date. Any earlier date will be rejected.

Note that the example expressions displayed in Table 8.4 work with both the Accept Value When edit option and the Permit Edit If edit option.

VALUE MUST ALWAYS BE VALID The Value Must Always Be Valid edit option is similar to Range Must Always Be Met. The only difference is that it applies to the expression specified in the Accept Value When option. Therefore, if you set Value Must Always Be Valid to Yes, you cannot leave the field blank when entering data through the custom form, and the value must meet the requirements defined in the Accept Value When option. If you set this option to No, you can leave the field blank when entering data through the custom form (by pressing ↵ to bypass the field), but any data entered must meet the Accept Value When requirements.

As with the Smallest and Largest Allowed Value options, if you've defined an expression for Accept Value When, you are not allowed to erase existing data for the field without specifying a valid value in its place—regardless of whether you set Value Must Always Be Valid to Yes or No. Again, however, you can use a different custom form that doesn't restrict the value of this field, or you can simply edit the data from the Control Center if you need to override the Accept Value When requirements for some reason.

UNACCEPTED MESSAGE The Unaccepted Message edit option lets you define a message that is displayed whenever an invalid value is entered into a field that uses the Accept Value When edit option. For example, if you created the DATEPAID field and Accept Value When edit option discussed in the previous section, you could also add an Unaccepted Message such as "Date must be today's date, or later."

Later, when you used the custom form to enter or edit data, an unacceptable entry into the DATEPAID field would cause dBASE to beep and display the message "Date must be today's date, or later (press SPACE)" at the bottom of the screen. You would need to press the space bar and enter a new date.

Note that you can use any character other than the double quotation mark (") in your message.

THE GO TO MENU

The Go To pull-down menu on the forms design screen works exactly as it does on the reports and labels design screen. The sample form letter in Chapter 7 provided an example of using the Go To menu to locate and replace all occurrences of a particular word on the design screen. You can use the same technique on the forms design screen.

COLORING CUSTOM FORMS

You've already seen how to select a box frame, field template, or any other area of a custom form on the forms design screen by pressing or clicking Select (F6). You can color any selected area by choosing Words ► Display on the forms design screen.

If you are using a monochrome monitor, you'll be given the options Intensity (to display letters in a bright boldface), Underline (to underline words), Reverse Video (to reverse the light and dark shades used for letters and their background), and Blink (to cause letters to blink on and off).

If you are using a color monitor, you will see the dBASE IV *electronic palette* for selecting a foreground and background color combination, as well as an option for blinking. (See the section "Changing the Display Colors" in Chapter 14 for information about selecting foreground and background colors).

Note that after you select a display attribute or color combination and return to the forms design screen, the selected area that you colored will still be highlighted, so your selection might not be readily apparent. To unselect the area and see the effects of your selection, press or click Select (F6) and then press the Esc key.

MULTIPLE-PAGE CUSTOM FORMS

A single dBASE IV database file can contain up to 255 fields per record. Needless to say, if you were to create a database with that many fields in it, you'd be hard pressed to squeeze all those fields onto a single screen. To solve this problem, dBASE IV lets you divide any custom form into several pages (or screensful) of fields.

Figure 8.9 shows a portion of a sample database, named TAXES.DBF, that contains 112 fields for entering income tax data. An accountant or tax preparer might create such a database to store income tax data. Each record in the database can hold enough data to fill in an income tax form for each client.

To enter and edit information in this database would require several pages of custom forms. For example, Figure 8.10 shows how the first page of the form might look on the screen, and Figure 8.11 shows how the second page on the form might appear. For convenience, the fields on each page are roughly organized to resemble the fields on the paper form.

To create multiple-page custom forms, you use the standard forms design screen that you used earlier in this chapter. Initially, the forms design screen displays only enough space to create a single page (on which you would use rows 1 through 21). However, you can use the PgDn and PgUp keys to scroll through additional pages on the forms design screen. A single custom form can actually contain over 1600 screen pages.

Structure for database: TAXES.DBF

Field	Field Name	Type	Width	Dec	Index
1	CLIENT_NO	Character	4		Y
2	LASTNAME	Character	15		N
3	FIRSTNAME	Character	15		N
4	MI	Character	1		N
5	ADDRESS	Character	25		N
6	CITY	Character	20		N
7	STATE	Character	2		N
8	ZIP	Character	10		N
9	PHONE	Character	13		N
10	SSN	Character	12		Y
11	SPOUSESSN	Character	12		N
12	OCCUPATION	Character	30		N
13	SPOUSEOCC	Character	30		N
14	ELECT_FUND	Logical	1		N
15	SP_ELECFND	Logical	1		N
16	FILESTATUS	Character	25		
17	SP_[illegible]				
					N
	_[illegible]_YR	Numeric	2		N
100	IRADEDUCT	Numeric	10	2	N
101	IRAPAY	Numeric	10	2	N
102	KEOGH	Numeric	10	2	N
103	PENALTY	Numeric	10	2	N
104	ALIMONYPD	Numeric	10	2	N
105	COUPLEWRK	Numeric	10	2	N
106	TAXWITHELD	Numeric	10	2	N
107	ESTPAYMNTS	Numeric	10	2	N
108	EARNEDINC	Numeric	10	2	N
109	EXTEN_PD	Numeric	10	2	N
110	EXCESS_SSN	Numeric	10	2	N
111	FUEL_CRDIT	Numeric	10	2	N
112	RIC_CREDIT	Numeric	10	2	N

Figure 8.9: A portion of the sample TAXES database

When using a completed form that contains multiple pages, you use the PgUp and PgDn keys to scroll forward and backward through individual pages. When you are at the last page of the form, pressing PgDn scrolls to the next record in the database. When you are at the first page, pressing PgUp scrolls back to the previous database record.

When you create your own multiple-page custom forms, it is a good idea to display useful identifying information on each page of the form. For example, Figure 8.11 displays the customer number and name from page 1 of the form so that you can see at a glance to which client the information on the screen refers.

You can repeat any field or fields on any page of a multiple-page form by positioning the cursor and pressing or clicking Add Field

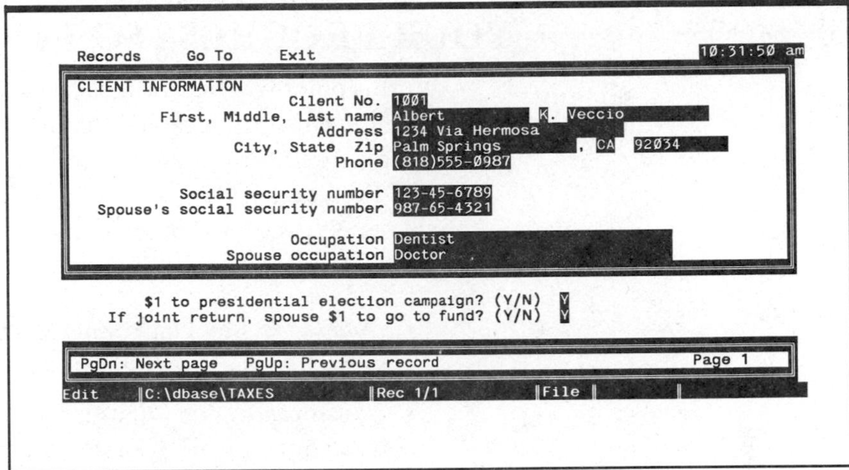

Figure 8.10: First page of form for entering tax data

```
Records     Go To     Exit                                  10:32:22 am
Client number: 1001   Albert Veccio
FILING STATUS: Married/joint          <- press space bar to view options
If married filing jointly, enter spouse name: Florence
If head of household: enter child's name:
If widow(er), enter year spouse died:        19
EXEMPTIONS Enter Y in boxes that apply:  Self: Y    Spouse: Y
Dependents         Under 5  Over 5 SSN  Relationship  Months home
Jason                 Y       - -       Son               12
                      N       - -
Pg Dn:  Next page  PgUp: Previous page                       Page 2
Edit   C:\dbase\TAXES      Rec 1/1      File
```

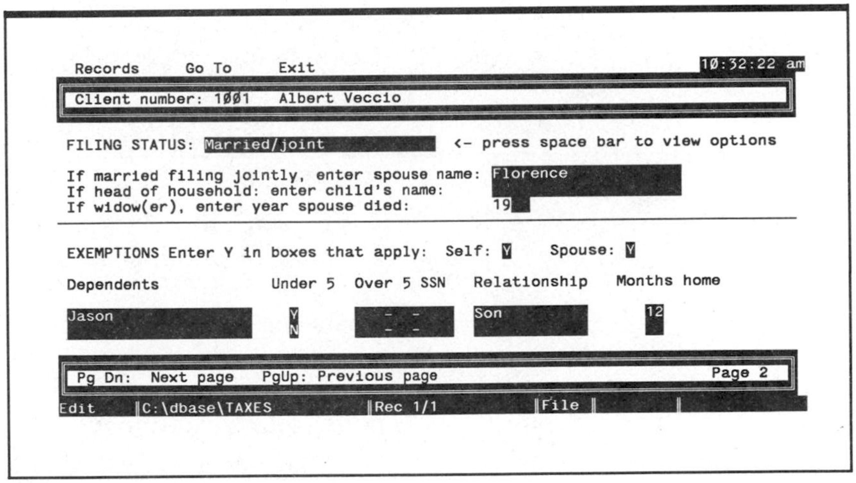

Figure 8.11: Second page of form for entering tax data

(F5) (or by double-clicking the mouse where you want to place the new field), and selecting the field name from the menu that appears. Note that because the field is repeated, there is no need to edit it on every page in the form. Therefore, you can set the Editing Allowed edit option to No for repeated fields and prevent the cursor from moving into the field highlight on page 2 and subsequent pages.

YOUR PROGRESS SO FAR

At this point you've learned a great deal about dBASE IV in general and have had quite a bit of hands-on experience in using some of the program's many features and capabilities. If you look at the dBASE IV Control Center now, you'll see that you have used five of the six panels presented in the Control Center to create, modify, and use various objects, as summarized here:

- *Data panel*: The Data panel lets you create, modify, and use a particular database and index (sort order).
- *Queries panel*: The Queries panel lets you create, modify, and use a query, which isolates particular records in the database, such as California residents or records within a particular range of dates.
- *Forms panel*: The Forms panel lets you create, modify, and use a custom form for entering and editing database data.
- *Reports panel*: The Reports panel lets you create, modify, and use a format for printing database data in a format that you specify.
- *Labels panel*: The Labels panel lets you create, modify, and use a format for printing labels.

Each panel uses a consistent set of keys and options for creating, modifying, and using an object, as summarized here:

- Highlighting <create> and pressing ↵ or double-clicking <create> in any panel lets you create a new object.
- Highlighting an existing file name within a panel and pressing or clicking Design (Shift-F2) takes you to a design screen, where you can modify an object.
- Highlighting an existing file name and pressing or clicking Data (F2) uses (or activates) the completed object.
- As an alternative to using the Design and Data keys or navigation line options, you can highlight any file name in any panel and press ↵ (or double-click on that file name) to see a

menu of options for using or modifying a particular object (if the Instruct setting is On).

Remember also that the menu bar at the top of any screen is accessible by pressing Menu (F10), by clicking the mouse on the menu bar, or by pressing the Alt key and the first letter of the option you want to use. Also, the navigation line at the bottom of the screen displays special keystrokes that you can use or options you can click with your mouse, along with instructions to guide you in your work with dBASE IV.

Before we move on to the sixth panel in the Control Center, Applications, let's take some time to round out the skills you've learned so far and increase your database management abilities. We'll begin with a discussion of the Numeric data type, which lets you add the power of calculations to your work with dBASE IV.

CHAPTER

9

Performing Calculations

Fast Track

To perform calculations with numbers, 304
use the arithmetic operators + (addition), – (subtraction), * (multiplication), / (division), and ^ (exponentiation).

To display calculated fields in reports, 310
position the cursor at the appropriate location on the reports design screen and press or click Add Field (F5), or double-click the mouse where you want to place the field. Select <create> from the CALCULATED submenu and enter a name and expression (formula) for the field.

To display totals or other summary information 313
about records in a report, move the cursor to the appropriate place in the Report Summary band and press or click Add Field (F5), or double-click the mouse where you want to place the field. Then select an option from the SUMMARY place and a field to summarize. Table 9.2 lists summary options.

To display subtotals in a report, 315
choose Band ► Add a Group Band in the report design screen. Select Field Value and the name of the field that defines the subtotal groups. Next, add summary fields to the Group Summary band, making sure to adjust the Reset Every option to the field that defines the subtotal groups.

To print a report with subtotals, 319
first index or sort the database on the field that defines the subtotal groups.

To remove repetitious data from a subtotal report, 324
move the field templates for the repeated values into the Group Intro band on the reports design screen.

To change the appearance of numbers or forms and reports, 327
highlight the field template on the design screen and press or click Add Field (F5), or just double-click the field template with your mouse. Then select either Template or Picture Functions and make your changes. (Table 9.3 lists numeric picture functions.)

To display the results of calculations in custom forms, 330
create a custom form and then create calculated fields using the same techniques as used in the reports design screen.

To perform calculations quickly, without using forms or reports, 332
use the queries design screen. Like the reports design screen, the queries design screen offers both calculated fields and summary operators such as Average, Count, Max (highest value), Min (lowest value), and Sum.

To calculate a date that is *x* number of days away, 343
add or subtract the number of days from a date.

To calculate the number of days between two dates, 343
subtract the earlier date from the later date.

To compare two fields in queries, 344
put an *example* (placeholder) into one field and use it in the filter condition in the other field. The placeholder can be any letter or word.

dBASE IV OFFERS GREAT POWER AND FLEXIBILITY for performing calculations in reports, forms, and queries. Whether you need to add 7.75 percent tax to sales transactions, print a subtotaled report of outstanding orders, list accounts receivable over 30 days past due, or count the customers in each state in a customer list, dBASE will help you get the information you need.

USING NUMERIC FIELDS

dBASE IV offers two different data types for numbers: Float (floating point) and Numeric. You can use all of the techniques discussed in this chapter with either type of number. The only difference between the two is the way dBASE handles them behind the scenes, which affects the type of number you use for a particular application.

THE NUMERIC DATA TYPE

The Numeric data type is best for most business applications, where numbers usually have a fixed number of decimal places. For example, sales quantities, such as 10 or 190, usually have no decimal places. Dollar amounts, such as $1.98, always have two decimal places. The Numeric data type is the most accurate for performing calculations with such numbers.

dBASE automatically displays extremely large numbers in scientific notation; for example, a 30-digit number might be displayed as .37789318629576E + 30.

THE FLOAT DATA TYPE

The Float data type is best for scientific applications that involve extremely large or extremely small numbers with no fixed number of decimal places. If a single field has a very large number, such as 123,456,789,876.1, in one record and a very small number, such as 0.00000000000012, in another, and you need to perform calculations on these numbers, then you should use the Float data type.

ARITHMETIC OPERATORS

dBASE IV offers the arithmetic operators shown in Table 9.1 for performing calculations. The relational operators that you've seen in earlier queries, such as < (less than), > (greater than), < = (less than or equal to), > = (greater than or equal to), = (equal), and # or <> (not equal), can also be used to compare numbers.

Table 9.1: Arithmetic Operators

Operator	Performs	Example
+	Addition	2 + 2 =4
–	Minus	5 – 3 =2
*	Multiplication	3*5 = 15
/	Division	10/2 =5
^ or **	Exponentiation	3^2 =9 3**2 =9
()	Grouping	(1 + 2)*5 =15 1 + (2*5) =11

ORDER OF PRECEDENCE

dBASE IV follows the standard mathematical order of precedence when performing calculations. That is, exponentiation takes place first, followed by multiplication and division, followed by addition and subtraction. Therefore, the formulas 2*5 + 1 and 1 + 2*5 both produce the same result, 11, because the multiplication takes place first.

When in doubt about order of precedence, use parentheses to group operations. For example, the formula (1 + 2)*5 results in 15, because the parentheses force the addition to take place before the multiplication. When using parentheses in a mathematical formula, you must make sure that the formula contains an equal number of opening and closing parentheses. Otherwise, dBASE responds with an error message, such as "Syntax error" or "Unbalanced parentheses."

NEGATIVE NUMBERS

To enter a negative number into a field, simply precede the number with a minus sign (hyphen) as you would in everyday arithmetic. For example, −10 is negative 10 (or minus 10).

SIZING NUMBERS

When you create a database with Numeric or Float data types (as you'll do in a moment), you need to define both a width and a number of decimal places for those fields. If you need only whole numbers, then you can set the number of decimal places to zero. For example, a numeric field with a width of four characters and zero decimal places can handle any number in the range −999 to 9999 (the minus sign requires a place in the width you specify).

When sizing numbers that require decimal places, remember that the decimal point takes up one digit in the width you assign. Therefore if you assign a width of nine characters and two decimal places to a field, then the field can hold any number in the range −99999.99 to 999999.99.

CREATING A SAMPLE DATABASE FOR PERFORMING CALCULATIONS

We'll create a database named ORDERS.DBF in this chapter to view techniques for performing calculations. Be sure that the LEARN catalog is in the Control Center. If necessary, select Catalog ► Use a Different Catalog and LEARN.CAT from the submenu that appears.

To create this database, select <create> from the Data panel on the Control Center and then type the information for each field, as shown in Figure 9.1. As you can see, the Qty field has a width of three characters and zero decimal places, and UNITPRICE has a width of nine characters and two decimal places. Notice also that the PARTNO field is marked Y for indexing.

Layout Organize Append Go To Exit 1:53:47 pm

Bytes remaining: 3969

Num	Field Name	Field Type	Width	Dec	Index
1	PARTNO	Character	5		Y
2	PARTNAME	Character	15		N
3	DATE	Date	8		N
4	QTY	Numeric	3	Ø	N
5	UNITPRICE	Numeric	9	2	N

Database C:\dbase\<NEW> Field 5/5

Change option to index on this field:Spacebar

Figure 9.1: Structure of the ORDERS database

You may have noticed that we stored fields for the quantity and unit price of each order in the ORDERS database, but not for the extended price (that is, the quantity times the unit price). That's because the extended price is the result of a calculation. It's best not to store the results of calculations in a database, for two reasons. First, any calculations can easily be performed while you are displaying data, so it's a waste of disk space to store the results of calculations in a database. Second, if you do store the results of calculations in a field, then any time you change a number in another field that affects the calculation, you'll have to make sure that all other calculated fields were also changed accordingly. This wastes time and increases the likelihood of errors.

After you've created the database structure, choose Layout ► Edit Database Description and enter the description **Outstanding orders**. Then choose Exit ► Save Changes and Exit and enter the file name **ORDERS** when prompted. You'll be returned to the Control Center, where you'll see the ORDERS database name in the Data panel.

To add some sample data to the database, highlight ORDERS in the Data panel, and press or click Data (F2). Use either the edit or browse screen to enter the records shown in Figure 9.2. Choose Exit ► Exit after entering the 10 records shown.

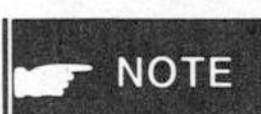

Because you *always* need to press ↵ after entering a value in dBASE IV, from now on this book will use instructions such as "enter **ABC**" instead of "type **ABC** and press ↵."

Use the Ditto key (Shift-F8) to save some typing when adding new records to the ORDERS database.

Records Organize Fields Go To Exit

PARTNO	PARTNAME	DATE	QTY	UNITPRICE
B-222	Banana Man	06/01/93	2	100.00
B-222	Banana Man	06/01/93	1	100.00
A-111	Astro Buddies	06/01/93	2	50.00
C-333	Cosmic Critters	06/01/93	1	500.00
A-111	Astro Buddies	06/02/93	3	50.00
A-111	Astro Buddies	06/05/93	4	50.00
B-222	Banana Man	06/15/93	1	100.00
C-333	Cosmic Critters	06/15/93	2	500.00
C-333	Cosmic Critters	06/15/93	1	500.00
C-333	Cosmic Critters	07/01/93	2	500.00

Browse | C:\dbase\ORDERS | Rec 10/10 | File

Figure 9.2: Sample data in the ORDERS database

PERFORMING CALCULATIONS IN REPORTS

If you highlight ORDERS in the Data panel and press or click Quick Report (Shift-F9) to print a report of its data, you'll see that the report already contains totals of the numeric fields QTY and UNITPRICE, as Figure 9.3 shows.

In most cases, you will probably want reports that offer a better format than Quick Report provides. For the ORDERS database, a column showing extended prices and a total of the extended prices would certainly be helpful. Let's start designing a report that provides this information.

1. Make sure the ORDERS database is open (its name should appear above the line in the Data panel).
2. Move the highlight to the Reports panel and select <create> or double-click <create> in that panel.
3. Choose Layout ► Quick Layouts.
4. Select Column Layout.

```
Page No.   1
07/08/93

PARTNO   PARTNAME          DATE          QTY     UNITPRICE

B-222    Banana Man        06/01/93        2        100.00
B-222    Banana Man        06/01/93        1        100.00
A-111    Astro Buddies     06/01/93        2         50.00
C-333    Cosmic Critters   06/01/93        1        500.00
A-111    Astro Buddies     06/02/93        3         50.00
A-111    Astro Buddies     06/05/93        4         50.00
B-222    Banana Man        06/15/93        1        100.00
C-333    Cosmic Critters   06/15/93        2        500.00
C-333    Cosmic Critters   06/15/93        1        500.00
C-333    Cosmic Critters   07/01/93        2        500.00
                                          19       2450.00
```

Figure 9.3: Quick report from the ORDERS database

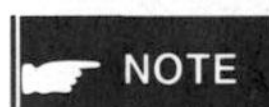

NOTE

Numeric fields in column reports are wider than the width defined in the database structure to accommodate totals at the end of each column. The field widths of other data types may be widened to match the width of the field name.

dBASE creates a report format that is identical to the format used for Quick Reports. Templates for all fields are spread across the Detail band, and templates for the totals of numeric fields appear in the Report Summary band. The names of the database fields, which appear as column headings in the printed report, appear within the Page Header band, as Figure 9.4 shows.

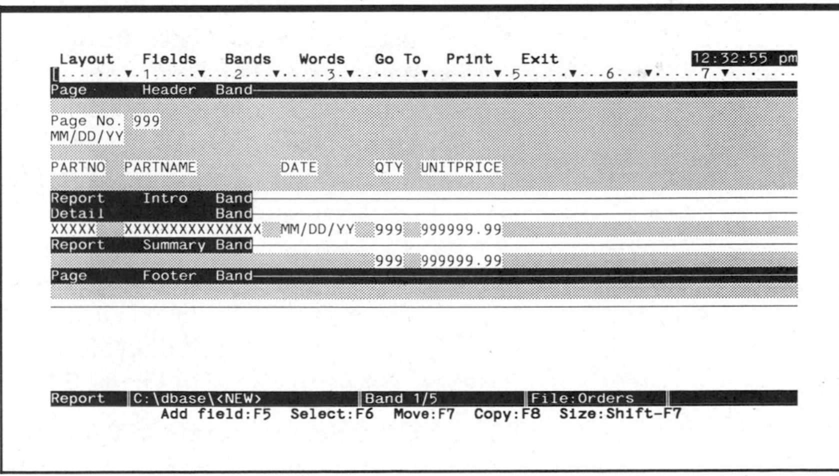

Figure 9.4: Initial column layout for a report

This example intentionally uses a database that has very few fields, so all the data will easily fit across one row on the screen and on one printed page. When you create columnar reports with larger databases, the fields might extend well beyond the right margin of the screen and printed page. You can move field templates (or remove them) using the basic techniques discussed in Chapter 7.

SETTING THE REPORT MARGINS

Before you begin arranging fields in the report, set the right margin for 8½-by-11-inch paper following these steps:

1. Choose Words ► Modify Ruler.
2. Press Tab eight times to move the cursor to column 64.
3. Type].
4. Press Ctrl-End or click the mouse.

Now you can proceed with adding calculated fields and arranging the report format.

ADDING A CALCULATED FIELD

Let's add a calculated field to the report format to display the extended price. The basic steps are the same as those used to place any other field: You position the cursor where you want the field to appear and then press Add Field (F5), or just double-click the mouse where you want to place the field. Here are the exact steps:

1. Move the cursor to column 55 in the Detail band (to the right of all other field templates within the Detail band), then press or click Add Field (F5). Alternatively, you can double-click the mouse in column 55 of the Detail band. You'll see a menu of options, as in Figure 9.5.
2. Select <create> from the CALCULATED column, because you want to create a calculated field.

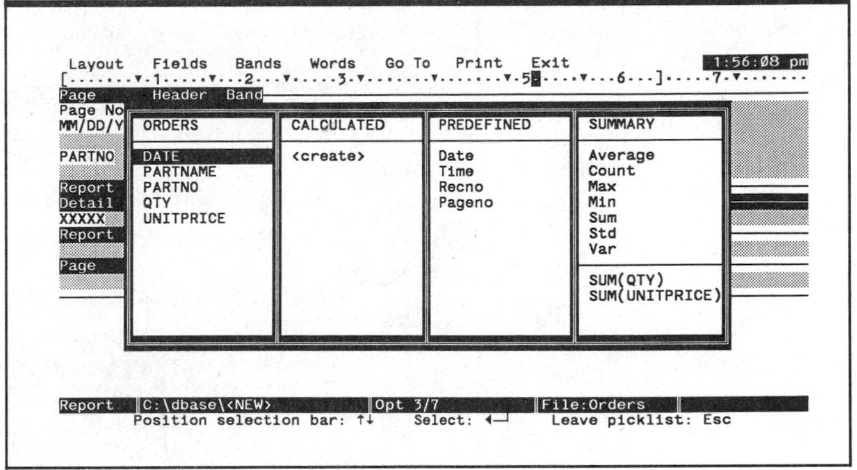

Figure 9.5: Options for placing fields in the report format

3. At this point, you are given options to define a name, description, expression, and display attributes for the calculated field.
4. Select Name and enter a name such as **EXTPRICE**.
5. Select Description and enter a plain-English description, such as **Extended price**. (The description is optional, but is useful for future reference.)
6. Select Expression and enter the expression **Qty * UnitPrice** to multiply the quantity by the unit price in this calculated field.

Your screen should now look like Figure 9.6. You could change the display attributes (that is, the template and picture functions) for the calculated field, but there is no need to do so right now (we'll discuss these options later in this chapter). Just press or click Accept (Ctrl-End) to leave the submenu.

Now you'll see the new calculated field template in the report format. You might also want to take a moment to rearrange the Page Header band, improve the column titles, and add a title for the new field, just to tidy things up, as in Figure 9.7.

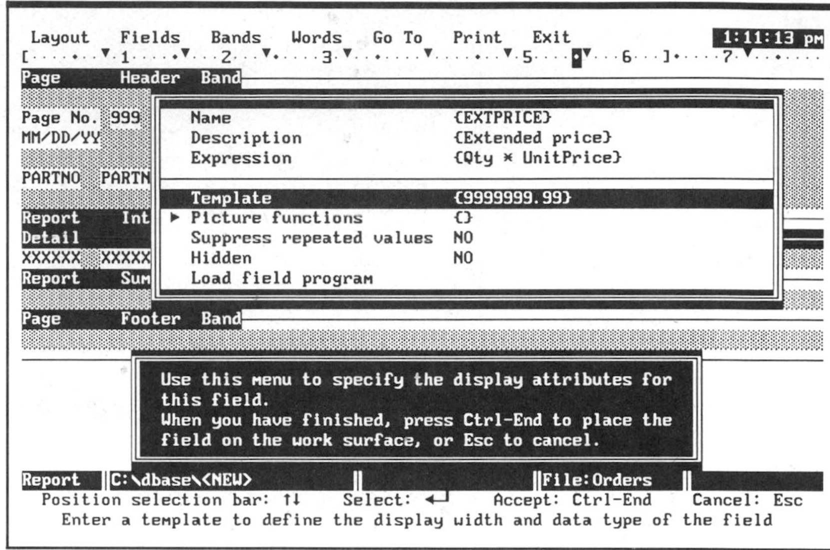

Figure 9.6: Calculated field defined

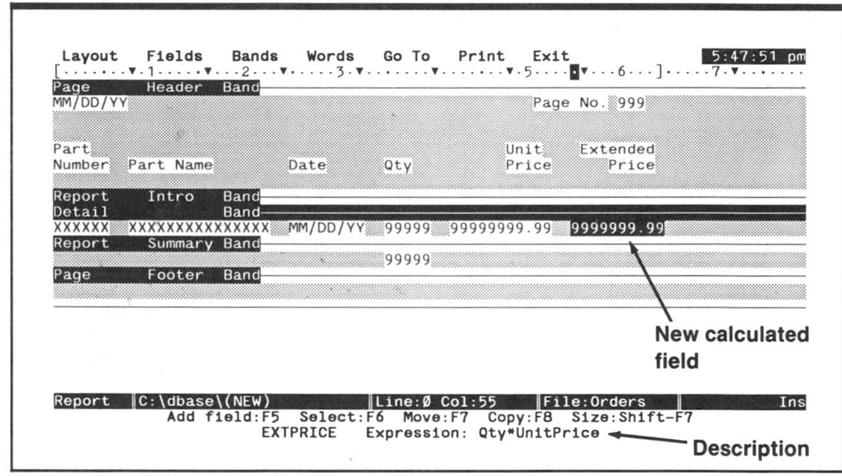

Figure 9.7: Calculated field added to the report format

Notice that when the cursor is in the calculated field template, the bottom line of the screen describes the field, as follows:

EXTPRICE   Expression: Qty * UnitPrice

This information can be helpful in the future, when you need to know what a field template contains.

CALCULATING TOTALS

To display the total of the extended price in the report, you need to use a *summary field*. A summary field summarizes the information in a group of records. The summary might be a total or subtotal, an average, a count, or some other calculation. Table 9.2 lists the summary options.

Table 9.2: Summary Field Options

Option	Operation
Average	Displays the average for a group of numbers
Count	Counts the number of records in a group
Max	Displays the largest value in a group
Min	Displays the smallest value in a group
Sum	Displays the total of values in a group
Std	Displays the standard deviation (a statistical measure) for a group
Var	Displays the variance (a statistical measure) for a group

Right now you need a summary field to total all the extended prices in the ORDERS database. You want this total to appear once at the end of the report, so you need to place it in the Report Summary band. You don't need the total of the UNITPRICE field that is currently in the format, so you can remove that now. Here are the steps to do so:

1. Move the cursor to the summary field template for the UNITPRICE field (the description at the bottom of the screen will show "Operation: SUM Summarize: UNITPRICE" when the cursor is in the correct template).

2. Press the Del key to remove the template.
3. Staying within the Report Summary band, move the cursor to column 55 and press Add Field (F5) or double-click your mouse in column 55 of that band.
4. You want a summary field that calculates a total (sum), so move the cursor to the SUMMARY column and select Sum or double-click Sum in that column.
5. Select Name and enter a name for the field (such as **SUMEXT**).
6. Select Description and enter the description **Sum of extended prices**.
7. Select Field to Summarize On and then select EXTPRICE from the submenu that appears (because you want to total the EXTPRICE field).
8. Press or click Accept (Ctrl-End).

The template for the summary field will appear on the screen. To improve the report format a bit, you can use equal bars to create a double line between the detail band and the totals. Follow these steps:

1. Press Home to move the cursor to column 0 in the Report Summary band or click the mouse at that location.
2. Press Ctrl-N to insert a blank line.
3. Place a string of equal signs above the 99999 and 9999999.99 templates, as in Figure 9.8.

Figure 9.8 shows the report format with the new summary field and the equal bars. Notice that when the cursor is within the template for the summary field, its name, the operation it performs, and the name of field it summarizes are displayed at the bottom of the screen, as follows:

```
SUMEXT   Operation: SUM  Summarize: EXTPRICE
```

(The name is optional in summary fields. If you don't create one, the Operation and Summarize information still appears at the bottom of the screen. In the Add Field menu that appears when you press F5, unnamed summary fields are displayed in the format SUM(QTY)—that is, sum-of-qty).

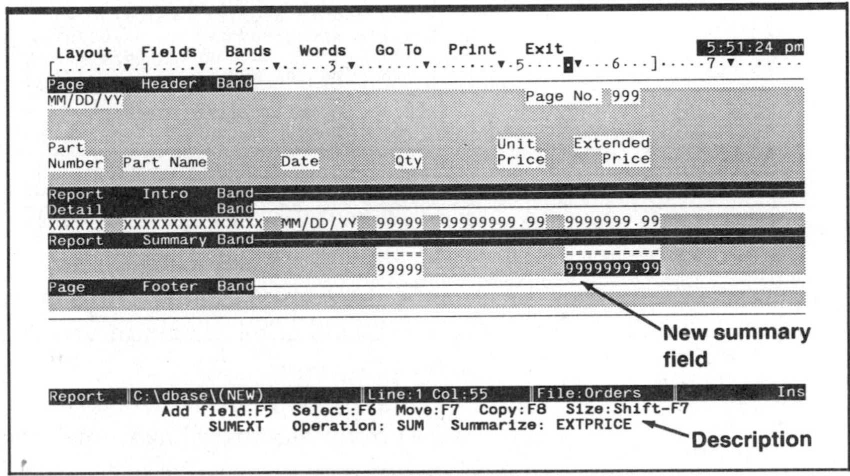

Figure 9.8: Summary field added to the report format

Use the usual technique now to save the report format: Choose Layout ► Edit Description of Report and enter a description such as **Total sales**. Then choose Exit ► Save Changes and Exit. When asked to name the report, enter **TOTALS**. After dBASE creates a program for printing the report, it returns you to the Control Center. From there, use the usual techniques to print the report (select its name from the Reports panel). The printed report will look like Figure 9.9.

CALCULATING SUBTOTALS

Suppose you want to print a report that shows not only overall totals, but also subtotals for each part number. To display subtotals, you need to add *group bands* to the report format. A group band tells dBASE to group similar items on the report. You can group records in any manner you wish. For instance, in the ORDERS database

```
07/08/93                                                    Page No.   1

Part                                                   Unit      Extended
Number   Part Name          Date            Qty       Price        Price

B-222    Banana Man         06/01/93          2      100.00       200.00
B-222    Banana Man         06/01/93          1      100.00       100.00
A-111    Astro Buddies      06/01/93          2       50.00       100.00
C-333    Cosmic Critters    06/01/93          1      500.00       500.00
A-111    Astro Buddies      06/02/93          3       50.00       150.00
A-111    Astro Buddies      06/05/93          4       50.00       200.00
B-222    Banana Man         06/15/93          1      100.00       100.00
C-333    Cosmic Critters    06/15/93          2      500.00      1000.00
C-333    Cosmic Critters    06/15/93          1      500.00       500.00
C-333    Cosmic Critters    07/01/93          2      500.00      1000.00
                                          =====               ==========
                                             19                  3850.00
```

Figure 9.9: The printed TOTALS report

you might want to group records by part number or date (or both). In the CUSTLIST database you could group customers by city, state, or zip code.

A group band actually consists of two parts: a Group Intro band, and a Group Summary band. Information in the Group Intro band is displayed once at the top of each group. For example, a report grouped by part number might display the group headings "Part number: A-111" for one group and "Part number: B-222" for the next. The Group Summary band displays its contents once at the bottom of each group. This is where you place summary fields to display subtotals.

Let's add a group band to the TOTALS report format to subtotal records by part number. Our goal will be to make the report format look like Figure 9.10. Here are the steps:

1. Make sure that ORDERS is still the database in use.
2. Move the highlight to TOTALS in the Reports panel and press or click Design (Shift-F2).
3. To insert a group band, move the cursor to the Report Intro band border or click on that band with your mouse (the indicator in the status bar will read "Band 2/5").
4. Choose Bands ► Add a Group band.
5. Select Field Value from the submenu.
6. Select PARTNO as the field to group by.

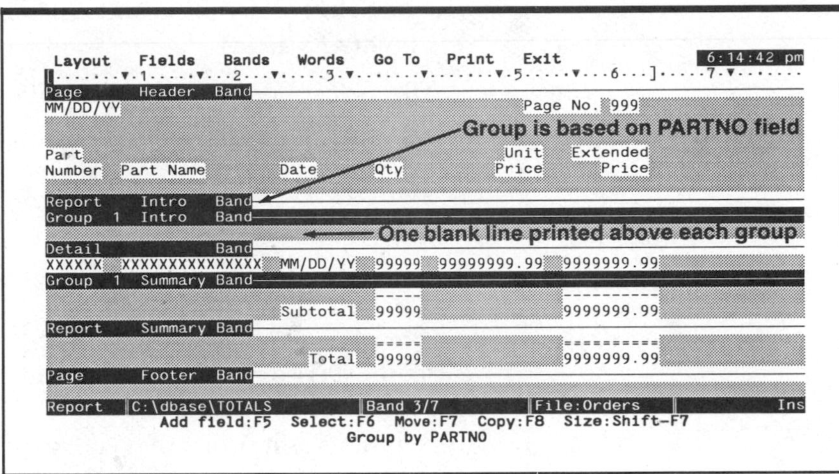

Figure 9.10: Report format for subtotals

You'll see the new group band appear in the report format. While the cursor is still on the group band, the message "Group by PARTNO" appears centered at the bottom of the screen. If you were to print the report now, however, you would not see any subtotals, because the Group Summary band is still empty. We'll rectify that situation right now by adding some summary fields.

If you need help placing hyphens and subtotal fields, use Figure 9.10 as a guide.

1. Press ↓ five times to move the cursor down to the blank line between the Group 1 Summary band and the Report Summary band, or click the mouse on that location.
2. Move the cursor to column 35 and place hyphens beneath the Qty (99999) and EXTPRICE (9999999.99) templates, (directly above the equal signs in the Report Summary band).
3. Press Ctrl-N to insert a blank line.
4. Move the cursor to line 1, column 35, directly below the hyphens you just entered, or click the mouse at that location.
5. Press Add Field (F5) or double-click the mouse at line 1, column 35 and select Sum from the SUMMARY column.
6. Select Name and enter a name for the field (such as **SUBQTY**).

7. Select Description and enter a description (such as **Subtotal of Qty field**).
8. Select Field to Summarize On and then select QTY.
9. Select Reset Every and then select PARTNO.
10. Select Template and press Backspace until the template reads 99999. Then press ↵.
11. Press or click Accept (Ctrl-End).

Step 9 is required so that dBASE will reset the subtotal to zero each time it encounters a new part number while printing the report. If the Reset Every option is set to REPORT, dBASE will accumulate the subtotals as it prints the report, giving you running totals rather than subtotals. Step 10 ensures that the template for the subtotal matches the template used elsewhere for the Qty field.

Let's add a subtotal field for the Extended Price field now.

1. Press → until the cursor is in column 55 (above the equal bars), or click the mouse at that location.
2. Press Add Field (F5), or double-click the mouse on column 55.
3. Select Sum from the SUMMARY column.
4. Select Name and enter **SUBEXT**.
5. Select Description and enter **Subtotal of extended price**.
6. Select Field to Summarize On and EXTPRICE from the submenu.
7. Select Reset Every and then PARTNO.
8. Press or click Accept (Ctrl-End).

Now your report will print subtotals as well as grand totals. You might want to add the words **Subtotal** and **Total** to the report format as well, as shown in Figure 9.10.

Rather than use this format to *replace* the previous TOTALS report, let's save this format as a new, separate file. That way, you'll still be able to use the TOTALS report format. Here are the steps:

1. Choose Layout ► Edit Description of Report.

2. Press Home or click the mouse on the T in total and then press Ctrl-Y to erase the previous description. Then enter the description **Subtotals by part number (requires PARTNO index)**. (This description will be explained in a moment.)
3. Choose Layout ► Save This Report
4. Press Backspace 10 times to remove the previous file name.
5. Type the new name **SUBTOTAL** and press ↵.
6. When dBASE finishes creating its program, choose Exit ► Abandon Changes and Exit.

In the last step, it was okay to select Abandon Changes and Exit because you had already saved your changes under a new file name. The original TOTALS report remains unchanged, and the new format is saved with the name SUBTOTAL. You can use this technique whenever you design a report that is similar to some existing report, so that you don't have to build each report format from scratch.

PRINTING SUBTOTALED REPORTS

Before you print the new subtotaled report, there is one catch you have to be aware of. The records in the printed report will be grouped properly only if the database is indexed (or sorted) on the field on which the grouping is based. Why? Because the report format tells dBASE only how to *display* the groups, not how to *create* the groups.

Let's assume that you printed the SUBTOTAL report without first using the PARTNO index to organize the records. dBASE would "see" the records in their unsorted order, like this:

B-222

B-222

A-111

C-333

A-111

A-111

B-222

C-333

Each time dBASE encounters a new part number while printing the report, it considers that record to be the start of a new group. Hence, it would print the first two records, with part number B-222, and then print subtotals for those two records before moving on to records containing part number A-111. It would print the record containing part number A-111 and a subtotal for that one record before moving on to the next part number. Then it would print the next record with part number C-333 and a subtotal for that one record, before moving on to the next record with part number A-111.

However, if you use an index to organize the records by part numbers, dBASE will "see" the data in this order before printing the report:

A-111

A-111

A-111

B-222

B-222

B-222

C-333

C-333

The sort order automatically groups similar records together. Hence, when dBASE prints a report from the data organized in this manner, it prints all the records containing A-111, and then a subtotal for those records, before moving on to the records with the next part number, B-222. Then it prints all the records with part number B-222, and a subtotal for those records, before moving on to the records with part number C-333.

So you need to organize the records in the ORDERS database into PARTNO order before printing the SUBTOTAL report. As you may recall, we indexed the PARTNO field when we designed the database structure, so now you just need to put that index into action. Here are the steps:

1. Highlight ORDERS in the Data panel.
2. Press or click Data (F2).
3. Choose Organize ► Order Records by Index.
4. Select PARTNO.
5. Press Ctrl-End to return to the Control Center.

Now you can print the SUBTOTAL report by selecting it from the Reports panel in the usual manner. The results should look something like Figure 9.11.

```
07/08/93                                                Page No.    1

Part                                                    Unit     Extended
Number  Part Name         Date            Qty          Price        Price


A-111   Astro Buddies     06/01/93          2          50.00       100.00
A-111   Astro Buddies     06/02/93          3          50.00       150.00
A-111   Astro Buddies     06/05/93          4          50.00       200.00
                                        -----                  ----------
                          Subtotal          9                      450.00

B-222   Banana Man        06/01/93          1         100.00       100.00
B-222   Banana Man        06/15/93          1         100.00       100.00
B-222   Banana Man        06/01/93          2         100.00       200.00
                                        -----                  ----------
                          Subtotal          4                      400.00

C-333   Cosmic Critters   06/01/93          1         500.00       500.00
C-333   Cosmic Critters   06/15/93          2         500.00      1000.00
C-333   Cosmic Critters   06/15/93          1         500.00       500.00
C-333   Cosmic Critters   07/01/93          2         500.00      1000.00
                                        -----                  ----------
                          Subtotal          6                     3000.00
                                        =====                  ==========
                             Total         19                     3850.00
```

Figure 9.11: Subtotaled report from the ORDERS database

It's often hard to remember to activate an index before printing a report with groups, probably because we expect dBASE to be smart enough to do this for us. No such luck. If you do forget, no harm done; the report will still be printed, but groups and subtotals will be in haphazard order. It helps to put a reminder in the description of the report format, as we did just before we saved the SUBTOTAL report. Then each time you highlight the report's name in the Control Center you'll be reminded that an index is required.

ORDER OF PRECEDENCE IN CALCULATIONS

When creating your own reports to perform calculations, keep in mind that there are four ways to perform calculations in report bands, and dBASE follows a certain order of precedence when performing calculations as summarized below:

Named	When you create a calculated field and give it a name (such as ExtPrice), the results of that calculation can be used as part of another calculation. These named calculated fields are calculated left-to-right, top-to-bottom within the band. Hence, if a calculated field uses the results of another calculated field, the second calculated field should be to the right of or below the first calculated field.
Unnamed	When you create a calculated field, you must provide an expression (such as Qty * UnitPrice), but the name is required only if another calculated field needs to use that name as part of its expression. Unnamed calculated fields are calculated last.
Hidden	When creating a calculated field, you have the option to change it to a Hidden field so that it can perform an intermediate calculation but not display the results of that calculation on the report. The hidden calculated fields in a band are always calculated first in a band, in the order in which they were created.
Summary	Summary fields, such as those used for subtotals and totals in this chapter, are calculated left to right, top to bottom within each band, along with the named calculated fields, unless the summary field is dependent on a calculated field. In that case, the summary field is calculated after all hidden and named calculated fields.

In practice, what this all boils down to is that how calculations are performed in a report depends both on the type of field performing the calculation, and its position within the band. You should always check the results of calculations in a printed report carefully, and make sure the proper data from the proper record is displayed on each page.

If you find that a value is being calculated incorrectly, try moving the field to the right of or below any other fields that its calculation depends on so that the other fields will be calculated first.

Or, if the calculated field is named, but does not need to be because no other fields depend on it, remove its name to convert it to an unnamed calculated field.

MANAGING REPORT BANDS

As you add new bands to your report format, your screen may become increasingly cluttered and difficult to read. You can close bands that you are not using at the moment by moving the cursor to the band border and pressing ↵, or by clicking your mouse on the band border. Just remember to reopen the band before you print the report, because closed bands do not print. To open a closed band, move the cursor to the band border and press ↵, or click on the band again. You can also choose Bands ► Open All Bands to open all closed bands.

To permanently remove a group band from a report format, place the cursor in the band's border or click the mouse on that border. Then press the Del key or choose Bands ► Remove Group. To change the field that a group is based on, move the cursor to the group band border, then choose Bands ► Modify Group.

FORMATTING REPORT BANDS

You can specify the pitch, quality, and spacing of lines for an individual band by moving the cursor to the band border and selecting the appropriate option from the Bands submenu. These are the same printer features that were discussed in Chapter 7; however, they affect only the current band when specified in this manner.

REMOVING REPETITIOUS FIELDS

In Figure 9.11, the part numbers and part names are repeated within each group. To display repetitious data only once in a group, move the appropriate field templates into the Group Intro band, as in Figure 9.12.

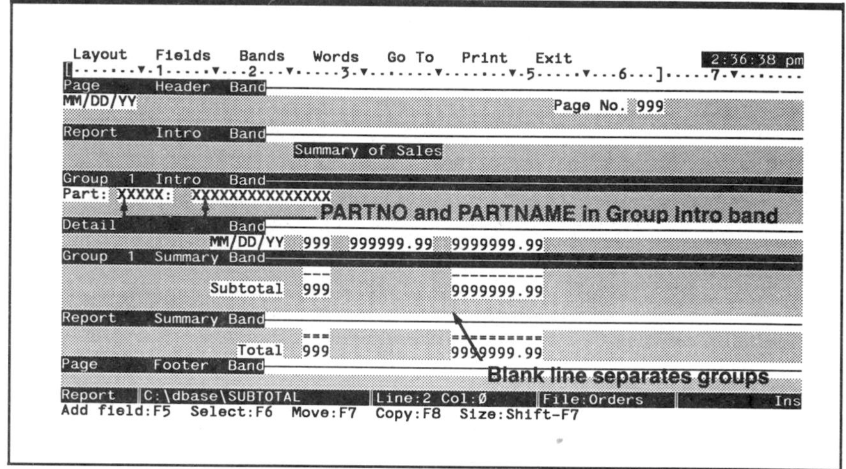

Figure 9.12: PARTNO and PARTNAME fields in the Group Intro band

Keep in mind that you cannot move the ghost image of a field from one report band to another. Before you press or click Move (F7), you must select the field you want to move and move the cursor to the new location for the field template. To try this for yourself, follow these steps:

1. At the Control Center, make sure the ORDERS database is still open (that its name appears above the line in the Data panel).
2. Highlight SUBTOTAL in the Reports panel and press or click Design (Shift-F2).
3. Press ↓ repeatedly, until the cursor appears in the Group 1 Intro band, or click the mouse inside that band.
4. Type **Part:** (including the colon).
5. Press ↓ and ← until the cursor is in the PARTNO field template or click on that template (the bottom of the screen will show the field name ORDERS->PARTNO when the cursor is properly positioned).

6. Press or click Select (F6).
7. Press → or move the mouse to the right until both the PARTNO and PARTNAME field templates are highlighted (the highlight should extend to column 23).
8. Press ↵ or click the mouse to complete the selection.
9. Press the ↑ and ← keys to move the cursor to the right of the newly typed word **Part:** (column 6), or click the mouse at that location.
10. Press or click Move (F7), and then press ↵ or click the mouse.
11. The move is now complete, but you may want to add a colon between the part number and the part name. To do so, repeatedly press → to move the cursor to column 12 (or click there) and type the colon (:).
12. Press the End key to move to the end of the field templates.
13. Press ↵ to insert a blank line in the Group 1 Intro band.

You may also want to remove the field name headings from the Page Header band using the usual Ctrl-Y key. To place the Summary of Sales heading, shown in Figure 9.12, in the Report Intro band, first move the cursor to the Report Intro band border and press ↵ to open the band (or click that band with your mouse). Press ↓, type the heading, and choose Words ► Position ► Center to center the heading. Add a blank line by pressing Ctrl-N with the cursor positioned at the right of the heading.

You might also wish to shift the contents of the Detail, Group1 Summary, and Report Summary bands to the left. You can press or click Select (F6) and Move (F7) to do so, but you must change each band independently because you cannot extend the selector highlight outside of the current band. Finally, add a blank line after the subtotals in the Group 1 Summary band. When you are finished formatting the report, follow these steps to save it with a new file name:

1. Choose Layout ► Save this Report.
2. When prompted, press the Backspace key six times to erase part of the original file name.

3. Type in the number **2** to change the file name to SUBTOT2.
4. Press ↵.
5. When dBASE finishes creating the program to print the report, choose Exit ► Abandon Changes and Exit.

When you return to the Control Center, remember that the database must still be sorted into part number order before you print the report. Use the same techniques that you used to print the SUBTOTAL report to print the new SUBTOT2 report.

Figure 9.13 shows a printed copy of the new report. Notice that the part number and part name are printed only once at the top of each subtotal group and that a single blank line beneath each subtotal separates the groups.

```
07/08/93                                              Page No.   1


                         Summary of Sales

Part: A-111:   Astro Buddies

                  06/01/93       2          50.00       100.00
                  06/02/93       3          50.00       150.00
                  06/05/93       4          50.00       200.00
                             -----                  ----------
                  Subtotal       9                      450.00

Part: B-222:   Banana Man

                  06/01/93       1         100.00       100.00
                  06/15/93       1         100.00       100.00
                  06/01/93       2         100.00       200.00
                             -----                  ----------
                  Subtotal       4                      400.00

Part: C-333:   Cosmic Critters

                  06/01/93       1         500.00       500.00
                  06/15/93       2         500.00      1000.00
                  06/15/93       1         500.00       500.00
                  07/01/93       2         500.00      1000.00
                             -----                  ----------
                  Subtotal       6                     3000.00

                             =====                  ==========
                     Total      19                     3850.00
```

Figure 9.13: Report printed by the format in Figure 9.12

HANDLING GROUPS AND PAGE BREAKS

Normally, if a particular group on the report continues to the next printed page, the Group Intro is not repeated on the new page. You can change this so that the Group Intro *is* repeated on the new page by changing the Group Intro on Each Page option on the Bands menu from No to Yes.

You can print groups successively, as in the examples in this chapter, or you can print each new Group or Detail band on a separate page. Move the cursor to the appropriate band border and then choose Band ► Begin Band on New Page. Change the setting to Yes to start each printed group on a new page.

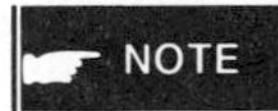

The templates in report formats are slightly larger than database field widths to provide extra space for totals.

NESTING GROUPS WITHIN GROUPS

You can *nest* group bands inside of each other to produce groups within groups. For instance, suppose you place a group band for PARTNO in the format of a report and then a group based on the DATE field within that group. You could then print a report that subtotals sales for particular products and, for each product, subtotal sales by date.

However, printing reports that have groups within groups requires complex indexes, and creating these can be tricky. Rather than opening up that can of worms right now, let's stay with the basic topic at hand. Chapter 12 will help you master complex indexes and report groupings.

FORMATTING NUMBERS

In Chapters 7 and 8, you saw how to use templates and picture functions to format Character and Logical fields in reports and forms. You can also format numbers, using similar techniques, when designing reports and forms.

NUMERIC TEMPLATES

When you place a numeric field in a report or form design, you'll see a template that reflects the width and decimal places assigned to the number in the database. For example, if a number is assigned a width of six digits and two decimal places, the template for that field will automatically be 999.99.

Unlike Character data, numeric data is never truncated to fit within the space provided by a template. When a number is too large for the space allotted, dBASE displays only asterisks. For example, the template 999 displays only numbers with three or fewer digits. It displays any larger number, such as 1,000, as asterisks (***). Therefore, if you change a template on a form or report format, be sure to specify enough digits to accommodate the largest possible number for the field or calculation.

NOTE

To change the format of an existing numeric template in a form or report design, move the cursor into the field template and press or click F5 or double-click that field template with your mouse.

To specify how many decimal places to display in printed numbers, insert a decimal point in the appropriate position in the template. dBASE will round the number to fit the template. For example, the template 99999 displays the value 12345.678 as 12346 (no decimal places displayed). The template 99999.99 displays the same value as 12345.68. The template 99999.9999 displays the value as 12345.6780.

To display numbers with embedded commas, such as 12,345 (rather than 12345), insert commas into the template wherever you want them to appear in the printed number. If you use the template 999,999.99 to display extended prices, then the value 3850.00 will be displayed as 3,850.00. The number 123.45 will still be displayed as 123.45, because it is not large enough to require a comma.

NUMERIC PICTURE FUNCTIONS

Numeric picture functions let you further refine the format of printed numbers. Whenever you add or modify a field template and select Picture Functions from the Display Attributes menu, you'll see the options shown in Figure 9.14. You can move the highlight to any option and press the space bar (or click the mouse on the option) to turn it on or off.

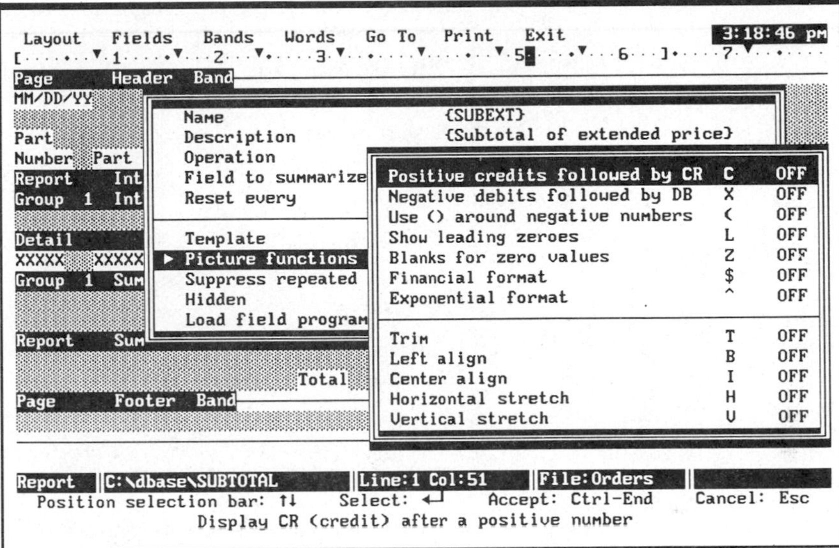

Figure 9.14: Numeric picture functions displayed in a menu

Table 9.3 shows picture functions that you can assign to numeric fields and calculations, and examples of how those functions affect the numbers 0, –123, and 98765.43. Each example assumes that the current template is 999,999.99.

Table 9.3: Numeric Picture Functions

Picture function	Symbol	Examples
Follow positive credits by CR	C	0.00 CR –123.00 98,765.43 CR
Follow negative debits by DB	X	0.00 123.00 DB 98,765.43
Use () around negative numbers	(	0.00 (123.00) 98,765.43
Show leading zeros	L	000000.00 –000123.00 098,765.43

Table 9.3: Numeric Picture Functions (continued)

Picture function	Symbol	Examples
Use blanks for zero values	Z	– 123.00 98,765.43
Use financial format	$	$0.00 $ – 123.00 $98,765.43
Use exponential format	^	.00000000000E + – .123 .123000000000000E + 3 .987654300000000E + 5

You can combine picture functions if you like. For example, combining C and X places CR after positive numbers and DB after negative numbers. Combining Z and (prints positive numbers normally, negative numbers in parentheses, and zeros as blank spaces (rather than as 0 or 0.00).

ADDING CALCULATED FIELDS TO FORMS

You can create calculated fields in custom forms using techniques similar to those used in reports. The calculated fields will be displayed on the form whenever you scroll through existing records in the database. However, the calculations are *not* updated on the screen automatically as you add or change data, so calculated fields on a custom form are of somewhat limited value.

As discussed in the previous chapter, you create a custom form by first opening the appropriate database and then selecting <create> from the Forms panel in the Control Center. Then you can choose Layout ► Quick Layout on the forms design screen to bring the field names and field templates into the new form.

To add a calculated field to a custom form, position the cursor where you want the field to appear and then press or click Add Field (F5) (or double-click the mouse where you want place the field). Select <create> from the CALCULATED column of the submenu that appears. You'll be given a menu of options to define the name, description, expression, template, and picture functions for the new field (exactly as when placing a calculated field in a report format).

Chapter 12 shows how to limit tax calculations to only taxable items in a database.

Figure 9.15 shows a form design for the ORDERS database. Notice that there are three calculated fields, each with its own expression. The expression Qty*UnitPrice displays the extended price. The expression 0.0775*(Qty*UnitPrice) displays the sales tax at 7.75 percent. The expression 1.0775*(Qty*UnitPrice) displays the total sale (the extended price with 7.75 percent tax added).

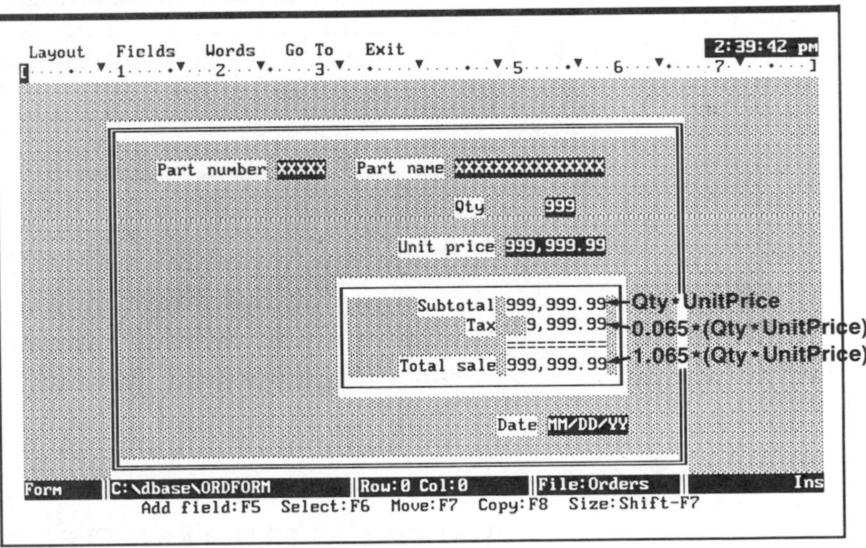

Figure 9.15: A form design with calculated fields

After you save the form design, you can select its name from the Forms panel in the Control Center to activate it. Figure 9.16 shows how the form design in Figure 9.15 appears when you use it to view records in the ORDERS database. As you can see, the form calculates and displays the subtotal, tax, and total sale for each record. As you scroll through records with the PgDn and PgUp keys, the calculations will adjust to new quantity and unit-price values.

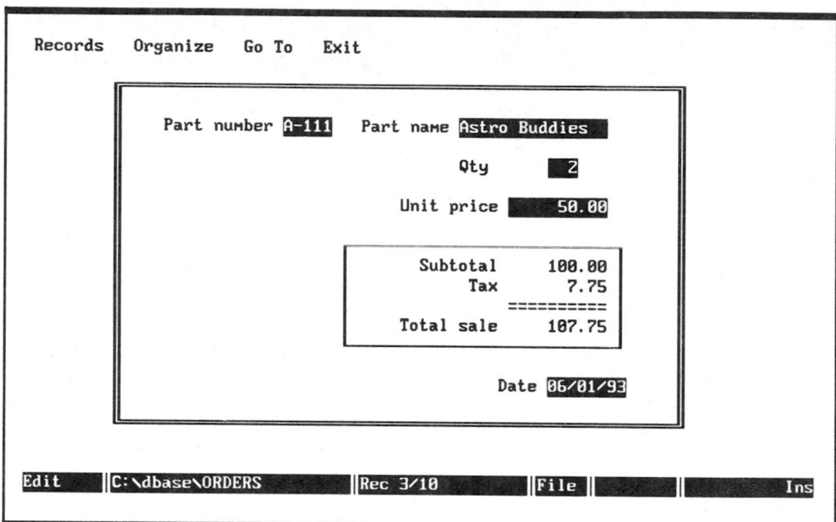

Figure 9.16: Custom form displaying calculations

PERFORMING CALCULATIONS ON THE FLY

You can use the queries design screen to perform some quick calculations without going through all the steps involved in creating a form or report format. This is useful when you just want to experiment with data and calculations and do not need a neatly formatted report.

USING CALCULATED FIELDS IN QUERIES

The general steps for performing calculations through queries are

- Create a query for the appropriate database.
- Choose Fields ► Create Calculated Field.
- Enter the expression (formula) required to perform the calculation, using database field names and arithmetic operators.

- Press Field (F5) to include the calculated field in the view skeleton so its results will be displayed.
- When prompted, enter a field name for the calculated field.
- Press or click Data (F2) as usual to see the results of the query.

To try an example for yourself using the ORDERS database, follow these steps:

1. Make sure that the ORDERS database is open (that its name appears above the line in the Data panel).
2. Select <create> from the Queries panel. This brings you to the query design screen.
3. Choose Fields ► Create Calculated Field. The screen displays a skeleton titled "Calc'd Flds."
4. Type the formula **Qty * UnitPrice** into the Calc'd Flds box (the cursor is already in position).
5. Press ↵ after typing in the formula.
6. Press F5 to move the calculated field to the view skeleton at the bottom of the screen.
7. When prompted, type in a name such as **ExtPrice** and press ↵.

Figure 9.17 shows the completed query. If the calculated field is scrolled off the right of your screen, you can press or click Next (F4) and then press the End key to view the right side of the view skeleton.

When you press or click Data (F2) to execute the query, the results will include a copy of the calculated field, as shown in Figure 9.18. The calculated field will appear in both the browse and edit screens. Remember that you can print the results of this or any other query simply by pressing Quick Report (Shift-F9) while the results are on the screen. To return to the query design screen, press Design (Shift-F2).

You can add up to 20 calculated fields to a query, simply by choosing Fields ► Create Calculated Field. Each new calculated field that you create will be added to the right of existing calculated fields.

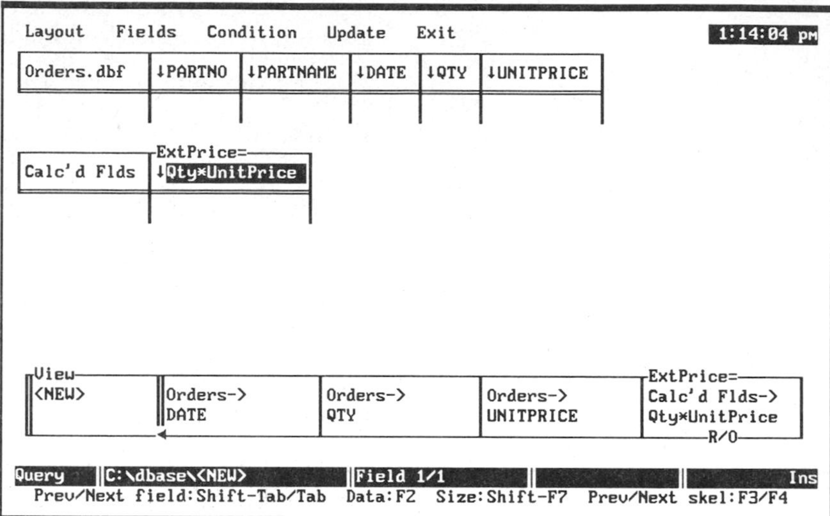

Figure 9.17: Calculated field in a query

Records Organize Fields Go To Exit

PARTNO	PARTNAME	DATE	QTY	UNITPRICE	EXTPRICE
B-222	Banana Man	06/01/93	2	100.00	200.00
B-222	Banana Man	06/01/93	1	100.00	100.00
A-111	Astro Buddies	06/01/93	2	50.00	100.00
C-333	Cosmic Critters	06/01/93	1	500.00	500.00
A-111	Astro Buddies	06/02/93	3	50.00	150.00
A-111	Astro Buddies	06/05/93	4	50.00	200.00
B-222	Banana Man	06/15/93	1	100.00	100.00
C-333	Cosmic Critters	06/15/93	2	500.00	1000.00
C-333	Cosmic Critters	06/15/93	1	500.00	500.00
C-333	Cosmic Critters	07/01/93	2	500.00	1000.00

Browse C:\dbase\EXTPRICE Rec 1/10 View

Figure 9.18: Results of query shown in Figure 9.17

USING FILTER CONDITIONS WITH NUMBERS

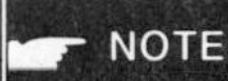

Remember: You press or click F3 and F4, or click the mouse on a skeleton, to move up and down from one skeleton to the next.

You can use filter conditions freely in queries containing calculated fields. The query in Figure 9.19 uses two filter conditions to display records that have A-111 in the PARTNO field *and* a value greater than 100 in the calculated ExtPrice field. (Both filter conditions are in the top row of their respective skeletons, so they are treated as an *AND* relationship.) The results of the query are shown in Figure 9.20.

Figure 9.21 shows a query that isolates records with extended price values in the range $100 to $200.

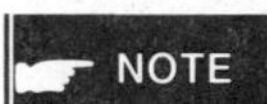

You'll learn more about the use of .AND. and .OR. in Chapter 16.

If you want to set up an OR query that uses fields from both the database file skeleton and a calculated field you need to create a *condition box* by choosing Condition ► Add Condition Box. Use the .AND. and .OR. operators to create AND and OR queries. For example, the query in Figure 9.22 displays records that have quantities greater than 3 or extended prices over $500.

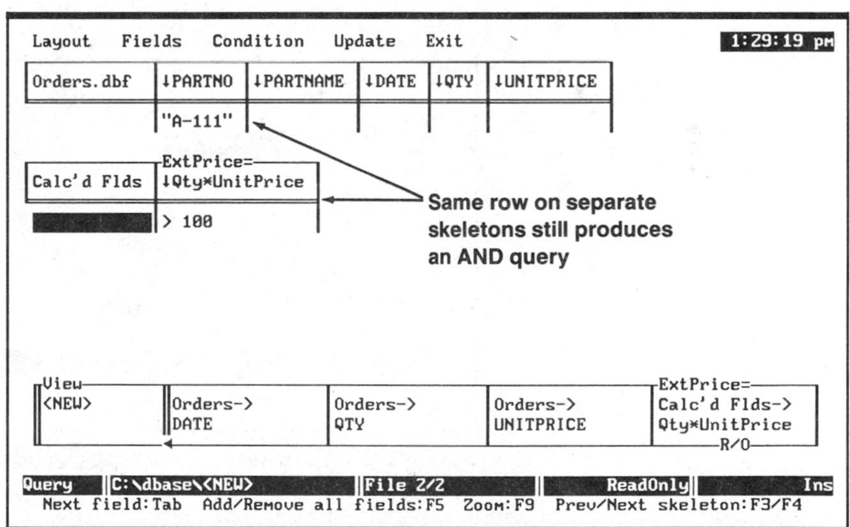

Figure 9.19: Filter conditions added to calculated field query

Records Organize Fields Go To Exit

PARTNO	PARTNAME	DATE	QTY	UNITPRICE	EXTPRICE
A-111	Astro Buddies	06/02/93	3	50.00	150.00
A-111	Astro Buddies	06/05/93	4	50.00	200.00

Browse C:\dbase\<NEW> Rec 5/10 View

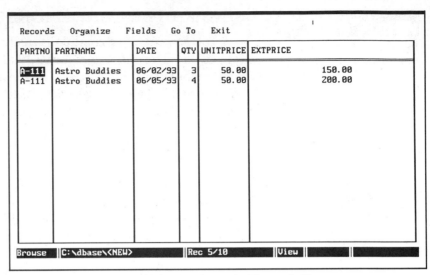

Figure 9.20: Results of the query shown in Figure 9.19

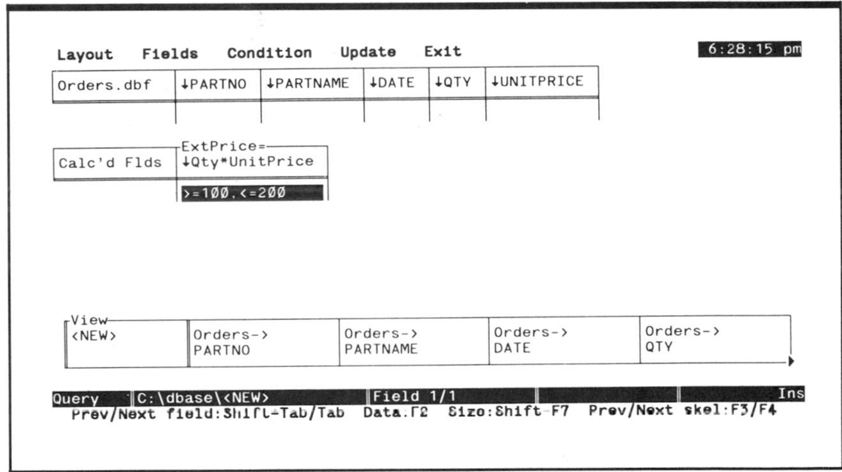

Figure 9.21: Query for records with extended prices in the range $100 to $200

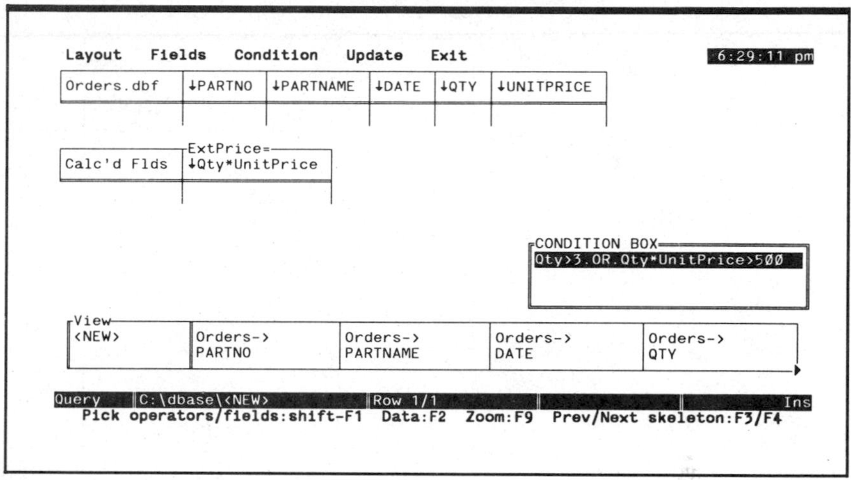

Figure 9.22: A sample OR query

REMOVING CALCULATED FIELDS

To remove a single calculated field from a query, move the cursor into that field in the Calc'd Flds skeleton, then choose Fields ► Delete Calculated Field.

To remove all of the calculated fields from a query, put the cursor into any calculated field in the Calc'd Flds skeleton and choose Layout ► Remove File from Query.

You can also use the Expression Builder (Shift-F1) to automatically insert a field name, operator, function, or QBE operator into any file skeleton, field, or condition box on the queries design screen, as discussed in Chapter 6.

USING SUMMARY OPERATORS

Like reports, queries offer summary operators. To use a summary operator in a query, you place its name beneath the box in the appropriate field. The summary operator must be spelled correctly, as listed in the left column of Table 9.4. The table also lists the data types with which each summary operator can be used.

Table 9.4: Summary Operators Used in Query Forms

Summary operator	Calculates	Data types
AVG or AVERAGE	Average	Numeric, Float
CNT or COUNT	Count	Numeric, Float, Character, Date, Logical
MAX	Highest value	Numeric, Float, Character, Date
MIN	Lowest value	Numeric, Float, Character, Date
SUM	Total	Numeric, Float

You can use summary operators with both database fields and calculated fields. Figure 9.23 shows a sample query that displays the sums of the QTY and UNITPRICE fields.

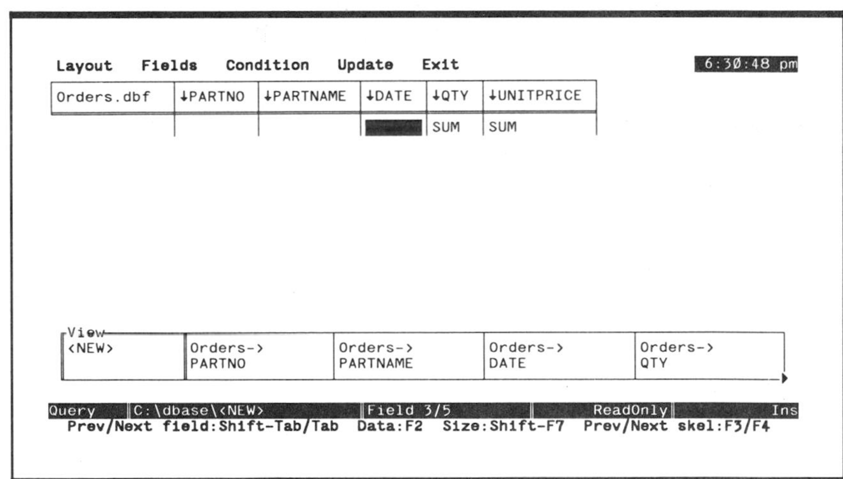

Figure 9.23: Query to sum the QTY and UNITPRICE fields

Figure 9.24 shows the results of the query. As you can see, only the summed fields are displayed. It would not make much sense to display any other fields, because the sums include all records, not just those for a particular part number or part name.

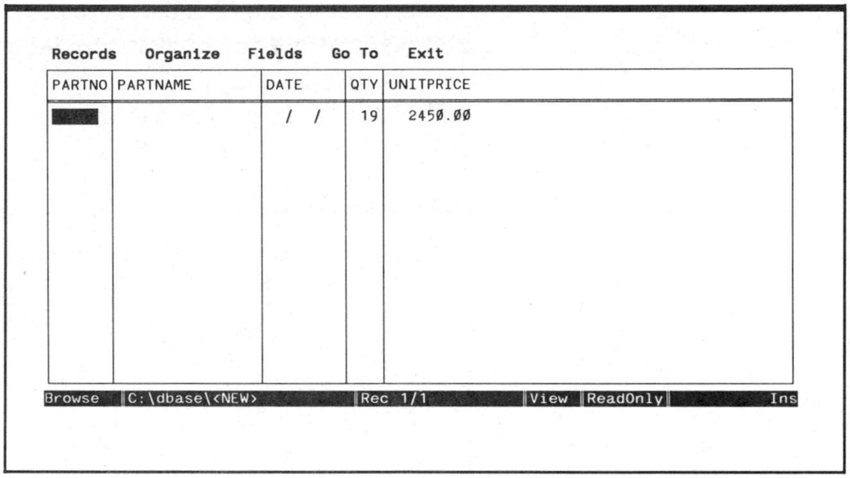

```
Records   Organize   Fields   Go To   Exit

PARTNO | PARTNAME | DATE | QTY | UNITPRICE
       |          | / /  |  19 |   2450.00

Browse  C:\dbase\<NEW>   Rec 1/1   View  ReadOnly   Ins
```

Figure 9.24: Results of the query shown in Figure 9.23

You can combine filter conditions and summary operators in separate fields or in the same field. When combining the two in a single field, separate them with a comma, as in Figure 9.25. (The query counts the number of records in the database with part number A-111.)

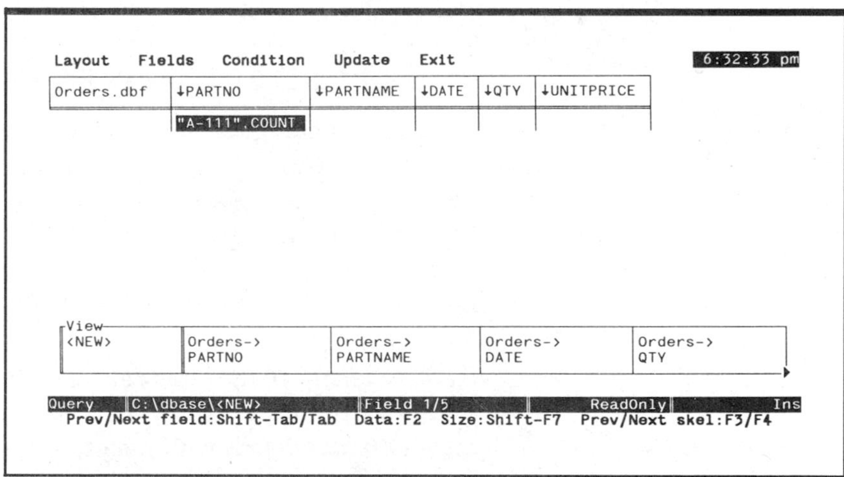

Figure 9.25: A query to count the number of records with A-111 in the PARTNO field

You can combine different summary operators in a single query. For example, the query in Figure 9.26 will display the highest (latest) date, the average quantity, and the lowest unit price. You could still use a filter condition, such as **A-111** in the PARTNO field, to limit the calculation to part number A-111.

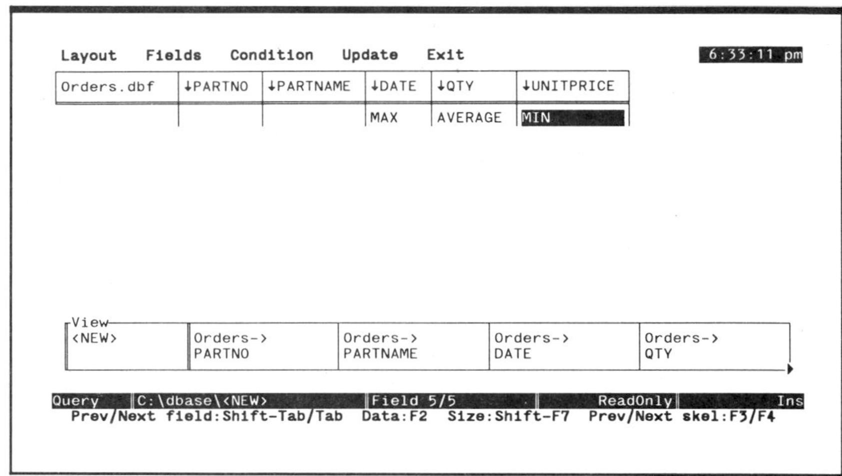

Figure 9.26: Summary operators combined in a query

GROUPS AND SUBTOTALS IN QUERIES

Unlike reports, queries don't require indexes to print subtotals or groups.

Queries can generate quick calculations that involve groups or subtotals, without the use of report formats or indexes. To group the results of a query, place the Group By operator in the field that you want records grouped by and include at least one summary operator to perform a calculation. Figure 9.27 shows an example query that groups records by the PARTNAME field and sums the QTY field for each group.

The results of the query are shown in Figure 9.28. Note that the results of the query show *only* the resulting summaries, and not the individual details within each group.

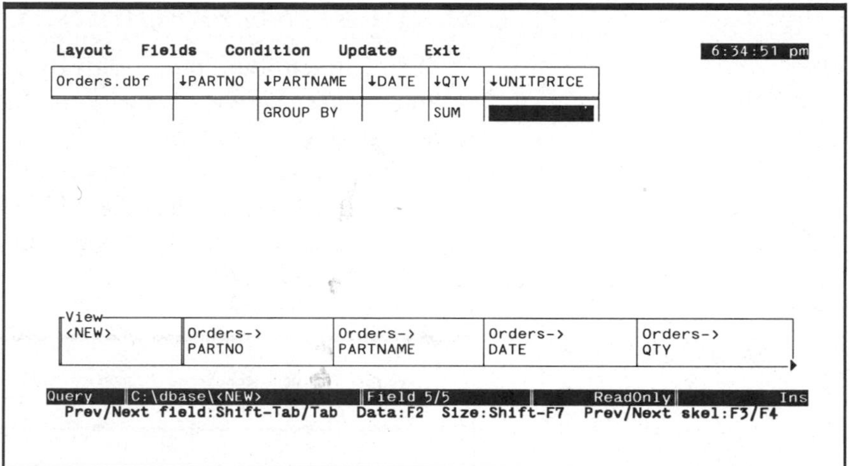

Figure 9.27: Query to subtotal QTY by part name

```
Records   Organize   Fields   Go To   Exit

PARTNO | PARTNAME        | DATE  | QTY | UNITPRICE
       | Astro Buddies   |  / /  |   9 |     .
       | Banana Man      |  / /  |   4 |     .
       | Cosmic Critters |  / /  |   6 |     .

Browse  C:\dbase\<NEW>   Rec 1/3   View  ReadOnly   Ins
```

Figure 9.28: Results of the query in Figure 9.27

By default, dBASE will sort the results of queries that use the Group By operator into ascending order, based on the Group By field. You can override this default sort order by choosing Fields ► Sort on this Field in the query design screen. For example, if the query in Figure 9.27 used Group By, Dsc1 in the PARTNO field, the results would have been displayed in descending order.

CALCULATING FREQUENCY DISTRIBUTIONS

You can combine the Group By and Count summary functions in a query to calculate a *frequency distribution* (a count of all records that have a specific value). For example, suppose that in the CUSTLIST database you want to know how many customers lived in each state.

First, you have to select the CUSTLIST database from the Control Center to open it. Then you must create a query like the one shown in Figure 9.29.

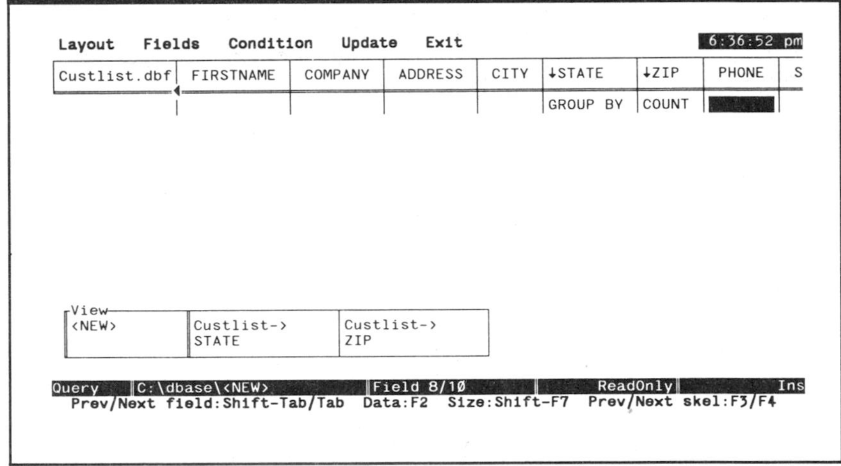

Figure 9.29: Frequency distribution query

Figure 9.30 shows the results of the query. Four people live in CA, and one person lives in each of the other states. (Obviously the results would be more impressive with a larger database.)

When performing frequency distributions, remember that the Group By operator, as opposed to the Count operator, is placed in the field of interest. To count how many people live in each city, place the Group By operator in the CITY field. To count the number of people in each zip code area, place the Group By field in the ZIP field. You can place the COUNT operator in any other field in the query design screen. To ensure that the results of the query are easy to read, include only the fields that contain the GROUP BY and COUNT operators in the view skeleton.

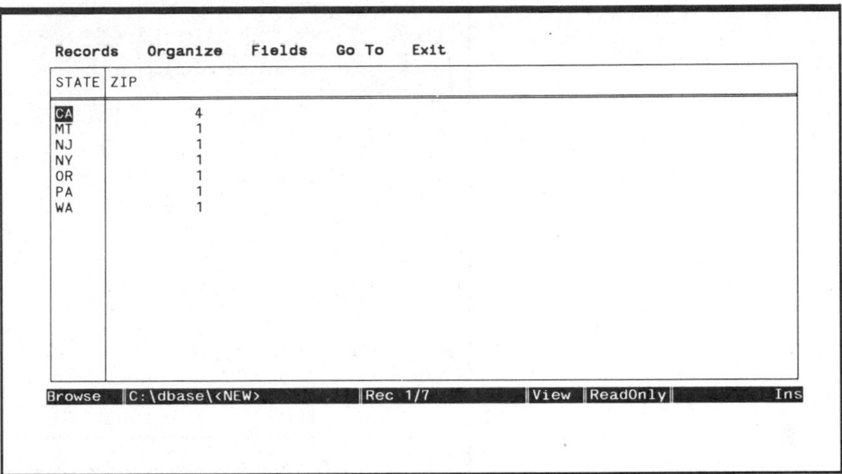

Figure 9.30: Results of the frequency distribution query

CALCULATING DATES

You can add a number to a date, or subtract a number from a date, to determine the date a certain number of days away. For example, the formula {01/01/93} +90 results in the date 04/01/93, the date that is 90 days past January 1, 1993. The formula {12/15/92}-60 results in 10/16/92, the date 60 days prior to December 15, 1992.

You can use this basic date arithmetic in queries. The query in Figure 9.31 uses a filter condition in the Date field of the ORDERS database to display records with dates "less than or equal to 9/12/93 minus 90 days." In English, that translates to dates that are 90 or more days before 9/12/93.

You can use the dBASE DATE( ) (today's date) function in place of a specific date in a query. If you replace the formula < = {9/12/93}-90} in Figure 9.31 with the formula < =DATE( )-90, the query will display records with dates that are 90 or more days before today. If you then save that query, you can simply select it from the Control Center at any time in the future to see records with dates from 90 or more days ago. This feature is very handy for accounts receivable.

You can also subtract one date from another to determine the number of days between two dates. For instance, the formula {12/15/93} – {12/01/93} results in the number 14, because 12/15/93 is 14 days

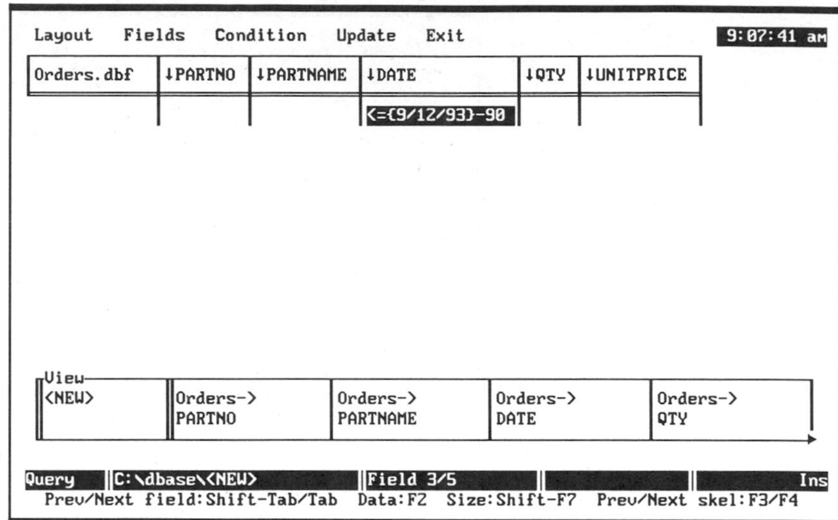

Figure 9.31: Request for records with dates 90 or more days before 09/12/93

"larger than" (that is, after) 12/01/93. The formula {01/01/93} – {03/01/93} results in –59, because 1/1/93 is 59 days "smaller than" (that is, before) 3/1/93.

This kind of date arithmetic can be very useful in databases that store starting and ending dates for projects. For instance, suppose a database contained two fields named STARTDATE and ENDDATE, and both are the Date data type. You could create a calculated field (either in a report or query) that used the expression ENDDATE – STARTDATE to quickly display the number of days between each starting and ending date.

COMPARING FIELDS

Once in a while, you might want to perform a query that compares values in one field to values in another field. Neither the CUSTLIST nor ORDERS database can provide a good example, but the database of stock prices shown in Figure 9.32 can. Suppose you want to isolate records from this database that have a difference of three or more dollars in the opening and closing stock prices.

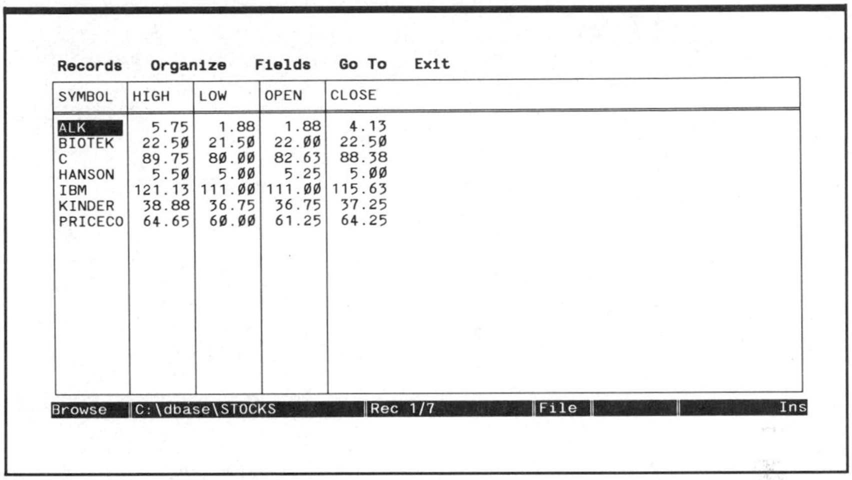

Records Organize Fields Go To Exit

SYMBOL	HIGH	LOW	OPEN	CLOSE
ALK	5.75	1.88	1.88	4.13
BIOTEK	22.50	21.50	22.00	22.50
C	89.75	80.00	82.63	88.38
HANSON	5.50	5.00	5.25	5.00
IBM	121.13	111.00	111.00	115.63
KINDER	38.88	36.75	36.75	37.25
PRICECO	64.65	60.00	61.25	64.25

Browse C:\dbase\STOCKS Rec 1/7 File Ins

Figure 9.32: Database of stock prices

To perform such a query, you need to use an *example*, or *placeholder*, in the query. The placeholder can be any letter or word (such as X, Y, or Zookie). Put the placeholder in one of the fields in the comparison and then use the placeholder in the filter condition of the other field in the comparison.

Figure 9.33 shows an example where several placeholders are used for comparisons and calculations. The placeholder for the OPEN field was typed in as StartofDay (though again, any letter or word would do). The CLOSE field uses the query expression >= *StartofDay + 3* to limit the resulting records being displayed to those in which the closing price is at least $3.00 higher than the opening price.

To calculate and display the difference between the opening and closing prices, a calculated field named CHANGE was also created and added to the View skeleton. As you can see, EndofDay was typed into the CLOSE field as an example (placeholder). Then the calculated field displays the result EndofDay-StartofDay, the difference between the closing and opening stock prices. Figure 9.34 shows the results of the query.

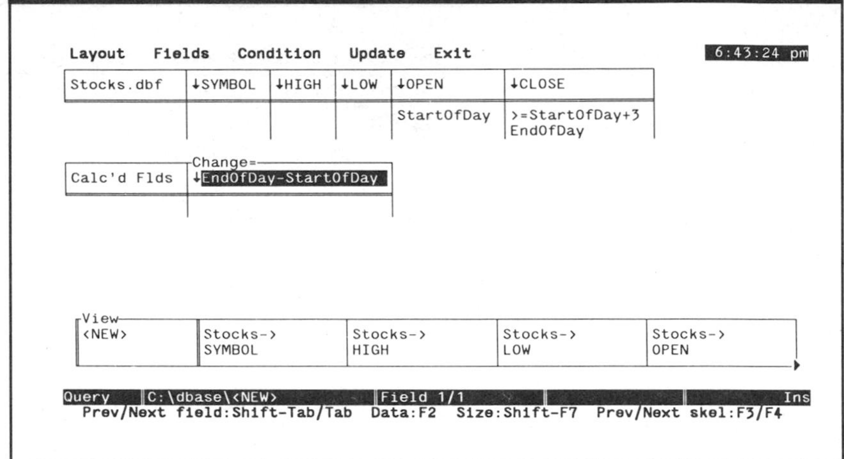

Figure 9.33: A query comparing two fields

Records **Organize** **Fields** **Go To** **Exit**

SYMBOL	HIGH	LOW	OPEN	CLOSE	CHANGE
C	89.75	80.00	82.63	88.38	5.75
IBM	121.13	111.00	111.00	115.63	4.63
PRICECO	64.65	60.00	61.25	64.25	3.00

Browse C:\dbase\<NEW> Rec 3/7 View Ins

Figure 9.34: Results of the query in Figure 9.33

NOTE

Examples (placeholders) are required only when comparing fields in filter conditions.

Returning to our date arithmetic, suppose you want to isolate records with 90 or more days between their starting and ending dates. You could put a placeholder in the STARTDATE field and a filter condition in the ENDDATE field that looks for ending dates that are 90 or more days "greater than" the starting date. Figure 9.35 shows such a query.

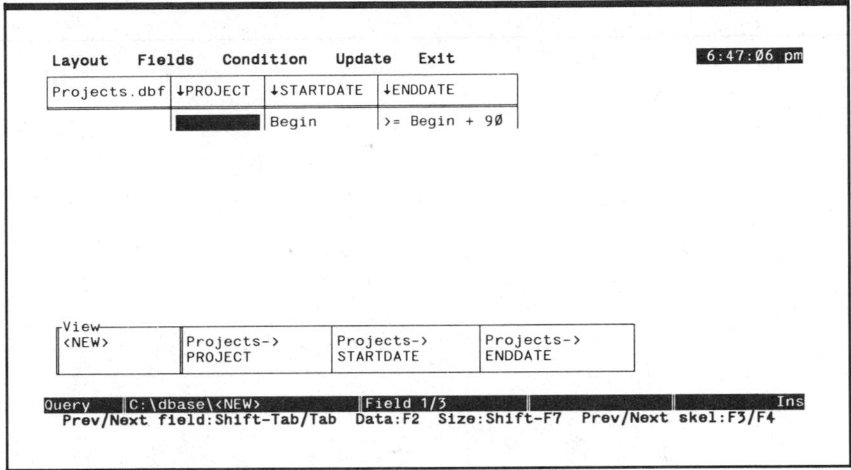

Figure 9.35: Query for records with ending dates 90 or more days past their starting dates

Figure 9.36 shows the results of this query, using a hypothetical database of projects.

Records Organize Fields Go To Exit

PROJECT	STARTDATE	ENDDATE
Design software	03/01/92	07/15/92
Write code	03/15/92	07/30/92
Write documentation	07/01/92	11/30/92
Fix bugs	08/01/92	01/15/93

Browse C:\dbase\<NEW> Rec 1/5 View Ins

Figure 9.36: Results of the query in Figure 9.35

You'll be learning still more features and capabilities of reports, forms, and queries in coming chapters. For now, you've seen a good portion of dBASE's math capabilities.

CHAPTER

10

Using Memo Fields to Store Documents

To enter or change data in a memo field, **354**
move the cursor into the memo field on the browse or edit screen and press Ctrl-Home (or double-click on the field). You'll be moved to the word-wrap editor.

To type information into a memo field, **357**
type as you normally would on a typewriter, but do not press ↵ until you get to the end of a paragraph. Lines within the paragraph will word-wrap automatically.

To create a memo window in a custom form, **359**
move the cursor into the memo field template on the forms design screen and press or click Add Field (F5) or double-click on that field. Change the Display As option to Window and select a border style for the window. Press or click Accept (Ctrl-End) to return to the design screen; then use Size (Shift-F7) and Move (F7) to size and position the window.

To use a memo window on a custom form, **361**
move the cursor into the memo window and press Ctrl-Home or Zoom (F9) , or double-click the mouse in the memo window.

To display memo fields in printed reports, **362**
first create the report by choosing Layout ► Quick Layouts ► Form Layout in the reports design screen. Adjust the width of the memo field template, as necessary, by pressing or clicking Size (Shift-F7), and leave the picture function set to Vertical Stretch ({V}).

IN SOME DATABASES, YOU MIGHT WANT TO STORE an entire written document with each database record. For example, you might want to store resumes in a personnel database. In a real estate office, you could store descriptions of each property in your database. You could store abstracts of journal articles in a database of scientific research references or reviews of performances in a music collection.

You can store a virtually unlimited amount of text in a *memo field.* A memo field can hold 1024 characters by 32,000 lines (over 32 million characters), or about 9000 single-spaced pages of text. dBASE offers many features for managing memo fields, including the dBASE IV *editor,* which provides tools for creating, changing, and formatting the text in a memo field.

GETTING STARTED

In this chapter we'll create a new catalog and database to demonstrate techniques for managing memo fields. The database will list references to journal articles and include an abstract of each article. Because most of the techniques you use in this chapter will be the same as those you've used in previous chapters, this chapter won't present step-by-step instructions for every object you create. If you need help with specific techniques in this chapter, refer to the appropriate chapter in this book.

To create a new catalog named RESEARCH, go to the Control Center and follow these steps:

1. Select Catalog ► Use a Different Catalog.
2. Select <create> from the submenu.
3. When prompted, type the catalog name **RESEARCH** and press ↵.

You should see the Control Center, with all the panels empty, and the name of the RESEARCH.CAT catalog centered near the top of the screen.

THE DATABASE STRUCTURE

To create a database structure for storing references, use the usual steps: select <create> from the Data panel of the Control Center and fill in field names and other information in the usual manner. Figure 10.1 shows the database structure that we'll use in this chapter. Note that the field named ABSTRACT is the memo data type. dBASE automatically assigns a width of 10 characters to the field. But don't worry; you can still enter thousands of pages of text in the memo field, as you'll soon see.

Layout Organize Append Go To Exit 11:51:54 am

Bytes remaining: 3732

Num	Field Name	Field Type	Width	Dec	Index
1	AUTHORS	Character	40		Y
2	TITLE	Character	65		N
3	JOURNAL	Character	65		N
4	VOLUME	Numeric	3	0	N
5	NUMBER	Numeric	3	0	N
6	DATE	Date	8		Y
7	PAGES	Character	9		N
8	KEYWORDS	Character	65		N
9	ABSTRACT	Memo	10		N

Database C:\dbase\REFERENC Field 9/9

Enter the field name. Insert/Delete field:Ctrl-N/Ctrl-U

Field names begin with a letter and may contain letters, digits and underscores

Figure 10.1: Database structure with a memo field

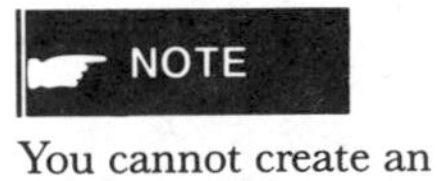

You cannot create an index of a memo field.

Also, as you can see in the figure, the AUTHORS and DATE fields are marked Y for indexing, so that you can easily display references in alphabetical order by name or in date order.

After you've created the database structure, choose Layout ► Edit Database Description and enter the description **References to journal articles**. Then choose Exit ► Save Changes and Exit. When prompted, type REFERENC as the file name and then press ↵. You'll be returned to the Control Center.

ENTERING DATA INTO MEMO FIELDS

To add or change memo field data, you first use the usual techniques for entering or changing database records. That is, make sure that REFERENC is highlighted in the Data panel and then press or click Data (F2). You'll notice that the memo field appears as a highlight with the word *memo* inside it. The word *memo* is used as a *marker* to remind you that this field can actually contain a much larger memo. Go ahead now and type the sample reference shown in Figure 10.2.

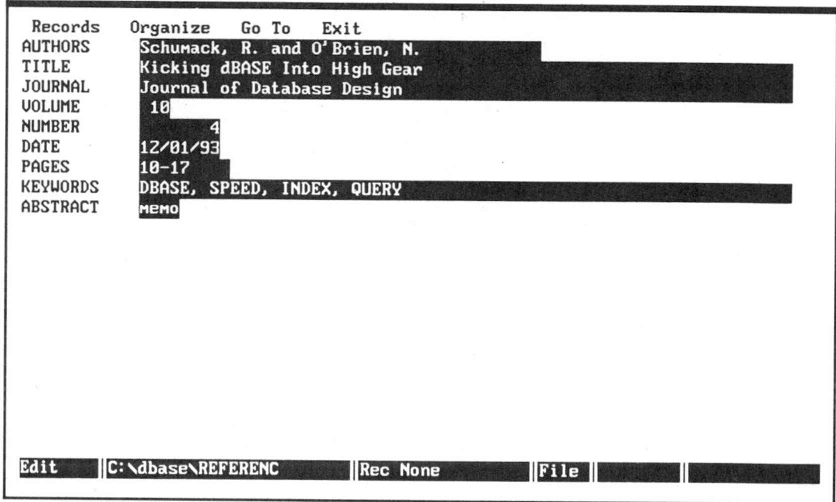

Figure 10.2: Partially completed reference

You can use any one of four techniques to enter text into the memo field:

- Move the cursor to the memo marker and press Ctrl-Home.
- Move the cursor to the memo marker and press Zoom (F9).
- Double-click the mouse on the memo marker.
- If the cursor is in the field directly above the memo field, pressing Next (F4) moves the cursor into the memo field, automatically preparing the screen for data to be added or modified.

If the cursor is in the field beneath the memo field, pressing Previous (F3) automatically takes you to the memo field editor.

In this example, the cursor is already in the memo field, so press Ctrl-Home. You'll be taken to the memo field editor, where you can enter your text.

USING THE MEMO FIELD EDITOR

The memo field editor is virtually identical to the word-wrap editor that you used in the reports design screen to create a form letter. Like a word processor, the memo field editor automatically *word wraps* long sentences into paragraphs, so that if you change something in a paragraph, the entire paragraph is reformatted automatically.

 TIP

Many of the alternative keystrokes shown in Table 10.1 are available in other dBASE editing modes as well. If you prefer the alternative keystrokes, feel free to try them at any time.

Most of the editing keys used with the memo field editor are identical to the editing keys you've already used to design reports and custom forms. These keys are listed in Table 10.1. Note that many operations provide alternative keystrokes. For example, to move the cursor right one space, you can press either → or Ctrl-D. The alternative keystrokes are identical to those in some popular word processing programs, such as WordStar. They are provided for dBASE IV users who are already familiar with such programs. You can also click the mouse to position the cursor anywhere within the memo field.

Table 10.1: Editing Keys Used in the Memo Field Editor

Keys	Alternative	Action
→	Ctrl-D	Moves cursor right one character
←	Ctrl-S	Moves cursor left one character
↓	Ctrl-X	Moves cursor down one line
↑	Ctrl-E	Moves cursor up one line
Ins	Ctrl-V	Toggles between Insert and Overwrite modes; when Insert mode is on, cursor appears as a blinking square, and when

Table 10.1: Editing Keys Used in the Memo Field Editor (continued)

Keys	Alternative	Action
		Insert mode is off, cursor appears as a blinking underline
Del	Ctrl-G	Deletes character at cursor
Ctrl-T		Deletes word to the right of the cursor
Ctrl-Backspace		Deletes word to the left of the cursor
Ctrl-Y		Deletes entire line
Backspace	Ctrl-H	Moves cursor left one character and erases along the way
↵	Ctrl-M	Marks end of a paragraph; adds a new blank line if Insert mode is on
Ctrl-N		Inserts a blank line, regardless of whether Insert mode is on
Home	Ctrl-Z	Moves cursor to beginning of line
End	Ctrl-B	Moves cursor to end of line
Ctrl-→	Ctrl-F	Moves cursor to beginning of next word
Ctrl-←	Ctrl-A	Moves cursor to beginning of previous word
PgDn	Ctrl-C	Scrolls down one screen or to bottom of existing text on the current page
PgUp	Ctrl-R	Scrolls up one screen or to top of existing text on the current page
Tab	Ctrl-I	Moves cursor to next tab stop
Shift-Tab		Moves cursor to previous tab stop
Ctrl-End	Ctrl-W	Saves changes and exits
Escape	Ctrl-Q	Abandons changes and exits

The top of the editor screen displays a menu bar and a ruler (see Figure 10.3). Within the ruler, the left bracket ([) shows the left margin, and the right bracket (]) shows the right margin. By default, the left margin is set at 0 and the right margin is set at 65, about the right width for printing on $8\frac{1}{2}$-by-11 inch paper with proper margins. The triangles show tab stops, which are used for indenting and outdenting memo field paragraphs.

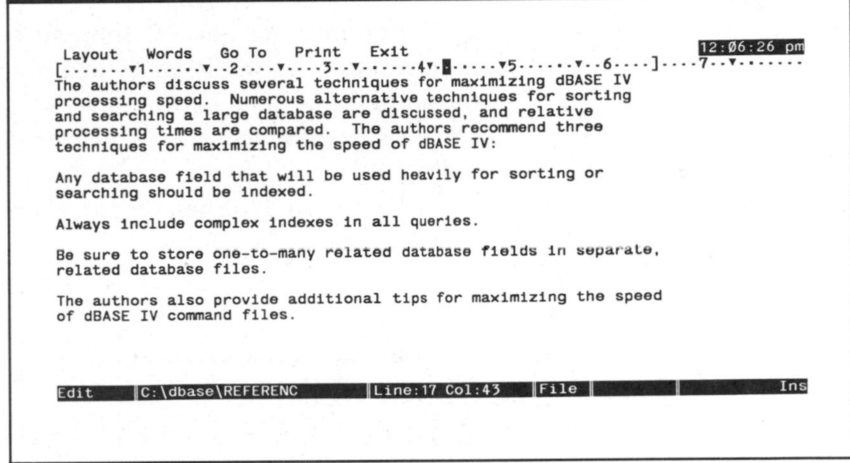

Layout Words Go To Print Exit
12:06:26 pm
The authors discuss several techniques for maximizing dBASE IV
processing speed. Numerous alternative techniques for sorting
and searching a large database are discussed, and relative
processing times are compared. The authors recommend three
techniques for maximizing the speed of dBASE IV:
Any database field that will be used heavily for sorting or
searching should be indexed.
Always include complex indexes in all queries.
Be sure to store one-to-many related database fields in separate,
related database files.
The authors also provide additional tips for maximizing the speed
of dBASE IV command files.
Edit
C:\dbase\REFERENC
Line:17 Col:43
File
Ins

Figure 10.3: Paragraph typed into a memo field

ENTERING PARAGRAPHS

When you type paragraphs of text into a memo field, the main point to keep in mind is that you do not press ↵ until you get to the end of a paragraph; unlike a conventional typewriter, dBASE automatically word wraps text within a paragraph when you attempt to type past the right margin. To enter the memo field text, type the first paragraph shown in Figure 10.3 without pressing ↵ until you get to the colon (:) at the end of the paragraph.

After you've finished typing the first paragraph, press ↵ twice before typing in the next two lines of text. Type the entire memo as shown in Figure 10.3, pressing ↵ twice at the end of each paragraph (wherever you see a blank line in the figure).

SAVING A MEMO FIELD

After you've finished entering your memo field, you can use either of the following techniques to save your work and return to the edit screen:

- Choose Exit ► Save Changes and Exit.
- Press Ctrl-End.

When you get back to the edit screen, you'll notice that the marker in the ABSTRACT field now reads "MEMO." When a memo field contains information, its marker is shown in uppercase letters, so you can tell when a memo field contains data without going to the editor.

After entering the first record, choose Exit ► Exit to return to the Control Center.

USING MEMO FIELDS IN CUSTOM FORMS

The standard edit and browse screens always indicate memo fields with markers. When you create your own custom forms, you can display memo fields as markers (as on the standard edit and browse screens), or you can display parts of memo fields in a *memo window*. The window technique is very handy because it lets you see at least a portion of the memo field while still viewing other fields in the database.

Figure 10.4 shows the first record in the REFERENC database displayed in a custom form, with the memo field displayed in a memo window. The memo window in this example shows the first few lines of the Abstract field. When you create your own custom forms with memo windows, you can make the memo window any size you wish.

To create a custom form with a memo window, start with the usual steps for creating a custom form. That is, make sure the appropriate database file is in use and then select <create> from the Forms panel. When you get to the forms design screen, choose Layout ► Quick Layout. Then you can use the techniques discussed in

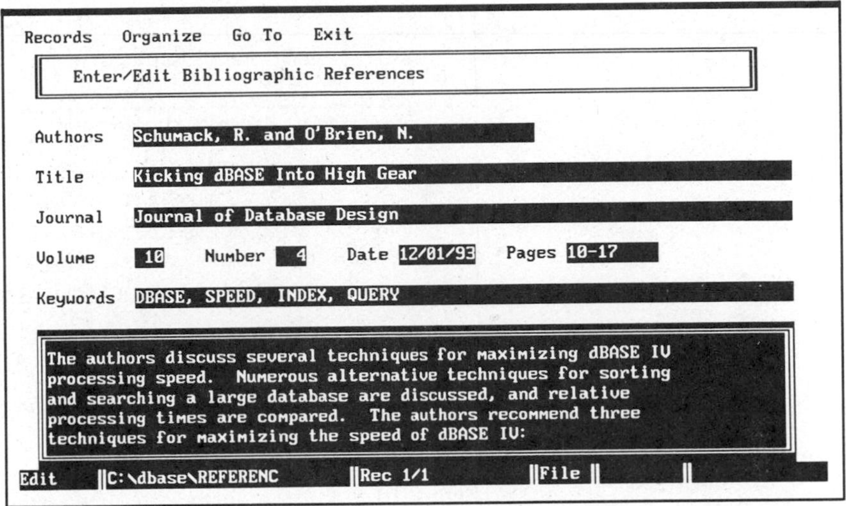
Records Organize Go To Exit
Enter/Edit Bibliographic References
Authors Schumack, R. and O'Brien, N.
Title Kicking dBASE Into High Gear
Journal Journal of Database Design
Volume 10 Number 4 Date 12/01/93 Pages 10-17
Keywords DBASE, SPEED, INDEX, QUERY
The authors discuss several techniques for maximizing dBASE IV
processing speed. Numerous alternative techniques for sorting
and searching a large database are discussed, and relative
processing times are compared. The authors recommend three
techniques for maximizing the speed of dBASE IV:
Edit C:\dbase\REFERENC Rec 1/1 File

Figure 10.4: A memo field displayed in a memo window

Chapter 8 to add, change, move, and copy field templates and text on the screen.

Initially, the memo field will be displayed as a marker on the custom form. If left as such, only the marker "memo" or "MEMO" will be displayed on your custom form (exactly as on the standard browse and edit screens). If you want to change the marker to a memo window, first rearrange all other fields on the form, leaving enough space to accommodate the memo window. For example, Figure 10.5 shows the current form with fields rearranged, a title added, and some blank space near the bottom where the memo field will be placed.

BUILDING A MEMO WINDOW

To create a memo window, you first change the memo field display format from Marker to Window and select a border for the window. Then you press or click Size (Shift-F7) and Move (F7) to size and move the window into position. Using the form in Figure 10.5 as a starting point, follow these steps to create a memo window:

1. Move the cursor to inside the memo field template (so that the cursor is on the first M in MEMO).

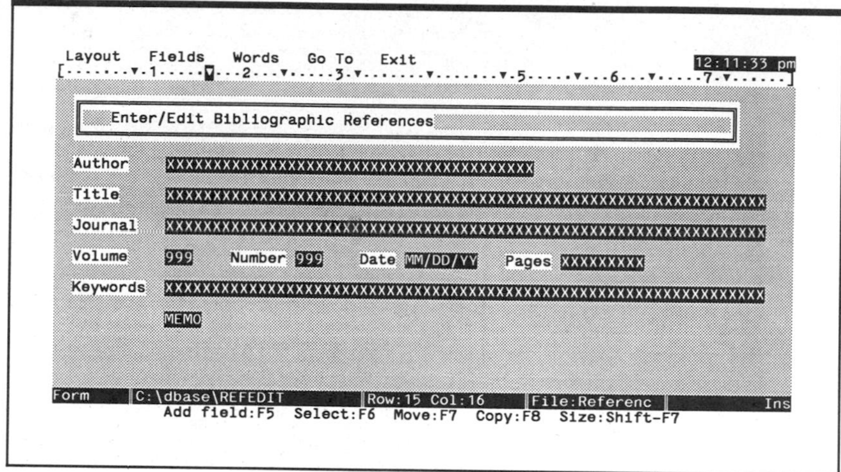

Figure 10.5: Custom form with memo field displayed as a marker

2. Press or click Add Field (F5) or double-click the memo field template.
3. Highlight the Display As option in the menu and press the space bar (or click that option) to change the setting to Window.
4. Select Border Lines.
5. Select any border type you wish (this example uses Double Line).
6. Press or click Accept (Ctrl-End) to leave the submenu.

When you return to the design screen, a large memo field window filled with X's will appear on the forms design screen.

Now you need to size and position the window. Here are the steps for this example:

1. Move the cursor to any position inside the memo window (or click the mouse inside that window).
2. Press or click Move (F7) and move the cursor to row 15, column 2 (as indicated in the center of the status bar near the bottom of the screen).
3. Press ↵ or click the mouse to complete the move.

4. Press or click Size (Shift-F7).
5. Use the ↑ and → keys (or move the mouse) to move the lower-right corner of the memo window to row 21, column 76.
6. Press ↵ or click the mouse to finish sizing the window.

After moving and sizing the memo window, press ↑ (or PgUp) as necessary to get back to the top of the screen. Figure 10.6 shows the memo window on the forms design screen. The window actually extends down to row 21, but you cannot see the bottom of the window in the figure because it is partially obscured by the status bar and navigation line of the design screen.

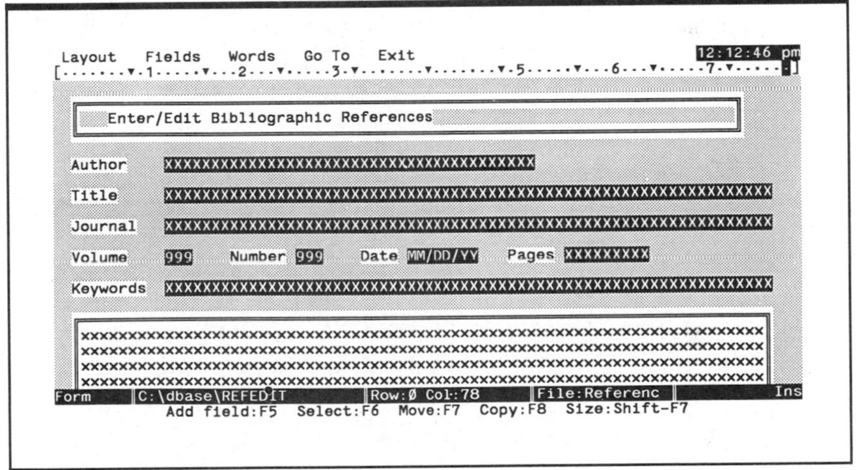

Figure 10.6: Memo window on the forms design screen

After placing the memo window, save the form by choosing Exit ► Save Changes and Exit. When prompted, assign a valid name to the form, such as **RefEdit**.

USING THE MEMO WINDOW

Now that you've created and saved the custom form, you can use it in the usual manner. That is, you can highlight its name in the Forms panel of the Control Center and press ↵, or double-click its name. Then select Display Data. You can edit existing records, or you can choose Records ► Add New Records to add new records.

To add or change the data in the memo window, move the cursor into the window and press Ctrl-Home or Zoom (F9), or double-click in the window, just as you would when a marker is displayed. To expand the memo window to full screen, press Zoom (F9). After making your changes, press Ctrl-End. You'll be returned to the custom form.

DISPLAYING MEMOS IN REPORTS

You can place memo fields in report formats just as you can any other database field. By default, the memo field will be displayed in a template 50 characters wide, using the Vertical Stretch picture function so that all text is word-wrapped within the allotted width.

To create a sample report, make sure that the REFERENC database is in use and then select <create> from the Reports panel. When you get to the reports design screen, choose Layout ► Quick Layouts ► Form Layout. Then use the usual keys and techniques to format the report.

Figure 10.7 shows a sample report format, which was initially created by choosing Layout ► Quick Layouts ► Form Layout. The usual editing keys and techniques were used to change text and to arrange the field templates. Notice that the Abstract field template is displayed as a series of 50 V's.

You cannot change the template assigned to a memo field. However, you can widen or narrow the memo field. To do so, move the cursor into the field template (or click on that template) and then press or click Size (Shift-F7). Use the ← or → key or your mouse to narrow or widen the template and then press ↵ or click the mouse when you are done. Later, when you print the report, all text in the memo field will be word-wrapped within the width of the field template on the report.

Because the Abstract field uses the Vertical Stretch picture function automatically (regardless of its setting), the text within the margin will extend downward when the report is printed. Remember to place at least one blank line beneath the memo field template in the Detail band if you want to print a blank line at the bottom of the memo field.

Figure 10.8 shows a single record printed from the sample report format. Note that the text in the memo field is word-wrapped within the default width of 50 characters.

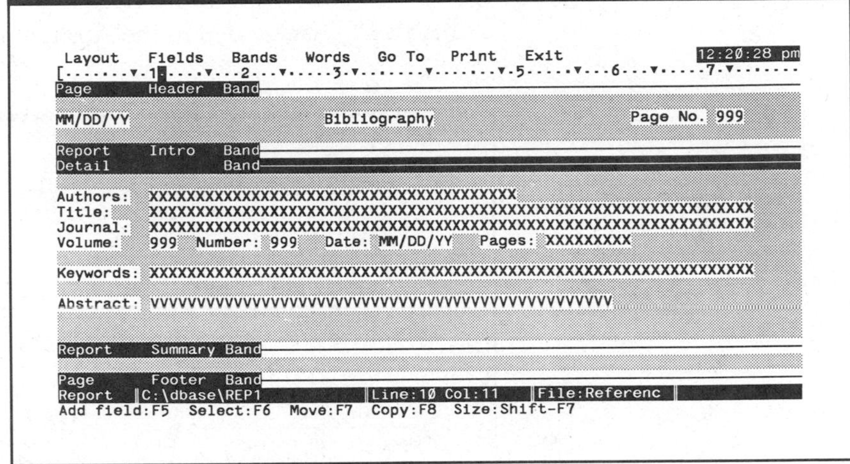

Figure 10.7: Sample report format with a memo field

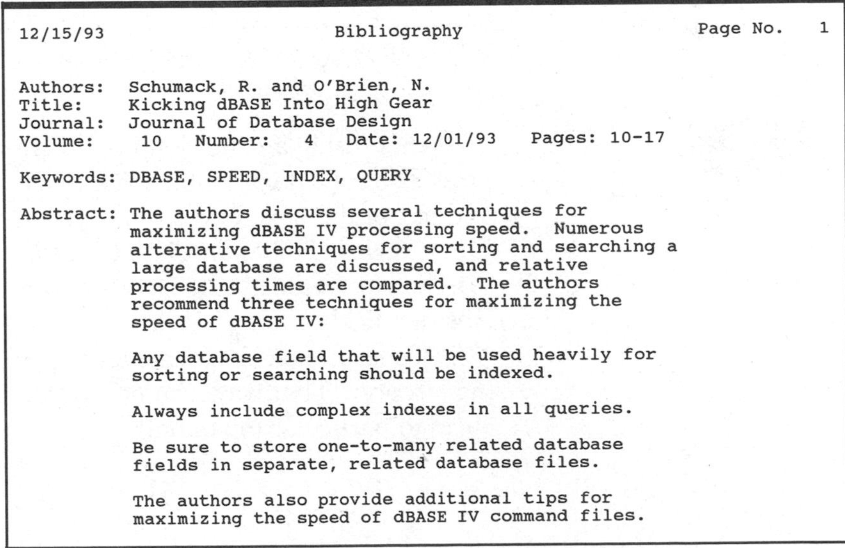

```
12/15/93                    Bibliography                    Page No.    1

Authors:  Schumack, R. and O'Brien, N.
Title:    Kicking dBASE Into High Gear
Journal:  Journal of Database Design
Volume:    10   Number:    4   Date: 12/01/93    Pages: 10-17

Keywords: DBASE, SPEED, INDEX, QUERY

Abstract: The authors discuss several techniques for
          maximizing dBASE IV processing speed.  Numerous
          alternative techniques for sorting and searching a
          large database are discussed, and relative
          processing times are compared.  The authors
          recommend three techniques for maximizing the
          speed of dBASE IV:

          Any database field that will be used heavily for
          sorting or searching should be indexed.

          Always include complex indexes in all queries.

          Be sure to store one-to-many related database
          fields in separate, related database files.

          The authors also provide additional tips for
          maximizing the speed of dBASE IV command files.
```

Figure 10.8: A printed record from the REFERENC database

QUERYING MEMO FIELDS

In the queries design screen, you can use the $ (embedded in) operator in a condition box to isolate records that have a particular word or group of words in the memo field. For example, Figure 10.9 shows a query that will search the REFERENC database for records with "dBASE IV" embedded in the Abstract field.

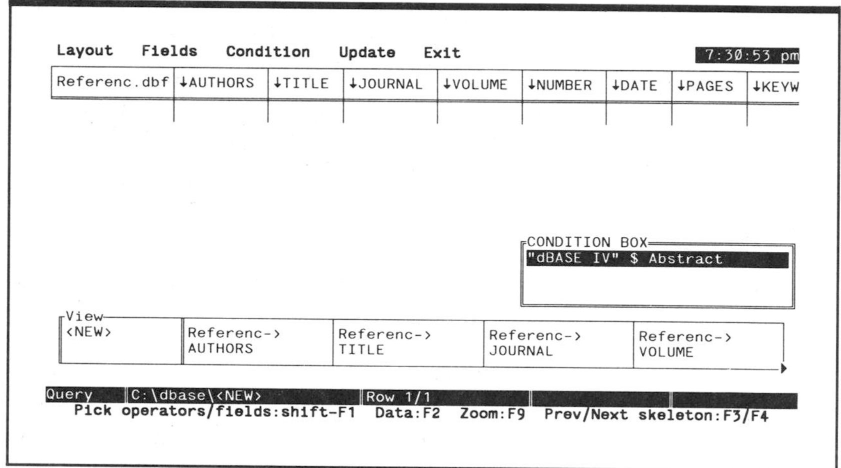

Figure 10.9: Query for records with "dBASE IV" in the Abstract field

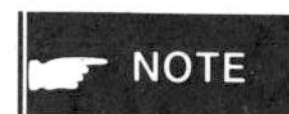

To create a condition box in the query design screen, choose Condition ► add Condition Box.

When using a condition box to create filter conditions, you can press Zoom (F9) or double-click in the condition box to zoom into and out of the box. Use .AND. and .OR. operators for AND and OR queries. For example, the filter condition in Figure 10.10 searches for records that have dBASE IV in the Keywords or the Abstract field.

Of course, you can create any query, save it, and use it for printing a report. That way, you can create bibliographies that list references to particular topics only.

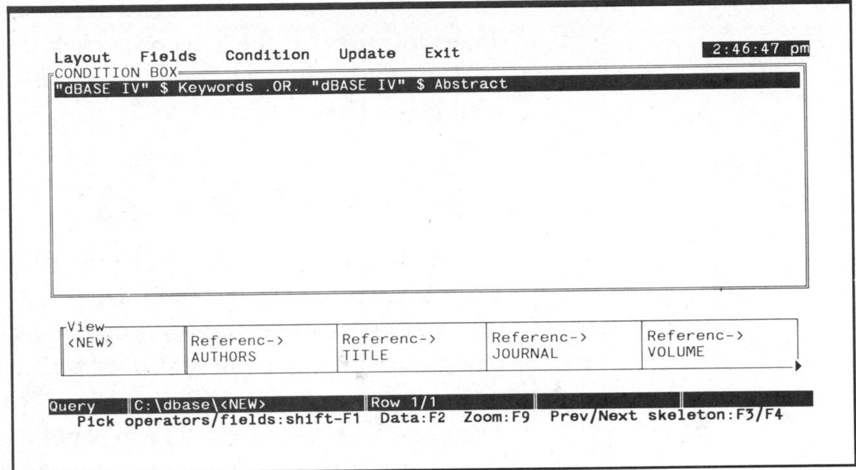

Figure 10.10: A complex query involving a memo field

MANAGING MEMO FIELD TEXT

You can use many techniques within the word-wrap editor to polish the format of your memo field data. This section discusses these techniques.

MOVING, COPYING, AND DELETING BLOCKS OF TEXT

To deselect a block of selected text, press Esc. The highlighting will disappear and you can then select a different block of text.

To move, copy, or delete a block of text, you must first select a block using the Select (F6) key. Position the cursor at the first character of the block you wish to select and press Select. Then use the arrow keys to extend the selection (the selected text will be highlighted). As an alternative to pressing an arrow key, you can press F6 a second time to select a word, or press F6 a third time to select an entire paragraph. Press ⟵ after highlighting the entire block of text. You can also use your mouse to select a block of text. Simply position the mouse pointer over the first character you want to select, then click the mouse button and drag to highlight the last character. After highlighting the text you want to select, release the mouse button.

To move or copy the selected block of text, move the cursor to the new location on the screen or click the mouse at the new location. Then press Move (F7) or Copy (F8). To delete the selected block, press the Del key.

FORCING PAGE BREAKS

When you print memo fields, dBASE will automatically start a new page when the current page is filled. If you prefer, you can force a page break to occur at a specific place in a memo field. To do so, position the cursor where you want a new page to begin. Then choose Words ► Insert Page Break. You'll see a dashed line across the screen where the new page will begin when the memo field is printed.

If you change your mind about the page break and want to delete it, just move the cursor to the dashed line and press Del.

COPYING TEXT FROM ONE MEMO FIELD TO ANOTHER

Suppose you want to use the text in one memo field in the memo field of another record. To do so, you need to copy the text from the source (original) memo field to a disk file. Then you need to move into the memo field of the target record (the one that is receiving the copy) and read in the file. Here are the basic steps:

1. Display the source record (the one that contains the memo field that you want to copy) on the edit screen.
2. Move the cursor to the memo field and press Ctrl-Home (or double-click the mouse in the field) to get to the editor.
3. Use the Select key (F6) or the mouse to highlight the block of text you want to copy (or all the text in the memo field, if you prefer).
4. Choose Words ► Write/Read Text File.
5. Select Write Selection to File from the submenu.
6. When prompted, enter a valid DOS file name (for example, you could enter **MEMCOPY**) but no extension. Then press ↵.

7. Press Ctrl-End to return to the edit screen.
8. Display the target record (the one you want to copy the text into) on the edit screen (or choose Records ► Add New Records to add a new record).
9. Move the cursor to the memo field of the target record and press Ctrl-Home (or double-click the mouse in the memo field of the target record).
10. Position the cursor where you want the incoming text to appear.
11. Choose Words ► Write/Read Text File.
12. Select Read Text from File from the submenu.
13. When prompted, enter the name of the file in which you stored the text (MEMCOPY, in this example), or press or click Available Files (Shift-F1) to see all file names with the .TXT extension and select a file from that list.
14. Press Ctrl-End to save the copied text.

Note that if you write the memo field text to a file that already exists, dBASE will beep and warn you that you are about to overwrite an existing file. If you are going to be copying memo field text often, you might want to reserve a special file name (MEMCOPY, for example) just for copying memo fields (dBASE automatically adds the extension .TXT to the file name you provide). That way, when dBASE warns that you are about to overwrite a file with the same name, you'll know that the existing file is the MEMCOPY file you created during the previous copy operation and can be safely overwritten.

FORMATTING PARAGRAPHS

You can indent a paragraph in a memo field by moving the cursor to the first character of the paragraph and pressing the Tab key. Each time you press the Tab key, the entire paragraph is indented by one tab stop. Pressing Shift-Tab has the opposite effect; it outdents the paragraph by one tab stop.

SOME TECHNICAL ASPECTS OF MEMO FIELDS

While you are using a database that contains a memo field, it will appear that you are working with a single database file, and that the memo field is just another field. But the actual events that are taking place behind the scenes are a little different than they look on the screen.

For instance, the contents of memo fields are not actually stored in the database file. Instead, they are stored in a separate file that has the same name as the database file, but the extension .DBT. For example, in this chapter, the file REFERENC.DBF holds all the fields except the memo field; the file REFERENC.DBT holds only the memo field.

The ABSTRACT field in the REFERENC.DBF database file contains a *pointer,* a special code that tells dBASE the location of the appropriate memo field in the separate .DBT file. The reason that memo fields are always assigned a width of 10 characters when you design a database is that this pointer occupies 10 characters in the record.

None of this information is particularly important to know unless you use commands outside of dBASE to copy, rename, or delete files. For example, if you were to use the DOS command **COPY REFERENC.DBF REFBAK.DBF** to copy the REFERENC.DBF database to a file called REFBAK.DBF, DOS would not automatically copy the REFERENC.DBT file in the process.

If you later tried to use REFBAK.DBF through dBASE, an error message would appear telling you that dBASE could not find the memo file and asking whether you want to create a new, empty memo file. In other words, dBASE is telling you that REFBAK.DBF has a memo field in it, but there is no file named REFBAK.DBT that contains the memos.

To avoid such errors, either use dBASE IV to copy, rename, and delete all files, or use the extension .DB? rather than .DBF when copying dBASE files in DOS. For example, entering the DOS command **COPY REFERENC.DB? REFBAK.DB?** automatically copies REFERENC.DBF and REFERENC.DBT to two files named REFBAK.DBF and REFBAK.DBT. See Chapter 14 for more information about managing files.

CHAPTER 11

Managing Groups of Records

To mark a record for deletion, 372
move the cursor to the appropriate record and press Ctrl-U or choose Records ► Mark Record for Deletion.

To temporarily delete, or *hide*, records marked for deletion, 373
choose Tools ► Settings in the Control Center and set the Deleted option to On.

To unmark records that are marked for deletion, 375
first set Deleted to Off. Then return to the browse or edit screen, position the cursor in the marked record, and press Ctrl-U or choose Records ► Clear Deletion Mark.

To permanently delete marked records from the database, 375
choose Organize ► Erase Marked Records on the database design, brouse, or edit screen.

To make a change to all records that meet a filter condition, 378

1. Create a query with the appropriate filter conditions.
2. Enter the word **REPLACE** beneath the file name in the file skeleton.
3. Enter the word **WITH** and the value or expression defining the replacement in the field that contains the values to be replaced.
4. Choose Update ► Perform the Update.

To mark all records that meet some filter condition, 386
set up the appropriate filter condition in a query and enter the word **MARK** beneath the file name in the file skeleton.

To unmark records that meet some filter condition, 386
set up the appropriate filter condition in a query and enter the word **UNMARK** beneath the file name in the file skeleton.

To unmark all records in a database, 387
choose Organize ► Unmark All Records from the database design, browse, or edit screen.

IN MANAGING YOUR DATABASE, YOU MAY SOMETIMES times want to perform an operation on an entire group of records. For example, you might want to raise the unit price of part B-222 by 10 percent in all records that contain this part number. This chapter discusses techniques for performing such tasks, as well as general techniques for hiding and deleting records and customizing the browse screen.

Once again, we'll use the database files in the LEARN catalog for demonstrations. If the LEARN catalog is not currently in the Control Center on your screen, choose Catalog ► Use a Different Catalog then select LEARN.CAT from the submenu that appears.

DELETING DATABASE RECORDS

There are two techniques for deleting database records. The first is to *mark* a record for deletion. This does not actually remove the record from the database, but instead allows you to hide, or temporarily delete, the record. You can bring marked records out of hiding and unmark them at any time.

The second method for deleting records is often called *packing*. Packing a database permanently removes from the database all records currently marked for deletion. Any records beneath a deleted record move up a notch to fill the void left by the deleted record (hence the term *packing*). There is no way to recover deleted records once you've packed the database.

MARKING RECORDS FOR DELETION

Whether you are using the edit or browse screen or a custom form, you use the same techniques to mark a record for deletion. First, use the usual arrow, PgUp, and PgDn keys, or the mouse, to move the cursor to the record you want to mark. Then use one of the following ways to mark the record:

- Choose Records ► Mark Record for Deletion.
- Press Ctrl-U.

Suppose Wilbur Watson has not placed an order in many months and you decide to delete him from the CUSTLIST database. Move to his record on the browse screen and type Ctrl-U to mark his record for deletion. The only indication that the record has been marked is the word "Del" in the status bar at the bottom of the screen. Figure 11.1 shows Wilbur Watson's record marked for deletion on the browse screen.

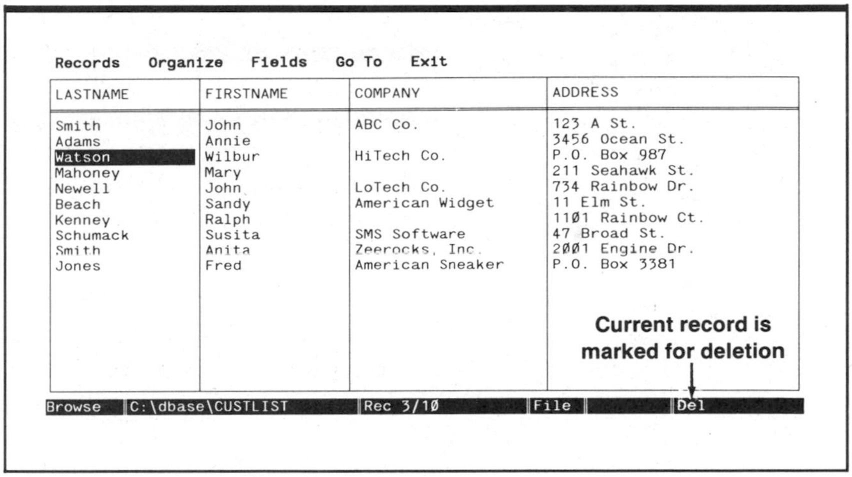

Records Organize Fields Go To Exit

LASTNAME	FIRSTNAME	COMPANY	ADDRESS
Smith	John	ABC Co.	123 A St.
Adams	Annie		3456 Ocean St.
Watson	Wilbur	HiTech Co.	P.O. Box 987
Mahoney	Mary		211 Seahawk St.
Newell	John	LoTech Co.	734 Rainbow Dr.
Beach	Sandy	American Widget	11 Elm St.
Kenney	Ralph		1101 Rainbow Ct.
Schumack	Susita	SMS Software	47 Broad St.
Smith	Anita	Zeerocks, Inc.	2001 Engine Dr.
Jones	Fred	American Sneaker	P.O. Box 3381

Current record is marked for deletion

Browse | C:\dbase\CUSTLIST | Rec 3/10 | File | Del

Figure 11.1: Watson's record marked for deletion

HIDING MARKED RECORDS

You can hide marked records without permanently deleting them. First you need to choose Exit ► Exit to return to the Control Center. At the Control Center, follow these steps:

1. Choose Tools ► Settings.
2. Highlight the Deleted option and press the space bar to change the option from Off to On (or click twice on that option with your mouse), as in Figure 11.2.
3. Choose Exit ► Exit to Control Center.

If you now highlight CUSTLIST in the data panel and press or click Data (F2) to view its records, you'll see that Wilbur Watson's

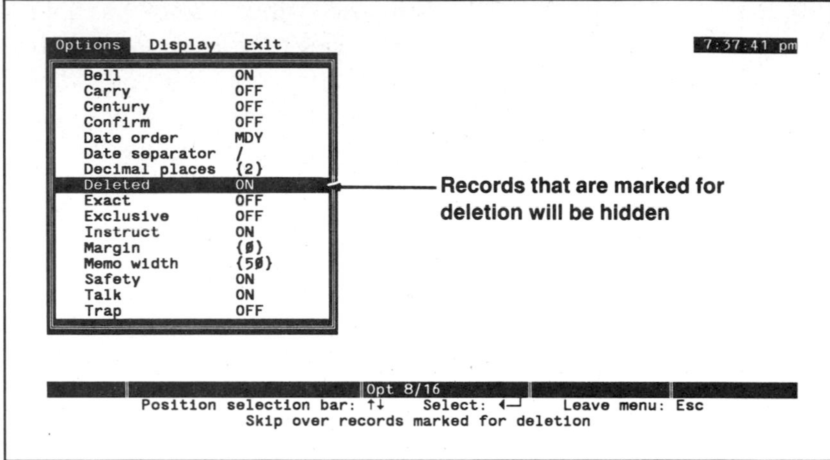

Figure 11.2: Deleted option set to On

record no longer appears, as Figure 11.3 shows. If you use the ↓ key to scroll through records, you might notice that the Rec indicator skips from 2 to 4 when you scroll from Adams to Mahoney. That's because Wilbur's record (number 3) still exists; it's just hidden for the time being.

Records Organize Fields Go To Exit

LASTNAME	FIRSTNAME	COMPANY	ADDRESS
Smith	John	ABC Co.	123 A St.
Adams	Annie		3456 Ocean St.
Mahoney	Mary		211 Seahawk St.
Newell	John	LoTech Co.	734 Rainbow Dr.
Beach	Sandy	American Widget	11 Elm St.
Kenney	Ralph		1101 Rainbow Ct.
Schumack	Susita	SMS Software	47 Broad St.
Smith	Anita	Zeerocks, Inc.	2001 Engine Dr.
Jones	Fred	American Sneaker	P.O. Box 3381

Browse C:\dbase\CUSTLIST Rec 4/10 File

Figure 11.3: Marked record hidden from view

BRINGING MARKED RECORDS OUT OF HIDING

WARNING

When the Deleted option is On, marked records are excluded from *all* dBASE operations, as though the records do not exist. Always remember to set the Deleted option to Off when you no longer need to hide marked records.

To bring marked records out of hiding, return to the Control Center and follow the same steps that you followed to hide the records, but change the Deleted setting from On back to Off. If you do so and then return to the browse screen, you'll see Wilbur's record once again. In addition, if you move the cursor to his record, you'll see that it is still marked for deletion.

UNMARKING RECORDS

To remove the mark for deletion from a record, first make sure that the Deleted option is set to Off (otherwise, you won't be able to see the marked record that you are trying to unmark). Then move the cursor to the record that you want to unmark and use one of these techniques:

NOTE

The Clear Deletion Mark option appears on the Records pull-down menu *only* if the current record is already marked for deletion. Otherwise, the option reads Mark Record for Deletion.

- Choose Records ► Clear Deletion Mark.
- Press Ctrl-U.

Notice that Ctrl-U acts as a toggle. That is, each time you press Ctrl-U, the current record's status changes from marked to unmarked. You'll see the Del indicator in the status bar appear or disappear each time you press Ctrl-U. For now, leave Wilbur's record marked for deletion.

ERASING MARKED RECORDS

Because packing the database permanently removes all marked records from the database, use this option with a good deal of caution. A good approach is to isolate all marked records and look at them on the browse screen before you pack the database. Use Ctrl-U or the Clear Deletion Mark option to unmark any records that you do not want permanently removed; *then* pack the database.

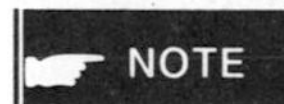
NOTE

Chapter 12 discusses dBASE functions in detail.

To isolate the records that are marked for deletion, you use a query, but place the filter condition in the condition box rather than in a specific field. (The condition box is like any other box on the query design screen, except that it takes into consideration the record as a whole, rather than a specific field.) Then place the dBASE function DELETED( ) in the condition box, which isolates records that are marked for deletion. Here are the steps:

1. Assuming that CUSTLIST is currently on the browse screen, mark both Watson and Kenney's records for deletion.
2. Return to the Control Center by choosing Exit ► Exit (or by pressing Ctrl-End).
3. Select <create> from the Queries panel.
4. Choose Condition ► Add Condition box.
5. Enter the function **DELETED( )** into the condition box, as in Figure 11.4.
6. Press or click Data (F2) to execute the query.

The browse screen appears, showing only those records that are marked for deletion, as in Figure 11.5. You can scroll through the records and use the Ctrl-U key or Clear Deletion Mark option to unmark any records that you do not want permanently removed.

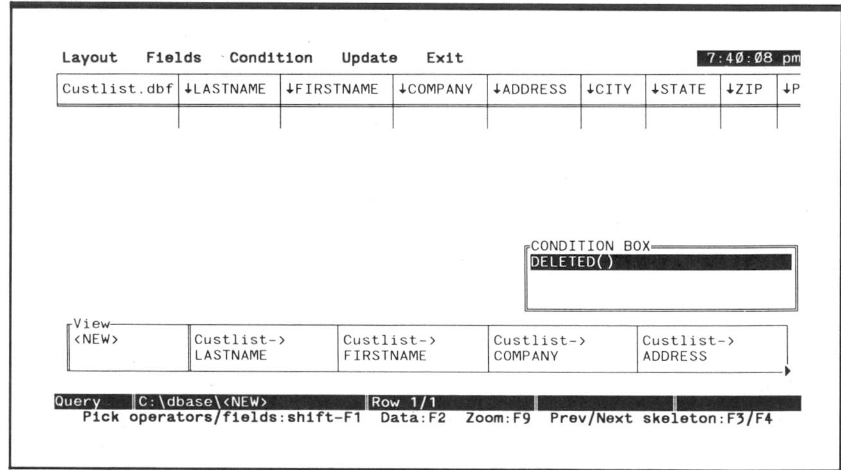

Figure 11.4: Query to isolate records marked for deletion

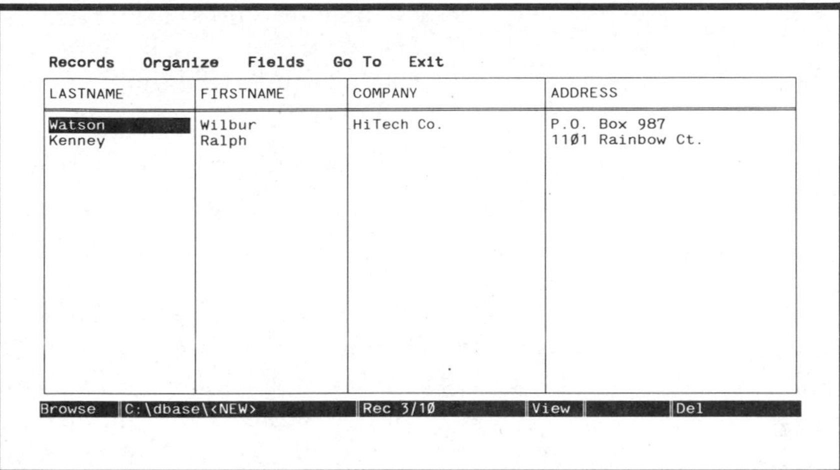

Figure 11.5: Marked records isolated on the browse screen

Note, however, that unmarking a record may not immediately remove it from the browse screen. However, the Del indicator will disappear from the status bar when you unmark a record. To be safe, you can switch back and forth from the query to the browse screen until you are certain only records that you want permanently removed are marked, as described in the following steps:

1. Move the cursor to Kenney's record and press Ctrl-U (so the Del indicator disappears).
2. Choose Exit ► Transfer to Query Design, or just press Design (Shift-F2) to return to the query design screen.
3. Execute the same query again, to double-check the marked records, by pressing or clicking Data (F2).

Now only Wilbur Watson's record should appear in the browse screen, because step 1 removed the deletion mark from Kenney's record. Assuming you want to leave Wilbur's record marked for deletion, go ahead and choose Exit ► Exit. dBASE will ask if you want to save the query that displays marked records. For now, select No to return to the Control Center.

To permanently erase all marked records from the database, you need to return to the browse/edit or database design screen and select

Erase Marked Records. Here are the steps:

1. Highlight CUSTLIST in the Data panel and press or click Data (F2).
2. Choose Organize ► Erase Marked Records.
3. When dBASE asks for confirmation, select Yes. A box will appear, indicating that the marked records are being erased.

If you view the data for the CUSTLIST database now, you'll see that Wilbur Watson's record is gone (press PgUp to view all remaining records). If you move the highlight to Mahoney's record you'll see that the record is now number 3, rather than number 4. All records following Watson's have moved up to fill the void left by the deletion. When you're done viewing the data, choose Exit ► Exit to return to the Control Center.

CHANGING SEVERAL RECORDS AT ONCE

Up to now, most of your changes to the database have involved a single record. With dBASE IV's *global editing* capability, you can extend that power to change several records simultaneously. For example, with global editing you can perform any of the following tasks in a single operation:

- Increase or decrease the unit price of all orders for part A-111 by 10 percent.
- Add or subtract 30 days from shipping dates for part number C-333.
- Mark or unmark for deletion all California residents' records.

The tool for performing global editing is the *update query.* You use the usual query design screen and filter conditions, but specify an update operator in the file skeleton. You can type the update operator directly beneath the file name in the skeleton, select it from a menu by choosing Update ► Specify Update Operation, or select it from the Expression Builder (as described in Chapter 6). The following update operators are discussed in this chapter:

REPLACE	Replaces the contents of fields that meet the filter condition with some new value
MARK	Marks for deletion those records that meet the filter condition
UNMARK	Unmarks those records that meet the filter condition

Unlike other queries, where you press Data (F2) to see the results, update queries require you to choose Update ► Perform the Update on the query design screen. Let's look at some examples using the ORDERS and CUSTLIST databases from the LEARN catalog.

REPLACING CHARACTER DATA

Suppose that product number B-222, Banana Man, is not doing well in the marketplace, and a corporate decision is made to change the product's name to Mondo Man. Your job is to change all references to Banana Man in the ORDERS database to Mondo Man. To change all the records without retyping them, follow these steps:

1. Open the Orders database by selecting ORDERS from the Data panel in the Control Center and Use File from the submenu.
2. Go to the query design screen by selecting <create> from the Queries panel in the Control Center.
3. To limit the update operation to part number B-222, enter the filter condition **"B-222"** (including the quotation marks) under the PARTNO field name in the file skeleton, as in Figure 11.6.
4. Press or click Data (F2) just to make sure you've isolated the appropriate records.

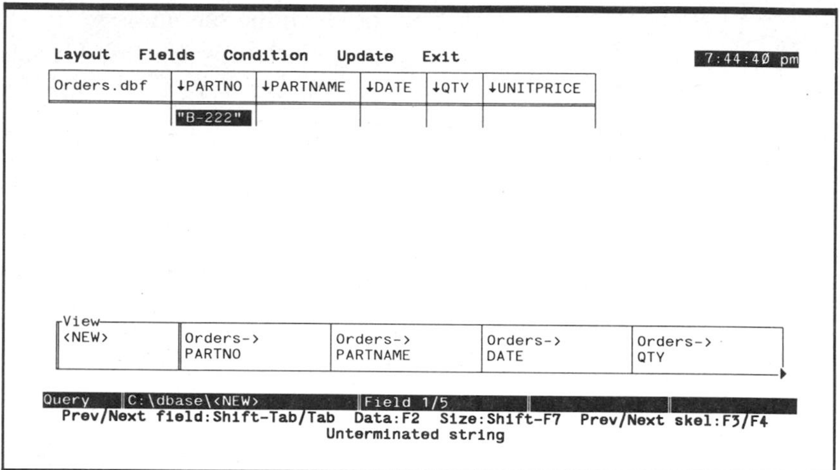

Figure 11.6: Filter condition for part number B-222

The browse screen should show only records with part number B-222 in the PARTNO field in the browse screen. This step may seem superfluous to you, since you already know that putting **"B-222"** under PARTNO in the query design screen will produce this result. However, when performing update queries, it's a good idea always to enter your filter condition first and test it by pressing or clicking Data (F2).

If you do not perform this step to test your filter condition, you might inadvertently change the wrong records. For example, suppose you created an update query to change part names to Mondo Man and simply forgot to include the filter condition that would limit changes to records with part number B-222. dBASE would not filter out other part numbers from the query. Hence, the update query would change *all* part names in the database to Mondo Man, and there would be no easy way to undo the erroneous (and extensive) change.

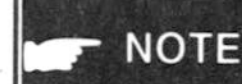

When executing update queries on your own important data, you can take the extra precaution of backing up your original database before making global changes. Chapter 14 tells you how to make backup copies.

In this example the filter condition is not too complex, so it's easy to be sure that the appropriate records are displayed. But when you start using REPLACE operators with very complex filter conditions, it's easy to make a mistake. Therefore, whenever you execute *any* update query, *always* enter the filter condition first and test that filter condition by pressing or clicking Data (F2). Scroll through the browse screen and make sure that *only* the records that you want to change are displayed.

If the appropriate records are not displayed, be sure to adjust the filter condition accordingly. Switch back to the query design screen by pressing Design (Shift-F2), modify the filter condition, and test the condition again by pressing or clicking Data (F2). Keep doing so until only the records that you want to change are displayed in the browse screen.

Assuming that your filter condition is accurate now, and only records for part number B-222 are displayed, follow these steps to change your basic query into an update query.

1. Press Design (Shift-F2) to return to the query design screen.
2. Press Shift-Tab to move the highlight to the space beneath the database name in the file, or click there with your mouse.
3. Type the update operator REPLACE and press ↵, or choose Update ► Specify Update Operation ► Replace Values in **ORDERS.DBF**. Alternatively, you can press Shift-F1 and select REPLACE from the QBE Operators column of the Expression Builder.
4. If dBASE tells you that it will delete the view skeleton, select Proceed. (You don't need the view skeleton because it is used to display data, and update queries do not *display* data, they *change* it.)
5. Move the highlight to the PARTNAME field.
6. Tell dBASE that you want to replace the current part name for product number B-222 *with* Mondo Man by typing **WITH "Mondo Man"** (including the quotation marks) in the highlighted area.
7. Press ↵.

Your query should now look like Figure 11.7. Notice that the query is actually quite descriptive. The word "Target" above the file name tells which database file is about to be changed (ORDERS.DBF in this case). The filter condition specifies records with B-222 in the PARTNO field. The update operation is to replace PARTNAME with Mondo Man (for records with B-222 in the PARTNO field).

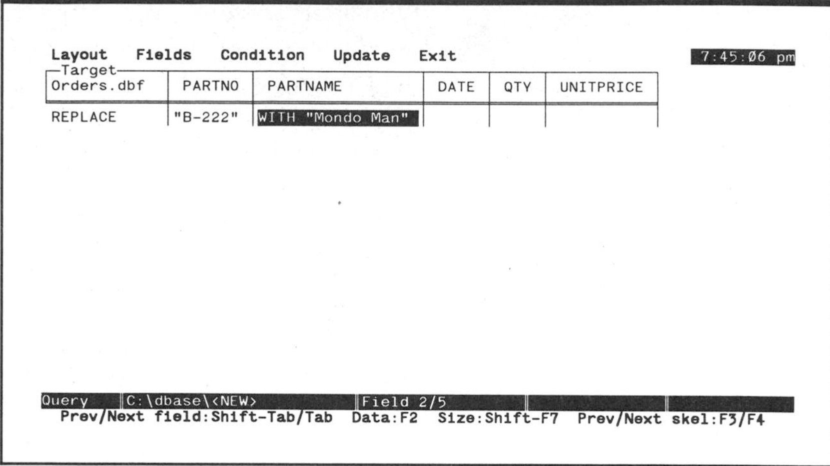

Figure 11.7: Query to replace the part number B-222 part name with Mondo Man

Now you are ready to actually execute the update query:

- Choose Update ► Perform the Update and wait a few seconds while dBASE does its work.

You may hear your computer's disk drive whirring or buzzing as dBASE makes the change. Update queries do not show any immediate results, so you need to return to the browse screen to see what happened. There is no need to save this query, because its job is done, so follow these steps:

1. When prompted, press any key to continue.
2. Choose Exit ► Abandon Changes and Exit.
3. When dBASE asks for confirmation before abandoning the query, select Yes.
4. When you get back to the Control Center, highlight ORDERS in the Data panel and press or click Data (F2).

As you'll see on the browse screen, and as Figure 11.8 shows, all part names for records with part number B-222 have been changed to Mondo Man. The change is complete and permanent. To return to the Control Center, select Exit ► Exit.

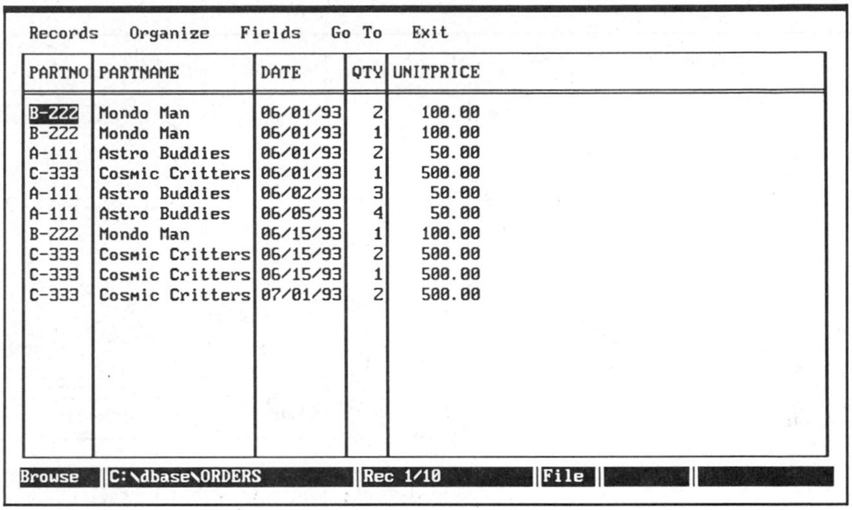

Records Organize Fields Go To Exit

PARTNO	PARTNAME	DATE	QTY	UNITPRICE
B-222	Mondo Man	06/01/93	2	100.00
B-222	Mondo Man	06/01/93	1	100.00
A-111	Astro Buddies	06/01/93	2	50.00
C-333	Cosmic Critters	06/01/93	1	500.00
A-111	Astro Buddies	06/02/93	3	50.00
A-111	Astro Buddies	06/05/93	4	50.00
B-222	Mondo Man	06/15/93	1	100.00
C-333	Cosmic Critters	06/15/93	2	500.00
C-333	Cosmic Critters	06/15/93	1	500.00
C-333	Cosmic Critters	07/01/93	2	500.00

Browse C:\dbase\ORDERS Rec 1/10 File

Figure 11.8: Banana Man changed to Mondo Man

CHANGING NUMERIC DATA

Suppose that the price of Astro Buddies (part number A-111) is increased by 10 percent on June 1, 1993. Your job is to add 10 percent to any orders for Astro Buddies that come in after June 1. To perform this task, you need to isolate records that have order dates later than 06/01/93 in the Date field *and* that have part number A-111 in the PARTNO field and then increase the UNITPRICE value by 10 percent for those records.

To begin, you need to set up the basic filter condition for the query, as in Figure 11.9. Note that the query isolates records that have A-111 in the PARTNO field and dates greater than 6/1/93 in the DATE field. Press Data (F2) to make sure that the filter conditions isolate the appropriate records. After testing the query, press Design (Shift-F2) to return to the query design screen.

Now you need to enter the REPLACE update operator under the file name in the file skeleton of the query design screen. Press Home, type the word **REPLACE**, and then press ↵. Select Proceed when dBASE reminds you that the view skeleton will be removed.

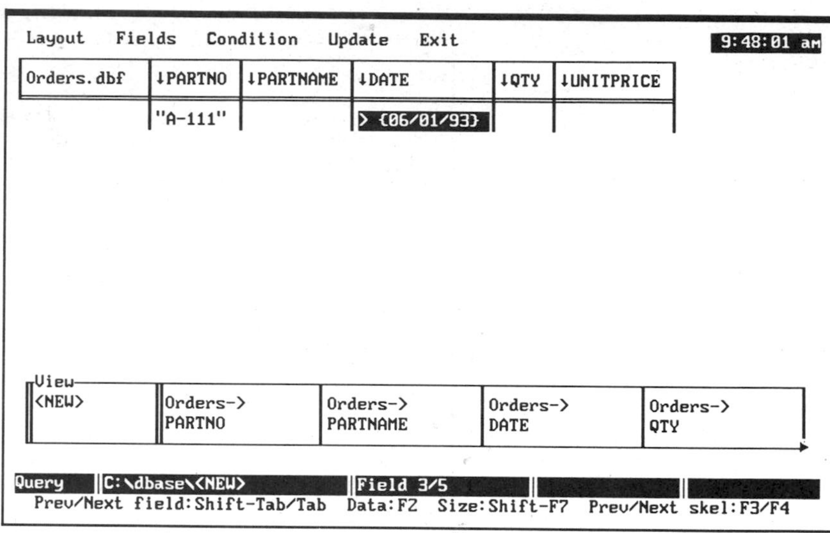

Figure 11.9: Query to isolate orders for A-111 after June 1

Now you need to tell dBASE to replace the current unit price with the current unit price plus 10 percent. Once again, you need to enter the key word WITH to perform the replacement. Also, in this case you are not just putting in a new value. Instead, you are increasing a value by 10 percent, so you want to multiply the current unit price by 1.10. Enter the expression WITH 1.10 * UNITPRICE under the UNITPRICE field name, as in Figure 11.10.

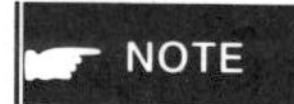

NOTE

An update query has no effect until you select Perform the Update.

Choose Update ► Perform the Update to make the change. As instructed on the screen, press any key, then press or click Data (F2) to view the results; you'll see that the appropriate unit prices have been increased by 10 percent, as Figure 11.11 shows.

If the field that you are changing in an update query is the same field that you are using for the filter condition, then enter the filter condition into the field first, test the basic query, and return to the query design screen. Then enter **"WITH"** and a replacement expression to the right of the filter condition, preceded by a comma.

TIP

Use the Zoom key (F9) or double-click the mouse as a toggle in the query design screen to zoom into and out of the current box.

For example, to add 30 days to the date 06/01/93 in the ORDERS database, first enter the filter condition {06/01/93} into the Date field on the query design screen. Press Data (F2) to test the query and then Design (Shift-F2) to return to the query. Then enter

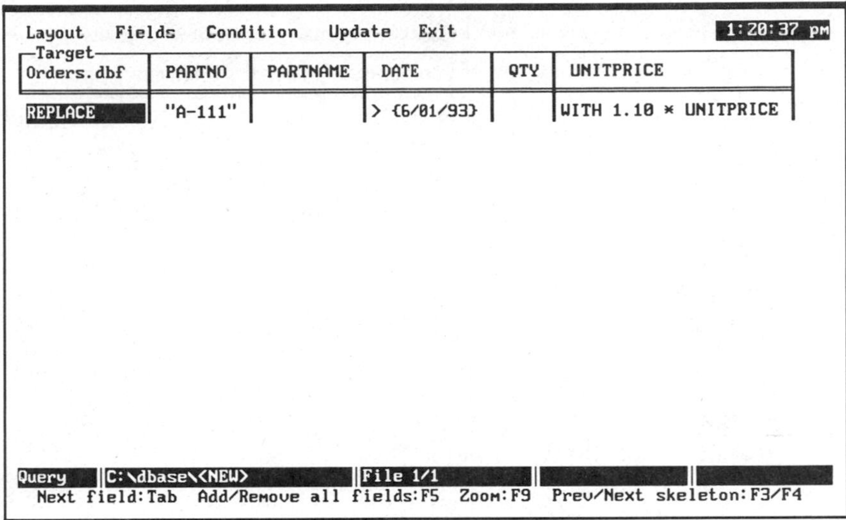

Figure 11.10: Query to increase the orders for part number A-111 after 6/1/93 by 10 percent

Records Organize Fields Go To Exit

PARTNO	PARTNAME	DATE	QTY	UNITPRICE
B-222	Mondo Man	06/01/93	2	100.00
B-222	Mondo Man	06/01/93	1	100.00
A-111	Astro Buddies	06/01/93	2	50.00
C-333	Cosmic Critters	06/01/93	1	500.00
A-111	Astro Buddies	06/02/93	3	55.00
A-111	Astro Buddies	06/05/93	4	55.00
B-222	Mondo Man	06/15/93	1	100.00
C-333	Cosmic Critters	06/15/93	2	500.00
C-333	Cosmic Critters	06/15/93	1	500.00
C-333	Cosmic Critters	07/01/93	2	500.00

Unit prices in two records increased by 10 percent

Browse | C:\dbase\ORDERS | Rec 1/10 | File

Figure 11.11: Results of update query in Figure 11.10

the REPLACE operator under the file name and the expression **,WITH Date + 30** next to the filter condition in the Date box, as in Figure 11.12.

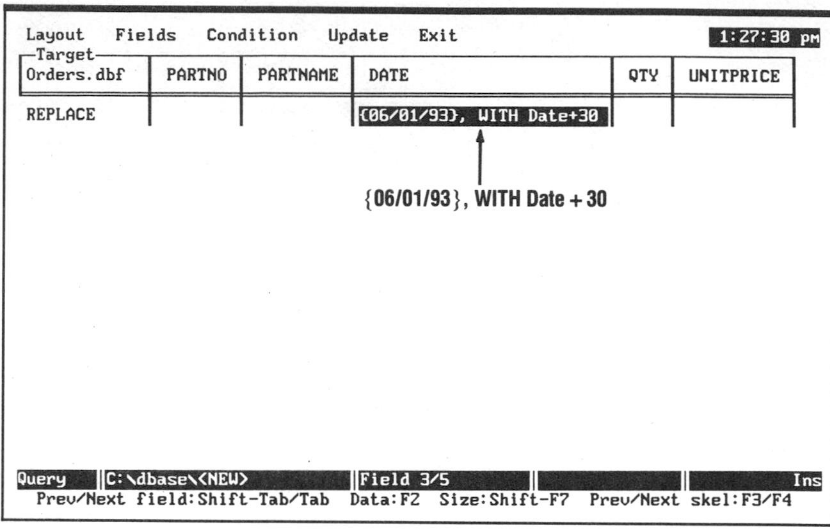

Figure 11.12: Filter condition and replacement value in one box

MARKING GROUPS OF RECORDS

To mark for deletion all records that meet some filter condition, enter the appropriate filter condition on the query design screen and test it. Then return to the query design screen and enter the update operator MARK under the field name in the skeleton. For example, Figure 11.13 shows a query to mark all records in the CUSTLIST database that have CA in the STATE field.

If you choose Update ► Perform the Update after setting up the query shown in Figure 11.13, dBASE will tell you how many records will be marked for deletion and ask if it's OK to mark them. Type **Y** and press ↵, then press any key. If you then press Data (F2), you will see California residents in the database. However, as you scroll through the records, you'll notice that the records of all California residents are marked for deletion. Of course, if you set Deleted to On (as discussed earlier in this chapter) and then view the data, the records for all California residents will be hidden, as in Figure 11.14.

If you change your mind about marking the records for deletion, type **N** and press ↵ (or press Esc), then press any key when dBASE asks if it's OK to mark the records. If you didn't catch yourself in time, just use the same query, but change MARK to UNMARK and perform the update again to unmark the records you just marked.

UNMARKING MULTIPLE RECORDS

To unmark records that meet some filter condition, use the UNMARK update operator in the file skeleton, as in Figure 11.15.

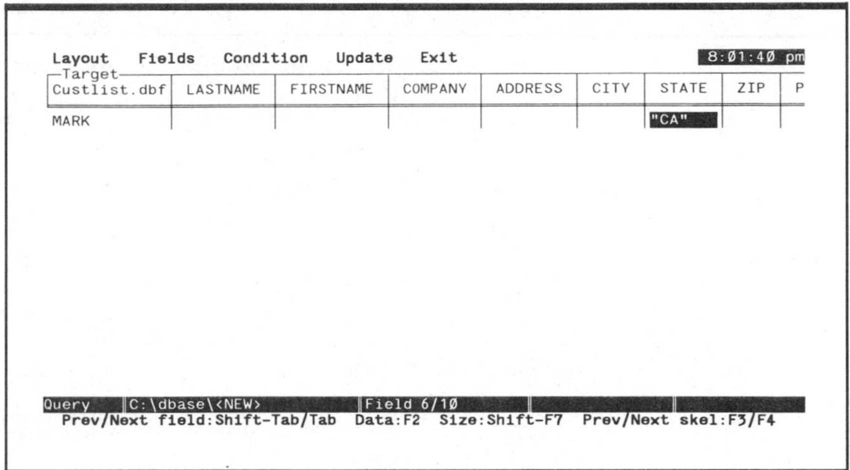

Figure 11.13: Query to mark all records that have CA in the STATE field

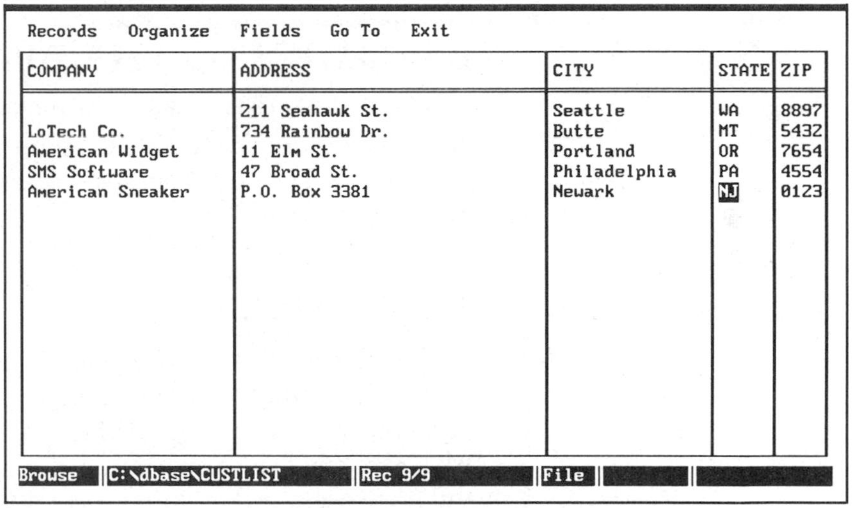

```
Records   Organize   Fields   Go To   Exit

COMPANY            ADDRESS             CITY           STATE  ZIP

                   211 Seahawk St.     Seattle        WA     8897
LoTech Co.         734 Rainbow Dr.     Butte          MT     5432
American Widget    11 Elm St.          Portland       OR     7654
SMS Software       47 Broad St.        Philadelphia   PA     4554
American Sneaker   P.O. Box 3381       Newark         NJ     0123

Browse  C:\dbase\CUSTLIST      Rec 9/9     File
```

Figure 11.14: Records for California residents are hidden

And of course, remember to choose Update ► Perform the Update.

To unmark all of the records in a database, you can either use the UNMARK update operator in a query with no filter conditions or choose Organize ► Unmark All Records in the database design, browse, or edit screen. If you use the latter method, the Deleted setting must be off.

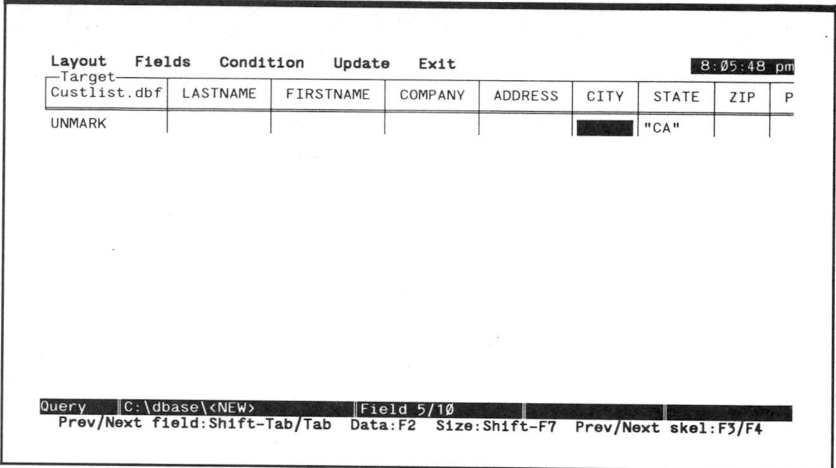

Figure 11.15: Query to unmark records

CUSTOMIZING THE BROWSE SCREEN

The browse screen offers several features to help you edit a database, which are particularly useful when you work with larger databases. All of these features are available from pull-down menus from the browse screen.

LOCKING FIELDS

The Fields ► Lock Fields on Left option lets you lock one or more fields at the left of the database so that they do not disappear when you scroll to the right. When you select this option, dBASE will ask how many fields you want to remain stationary. Enter a number and press ↵.

Figure 11.16 shows the CUSTLIST database on the browse screen with the two fields, LASTNAME and FIRSTNAME, locked. Notice that the cursor is scrolled all the way to the PAID field, but the two locked fields, LASTNAME and FIRSTNAME, are still on the screen.

Records Organize Fields Go To Exit

LASTNAME	FIRSTNAME	STATE	ZIP	PHONE	STARTDATE	PAID
Smith	John	CA	92067	(619)555-1234	11/15/92	T
Adams	Annie	CA	92001	(714)555-0123	01/01/93	F
Mahoney	Mary	WA	88977	(206)555-8673	12/01/92	T
Newell	John	MT	54321	(303)555-6739	12/15/92	T
Beach	Sandy	OR	76543	(717)555-0898	12/15/92	T
Kenney	Ralph	CA	96607	(213)555-9988	12/30/92	F
Schumack	Susita	PA	45543	(202)555-9720	12/30/92	T
Smith	Anita	CA	92220	(415)555-9854	01/01/93	T
Jones	Fred	NJ	01234	(202)555-0987	01/15/93	Y

Browse | C:\dbase\CUSTLIST | Rec 1/9 | File

Figure 11.16: LASTNAME and FIRSTNAME fields locked on the browse screen

FREEZING A FIELD

The Field ► Freeze Field option lets you isolate a particular field on the browse screen. When you select this option, dBASE asks for the name of the field to freeze. Type the field name and press ↵.

The highlight will move to the field you've named and cannot be moved out of that field, either by pressing keys on the keyboard or by clicking the mouse. Pressing Tab and Shift-Tab moves the highlight up and down, rather than across fields. To unfreeze the field, select the option again and press the Backspace key repeatedly to remove the field name.

BLANKING A FIELD OR RECORD

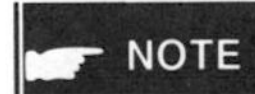

The Blank Record option leaves an empty record in a database. It does not mark or delete the record.

To empty the contents of a field, move the cursor to the appropriate field and choose Fields ► Blank Field. To empty all the fields in a record, choose Records ► Blank Record. If you accidentally blank the wrong field or record, choose Records ► Undo Change to Record.

SIZING COLUMNS

You cannot resize the last (rightmost) field on the browse screen.

You can expand or contract the size of a column on the browse screen by moving the highlight to the appropriate column and choosing Fields ► Size Field, or by pressing Size (Shift-F7). Next, use the → or ← key (or move your mouse to the right or left) to widen or narrow the field. Finally, press ↵ or click the mouse.

Alternatively, you can move the mouse pointer to the right vertical border of the column you want to resize (just to the right of the field name and above the double line that separates the field name from the first record), then drag the vertical border to the right or left to widen or narrow the column. Release the mouse button when the column is properly sized.

PREVENTING AUTOMATIC RE-SORT

When you are using an index to maintain a sort order on the browse screen, changing values in the index field causes the records to be re-sorted. (You saw an example of this in Chapter 5 when you changed Adams's last name to Zastrow.)

If you do not want the cursor to follow records to their new sorted positions while you are editing, choose Records ► Follow Record to New Position and change its setting from Yes to No.

LOCKING RECORDS

If you are using dBASE IV on a network, other users working on the same database may change information in the database while you are viewing it. To prevent other users from changing the data in a record while you are viewing it, choose Record ► Record Lock. The record will remain locked until you move the highlight to a different record.

At this point, you can create and manage just about any database, because you know all the basic techniques. Occasionally, though, you may need a sort order, report grouping, or calculation more complex than those we've discussed so far. No matter how complex a particular operation is, a dBASE function can probably handle it, as you'll see in the next chapter.

CHAPTER

12

Using Functions to Control Your Data

To combine fields of different data types in index expressions, 396
use the DTOS( ) function to convert Date data and the STR( ) function to convert Numeric or Float data to the Character data type.

To reverse the order of a date or numeric field 399
in an index expression, subtract the field value from the largest possible value for the field. For example, the index expression PARTNO + STR(999-QTY,3) displays records in ascending part number order and in descending quantity order within each part number.

To use a dictionary, rather than an ASCII, sort order 403
for an indexed Character field, use an index expression such as UPPER(LASTNAME + FIRSTNAME) that converts all letters to uppercase.

To group records in a report based on month, 412
use the expression CMONTH(<*date-field-name*>) as the group expression on the reports design screen and an index that displays records sorted into date order.

To group records based on the first letter in a Character field, 413
use the grouping expression LEFT(<*character field name*>,1) in the report design and an index that displays records in sorted order by the Character field.

To create calculated fields that make decisions 418
in queries, reports, and forms, use the IIF( ) function. For example, if a field named Taxable contains T for taxable items and F for nontaxable items, then the expression IIF(Taxable, 0.0775*ExtPrice, 0) returns 7.75 percent of the field named

ExtPrice for records that have T in the Taxable field, and 0 for records that have F in the Taxable field.

To include Logical fields in an index expression, 423
you can use the IIF( ) function to convert logical T and F to letters. For example, the index expression IIF(Paid,"T","F") +LASTNAME +FIRSTNAME displays records sorted into two groups: paid and unpaid. Within each group, records are displayed in alphabetical order by name.

When nesting functions in complex expressions, 425
be sure to use appropriate open and closing parentheses for each function: for example, SQRT(ABS(<*field-name*>)).

To solve rounding problems in reports, 428
use the rounding function ROUND (*value, decimal places*). For example, use ROUND (Amount,2) to round the value in the Amount field to 2 decimal places.

dBASE IV OFFERS MANY FUNCTIONS TO HELP YOU refine your queries, forms, and reports. A *function* is a predefined procedure that performs an immediate operation on one data item. All functions use the same basic syntax: a word or abbreviation followed by a pair of parentheses. You've already seen a few functions in action: DATE( ), which returns the current date, and DELETED( ), which can be used in a query to isolate records that are marked for deletion.

Some dBASE IV functions require one or more *arguments:* data to operate on, which is enclosed in parentheses. For example, the PAYMENT( ) function, which calculates the payment on a loan, requires three arguments: *principal, interest,* and *term.* The arguments are always separated by a comma. Hence, if a database contained loan parameters in three fields named Principal, Interest, and Term, then a calculated field containing the expression PAYMENT(Principal,Interest,Term) would display the payment for each record.

All functions *return* a value. The DATE( ) function returns the current date. The DELETED( ) function returns T if a record is marked for deletion, and F if it is not. In the expression PAYMENT(Principal,Interest,Term), the PAYMENT function returns the payment on the loan.

When speaking, it is common to use the word *of* between a function and its argument. For example, the SQRT( ) function returns the square root *of* a number. For the expression SQRT(81), you could say "the square root of 81."

dBASE offers over 150 functions, though many of these are used only in dBASE IV programming (a topic we'll discuss in Chapter 17). This chapter focuses on functions that are useful for refining your queries, forms, reports, and sort orders.

REFINING SORT ORDERS

As you may recall from Chapter 5 and examples since then, you can use an index to control the order in which records are displayed and printed. In case you've forgotten, the basic procedure for creating an index is summarized below:

- In the Data panel of the Control Center, highlight the name of the database that you want to use.
- Press or click Data (F2).
- Choose Organize ► Create New Index.
- Select Name of Index and type in a valid name (up to eight letters, no spaces or punctuation, and no file name extension). Press ↵.
- Select Index Expression, and type in the index expression, or press or click Shift-F1 to access the Expression Builder. Press ↵ after defining your index expression.
- Press Ctrl-End when done.

You can see the new sort order immediately if you are at the browse screen. (If you are at the edit screen, just press F2 to switch to the browse screen.)

Once you create an index, you need not re-create it in the future. Instead, simply select it from the Organize pull-down menu. Once again, as a quick reminder, the basic steps are as follows:

- If you are at the Control Center, highlight the database name in the Data panel and press or click Data (F2) to get to the browse or edit screen.
- Choose Organize ► Order Records by Index.
- Move the highlight to the index you want to activate to control the sort order. As you scroll through the index names, the expression for each index is displayed to the left of the menu. (The Natural Order option means "no index"; records are displayed in the order they were entered into the database.)
- Press ↵ to make your selection and return to the edit/browse screen.

TIP

As an alternative to scrolling through the list of index entries and pressing ↵, you can double-click on the index you want to use. You can also type the first letter (or the first few letters) of the index name to quickly move the highlight to that index; then press ↵.

Chapter 5 also discussed how you can do a sort within a sort using an index by combining two or more fields in the index expression. The index expression LASTNAME + FIRSTNAME, for example, could be used to display records in alphabetical order by last name and by first name within last names (for example, Ann Smith would come before Bob Smith, as in the phone book).

This technique of combining fields to produce a sort within a sort works fine *only* if the fields involved are the Character data type. If you try to mix data types, dBASE just beeps and displays the error message "Data Type Mismatch" while you are creating the index expression.

NOTE

The term *string* is short for "character string," and is just a shortcut way of referring to text stored as the Character data type.

For example, in the CUSTLIST database, LASTNAME is a Character field, while STARTDATE is a Date field. If you tried to create an index based on LASTNAME + STARTDATE, dBASE would reject your entry because you cannot mix the two data types. (The reason that you cannot combine data types has to do with how the computer and dBASE store information, but we need not get into all of that here.) However, you *can* mix data types in an index expression if you convert all the data types in the expression to Character data, and dBASE offers several *conversion functions* that allow you to do precisely that. Two of the most widely used functions are DTOS (Date to String) and STR (string), discussed in the next two sections.

COMBINING DATE AND CHARACTER DATA

To combine the Date and Character data types, you use the DTOS (Date to String) function. This function converts a date to a character string in the format *yyyymmdd.* For example, DTOS ({12/31/93}) would convert 12/31/93 to 19931231, which is the correct format for sorting dates. (Because you are using DTOS in an index expression, the converted date is used only within the index; you never actually see the date in yyyymmdd format.)

As an example, suppose you have a database of medical patients and appointment dates; the patient names are stored in Character fields LASTNAME and FIRSTNAME, and the appointment dates are stored in a Date field named APTDATE. You want to display the records with patients listed in alphabetical order by last and first name, and then in chronological order by appointment date for each patient.

You will note that you cannot use the index expression LASTNAME + FIRSTNAME + APTDATE because you'd be mixing data types. However, if you use the index expression LASTNAME + FIRSTNAME + DTOS(APTDATE) after choosing Organize ► Create New Index ► Index Expression, dBASE will accept your entry and display records in the order you want.

As another example, if you used the index expression DTOS (APTDATE) + LASTNAME + FIRSTNAME, dBASE would display the records in chronological order by date. Within each date, the names would be alphabetized.

COMBINING NUMERIC AND CHARACTER DATA

The STR function lets you convert data stored as the Numeric or Float data type to the Character data type. This function uses the general format

STR(*number*,*length*,*decimals*)

The following list describes the arguments in this format:

number An actual number or the name of the field or memory variable that contains Numeric or Float data

length The total length of the converted data. (If you leave this argument out, dBASE assigns a length of 10.)

decimals The number of decimal places that dBASE rounds to when converting the data. (If you leave this argument out, dBASE uses 0 decimal places. You must specify a length if you want to specify the number of decimal places.)

When using STR to convert data for sorting purposes, you'll usually want to use the same *length* and *decimals* as specified in the database structure. Let's look at some examples.

NOTE

The structure of the ORDERS database is shown back in Figure 9.1 near the beginning of Chapter 9.

The ORDERS database you created in Chapter 9 contains two Numeric fields—QTY, with a length of 3 and no decimal places, and UNITPRICE, with a length of 9 and two decimal places. The PARTNO field in that database is the Character data type.

Now, suppose you want to display records from that database in part code (PARTNO) order, and by quantity within each part code.

You cannot use the expression PARTNO + QTY because the data types are different. However, if you use the index expression PARTNO + STR(QTY,3), dBASE will accept the index expression and display records in the order you wish.

Suppose you wanted to view records in price (UNITPRICE) order and alphabetically by part code within each identical unit price. The index expression in this case would need to be STR(UNITPRICE,9,2) + PARTNO.

COMBINING DATES AND NUMBERS

If you are combining both dates and numbers in an index expression, convert both to the Character data type. For example, if you want to sort records in the ORDERS database in date order and then by quantity within each date, you should use the index expression DTOS(DATE) + STR(QTY,3). If you want to sort records by date and then by part number within each date and then by quantity within each part number, you should use the index expression DTOS(DATE) + PARTNO + STR(QTY,3).

MIXING ASCENDING AND DESCENDING ORDERS

Whenever you create an index, dBASE gives you the opportunity to specify the entire sort in either ascending or descending order. In some situations, you might want to combine ascending and descending sort orders. For example, suppose you want to display records from the ORDERS database in *ascending* part number order (for example, A-111 to C-333), but within each part number, you want records displayed in *descending* quantity order (largest to smallest), like this:

PARTNO	QTY
A-111	4
A-111	3
A-111	2
B-222	2

PARTNO	QTY
B-222	1
B-222	1
C-333	3
C-333	2
C-333	1

You need to index on the *inverse* of the quantity by subtracting each quantity from the largest possible quantity. Recall that the QTY field has a width of 3, with no decimal places, so the largest possible number in QTY is 999. Because you are combining this value with PARTNO, the result has to be converted to Character data. Hence, the appropriate index expression is PARTNO + STR (999 – QTY,3). (You would still select ASCENDING as the overall sort direction, to make sure the part numbers are in ascending order.)

Recall that the UNITPRICE field has a width of 9 and two decimal places. Hence, the largest possible number in the UNITPRICE field is 999999.99. Therefore, to display the unit price field in descending order within an ascending index, you would invert the unit prices with the basic formula 999999.99 – UNITPRICE. To convert this to a Character string, you can use the STR function with a width of 9 and two decimal places, like this: STR(999999.99 – UNITPRICE,9,2).

You can reverse the order of dates within an ascending index order by subtracting each date from the latest possible date in the field. For example, suppose you want to list records in ascending part number order, but in descending order by date, as follows:

```
A-111   07/01/93
A-111   06/15/93
A-111   06/01/93

B-222   07/01/93
B-222   06/15/93
B-222   06/14/93
```

C-333 06/15/93
C-333 06/10/93
C-333 06/01/93

Here, we'll assume that the latest possible date is 12/31/1999. Hence, the entire index expression is PARTNO + STR({12/31/99} – DATE)—again using an ascending order for the overall index. Note that, in this case, the STR( ) function is used to convert the numeric result of subtracting two dates to the Character data type.

There is no reliable technique for inverting Character data. For example, you cannot subtract peoples' last names from ZZZZZZ to invert the sort order. To display records in descending order in a Character field, you must select descending as the overall sort order for the index. But you can still invert a Date or Numeric field to present their sort orders in the opposite direction.

Just remember that an inverted Numeric or Date field is always displayed in the opposite order of the overall index. That is, the expression PARTNO + STR(999 – QTY,3) displays part numbers in ascending order and quantities in descending order when the overall index order is ascending. However, this same index expression displays part numbers in descending order and quantities in *ascending* order when the overall sort order is descending.

SORTING BY THE RESULTS OF CALCULATIONS

We stored quantities and unit prices of transactions in the ORDERS database, but we did not store the extended price. Suppose you want to display records in the ORDERS database in extended price order (that is, from the smallest total sale to the largest, or vice versa). To do so, you index on a calculated field, just as you display the extended price as a calculated field.

The TOTALS report is shown in Figure 9.9 in Chapter 9.

To display records in extended-price order from smallest to largest total sale, you use the index expression QTY*UNITPRICE and ascending as the overall sort order. To display records in order from largest to smallest extended price, you use the same index expression, but descending as the overall sort order. (To see the results of the index, you need to use a query or report format, such as TOTALS, that includes a calculated field to display the extended price.)

What if you want to display records sorted by part number and by extended price within each part number? You need to convert the results of the calculation QTY*UNITPRICE to a Character data type. To ensure an adequate width in the Character field, use the sum of the widths within the STR function. QTY has a width of 3, and UNITPRICE has a width of 9, so within the STR function, you specify a width of 12.

For example, to display records in ascending part number and extended price order, you use the index expression PARTNO + STR(QTY*UNITPRICE,12,2). To display records in ascending part number order and descending extended-price order, you use the following index expression instead: PARTNO + STR(999999999.99 – QTY*UNITPRICE,12,2). This index produces the sort order shown here, where part numbers are sorted into ascending order, and extended prices are sorted into descending order within each part number:

```
A-111     220.00
A-111     165.00
A-111     100.00

B-222     200.00
B-222     200.00
B-222     100.00

C-333    1000.00
C-333    1000.00
C-333     500.00
C-333     500.00
```

SORTS-WITHIN-SORTS WITH NUMBERS

If you want to combine numbers in an index to obtain a sort within a sort, convert both numeric fields to the Character data type.

Otherwise the index will contain the sum of the two numeric fields—that is, the result of a calculation—rather than a combination of the two fields.

For example, suppose you had a database with the following floor numbers and office numbers stored in two fields named FLOOR and ROOM:

ROOM	FLOOR
1	1
1	2
1	3
1	4
2	1
2	2
2	3

If you created an index based on the expression FLOOR +ROOM, the index would contain the *sums* of the room and floor numbers and would therefore display the FLOOR and ROOM column in the order shown here:

FLOOR + ROOM	FLOOR	ROOM
2	1	1
3	1	2
3	2	1
4	1	3
4	2	2
5	1	4
5	2	3

To obtain a correct sort-within-sort order, you would convert both numeric fields to character strings using the index expression STR(FLOOR,1,0) + STR(ROOM,1,0). The resulting index would contain character strings that combine the numeric digits (shown in quotes) and would yield the sort order, as shown here:

STR(FLOOR,1,0,) + STR(ROOM,1,0)	FLOOR	ROOM
"11"	1	1
"12"	1	2
"13"	1	3
"14"	1	4
"21"	2	1
"22"	2	2
"23"	2	3

DICTIONARY SORTS VIA INDEX

Chapter 5 discussed the difference between dictionary sorts and ASCII sorts. Indexes use the ASCII method, in which all lowercase letters are considered to be "larger than" all uppercase letters. Hence, an index of the LASTNAME field puts a name such as van der Pool after Zastrow in a sort order.

To get around this problem, you can convert all values in a Character field to uppercase using the UPPER( ) function in the index expression. For example, the index expression UPPER(LASTNAME) creates the following sort order (even though the names in the actual database are stored with both uppercase and lowercase letters):

ADAMS

BAKER

CARLSON

MILLER

VAN DER POOL

WILSON

ZASTROW

Remember that only the index contains words converted to uppercase; the names in the actual database are still in their original format. If you want to combine first and last names in the sort order, place the usual expression in the UPPER( ) function, like this: UPPER(LASTNAME + FIRSTNAME).

SEARCHING COMPLEX INDEXES

When you are using an index to display records in the browse or edit screen, you can choose Go To ► Index Key Search to quickly look up a value. However, keep in mind that this option searches the *index,* not the actual database file. Therefore, any special techniques that you used in creating the index must be used when searching the index.

For example, suppose you used the index expression UPPER(LASTNAME + FIRSTNAME) to sort the CUSTLIST database and that index is in effect while you are at the browse screen. You want to quickly locate the first Smith record, so you choose Go To ► Index Key Search. dBASE displays the index expression and allows you to type a value to search for.

When you see the expression UPPER(LASTNAME + FIRSTNAME), remember that all the values in the index are in uppercase, so whatever you want to search for must be specified in uppercase. Therefore, you would enter **SMITH**, rather than **Smith** in this case (as shown in Figure 12.1) to locate the first Smith record.

Suppose you had organized records in the ORDERS database into descending DATE order and ascending PARTNO order within each date, using the index expression STR({12/31/1999} – DATE) + PARTNO. If you want to search this index for a particular date, you need to convert that date in exactly the same manner that you converted the dates in the index. That is, to search for the first record with

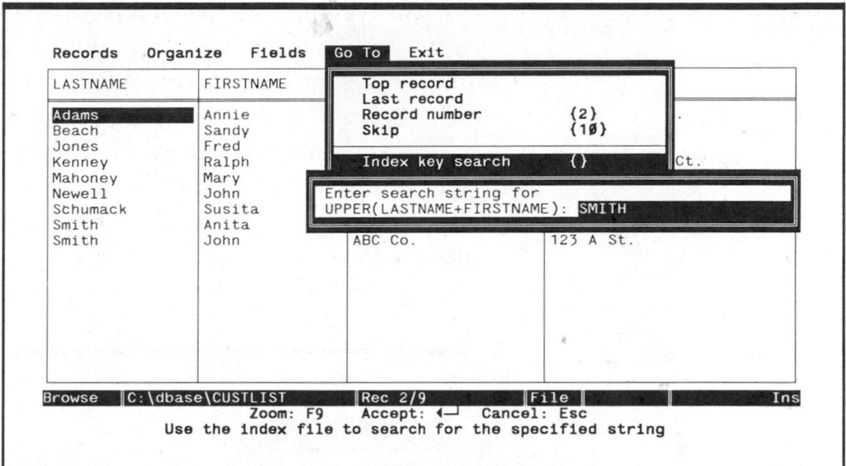

Figure 12.1: An index search for the first Smith record

06/01/93 in the date field, you would need to enter STR({12/31/1999} – {06/01/93}) as the Index Key Search value.

Unfortunately, the Index Key Search option may not provide enough space for entering such a large, complex expression. To get around this problem, you could create one index with the complex expression STR({12/31/1999} – DATE) + PARTNO to define a sort order only, and another index with the simple field name DATE for searching. Then, when searching for dates, you could use the index with the simpler expression so that you do not need to convert the date for searching.

FUNCTIONS AND REPORT GROUPINGS

Chapter 9 touched on some potential problems of using groups within groups in report formats; for instance, when you need a complex index to presort a database into the groups specified in the report format. As you may recall, groups within groups require an index that matches the grouping. For example, if group 1 is based on the PARTNO field and group 2 is based on the DATE field, then the index expression must be PARTNO + DATE.

This problem is easily solved by using functions in your index expression. Even though you cannot index on PARTNO + DATE, you can certainly index on PARTNO + DTOS(DATE) to create the index that the report grouping requires.

As an example, Figure 12.2 shows a report format that prints records from the ORDERS database grouped by part number and by date within each part number. The group-2 summary band displays the subtotal for each date within each part number. The group-1 summary band prints a subtotal for each part number.

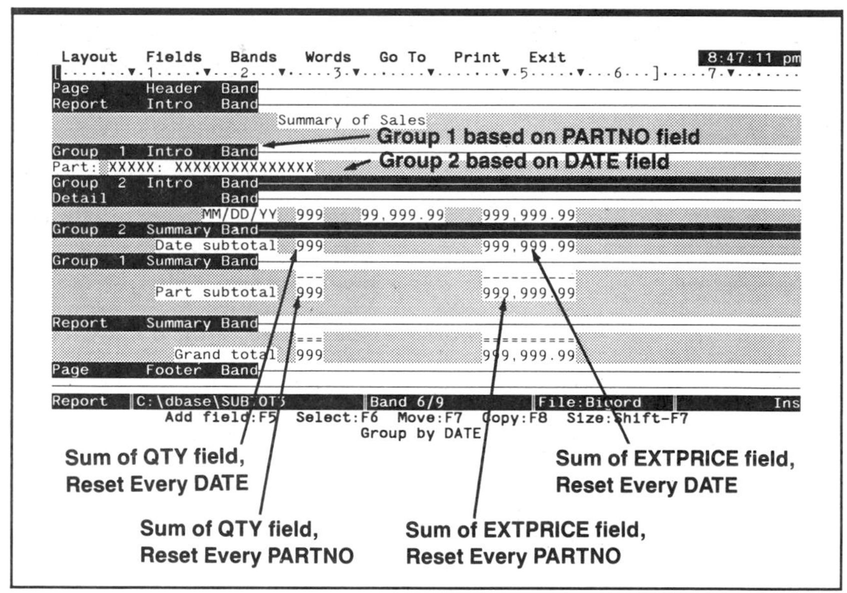

Figure 12.2: Report format to subtotal by date within parts

Note that to create such a report, you would need to choose Bands ► Add a Group Band twice, basing the outermost band on the PARTNO field and the innermost band on the DATE field.

Before printing the report, you need an index with an expression that matches the group order. That is, the report uses PARTNO as group 1 and DATE as group 2, so you need the index expression PARTNO + DTOS(DATE).

Here are the general steps you would go through to create the index:

- If you are still at the reports design screen, save your report format by pressing Ctrl-End or choosing Exit ► Save Changes and Exit.
- At the Control Center, highlight the database name (ORDERS in this example) in the Data panel.
- Press or click Data (F2) to get to the edit/browse screens.
- Choose Organize ► Create New Index, and enter a valid index name (such as PARTDATE in this example).
- Select Index Expression and enter the appropriate index expression—PARTNO + DTOS(DATE) in this example, as in Figure 12.3.
- Press Ctrl-End when done.

In the future, whenever you print the report, you'll need to first activate the PARTDATE index. In this particular case, that index is active because you just created it, but in future dBASE sessions you'll need to activate the index before printing the report. So the complete

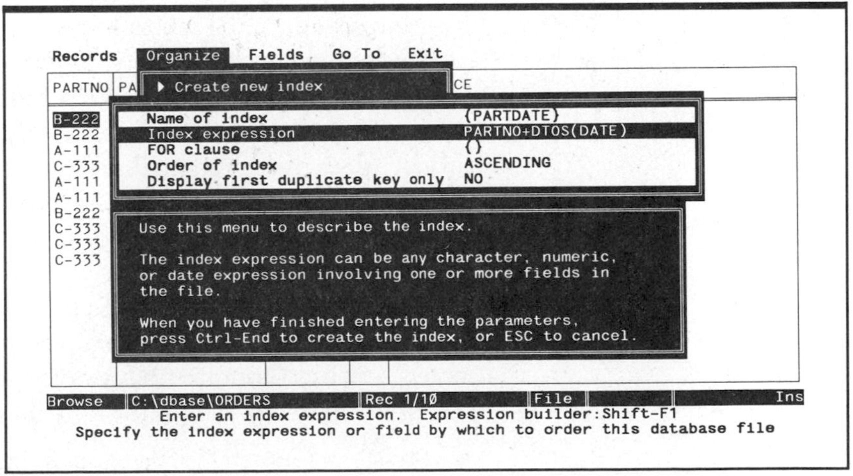

Figure 12.3: Index for report with part number and date subtotals

steps for printing the report in the future would be as follows:

- Highlight the name of the database in the Data panel at the Control Center (ORDERS in this example).
- Press or click Data (F2) to get to the edit/browse screens.
- Choose Organize ► Order Records by Index.
- Select the appropriate index for the report (PARTDATE in this example).
- Press Ctrl-End or choose Exit ► Exit to get back to the Control Center.
- In the Reports panel, highlight the name of the report you want to print (SUBTOT2 in this example) and press ↵, or double-click on that report.
- Select Print Report and whatever options you wish from the Print menu options.

Figure 12.4 shows the printed SUBTOT2 report using some hypothetical data that aren't actually in the ORDERS database right now. But what's important here is the grouping (sort order). As you can see, the records are grouped by part number, and within each part number, records are sorted by date. And it's the combination of the group bands in the report format and the sort order of the PARTCODE index that allows the records to be displayed in that manner.

Now let's suppose that after printing the first copy of the report you decide you would rather display the records in *descending* (latest to earliest) date order rather than in ascending order by date. Would you need to change the report format? No—because the groups will still be based on the same two fields, PARTNO, and within each PARTNO, DATE.

What you need to change is the sort order, which means changing the index. Hence, you'd want to get back to the browse or edit screen, choose Organize ► Modify Existing Index, select PARTDATE as the index to modify, and change the index expression to

```
PARTNO + STR({12/31/1999}-DATE)
```

```
                       Summary of Sales

Part: A-111:   Astro Buddies
                 06/01/93    2         50.00           100.00
                 06/01/93    4         50.00           200.00
                 06/01/93    2         50.00           100.00
                 06/01/93    4         50.00           200.00
                 06/01/93   10         50.00           500.00
            Date Subtotal   22                       1,100.00
                 06/15/93    3         50.00           150.00
                 06/15/93    4         50.00           200.00
                 06/15/93    5         50.00           250.00
                 06/15/93    3         50.00           150.00
            Date Subtotal   15                         750.00
                           ---                     ----------
            Part Subtotal   37                       1,850.00

Part: B-222:   Mondo Man
                 06/01/93    2        100.00           200.00
                 06/01/93    2        100.00           200.00
                 06/01/93    8        100.00           800.00
                 06/01/93   10        100.00         1,000.00
                 06/01/93    1        100.00           100.00
            Date Subtotal   23                       2,300.00
                 06/15/93    1        100.00           100.00
                 06/15/93    5        100.00           500.00
                 06/15/93    1        100.00           100.00
                 06/15/93    1        100.00           100.00
                 06/15/93    6        100.00           600.00
            Date Subtotal   14                       1,400.00
                           ---                     ----------
            Part Subtotal   37                       3,700.00

Part: C-333:   Cosmic Critters
                 06/01/93    1        500.00           500.00
                 06/01/93    2        500.00         1,000.00
                 06/01/93    1        500.00           500.00
                 06/01/93    1        500.00           500.00
                 06/01/93    2        500.00         1,000.00
                 06/01/93    1        500.00           500.00
            Date Subtotal    8                       4,000.00
                 06/15/93    3        500.00         1,500.00
                 06/15/93    2        500.00         1,000.00
                 06/15/93    6        500.00         3,000.00
                 06/15/93    4        500.00         2,000.00
                 06/15/93    8        500.00         4,000.00
                 06/15/93    2        500.00         1,000.00
                 06/15/93    1        500.00           500.00
            Date Subtotal   26                      13,000.00
                           ---                     ----------
            Part Subtotal   34                      17,000.00

                           ===                     ==========
              Grand Total  108                      22,550.00
```

Figure 12.4: Sample report grouped by part number and date

so that dates will be displayed in descending order. Press Ctrl-End until you get back to the Control Center to save the change.

In the future, when you activate the PARTCODE index and print the report, the records would be listed in the order shown in

Figure 12.5, with later dates preceding earlier dates within each part number group.

The important thing to remember is that the group bands in a report format do not *force* a particular sort order on a database, they just *use* the current sort order to group data. If the database records are in random (or natural) order when you start printing the report, they'll be in random order in the printed report. Remember, it's entirely up to you to remember to activate the appropriate index at the browse or edit screen prior to printing the report.

Actually, there are three alternatives to having to remember to activate an index yourself before printing a grouped report, though two of them involve topics that we have not yet discussed:

- Before you create the report format, create a query that sorts data into the order you need (as discussed in Chapter 6), then use that query to design the report and to print the report in the future (Chapter 7).
- Record the keystrokes required to activate the index and print the report in a keystroke macro so you need not repeat all of those keystrokes in the future (see Chapter 14).
- Create a command file that sets up the sort order and prints the report. (Command files are discussed in Chapters 17 and 18).

Just keep these three alternatives in mind for the time being—there's no need to try any of them out right now. Instead, let's get back to the main topic at hand, using dBASE functions.

MORE COMPLEX GROUPINGS

There is no limit to the number of group bands that you can place in a report format. Just be certain to use the appropriate index expression to print the report. For example, suppose you have a database that includes fields named SALESREP, PARTNUMBER, DATE, QTY, and UNITPRICE and you want to print a report with subtotals by sales representative, by date within each sales representative, and by part number within each date. Furthermore, you want records displayed in descending order by quantity within each date.

```
                    Summary of Sales

Part: A-111:  Astro Buddies
                 06/15/93    3          50.00          150.00
                 06/15/93    4          50.00          200.00
                 06/15/93    5          50.00          250.00
                 06/15/93    3          50.00          150.00
            Date Subtotal   15                         750.00
                 06/01/93    2          50.00          100.00
                 06/01/93    4          50.00          200.00
                 06/01/93    2          50.00          100.00
                 06/01/93    4          50.00          200.00
                 06/01/93   10          50.00          500.00
            Date Subtotal   22                       1,100.00
                           ---                     ----------
            Part Subtotal   37                       1,850.00

Part: B-222:  Mondo Man
                 06/15/93    1         100.00          100.00
                 06/15/93    5         100.00          500.00
                 06/15/93    1         100.00          100.00
                 06/15/93    1         100.00          100.00
                 06/15/93    6         100.00          600.00
            Date Subtotal   14                       1,400.00
                 06/01/93    2         100.00          200.00
                 06/01/93    2         100.00          200.00
                 06/01/93    8         100.00          800.00
                 06/01/93   10         100.00        1,000.00
                 06/01/93    1         100.00          100.00
            Date Subtotal   23                       2,300.00
                           ---                     ----------
            Part Subtotal   37                       3,700.00

Part: C-333:  Cosmic Critters
                 06/15/93    3         500.00        1,500.00
                 06/15/93    2         500.00        1,000.00
                 06/15/93    6         500.00        3,000.00
                 06/15/93    4         500.00        2,000.00
                 06/15/93    8         500.00        4,000.00
                 06/15/93    2         500.00        1,000.00
                 06/15/93    1         500.00          500.00
            Date Subtotal   26                      13,000.00
                 06/01/93    1         500.00          500.00
                 06/01/93    2         500.00        1,000.00
                 06/01/93    1         500.00          500.00
                 06/01/93    1         500.00          500.00
                 06/01/93    2         500.00        1,000.00
                 06/01/93    1         500.00          500.00
            Date Subtotal    8                       4,000.00
                           ---                     ----------
            Part Subtotal   34                      17,000.00

                           ===                     ==========
              Grand Total  108                      22,550.00
```

Figure 12.5: Parts in ascending order, dates in descending order

In the report format, SALESREP would be the group-1 field, DATE would be the group-2 field, and QTY would be the group-3 field. The basic index expression for the report groups would be SALESREP + DTOS(DATE) + PARTNO. However, to ensure that quantities are displayed in descending order within each part number, the complete index expression would be SALESREP + DTOS(DATE) + PARTNO + STR(999 – QTY,3).

GROUPING BY EXPRESSION

Choosing Bands ► Add a group Band displays three options: Field Value, Expression Value, and Record Count. As you've seen, selecting Field Value lets you specify a particular field to group by, such as PARTNO in the SUBTOTAL report.

The Expression Value option lets you group by an expression rather than a field. The expression you enter can be a combination of Character fields joined with a plus sign, such as LASTNAME + FIRSTNAME, in which case each group would consist of people with the same last and first names. You can also use expressions with functions in them, just like the index expressions discussed earlier. There are a few functions, however, that are especially useful for report groupings, as summarized in Table 12.1.

Table 12.1: Functions Used in Grouping

Function	Returns	Used with data type
CMONTH( )	The month of a date	Date
YEAR( )	The year of a date	Date
CDOW( )	The day of the week	Date
LEFT( )	Leftmost characters	Character

GROUPING BY MONTH Suppose you want to group records in a report by month, regardless of the particular day. If you use Date alone as the grouping field, your report will display a separate group for each specific date. However, if you use the expression value CMONTH(DATE) to determine groups, all of the records for January will be grouped together, followed by all of the records for February, and so forth. Figure 12.6 shows a sample report format that uses the CMONTH( ) function for grouping.

```
Layout   Fields   Bands   Words   Go To   Print   Exit                    10:57:14 pm
[........▼.1......▼...2...▼......3.▼........▼........▼.5.....▼...6...▼....]7.▼......
Page        Header   Band
MM/DD/YY                                                          Page No. 999
                       Part                         Unit          Extended
           Date        Number  Part Name      Qty   Price         Price
Report      Intro    Band

Group   1   Intro    Band
Month: XXXXXXXXXXXXXXXXXXXXXXXX

Detail               Band
         MM/DD/YY  XXXXXX XXXXXXXXXXXXXXX 999 99,999.99 99,999.99
Group   1   Summary  Band
                                             ---            ---------
                          Month subtotal     999            99,999.99

Report      Summary  Band
                                             ===            =========
                        Year to date total   999            99,999.99
Page        Footer   Band
Report   C:\dbase\MONTHORD         Band 1/7          File:Bigord            Ins
            Add field:F5  Select:F6  Move:F7  Copy:F8  Size:Shift-F7
```

Group Intro is a calculated field containing CMONTH(DATE)

Figure 12.6: Sample report format for grouping records by month

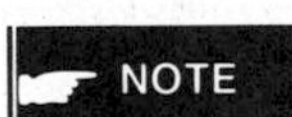

When you subtract two dates, the result is a number; the STR( ) function here converts that result to character data.

Before printing the report, you need to activate an index that puts the records in date order. This could be a simple index of the DATE field or a complex index using DTOS(DATE) combined with another field, just so long as the records are presorted into date, or month, order. Figure 12.7 shows a sample report printed by this format, using DATE as the field for the index.

Be sure to type both a comma and a space after the LASTNAME field in the report format shown in Figure 12.8, and to set the Trim picture function for the LASTNAME field to On. If you omit the space before the FIRSTNAME field, or do not trim the LASTNAME field, your report will include extra blank spaces after the comma or after the last name.

GROUPING BY FIRST LETTER With Character fields, you can use the LEFT( ) function to group records by the leading characters in each field. To use the LEFT function, you must include both the field name and the number of characters within the parentheses. For example, suppose you want to print a customer list grouped by the first letter in people's last names (that is, all the A's, then all the B's, and so forth). To do so, you need to base the grouping on the expression LEFT(LASTNAME,1), with the 1 indicating that only the first letter is to be used for breaking groups. Figure 12.8 shows a sample report format to group records by the first letter in the LASTNAME field.

Once again, before printing the report, you need to put the records into alphabetical order. You can use any index expression that is appropriate here, such as LASTNAME or LASTNAME +FIRSTNAME. Figure 12.9 shows a sample printed report that

```
03/15/93                                                     Page No.    1

            Date        Part      Part Name             Qty   Unit        Extended
                        Number                                Price        Price
Month: January

            01/01/93    B-222     Mondo Man               2     100.00      200.00
            01/05/93    B-222     Mondo Man               2     100.00      200.00
            01/09/93    A-111     Astro Buddies           2      50.00      100.00
            01/11/93    C-333     Cosmic Critters         1     500.00      500.00
            01/12/93    A-111     Astro Buddies           4      50.00      200.00
            01/15/93    A-111     Astro Buddies           2      50.00      100.00
            01/20/93    B-222     Mondo Man               8     100.00      800.00
            01/21/93    C-333     Cosmic Critters         2     500.00    1,000.00
            01/30/93    C-333     Cosmic Critters         1     500.00      500.00
                                                        ---               ---------
                                    Month subtotal       24               3,600.00
Month: February

            02/02/93    C-333     Cosmic Critters         1     500.00      500.00
            02/11/93    A-111     Astro Buddies           4      50.00      200.00
            02/12/93    A-111     Astro Buddies          10      50.00      500.00
            02/12/93    A-111     Astro Buddies           4      50.00      200.00
            02/15/93    A-111     Astro Buddies           3      50.00      150.00
            02/20/93    B-222     Mondo Man              10     100.00    1,000.00
            02/21/93    B-222     Mondo Man               1     100.00      100.00
                                                        ---               ---------
                                    Month subtotal       33               2,650.00
Month: March

            03/01/93    A-111     Astro Buddies           5      50.00      250.00
            03/03/93    C-333     Cosmic Critters         2     500.00    1,000.00
            03/05/93    A-111     Astro Buddies           3      50.00      150.00
            03/05/93    C-333     Cosmic Critters         1     500.00      500.00
            03/09/93    B-222     Mondo Man               5     100.00      500.00
                                                        ---               ---------
                                    Month subtotal       16               2,400.00

                                                        ===               =========
                               Year to date total        73               8,650.00
```

Figure 12.7: Orders subtotaled by month

used the LASTNAME + FIRSTNAME index expression and the format shown in Figure 12.8.

Suppose you want to group customers by a general zip code area, such as all the 91's followed by the 92's, the 93's, and so forth. If the zip codes are stored as the Character data type in a field named ZIP, then the expression for grouping is LEFT(ZIP,2). In this case, you need to activate an index of the ZIP field before printing the report.

GROUPING BY RECORD COUNT

You can group records by record count, which simply separates printed rows into equal-sized blocks. To do so, choose Bands ► Add

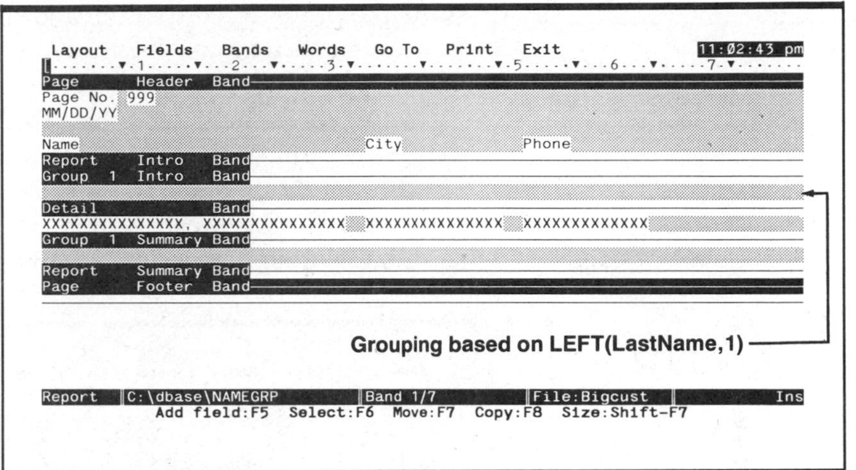

Figure 12.8: Report format to group letters by first letter of last name

```
Page No.  1
08/01/93

Name                     City              Phone

Adams, Annie             Santa Monica      (714)555-0123
Adroit, Bob              Palm Springs      (714)555-9987
Agajaninan, Rob          Oakland           (415)787-5233
Amanda, Rhonda           Newark            (217)555-0990
Anastasie, Steve         Hatboro           (215)543-9283
Atritia, Ted             Buffalo           (208)756-9320


Beach, Sandy             Portland          (717)555-0898
Boon, Lenny              New Orleans       (606)551-1212
Byers, Bob               Torrance          (213)756-9320


Carlyle, Tim             Glendora          (818)550-3345
Caruthers, Candy         Ocean Beach       (619)465-3968
Casanova, Juan           Azusa             (818)776-5464
Coulter, Lou             San Diego         (619)225-0998
Cuisine, Zeke            Carmel            (404)649-2453


Davis, Randi             Newport Beach     (714)564-3648
Delorrio, Maria          Orange            (818)555-0989
Devine, Deedra           Santa Ana         (714)800-5434
Dillon, Jack             Indianapolis      (317)800-5434
Divin, Adam              Los Angeles       (213)655-8956
```

Figure 12.9: Names grouped by first letter

a Group Band ► Record Count and enter the number of records you want within each group. Figure 12.10 shows a sample report format with grouping based on groups of five records.

Figure 12.11 shows a sample report printed by the previous format. Notice that the records are organized into groups of five, regardless of their contents. As usual, the number of blank spaces that appears between each group is determined by the number of blank lines within the group band in the report design.

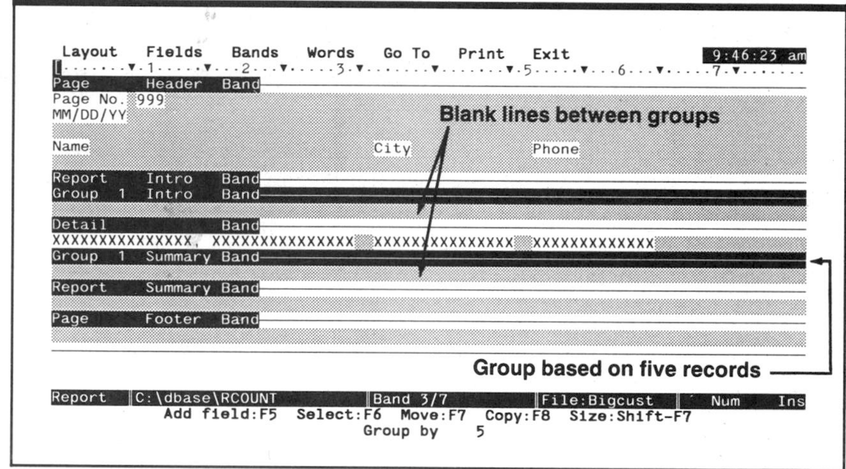

Figure 12.10: Sample report format with records grouped by count

A DECISION-MAKING FUNCTION

One of dBASE IV's most powerful and versatile functions is IIF( ) (an abbreviation for immediate IF). This function makes a spur-of-the-moment decision about which of two alternative actions to take. The plain English syntax for this function is

IIF(*this-is-true*,*do-this*,*otherwise-do-this*)

The first argument must be either the name of a Logical field (which is always either true or false) or an expression with a true or false result. For example, the expression PARTNO = "A-111" is

```
Page No.  1
01/01/93

Name                      City               Phone


Adams, Annie              Santa Monica       (714)555-0123
Adroit, Bob               Palm Springs       (714)555-9987
Agajaninan, Rob           Oakland            (415)787-5233
Amanda, Rhonda            Newark             (217)555-0990
Anastasie, Steve          Hatboro            (215)543-9283


Atritia, Ted              Buffalo            (208)756-9320
Beach, Sandy              Portland           (717)555-0898
Boon, Lenny               New Orleans        (606)551-1212
Byers, Bob                Torrance           (213)756-9320
Carlyle, Tim              Glendora           (818)550-3345


Caruthers, Candy          Ocean Beach        (619)465-3968
Casanova, Juan            Azusa              (818)776-5464
Coulter, Lou              San Diego          (619)225-0998
Cuisine, Zeke             Carmel             (404)649-2453
Davis, Randi              Newport Beach      (714)564-3648


Delorrio, Maria           Orange             (818)555-0989
Devine, Deedra            Santa Ana          (714)800-5434
Dillon, Jack              Indianapolis       (317)800-5434
Divin, Adam               Los Angeles        (213)655-8956
Jones, Fred               Newark             (202)555-0987
```

Figure 12.11: Report with groups of five records

either true or false, because a specific PARTNO either is or is not equal to "A-111." The expression QTY>10 also results in either a true or a false value, because a specific QTY either is or is not greater than 10.

The other two arguments (both are required) in an IIF function can be any expression; these arguments usually reflect the contents of a calculated field. To see how IIF works, we'll create a query that adds 7.75 percent sales tax only to taxable items in the ORDERS database.

USING IIF IN A QUERY

Suppose that the ORDERS database contains a Logical field named TAXABLE, which contains T if a particular transaction is taxable and F if the transaction is not taxable. Figure 12.12 shows the structure of the ORDERS database with this field added.

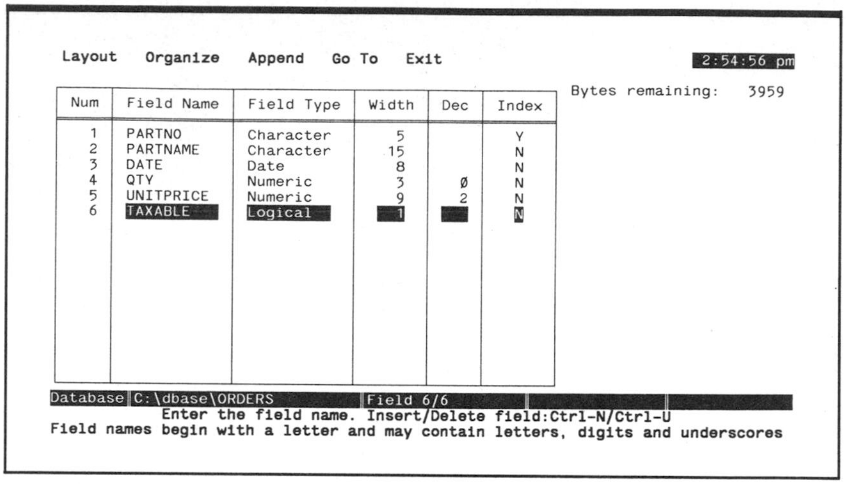

Layout Organize Append Go To Exit 2:54:56 pm

Bytes remaining: 3959

Num	Field Name	Field Type	Width	Dec	Index
1	PARTNO	Character	5		Y
2	PARTNAME	Character	15		N
3	DATE	Date	8		N
4	QTY	Numeric	3	0	N
5	UNITPRICE	Numeric	9	2	N
6	TAXABLE	Logical	1		N

Database C:\dbase\ORDERS Field 6/6

Enter the field name. Insert/Delete field:Ctrl-N/Ctrl-U

Field names begin with a letter and may contain letters, digits and underscores

Figure 12.12: TAXABLE field added to the ORDERS database

Within the ORDERS database records, transactions involving part numbers A-111 and C-333 are marked as taxable, and those involving part number B-222 are marked as not taxable. Figure 12.13 shows the ORDERS database with the TAXABLE field filled in.

Now suppose you want to execute a query that calculates tax. Select <create> from the Queries panel and then choose Fields ►

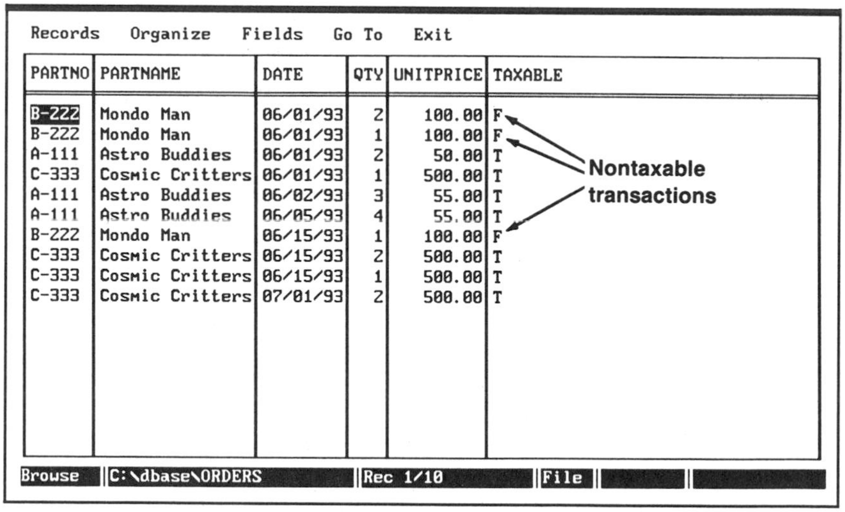

Records Organize Fields Go To Exit

PARTNO	PARTNAME	DATE	QTY	UNITPRICE	TAXABLE
B-222	Mondo Man	06/01/93	2	100.00	F
B-222	Mondo Man	06/01/93	1	100.00	F
A-111	Astro Buddies	06/01/93	2	50.00	T
C-333	Cosmic Critters	06/01/93	1	500.00	T
A-111	Astro Buddies	06/02/93	3	55.00	T
A-111	Astro Buddies	06/05/93	4	55.00	T
B-222	Mondo Man	06/15/93	1	100.00	F
C-333	Cosmic Critters	06/15/93	2	500.00	T
C-333	Cosmic Critters	06/15/93	1	500.00	T
C-333	Cosmic Critters	07/01/93	2	500.00	T

Nontaxable transactions

Browse C:\dbase\ORDERS Rec 1/10 File

Figure 12.13: Transactions marked as taxable or nontaxable

Create Calculated Field for each calculated field that you wish to add. Be sure to name each calculated field and move a copy of each field into the view skeleton (by pressing F5). If you want to use a calculated value in another calculated field's expression, place an example in the box beneath the expression.

Figure 12.14 shows a query with three calculated fields. The first, named ExtPrice, calculates the extended price before taxes using the usual expression Qty*UnitPrice. The second calculated field, named Tax, contains the expression IIF(Taxable,0.0775*EPrice,0). In English, this expression says, "If the taxable field is T in this record, then display 7.75 percent times the extended price; otherwise display zero." (That is, if the Taxable field is F for a particular record, then the tax to be added is 0.)

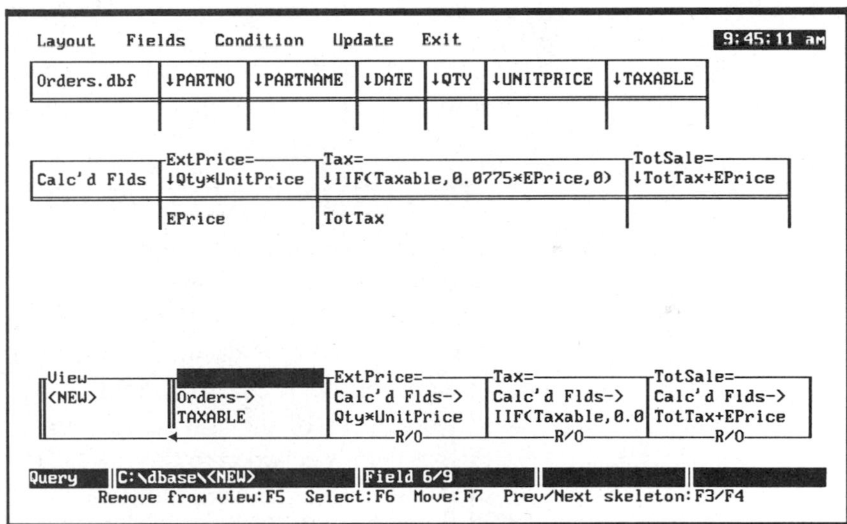

Figure 12.14: Query to calculate taxes for taxable transactions

The third calculated field, TotSale, calculates the total sale by adding the tax to the extended price using the expression TotTax +EPrice. TotTax, in turn, is used as an example in the calculated Tax field. Figure 12.15 shows the results of the query (compressed and reorganized so that you can see all the data) after you press Data (F2). Of course, you can enter any filter conditions you wish into the

Records Organize Fields Go To Exit

PARTNO	QTY	UNITPRICE	TAXABLE	TAX	TOTSALE
B-222	2	100.00	F	0.00	200.00
B-222	1	100.00	F	0.00	100.00
A-111	2	50.00	T	7.75	107.75
C-333	1	500.00	T	38.75	538.75
A-111	3	50.00	T	11.63	161.63
A-111	4	50.00	T	15.50	215.50
B-222	1	100.00	F	0.00	100.00
C-333	2	500.00	T	77.50	1077.50
C-333	1	500.00	T	38.75	538.75
C-333	2	500.00	T	77.50	1077.50

Browse | C:\dbase\<NEW> | Rec 1/10 | View

Figure 12.15: Results of tax-calculation query

query to confine this display to only certain records (such as part number A-111).

USING IIF IN A REPORT FORMAT

Suppose you wish to develop a report format that shows the tax, and the total sale price including the tax, for each transaction. Just as in the preceding sample query, the calculated fields in the report design will need to "decide" whether to tax transactions based on the contents of the TAXABLE field.

Figure 12.16 shows a sample report format (assuming the TAXABLE field was added to the ORDERS database, as discussed previously). A calculated field, named EXTPRICE, calculates and displays the extended price using the expression QTY*UNITPRICE.

To the right of the Extended Price column, notice the calculated field named TAX, which uses the expression IIF(TAXABLE,0.0775 *EXTPRICE,0) to display the tax. The template for the field was reduced to 999.99, and the Blanks for Zero Values picture function was set to On so the report would display blanks in place of the number 0.

To the right of the TAX column in the detail band is a calculated field named TOTSALE that uses the expression EXTPRICE

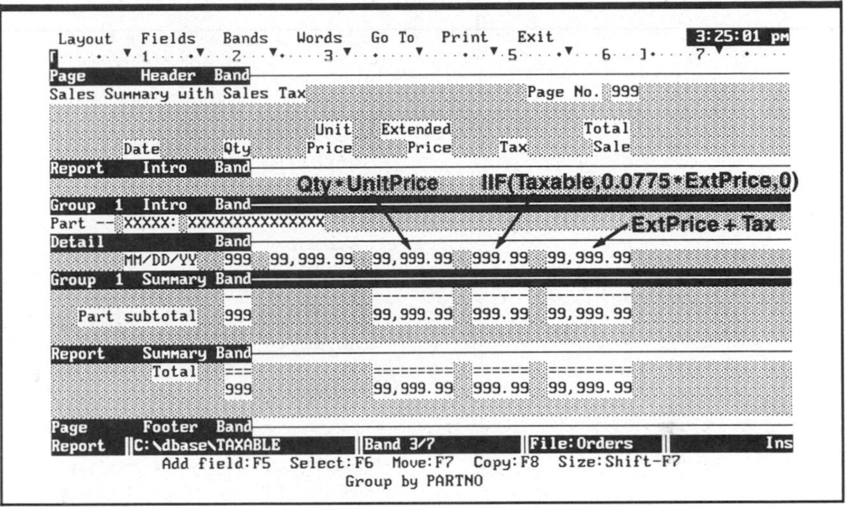

Figure 12.16: Report format that calculates tax on taxable items

+TAX to calculate the total sale. (Hence, if tax is zero, no tax is added to the total.) Summary fields using the Sum operator total the EXTPRICE, TAX, and TOTSALE columns within each group (based on the PARTNO field) and at the end of the report.

Figure 12.17 shows an example of the printed report. Note that no tax is added to transactions involving part number B-222. Blanks, rather than zeroes, are displayed in the Tax column for those parts because the {Z} Picture function was assigned to the calculated TAX field in the report format. (Because the report is also grouped by part number, you must activate the PARTNO index before printing the report.)

USING IIF IN CUSTOM FORMS

You can use the IIF function in a custom form in exactly the same way you would in either a query or report format. Simply place a calculated field on the form design screen and use the IIF function as you normally would. For example, Figure 12.18 shows a form on the forms design screen with calculated fields to display the tax (assuming, once again, that the TAXABLE field has already been added to the ORDERS database).

Sales Summary with Sales Tax — Page No. 1

	Date	Qty	Unit Price	Extended Price	Tax	Total Sale
Part -- A-111: Astro Buddies						
	06/01/93	2	50.00	100.00	7.75	107.75
	06/02/93	3	50.00	150.00	11.63	161.63
	06/05/93	4	50.00	200.00	15.50	215.50
		---		---------	------	---------
Part subtotal		9		450.00	34.88	484.88
Part -- B-222: Mondo Man						
	06/01/93	2	100.00	200.00	0.00	200.00
	06/01/93	1	100.00	100.00	0.00	100.00
	06/15/93	1	100.00	100.00	0.00	100.00
		---		---------	------	---------
Part subtotal		4		400.00	0.00	400.00
Part -- C-333: Cosmic Critters						
	06/01/93	1	500.00	500.00	38.75	538.75
	06/15/93	2	500.00	1,000.00	77.50	1,077.50
	06/15/93	1	500.00	500.00	38.75	538.75
	07/01/93	2	500.00	1,000.00	77.50	1,077.50
		---		---------	------	---------
Part subtotal		6		3,000.00	232.50	3,232.50
Total		===		=========	======	=========
		19		3,850.00	267.38	4,117.38

Figure 12.17: Sample report with tax calculations

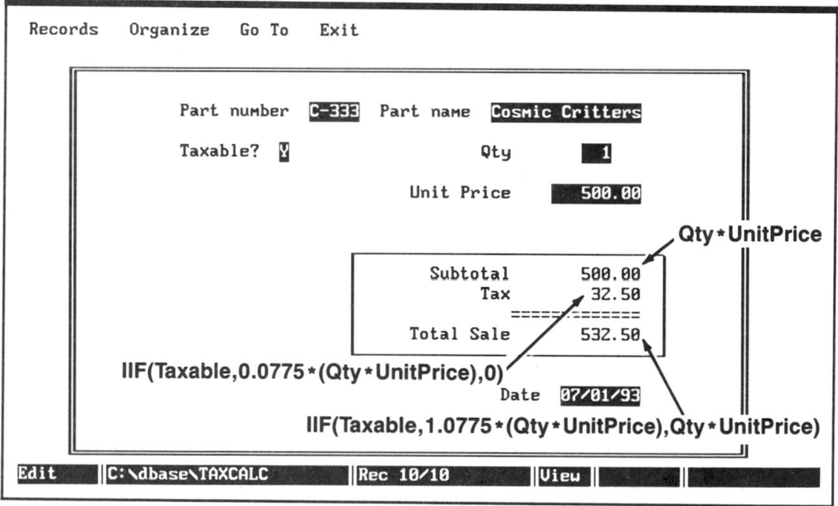

Figure 12.18: Custom form with tax calculations

INDEXING LOGICAL FIELDS

Earlier you learned that you cannot include Logical fields in index expressions. However, just as with the Numeric and Date fields, if you convert the Logical field to the Character data type within the index expression, you most certainly can index on Logical fields. Just use the IIF function to convert the logical values T or F to the letter "T" or "F".

For example, the CUSTLIST database includes a Logical field named PAID. Suppose you want to sort this database into customers who have paid and customers who have not and then display the names in each group in alphabetical order. You would use the usual techniques to create an index, using the index expression IIF (PAID,"T","F") + LASTNAME + FIRSTNAME. After you choose Organize ► Order Records by Index to activate the new index and press Data (F2) to view your data, you'll see all customers who have not paid listed before all those who have paid (because the letter "F" is "less than" the letter "T").

If you want to place the trues before the falses in the sort order, use a "lower" letter for the trues. For example, the index expression IIF(Paid,"A","Z") + LASTNAME + FIRSTNAME would place all those who have paid before those who have not. (Remember, though, that if you wanted to search the Paid field using an index search, you would need to search for the letter "A" to find a T value, and the letter "Z" to search for an F value.)

Of course, once you create an index based on the Paid field, you can create a report format that groups the customers into two lists: those who have paid and those who have not. Figure 12.19 shows an example format. Note the use of a calculated field in the Detail band to display the paid status of each customer in the group. If the customer that is about to be printed has paid, the word "Paid" is printed under the Status column of the report. If the customer hasn't paid, the words "Not Paid" are printed under that column.

Figure 12.20 shows the printed report based on the index expression IIF(Paid,"A","Z") + LASTNAME + FIRSTNAME, which, as discussed earlier, lists customers who have paid before those who have not paid.

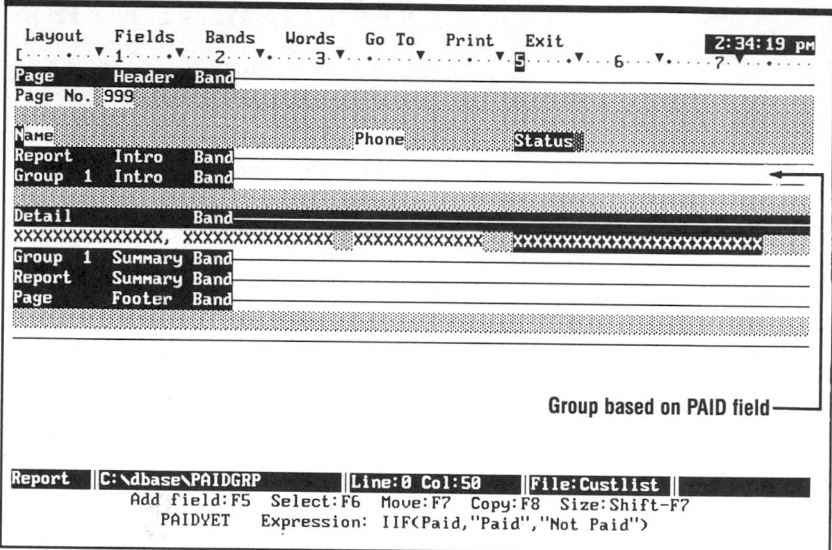

Figure 12.19: Report format that groups on the PAID field

```
Page No.   1

Name                                  Phone           Status

Beach, Sandy                          (717)555-0898   Paid
Jones, Fred                           (202)555-0987   Paid
Mahoney, Mary                         (206)555-8673   Paid
Newell, John                          (303)555-6739   Paid
Schumack, Susita                      (202)555-9720   Paid
Smith, Anita                          (415)555-9854   Paid
Smith, John                           (619)555-1234   Paid

Adams, Annie                          (714)555-0123   Not Paid
Kenney, Ralph                         (213)555-9988   Not Paid
```

Figure 12.20: Report grouped by the contents of the PAID field

Now, you may be wondering how the group heading was able to decide whether the PAID field was T or F, when the index "cheated" by converting these to the letters "A" and "Z." Remember, the index defines only the order in which records are displayed. As dBASE prints the report, it always looks at the original database data to decide when to end one group and start another. Hence, it does not matter how you convert the values in the index, so long as the index puts the records into the appropriate sort order for the grouping.

NESTING FUNCTIONS

You can nest functions within each other to combine their power. However, when you do so, you must make sure that each function has its appropriate number of opening and closing parentheses and that the parentheses are properly placed.

For example, the SQRT( ) function returns the square root of a positive number; thus, the expression SQRT(81) returns 9. You cannot take the square root of a negative number, so attempting to perform a calculation such as SQRT(–81) would cause dBASE to display an error message such as "Execution error on SQRT( ) : Negative." To avoid such errors, you could nest the ABS( ) (absolute value) function within the SQRT( ) function to convert any negative number to a positive number.

Hence, the expression SQRT(ABS(–81)) returns 9, because the ABS function converted the –81 to 81 before the SQRT function did its work. (dBASE always works from the innermost to the outermost function when functions are nested.) Note that the expression SQRT (ABS(–81) will generate a syntax error rather than the result you want because it contains two opening parentheses, but only one closing parenthesis. One of the functions is missing a closed parenthesis.

The expression SQRT(ABS)(–81) will also generate an error, even though there are an equal number of parentheses. The error in this case is that the ABS function is not fully nested within the SQRT function. The inner function, ABS(–81), must be fully nested within the outer function, SQRT, like this:

```
SQRT( ABS( – 81) )
```

When nesting functions, it is also important to remember that the inner function must return the correct data type for the outer functions. For example, the LEFT( ) function operates only on the Character data type. Therefore the expression LEFT(DATE( ),2) would produce an error, because the DATE( ) function returns the Date data type. On the other hand, the expression LEFT(DTOS (DATE( )),4) is valid because DTOS( ) converts the results of the DATE( ) function to the Character data type (for instance, "19930101") before the LEFT( ) function returns the four leftmost characters ("1993").

QUERIED INDEXES

Up to this point, you've seen how indexes can be used to control the sort order of records, and how queries can be used to display only certain types of records. You've also seen that queries can be used to control the sort order of records, using the Asc or AscDict operators.

At the risk of confusing things, perhaps now is a good time to mention that indexes can actually be used for simple queries. For example, you can create an index that includes only records that have CA in the STATE field. Whenever you activate that index, records without CA in the STATE field will be "invisible."

Now you may be thinking, "If queries can do sorts, and indexes can do queries, why have both?" There are several answers to this question. But suffice it to say for now that indexes only let you do rudimentary querying, and do not offer all the features of the queries design screen such as file linking, a view skeleton, and so forth.

To create a "query" index, you need to create an index expression and a *FOR clause* for that index. You can do so either after choosing Organize ► Create New Index or Organize ► Modify Existing Index (at the edit, browse, or database design screen). After selecting the FOR Clause option, you can press Shift-F1 to access the Expression Builder if you want help creating your expression.

The expression you use in a FOR clause should follow the general syntax shown below:

fieldname operator value

The arguments in this syntax are described below:

fieldname	The name of the field to be queried
operator	The comparison method, such as = (equal), <> (not equal), > (greater than), < (less than), $ (embedded in), and so forth, as discussed in Chapter 6
value	The value being searched for such as "CA" or {12/31/93} or 123.45, using the same data type delimiters described in Chapter 6

For example, if you wanted your index to include only CA residents, the FOR clause expression would be

STATE = "CA"

as shown in Figure 12.21.

Whenever you use this index to organize your database records (by choosing Organize ► Order Records by Index), only records with CA in the STATE field will be displayed. (In this example, the records will be in alphabetical order by name.)

If you wanted to create an index that includes only records with today's date in a Date field named STARTDATE, the FOR clause expression would be:

STARTDATE = DATE( )

If you wanted to create an index that displays only records that have a value of $1,000.00 or more in a Numeric field named PRICE, you would use the expression:

PRICE >= 1000

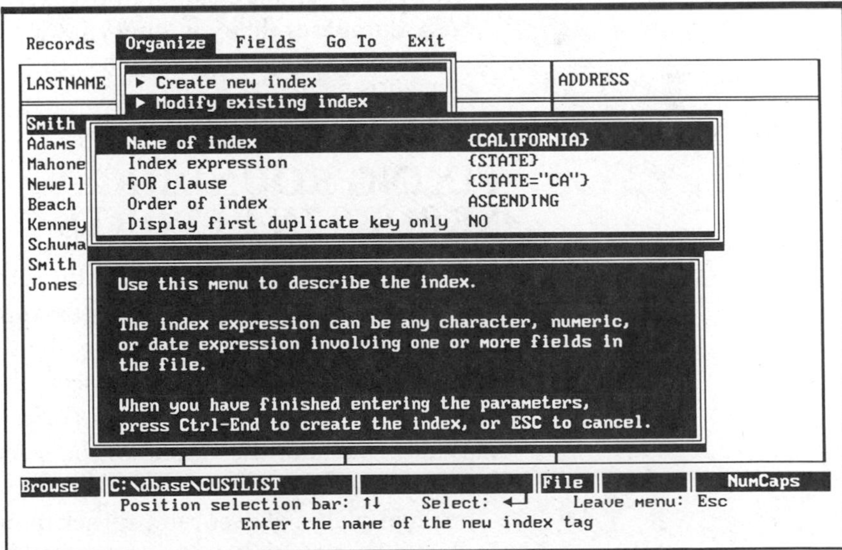

Figure 12.21: Creating an index for CA residents only

What's the advantage of using a FOR clause with an index to "query" a database? At this point, there really is none other than the fact that you could instantly activate the "query" from the browse or edit screen by activating the index from the Organize pull-down menu—thereby eliminating the need to go to the queries design screen.

However, you will probably find it easier and less confusing to stick with the queries design screen, for now, to perform your queries. Later, if you get into programming with dBASE IV (starting in Chapter 17) you may find some interesting applications of this feature.

SPEEDING UP SUBSEQUENT QUERIES

dBASE IV sometimes creates temporary indexes during a query, then deletes those indexes after the query is finished to conserve disk space. If you want to keep those indexes around to speed up subsequent executions of the same query, or any other query that uses the same index characteristics, you can choose Fields ► Keep Speedup Indexes and change that option to Yes. This feature is most useful for large databases that you query frequently.

FIXING ROUNDING ERRORS IN REPORTS

A problem in many computer programs (not just dBASE IV) concerns rounding errors. The basic problem is that, even though the screen or printed report displays the results of calculations with two (or whatever) fixed decimal places, the results of those calculations are stored in memory with 15 (or so) decimal places of accuracy. When you total the results of the calculations in a report, the total might be off by a bit because the summing formula uses the full 15 decimal places of accuracy, rather than the fixed number of decimal places displayed on the screen.

Let's look at an example. Suppose you have a database that contains two fields, named Amount and Discount. Both fields are

Numeric; Amount has two decimal places, Discount has one decimal place, as shown below:

Record#	AMOUNT	DISCOUNT
1	123.41	9.1
2	123.41	9.8
3	123.41	10.0
4	123.41	10.1
5	123.41	10.5
6	123.41	12.0
7	123.41	15.5

Now let's say you create a report format that uses the formula below in a calculated field to calculate the Amount field discounted by the value in the Discount field:

```
Amount – ((Discount/100)*Amount)
```

The same report also uses a summary field to sum the results of the calculated field. When you print the report, the end result might end up looking like this:

```
    Amount    Disc. %      Total
  ----------  -------   ----------
    123.41       9.1     112.18
    123.41       9.8     111.32
    123.41      10.0     111.07
    123.41      10.1     110.95
    123.41      10.5     110.45
    123.41      12.0     108.60
    123.41      15.5     104.28
--------------------
    863.87   768.84
```

If you total up the amounts in the rightmost column, you'll see that the final total is off by a penny. It should be 768.85, not 768.84. The "missing penny" is bound to drive any accountant batty.

To fix the problem, you need to use the ROUND function to round the results of any operations involving multiplication or division to the same number of decimal places used in the total (two decimal places in this example). The ROUND function requires the basic syntax

ROUND (*value,decimal places*)

where *value* is a number or a formula that results in a number that you want rounded; and *decimal places* is the number of decimal places to round to.

To fix the rounding error in the example shown above, you would replace the formula **Amount – ((Discount/100)*Amount)** in the report format with the formula:

```
ROUND(Amount – ((Discount/100)*Amount),2)
```

Here, the original formula is used as the *value* in the round function, and the 2 specifies that the result be rounded to two decimal places of accuracy.

Figure 12.22 shows a sample report format with the formula in place. The calculated field in the report Detail band is currently highlighted. It's a Calculated field, named DiscAmt. You can see the formula used in this calculated field next to Expression near the bottom of the screen.

The Report Summary band contains Summary fields to sum the Amount field, and the calculated DiscAmt field (no rounding is required in the summary calculations). When you print this modified version of the report, the outcome is:

Amount	Disc. %	Total
----------	-------	----------
123.41	9.1	112.18
123.41	9.8	111.32
123.41	10.0	111.07
123.41	10.1	110.95

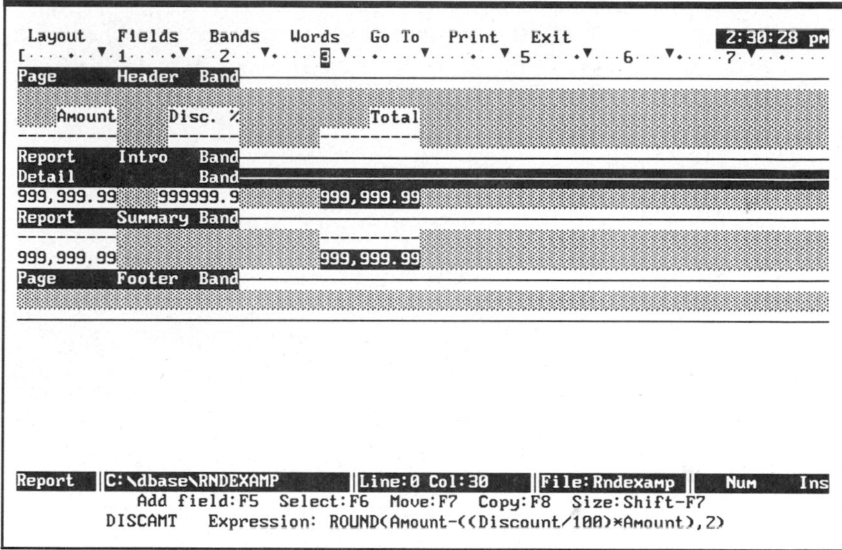

Figure 12.22: Sample report format with the ROUND function used in a calculated field to prevent rounding errors in the total

Amount	Disc. %	Total
123.41	10.5	110.45
123.41	12.0	108.60
123.41	15.5	104.28

863.87	768.84	

This is probably more of what you had in mind in the first place!

MORE ON FUNCTIONS

This chapter has introduced some of dBASE IV's many functions and provided some practical suggestions for using them in your work. For a quick reference to all of dBASE IV's functions, see Appendix E.

CHAPTER

13

Managing Related Database Files

To create databases that have a one-to-many relationship 437
among fields, put a common field with the same name, data type, width, and decimal places in each database.

To view data from two databases simultaneously, 438
set up a query that uses an identical example to link the two databases on the common field.

To print reports from multiple related databases, 453
save the query that links the databases and use it as the basis for the report design.

To print reports grouped by a particular field from a view, 454
use sorting operators in the appropriate fields of the query.

To link more than two files, 456
place a file skeleton for each database in the query and use matching examples to link the common fields.

To execute automatic updating, 464
as when you subtract items sold from the in-stock quantity in an inventory database, use a REPLACE query with an example to link the common fields, placeholders for values being added or subtracted, and expressions in the target file skeleton to perform the appropriate calculation.

UP TO NOW, WE HAVE FOCUSED ON WORKING WITH A single database at a time. Now it's time to add a new dimension to your database management skills by learning to manage multiple *related* files. But before we discuss the specific techniques involved, let's discuss *database design theory*.

DATABASE DESIGN

In most business applications, it is simply not practical to store all information in a single database file. Suppose, for instance, that you want to store accounts receivable information for customer charge account transactions in which a customer can charge any number of items in a month. You can attempt to store the accounts receivable information in a single database file using either one record per transaction or one record per customer. Neither of these approaches is satisfactory, however.

If you base each record on a single charge transaction, as in Figure 13.1, the database will store the correct information, but the database will not be efficient or convenient to use because

- Repeating names and addresses wastes a lot of disk space.
- If the person entering the information has to retype the name and address for every order, much time is wasted.
- If a customer changes address, this change must be made in many different records.

```
LastName FirstName Address      City       State Zip    Amount         Date
---------------------------------------------------------------------------
Smith    John      123 A St.    San Diego  CA     92067  $276.69    01/01/93
Smith    John      123 A St.    San Diego  CA     92067  $600.26    01/01/93
Smith    John      123 A St.    San Diego  CA     92067  $962.91    01/01/93
Smith    John      123 A St.    San Diego  CA     92067  $291.88    02/02/93
Smith    John      123 A St.    San Diego  CA     92067  $972.70    02/02/93
Beach    Sandy     11 Elm St.   Portland   OR     76543  $331.00    01/01/93
Beach    Sandy     11 Elm St.   Portland   OR     76543  $100.63    01/01/93
Beach    Sandy     11 Elm St.   Portland   OR     76543  $698.52    01/01/93
Beach    Sandy     11 Elm St.   Portland   OR     76543  $183.15    02/02/93
Beach    Sandy     11 Elm St.   Portland   OR     76543  $217.41    02/02/93
```

Figure 13.1: A poorly designed accounts receivable database

If you base each record on a customer, rather than a transaction, and use multiple fields for charge transactions, you eliminate the problem of repeated names and addresses. Figure 13.2 shows an example in which charge amounts are stored in fields named Amount1, Amount2, and Amount3, and dates are stored in similarly named fields. This second design, however, has a different set of problems:

- There is a limit to the number of fields that a database record can have, so there is a limit to the number of charges a customer can make.
- If you want to query for all charge transactions that occurred, for example, on 01/01/93, you would need to include each Date field in the query (Date1 =01/01/93 or Date2 =01/01/93 or Date3 = 01/01/93 . . . and so on).
- You could not easily distinguish charges that have been invoiced or paid from those that have not.

LastName	FirstName	Address	City	State	Zip	Amount1	Date1	Amount2	Date2	Amount3	Date3
Smith	John	123 A St.	San Diego	CA	92067	$468.39	01/01/93	$926.61	01/01/93	$ 54.66	01/01/93
Adams	Annie	3456 Ocean St.	Santa Monica	CA	92001	$702.02	01/01/93	$253.07	01/01/93	$684.76	01/01/93
Mahoney	Mary	211 Seahawk	Seattle	WA	88977	$632.50	01/01/93	$351.02	01/01/93	$702.53	01/01/93
Newell	John	734 Rainbow	Butte	MT	54321	$665.33	01/02/93	$892.19	01/02/93	$294.24	01/02/93
Beach	Sandy	11 Elm St.	Portland	OR	76543	$ 75.96	01/02/93	$970.92	01/02/93	$ 99.69	01/02/93
Kenney	Ralph	1101 Rainbow	Los Angeles	CA	96607	$582.68	01/02/93	$307.47	01/02/93	$523.95	01/02/93
Schumack	Susita	47 Broad St.	Philadelphia	PA	45543	$990.16	01/03/93	$598.00	01/03/93	$943.32	01/03/93

Figure 13.2: A second poor design for the accounts receivable database

At the heart of this accounts receivable problem is the fact that there is a natural *one-to-many* relationship between customers and their charges. Any *one* customer may have *many* charges, and in fact may have any *unpredictable* number of charges.

The best way to store information when there is a one-to-many relationship involved is to place the information on two separate databases in such a manner as to minimize repetition of information. Hence, the best way to store information about customers and their charges is to use two separate database files: one for names and addresses and another for charge transactions. That way, you will not need to repeat information unnecessarily, and the number of charge transactions that a customer can make will not be limited.

However, separating customers and their transactions into two separate database files does create one new problem. How do you ensure that each charge in the charge transaction database is billed to the correct customer? The solution to this problem is the *common field.*

RELATING DATABASE FILES

If you store customer information in one database and charges in another, you need some way to *relate* each charge to the appropriate customer. To do this, you create a common field: a field that exists in both databases. This field must contain information that is unique to each customer. If the linking information is not unique to each customer, problems will arise.

For example, if you use the customer's last name to link charges to customers, dBASE can look at any single charge and link it to a specific customer, such as Smith. But what if there are two or more Smiths? How does dBASE decide which Smith gets the bill?

You could use two fields, LastName and FirstName in the Charges database to specify which customer a charge belongs to, but you still run into the same problem if there are two customers named John Doe. You could further clarify who a charge belongs to by adding the Address field to the Charges database, but by this point, you're back to repeating too much information from the Customer database in the Charges database.

The best way to solve this problem of relating the two databases is to assign each customer a unique customer number, or code, and to store this code with each record in the Charges database. As long as no two customers have the same customer number, there can be no confusion about who is responsible for each charge transaction.

Figure 13.3 shows an example in which a field named CUSTNO exists in both the CHARGES database and the CUSTOMER database. Notice that each customer has a unique customer number, so there is no doubt about who gets billed for charges to customer number 1002, or any other number.

CUSTOMER database

CustNo	LastName	FirstName	Address	City	State	Zip
1001	Smith	John	123 A St.	San Diego	CA	92067
1002	Adams	Annie	3456 Ocean St.	Santa Monica	CA	92001
1003	Mahoney	Mary	211 Seahawk	Seattle	WA	88977
1004	Newell	John	734 Rainbow	Butte	MT	54321
1005	Beach	Sandy	11 Elm St.	Portland	OR	76543
1006	Kenney	Ralph	1101 Rainbow	Los Angeles	CA	96607
1007	Schumack	Susita	47 Broad St.	Philadelphia	PA	45543

CHARGES database

CustNo	Amount	Date
1001	$468.39	01/01/93
1001	$702.02	01/01/93
1001	$632.50	01/01/93
1001	$665.33	01/02/93
1002	$75.96	01/02/93
1002	$582.68	01/02/93
1002	$990.16	01/03/93
1002	$926.61	01/01/93
1003	$253.07	01/01/93
1003	$351.02	01/01/93

Figure 13.3: The best way to store accounts receivable data

Of course, the design shows only a basic structure for the accounts receivable application. Realistically, you would probably want to store more information about each charge, such as the item purchased, the quantity, and the unit price. You could certainly add such fields to the CHARGES database.

In an accounts receivable system, you also need to keep track of payments. But this is no problem now, because you can just create a third database, perhaps named PAYMENTS, and use the CUSTNO field to identify the customer to which each payment belongs. The following small sample database presents an example:

CustNo	CheckNo	AmtPaid	DatePaid
1001	285	$100.00	01/30/93
1002	998	$300.00	01/29/93
1003	335	$ 50.00	02/01/93

As you can see, it's quite easy to see which customer made each payment in this database, because the CustNo field clearly links each payment to a specific customer.

There is always the temptation to kill two birds with one stone by putting hidden meaning into common fields that relate two files. For example, you might assign each customer a code such as SD41293, where SD stands for San Diego, 4 stands for an excellent credit rating, and 1293 stands for a starting date. But if you try to use a scheme like this and end up with two or more San Diego residents with credit ratings of 4 and start dates of 12/93, you have a problem on your hands. When you enter a charge transaction for customer number SD41293, dBASE will not know to *which* customer SD41293 the transaction belongs.

Using an arbitrary and meaningless number is the best (albeit most impersonal) way to relate two files. For example, if you have fewer than 9,000 customers, assign those customers numbers in the range 1001 to 9999. Starting at 1001 ensures that each customer has a four-digit number, which adds consistency to the numbering scheme.

CREATING MULTIPLE RELATED DATABASES

When developing multiple related databases, you create each separate database using the same techniques you've used elsewhere in this book. That is, you select <create> from the Data panel in the Control Center and define each field. But you need to be sure that each of the related databases includes a field that has the same name, data type, width, and decimal places in both files. It also is a good idea to index this field in both databases, as this will speed up later operations.

To see how multiple related databases work, we'll modify the CUSTLIST and ORDERS databases in the LEARN catalog to link orders to customers. Be sure dBASE IV is up and running on your computer right now and that the LEARN catalog is in the Control Center.

1. Highlight CUSTLIST in the Control Center Data panel and press or click Design (Shift-F2).
2. Press Esc to leave the Organize menu and then press Ctrl-N to insert a new field.

3. Enter a new field named **CUSTNO**, with the **Numeric** data type, a width of **4**, **0** decimal places, and **Y** in the index column, as shown in Figure 13.4.
4. Press Ctrl-End to complete the addition.
5. When dBASE asks for permission to make the change, select Yes.

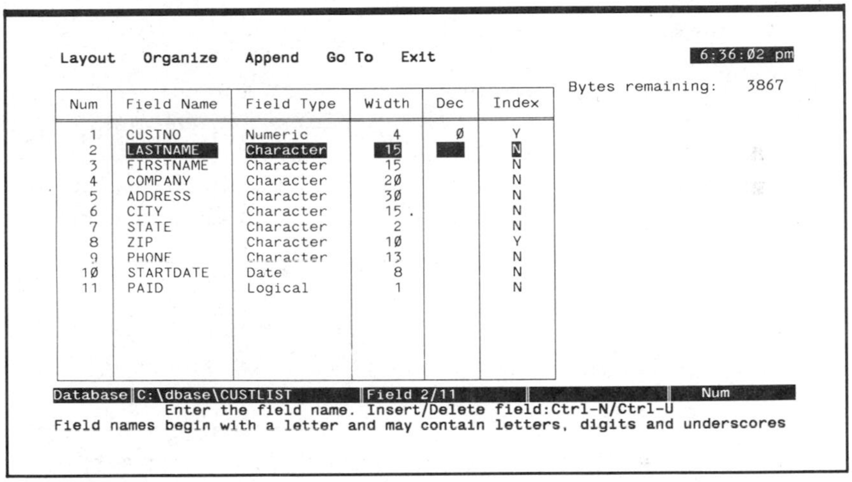

Layout Organize Append Go To Exit 6:36:Ø2 pm

Bytes remaining: 3867

Num	Field Name	Field Type	Width	Dec	Index
1	CUSTNO	Numeric	4	Ø	Y
2	LASTNAME	Character	15		N
3	FIRSTNAME	Character	15		N
4	COMPANY	Character	2Ø		N
5	ADDRESS	Character	3Ø		N
6	CITY	Character	15		N
7	STATE	Character	2		N
8	ZIP	Character	1Ø		Y
9	PHONE	Character	13		N
1Ø	STARTDATE	Date	8		N
11	PAID	Logical	1		N

Database C:\dbase\CUSTLIST Field 2/11 Num

Enter the field name. Insert/Delete field:Ctrl-N/Ctrl-U

Field names begin with a letter and may contain letters, digits and underscores

Figure 13.4: CUSTNO field added to the CUSTLIST database

The next step is to assign a number to each customer. You could go the browse or edit screen and do this record by record—but you also can take a shortcut:

1. Select <create> from the Queries panel of the Control Center.
2. Type the update operator **REPLACE** beneath the file name in the file skeleton and press ↵.
3. Select Proceed when dBASE warns you about removing the view skeleton.
4. Press Tab and enter the update expression **WITH RECNO( ) + 1000** under the CUSTNO field name, so your screen looks like Figure 13.5.

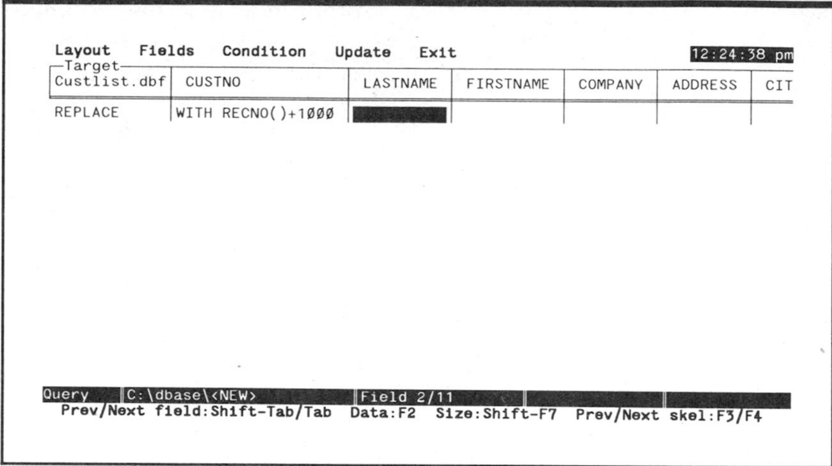

Figure 13.5: Query to add customer numbers

5. Choose Update ► Perform the Update.
6. When the update is complete, press any key, then press or click Data (F2) to see the results.

Your screen should look like Figure 13.6 now, where each customer has a unique number starting at 1001. The update query told dBASE to replace the current (empty) contents of the CUSTNO field with the record number (using the RECNO( ) function) plus 1000, so the customers now have numbers 1001, 1002, 1003, and so forth. (Again, this is just a shortcut for your convenience; you could just as well have typed these numbers into the blank field from the browse or edit screen.)

Now let's modify the ORDERS database. Leave the current browse screen by pressing Esc and selecting No when dBASE asks if you want to save the query. When you get back to the Control Center, follow these steps to add a CUSTNO field to the ORDERS database:

1. Highlight ORDERS in the Data panel and press or click Design (Shift-F2) to get to the database design screen.
2. Press Esc, and then Ctrl-N to insert a new field.

3. Add the CUSTNO field, using the exact same field name, data type, width, decimals, and index option as used in the CUSTLIST database, as shown in Figure 13.7.
4. Press Ctrl-End and select Yes when prompted.

Records Organize Fields Go To Exit

CUSTNO	LASTNAME	FIRSTNAME	COMPANY	ADDRESS
1001	Smith	John	ABC Co.	123 A St.
1002	Adams	Annie		3456 Ocean St.
1003	Mahoney	Mary		211 Seahawk St.
1004	Newell	John	LoTech Co.	734 Rainbow Dr.
1005	Beach	Sandy	American Widget	11 Elm St.
1006	Kenney	Ralph		1101 Rainbow Ct.
1007	Schumack	Susita	SMS Software	47 Broad St.
1008	Smith	Anita	Zeerocks, Inc.	2001 Engine Dr.
1009	Jones	Fred	American Sneaker	P.O. Box 3381

Browse C:\dbase\CUSTLIST Rec 1/9 File

Figure 13.6: A number assigned to each customer

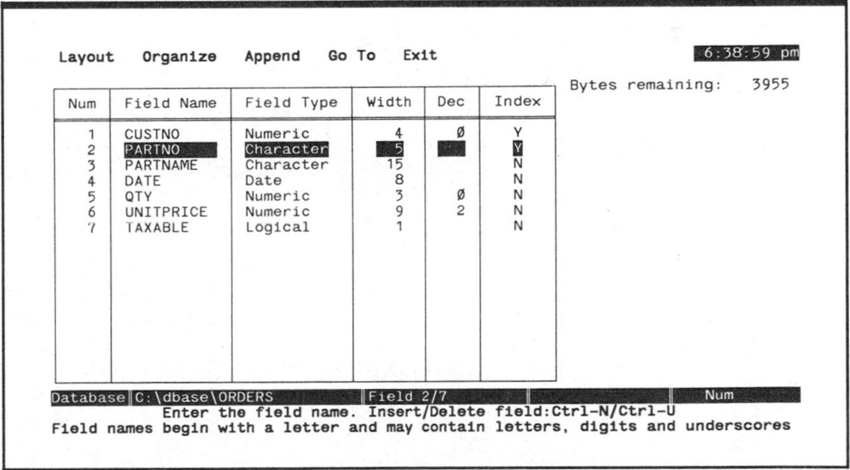

Figure 13.7: CUSTNO field added to the ORDERS database

5. To deactivate the CUSTNO index before adding new records, press ↵ and select Close File.

After you've added the indexed CUSTNO field, you must close the file to deactivate the index so that dBASE will not re-sort records as you enter customer numbers later.

Choose Organize ► Order Records by Index, then Natural Order to prevent record re-sort while adding customer numbers.

Now you need to assign each order in the ORDERS database to a customer. Follow these steps:

1. Highlight ORDERS and press or click Data (F2) to get to the browse screen. (If the edit screen appears instead, press F2 again.)
2. Press PgUp to make sure you are at the topmost record in ORDERS.
3. Type customer numbers, as in Figure 13.8.

Records Organize Fields Go To Exit

CUSTNO	PARTNO	PARTNAME	DATE	QTY	UNITPRICE	TAXABLE
1001	B-222	Mondo Man	06/01/93	2	100.00	F
1002	B-222	Mondo Man	06/01/93	1	100.00	F
1001	A-111	Astro Buddies	06/01/93	2	50.00	T
1001	C-333	Cosmic Critters	06/01/93	1	500.00	T
1002	A-111	Astro Buddies	06/02/93	3	55.00	T
1003	A-111	Astro Buddies	06/05/93	4	55.00	T
1003	B-222	Mondo Man	06/15/93	1	100.00	F
1004	C-333	Cosmic Critters	06/15/93	2	500.00	T
1005	C-333	Cosmic Critters	06/15/93	1	500.00	T
1006	C-333	Cosmic Critters	07/01/93	2	500.00	T

Browse | C:\dbase\ORDERS | Rec 1/10 | File

Figure 13.8: Customer numbers added to the ORDERS database

4. If the "Add New Records" prompt appears after you enter the last customer number, type **N** for No.
5. Choose Exit ► Exit after entering customer numbers for orders.

At this point, you have assigned each customer in the CUSTLIST database a unique customer number. Also, you've assigned transactions in the ORDERS database to individual customers. That's *all* you've done. dBASE does not yet "know" that the

CUSTNO field in ORDERS is in any way related to the CUSTNO field in the CUSTLIST database. However, as you will see in a moment, you can use the common CUSTNO field to create a view that links records from the two databases.

Before we create a view, however, let's clarify one point. You may have noticed that the ORDERS database contains repeated information: PARTNAME and UNITPRICE are repeated for each part number. You may wonder whether you can create a third database with information about parts, including part number, part name, and unit price, and then include only the part number in the ORDERS database to avoid the repetitions. The answer is yes, you can.

For now, however, we will focus on techniques for managing just two related database files. Once you've learned how to manage two related databases, you'll see that managing three or more is just as easy.

COMBINING INFORMATION FROM RELATED DATABASES

Suppose you want to view all the records in the ORDERS database, with the name of the customer who placed each order. You need some information from ORDERS and some from CUSTLIST to accomplish this. Therefore, you need to create a view that links the two databases by their common field, CUSTNO. A view essentially is a query that includes two or more file skeletons and an *example* (or *placeholder*) to relate the common fields. The example used in the query design screen must show dBASE that records with identical values in the common field on both databases are related. Let's build a view now to link ORDERS and CUSTLIST, following these steps:

1. If the ORDERS database is not currently in use (above the line in the Data panel), highlight its name and press ↵ (or double-click its name), then select Use File from the submenu that appears.

> **NOTE**
>
> Basic techniques for using the query design screen were presented in Chapter 6.

2. To start building the view, select <create> in the Queries panel which brings you to the query design screen.

3. Choose Fields ► Include Indexes to change the setting to Yes (a ▲ symbol appears next to the indexed fields).

4. Now, to bring a file skeleton of the CUSTLIST database into the design screen, choose Layout ► Add File to Query.
5. Select CUSTLIST.DBF from the submenu that appears.
6. Activate the CUSTLIST index by choosing Fields ► Include Indexes.
7. To tell dBASE that the two databases are related through the CUSTNO field, press Tab to move the highlight to the CUSTNO field in the CUSTLIST file skeleton, or click on the empty box just below that field name.
8. Choose Layout ► Create Link by Pointing. (Note that the placeholder LINK1 appears in the box, and instructions appear at the bottom of the screen.)
9. Press or click Choose File (F3) to move to the ORDERS database file skeleton, then press Tab to move the highlight to the CUSTNO field in that file skeleton.
10. Press ↵ to complete the link.

The Create Link by Pointing menu option uses LINK1 as the placeholder, but you can type any letter or word into the common fields, so long as you use the same letter or word in both file skeletons.

dBASE adds the placeholder LINK1 to the CUSTNO field of each file skeleton. The query presents an example to dBASE, where the CUSTNO field from each database contains the same placeholder. dBASE will follow this example when you execute the query and will display records that have the same value in the CUSTNO field.

Before you execute the query, you need to adjust the view skeleton to include fields from both databases. As you may recall, the view skeleton defines which fields will be displayed in the results of the query. At the moment, the view skeleton includes only fields from the ORDERS database. To view the customer's name with each order, you need to include the LASTNAME and FIRSTNAME fields from the CUSTLIST database in the view skeleton. Follow these steps to include those fields and rearrange the view skeleton:

1. Press or click Next Skel (F4) to move the highlight to the CUSTLIST database file skeleton, then press the Tab (or Shift-Tab) key as necessary to move the highlight to the LASTNAME box. Alternatively, you can click the mouse in the LASTNAME box of the CUSTLIST database file skeleton.

2. Press F5 to copy the field to the view skeleton (an arrow appears next to the field name after you press F5, indicating that the field is now included in the view skeleton).
3. Press Tab to move the highlight to the FIRSTNAME box, or click in that box.
4. Press F5 to copy it to the view skeleton.
5. Now, to display customer names next to the customer numbers, you need to rearrange the view skeleton. First press or click Next Skel (F4) to move the highlight to the view skeleton, or click the mouse on the horizontal line just above any of the field names in the view skeleton.
6. Press End to quickly move the highlight to the end of the view skeleton.
7. Press or click Select (F6) and then press Shift-Tab to highlight the LASTNAME and FIRSTNAME boxes.
8. Press ↵ to finish highlighting.
9. Press Home to quickly move the highlight to the beginning of the view skeleton.
10. Press or click Move (F7), then press ↵ to move the selected boxes, LASTNAME and FIRSTNAME, to the right of the CUSTNO box.

NOTE

Remember, a ▲ in the file skeleton indicates that the field is indexed and Include Indexes on the Fields pull-down menu is set to YES. A ↓ in the file skeleton indicates that the field is included in the view skeleton (by pressing F5).

At this point, your query should look like Figure 13.9. Notice that the view skeleton shows both the database and field name in each box. The box containing Orders – >CUSTNO will display the CUSTNO field from the ORDERS database. The Custlist – >LASTNAME and custlist – >FIRSTNAME boxes will display the LASTNAME and FIRSTNAME fields from the CUSTLIST database. (Some additional fields are beyond the right edge of the display.)

When you've completed the query, press Data (F2) to execute it. A browse screen will appear showing all the fields that you specified in the view skeleton. Figure 13.10 shows an example with LASTNAME and FIRSTNAME from the CUSTLIST database and CUSTNO, PARTNO, PARTNAME, QTY, and UNITPRICE from the ORDERS database. (If your screen shows other fields, use the Tab key to scroll horizontally through the browse screen.)

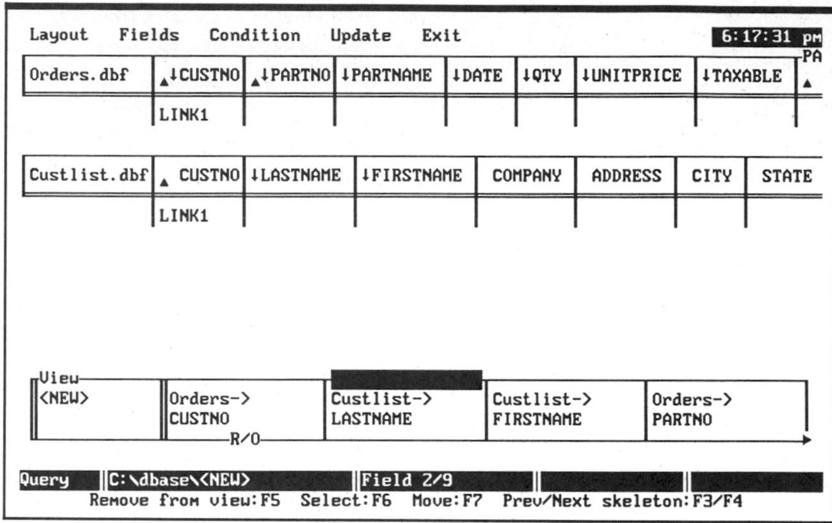

Figure 13.9: Query to link ORDERS and CUSTLIST

Records Organize Fields Go To Exit

CUSTNO	LASTNAME	FIRSTNAME	PARTNO	PARTNAME	QTY	UNITPRICE	TA
1001	Smith	John	B-222	Mondo Man	2	100.00	F
1001	Smith	John	A-111	Astro Buddies	2	50.00	T
1001	Smith	John	C-333	Cosmic Critters	1	500.00	T
1002	Adams	Annie	B-222	Mondo Man	1	100.00	F
1002	Adams	Annie	A-111	Astro Buddies	3	55.00	T
1003	Mahoney	Mary	A-111	Astro Buddies	4	55.00	T
1003	Mahoney	Mary	B-222	Mondo Man	1	100.00	F
1004	Newell	John	C-333	Cosmic Critters	2	500.00	T
1005	Beach	Sandy	C-333	Cosmic Critters	1	500.00	T
1006	Kenney	Ralph	C-333	Cosmic Critters	2	500.00	T

Browse C:\dbase\<NEW> Rec 1/9 View Num

Figure 13.10: Data from CUSTLIST and ORDERS combined in a view

The browse screen makes it appear as though a single database contains repetitive customer names with each order. However, we know that there is actually no such database; the browse screen is just presenting information from two related database files *as though* the names were stored repeatedly. As you'll see, you can use a view such as this to print invoices. That is, you can print customer names and addresses from the CUSTLIST database, along with transactions from the the ORDERS database.

When a browse or edit screen is displaying a view, you can often make changes. But do so with care, because your changes will affect the underlying database. For example, if you change any of the part numbers in the view, those changes affect the ORDERS database. Likewise, if you change a customer's last name in the view, you'll see those changes in the CUSTLIST database.

Not all data displayed through a view can be changed on the browse or edit screen, however. If you look back at Figure 13.9, you'll see "R/O" below the CUSTNO field in the view skeleton. "R/O" means the field is read-only, and that you cannot update it on the browse or edit screen. Likewise, after running certain queries, you will see "ReadOnly" in the status line of the browse or edit screen, which indicates that you cannot update *any* data in the view because all the fields are read-only. Figure 13.20 shows an example of a view that will not allow you to update any data.

Fortunately, you don't have to remember which fields can be updated and which cannot because dBASE will beep and ignore your keystrokes if you do try to change a read-only field.

INCLUDING EVERY RECORD

As you can see in Figure 13.10, the view presents only records that have a common CUSTNO in both the CUSTLIST and ORDERS databases. Customers numbered 1007 to 1009 are not included in the view, because these individuals had no records in the ORDERS database. However, in some situations you *might* want to include all records from a database file, even if the related file contains no information for some of the records.

To include all records from a file in a view, use the *Every* operator in the query, placing it before the linking example in the appropriate file skeleton (the file skeleton for the database that is not having all its records displayed: CUSTLIST in this example). Follow these steps to make this change:

1. Choose Exit ► Transfer to Query Design.
2. Press or click F3, then move the highlight to the CUSTNO field in the CUSTLIST file skeleton (or click on that field with your mouse).
3. Change the entry to **Every LINK1**, as shown in Figure 13.11 (you can type over the existing entry or insert the word Every if Insert mode is on).
4. Press Data (F2) to execute the query.

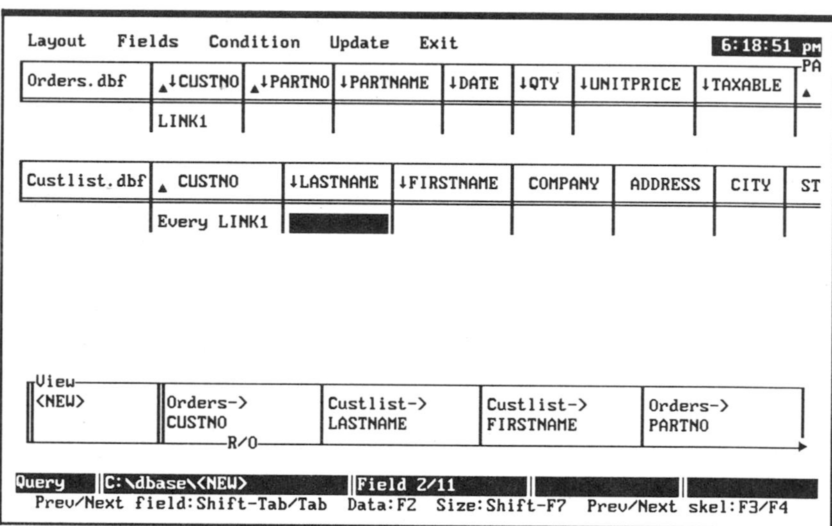

Figure 13.11: Query to include all records from CUSTLIST

Figure 13.12 shows the results of the query. Notice that even though there are no orders for Susita Schumack, Anita Smith, or Fred Jones, their records are included in the view. Fields from the ORDERS database for these customers are empty, because there is no related information. (The CUSTNO field contains blanks because the view skeleton shows Orders – >CUSTNO. If you changed the view skeleton to show CustList – >CUSTNO, then customer numbers for these three individuals would be displayed.)

Records Organize Fields Go To Exit

CUSTNO	LASTNAME	FIRSTNAME	PARTNO	PARTNAME	QTY	UNITPRICE	TA
1001	Smith	John	B-222	Mondo Man	2	100.00	F
1001	Smith	John	A-111	Astro Buddies	2	50.00	T
1001	Smith	John	C-333	Cosmic Critters	1	500.00	T
1002	Adams	Annie	B-222	Mondo Man	1	100.00	F
1002	Adams	Annie	A-111	Astro Buddies	3	55.00	T
1003	Mahoney	Mary	A-111	Astro Buddies	4	55.00	T
1003	Mahoney	Mary	B-222	Mondo Man	1	100.00	F
1004	Newell	John	C-333	Cosmic Critters	2	500.00	T
1005	Beach	Sandy	C-333	Cosmic Critters	1	500.00	T
1006	Kenney	Ralph	C-333	Cosmic Critters	2	500.00	T
	Schumack	Susita				.	
	Smith	Anita				.	
	Jones	Fred				.	

Browse C:\dbase\<NEW> Rec 1/9 View

Figure 13.12: Results of query for Every customer

ADDING FILTER CONDITIONS

If a query includes both a filter condition and an Every operator, the filter condition takes precedence.

You can still place any filter condition in the query to isolate records that meet some search criterion. If the filter condition is based on one of the linking fields, enter the LINK example first, followed by a comma and the filter condition. For example, the query shown in Figure 13.13 limits the display to orders for customer number 1002. Figure 13.14 shows the results of this query.

You can place filter conditions in any other field boxes in the usual manner and use the rows from each skeleton to create *AND* and *OR* relationships. For example, placing **"CA"** (with the quotation marks) in the STATE field of the CUSTLIST database limits output to California residents. Placing **"CA"** in the top row of the CUST-LIST file skeleton and **"A-111"** in the top row of the ORDERS skeleton, under the PARTNO field, limits the display to records that

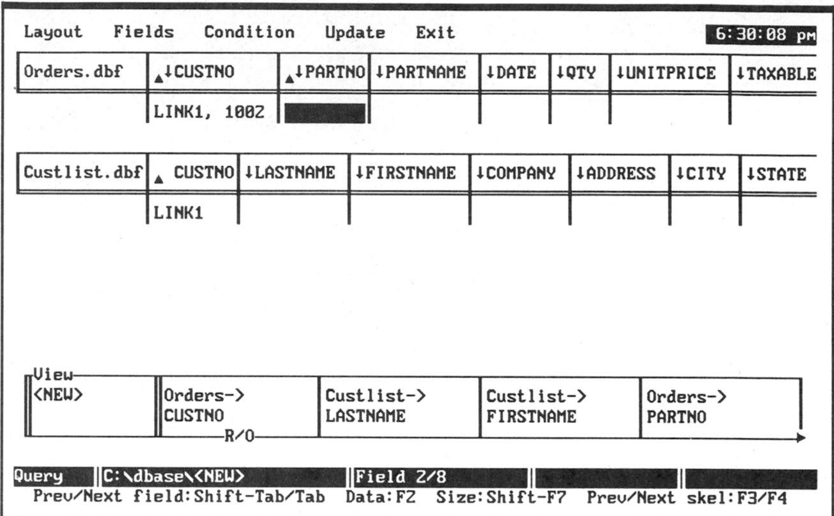

Figure 13.13: Query combining a filter condition and linking examples

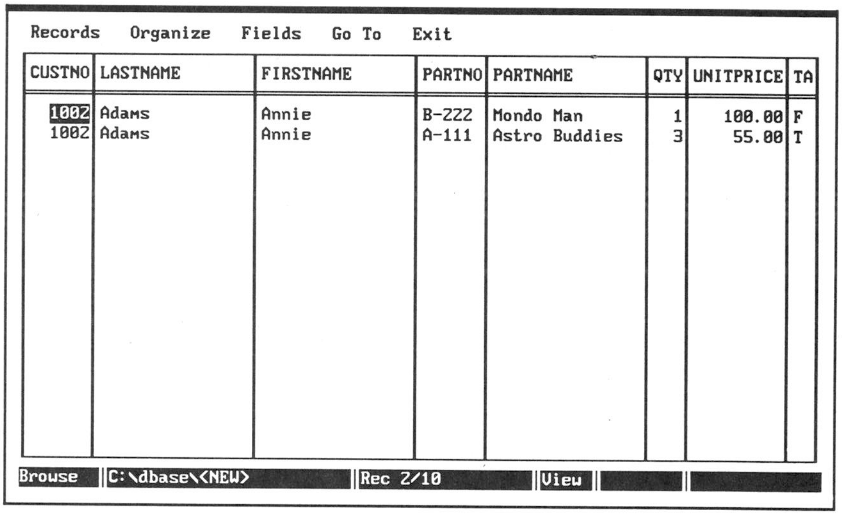

Records Organize Fields Go To Exit

CUSTNO	LASTNAME	FIRSTNAME	PARTNO	PARTNAME	QTY	UNITPRICE	TA
1002	Adams	Annie	B-222	Mondo Man	1	100.00	F
1002	Adams	Annie	A-111	Astro Buddies	3	55.00	T

Browse C:\dbase\<NEW> Rec 2/10 View

Figure 13.14: Results of query for orders by customer 1002

have CA in the STATE field *and* A-111 in the PARTNO field. Placing **"CA"** in the first row of the CUSTLIST skeleton and **"A-111"** in the second row of the ORDERS skeleton displays records that have CA in the STATE field *or* A-111 in the PARTNO field.

PRINTING REPORTS FROM RELATED DATABASES

To print a report from two databases, you first need to create a query that links the databases. Also, make sure that all the fields that you need in the printed report are included in the view skeleton. If the report that you want to print involves any groups, be sure to choose Fields ► Sort on This Field on the query screen to arrange the records into proper order for the grouping.

Figure 13.15 shows an example query, which we'll use to design a report to print invoices. The LINK1 placeholder is included to set up the link between CUSTLIST and ORDERS based on the common CUSTNO field. The Every operator ensures that all customers will be included in the view (though you could omit this operator if you wanted to print invoices for only those individuals who have outstanding orders).

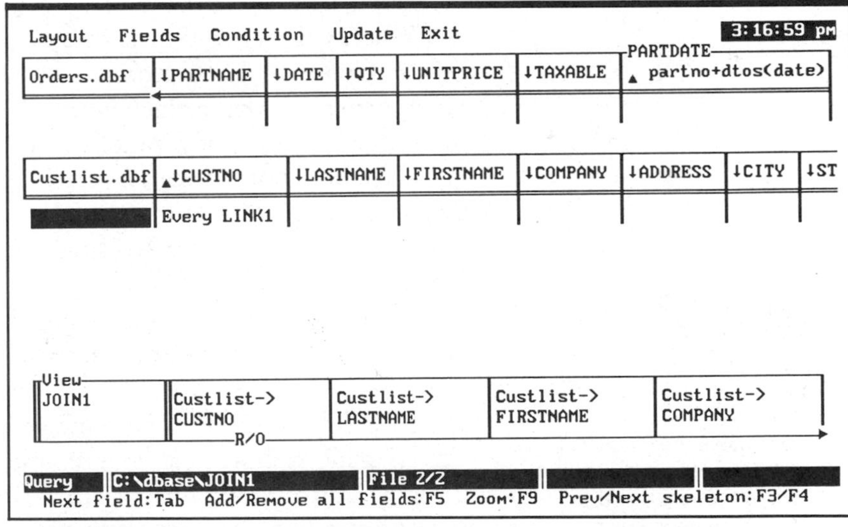

Figure 13.15: View to print a report

Using the Asc1 operator in the Orders ->CUSTNO field ensures that the orders are sorted into customer number order. (The sort is particularly important in this case because, when printing invoices, a group band based on customer number is needed to print each customer's charges on a single invoice.)

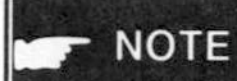
NOTE

To quickly put all fields from CUSTLIST into the view skeleton, first remove Orders – >CUSTNO by highlighting it and pressing F5. Then put the highlight beneath CustList.DBF and press F5.

NOTE

When you test this query, notice that the status line on the edit or browse screen indicates ReadOnly to remind you that you can't update *any* of the fields in this view.

TIP

To move the cursor to field templates that are off the right edge of the screen, move the cursor into the detail band and press End to move to the rightmost template or Ctrl-→ to move to the next template.

All fields from both database file skeletons, except Orders ->CUSTNO, are included in the view skeleton. Orders -> CUSTNO is not included in the view skeleton because, as you saw in an earlier example, this field is blank when displaying customers for which there are no charge transactions. We want to print a customer number on each invoice, so the query uses the CUSTNO field from the CUSTLIST database (which contains all customer numbers).

After creating the query and testing it by pressing Data (F2), press Design (Shift-F2) or choose Exit ► Transfer to Query Design to return to the query design screen. Then choose Layout ► Edit Description of Query and enter a description such as **View to link ORDERS and CUSTLIST**. Then choose Exit ► Save Changes and Exit. When prompted, enter the file name **JOIN1**.

Next, you need to use the view as the basis for building a report format. If JOIN1 is not already above the line in the Queries panel, highlight its name and press ↵ (or double-click on the name), and select Use View. Then highlight <create> in the Reports panel and press ↵ (or double-click on <create>).

When you get to the reports design screen, choose Quick Layouts ► Column Layout from the opened Layout menu to start with a column layout. The initial layout will include all fields that are in the view (though some may initially be off the right edge of your screen). As far as the reports design screen is concerned, a view is no different from a database file, so you are now free to use the same techniques you've used previously with single database files to design a report format to your liking.

To ensure that charges for a single customer are grouped together on one invoice, move the cursor to the Report Intro band (Band 2/5) and choose Bands ► Add a Group Band. Select Field Value and then CUSTNO as the field to base the groups on.

To print each invoice on a separate page, leave the cursor in the Group 1 Intro band border. Then choose Bands ► Begin Band on New Page and set the option to Yes.

Figure 13.16 shows a sample report format after adding, rearranging, and deleting some field templates, and closing the Report Summary and Page Footer bands (those bands have scrolled off the screen in the sample figure).

Notice the customer information in the figure: All fields are trimmed (using the Trim picture function), there's a space between the FIRSTNAME and LASTNAME fields on the first line of customer information, and the last line of customer information includes a comma and a space after the CITY field, and two spaces after the STATE field. By typing text (blank spaces and a comma in this case) between fields and trimming the fields, we avoid unsightly gaps between fields in the printed invoice report.

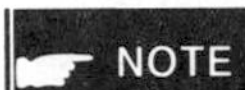

You could also use the IIF function in a calculated field to display the tax and total sale in this report, using techniques discussed in the previous chapter.

The field template furthest to the right of the detail band is a calculated field named ExtPrice, based on the expression Qty*UnitPrice. The template beneath that one is a summary field that sums the ExtPrice field. Be sure to set Reset Every to CUSTNO for this summary field so that the total is reset to zero for each customer.

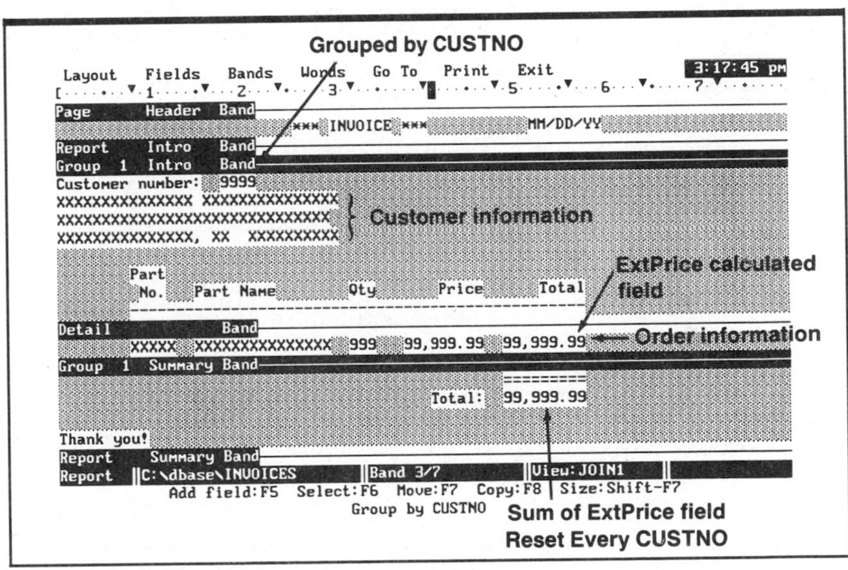

Figure 13.16: Report format for printing invoices

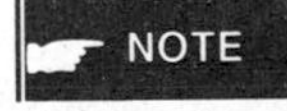

The sample application in Chapter 21 also prints invoices.

After creating the report format, choose Exit ► Save Changes and Exit to save it. Enter **INVOICES** as the file name when prompted. When you get back to the Control Center, you can select INVOICES from the Reports panel to print the invoices. Figure 13.17 shows an invoice printed from the report format.

```
                                   *** INVOICE ***              07/30/93
Customer number:  1003
Mary Mahoney
211 Seahawk St.
Seattle, WA  88977

        Part
         No.   Part Name         Qty        Price      Total
        ------------------------------------------------------
        A-111  Astro Buddies       4        55.00     220.00
        B-222  Mondo Man           1       100.00     100.00
                                                     =========
                                           Total:     320.00

Thank you!
```

Figure 13.17: An invoice printed from the JOIN1 view

USING FORMS WITH RELATED FILES

Remember dBASE beeps and ignores your keystrokes if you try to change data in a read-only field.

Just as you can use the fields in a view to lay out a report format, you can use a view to lay out a custom form. And in many cases, you can even use that custom form to change the data. As long as the status line of the custom form doesn't indicate "ReadOnly," and the field isn't marked with "R/O" on the view skeleton of the query design screen, you're free to change data through your custom form. In cases where you're not allowed to change the data, the custom form is still useful for viewing data on the screen.

The sample business management application in Chapter 20 demonstrates some advanced techniques for creating and using custom forms that access multiple related database files.

LINKING MORE THAN TWO FILES

A common field is also known as a linking field or a key field.

Linking three or more files is no more difficult than linking two. Just be sure that you include proper common fields so that you can set up the links. For example, Figure 13.18 shows a modified version of the CUSTLIST and ORDERS databases with a third database, named PARTLIST, added. The PARTLIST database contains information about the product inventory.

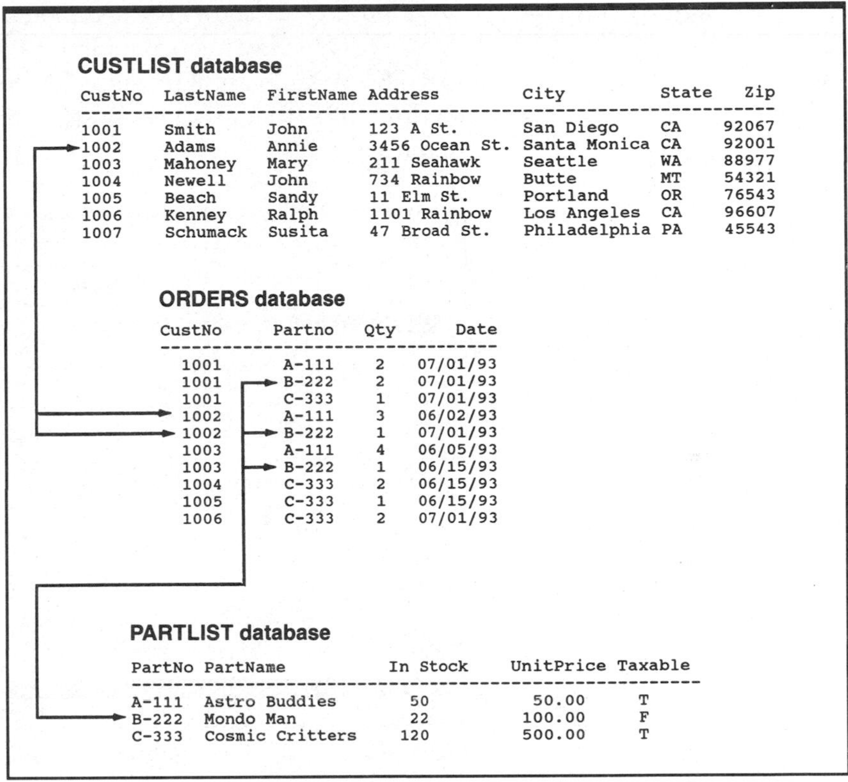

CUSTLIST database

CustNo	LastName	FirstName	Address	City	State	Zip
1001	Smith	John	123 A St.	San Diego	CA	92067
1002	Adams	Annie	3456 Ocean St.	Santa Monica	CA	92001
1003	Mahoney	Mary	211 Seahawk	Seattle	WA	88977
1004	Newell	John	734 Rainbow	Butte	MT	54321
1005	Beach	Sandy	11 Elm St.	Portland	OR	76543
1006	Kenney	Ralph	1101 Rainbow	Los Angeles	CA	96607
1007	Schumack	Susita	47 Broad St.	Philadelphia	PA	45543

ORDERS database

CustNo	Partno	Qty	Date
1001	A-111	2	07/01/93
1001	B-222	2	07/01/93
1001	C-333	1	07/01/93
1002	A-111	3	06/02/93
1002	B-222	1	07/01/93
1003	A-111	4	06/05/93
1003	B-222	1	06/15/93
1004	C-333	2	06/15/93
1005	C-333	1	06/15/93
1006	C-333	2	07/01/93

PARTLIST database

PartNo	PartName	In Stock	UnitPrice	Taxable
A-111	Astro Buddies	50	50.00	T
B-222	Mondo Man	22	100.00	F
C-333	Cosmic Critters	120	500.00	T

Figure 13.18: Database design with three related files

TIP

As an alternative to creating a link by pointing, you can type the example text yourself (taking care to type exactly the same text in both linked fields). For instance, you can create a link by typing LINK1 in the CUSTNO fields of both the CUSTLIST and ORDERS file skeletons; likewise, you can create a second link by typing LINK2 in the PARTNO fields of both the ORDERS and PARTLIST file skeletons.

PARTNO is the common field that links the PARTLIST database to the ORDERS database. It has the same name, data type, width, decimal places, and index option as the PARTNO field in the ORDERS database, as is required when creating a common field.

To set up a query to link the three files, you need to include file skeletons for all three files (using the usual Fields ► Include Indexes option to include the indexes for each database and the Layout ► Add File to Query option to add each new skeleton). Choose Layout ► Create Link by Pointing to set up the link between CUSTLIST and ORDERS and then choose Layout ► Create Link by Pointing a second time to set up the link from ORDERS to PARTLIST. (dBASE will automatically use LINK2 as the placeholder for the second link.)

Figure 13.19 shows the completed query. Note that in the figure, Asc1 will display records sorted by the CUSTNO field in the ORDERS database. The view skeleton includes selected fields from all three files (though some fields are beyond the left and right edges of the screen).

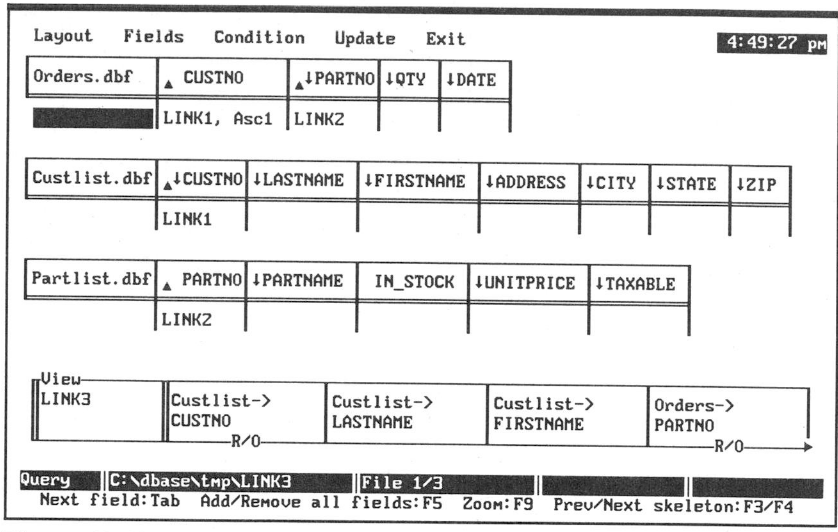

Figure 13.19: View linking three related files

Figure 13.20 shows the results of the query. Just as in the example with two databases, the customer's name, the part number, the part name, the unit price, and other information for each order is readily available and appears to be on one database. Of course, you can save this query and use it as the basis for developing report formats.

THE MANY-TO-MANY DESIGN

The preceding example has actually brought us into the realm of another common database design based on a *many-to-many* relationship. Whereas there is a one-to-many relationship between customers and orders (every one customer may place many orders) and

```
Records   Organize   Fields   Go To   Exit

CUSTNO LASTNAME   FIRSTNAME  PARTNO PARTNAME         QTY UNITPRICE TA
  1001 Smith      John       A-111  Astro Buddies      2     50.00 T
  1001 Smith      John       B-222  Mondo Man          2    100.00 F
  1001 Smith      John       C-333  Cosmic Critters    1    500.00 T
  1002 Adams      Annie      A-111  Astro Buddies      3     50.00 T
  1002 Adams      Annie      B-222  Mondo Man          1    100.00 F
  1003 Mahoney    Mary       A-111  Astro Buddies      4     50.00 T
  1003 Mahoney    Mary       B-222  Mondo Man          1    100.00 F
  1004 Newell     John       C-333  Cosmic Critters    2    500.00 T
  1005 Beach      Sandy      C-333  Cosmic Critters    1    500.00 T
  1006 Kenney     Ralph      C-333  Cosmic Critters    2    500.00 T

Browse  C:\dbase\tmp\LINK3   Rec 1/10   View  ReadOnly
```

Figure 13.20: Results of view linking three databases

a one-to-many relationship between Orders and Parts (each part may appear in many different orders), there is a many-to-many relationship between customers and parts—that is, many customers can order many different parts.

This type of relationship occurs quite often in applications that involve scheduling. For example, a school offers many different courses, and each course is attended by many different students. To set up a database design for such an application, you need three database files: one to list students, one to list courses, and one to list student's numbers and the courses in which they are enrolled. The design assumes that each student and each course has a unique number.

Figure 13.21 shows the three databases and the links among them. The common field between STUDENTS and LINKER is StudentID, a Character field that is 11 spaces wide in both databases. The common field linking COURSES to LINKER is CourseID, a Character field that is 5 spaces wide in both databases.

In Figure 13.21, you can see that course identifiers use a department abbreviation combined with a number (for example, Bi101). In a sense, this identification scheme goes against earlier advice about using arbitrary identifiers in common fields. However, in this particular case, so long as the school makes certain that each department has a

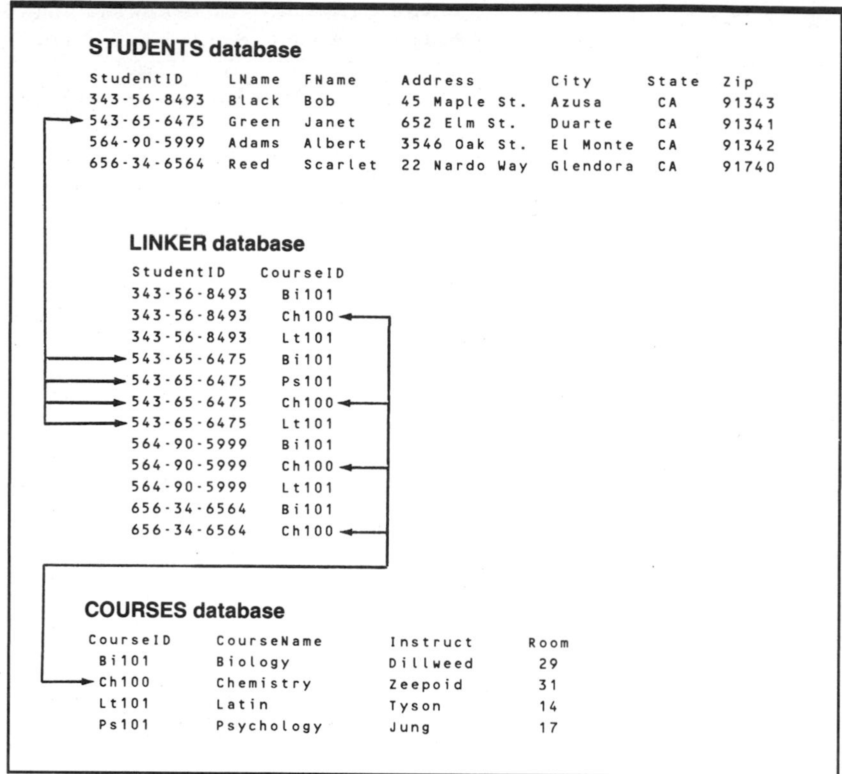

STUDENTS database

StudentID	LName	FName	Address	City	State	Zip
343-56-8493	Black	Bob	45 Maple St.	Azusa	CA	91343
543-65-6475	Green	Janet	652 Elm St.	Duarte	CA	91341
564-90-5999	Adams	Albert	3546 Oak St.	El Monte	CA	91342
656-34-6564	Reed	Scarlet	22 Nardo Way	Glendora	CA	91740

LINKER database

StudentID	CourseID
343-56-8493	Bi101
343-56-8493	Ch100
343-56-8493	Lt101
543-65-6475	Bi101
543-65-6475	Ps101
543-65-6475	Ch100
543-65-6475	Lt101
564-90-5999	Bi101
564-90-5999	Ch100
564-90-5999	Lt101
656-34-6564	Bi101
656-34-6564	Ch100

COURSES database

CourseID	CourseName	Instruct	Room
Bi101	Biology	Dillweed	29
Ch100	Chemistry	Zeepoid	31
Lt101	Latin	Tyson	14
Ps101	Psychology	Jung	17

Figure 13.21: Three related databases used for scheduling

unique abbreviation, and that each course in each department has a unique number, then each course will be ensured a unique code.

Figure 13.22 shows a query to display information from the three files, with records sorted by the StudentID field in the LINKER database. The view skeleton includes some fields from all three files (several fields are beyond the right edge of the screen). Note that all of the linking fields are indexed (as indicated by the ▲ symbol).

You could press F2 to see the immediate results of the query. Optionally, you could save the query and use it as a basis for creating the report format shown in Figure 13.23. In this report, the group band is based on the StudentID field.

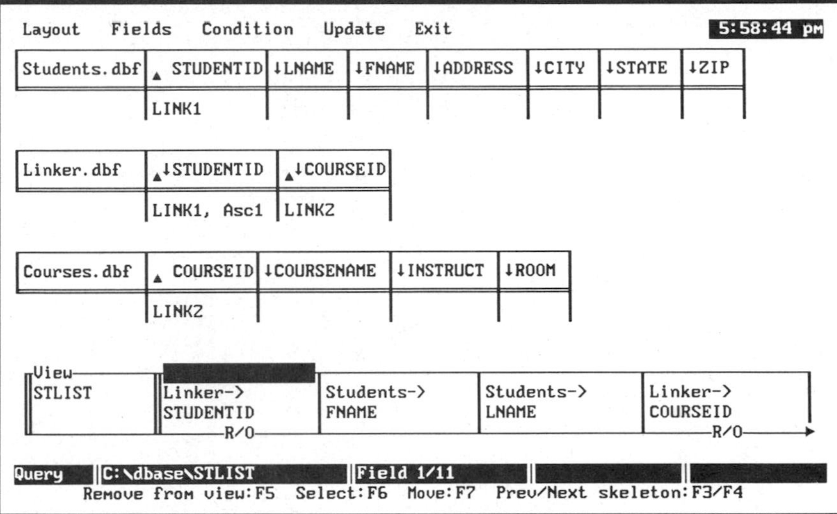

Figure 13.22: Query to display data from many-to-many related files

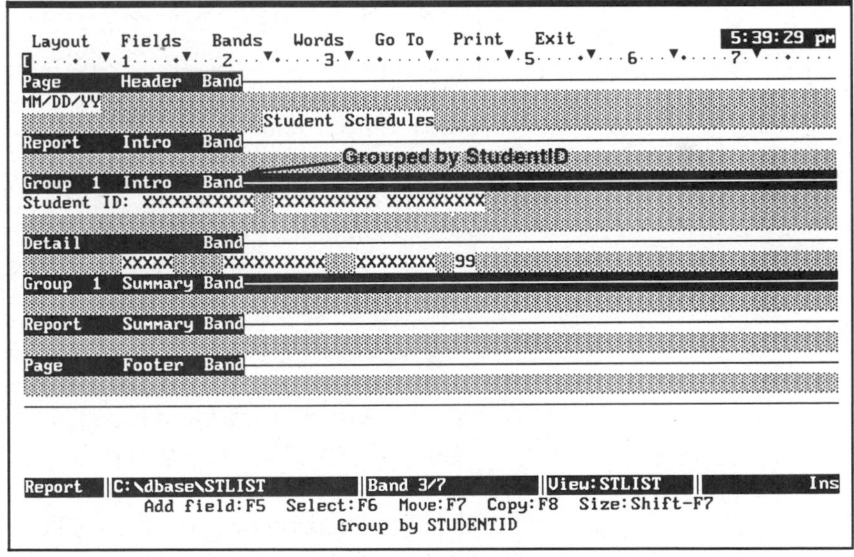

Figure 13.23: Report format to display students and courses

Figure 13.24 shows the output from the report format. Because the query sorts records into StudentID order, student numbers are printed in ascending order and grouped according to the group band field, StudentID.

```
07/21/93
                          Student Schedules

Student ID: 343-56-8493  Bob Black

            Bi101     Biology       Dillweed  29
            Ch100     Chemistry     Zeepold   31
            Lt101     Latin         Tyson     14

Student ID: 543-65-6475  Janet Green

            Bi101     Biology       Dillweed  29
            Ps101     Psychology    Jung      17
            Ch100     Chemistry     Zeepold   31
            Lt101     Latin         Tyson     14

Student ID: 564-90-5999  Albert Adams

            Bi101     Biology       Dillweed  29
            Ch100     Chemistry     Zeepold   31
            Lt101     Latin         Tyson     14

Student ID: 656-34-6564  Scarlet Reed

            Bi101     Biology       Dillweed  29
            Ch100     Chemistry     Zeepold   31
```

Figure 13.24: Report grouped by students

If you want a list of courses and the students enrolled in each, you set up the links in the query design screen, as usual, and base the sort order on the CourseID field in the LINKER database. Figure 13.25 shows the appropriate query. (Once again, some of the fields included in the view skeleton are off the right edge of the screen.)

Using this query as the basis for a report design, you could create a format with a group band based on the CourseID field, as shown in Figure 13.26. The actual report printed by the format is shown in Figure 13.27.

The two preceding examples illustrate the importance of selecting an appropriate sort field in the queries design screen if you want to print the results in a grouped report. To print a report with records grouped by students, the results of the query must be sorted by student number. To print a report with records grouped by courses, the results of the query must be sorted by course number.

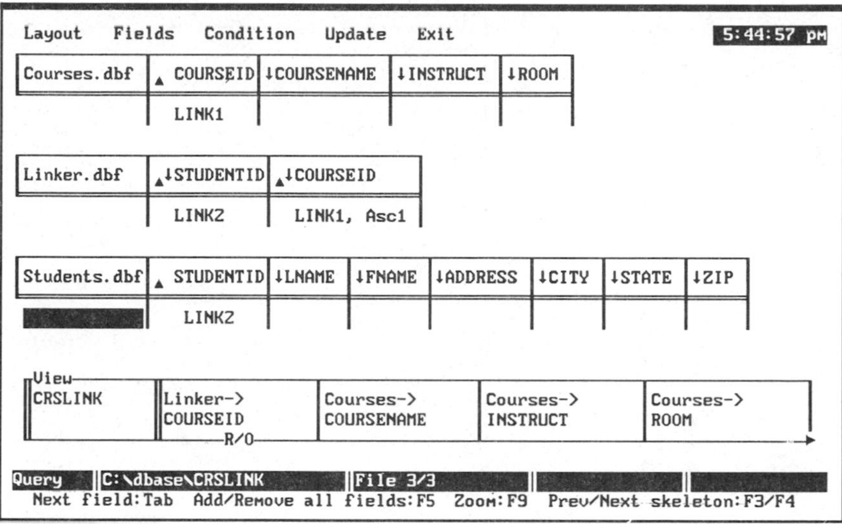

Figure 13.25: Query to list course schedule in CourseID order

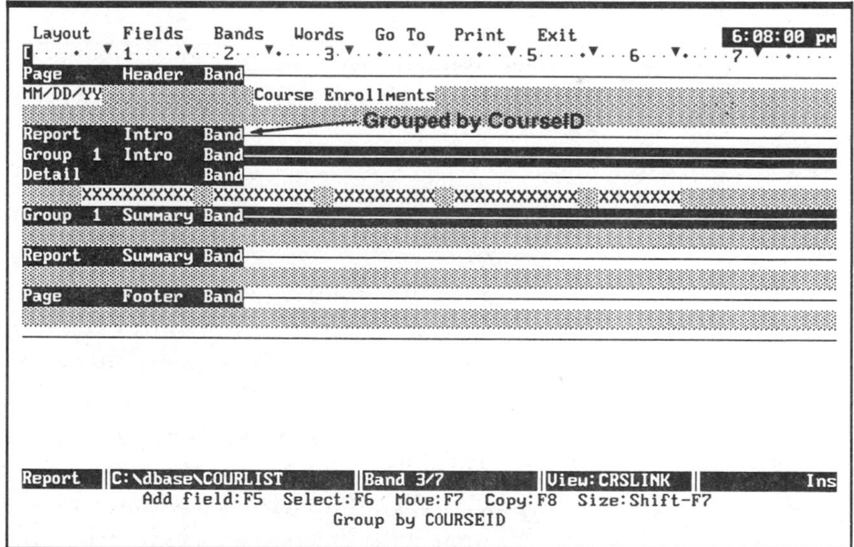

Figure 13.26: Report format to print course list

```
07/21/93                 Course Enrollments

Course number: Bi101  Course name: Biology
Instructor: Dillweed         Room:  29

      343-56-8493  Black       Bob          45 Maple St.  Azusa
      543-65-6475  Green       Janet        652 Elm St.   Duarte
      564-90-5999  Adams       Albert       3346 Oak St.  El Monte
      656-34-6564  Reed        Scarlet      22 Nardo Way  Glendora

Course number: Ch100  Course name: Chemistry
Instructor: Zeepold          Room:  31

      343-56-8493  Black       Bob          45 Maple St.  Azusa
      543-65-6475  Green       Janet        652 Elm St.   Duarte
      564-90-5999  Adams       Albert       3346 Oak St.  El Monte
      656-34-6564  Reed        Scarlet      22 Nardo Way  Glendora

Course number: Lt101  Course name: Latin
Instructor: Tyson            Room:  14

      343-56-8493  Black       Bob          45 Maple St.  Azusa
      543-65-6475  Green       Janet        652 Elm St.   Duarte
      564-90-5999  Adams       Albert       3346 Oak St.  El Monte

Course number: Ps101  Course name: Psychology
Instructor: Jung             Room:  17

      543-65-6475  Green       Janet        652 Elm St.   Duarte
```

Figure 13.27: Report grouped by course list

AUTOMATIC UPDATING

In many business applications, you'll want dBASE to automatically update information in one database file based on information in another database file. For example, suppose you have a database for your master inventory that includes the in-stock quantity of each item. A second database stores orders or sales transactions, including the part number and quantity of each item sold. To calculate the true in-stock quantity for each product in the inventory, you need to subtract the quantities sold from the in-stock quantities.

To understand how automatic updating works, assume that you have three database files, named MASTER, SALES, and PURCHASE. The MASTER database stores information about each item in the inventory, including the part number, part name, in-stock quantity, unit price, and reorder point, as well as other useful information. Figure 13.28 shows the database structure on the database design screen. Note that the PARTNO field is indexed. Figure 13.29 shows some sample records in the database.

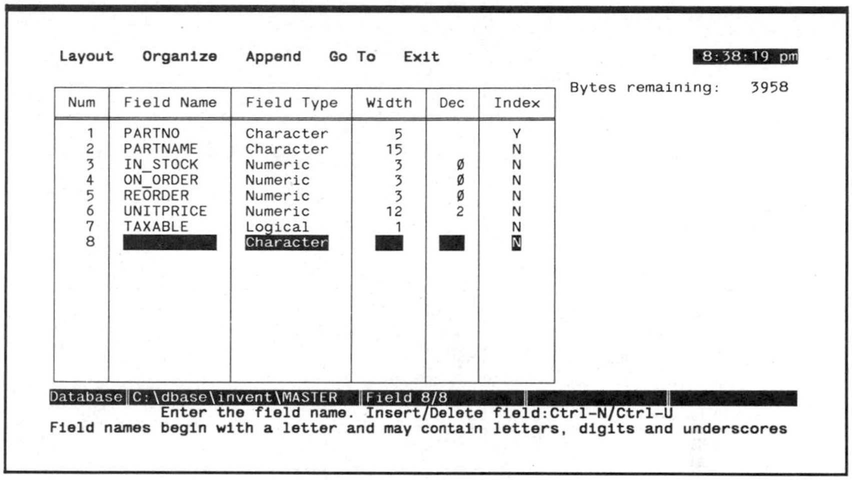

Layout Organize Append Go To Exit 8:38:19 pm

Bytes remaining: 3958

Num	Field Name	Field Type	Width	Dec	Index
1	PARTNO	Character	5		Y
2	PARTNAME	Character	15		N
3	IN_STOCK	Numeric	3	Ø	N
4	ON_ORDER	Numeric	3	Ø	N
5	REORDER	Numeric	3	Ø	N
6	UNITPRICE	Numeric	12	2	N
7	TAXABLE	Logical	1		N
8		Character			N

Database C:\dbase\invent\MASTER Field 8/8

Enter the field name. Insert/Delete field:Ctrl-N/Ctrl-U

Field names begin with a letter and may contain letters, digits and underscores

Figure 13.28: Structure of the MASTER database

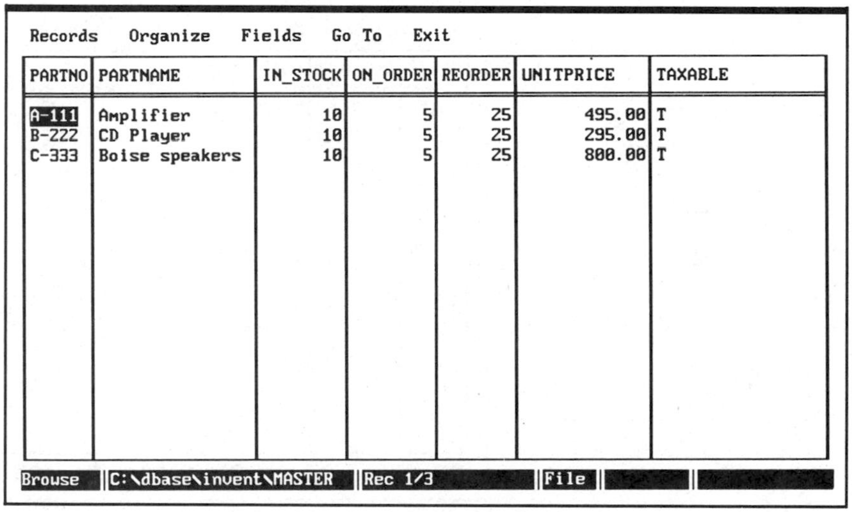

Records Organize Fields Go To Exit

PARTNO	PARTNAME	IN_STOCK	ON_ORDER	REORDER	UNITPRICE	TAXABLE
A-111	Amplifier	10	5	25	495.00	T
B-222	CD Player	10	5	25	295.00	T
C-333	Boise speakers	10	5	25	800.00	T

Browse C:\dbase\invent\MASTER Rec 1/3 File

Figure 13.29: Sample data in the MASTER database

Individual sales transactions are stored in the database named SALES. Figure 13.30 shows the structure of the SALES database. The PARTNO field is indexed and is the common field that will be used to link sales transactions to items in the MASTER database. Figure 13.31 shows some sample records in the database.

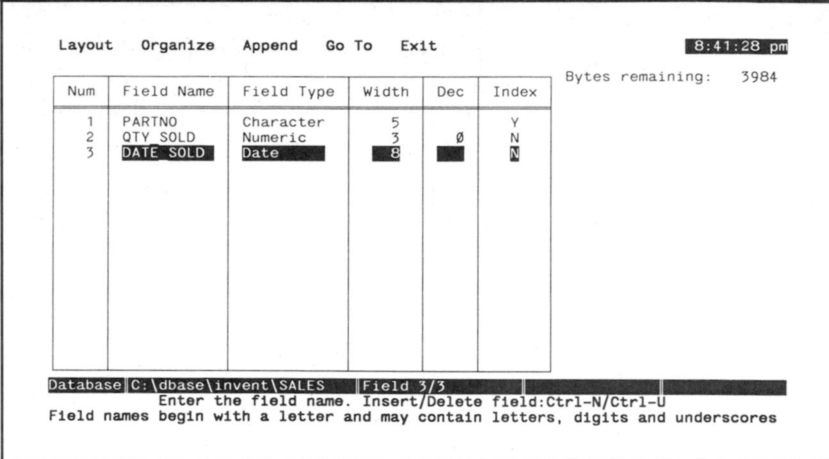

Figure 13.30: Structure of the SALES database

Records Organize Fields Go To Exit

PARTNO	QTY_SOLD	DATE_SOLD
A-111	1	01/01/93
A-111	1	01/01/93
A-111	1	01/01/93
A-111	5	01/01/93
B-222	1	01/01/93
B-222	1	01/01/93
B-222	1	01/01/93
C-333	1	01/01/93
C-333	1	01/01/93
C-333	1	01/01/93
C-333	1	01/01/93

Browse | C:\dbase\invent\SALES | Rec 1/11 | File

Figure 13.31: Sample sales transactions in the SALES database

The business purchases items to sell. All completed purchase transactions, for this example, are stored in the database named PURCHASE. Figure 13.32 shows the structure of the PURCHASE database. Figure 13.33 shows some sample records in the database.

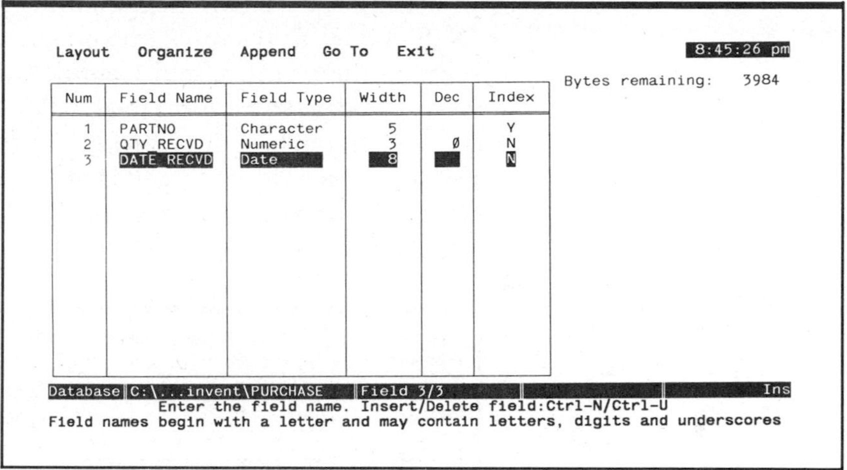

Figure 13.32: Structure of the PURCHASE database

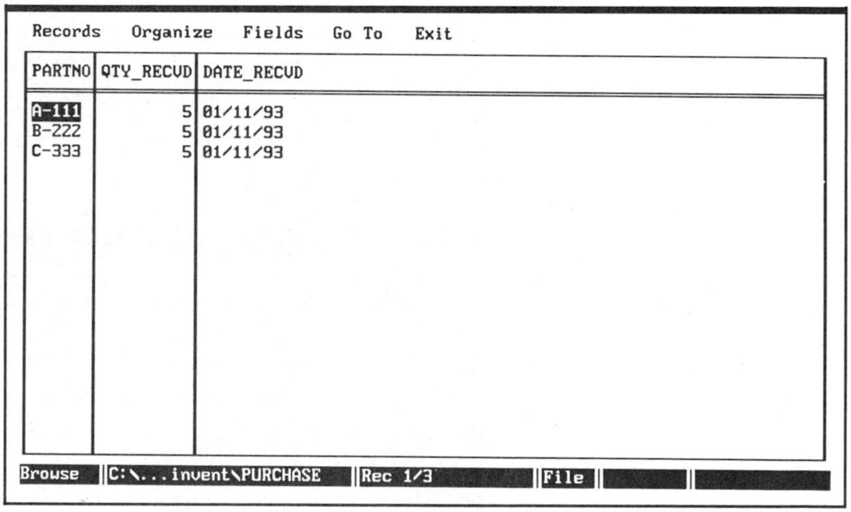

```
Records   Organize   Fields   Go To   Exit

PARTNO  QTY_RECVD  DATE_RECVD
A-111           5  01/11/93
B-222           5  01/11/93
C-333           5  01/11/93

Browse  C:\...invent\PURCHASE  Rec 1/3  File
```

Figure 13.33: Sample data in the PURCHASE database

To subtract the quantities of items sold in the SALES database from IN_STOCK quantities in the MASTER database, you need to create an UPDATE query that links the two databases. Figure 13.34 shows a sample query that will do the job. Notice that the MASTER file (the one containing the REPLACE operator) is the target of the replacements.

The QTY_SOLD field contains the placeholder, Sold. The IN_STOCK field uses the expression WITH In_Stock – Sold to subtract the quantity sold from the quantity in stock. When you choose Update ► Perform the Update to execute this query, dBASE will step through each record in the nontarget database (SALES), look for a record in the target database (MASTER) that has the same part number (because LINK1 sets up the link), and then perform the WITH calculation in the IN_STOCK field.

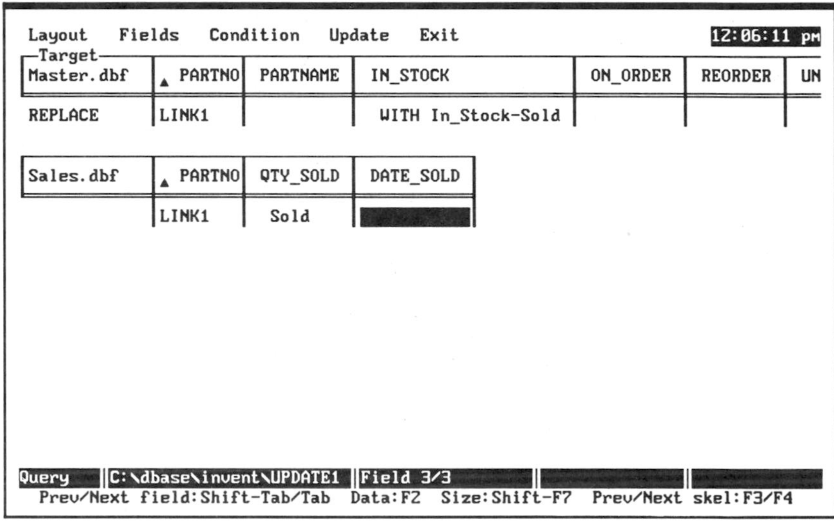

Figure 13.34: Query to subtract sold quantities from in-stock quantities

After dBASE executes the update, the MASTER database will contain the information shown in Figure 13.35. Notice that there are now two amplifiers in stock, because eight were sold. The in-stock quantities for CD players and Boise speakers have also been adjusted.

To update the MASTER database using the quantities in the PURCHASE database, you need to add the quantities received to the in-stock quantities and subtract the quantities received from the on-order quantities. (Presumably, the items received were previously on order, but now that they have been received, the on-order quantity needs to be decreased accordingly.)

The query to perform the update appears in Figure 13.36. The REPLACE update operator specifies a replacement update.

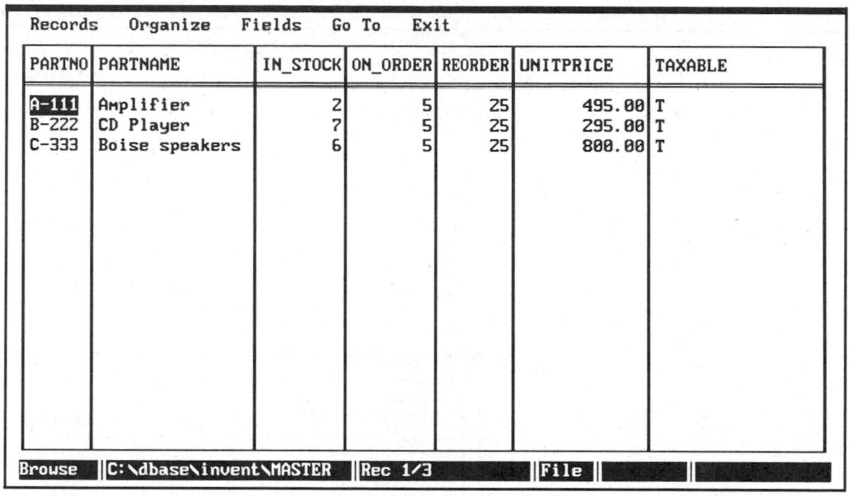

Records Organize Fields Go To Exit

PARTNO	PARTNAME	IN_STOCK	ON_ORDER	REORDER	UNITPRICE	TAXABLE
A-111	Amplifier	2	5	25	495.00	T
B-222	CD Player	7	5	25	295.00	T
C-333	Boise speakers	6	5	25	800.00	T

Browse ‖C:\dbase\invent\MASTER ‖Rec 1/3 ‖File ‖

Figure 13.35: Sales quantities subtracted from in-stock quantities

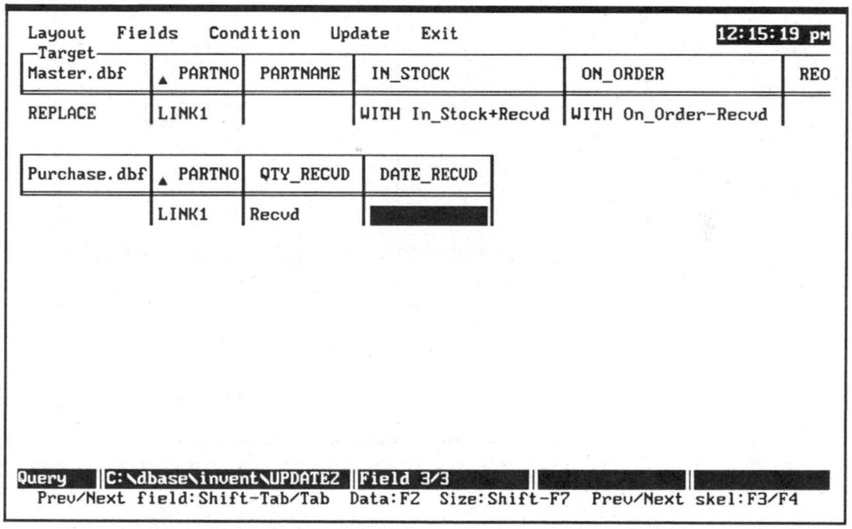

Layout Fields Condition Update Exit 12:15:19 pm

Target

Master.dbf	PARTNO	PARTNAME	IN_STOCK	ON_ORDER	REO
REPLACE	LINK1		WITH In_Stock+Recvd	WITH On_Order-Recvd	

Purchase.dbf	PARTNO	QTY_RECVD	DATE_RECVD
	LINK1	Recvd	

Query ‖C:\dbase\invent\UPDATE2 ‖Field 3/3 ‖ ‖

Prev/Next field:Shift-Tab/Tab Data:F2 Size:Shift-F7 Prev/Next skel:F3/F4

Figure 13.36: Query using PURCHASE to update MASTER

The word *Recvd* is a placeholder for the value in the QTY_RECVD field. The expression WITH In_Stock + Recvd replaces the in-stock value with its current value plus the quantity received. The expression WITH On_Order – Recvd replaces the on-order value with its current value minus the quantity received. Again, because the

PARTNO fields in the two file skeletons contain the same LINK1 placeholder, the replacement takes place only in the MASTER file record that has the same part number as the record in the SALES database.

After you create the query and execute it by choosing Update ► Perform the Update, the MASTER database will contain the information shown in Figure 13.37. Seven amplifiers are now in stock, and none are on order, because five were received. The other records have been updated as well.

Records Organize Fields Go To Exit

PARTNO	PARTNAME	IN_STOCK	ON_ORDER	REORDER	UNITPRICE	TAXABLE
A-111	Amplifier	7	0	25	495.00	T
B-222	CD Player	12	0	25	295.00	T
C-333	Boise speakers	11	0	25	800.00	T

Browse | C:\dbase\invent\MASTER | Rec 1/3 | File

Figure 13.37: MASTER database after updating from the PURCHASE database

HANDLING OLD TRANSACTIONS

One issue that arises when you print invoices and perform automatic updating is how to handle old transactions that have already been printed on invoices and used in updates. For example, after dBASE has completed the updates from the SALES and PURCHASE databases, both the SALES and PURCHASE databases will still contain the same data. dBASE has no way of knowing that their records have already been used in an update. Therefore, each time you perform the update in the future, these same quantities will be added to, and subtracted from, the IN_STOCK and ON_ORDER values in the MASTER database.

Of course, each time this happens, the IN_STOCK and ON_ORDER quantities become less accurate. It's up to you to develop a scheme to prevent this from happening. There are several techniques you can use. You can flag the records as having already been used, or not used, in an update, or you can move updated transactions from the SALES and PURCHASE databases to history files that contain only *posted* transactions (that is, transactions already used in an update).

Either technique, unfortunately, takes several steps to accomplish and is therefore prone to errors if each step is not fully completed. The safest way to ensure that all steps are handled properly is to combine them into a *batch process*, so that pressing a single button performs the entire update operation, including handling posted transactions. You'll see how to do this in Chapters 19 through 21, where we develop a complete inventory management system.

CHAPTER 14

Techniques for Managing Your Workspace

To create a catalog, use a different catalog, or add or delete catalog file names, use options from the Catalog pull-down menu that appears above the Control Center. **477**

To manipulate files via DOS, choose Tools ► DOS Utilities at the Control Center. **480**

To view the directory tree on the hard disk, press Zoom (F9) from the DOS utilities screen. **482**

To mark groups of files on the DOS utilities screen, first choose Files ► Display Only and enter a wildcard pattern to qualify a particular kind of file for inclusion. Then choose Mark ► Mark All. You can repeat this process to include additional categories until all the files that you wish to perform an operation on are marked. **484**

To copy, delete, rename, or move a file or group of files, use options on the Operations pull-down menu on the DOS utilities screen. **484**

To change the default drive and directory for storing and retrieving dBASE files, choose DOS ► Set Default Drive: Directory on the DOS utilities screen. **491**

To enter DOS commands without leaving dBASE IV, choose DOS ► Perform DOS Command or DOS ► Go to DOS on the DOS utilities screen. **491**

To change environmental settings for the current session— for example, to change the date format choose Tool ► Settings at the Control Center and highlight the Options menu. **492**

To change screen colors for the current dBASE session, 495
choose Tools ► Settings at the Control Center, highlight or click on the Display option, then select a part of the screen to color. Select a foreground and background color combination from the colors listed.

To change the structure of a database that contains records, 496
highlight the name of the database in the Data panel and press or click Design (Shift-F2). If you plan to remove or change any field names, make a copy of the database first.

THIS CHAPTER PRESENTS GENERAL TECHNIQUES for managing catalogs, files, and settings, as well as techniques for interfacing with DOS. Many of the tasks discussed in this chapter are referred to as housekeeping chores, because they help you keep your files in order. Housekeeping chores that you'll want to perform on your computer from time to time include

- Finding particular files
- Erasing outdated files
- Copying files to floppy disks as backup copies or for use on another computer
- Changing the names of files
- Deleting unnecessary files to conserve disk space

You may find that you need to use only a few of the techniques presented in this chapter. Therefore, don't worry about trying all of them. Instead, you can just become familiar with the options available to you and then refer to this chapter later as necessary.

MANAGING CATALOGS

As discussed in Chapter 2, a catalog is a tool for helping you keep the names of files that belong together visible in the Control Center. Any time you create a file (be it a database file, report format, custom screen, or whatever), dBASE automatically adds thc filc namc that you assign the file to the current catalog, and that name appears in the Control Center. (You've already seen many examples of this.)

TIP

To avoid confusing *catalogs* and *directories*, remember that a directory (or subdirectory) is a place on the disk where files are stored, and a catalog is simply a list of file names.

Because a catalog consists of only the names of files, you can include the same file in more than one catalog. As you create and work with multiple catalogs, you may eventually want to add, change, or delete file names in a catalog. The Catalog pull-down menu in the Control Center offers all the techniques you'll need to manage catalogs.

CREATING A NEW CATALOG

To create a new catalog, start at the Control Center, choose Catalog ► Use a Different Catalog, and then select <create> from the submenu that appears. When the screen asks for a name, type a valid file name (eight letters maximum, no spaces) and press ↵. That new catalog will become the current catalog, and the panels in the Control Center will be empty. Any new files that you create while using the new catalog will be listed in the catalog automatically.

SELECTING A CATALOG

When working with multiple catalogs, you can switch from one to another by starting at the Control Center, then choosing Catalog ► Use a Different Catalog. Select the name of the catalog that you want to use from the submenu of catalog names that appears.

CHANGING A CATALOG DESCRIPTION

To change the description of a catalog, choose Catalog ► Edit Description of Catalog. Use the usual editing keys to change the description (or type a new description) and press ↵. The description of the catalog appears when you scroll through catalog names after selecting Use a Different Catalog.

ADDING FILE NAMES TO A CATALOG

Suppose you create a file while using one catalog and want that file name to appear in a different catalog. To add a file name to a catalog, select the catalog to which you want to add the file name and then move the highlight to the panel that describes the type of file that you want to add. For example, if you are adding a database file name to the current catalog, move the highlight to the Data panel. Similarly, if you're adding a report file name, move the highlight to the Reports panel.

Next, choose Catalog ► Add File to Catalog. A submenu will list all files in the current directory that match the type of file you are adding (for example, all .DBF files if the highlight is in the Data panel). The submenu will also list options to change to a different disk drive, to the parent directory, or to another subdirectory. If necessary, switch to the appropriate directory to locate the file name. Then select the file name from the submenu.

You can either edit the description of the file or just press ↵ to use the current description. The name of the file will appear in the appropriate panel of the Control Center.

NOTE

Chapter 17 lists other dBASE file name extensions and the types of files they represent.

If you are adding a query, form, report, or label file name to the current catalog, the submenu will display every file name with every extension (such as CUSTFORM.FRM and CUSTFORM.SCR). You need select only one of these multiple names, using the appropriate extension, as listed here.

File type	Extension to select
Query	.QBE
Update query	.UPD
View query	.QBE
Form	.SCR
Report	.FRM
Labels	.LBL
Application	.APP

Note that if you add the name of a file that is stored on a floppy disk to a particular catalog, that floppy disk must be in its disk drive whenever you use that catalog; adding a file name to a catalog does not copy the file to the current drive or directory. If you do want to copy the file from the floppy disk onto your hard disk, use the copying techniques discussed later in this chapter and then add the file name to the hard disk catalog.

REMOVING FILE NAMES FROM A CATALOG

To remove a file name from the current catalog, first highlight the file name that you wish to remove. Then choose Catalog ► Remove

Highlighted File from Catalog, or press the Del key. dBASE will double-check your request by asking

> Are you sure you want to remove
> this file from the catalog?
>
> No Yes

Select Yes if you do want to delete the file. Next, dBASE will ask,

> Do you also want to delete
> this file from the disk?
>
> No Yes

If you select No, then the file name is removed from the catalog, but the file remains intact on the disk (and its name can be added to some other catalog). If you select Yes, then the file is permanently removed from the disk and cannot be recovered. (So use this option with caution!)

dBASE will not let you delete an open database or query from the catalog or the hard disk. Suppose, for example, that you are currently using a database named OLDCUSTS (that is, OLDCUSTS appears above the horizontal line in the Data panel). If you try to delete that database from the catalog, you'll see the message "Cannot erase open file" after dBASE asks if you're sure you want to remove the file from the catalog. To solve this problem, press any key to continue. Then press ↵ and select Close File (or Close View if you're closing a query) from the submenu that appears. Now you can highlight OLDCUSTS in the Data panel and delete the database as described above.

NOTE

Appendix H lists all the file extensions used by dBASE.

Here's one other interesting point about removing file names from a catalog. When you delete a file from the catalog and the hard disk using Catalog ► Remove Highlighted File from Catalog (or the Del key), dBASE doesn't automatically remove *all* the files that are associated with the file you removed. For example, if you remove a report named CUSTRPT from the catalog and the hard disk, dBASE only removes the file named CUSTRPT.FRM. It does not automatically remove the related CUSTRPT.FRG file, which is the actual program file generated when you saved the report. Likewise, if you remove an indexed database named OLDCUSTS, dBASE removes only the OLDCUSTS.DBF file, leaving behind the OLDCUSTS.MDX (database index) file. To remove those files, you must use techniques described later in this chapter under "Managing Files."

CHANGING A FILE DESCRIPTION

To change the description that you've assigned to a file, first highlight the file name in the Control Center. Then choose Catalog ► Change Description of Highlighted File. Use the usual arrow and Backspace keys, or your mouse, to position the cursor and erase, as needed, and then save the new description by pressing ↵. The new description will appear below the Control Center panels whenever the file name is highlighted.

CHANGING THE NAME OF THE CURRENT CATALOG

If you start dBASE IV from a directory that contains no catalogs, it will automatically create a catalog named UNTITLED.CAT that includes all of the dBASE IV database files on the current directory. To change the name of the current catalog, choose Catalog ► Modify Catalog Name. Press Backspace as needed to erase the current name and then enter the new name. (You need not enter the .CAT extension; dBASE will add it automatically. Do not enter a different extension.)

NOTE

Appendix A discusses basic DOS concepts and is especially useful for dBASE users new to computers.

MANAGING FILES

The computer's disk operating system (DOS) handles all basic file management tasks, including saving, retrieving, copying, moving, and deleting files, as well as managing directories. dBASE IV lets you interact with DOS to manage files on your own via the DOS utilities screen.

Whereas the Catalog pull-down menu lets you manage the file *names* that appear in a catalog, the DOS utilities screen offers options for actually manipulating files, including techniques for copying, moving, deleting, and renaming files. To get to the DOS utilities screen, start at the Control Center and choose Tools ► DOS Utilities. You will see a box containing a *file list* that includes all subdirectory names (directories beneath the current directory) and files, as in Figure 14.1. (Of course, many of the file and subdirectory names on your screen will be different.)

```
DOS   Files   Sort   Mark   Operations   Exit                         5:16:32 pm
                              C:\DBASE
 Name/Extension      Size    Date & Time           Attrs     Space Used

 <parent>           <DIR>    Feb 18,1992   1:27p   ****
 DBTUTOR            <DIR>    Feb 18,1992   1:40p   ****
 INVENT             <DIR>    Mar  1,1993  11:50a   ****
 MEMBERS            <DIR>    Feb 18,1992   2:59p   ****
 SAMPLES            <DIR>    Feb 18,1992   1:40p   ****
 SQLHOME            <DIR>    Feb 18,1992   1:34p   ****
 TMP                <DIR>    Feb 28,1993   4:19p   ****
 BIGCUST  DBF         320    Feb 28,1993   4:50p   a***          4,096
 BIGCUST  DBK         148    Feb 28,1993   4:41p   a***          4,096
 BIGCUST  MBK       4,096    Feb 28,1993   4:41p   a***          8,192
 BIGCUST  MDX       4,096    Feb 28,1993   4:50p   a***          8,192

Total  <marked>              0  (   0 files)                         0
Total  <displayed>   5,758,341  ( 249 files)                 6,397,952

 Files: *.*                                            Sorted by: Name

DOS util ||C:\DBASE                                                    Num
       Position selection bar: ↑↓   Mark file: ←┘   Directories: F9
```

Figure 14.1: The DOS utilities screen

The current drive and directory, C:\DBASE in this example, are displayed at the top of the box. Within the file list, the Name/Extension column lists subdirectory names enclosed in < > brackets (for instance, <DBTUTOR>) and file names. The Size column displays the number of characters in the file (or <DIR> for subdirectory names). The Date & Time column shows the date and time that the file was created or last changed.

The Attrs (Attributes) column lists the DOS attributes assigned to each file, in the order Archive, Hidden, Read-Only, and System. (These attributes need not concern you just now.) The Space Used column shows how much real disk space the file occupies. This information differs from that in the Size option because the computer stores files in clusters, which have some minimal size. For example, if your computer uses a cluster size of 4,096 bytes, then even the smallest file occupies at least 4,096 bytes.

The Total Marked information at the bottom of the box lists the total size and number of files that are currently marked (zero in the figure). The Total Displayed information lists the size and number of files displayed. Use the PgUp, PgDn, Home, and End keys to scroll through file names.

The indicator "Files:*.*" means that all files are currently displayed. (The *.* wildcard pattern means "files with any name, followed by any extension.") The "Sorted by: Name" indicator means that file names are currently sorted by name (though subdirectory names are listed above file names).

TEMPORARILY CHANGING DIRECTORIES

You can use the ↑ and ↓ keys or your mouse to move the highlight through the file list. To switch to a subdirectory, select the subdirectory name using the usual technique of highlighting and press ↵, or click the subdirectory with your mouse. To switch to the parent directory, select <parent>.

To get a better view of the overall directory structure, press Zoom (F9). dBASE then presents the directory structure in a tree format, as in the example in Figure 14.2. Note that subdirectory names are indented beneath the name of their parent directory. The current directory is indicated by a pointer to the left of the directory name.

To switch to any directory or subdirectory while the directory tree is displayed, highlight the appropriate name and press ↵, or click that name with your mouse. The file list will appear, showing the names of files on the new current directory.

You can also switch to a new drive and directory by choosing Files ► Change Drive: Directory. When you select this option, you'll be given the opportunity to enter a new drive and directory or press Pick (Shift-F1) to view the directory tree.

Note that the techniques discussed in this section affect only the DOS utilities screen display. When you return to the Control Center, the directory that was in effect before you went to the DOS utilities will still be in effect.

The DOS ► Set Default Drive: Directory option lets you permanently change the default directory.

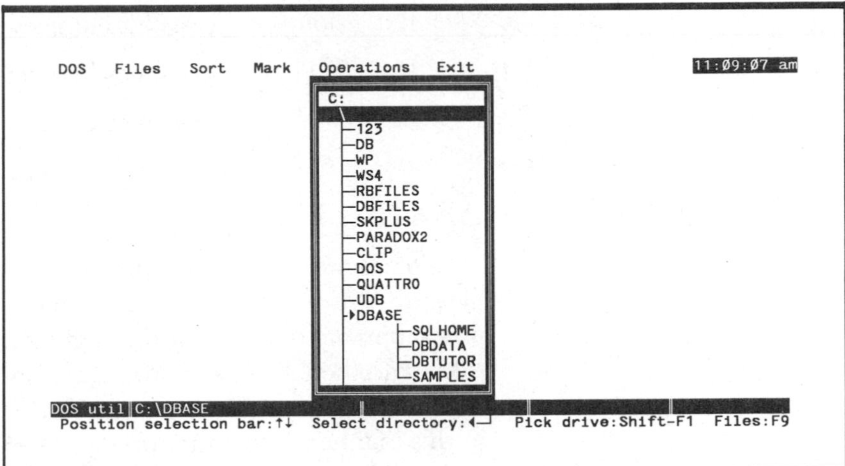

Figure 14.2: Sample directory tree

SELECTING FILES TO DISPLAY

You can limit the file names displayed on the DOS utilities screen to only those that match some wildcard pattern. As with searches, you can use **?** to stand for any single character and * to stand for any group of characters. To change the wildcard pattern, choose Files ► Display Only and type the new wildcard pattern.

For example, to view only database file names (those with the extension .DBF), change the wildcard pattern to ***.DBF**. To view only file names that begin with the letters CUST, change the wildcard pattern to **CUST*.***. Note that subdirectory names and the <parent> option are still displayed, regardless of the wildcard pattern you use.

SORTING FILE NAMES

The Sort pull-down menu lets you select a sort order for viewing file names. When you highlight Sort on the menu bar, you'll be given a menu of choices:

Name — Lists files alphabetically by file name (the default setting)

Extension	Lists files alphabetically by extension
Date & Time	Lists files in ascending order by date and time
Size	Lists files by size, from smallest to largest

MARKING FILES

Sometimes you may want to perform operations on groups of files. dBASE provides several techniques for marking files. The simplest approach is to scroll the highlight to the file that you want to mark and then press ↵. You can also mark a file with your mouse by clicking on that file name. You can mark as many files as you wish in this manner. (Note that pressing ↵ or clicking the mouse works as a toggle: Each time you perform this action, you either mark or unmark the current file.)

You can also use options from the Mark pull-down menu to mark and unmark records. The Mark All option marks all currently displayed file names. Hence, if the wildcard pattern CUST*.* is in effect and you select Mark All, then all files beginning with the letters CUST will be marked. Changing the wildcard pattern does not affect the marks (though the marked files may temporarily disappear from the list until you again enter a *.* wildcard pattern), so you can mark several groups of files by changing the wildcard pattern and selecting Mark All.

The Unmark All option on the Mark pull-down menu unmarks all currently displayed file names. The Reverse Marks option swaps the file marks, so that unmarked files are marked, and marked files become unmarked. This option is handy when, for example, you want to copy two groups of files to two floppy disks. You could mark one set of files and copy those files to one floppy disk. Then you could reverse the marks and copy the now-marked files to another floppy disk.

COPYING, MOVING, DELETING, AND RENAMING FILES

To copy, delete, move, or rename files, select the appropriate option on the Operations pull-down menu. You'll first see a submenu with these options:

Single File	Includes only the currently highlighted file name in the operation
Marked Files	Includes all currently displayed marked files in the list in the operation
Displayed Files	Includes only the currently displayed files in the operation

Note that the phrase "currently displayed" as used here refers to all files that match the current wildcard pattern. Hence, any file names that are not visible at the moment simply because they are scrolled off the bottom of the screen are still included in the operation. The Marked Files option includes only marked files that are currently displayed (that is, marked files that match the current wildcard pattern).

If the highlight is on a directory name when you choose a group of files for an operation and you select Single File, then the operation will be performed for all files in that directory.

After you've selected the files to include in the operation, you'll be given further information and options relevant to that operation, as discussed in the following sections.

COPYING FILES If you selected Copy as the file operation, you will be prompted to specify the destination and file names for the copy operation. Enter the appropriate disk drive and directory for the copy operation and press ↵. For example, to copy files to a floppy disk in drive A, delete the current destination and type the new destination **A:** (be sure to type the colon). Then press ↵.

If you are copying a single file, its name will be displayed as the name for the copied file. You can change that name (so that the copied file has a different name than the original file) or press ↵ to use the same name. If you are copying a group of files, enter *.* as the destination file name to ensure that copied files have the same names as the original files.

If you prefer, you can assign new names to the copied files. In the destination file name, use a combination of the new name (for that part of the file name that you want to change) and a wildcard (for the part that you want to remain the same). For example, suppose you mark the files CUSTLIST.DBF and CUSTLIST.MDX as the file group to copy. If you enter **CUSTBAK.*** as the destination file name, the copied files will have the names CUSTBAK.DBF and CUSTBAK.MDX.

If you want to place copied files in thc same directory as the original files, you must specify a new name for the copied files (a directory cannot have two files with the same name). For example, suppose you want to copy C:\DBASE\ORDERS.DBF and C:\DBASE\ORDERS.MDX to two backup files in the same directory. You would keep the destination for the copy as C:\DBASE, but enter a file name with a wildcard character, such as **OLDORDER.***, so that the copies would have the file names OLDORDER.DBF and OLDORDER.MDX.

When you have finished filling in the destination and file name for the copy, press or click Ctrl-End to begin the copy operation. Note that you can also copy a single file by highlighting its name in the files list and pressing Copy (F8).

WARNING

Before deleting all marked or displayed files, use PgDn and PgUp to scroll through the file list to make certain that you know exactly which files will be deleted. Also, make sure that the highlight is not on a subdirectory name when you select Delete; otherwise you might inadvertently delete the entire directory.

Using * rather than a specific file name helps to ensure that all the appropriate files are copied. For example, if a database contains a memo field, the memos are stored in a separate file with the extension .DBT. Therefore, if you named the database REFERENC, and copied REFERENC.*, you'd be sure that all the appropriate files, REFERENC.DBF, REFERENCE.DBT, and REFERENCE.MDX, were copied.

Keep in mind that when you copy files, the copies are stored in the directory you specified, but in no particular catalog. When you've completed your Copy operation, you'll need to either select an existing catalog, or create a new catalog to put the filc namcs in. Then add the file names as discussed in "Managing Catalogs" earlier in this chapter.

DELETING FILES If you select Delete as the operation, dBASE displays the options Proceed and Cancel. If you are sure you want to delete all the files described, select Proceed. But use this option with caution, because once you delete a file, you cannot retrieve it. If you are unsure about deleting the files, select Cancel.

You can also delete any single file by moving the highlight to the appropriate file name in the file list and pressing Del. You'll still be given the option to proceed or cancel.

Keep in mind that dBASE does not allow you to delete active databases or query files. This problem is easily solved by closing the open file. Simply return to the Control Center by choosing Exit ► Exit to Control Center from the DOS utilities menu, then highlight the database or query you want to delete and press ↵ (or double-click that database or query). Now select Close File (for databases) or Close View (for queries) from the submenu that appears. With that done, you can return to the DOS utilities screen and delete the database or query files as usual.

MOVING FILES The Move option lets you move a file from one disk drive directory to another. This option works in the same manner as Copy, except that the original file is deleted from its original drive and directory after being copied to its new destination. The general technique used is identical to that used for copying. After you select the option, you specify a disk drive or directory to move the file to or press Pick (Shift-F1) to select a new directory from the directory tree.

After specifying the disk drive and directory to move the file to, you'll be prompted to enter a new name for the moved file. If you are moving a single file, its name will be displayed, and you can just press ↵ to retain the name. If you are moving a group of files, enter the wildcard patterns *.* to move all files and retain their current names. Press or click Ctrl-End after responding to both prompts (or press Esc to abort the operation).

You can also move a single file by highlighting its name in the file list and pressing Move (F7).

RENAMING FILES The Rename option lets you change the name of a file, group of files, or a subdirectory. When you select this option, you'll be prompted to enter the new name. If you are renaming a group of files, be sure to use a wildcard character in the new file name. For example, if you want to rename all files named CUSTBAK to OLDCUST, enter **OLDCUST.*** as the new file name. Each file previously named CUSTBAK will be renamed OLDCUST, but will still have the original extension. (Hence, CUSTBAK.DBF becomes OLDCUST.DBF, and CUSTBAK.MDX becomes OLD-CUST.MDX.)

If the new name that you assign to a file is the same as an existing file name, an information box will warn you that the existing file will be erased. The screen will display options to overwrite the existing file or to skip the renaming operation. Unless you are absolutely sure that you wish to replace the currently named file with the new one, select Skip.

HANDLING MISSING OR MISMATCHED INDEXES

It turns out that dBASE performs a number of housekeeping tasks behind the scenes when you work with databases. One of these tasks involves keeping track of database files and their associated indexes. For example, the CUSTLIST database file is named CUSTLIST.DBF, and its associated file of indexes is named CUST-LIST.MDX. (You may also have a CUSTLIST.DBK file, which is the backup file for that database, and a CUSTLIST.MBK file, which is the backup file for the CUSTLIST index.)

Suppose you want to copy or rename the CUSTLIST database to CUSTNEW. The first steps are straightforward, and use methods you have just learned:

1. From the Control Center, choose Tools ► DOS Utilities.
2. Choose Files ► Display Only, then type **CUSTLIST.*** and press ↵.
3. Choose Mark ► Mark All.
4. Choose Operations ► Copy (or Rename). Then select Marked Files.
5. Press ↵ to use the same directory, then type **CUSTNEW.*** and press ↵ to specify the new file names. Press or click Ctrl-End to perform the copy.
6. Exit to the Control Center by choosing Exit ► Exit to Control Center.

Now add CUSTNEW to the catalog by moving the highlight to the Data panel and choosing Catalog ► Add File to Catalog. Highlight CUSTNEW.DBF in the list that appears and then press ↵ (or double-click that file name). Now enter a new description. So far so good. But here's the problem: If you now highlight CUSTNEW and press or click Data (F2) to view the database, you see the message "Production .MDX file not found: CUSTNEW.mdx" along with the options Cancel, Proceed, and Help. At this point, you should choose Cancel. (If you choose Proceed instead of Cancel when you see the error message, the data will display on the edit or browse screen as usual, but you won't be able to add, modify, or use an index. In fact, if you try to create a new index, you'll get the message "MDX file doesn't match database. Press any key to continue...".)

All of this may seem very cryptic, but fortunately there's a relatively simple solution. Here are the steps to follow after adding the new or renamed database to the catalog:

1. Return to the Control Center if you're not there already and choose Tools ► DOS Utilities.
2. Highlight the index file for the new or renamed database and then press Del. In this example, highlight CUSTNEW.MDX and press Del. When prompted, select Proceed to delete the index file.
3. Return to the Control Center by choosing Exit ► Exit to Control Center.
4. Now, create all the indexes for the database using techniques described in Chapter 5. For example, highlight CUSTNEW in the Data panel of the Control Center, press or click Data (F2), then choose Organize ► Create New Index and define an index for the database. Repeat this step for each new index you want to create.

NOTE

If your database also includes an index backup file ending in .MBK, you can mark both the .MDX and .MBK files, then choose Operations ► Delete ► Marked Files to delete both index files at once.

MAKING BACKUP COPIES OF IMPORTANT FILES

To see how to use the DOS utilities screen as a tool for making backup copies of important files, we'll go through the steps necessary to

Use the general techniques described in this section to make backup copies of all your database files from time to time. That way, if you ever inadvertently lose any files from your hard disk, you can just copy the backup files from the floppy disks back onto your hard disk.

copy the CUSTLIST and ORDERS databases to a formatted disk in drive A. (This example assumes that you have a formatted disk with at least 51K of blank space on it readily available, and that your floppy disk drive is named A. If you need help creating a formatted floppy disk, see the FORMAT command in your DOS manual. But be careful when using the format command, because it permanently erases any files already on the disk.)

From the Control Center, choose Tools ► DOS Utilities. When the file list appears, choose Files ► Display Only and change the wildcard pattern to **CUSTLIST.***. Then choose Mark ► Mark All to mark the files named CUSTLIST.DBF, CUSTLIST.MDX, and several other files beginning with CUSTLIST (the .MDX file contains the indexes for CUSTLIST.DBF). You may have to press PgDn a few times to see the marked file names.

Next, choose Files ► Display Only and change the wildcard pattern to **ORDERS.***. Once again, choose Mark ► Mark All. Choose Files ► Display Only again and change the wildcard pattern to *.* (or just press Ctrl-Y to blank the option; dBASE will change the pattern to *.* after you press ↵).

If you use the PgDn and PgUp keys now to scroll through the files list, you'll see that the CUSTLIST and ORDERS files are the only ones marked. Also, beneath the file list you can see that the total amount of space used by the marked files is about 51,200 bytes (about 50K, because a kilobyte contains 1,024 characters).

To begin the copy operation, first place the floppy disk in drive A. Then choose Operations ► Copy ► Marked Files. Press Ctrl-Y to erase the current drive and directory names suggested by the prompt and then enter the destination drive, **A:**. Then press ↵ and enter *.* as the file name, so that copied files retain their same names and extensions. To perform the copy operation, press or click Ctrl-End.

dBASE will begin copying all the marked files onto the disk in drive A. Note that if the disk already contains copies of these files, you will be given the option to overwrite (replace) the current file or skip (not copy) the file with the currently displayed name.

To verify the copy operation, choose Files ► Change Drive: Directory and change the setting to **A:**. After you press ↵, you should see the names of the copied files on the disk in drive A. (If there are other files on the floppy disk in drive A, you may need to use PgDn and PgUp to scroll through the file list.)

To return to the C:\DBASE directory, choose Files ► Change Drive: Directory once again and replace A: with **C:\DBASE**. Then press ↵. Files from the C:\DBASE drive and directory will be displayed in the file list once again.

CHANGING THE DEFAULT DRIVE AND DIRECTORY

To change the default drive and directory for *all* operations in the current dBASE session, start at the Control Center and choose Tools ► DOS Utilities, then choose DOS ► Set Default Drive: Directory. You can then either type the name of the new drive and directory to log on to or press Pick (Shift-F1) to select an option from the directory tree.

Note that this change tells dBASE to look for and save all files on the new drive and directory. It does not immediately affect the current files list. (To view files on the new default drive and directory, you need to choose Files ► Change Drive: Directory and type or select the name of the new default drive and directory.)

After you leave the DOS utilities screen and return to the Control Center, you'll see that dBASE is logged on to the new drive and directory (the catalog name centered above the Control Center will include the current drive and directory). dBASE will search only this new default directory for any files that you request. Any new files that you create also will be saved on the new drive and directory.

ACCESSING DOS

dBASE IV offers two techniques for accessing DOS commands without quitting dBASE. Both are available by starting at the Control Center and choosing Tools ► DOS Utilities, then choosing DOS from the menu.

The Perform DOS Command option lets you enter a single DOS command. When the DOS command completes its job, you'll be prompted to press any key to return to dBASE IV.

The Go to DOS option on the DOS pull-down menu temporarily leaves dBASE IV and displays the DOS prompt. If any marked files are currently in the file list, dBASE will warn you that all marked files will be unmarked and ask whether you want to proceed or to cancel the operation.

Whenever you select Go to DOS, be sure to return to dBASE IV and exit dBASE in the usual manner before turning off your computer.

If you select Proceed, you'll be taken to the DOS prompt, with dBASE IV suspended in memory. You can enter whatever DOS commands you wish. To return to dBASE IV, type the command **EXIT** at the DOS prompt and press ←┘, as instructed on the screen.

CHANGING ENVIRONMENTAL SETTINGS

In previous chapters, you saw how to use the Settings submenu to turn the Instruct and Deleted options on and off. This section discusses the other options on the Settings submenu. To get to the Settings menu from the Control Center, choose Tools ► Settings.

CHANGING OPTIONS

To permanently change a setting so that it affects all future dBASE IV sessions, use the DBSETUP program discussed in Appendix B.

When you first select Settings, you'll see the Options pull-down menu, which displays a list of the most commonly used settings, as shown in Figure 14.3. The effects of changing the settings are summarized in Table 14.1. Note that changing these settings affects only

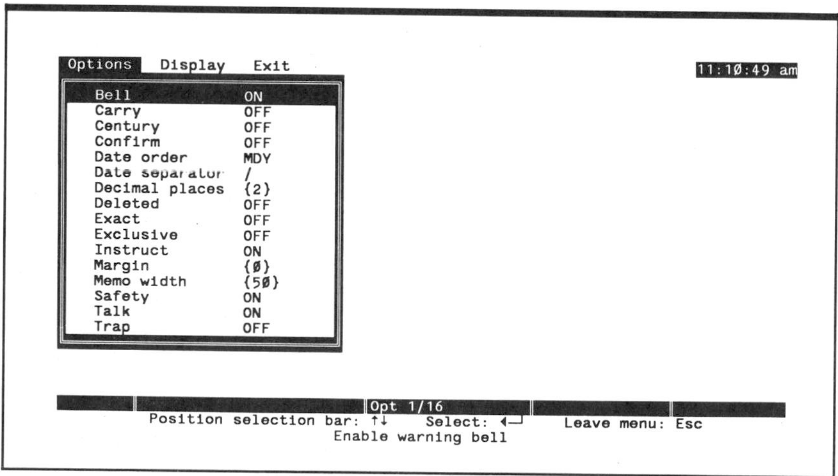

Figure 14.3: The Settings Options submenu

Table 14.1: Settings Options

Option	Effect of settings
Bell	When on, beeps whenever a field on an edit screen or custom form is filled or an error occurs. When off, doesn't beep.
Carry	When on, copies all information from the current record to the next new record while you are entering new data. When off, starts each new record with blank fields.
Century	When off, displays dates with two-digit years (for example, 12/31/93). When on, displays dates with four-digit years (for example, 12/31/1993).
Confirm	When off, automatically moves the cursor to the next field when you fill a field during data entry or editing. When on, keeps the cursor in the current field until the ↵ key is pressed.
Date Order	Lets you determine the order of month, day, and year in date displays (press the space bar to scroll through the options). Options are MDY (12/31/93), DMY (31/12/93), and YMD (93/12/31).
Date Separator	Determines the character used in date displays (space bar scrolls through options). Slash (/) displays dates as 12/31/93, hyphen (-) displays dates as 12-31-93, and period (.) displays dates as 12.31.93. Can be used in conjunction with Date Order to create various international date formats (for example, 93.12.31).
Decimal Places	Determines the number of decimal places displayed in the results of calculations, in the range 0 to 18. The default setting is 2.
Deleted	When off, displays records that are marked for deletion. When on, hides from view, and from all operations, records marked for deletion.

Table 14.1: Settings Options (continued)

Option	Effect of settings
Exact	When off, matches strings of different lengths in a search. When on, matches only strings of the same length. Hence, when Exact is off, a search for **"AB"** locates "ABC Co." When on, a search for **"AB "** matches only "AB ".
Exclusive	When off, lets other network users access the file you are currently using. When on, does not let other network users access the file you are currently using.
Instruct	When on, displays information boxes each time you use a feature for the first time. When off, does not display information boxes.
Margin	Adjusts the left margin for all printed output, as measured in characters. Thus, entering **10** adds a one-inch margin to the left side of the page (assuming that 10 characters to the inch are printed).
Memo Width	Adjusts the default width of memo field displays during certain operations. Can accept a value in the range 5 to 255. (Widths defined in custom forms and reports override this setting.)
Safety	When on, displays a warning before dBASE overwrites an existing file and provides an option to cancel the operation. When off, displays no warning and immediately overwrites the existing file.
Talk	When on, displays results of various dBASE operations on the screen. When off, does not display results on the screen (used mainly in custom programming).
Trap	In custom programming, determines whether the dBASE IV debugger is activated when an error occurs in a program.

the current dBASE IV session. When you exit and then return to dBASE IV later, the original settings will be in effect.

CHANGING THE DISPLAY COLORS

The color options available to you depend on the type of color monitor you have.

If you have a color monitor, you can use the options on the Display pull-down menu to change display colors. The Display pull-down menu provides a list of areas to color. When you select an area, you'll see a list of possible foreground and background colors for that area, as shown in Figure 14.4.

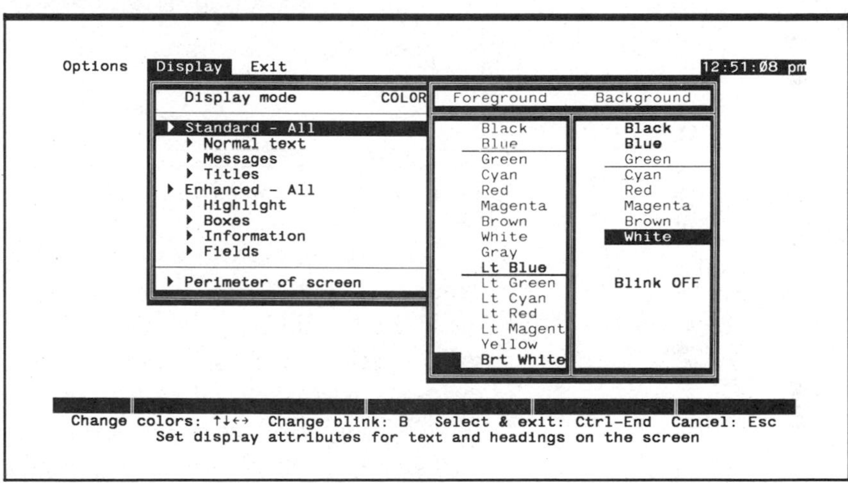

Figure 14.4: Display menu and color options

When creating a custom form, you can also select colors that affect only that form, as discussed in Chapter 8.

The Standard – All option affects the general color of text and background on normal (that is, unhighlighted) sections of the screen. The Enhanced – All option sets the general color for all highlighted text, such as text in the menu, status bar, and input fields of a custom form. You can color more specific areas by selecting options under Standard – All and Enhanced – All. Some examples of these specific areas are shown in Figure 14.5.

After you select an area to color, the menu of foreground and background options appears. A small square indicates the current foreground color. You can use ↑ and ↓ to scroll up and down and select a different foreground color.

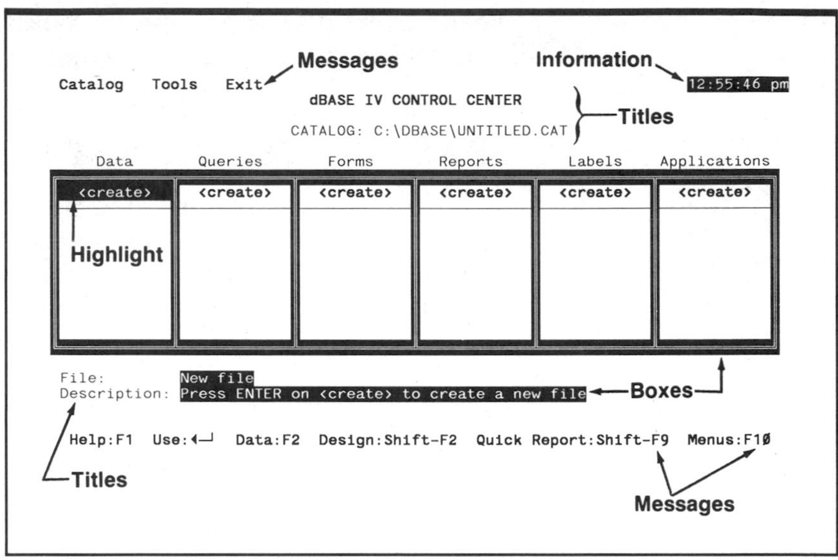

Figure 14.5: Some areas that can be colored

> NOTE
>
> You can also change the foreground or background color by clicking your mouse on the color you want. Each time you click on a foreground or background color option, the screen will adjust to show the color combinations you have chosen.

After selecting a foreground color, press → to move the background options. Once again, you can scroll through color options using the ↑ and ↓ keys. As you scroll through foreground and background colors, the screen adjusts to show color combinations. For example, if you select Lt Cyan as your foreground color and then scroll through background colors, you'll see Lt Cyan displayed with all possible backgrounds in the Background column and the currently highlighted background color behind all foreground colors in the Foreground column.

You can switch back and forth between the Background and Foreground columns and try different combinations until you find one you like. When you do, press or click Ctrl-End. You can color as many areas as you wish and then choose Exit ► Exit to Control Center.

> NOTE
>
> Colors that you select under the Settings menu affect only the current dBASE session. To change the colors used in all dBASE sessions, use the DBSETUP program discussed in Appendix B.

MODIFYING A DATABASE STRUCTURE

You can change the structure of a database at any time, regardless of how many records are in that database. To do so, highlight the name of the database in the Control Center and press or click Design (Shift-F2).

You'll see the structure of the database on the database design screen. There you can change any field definitions, add new fields below existing ones, delete a field with Ctrl-U, or insert a new field with Ctrl-N.

As soon as you enter the database design screen, dBASE IV makes a temporary copy of the records in the current database. After you save your changes, dBASE attempts to copy records from the temporary database back into the original database. It will be successful at doing so only if you use a little caution while changing the database structure, as discussed here.

As an added precaution, make your own backup copy of a database before changing its structure, using the techniques described earlier in this chapter.

If you delete a field from the database structure, keep in mind that you are also deleting all the data in that field. In other words, if you have a database with 10,000 names and addresses in it and you delete the City field from that database structure, you have just lost all the cities that were in that field. To get them back you have to type each one in again by hand—not a pleasant task!

To change the position of a field in the database structure, first note the exact spelling of the field name, the data type, the width, and the number of decimal places. Then delete the field from its current position using the Ctrl-U key. Use Ctrl-N to insert a new blank field, or add the new field beneath the existing field names. Be sure to use the same spelling, data type, width, and number of decimal places. Do not perform any other operations at this time; save your changes and exit immediately.

You can change the name of a field *only* if you do not add, change, move, or delete any fields during the same operation. If you change field names and rearrange fields in the same operation, dBASE will become confused, and there is no telling how things might be arranged after you save your changes.

Again, your best bet is to use the DOS utilities screen to make a copy of the entire database before you even begin to modify its structure.

SAVING TIME WITH KEYSTROKE MACROS

Some operations require many keystrokes to accomplish. As an alternative to rekeying each time you want to perform one of these operations, you can record all the necessary keystrokes in a *keystroke macro,* and then play them back at any time. To demonstrate, we'll record the keystrokes required to display the names of all database (.DBF) files in the list of DOS utilities.

RECORDING KEYSTROKES

If you're using a mouse with dBASE, you may be surprised to see what happens when you record your first keystroke macro: The mouse pointer disappears completely and the mouse is temporarily disabled. That's because, as the name implies, *keystroke macros* record only keystrokes, not mouse movements or clicks. Therefore, you cannot use your mouse to open menus or make selections while recording a macro. Of course, once you finish recording your keystroke macro, dBASE restores the full capabilities to your mouse and you can use it in the usual manner.

Now, assuming that the Control Center is currently displayed on your screen, follow these steps to start recording keystrokes:

1. Choose Tools ► Macros.
2. Select Begin Recording.
3. A submenu will appear, as in Figure 14.6, instructing you to choose the key that will activate the macro once it is recorded.

While macros are one of the main tools for creating applications in word processors and spreadsheets, they play a minor role in database management. Therefore, it's not essential to invest a lot of time in learning about keystroke macros in dBASE IV.

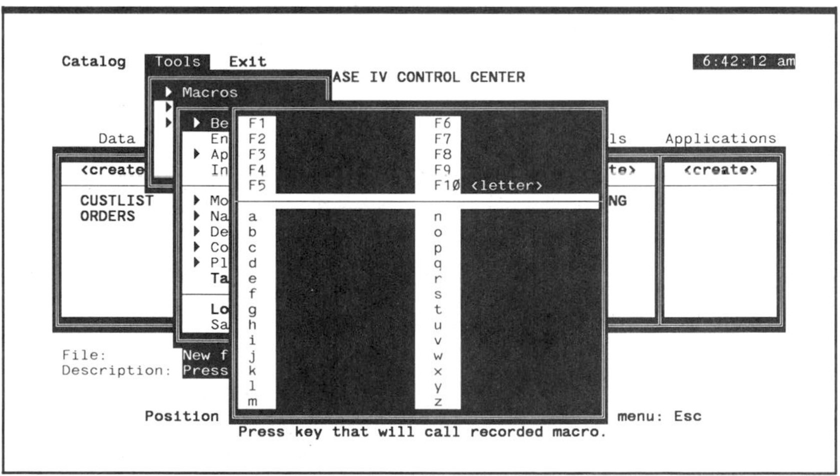

Figure 14.6: Submenu of keystroke macros

4. You can pick any letter key or function key to call your macro; for this example, type the letter D as your choice. (After you record a macro, its name is listed in the macro submenu.)
5. The navigation line informs you that keystrokes are now being recorded, so you can type the keystrokes that you want to save.
6. Press Alt-T to access the Tools pull-down menu.
7. Type D to select DOS Utilities.
8. Press Alt-F to access the Files pull-down menu.
9. Type the letter D to select Display Only.
10. Press Ctrl-Y to erase the current entry.
11. Type ***.DBF** and press ↵ to display the names of database files only. (The screen will continue to display the names of directories as well.)
12. Press PgDn as many times as necessary to view the names of database (.DBF) files.
13. Assuming that you want your recorded keystrokes to stop at this point, press Shift-F10, and select End Recording.

The navigation line now informs you that macro recording has stopped. To return to the Control Center, choose Exit ► Exit to Control Center.

PLAYING BACK RECORDED KEYSTROKES

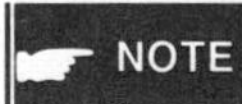

NOTE

Macro means *large* (the opposite of *micro*); a *keystroke macro* is a single keystroke that plays back many keystrokes—that is, a "large keystroke."

Now let's suppose that you want to view the names of all .DBF files on the current directory. You need not enter all the usual keystrokes to do so. Instead, just play back your recorded keystrokes by following these steps:

1. Choose Tools ► Macros.
2. Select Play from the submenu that appears.
3. Type the letter D to play back the macro that you just created.

4. dBASE IV plays back the recorded keystrokes, leaving you at the DOS utilities screen with the names of all .DBF files displayed.

Once the recorded keystrokes are all played back and dBASE IV returns to normal, you can either do more work in the DOS utilities screen, or choose Exit ► Exit to Control Center.

SAVING KEYSTROKE MACROS

When you first save recorded keystrokes in a macro, they are only stored in RAM, not on disk. If you want to save a keystroke macro for all future sessions in your work with dBASE IV, you must save the macro in a *macro library* on disk. To do so, follow these steps:

1. Start at the Control Center and choose Tools ► Macros.
2. Select Save Library from the submenu that appears.
3. Enter a valid DOS file name with no extension (such as MYMACROS), and press ↵.

A single macro library can contain up to 34 macros. When you want to use a saved macro or add more macros to an existing macro library, you must first be sure that that macro library is loaded.

LOADING A MACRO LIBRARY

To reload a saved macro library into RAM, follow these steps:

1. From the Control Center, choose Tools ► Macros.
2. Select Load Library.
3. Select the macro library name from the submenu that appears.

Now you can either play one of the previously recorded macros by selecting Play, or you can create a new macro by selecting Begin Record and a name (key) for the macro. Optionally, press Esc to return to the Control Center. The loaded macro library stays loaded for the duration of the current dBASE session or until you load a different macro library.

AVOIDING COMMON MACRO ERRORS

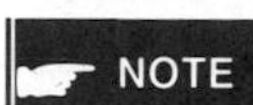

Remember that your mouse is disabled when you record a macro.

If your recorded macro accesses pull-down menus, use Alt-<*first letter*>, rather than F10, to access the pull-down menus, when you record macro keystrokes. Alt-<*first-letter*> always pulls down a specific menu, whereas F10 pulls down the last-used menu. This is why you used Alt-T and Alt-F to pull down menus while recording keystrokes in the preceding example. If you use F10 to pull down a menu while recording keystrokes, the recorded F10 keystroke may pull down a different menu when you play back the macro.

Similarly, when selecting options from pull-down menus, type the first letter of the option, rather than highlighting and pressing ↵, to select the option. In this way, you ensure that the macro will not select the wrong option because the highlighter is in a different position during playback than it was when you recorded the macro.

If you want the macro to select an option from a panel in the Control Center, or a submenu of file or field names, type out the name rather than just highlighting it. Submenus of file and field names change as you add and delete objects, so the position of a field or file name in a submenu may vary. If you type out the file or field name while recording keystrokes, you need not be concerned about its position when you later use the macro.

RECORDING KEYSTROKES WITHOUT THE TOOLS MENU

Suppose that you regularly create form letters and at the top of each new letter you always type your own name and address. To save time, you decide to record the keystrokes required to type this information. First, you go to the reports design screen and create a blank Mailmerge report format.

When you are ready to start recording keystrokes, the first thing you notice is that there is no Tools pull-down menu on the reports design screen. So how do you record your keystrokes? Easy—you use the shortcut method of pressing Shift-F10. Doing so displays a sort of "mini-macros" menu with these options:

Begin Recording   Cancel

To start recording your keystrokes, select Begin Recording. The screen displays the message "Press the key that will call this macro." Press any letter key or function key. If you select one that is already assigned to a macro, the screen displays the message "Do you really want to overwrite <letter>? (Y/N)." If you select No, the operation is canceled and you can start over. If you select Yes, dBASE begins recording keystrokes immediately. When you've finished recording your keystrokes, type Shift-F10 and select End Recording.

To save the recorded macro in the current macro library, you will eventually need to return to the Control Center. Choose Tools ► Macros, and then select Save Library from the submenu.

PLAYING BACK MACROS WITHOUT THE TOOLS MENU

To play back a recorded macro without using the Tools menu, press Alt-F10. You will be asked to "press an alphabetic key of the macro to play back." Type the letter name you assigned to the keystroke macro to start playing it back.

NAMING KEYSTROKE MACROS

Initially, all macros have only the single-letter name that you assign to them. If you need a reminder as to what a particular macro does, you can add an additional name. To do so, choose Tools ► Macros, then select Name from the submenu. Type the letter name of the macro to which you want to add a name. You'll be prompted to enter a macro name up to 10 letters long. The additional macro name appears in the list of existing macros for the current library, but you still use the single-letter name to play back the macro.

INSTANT MACROS

When you assign one of the function keys to a macro, you can play back that macro by simply holding down the Alt key and pressing the appropriate function key. For example, if you assign F5 as the macro name (by pressing the F5 function key) when you begin recording a macro, you can play back the macro by simply pressing Alt-F5.

ADDING TO A MACRO

You can add more recorded keystrokes to a macro by selecting the Append to Macro option from the Macros menu. When you select this option, you'll see a list of existing macros. Press the name of the macro that you want to add more keystrokes to. You'll see a prompt at the bottom of the screen indicating that the keystrokes are being recorded. Type the keystrokes that you want to record, then press Shift-F10 and E.

When you play back the macro, it will perform all of its original keystrokes, then all of the ones that you just added to it.

MAKING A MACRO PAUSE

You might want to create a macro that performs a series of keystrokes, pauses for some unique entry, then continues playing back additional keystrokes. For example, you might want to create a macro that takes you from the Control Center to the screen for selecting an existing index. Then it pauses while you select an index, and then takes you back to the Control Center.

To create such a macro, you record the keystrokes as you normally would. Then when you get to the place where you want the macro to pause, press Shift-F10 and select Input User-Input Break. Then continue recording the remaining keystrokes for the macro. When you've finished, stop recording keystrokes in the usual manner—by pressing Shift-F10 and selecting End Record.

When you play back the macro, the message "Macro Playback suspended, press Shift-F10 to resume macro playback" appears in a window on the screen when the input break is reached. You can type or press any keys you wish (for example, move the highlighter to a menu option), then press Shift-F10 to resume the macro playback.

EDITING A KEYSTROKE MACRO

Sometimes when you create a macro or append keystrokes to an existing macro, you make mistakes, and when you play back the macro, the mistakes are also played back. One way to fix such mistakes would, of course, be to re-record all the keystrokes. But dBASE also offers an alternative way to fix macro problems; you can edit the recorded keystrokes directly. To edit a keystroke macro, you follow these general steps:

- At the Control Center, choose Tools ► Macros.
- Select Modify.
- Press the "macro name" key (for example, type B to edit macro B).

At this point, you'll see the contents of the macro on an edit screen, similar to the edit screen used to edit memo fields. For example, Figure 14.7 shows the macro editing screen for the "D" macro created earlier. Any text that the macro types directly (such as the "*.DBF" shown in Figure 14.7) is displayed simply as text. You can use the usual arrow keys or your mouse to move the cursor on the screen, and the usual Del, Backspace, and other keys to make changes and corrections to the contents of your keystroke macros.

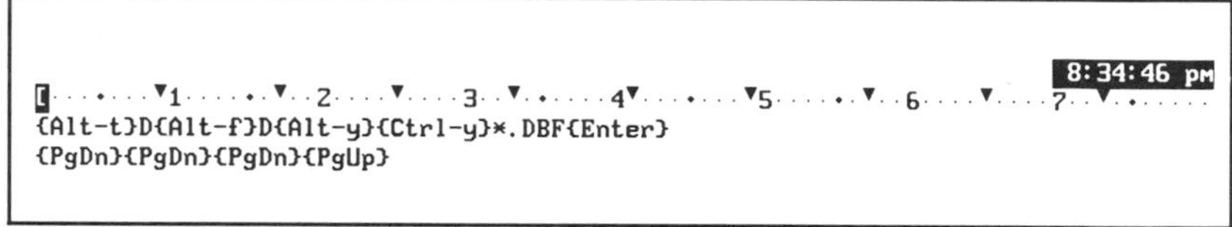

Figure 14.7: The macro editing screen resembles the editing screen for memo fields.

The menu options for editing memo fields are discussed in Chapter 10.

You can also press the F10 key to display the macro editor's menu bar, which offers the same options as the menu bar for editing memo fields. Figure 14.8 shows the menu bar, with the Exit menu pulled down. The menu bar disappears after you choose an option from one of its menus, but you can easily redisplay it by pressing F10 again.

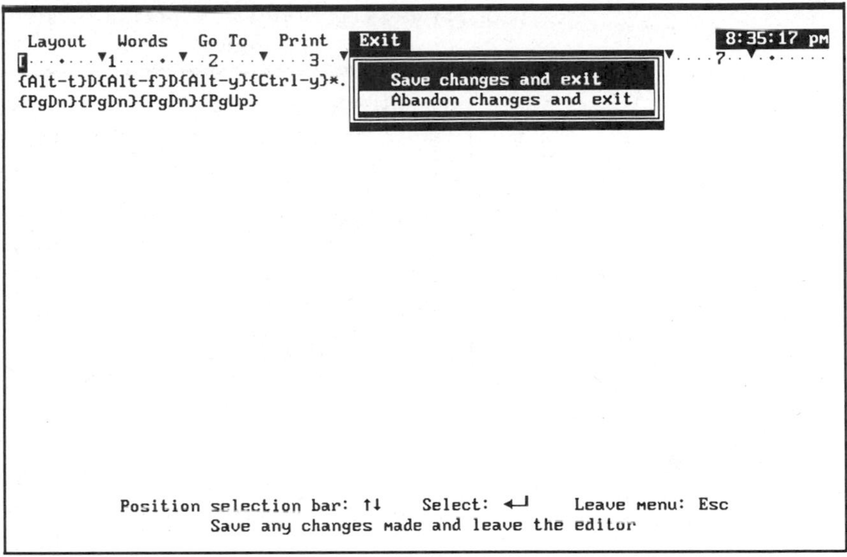

Figure 14.8: Press the F10 key to activate the menu bar on the macro editing screen.

Within a keystroke macro, special keys, like ↵, →, PgUp, and so forth, are displayed within curly braces, as shown in Table 14.2. If you wish to add a special keystroke (or input break command) to your macro while editing it, you must use the format shown in the second column of that table (upper/lowercase is not important—{LEFTARROW}, {LeftArrow}, and {leftarrow} are all the same).

Table 14.2: Names of special keys/commands in keystroke macros.

Keystroke	Macro Symbol
↵	{Enter}
Esc	{Esc}
←	{leftarrow}
→	{rightarrow}
↑	{uparrow}
↓	{downarrow}
Delete (Del)	{Del}

Table 14.2: Names of special keys/commands in keystroke macros. (continued)

Keystroke	Macro Symbol
Insert (Ins)	{Ins}
Backspace	{Backspace}
Tab	{Tab}
Page Up (PgUp)	{PgUp}
Page Down (PgDn)	{PgDn}
Home	{Home}
End	{End}
Ctrl	{Ctrl-
Shift	{Shift-
Alt	{Alt-
F1, F2...	{F1}, {F2}...{{}
User Input Break	{InpBreak}

Because the Alt, Shift, and Ctrl keys are always used in conjunction with another key, the two keys are shown together between one pair of braces. For example, the keystroke combination Alt-F5 is represented as {Alt-F5}.

If you want a macro to actually type a left curly brace, you must use {{} to represent this. Otherwise, dBASE "thinks" that the { is the first character to a special key.

When you've finished modifying your keystroke macro, press Ctrl-End to save your changes (or press Esc to abandon those changes).

DELETING A MACRO

To delete a macro from a macro library, first stop recording keystrokes (if you have not already) by pressing Shift-F10 and typing E. Then, choose Tools ► Macros ► Delete from the Control Center. Then press the name of the macro, for example A or the F5 key, and type Y (for Yes) when dBASE asks for confirmation.

CHAPTER 15

Introducing Applications

Fast Track

An application is a group of database objects 510

linked together by a custom menu system. Unlike a catalog, which displays the names of related database objects, an application "hides" the names of objects from the user and lets the user interact with the database through a menu of actions (such as Add New Records or Print a Report).

To develop a quick application 514

for a single database, custom screen, report format, and mailing label format,

1. Select <create> from the Applications panel of the Control Center.
2. Select Applications Generator from the submenu and fill in the Application Definition form.
3. Choose Application ► Generate Quick Application.
4. Fill in the names of the objects to be used by the application and press or click Ctrl-End.

To use a completed application, 516

highlight the application name in the Applications panel of the Control Center and press ↵, or double-click the application name. Then select Run Application from the dialog box that appears.

When developing larger applications of your own, 519

it's best to break the overall project into a series of steps:

1. Define the goals of the application.
2. Design and create the database objects.

3. Design a menu structure.
4. Build the application.
5. Test and refine the application as necessary.

THIS CHAPTER INTRODUCES YOU TO dBASE IV APplications and to the dBASE IV Applications Generator. In this chapter, we'll discuss applications in general and generate a sample application to give you some hands-on experience. Later in the chapter, we'll discuss techniques for designing and developing larger applications.

WHAT IS AN APPLICATION?

An *application* is a customized menu system that simplifies access to database files, forms, reports, queries, and other related database objects. Unlike the Control Center, which simply displays the names of files in a catalog, an application lets you build a menu system that is based on *actions*, rather than file names.

To clarify the difference between a catalog and an application, suppose you develop several databases, forms, views, and so forth to manage an inventory, and you include them in a single catalog. Figure 15.1 shows how the file names might appear in the Control Center. If you, personally, had created all these files, managing the inventory might be easy because of your knowledge of how to select items from the Control Center, what each file in the panels stands for, how to use dBASE menus, and so on.

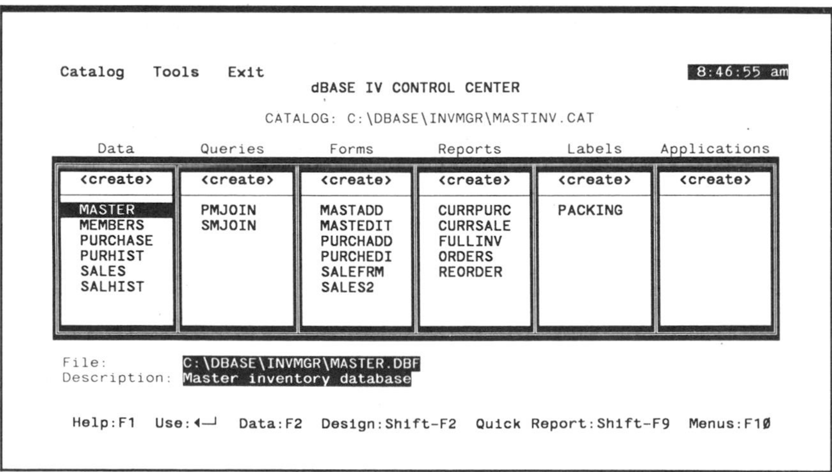

Figure 15.1: A sample catalog for managing an inventory

But suppose that you wanted someone else, perhaps an employee, to use all the files in the catalog to manage the inventory. If this person (whom we will refer to as the *user*) had no prior computer experience, you might need to invest quite a bit of time teaching him or her the basics of dBASE IV and the purpose of each file in the Control Center.

An application, on the other hand, would be much easier for the novice to learn. To start with, your application could bypass the Control Center altogether and display a personalized *sign-on banner*, as in Figure 15.2.

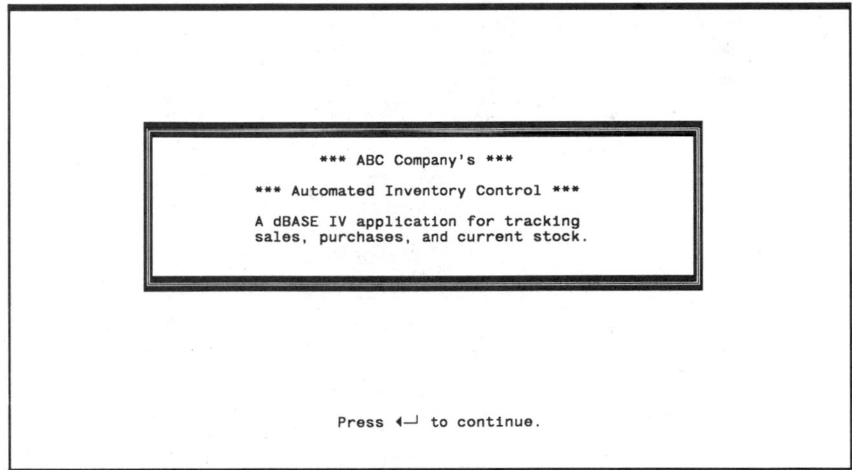

*** ABC Company's ***
*** Automated Inventory Control ***
A dBASE IV application for tracking
sales, purchases, and current stock.
Press ↵ to continue.

Figure 15.2: Sign-on banner for the inventory application

After pressing ↵, the novice user would see a custom menu (that you designed) dedicated to managing the inventory. This custom menu system would replace the dBASE IV menus and provide options specifically geared toward managing the inventory. Figure 15.3 shows a menu for the sample inventory application with a custom pull-down menu for managing the master inventory displayed.

Notice that the application menu clearly defines specific jobs involved in managing the inventory. From the Master Inventory pull-down menu, currently displayed on the screen, the user can add new products, change or delete products, browse through the

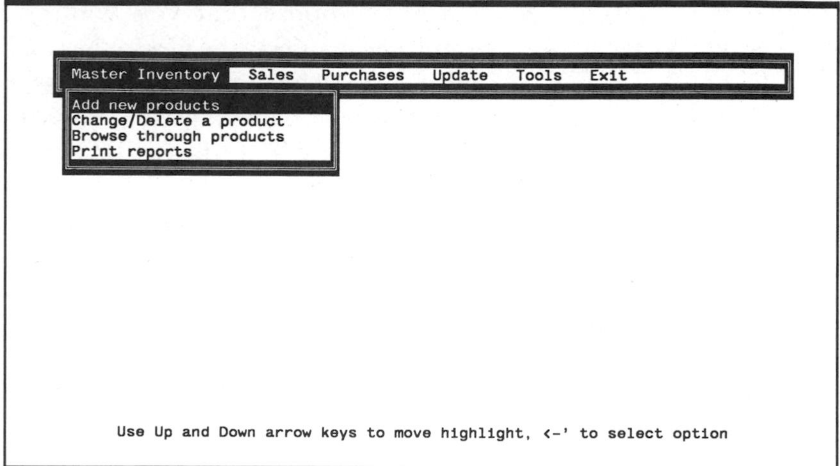

Figure 15.3: Custom menu for managing the inventory

inventory, or print reports. The pull-down menus under Sales and Purchases offer these same basic options for managing sales transactions and purchases.

The user does not need to know anything about the underlying files, forms, reports, or views or even that such things exist. All the user really needs to know is how to move through the menus and how to select items. The application menus operate in a manner that is similar to the dBASE IV menus. That is, the user can move the highlight across the menu bar or up and down a pull-down menu to highlight any option. Pressing ↵ selects the currently highlighted option. Similarly, if the computer is equipped with a mouse, the user can click the mouse on the menu bar to open a pull-down menu, then click the mouse on the desired option to select that option.

When you create an application, you can further simplify matters for the user by adding descriptive text to menus. For example, Figure 15.4 shows the pull-down menu for the Update option in the inventory management application. The first two items, Cancel and Proceed, are actual menu options. The underline and text beneath describe what the Update option does and cannot be highlighted or selected.

Like the dBASE IV menus, the application menu system can include submenus. For example, Figure 15.5 shows such a menu that appears when the user opts to print a report.

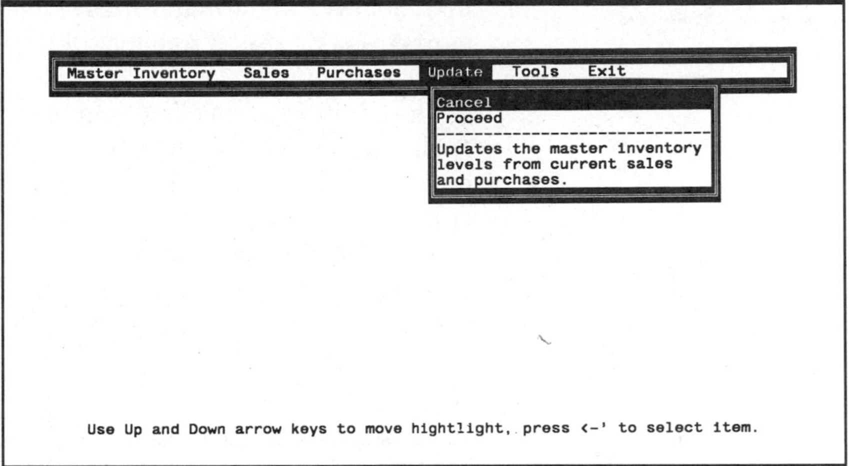

Figure 15.4: Pull-down menu with descriptive text

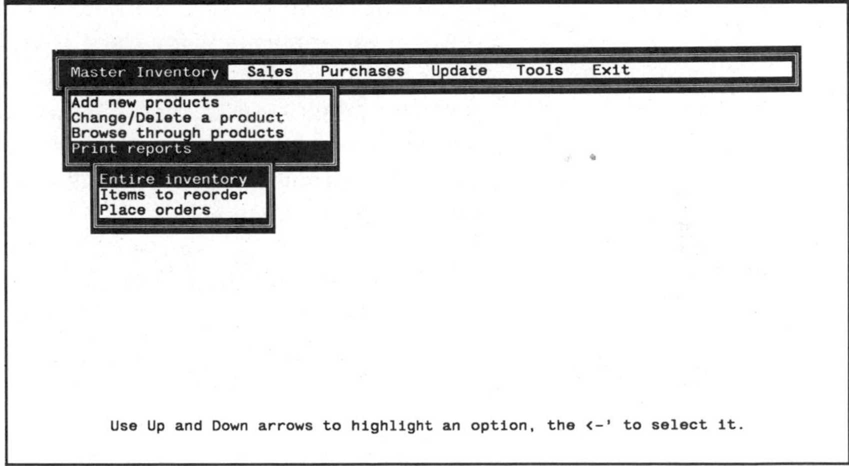

Figure 15.5: Submenu for printing reports

You can also create custom help screens for your application, which the user will see when he or she presses Help (F1), and you can customize the messages that appear at the bottom of the screen as the user scrolls through menu options and makes selections.

When the user is finished using the inventory application, he or she can select Exit from the menu bar and be returned to the DOS prompt, without ever seeing the Control Center. In fact, the user need not even know that dBASE IV is involved, or that such a thing as dBASE IV exists! From the user's perspective, only the inventory application itself exists.

In addition to meeting your own needs, some of your custom applications may meet the needs of others as well. For example, suppose you own a construction company, and you develop a very powerful and easy-to-use application for managing time, materials, and accounts. If the application is useful for others in the construction business, you could market your application, perhaps sell hundreds of copies, and turn quite a profit.

DEVELOPING A QUICK APPLICATION

To give you some hands-on experience in using a completed application, we'll use the dBASE IV Applications Generator to develop an application for the LEARN catalog. The Applications Generator is similar to the design screens you used to create report formats, label formats, and custom forms, except that it lets you develop an entire application. We'll use the *quick application* technique to create a simple application. Follow these steps to begin generating the sample application:

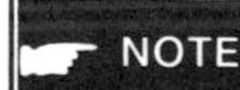

This example assumes you've already created the database, forms, report, and label formats described in Chapters 3–8.

1. Make sure the LEARN catalog is displayed in the Control Center.
2. Move the highlight to the Applications panel and select <create>.
3. From the dialog box that appears, select Applications Generator.
4. When the Application Definition form appears, fill it in as shown in Figure 15.6 (we'll discuss this form in detail in Chapter 16).
5. Press or click Ctrl-End after completing the form.

dBASE now displays the Applications Generator work surface. Like other work surfaces, it has a menu bar and pull-down menus. Initially, the Applications Generator work surface looks like Figure 15.7.

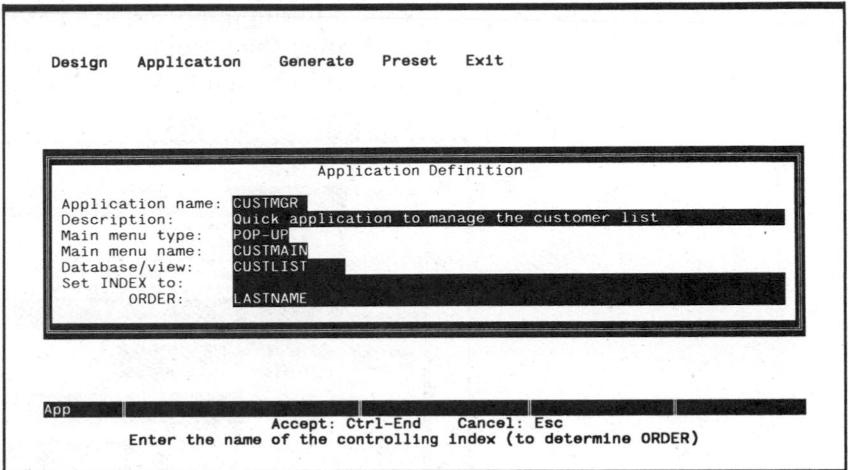

Figure 15.6: Completed Application Definition form

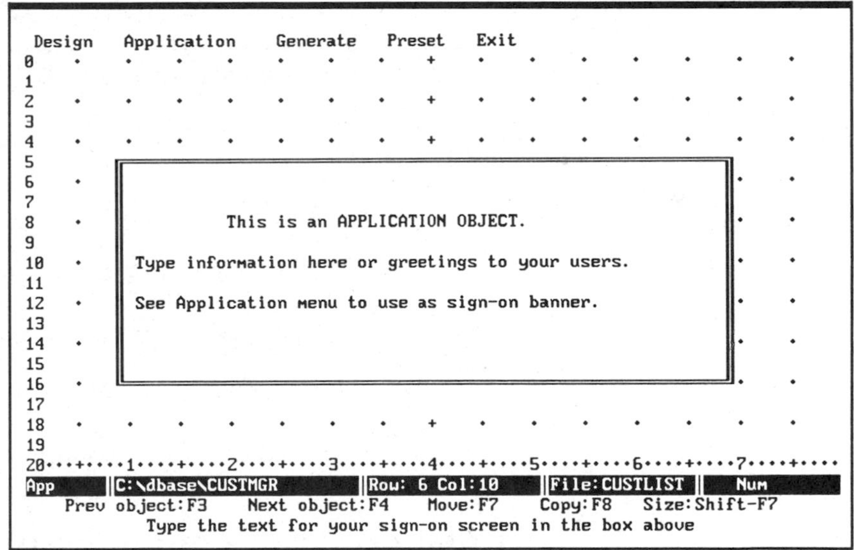

Figure 15.7: The Applications Generator work surface

USING A QUICK APPLICATION

Your next step is to create a quick application:

1. Choose Application ► Generate Quick Application.

2. Fill in the quick application form as shown in Figure 15.8. Rather than typing file names, you can press Pick (Shift-F1) to select them from a submenu.

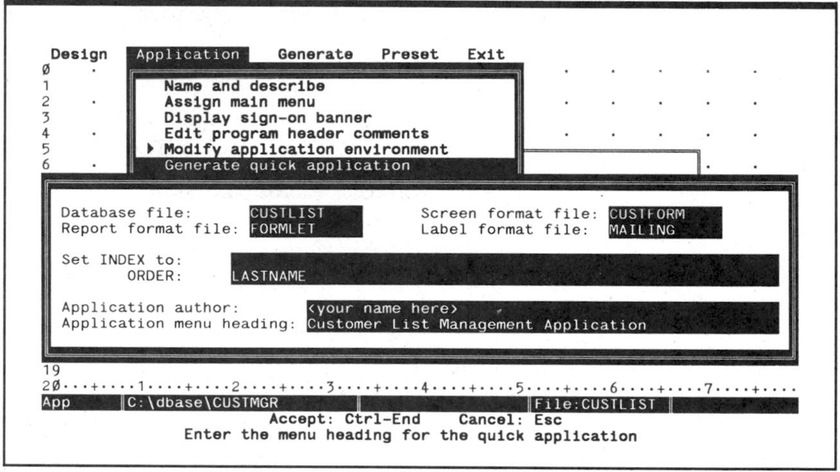

Figure 15.8: Quick application form filled out

3. Press or click Ctrl-End after filling in the quick application form.
4. Select Yes from the dialog box that appears.
5. After the Applications Generator writes the program for the application, you'll see the prompt, "Generation is complete. Press any key . . . " Press a key or click the mouse.
6. Choose Exit ► Save All Changes and Exit.

You have finished creating the sample application.

RUNNING THE APPLICATION

When you return to the Control Center, you'll see the name of your application in the Applications panel. To run the application, follow these simple steps:

1. Highlight the name of the application in the Applications panel and press ↵, or double-click on the application name.

2. Select Run Application from the submenu that appears.
3. Select Yes when dBASE asks for verification.

After a few seconds the application main menu appears on the screen, as shown in Figure 15.9. The quick application technique does not create a menu bar with pull-down menus. Instead, it presents a smaller sign-on banner at the top of the screen and a single pop-up menu centered on the screen. The pop-up menu is identical to a pull-down menu, except that it is not directly attached to a menu-bar option.

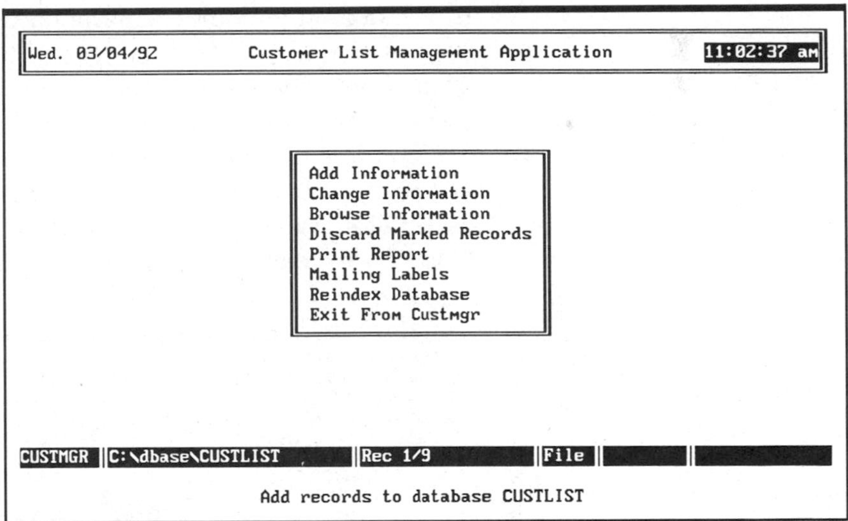

Figure 15.9: The quick application main menu

Feel free to experiment with the application. The Add and Change options will take you to the CUSTFORM form, where you can add or edit records. The Browse option will take you to the familiar browse screen. Exiting these screens returns you to the application main menu, where you can select another option.

The Discard Marked Records option packs the database (that is, permanently erases records that are marked for deletion). The Print Report option and Mailing Labels option behave a little differently than they usually do in dBASE. The screen shows the names and data types of each field in the database. A pop-up menu in the center of the screen provides options for locating a starting record, as shown in Figure 15.10.

To start printing a report from the first record, select GOTO Record and then Top from the submenu. Then choose Done Positioning and select an output option from the Send to . . . submenu that appears. You may also want to experiment with the SEEK and LOCATE commands, but don't be too concerned with these right now. When you develop your own applications later, you'll probably want to devise other techniques for printing reports.

Because indexes are susceptible to power failures and other disasters that occasionally strike computers, the Reindex Database option is included on the quick application main menu. When you create your own applications, it's a good idea to include such an option. That way, if some catastrophe erases your indexes, you can repair them immediately using a simple menu selection.

Feel free to experiment with the sample application as much as you wish, but don't worry about mastering or understanding every aspect of it. When you've finished experimenting, select Exit From CustMgr to return to the Control Center.

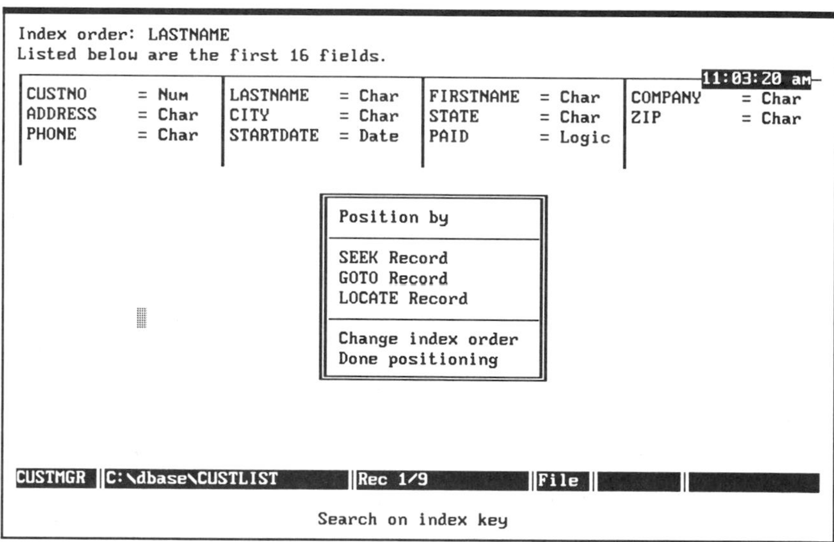

Figure 15.10: Quick application printing technique

DEVELOPING LARGER APPLICATIONS

The quick application technique generates only the simplest possible application, but it has allowed us to experiment with a sample application. In the future, you may want to create some more sophisticated and powerful applications of your own. However, before you start pounding the keyboard to bring your great application idea to fruition, you should take some time to design the end product.

You can think of the application development process as several separate tasks, as follows:

- Define the goals of the application.
- Design and create the objects (that is, databases, forms, and reports) of the application.
- Design a menu structure for the application.
- Build the application using the Applications Generator.
- Test and refine the finished application as necessary.

The following sections discuss each of thesc tasks in more detail, breaking them into a series of steps. (The next chapter uses these same steps to actually build a very powerful membership management system.) Keep in mind that application development is seldom linear; it is usually a series of refinements. You need not rigidly follow the steps that are described here; you can backtrack and make changes along the way.

STEP 1: DEFINE THE GOALS OF THE APPLICATION

The first step in building an application is simply to jot down some notes about what you want the application to do. If you are automating an existing manual system, analyze the manual system and get copies of forms and reports that are currently used in the system. Note what information is currently stored in manual files (such as Rolodexes, index cards, forms, and so forth). This information will help you design the databases.

If you are writing the application for a client, find out in as much detail as possible what the client wants. Given your knowledge of dBASE and its capabilities, you can offer suggestions to make the client's work easier.

As you make notes, start with a broad description of your goal, such as this:

> Develop an order entry and inventory management application.

Then refine the broad definition into specific goals and features, focusing on the fundamental aspects of database management: database structure, sorting and searching requirements, types of reports needed, and specific types of updating or other processes that are required. For example, you can refine the description of your goal as follows:

> Develop an order entry and inventory management application that
>
> - Stores the current product inventory, sales transactions, and purchases for ABC Company
> - Allows users to sort any database into part number order and search for any part number
> - Allows users to print the entire inventory, a reorder report, orders that need to be placed, a sales summary, and a purchases summary
> - Updates current in-stock and on-order quantities by quantities sold and quantities received from the Sales and Purchases database
> - Provides utilities for backing up the databases, copying the application, and repairing corrupted indexes

As you refine the written definition, try to break the overall goal of the application into smaller, more manageable tasks. That way, each task becomes a smaller goal in itself. It's much easier to achieve a big goal (for example, to create a large application) if you break it into a series of smaller, more manageable goals.

STEP 2: DESIGN AND TEST THE DATABASES

The next step is to determine which fields are required to store the information needed in the application. To ensure the most efficient database design, you may need to use several related database files. In Chapter 13, you saw how trying to combine customer names and addresses with each charge transaction in an accounts receivable database led to a great deal of repeated information.

To eliminate redundancy, customer information and charge transactions were stored on two separate databases, and the two database files were linked by a common field named CustNo. To ensure that there would be no errors in linking charges to customers, each customer was assigned a unique customer number.

When designing your own database structures, use these same techniques to structure the databases for your application. If you need a reminder about one-to-many and many-to-many database designs, refer to Chapter 13.

After you have decided what information needs to be stored in the database file (or files), create each one in the usual manner (by selecting <create> from the Data panel of the Control Center). Index any common fields that relate two or more database files as well as any fields that will be used regularly for sorting or for quick lookups, to speed these operations. After creating each database file, enter some sample data so you can test the components of the application as you build them.

STEP 3: DESIGN THE VIEWS

If any forms or reports in your query will require data from two or more related database files, create the views to link the files, using the usual techniques (start by selecting <create> from the Queries panel of the Control Center). For maximum speed, always include indexes in each file skeleton by choosing Fields ► Include Indexes in the query design screen.

Remember to choose Layout ► Create Link by Pointing (or create identical placeholders) to link the common fields. Also, if the output of a printed report is to be sorted or grouped, use the appropriate sorting operators in the query design screen. Test the view to ensure that it links the files in the proper manner. When you are certain that the view works, save it and assign it a name.

You need not be concerned about creating simple search queries, such as those that isolate all New York residents or records with a particular range of dates. You can enter appropriate filter conditions while developing the application, without using a query. You'll see how to do this in the next chapter.

STEP 4: DESIGN THE FORMS

The next step is to design and create the custom forms used by the application. If a form needs to use data from two or more database files, be sure to build the form from a view rather than a database.

When designing forms for complex applications, use the techniques listed here to simplify the user's work:

- If information being typed on the screen is coming from an existing paper form, try to make the form on the screen resemble the paper form. Most important, be sure that the order of fields (left to right and top to bottom) on the screen form matches the order of fields on the manual form.
- Always place the most important information near the center of the screen, as this is where the user always looks first.
- Be consistent when placing similar information on different forms. For example, if each form displays the current date and time, always place that information in a particular corner of the screen.
- If a large database requires several screens full of information to add or edit a record, repeat some identifying information on each screen. For example, suppose a database accepts all information necessary to fill in a tax form, and the user needs to use several screens to enter all the information. If the taxpayer's name appears on each screen, the user will not have to scroll back to the first screen to remember the current taxpayer's name.
- Use templates and validation techniques to trap faulty entries before they are stored in the database.

- Use boxes, lines, and graphics characters (such as arrows) to enhance the form, but don't clutter the form. A form with open space is easier to comprehend than an overcrowded form.

After you've created each form, test it by entering and editing some data. When you are satisfied that all forms are working as expected, you can move on to the next step.

STEP 5: DESIGN THE REPORTS

The next step is to create the report and mailing label formats for the application. Use the usual reports and labels design screens to create these. Use each format to print some sample data. When you are satisfied with each report and label format, you can start on the next step.

STEP 6: DESIGN THE MENU STRUCTURE

Before you fire up the Applications Generator, take some time to design the menu structure for your application on paper. Place main menu-bar options across the top row of the design and pull-down menus (or submenus) beneath the menu bar in a hierarchical manner.

Figure 15.11 shows a menu structure for an inventory application like the one presented earlier in this chapter. Note the hierarchical structure, from the general to the specific, for the pull-down menus. That is, under the general option of Master Inventory are several options for managing that information. Beneath the Print Reports menu option is a submenu of specific reports to choose from.

When you actually begin to develop the application, you will need to assign valid DOS file names (eight letters maximum, no spaces) to each menu in your application. You might want to note the menu names on your design to help you keep track of them later. Figure 15.12 shows an example.

You might also want to jot down some notes about the databases, objects, and actions associated with each menu option. Later, when you start developing the application, these notes will help you remember all of the details. Figure 15.13 shows an example with the menu and submenu under the Master Inventory option.

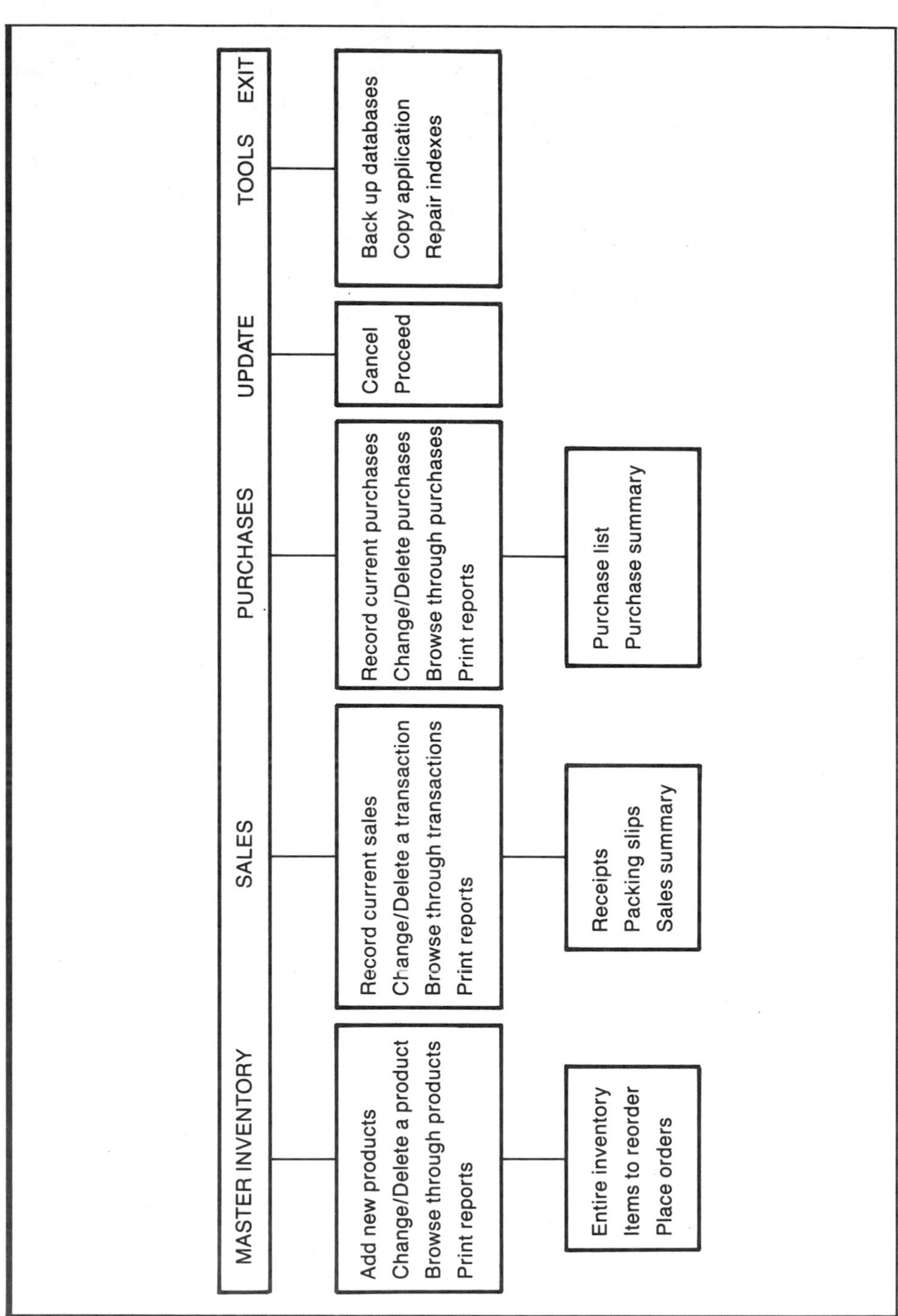

Figure 15.11: Sample menu structure

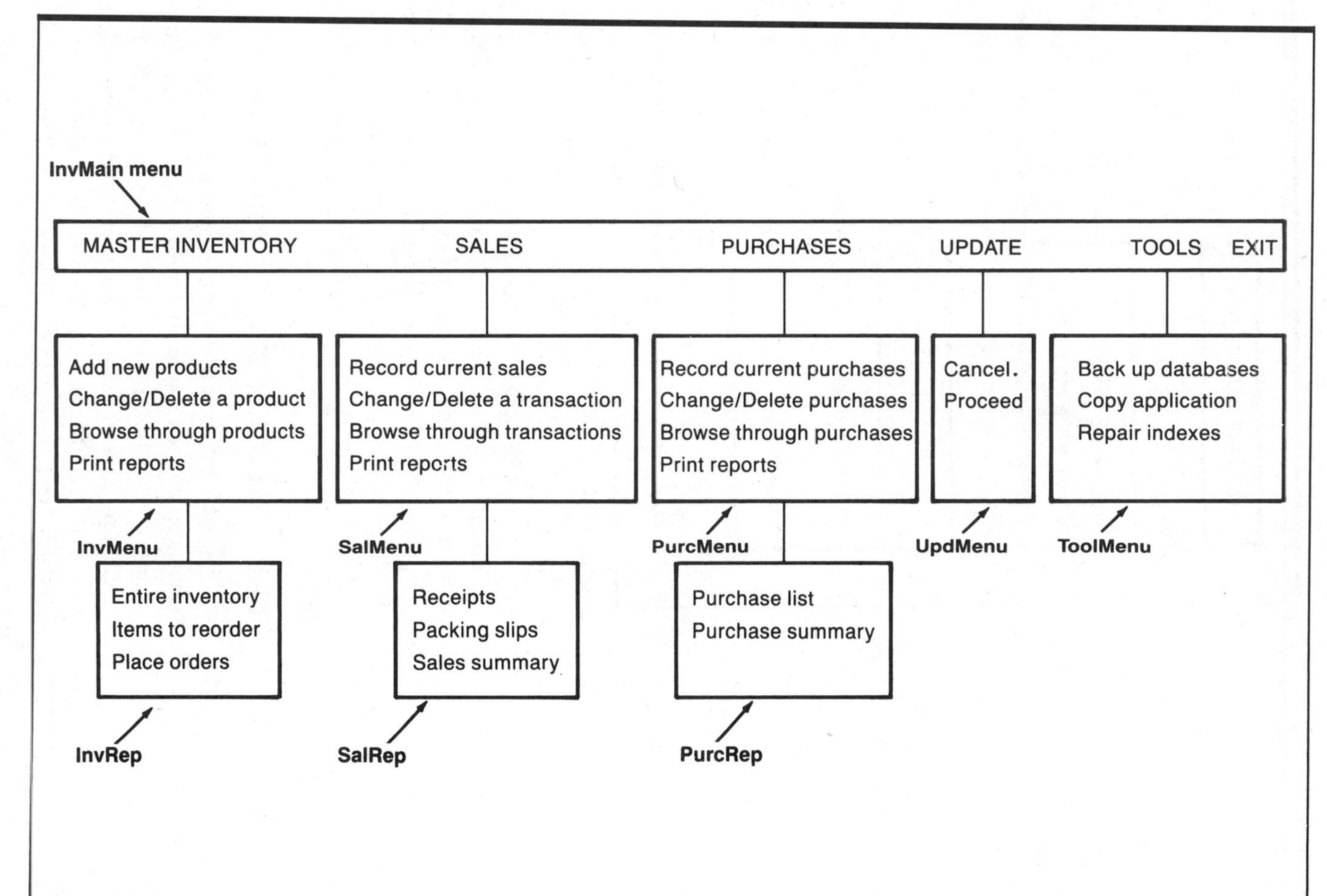

Figure 15.12: File names assigned to menus

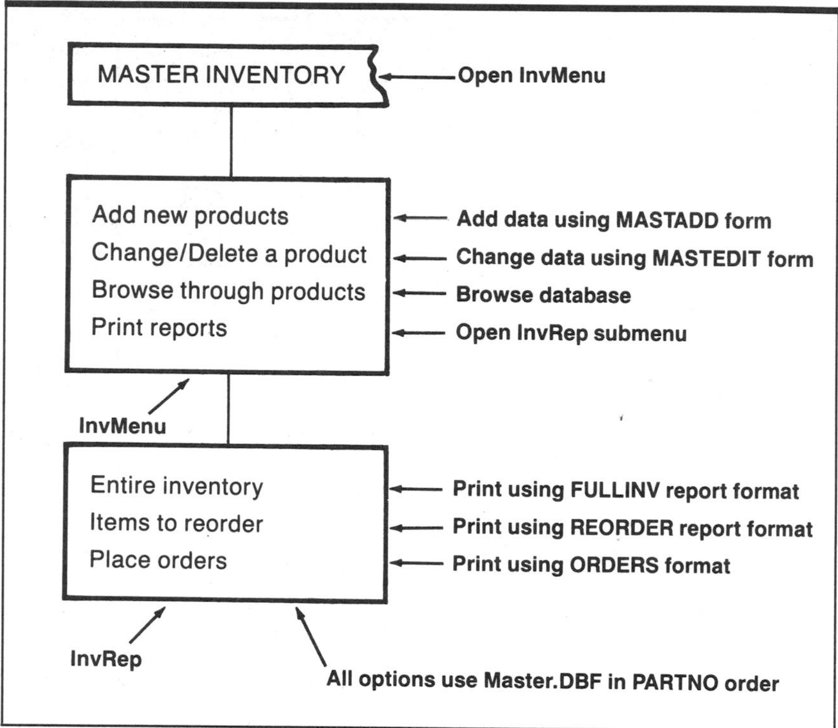

Figure 15.13: Notes about objects used at each menu option

In the example, the Master Inventory option opens the menu named InvMenu. The Add New Products option lets the user add new records using a custom form named MASTADD. The Print Reports option opens a submenu named InvRep. The Items to Reorder option prints a report using a format named REORDER. All options use the MASTER.DBF database in PARTNO order.

STEP 7: DESIGN BATCH PROCESSES

A *batch process* is a series of operations assigned to a single menu selection. For example, suppose you want your application to provide a menu option that copies all database files and their indexes to the floppy disk in drive A. Furthermore, assume that the application (like the inventory example) uses three databases: MASTER.DBF, SALES.DBF, and PURCHASE.DBF. When the user selects the

Backup option, the application must perform three steps:

Copy MASTER.* to A:
Copy SALES.* to A:
Copy PURCHASE.* to A:

(The * wildcard is used to ensure that the .MDX index files are copied with each .DBF database file.) To design a batch process such as this, assign an eight-letter file name to the process and list the required steps in English. Figure 15.14 shows an example. The Backup Database option is attached to a batch process named BACKUP.

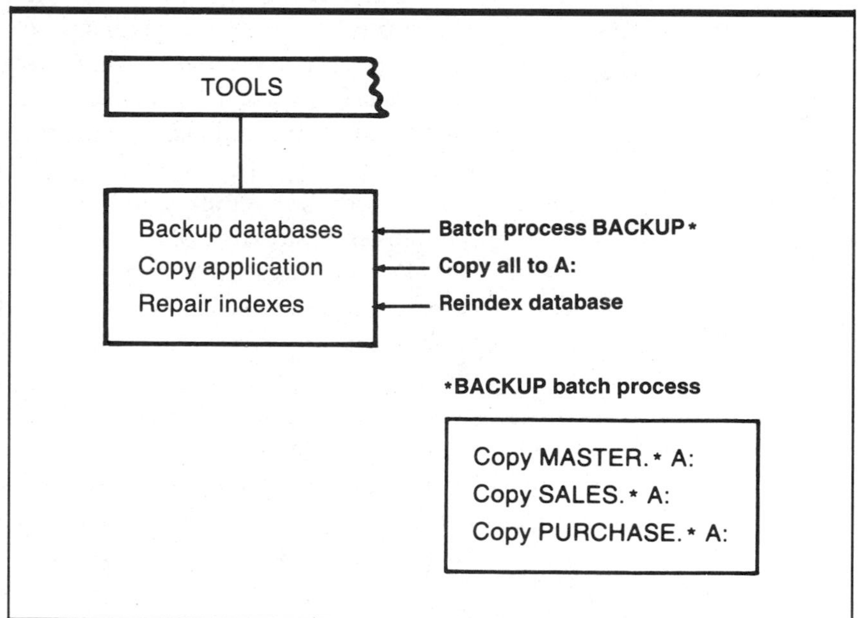

Figure 15.14: Batch process defined and assigned to a menu option

Batch processes can become quite sophisticated and complex. But don't be too worried right now if you are not sure what types of batch operations are possible. As you gain more experience with the Applications Generator in the chapters that follow, you'll find it much easier to develop batch processes of your own.

STEP 8: DEVELOP, TEST, AND REFINE

After you have a created all the appropriate objects for your application and designed your menu structure, you can begin using the Applications Generator to develop the application. The Applications Generator will allow you to "draw" each menu and attach an action to each menu option.

After you create the application, use it and check to make sure that everything works as expected. Sometimes, developing an application is an iterative process. You start with a design, develop the application, and then use the application for a while. After a time, you might decide to make some improvements and changes. You can do so, again using the Applications Generator to modify the existing application. You can repeat this process of testing and refining several times until you create a satisfactory (if not perfect) application.

When you are completely satisfied with the application, you may want to add some embellishments, such as custom help screens, messages, and colors. It's easiest to add these embellishments after you are finished with the overall application. That way, you won't need to concentrate on these extras while you are refining your application.

The steps presented here offer a somewhat simplified version of *program design.* If you should ever start developing large, complex applications on your own, you might want to look into this topic in more detail, either in a book devoted to program design and development or in an advanced book on dBASE IV programming and application development.

For the time being, however, the basic techniques discussed here should be sufficient to get you started. In the next chapter, we'll develop a sophisticated application, following the steps discussed in this chapter so you can see them in action.

CHAPTER

16

A Membership Management Application

To develop an application using the Applications Generator, 548
you need to perform seven steps:

1. Define the application name and default settings.
2. Create a sign-on banner for the application.
3. Create the menu bar and pull-down menus.
4. Attach actions to each menu option.
5. Create batch processes (if any are required).
6. Generate the application.
7. Save all changes and exit.

To begin developing an application, 549
select <create> from the Applications Generator panel of the Control Center, select Applications Generator from the submenu, and then fill in the application name and default settings.

To create a horizontal bar menu for an application, 552
choose Design ► Horizontal Bar Menu on the applications design screen.

To enter options into a horizontal bar menu, 552
position the cursor where you want the option to appear, press F5, type the option, and press F5 again.

To create pop-up or pull-down menus for an application, 554
choose Design ► Pop-Up Menu on the applications design screen.

To resize or move a pop-up or pull-down menu frame, **554**

press or click Size (Shift-F7) and move (F7); or drag the right or bottom frame border (or the lower right-hand corner) to resize, or the top or left frame border to move.

To assign actions to items in your custom menus, **561**

make sure the custom menu is the current object, highlight the menu option to be assigned an action, then choose Item ► Change Action.

To create a batch process, **580**

choose Design ► Batch Process on the applications design screen, select <create>, type the name and description of the batch process, then list the steps (in plain English) that the process is to perform. Then assign actions to each step in the process, using the same techniques that you use to assign actions to menu options.

Whenever you create or modify an application, **587**

you must generate the application code. To do so, choose Generate ► Select Template and specify MENU.GEN as the template to use. Then select Begin Generating from the same menu.

After generating (or regenerating) an application, **596**

Choose Exit ► Save All Changes and Exit to return to the Control Center.

THIS CHAPTER PRESENTS A COMPLETE EXAMPLE OF application design and development. Starting from scratch and following the basic steps of application design and development discussed in the previous chapter, we will develop an application to manage a membership database. First, we'll define the goals of the application, and then we'll develop the various objects, such as the database, custom forms, and report formats. Next, we will design a menu system, and finally we'll use the Applications Generator to create the finished product.

This chapter assumes that you are now familiar enough with the database, labels, reports, and forms design screens to create these objects with minimal assistance. Of course, when you start using the Applications Generator later in the chapter, step-by-step instructions will be provided. The techniques that you learn here will help you build your own applications, as well as the larger, more complex business management application presented in Chapter 21.

CREATING A SUBDIRECTORY FOR THE APPLICATION

To keep individual applications from becoming entangled, it's a good idea to create each new application on a unique subdirectory. In this chapter, you'll store the membership application on a subdirectory named \DBASE\MEMBERS on the hard disk. Follow these steps to create and switch to this new directory:

1. If you are currently running dBASE IV, return to the Control Center and choose Exit ► Quit to DOS.
2. At the DOS prompt, type the command **MD\DBASE \MEMBERS** and press ↵. (If the error message "Unable to Create Directory" appears, the directory already exists—proceed with step 3.)
3. To log on to the new directory, type the command **CD \DBASE\MEMBERS** and press ↵.

If the subdirectory name \DBASE\MEMBERS does not appear next to the C> prompt, type the command **PROMPT PG** and press ↵. This DOS command will display the directory name.

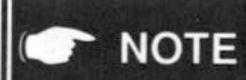

Appendix A discusses DOS commands, directories, and paths in more detail.

You should be able to run dBASE IV from the directory by entering the usual command **DBASE** (followed by ↵, of course). If the error message "Bad Command or File Name" appears, your PATH setting does not include the directory on which dBASE IV is stored. You can run dBASE by including the path in the command. For example, if dBASE IV is stored on the \DBASE directory, you can enter the command **\DBASE\DBASE** (or substitute the correct directory name in place of the first DBASE).

Remember that whenever you wish to use the membership system in the future, you must be logged on to the \DBASE\MEMBERS directory. To do so, you can use the command **CD\DBASE\MEMBERS** at the DOS prompt (before you run dBASE). If dBASE is already running, you can log on to the \DBASE\MEMBERS directory by choosing Tools ► DOS Utilities from the Control Center menu. Then choose DOS ► Set Default Drive:Directory and enter **C:\DBASE\MEMBERS** as the new default directory.

GOALS OF THE MEMBERSHIP APPLICATION

The membership application will be designed to allow the membership committee of a computer user's group to automate tasks that they currently perform manually. The application will allow the group to do the following:

- Store members' names and addresses, membership starting and expiration dates, and other useful information
- At any time during the month—

  Add, change, and delete members' records

  Print a current membership roster, alphabetized by name

  Print mailing labels, sorted by zip code, for each active member

  Update records when a membership is renewed

- At any time during the month, perform the following basic housekeeping tasks:

  Change the system date

  Make a backup copy of the database

  Copy the entire application to a diskette

  Repair corrupted indexes

- The application will also automate printing of the following monthly form letters:

  Welcome letters and mailing labels for new members

  Renewal reminders and labels for memberships that expire next month

  Overdue notices and labels for memberships that expired in the previous month

TIP

If you would like to take a look at the completed application, refer to the section "Testing the Application" near the end of this chapter.

At this point, you might want to start refining each feature of the application by sketching on paper a database design and a form design and draft form letters. However, in this chapter we'll design and create simultaneously to save some space and time. If you have not done so already, log on to the \DBASE\MEMBERS directory and get dBASE IV up and running, so the Control Center is displayed on your screen.

DESIGNING THE MEMBERSHIP APPLICATION DATABASE

The membership application database, named MEMBERS.DBF, is structured to manage information about each group member. You can create this database structure now by selecting <create> from the Data panel on the Control Center. Type the field information as shown in Figure 16.1 (of course, you can't type the description of each field). Note that the ZIP field is marked Y for indexing. After completing the structure, choose Exit ► Save Changes and Exit and assign the file name MEMBERS to the database.

Num	Field Name	Type	Width	Dec	Index	Description
1	TITLE	Character	4		N	Mr./Mrs. title
2	FIRSTNAME	Character	12		N	First name
3	MI	Character	2		N	Middle initial
4	LASTNAME	Character	12		N	Last name
5	COMPANY	Character	25		N	Company
6	DEPARTMENT	Character	25		N	Department
7	ADDRESS	Character	32		N	Address
8	CITY	Character	20		N	City
9	STATE	Character	2		N	State
10	ZIP	Character	10		Y	Zip code
11	PHONE	Character	13		N	Phone number
12	EXTENSION	Character	4		N	Phone extension
13	STATUS	Character	8		N	Membership status
14	STARTDATE	Date	8		N	Starting date
15	EXPIRES	Date	8		N	Next expiration date
16	CURRENT	Logical	1		N	Is memberhip current?
17	RENEWED	Logical	1		N	Renewed this month?

Figure 16.1: Structure of the MEMBERS database

CREATING AN ALPHABETICAL SORT ORDER

To create a complex index for alphabetizing names, highlight the MEMBERS database name in the Data panel of the Control Center and press or click Data (F2). Choose Organize ► Create New Index to create a complex index with these characteristics:

Name of index	LASTNAME
Index expression	LASTNAME + FIRSTNAME + MI
FOR clause	
Order of index	ASCENDING
Display first duplicate key only	NO

Press or click Ctrl-End after defining the index. Then choose Exit ► Exit to return to the Control Center.

CREATING A CUSTOM FORM FOR THE MEMBERSHIP SYSTEM

The membership application will use a custom form, named MEMFORM, to allow the user to enter and edit membership data.

Use the MEMBERS database and select <create> from the Forms panel to create the form. Use the usual editing techniques to arrange the fields as in Figure 16.2. (Note that a small portion of the custom form is below the bottom of the screen; you'll see the missing portion in the next figure.)

Some of the fields in the form can be improved by specialized templates or picture functions. These fields are listed in Table 16.1 (those not listed use the default template and picture function and do not need to be changed). Remember: To change a template or picture function, move the cursor into the field template and press or click Add Field (F5), or double-click that field template.

The STARTDATE, EXPIRES, and CURRENT fields use Edit Options to display default (suggested) values. To assign a default value, move the cursor into the field template and press or click Add Field (F5), or double-click that field template. Then choose Edit Options ► Default Value, enter the default value, and press or click Ctrl-End. The STARTDATE field uses the default value DATE() to display the current date. The EXPIRES field uses the current date plus one year, DATE() + 365, as the default value. Because most members pay immediately when they join, the CURRENT field uses a default value of .T. (for true).

Note that the RENEWED field is not included on the form. This field is used in a browse screen to *flag* (identify) members who have

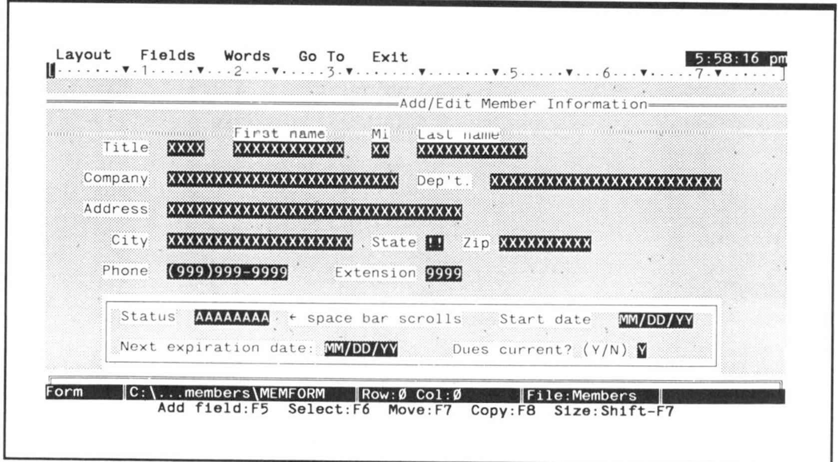

Figure 16.2: MEMFORM form for the membership application

Table 16.1: Templates and Picture Functions in MEMFORM

Field	Template	Picture function
STATE	!!	
PHONE	(999)999-9999	
EXTENSION	9999	
STATUS	AAAAAAAA	Multiple choice {M} with options REGULAR, OFFICER
CURRENT	Y	

renewed their membership. You'll see the RENEWED field put to use later.

After you create the form, save it and assign the name MEMFORM. When you get back to the Control Center, highlight MEMFORM in the Forms panel and press or click Data (F2). You should see the form appear on the screen as in Figure 16.3. Note that the default starting date on your screen will match the current date, and the default expiration date will be one year beyond the current date.

To test the form, let's add a sample record. When entering data in the STATUS field, you should be able to switch from REGULAR to OFFICER and back again by pressing the space bar. Now enter the following record (regardless of the suggested start and expiration dates that appear on the screen, enter the start and expiration dates in the example shown here):

```
Mr. Andy A. Adams
ABC Technology
Engineering Dep't
13307 Artesia Ave
Los Angeles     CA     90165
(818)555-0101  Extension 123
Status: REGULAR                  Start date: 01/01/93
Next expiration date:01/01/94    Dues current? Y
```

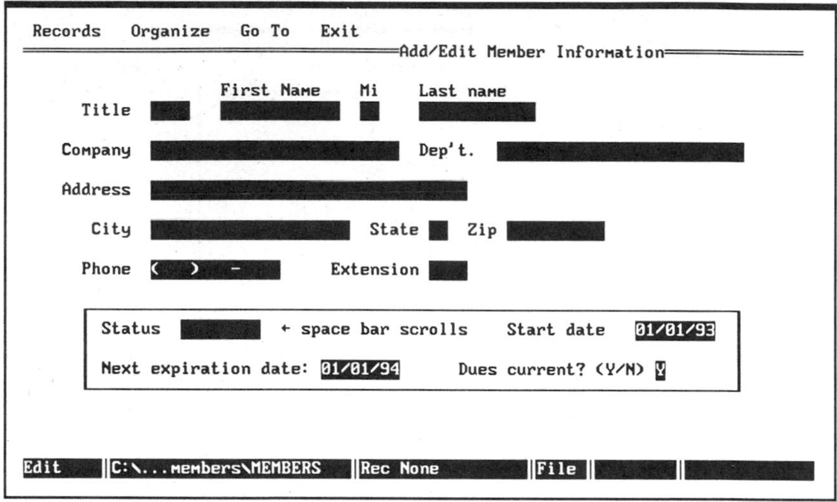
Records Organize Go To Exit
Add/Edit Member Information
Title First Name Mi Last name
Company Dep't.
Address
City State Zip
Phone ( ) - Extension
Status ← space bar scrolls Start date 01/01/93
Next expiration date: 01/01/94 Dues current? (Y/N) Y
Edit C:\...members\MEMBERS Rec None File

Figure 16.3: MEMFORM form ready to accept data

After entering the sample record, choose Exit ► Exit to return to the Control Center. Now you can begin developing the reports that the application will use.

CREATING MEMBERSHIP APPLICATION REPORTS

The membership application in this example uses four report formats, three of which are form letters. Create each of the report formats using the usual <create> option from the Reports panel of the Control Center. Use the MEMBERS database as the basis for each report format.

The first report format, named ROSTER, will display a list of all members. Use the usual editing techniques on the reports design screen to format the report to your liking. Figure 16.4 shows an example, where the fields are arranged as shown here:

```
LASTNAME, TITLE FIRSTNAME MI
COMPANY
DEPARTMENT
ADDRESS
CITY, STATE ZIP PHONE EXTENSION
```

Status: STATUS Current?: CURRENT
Start Date: STARTDATE Expiration Date: EXPIRES

A single blank line is included in the Detail band to separate printed records. Choose Exit ► Save Changes and Exit after completing the format.

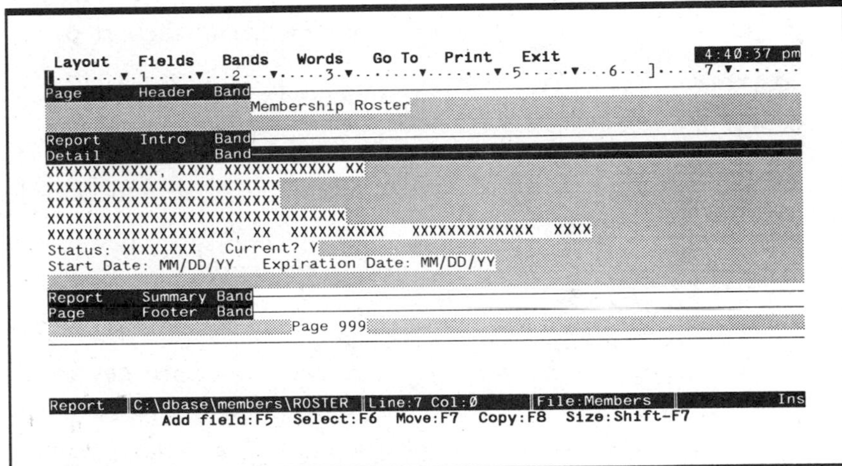

Figure 16.4: Format of the ROSTER report

If you forget to set the report margin ahead of time, you can select all the field templates and text in a band (by pressing F6 or using your mouse), then choose Words ► Modify Ruler as usual.

The other three reports are form letters, each of which uses an identical name and address format near the top of the letter. To speed the development of the form letters, first select <create> from the Reports panel in the Control Center. Before inserting any fields into the report, you should set the right margin to 65. To set the margin, choose Words ► Modify Ruler, then press the Home key to move the cursor to the beginning of the ruler. Press the Tab key eight times to move the cursor to 65 on the ruler, press the] key to set the right margin, then press Ctrl-End.

Now choose Layout ► Quick Layouts ► Mailmerge Layout. Using the usual techniques, arrange the fields as shown in the next example. (The MM/DD/YY template is for the current date, which you can place by pressing or clicking Add Field (F5) and selecting Date from the PREDEFINED column of the menu that appears.)

MM/DD/YY
TITLE FIRSTNAME MI LASTNAME

```
COMPANY
DEPARTMENT
ADDRESS
CITY, STATE ZIP

Dear FIRSTNAME:
```

After arranging the fields as shown, make three copies of the current format by following these steps:

1. Choose Layout ► Save This Report.
2. Enter **WELCOME** as the report name and press ↵.
3. Choose Layout ► Save This Report.
4. Use the Backspace key to erase WELCOME.FRM; then enter **RENEWAL** as the report name and press ↵.
5. Choose Layout ► Save This Report.
6. Use the Backspace key to erase RENEWAL.FRM; then enter **OVERDUE** as the report name and press ↵.
7. Choose Exit ► Abandon Changes and Exit, then select Yes.

When you return to the Control Center, you can complete each form letter by highlighting its name in the Control Center and pressing or clicking Design (Shift-F2). Figures 16.5, 16.6, and 16.7 show examples of three form letters. (Most of each letter is scrolled off the bottom of the screen, but you'll undoubtedly want to create your own form letters anyway.)

After creating each report format, you can print a test copy by highlighting the report name in the Control Center and pressing ↵, or by double-clicking the report name. Then select Print Report and either Begin Printing or View Report on Screen from the Print submenu.

CREATING A MAILING LABEL FORMAT

The application also needs a format for printing labels. Select <create> from the Labels panel in the Control Center and arrange

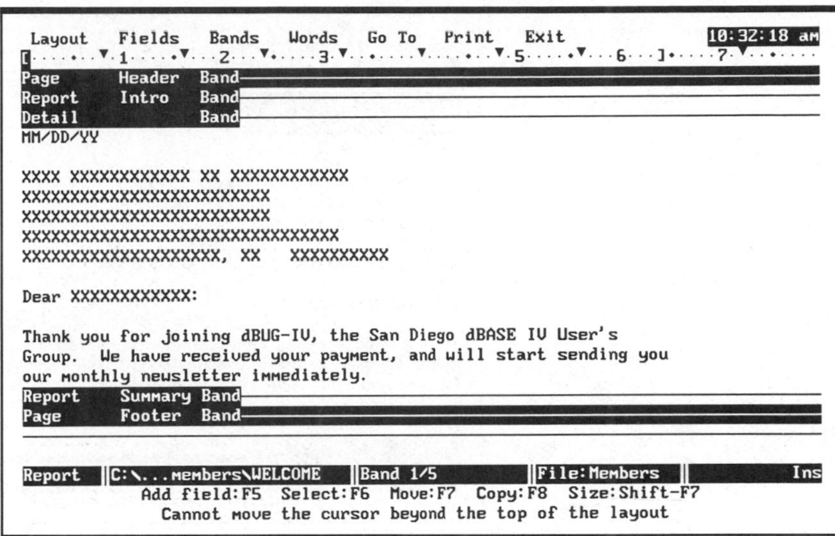

Figure 16.5: Format for the WELCOME letter

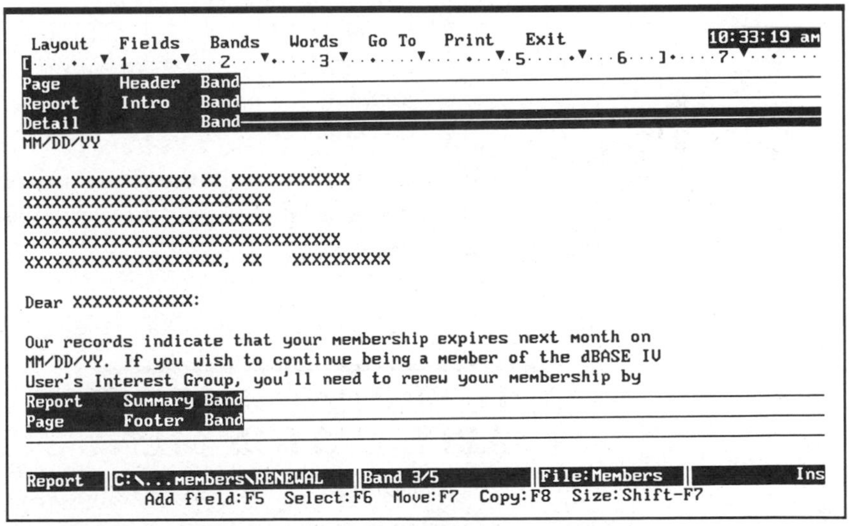

```
Layout   Fields   Bands   Words   Go To   Print   Exit          10:33:19 am
Page      Header  Band
Report    Intro   Band
Detail            Band
MM/DD/YY

XXXX XXXXXXXXXXXX XX XXXXXXXXXXXX
XXXXXXXXXXXXXXXXXXXXXXXXX
XXXXXXXXXXXXXXXXXXXXXXXXX
XXXXXXXXXXXXXXXXXXXXXXXXXXXXXXXX
XXXXXXXXXXXXXXXXXXXX, XX   XXXXXXXXXX

Dear XXXXXXXXXXXX:

Our records indicate that your membership expires next month on
MM/DD/YY. If you wish to continue being a member of the dBASE IV
User's Interest Group, you'll need to renew your membership by
Report    Summary Band
Page      Footer  Band

Report  C:\...members\RENEWAL  Band 3/5  File:Members        Ins
            Add field:F5  Select:F6  Move:F7  Copy:F8  Size:Shift-F7
```

Figure 16.6: Format for the RENEWAL letter

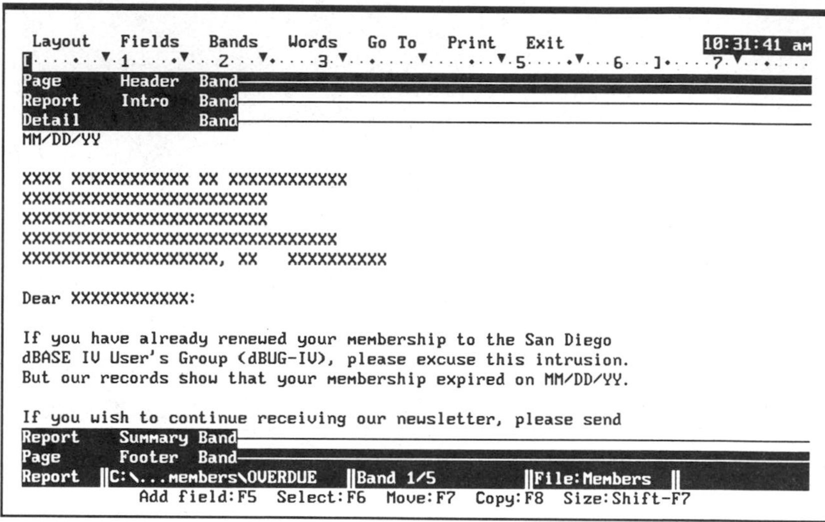

Figure 16.7: Format for the OVERDUE letter

the fields as follows:

TITLE FIRSTNAME MI LASTNAME
COMPANY
DEPARTMENT
ADDRESS
CITY, STATE ZIP

Save the format using the file name MEMLABEL and then test it by printing a label, using the same basic technique you use to print reports.

DESIGNING THE MEMBERSHIP APPLICATION MENU STRUCTURE

Now that you've created and tested all the objects for the membership application, you can begin designing the menu structure. (Some people prefer to design the menu structure early in the design phase so that they can refine the written definition before creating any objects. There is certainly no harm in doing so.)

TIP

If you have a copy machine nearby, you might want to copy Figures 16.8 and 16.9 and keep them in front of you as you develop the application to help you keep track of each menu and menu option.

Figure 16.8 shows the menu structure for the membership application, including the names in the horizontal bar menu and the pull-down menus. Figure 16.9 shows the menu structure with the names of objects, sort orders, filter conditions, and the batch process defined. (At this point, filter conditions are in plain English; for example, "new members" is a filter for printing welcome letters.)

DESIGNING THE MEMBERSHIP APPLICATION BATCH PROCESS

NOTE

When entering logical values into a field, you type T for True and F for False (or Y for True and N for False). Likewise, logical values display as T, F, Y, or N on edit and browse screens, forms, and reports. However, if you are specifying a logical value in a query, defining an application in the Applications Generator, or working at the dBASE dot prompt, you must type .T. for True and .F. for False (with periods before and after) to prevent dBASE from confusing the logical value with a variable name.

The membership application uses a single batch process, named RENEW.BCH, to help the user renew memberships (dBASE automatically adds the .BCH extension). The batch process performs four operations to automate the task of updating memberships each month. To see what each operation in the process does, assume that the current date is February 28, 1994, and the database contains the following four records (only relevant fields are used in this example). Note that Andy Adams' CURRENT field is already marked F, because his membership expired last month:

LASTNAME	FIRSTNAME	STARTDATE	EXPIRES	CURRENT	RENEWED
Adams	Andy	01/01/93	01/01/94	F	F
Baker	Bob	02/01/93	02/01/94	T	F
Carlson	Cara	02/28/93	02/28/94	T	F
Davis	Deedra	03/31/93	03/31/94	T	F

The batch process performs four operations.

OPERATION 1: FLAG EXPIRED MEMBERSHIPS

The first operation in the batch process automatically changes the CURRENT field to F for all memberships that have expired. Again, given that the current date is 02/28/94, this operation will modify two

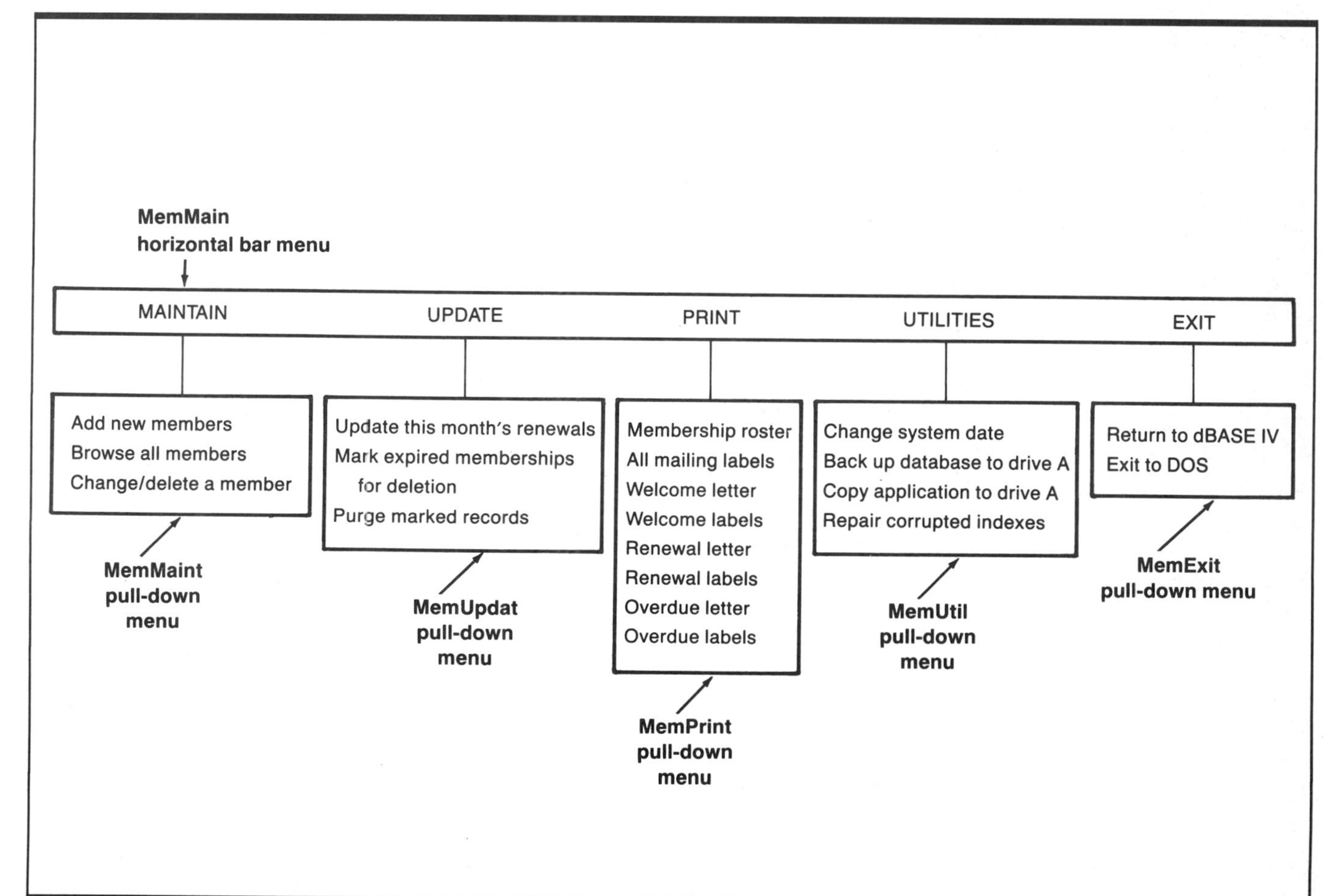

Figure 16.8: Menu structure for the membership application

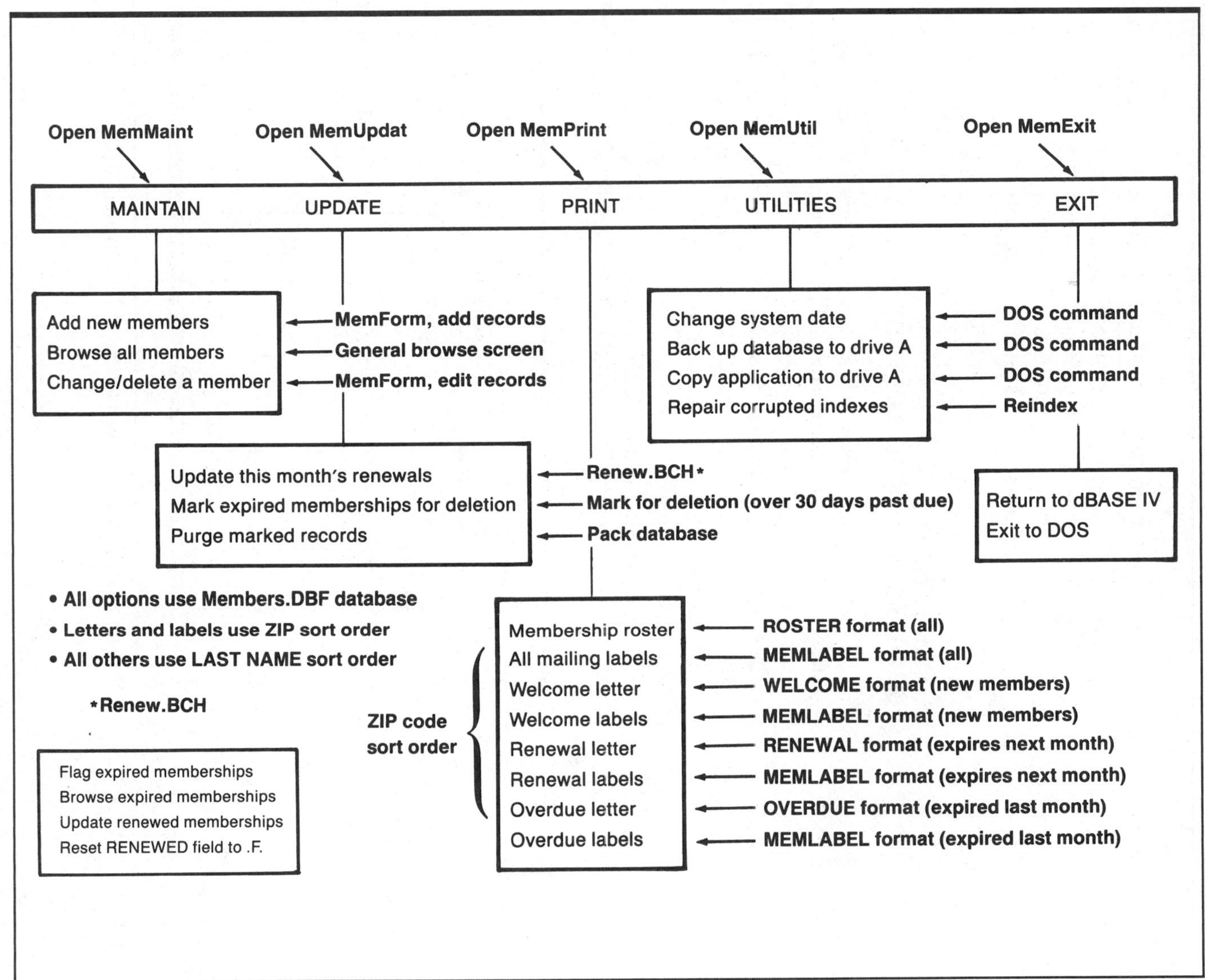

Figure 16.9: Objects, filters, sort orders, and batch processes sketched out

of the four records, bringing the CURRENT field up to date in all records, as follows:

LASTNAME	FIRSTNAME	STARTDATE	EXPIRES	CURRENT	RENEWED
Adams	Andy	01/01/93	01/01/94	F	F
Baker	Bob	02/01/93	02/01/94	F	F
Carlson	Cara	02/28/93	02/28/94	F	F
Davis	Deedra	03/31/93	03/31/94	T	F

OPERATION 2: BROWSE EXPIRED MEMBERSHIPS

The next operation in the batch process displays only expired memberships on a browse screen. The user, who presumably has payments from all renewed members, can then change the RENEWED field from F to T for members who have renewed. For convenience, the cursor is locked into the RENEWED field, and the field is displayed to the left of other fields. Figure 16.10 shows the browse screen with some sample data.

Suppose Adams and Baker have renewed their memberships, so the user changes the F to T in the RENEWED field for each of their

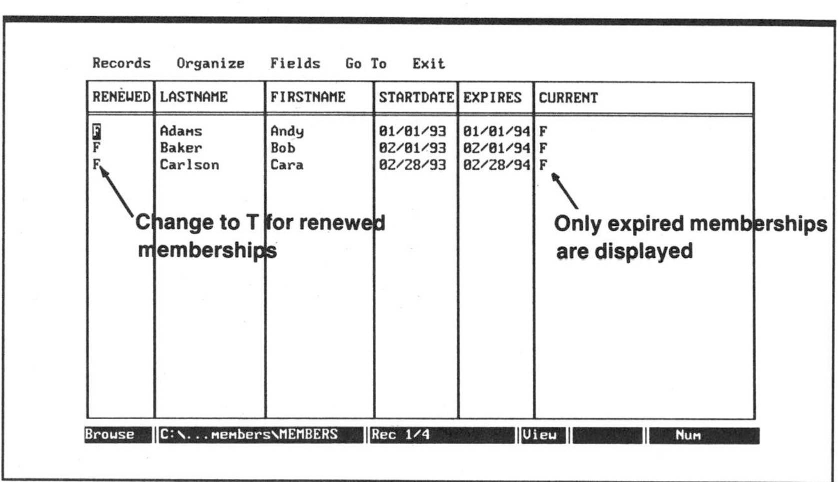

Figure 16.10: Browse screen for indicating renewed memberships

records and then saves these changes. The database now contains the following data:

LASTNAME	FIRSTNAME	STARTDATE	EXPIRES	CURRENT	RENEWED
Adams	Andy	01/01/93	01/01/94	F	T
Baker	Bob	02/01/93	02/01/94	F	T
Carlson	Cara	02/28/93	02/28/94	F	F
Davis	Deedra	03/31/93	03/31/94	T	F

OPERATION 3: UPDATE RENEWED MEMBERSHIPS

Now that the database has been saved with renewed memberships marked with a T, the third operation in the batch process automatically marks the appropriate CURRENT fields as T and extends the expiration dates by one year (to 1995) as follows:

LASTNAME	FIRSTNAME	STARTDATE	EXPIRES	CURRENT	RENEWED
Adams	Andy	01/01/93	01/01/95	T	T
Baker	Bob	02/01/93	02/01/95	T	T
Carlson	Cara	02/28/93	02/28/94	F	F
Davis	Deedra	03/31/93	03/31/94	T	F

OPERATION 4: RESET RENEWED FIELD TO FALSE

All records with renewed memberships now have T in the CURRENT field and have had their expiration dates extended by a year. The user can now deposit the payments and need not be concerned about these memberships for another year. (They won't even appear on the updating browse screen for another year.)

However, the batch process is not quite complete, because even though the third operation in the batch process completed the renewal process, those records still have T in the RENEWED field. If the user were to run this batch process again, those records would have their expiration dates extended by *another* year (in this case, to 1996). To prevent this mistake, the fourth operation in the batch process resets all the values in the RENEWED field to F, as follows:

LASTNAME	FIRSTNAME	STARTDATE	EXPIRES	CURRENT	RENEWED
Adams	Andy	01/01/93	01/01/95	T	F
Baker	Bob	02/01/93	02/01/95	T	F
Carlson	Cara	02/28/93	02/28/94	F	F
Davis	Deedra	03/31/93	03/31/94	T	F

Now the database is accurate for the current month and ready for next month's updates. Adams and Baker need not be renewed again until next year. When March rolls around and the user repeats the batch operation, Carlson and Davis will appear on the browse screen for possible renewal. The user will identify those members (if any) that have renewed by placing T in the RENEWED field, and the batch process will once again update all appropriate memberships for the month of March.

You'll see how to create and use this batch process later in this chapter. Let's go ahead now and start developing the application.

DEVELOPING THE APPLICATION

Now that you have created the database, forms, label, and report formats for the membership application and planned the batch process, you can use the Applications Generator to develop the application. Developing the application involves a series of steps:

- Define the application name and default settings.
- Create a sign-on banner for the application (this step is optional).
- Create the menu bar and pull-down menus.
- Attach *actions* to each menu option.
- Create batch processes.
- Generate the application.
- Save all changes and exit.

NOTE

If you do exit dBASE now, remember to log on to the \DBASE\MEMBERS subdirectory before resuming your work on the application later.

Completing all of the necessary steps might take quite a bit of time, particularly in large applications that contain many menu options. In the sections that follow, you'll complete the first three steps and then take a break. Still, it may take half an hour or more for you to complete those steps, so if you are pressed for time at the moment, you may want to start developing the application later.

To get started, follow these steps:

1. Select <create> from the Application panel in the Control Center.
2. Select Applications Generator from the submenu.

DEFINING THE APPLICATION

The first dialog box to appear when you enter the Applications Generator will ask for the application definition. You need to name the application, using a valid DOS file name. For this example, we'll use the name MEMMGR (an abbreviation for Membership Manager). You also need to enter a name for the main menu, which will be MEMMAIN in this example.

At this step, you need to assign a default database, index file, and sort order. These default settings will be used by all menu selections, except those that you specifically change. For example, the membership application will use the default alphabetical sort order for edit screens, browse screens, and the membership roster. But menu options that print form letters and mailing labels will override the default setting and use zip code order.

Figure 16.11 shows the completed application definition for the membership application. Press or click Ctrl-End after you complete the definition.

THE APPLICATION DESIGN SCREEN

After you have saved the application definition, you'll be taken to the application design screen. Here is where you will create the *application objects* that make up the application. The application objects include the menus, batch processes, and optional sign-on banner.

Currently, the sign-on banner is centered on the design screen, as shown in Figure 16.12.

Like other dBASE IV design screens, the application design screen has a menu bar at the top and pull-down menus. However, unlike other dBASE IV menus, this menu bar changes from time to time to reflect the type of object that you are creating at the moment. At first, this can be a little confusing, but as you develop the membership application in this chapter, you'll see how and when the changes occur.

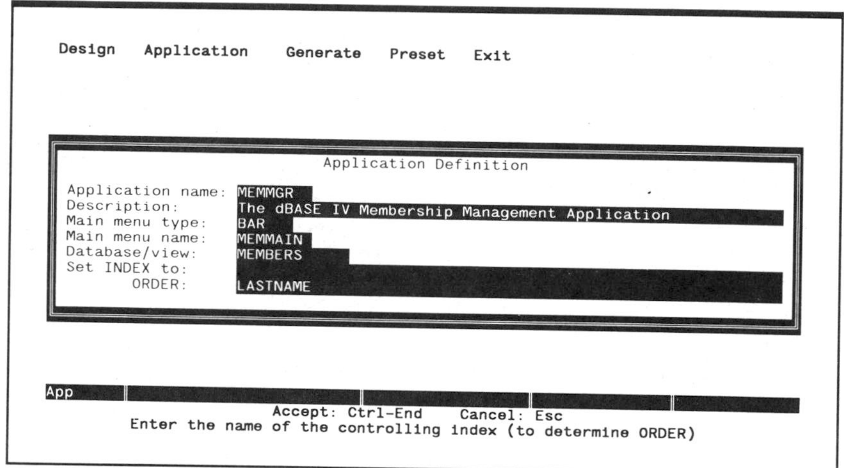

Figure 16.11: Completed application definition

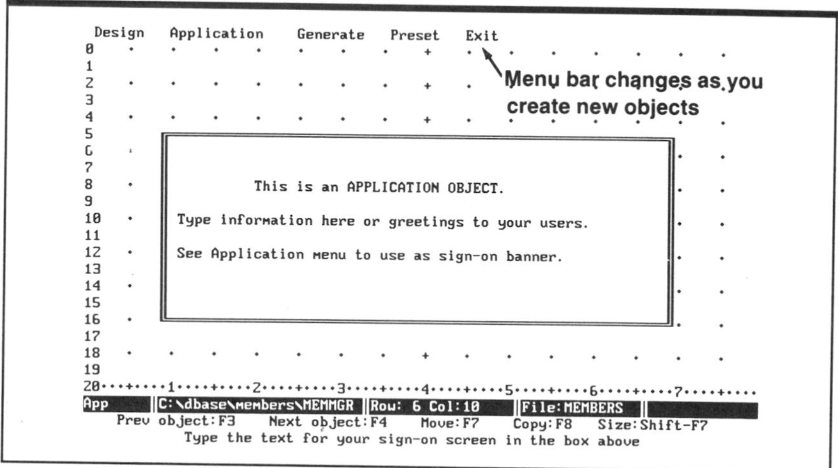

Figure 16.12: The application design screen

THE SIGN-ON BANNER

You can use the application object that is currently on the design screen as a sign-on banner, which will appear each time the user runs the completed application. Use Ctrl-Y to delete the text that is currently in the box and type your own sign-on information. You can type the application title, a description, author name, copyright notice, or any other text in the sign-on banner. You can use the usual editing keys to make changes if necessary.

You can also resize and move the frame that contains the sign-on banner (as well as most other objects that you create). To change the size of the frame, press or click Size (Shift-F7). The border will blink. Use the arrow keys to expand or reduce the size of the box; then press ↵ when you are done. To move the box, press or click Move (F7) and then use the arrow keys to move the box to a new location. Press ↵ to complete the move operation.

> **NOTE**
> When you size the frame, pressing → or ← moves the right side of the frame out or in, respectively. Pressing ↑ or ↓ moves the bottom of the frame up or down, respectively.

You can also resize or move the frame with your mouse by dragging the frame borders. To resize the frame, move the mouse pointer to the right or bottom border, or to the lower right-hand corner, and drag. If you're sizing from the right border, you can drag to the left or right to adjust the frame width. If you're sizing from the bottom border, you can drag up or down to adjust the frame height. And if you're sizing from the lower right-hand corner, you can drag diagonally to adjust the frame height and width at the same time. When you're finished sizing, release the mouse button.

To move the frame, move the mouse pointer to the top or left border and drag the mouse in whatever direction you want the frame to move; release the mouse button when the frame is positioned properly.

The border will blink as you drag the mouse, as it does when you're resizing or moving the frame with the arrow keys.

Figure 16.13 shows a suggested sign-on banner for the membership application. In this example, the box has been reduced slightly in size and moved up a few rows. Once you've completed the banner, you need to make a few menu selections to ensure that it is displayed when the user starts up the application. Here are the steps to do so:

1. Choose Application ► Display Sign-On Banner.
2. Select Yes from the options that appear.

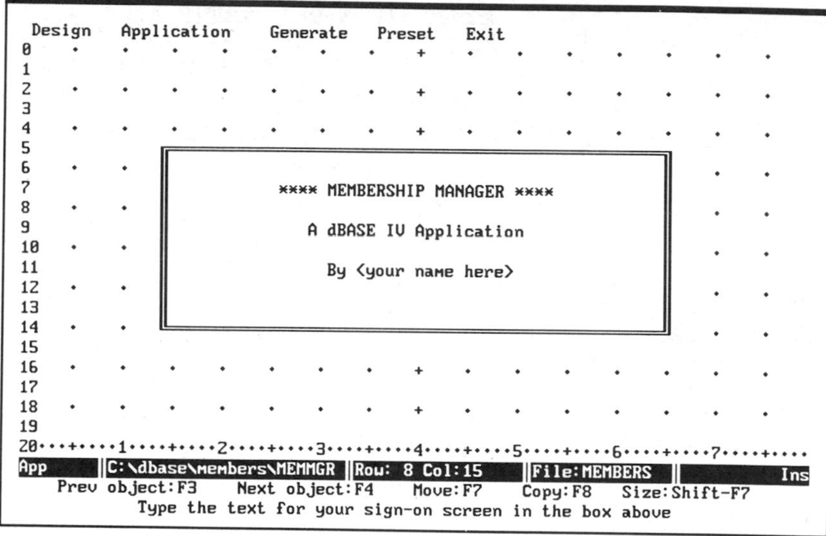

Figure 16.13: Sign-on banner for the membership application

CREATING THE HORIZONTAL BAR MENU

Next you can create the horizontal bar menu (the main menu) that appears across the top of the screen when the user runs the application. (In Figure 16.8, this is the horizontal menu named MEMMAIN.) To create the menu, follow these steps:

1. Choose Design ► Horizontal Bar Menu.
2. Select <create> from the submenu that appears.
3. In the dialog box that appears, enter **MEMMAIN** as the menu name.
4. Enter **Membership application main menu** as the description.
5. Leave the message line prompt blank for now.
6. Press or click Ctrl-End when you are done.

Now you can place menu options inside the menu bar. To enter an option, press the F5 key, type the option text, then press F5 again.

NOTE

After you have created the horizontal bar menu, it becomes the current object, and the second option in the Application Design menu changes from Application to Menu.

Here are the steps to enter the menu options Maintain, Update, Print, Utilities, and Exit:

1. Press F5, type **Maintain**, and press F5 again.
2. Press the space bar three times, press F5, type **Update**, and press F5 again.
3. Press the space bar three times, press F5, type **Print**, and press F5 again.
4. Press the space bar three times, press F5, type **Utilities**, and press F5 again.
5. Press the space bar three times, press F5, type **Exit**, and press F5 again.

You've now finished the membership application main menu. To see how the menu will appear when the user actually runs the application, you can remove the application design screen menu and status bar by pressing Zoom (F9). After you do so, your screen should look like Figure 16.14. (Press Zoom again to bring back the application design screen menu and status bar.)

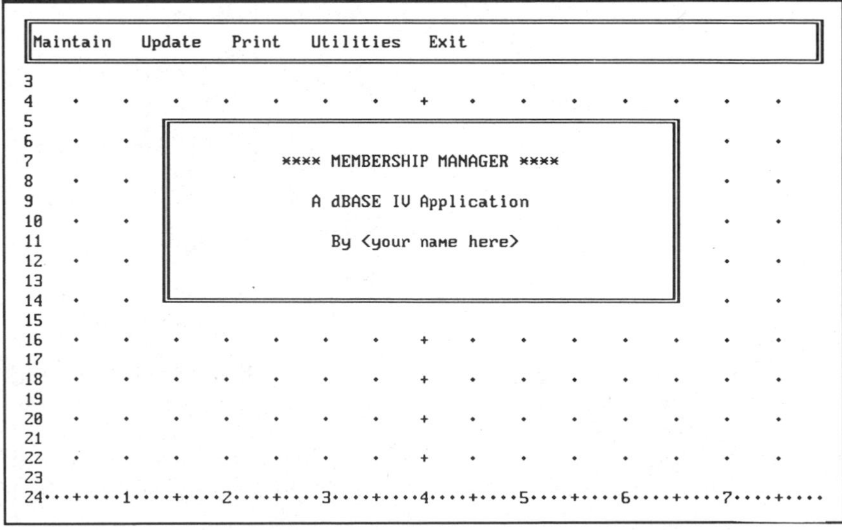

Figure 16.14: Horizontal bar menu for the membership application

CREATING THE PULL-DOWN MENUS

The Design ► Pop-Up Menu option is used to create both pop-up and pull-down menus.

Creating the pull-down menu for each main menu option is the next step. (The options on each pull-down menu were defined in Figure 16.8.) The general procedure to create each pull-down menu is the same: You start with a blank pop-up menu, increase its size as necessary, and then type menu options and optional text. You can then resize the menu to tighten the frame around the options and move the menu to where you want it to appear when the user runs the application. Remember that you can use the keyboard or the mouse to resize or move the menu frame, as described earlier under "The Sign-On Banner." However, for convenience, we'll stick with the keyboard method in the next few exercises.

THE MAINTAIN PULL-DOWN MENU Follow these steps to create the pull-down menu for the application's Maintain option:

1. Choose Design ► Pop-Up Menu.
2. Select <create> from the submenu.
3. Enter **MEMMAINT** as the menu name.
4. Leave the other options blank for the time being.
5. Press or click Ctrl-End.
6. Press or click Size (Shift-F7) and press → five times to widen the box. Then press ↵.
7. Type the option **Add new members** and press ↵.
8. Type **Browse all members** and press ↵.
9. Type **Change/delete a member**.
10. Press or click Size (Shift-F7) again and press ↑ five times to remove blank lines in the box. Press ↵.
11. Press or click Move (F7) and select Entire Frame to begin moving the menu.
12. Use the arrow keys to move the menu to beneath the Maintain option, as in Figure 16.15. Press ↵ after completing the move.

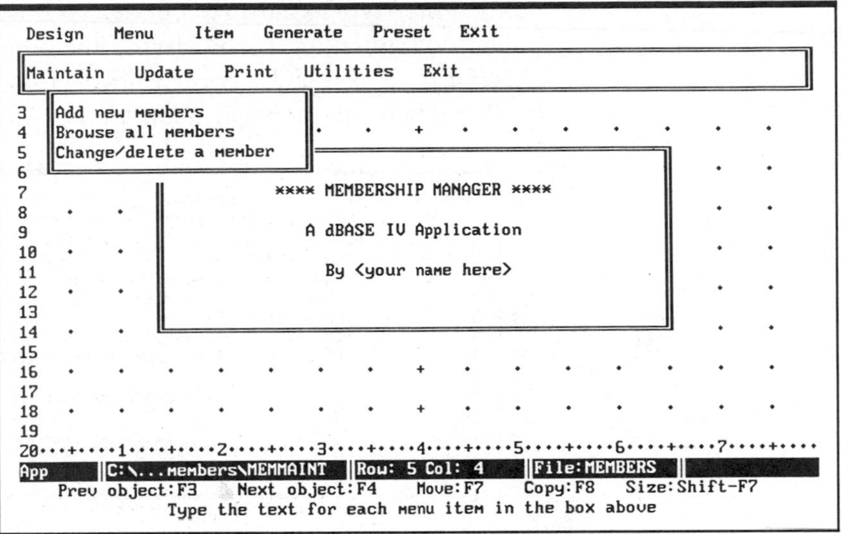

Figure 16.15: The Maintain pull-down menu in place

After completing the MEMMAINT pull-down menu, save it and put it away (hide it temporarily to reduce screen clutter) by choosing Menu ► Put Away Current Menu. When prompted, select Save Changes.

THE UPDATE PULL-DOWN MENU To create the pull-down menu for the application Update option, use the same general techniques as you used for the Maintain option to get started. That is, choose Design ► Pop-Up Menu and <create> from the submenu. Enter **MEMUPDAT** as the name of the menu. You can leave the description and message line prompt blank for the time being and just press or click Ctrl-End.

When the menu frame appears, you'll need to enlarge it (by pressing or clicking Shift-F7) to accommodate all the options (you can resize the menu frame at any time, so you don't need to worry about getting the frame right the first time). Then type the following items and text:

Update this month's renewals
Mark expired memberships for deletion
Purge marked records

After typing all three options, you can press or click Size (Shift-F7) to tighten the frame around the options if necessary. Then press or click Move (F7), select Entire Frame, and align the completed menu beneath the application Update option, as in Figure 16.16.

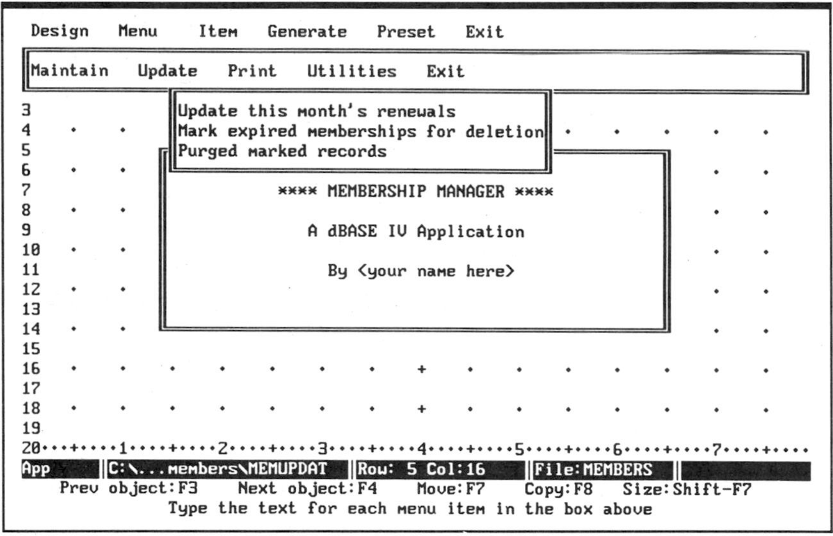

Figure 16.16: The Update pull-down menu in place

Once again, to reduce screen clutter and save the new menu, choose Menu ► Put Away Current Menu and select Save Changes when prompted.

THE PRINT PULL-DOWN MENU Now you can create the pull-down menu for the Print option of the membership application. Start with the usual steps: Choose Design ► Pop-Up Menu, select <create> from the submenu, and enter **MEMPRINT** as the name of the menu. Press or click Ctrl-End to leave other options blank.

Press or click Size (Shift-F7) to enlarge the initial frame to accommodate the menu options and then type the options and text shown here (use hyphens for the dividing line):

```
Membership roster
All mailing labels
Welcome letters
Welcome labels
```

Renewal letters
Renewal labels
Overdue letters
Overdue labels

Complete all options
on the Update menu
before printing
monthly letters.

After completing the pull-down menu, resize it (using Shift-F7 or your mouse) to tighten the frame around the options. Then move it (using F7 or your mouse) so that it is aligned beneath the Print option on the application horizontal bar menu, as shown in Figure 16.17.

After completing the MEMPRINT pull-down menu, choose Menu ► Put Away Current Menu ► Save Changes.

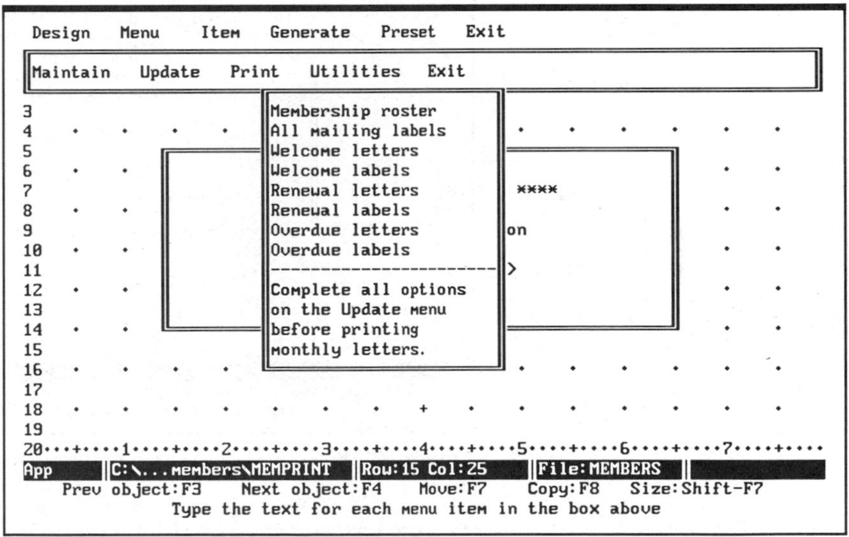

Figure 16.17: The Print pull-down menu in place

THE UTILITIES PULL-DOWN MENU To create the pull-down menu for the application Utilities option, choose Design ► Pop-Up Menu and select <create> from the submenu. Enter **MEMUTIL** as the menu name and press or click Ctrl-End to leave the other options blank. Use Shift-F7 or your mouse to widen the blank frame and then fill in the options as follows:

Change system date
Back up database to drive A
Copy application to drive A
Repair corrupted index

When you are done, use Shift-F7 or your mouse again, if necessary, to tighten the frame around the menu options and then use Move (F7) or your mouse to reposition the menu beneath the Utilities option, as shown in Figure 16.18.

Choose Menu ► Put Away Current Menu ► Save Changes to save your work and clear some work space.

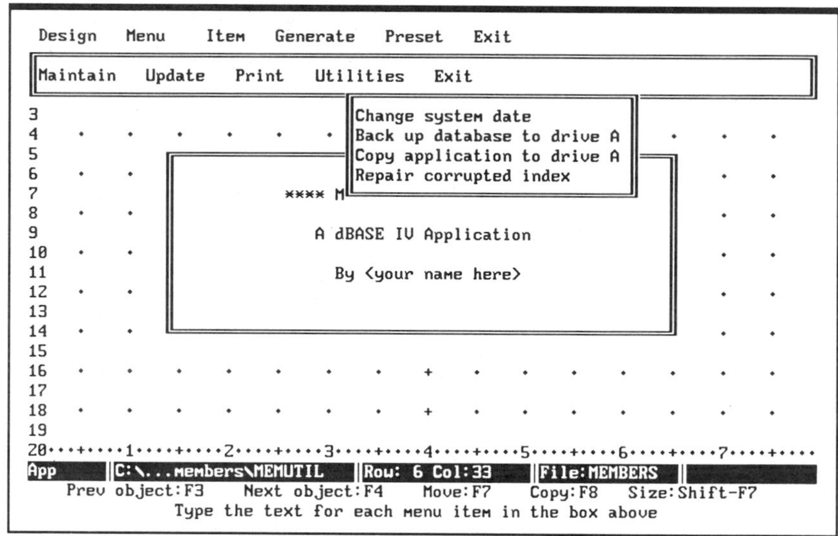

Figure 16.18: The Utilities pull-down menu in place

THE EXIT PULL-DOWN MENU Finally, use the usual techniques to create the pull-down menu for the application Exit option. That is, choose Design ► Pop-Up Menu and select <create> from the submenu. Enter the name **MEMEXIT** and press or click Ctrl-End to leave all other options blank for the time being. Fill in the box with these two options:

Return to dBASE IV
Exit to DOS

Size the frame for a tight fit and move the frame to the appropriate location beneath the Exit option on the menu bar, as in Figure 16.19.

SELECTING THE CURRENT OBJECT

Before putting away the Exit menu, you might want to experiment with Previous Object (F3) and Next Object (F4) for a moment. Whenever there are multiple objects on the applications design screen, these options allow you to scroll from one application object to the next.

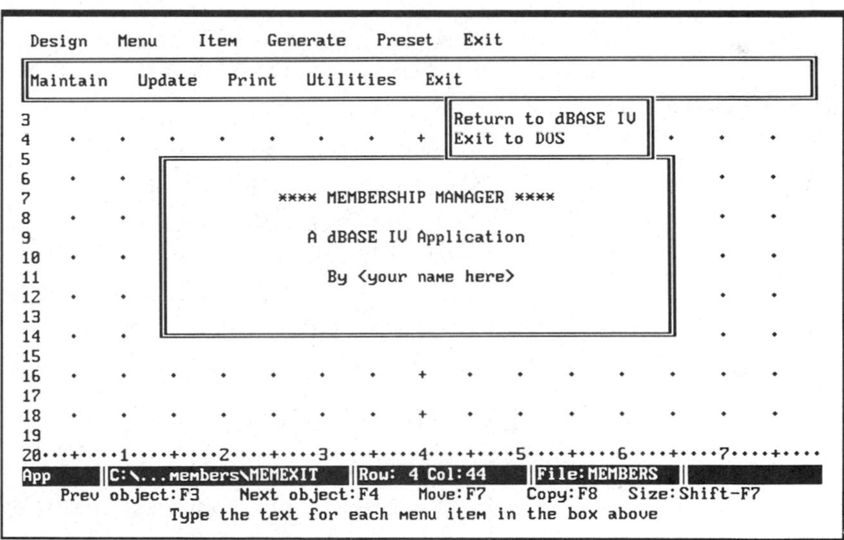

Figure 16.19: The Exit pull-down in place

If you press or click either F3 or F4 repeatedly now, you'll notice that the current object switches among the pull-down menu, the horizontal bar menu, and the sign-on banner. The *current* object always has its frame highlighted and overlays any other objects on the screen. Alternatively, you can just click your mouse on an object to make it the current object.

To bring a hidden object (one that you've already put away) back to the design screen, select the type of object you want to bring back from the Design pull-down menu and then select the object name from the submenu. For example, to bring the MEMPRINT pop-up menu to the design screen, choose Design ► Pop-Up Menu and select MEMPRINT from the submenu. The MEMPRINT menu appears on the design screen and automatically becomes the current object.

You can resize, move, or change the current object at any time, using the same techniques you used to create the object. If the current object is a pop-up (or pull-down) menu, you can delete an option by highlighting it and pressing Ctrl-Y. To insert a new option, increase the size of the box as necessary, position the highlight to where you want to insert an option, and press Ctrl-N. You may want to experiment a bit with these options now and correct any mistakes you made while developing the menus.

PUTTING AWAY ALL OBJECTS

Exit ► Save Changes and Exit also save all application objects. . .

You can save and put away all of the objects in an application by choosing Menu ► Clear Work Surface or Application ► Clear Work Surface. Go ahead and select that option now. dBASE will ask whether you want to save changes made to each unsaved object before dBASE puts it away. In this case, select Save Changes for each object. Note that the sign-on banner is always displayed on the design screen and cannot be put away.

TAKING A BREAK

Now you have created the entire menu structure for the membership application. Your next step will be to assign actions to each menu option. But first you might want to take a break. To do so, choose Exit ► Save All Changes and Exit. You'll be returned to the Control Center, where you can exit dBASE in the usual manner before turning off the computer.

To resume your work later, first make sure to switch to the C:\DBASE\MEMBERS directory; then run dBASE IV in the usual manner. Highlight MEMMGR in the Application panel at the right side of the Control Center and then press or click Design (Shift-F2). You'll be returned to the application design screen, with the sign-on banner displayed in the center of the screen. Other objects will be hidden.

You can use the techniques discussed here to take a break and then resume your work at any time as you complete the application in the following sections.

ASSIGNING ACTIONS TO MENU ITEMS

Your next step is to attach actions to each menu option in the application. The general procedure is to highlight the option to which you want to attach an action, choose Item ► Change Action, and then select an appropriate action. In this section, we'll attach actions to all menu options in the membership application.

ATTACHING MENU-BAR ACTIONS

We'll start by attaching actions to the options in the application horizontal bar menu. First, you must reveal the horizontal bar menu and make it the current object by following these steps:

1. Choose Design ► Horizontal Bar Menu.
2. Select MEMMAIN from the submenu.

Now you can assign actions to each option on the horizontal menu. Let's start with the Maintain option.

ASSIGNING AN ACTION TO THE MAINTAIN OPTION If the user selects the Maintain option from the horizontal bar menu, you want the application to display the MEMMAINT pull-down menu. Here are the steps to assign the appropriate action:

1. Choose Item ► Change Action.
2. Select Open a Menu as the action.
3. Press the space bar or click the mouse in the Menu Type box until the Pop-Up option appears; then press ↵.

4. Type the name of the appropriate pull-down menu (**MEMMAINT**) or press Pick (Shift-F1) and select MEMMAINT from the submenu that appears.
5. Press or click Ctrl-End.

While the Item pull-down menu is displayed, you can use the PgUp and PgDn keys or click those options on the navigation line to scroll through options on an application menu.

At this point, you'll be returned to the Item pull-down menu. Take a moment to look at the status bar near the bottom of the screen. You'll notice that in the center it displays the current menu option, Maintain. Whenever you assign an action to a menu option, take a quick look at the option displayed in the status bar to make sure you are working with the correct menu option.

ASSIGNING AN ACTION TO THE UPDATE OPTION When the user selects UPDATE from the application main menu, you want the application to display the MEMUPDAT pull-down menu. Here are the steps to assign the appropriate action:

1. Press or click PgDn so that the Update option is current (it appears centered in the status bar near the bottom of the screen).
2. Select Change Action.
3. Select Open a Menu.
4. Press the space bar or click the mouse in the Menu Type box until the Pop-Up option is displayed; then press ↵.
5. Press Pick (Shift-F1) and select MEMUPDAT as the menu to attach.
6. Press or click Ctrl-End.

Repeat steps 1 to 6 for the Print, Utilities, and Exit menu options. Substitute the appropriate menu option in step 1 and, in step 5, the pull-down menu name for each bar menu option, as listed here (you can refer to Figure 16.8 for a visual display).

Menu option (step 1)	Pull-down menu name (step 5)
Print	MEMPRINT
Utilities	MEMUTIL
Exit	MEMEXIT

When you are finished, press Ctrl-End to leave the Item menu and return to the application design screen.

CONVERTING POP-UP MENUS TO PULL-DOWN MENUS

Even though pop-up menus and pull-down menus are formatted identically, they behave in slightly different ways. Pop-up menus are not displayed until the user *selects* the higher-level menu item by highlighting and pressing ↵, or by clicking that item with the mouse. Pull-down menus, on the other hand, are displayed as soon as the higher-level menu option is highlighted (the user need not press ↵ to see the pull-down menu).

To convert the pop-up menus beneath the membership application bar menu to pull-down menus, follow these simple steps:

1. Choose Menu ► Attach Pull-Down Menus.
2. Select Yes from the submenu that appears.

When you attach pull-down menus to a menu bar, the pull-down menus automatically *inherit* many characteristics of the menu bar, including the database in use, index and order in use, and colors. You can, however, override any of these inherited characteristics, as you'll see later.

ASSIGNING ACTIONS TO THE MAINTAIN MENU

Now you need to begin attaching actions to the pull-down menus. (These actions were summarized previously in Figure 16.9.) Before you can assign actions to the Maintain pull-down menu, you need to take it out of hiding by following these steps:

1. Choose Design ► Pop-Up Menu.
2. Select MEMMAINT from the submenu.

You'll see the Maintain pull-down menu appear on the screen with its frame highlighted, indicating that it is the object currently in use. Now you can assign an action to each menu option.

ADD NEW MEMBERS The Add New Members option allows the user to add (*append*) new records to the MEMBERS database, using the MEMFORM custom screen you created earlier. Follow these steps:

1. Choose Item ► Change Action.
2. Select Edit Form (Add, Delete, Edit) from the submenu.
3. Press Pick (Shift-F1) and select MEMFORM as the form to use to add records.
4. When the cursor is in the Mode box, press the space bar or click the mouse, if necessary, to change the option to APPEND.
5. Leave all other options at their default values, as shown in Figure 16.20.
6. Press or click Ctrl-End.

BROWSE ALL MEMBERS The second option on the Maintain pull-down menu, Browse All Members, allows the user to change

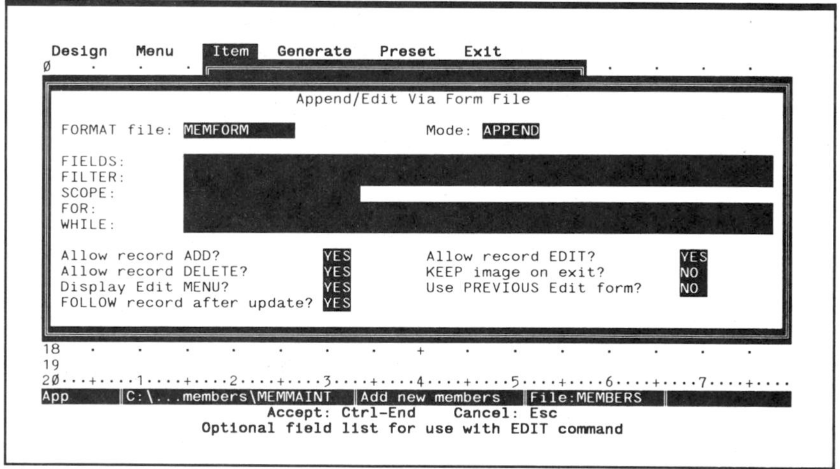

Figure 16.20: Append/Edit Form for the Add New Members option

the MEMBERS database through a browse screen. (This is a general-purpose browse screen, unlike the browse screen displayed during membership renewals, which displayed only expired memberships.) Here are the steps to attach the appropriate action to the menu option:

1. Press or click PgDn to move to the next menu option (Browse All Members should appear in the center of the status bar).
2. Select Change Action.
3. Select Browse (Add, Delete, Edit).
4. Press ↵ five times to move to the FORMAT File option, or click the mouse on the empty box next to that option.
5. Press Pick (Shift-F1) and select MEMFORM as the related format file.
6. Press or click Ctrl-End to leave all other settings at their default values.

In the previous steps, you directed the Applications Generator to display the data on a browse screen when the user selects Browse All Members. However, steps 4 and 5 told the Applications Generator to use the MEMFORM custom screen. This creates a contradiction, because the browse screen displays multiple database records in rows and columns, and the MEMFORM screen displays a single record at a time.

dBASE resolves this contradiction by displaying the browse screen as usual, but using any special templates, picture functions, and edit options defined for the MEMFORM custom form. For example, even though the data is displayed on a browse screen, the user will still be able to press the space bar to scroll through the REGULAR and OFFICER options in the STATUS field, because you defined this as a multiple-choice field in the MEMFORM custom form (see Table 16.1).

All other features that you added to the MEMFORM custom form, such as default dates, will also be carried over to the browse screen, because you specified MEMFORM as the FORMAT file for the browse screen. You'll have a chance to test this later when you use the completed application.

CHANGE/DELETE A MEMBER Now you need to assign an action to the third item on the Maintain menu, Change/Delete a Member. This option displays a single record from the MEMBERS database on the MEMFORM custom screen and allows the user to make changes. Here are the steps to assign the menu action:

1. Press or click PgDn to display Change/Delete in the status bar.
2. Select Change Action.
3. Select Edit Form (Add, Delete, Edit).
4. Type or select (using Pick, Shift-F1) MEMFORM as the form to use.
5. In the Mode box, specify Edit as the mode (pressing the space bar or clicking the mouse if necessary).
6. Press or click Ctrl-End to complete the operation and leave all other settings at their default values.

Now you have assigned actions to all three items on the Maintain pull-down menu. You can save and put away that menu now by following these steps:

1. Choose Menu ► Put Away Current Menu.
2. Select Save Changes from the submenu.

ASSIGNING ACTIONS TO THE UPDATE MENU

Now you need to assign actions to the application Update pull-down menu. First, take that menu out of hiding and make it the current object by following these steps:

1. Choose Design ► Pop-Up Menu.
2. Select MEMUPDAT from the submenu.

The Update pull-down menu appears on the application design screen, and you are ready to assign actions to its options.

UPDATE THIS MONTH'S RENEWALS As discussed earlier in the chapter, the Update This Month's Renewals option automates the steps involved in updating renewed memberships. When the user selects this option, the application executes a batch process named RENEW.BCH (dBASE adds the file extension .BCH). We'll create the actual batch process later, but you can assign the action to the menu option. Here are the steps:

1. Make sure that the Update This Month's Renewals option is highlighted in the pull-down menu.
2. Choose Item ► Change Action.
3. Select Run Program.
4. Select Execute BATCH Process.
5. Type the batch process name **RENEW** and press ↵.

Now you can move on and assign the action to the next menu option.

MARK EXPIRED MEMBERSHIPS FOR DELETION The Mark Expired Memberships for Deletion option marks for deletion all records of members whose membership expired 60 or more days ago (and was never renewed). The option performs this task automatically for the entire database, so that the user need not scroll through and mark these records one at a time. Here are the steps to assign the appropriate action to the menu option:

1. Press or click PgDn to move to the Mark Expired Memberships for Deletion option.
2. Select Change Action.
3. Select Perform File Operation.
4. Select Mark Records for Deletion.
5. Enter the expression **DATE()–Expires>60 .AND. .NOT. Current** as the FOR option, as shown in Figure 16.21.

The expression that you entered as the FOR option acts as a filter condition, just like the filter conditions you created in queries in Chapter 6. As with queries, the expression must result in a true or false verdict, as in the expression PartNo = "A-111" or Qty < 10.

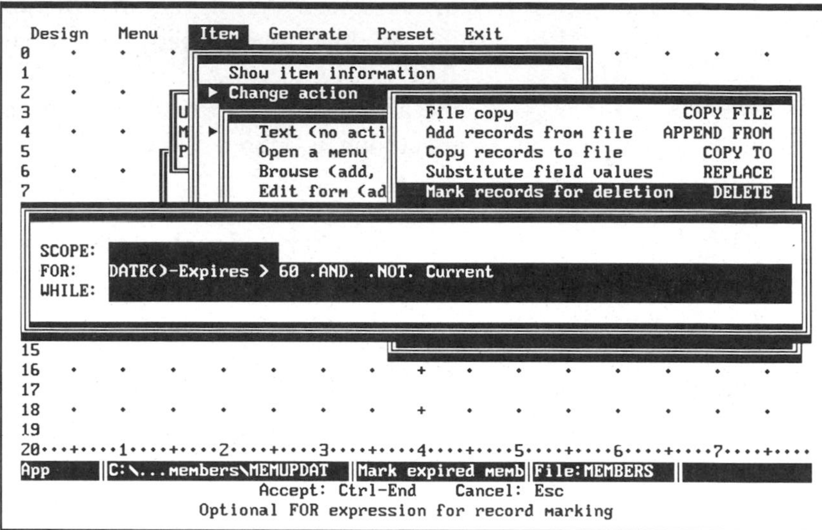

Figure 16.21: FOR condition for marking expired memberships

However, when using the Applications Generator, you do not stagger filter conditions onto separate rows to create AND and OR queries. Instead, you use the operator .AND. for an AND condition and the operator .OR. for an OR condition.

You can also use the .NOT. operator, which, when used with the Logic data type, means that the result of the expression should be false, rather than true.

Logical data types always contain either a true or a false value, so you need not use a complete expression to test this particular data type. Just using the logical field name, such as CURRENT, implies the expression CURRENT = .T. Using the .NOT. operator in front of the Logical field's name, as in the expression .NOT. CURRENT, is the same as using the expression CURRENT = .F.

In this particular example, the expression used as the FOR condition, DATE()-Expires>60 .AND. .NOT. Current, specifies records with membership expiration dates that are 60 or more days "less than" (earlier than) the current date and in which membership has not been renewed (that is, the CURRENT field contains F). When the user selects this menu option, the application will automatically mark such records for deletion.

To permanently delete records that are marked for deletion, the user needs to select the next menu option, Purge Marked Records.

To make complex expressions more readable, it is common practice to type function names, such as DATE(), in all uppercase letters and field names, such as Expires, with only the first letter capitalized. However, you can use whatever upper- and lowercase conventions you wish.

Before moving on to the next menu option, however, press or click Ctrl-End to save the current menu action.

PURGE MARKED RECORDS The next item on the Update menu is Purge Marked Records. This option packs the database, permanently removing all records that are marked for deletion. This purging includes records that were marked in the previous operation, as well as any that were marked by the user (using Ctrl-U) while editing or browsing. To assign an action to this option, follow these steps:

1. Press or click PgDn to move to the Purge Marked Records option (check the status bar to be sure you have the correct option).
2. Select Change Action.
3. Select Perform File Operation.
4. Select Discard Marked Records.
5. Select OK when prompted.

That completes the actions for the Update pull-down menu for the time being, until later when we create the RENEW.BCH batch process. For now, choose Menu ► Put Away Current Menu ► Save Changes.

ASSIGNING ACTIONS TO THE PRINT MENU

The Print pull-down menu in the membership application presents options for printing reports and mailing labels. To assign actions to these menu options, first make the Print menu the current object by following these steps:

1. Choose Design ► Pop-Up Menu.
2. Select MEMPRINT from the submenu.

MEMBERSHIP ROSTER The Membership Roster option allows the user to print a list of all members, using the format you created earlier and named ROSTER. To assign the appropriate action to this menu, follow these steps:

1. Choose Item ► Change Action.
2. Select Display or Print.
3. Select Report.
4. Press Pick (Shift-F1) and select ROSTER.
5. Press ↵ to leave the HEADING box blank.
6. Complete other print options as follows (all are multiple-choice options that you can scroll through by pressing the space bar or clicking the mouse):

If you change Send Output to ASK AT RUNTIME, the user can decide where to send output.

Report format:	FULL DETAIL
Heading Format:	INCLUDE DATE AND PAGE
Before printing:	SKIP TO NEW PAGE
Send output to:	PRINTER

7. Press or click Ctrl-End when you are done.

ALL MAILING LABELS The second option on the Print menu lets the user print all mailing labels. It uses the MEMLABEL format that you created earlier. Here are the steps to assign the action:

1. Press or click PgDn to scroll to the All Mailing Labels menu option.
2. Select Change Action.
3. Select Display or Print.
4. Select Labels.
5. Press Pick (Shift-F1) and select MEMLABEL.
6. Set the Send Output To option to PRINTER.
7. Set the Print Sample? option to Yes.
8. Press or click Ctrl-End.

WELCOME LETTERS The Welcome Letters option on the Print menu prints the WELCOME form letter for new members who joined this month. To assign the action to this menu option,

1. Press or click PgDn to move to the Welcome Letters option.
2. Select Change Action.
3. Select Display or Print.
4. Select Report.
5. Press Pick (Shift-F1) and select Welcome from the Pick menu.
6. Fill in other options as shown in Figure 16.22.

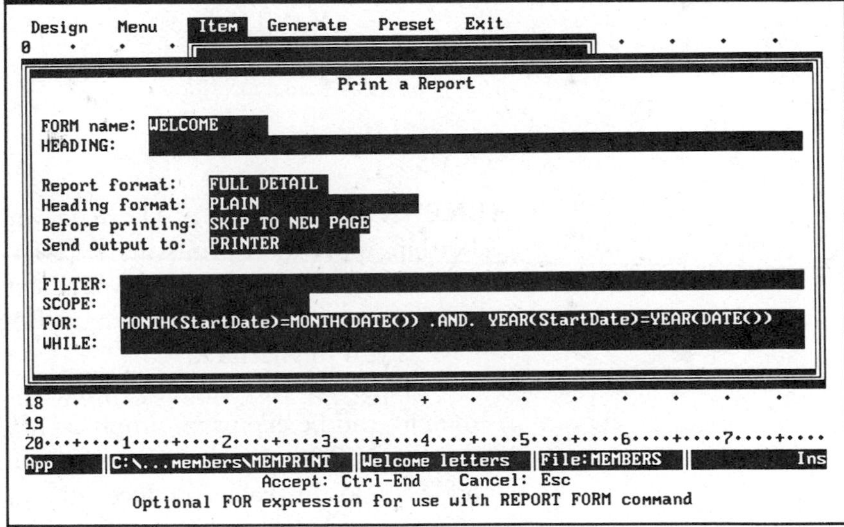

Figure 16.22: Dialog box for printing welcome letters

Be sure to notice the filter condition used with the FOR box in the dialog box: MONTH(StartDate) = MONTH(DATE()) .AND. YEAR(StartDate) = YEAR(DATE()). This filter condition limits printing of the welcome letters to members who joined in the current month of the current year (that is, this month's new members). Press or click Ctrl-End after completing the dialog box.

WELCOME LABELS The Welcome Labels option prints a mailing label for each letter that the Welcome Letters option printed. It uses the MEMLABEL format and the same filter condition that the Welcome Letters option uses. To assign the action, follow these steps:

1. Press or click PgDn to move to the Welcome Labels option.
2. Select Change Action.
3. Select Display or Print.
4. Select Labels.
5. Press Pick (Shift-F1) and select the MEMLABEL format.
6. In the FOR box, enter the same filter condition used in Figure 16.22:

   MONTH(StartDate) = MONTH(DATE()) .AND.

   YEAR(StartDate) = YEAR(DATE())

7. Press or click Ctrl-End.

RENEWAL LETTERS The Renewal Letters option in the membership application prints the RENEWAL form letter for each person whose membership will expire next month. Unfortunately, defining "next month" in terms that dBASE will understand is not as easy as you might think.

First, for the months January through November, "next month" can be expressed simply as MONTH (DATE()) + 1, because the MONTH() function returns a number between 1 and 12, and adding 1 to this value produces the number for the next month (for example, in January, the expression MONTH (DATE()) + 1 produces 2, the month number for February). However, in December, the expression MONTH(DATE()) + 1 produces 13, obviously not the month number for January.

To solve this problem, you can divide the month number by 12 and then add one to the *modulus* (the remainder after division) to determine the next month. This approach works because dividing any number below 12 by 12 produces a modulus that equals the current month. For example, 1/12 produces zero and a modulus of 1. Dividing February, month 2, by 12 produces zero and a modulus of 2. Dividing the twelfth month, December, by 12 (12/12) produces 1 and a modulus of zero; adding 1 to zero produces 1, the month after December.

The dBASE MOD() function returns the modulus of one argument divided by a second argument. Hence, the expression MOD (MONTH(DATE()),12) + 1 always returns the number of the next month, even in December. But this does not solve all problems for the membership application, because renewal letters should be sent only to people whose memberships expire in the next month of the current year.

Once again, however, you cannot use the simple expression YEAR(DATE()) to specify the current year, because in December, next month is also next year (that is, the month following December 1993 is January 1994). But if you divide any month number from January to November (month number 1 to 11) by 12, the integer portion of the division is zero (for example, 11/12 = 0 if you exclude the decimal portion of the result). Dividing December (month 12) by 12 (12/12), however, produces 1. If you add the integer portion of the results of the division to the current year, the result will be the appropriate year.

To isolate the integer portion of a number (with the decimal value completely removed), you use the dBASE INT() function. Therefore, the complete expression used for isolating appropriate years in the EXPIRES field is YEAR(Expires) = YEAR(DATE()) + INT (MONTH(Expires)/12).

Actually, there is a third problem to contend with. The space allotted for a FOR filter condition in the Applications Generator does not provide enough room for the complete expression that renewal letters require: MONTH (Expires) = MOD(MONTH(DATE()),12) + 1 .AND.YEAR(Expires) = YEAR(DATE()) + INT(MONTH (Expires)/12). But, as you may have guessed, there is a way around this limitation too, as you'll see in a moment. Let's get back on track now and assign the appropriate action to the Renewal Letters menu option, following these steps:

1. Press or click PgDn until Renewal Letters appears in the status bar.
2. Select Change Action.
3. Select Display or Print.

4. Select Report.
5. Type the report format name **RENEWAL**, or press Pick (Shift-F1) and select RENEWAL from the Pick submenu.
6. Fill in the rest of the Print a Report Dialog box as shown in Figure 16.23.

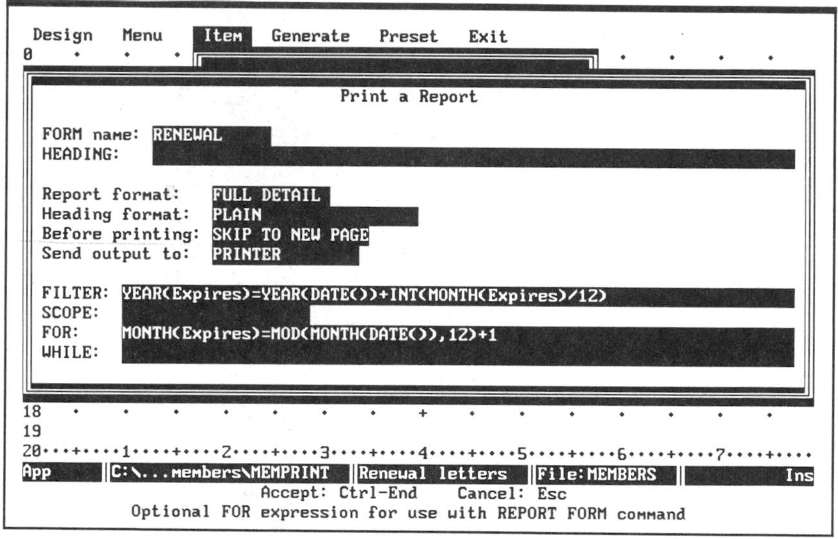

Figure 16.23: Dialog box for printing renewal letters

As you can see in the dialog box, both the FILTER and FOR options contain filter conditions. The FILTER condition YEAR(Expires) = YEAR(DATE()) + INT(MONTH(Expires)/12) isolates records that have the appropriate expiration year (the current year for the months January through November and the next year for December). The FOR condition MONTH(Expires) = MOD (MONTH(DATE()),12) + 1 isolates records that have expiration dates in the next month. The FOR and FILTER options are additive, so placing filter conditions in both is equivalent to placing the single long filter condition YEAR(Expires) = YEAR(DATE()) + INT(MONTH(Expires)/12).AND.MONTH(Expires) = MOD (MONTH(DATE()),12) + 1 into the FOR (or FILTER) condition box.

After filling in the dialog box (paying close attention to parentheses in the expressions), press or click Ctrl-End.

RENEWAL LABELS Mailing labels for the renewal letters can be printed using the usual MEMLABEL format and the same filter condition as is used to print renewal letters. Follow these steps to assign an action to the application Renewal Labels menu option:

1. Press or click PgDn to move to the Renewal Labels menu option.
2. Select Change Action.
3. Select Display or Print.
4. Select Labels.
5. Fill in the Print Labels dialog box as shown in Figure 16.24.
6. Press or click Ctrl-End after filling in the dialog box.

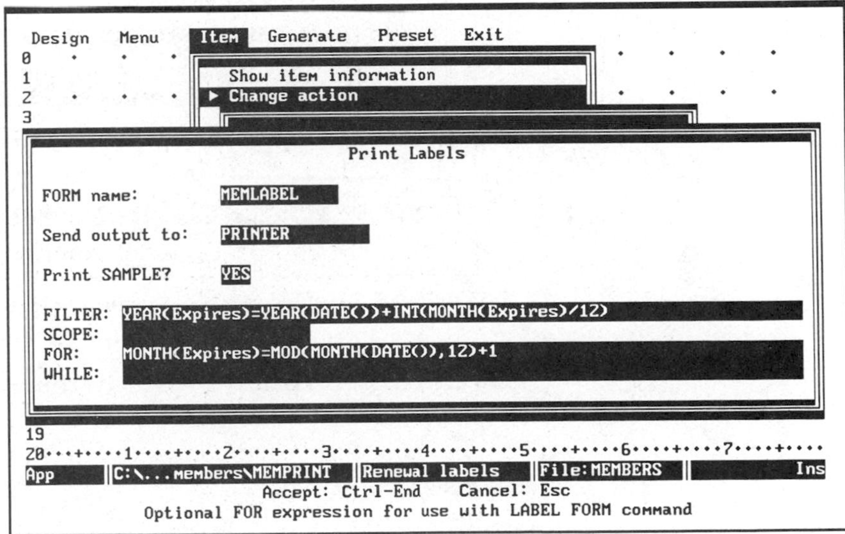

Figure 16.24: Dialog box for printing renewal labels

OVERDUE LETTERS The Overdue Letters option prints the OVERDUE form letter for people whose memberships expired 30 or more days ago, and who have still not renewed. Here are the steps to assign the action to the menu option:

1. Press or click PgDn to make Overdue Letters the current menu option.

2. Select Change Action.
3. Select Display or Print.
4. Select Report.
5. Fill in the screen as shown in Figure 16.25.
6. Press or click Ctrl-End.

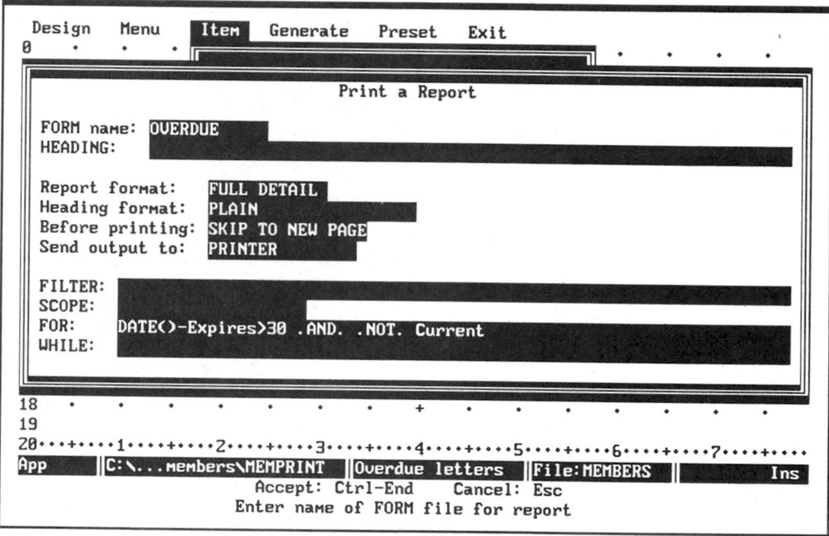

Figure 16.25: Dialog box for printing overdue letters

OVERDUE LABELS The Overdue Labels option prints mailing labels for the overdue letters. It uses the MEMLABEL format and the same filter condition as the overdue letter. Here are the steps to assign the action:

1. Press or click PgDn to make Overdue Labels the current menu option.
2. Select Change Action.
3. Select Display or Print.
4. Select Labels.
5. Enter **MEMLABEL** as the label format.

6. Enter **DATE()-Expires>30.AND..NOT.Current** as the FOR condition.
7. Press or click Ctrl-End.

This completes the menu options for the Print menu. To save the menu and put it away, choose Menu ► Put Away Current Menu ► Save Changes.

ASSIGNING ACTIONS TO THE UTILITIES MENU

To assign actions to the Utilities menu, first make it the current menu by following these steps:

1. Choose Design ► Pop-up Menu.
2. Select MEMUTIL from the submenu.

Now you can assign actions to the Utilities menu options.

CHANGE SYSTEM DATE The Change System Date option allows the user to change the current (system) date without exiting the application. It does so by running the external DOS command, DATE. Here are the steps to assign the action to this option:

1. Choose Item ► Change Action.
2. Select Run Program.
3. Select Run DOS Program.
4. Next to the prompt "Program:" enter the command **DATE**.
5. Press or click Ctrl-End.

BACK UP DATABASE TO DRIVE A The Back Up Database to Drive A option uses the DOS command COPY MEMBERS.* A: to copy MEMBERS.DBF and MEMBERS.MDX to a diskette in drive A. Here are the steps to assign the action:

1. Press or click PgDn to move to the Back Up Database menu option.

2. Select Change Action.
3. Select Run Program.
4. Select Run DOS Program.
5. In the dialog box, enter **COPY** as the program name.
6. Enter **MEMBERS.* A:** in the parameters box.
7. Press or click Ctrl-End.

COPY APPLICATION TO DRIVE A The Copy Application to Drive A command copies all files on the \DBASE\MEMBERS directory to a floppy disk in drive A. This option can be used both for making backup copies and for making extra copies to give to others to use. Here are the steps for assigning the action:

1. Press or click PgDn to move to the Copy Application to Drive A option.
2. Select Change Action.
3. Select Run Program.
4. Select Run DOS Program.
5. Enter **COPY** as the name of the program to run.
6. Enter ***.* A:** as the parameters.
7. Press or click Ctrl-End.

REPAIR CORRUPTED INDEX Repair Corrupted Index helps the user to recover from power outages and other situations that can corrupt indexes. To assign the action to this menu option, follow these steps:

1. Press or click PgDn to move to the Repair Corrupted Index menu option.
2. Select Change Action.
3. Select Perform File Operation.
4. Select Reindex Database.
5. Select OK.

That completes the actions for the Utilities menu. Choose Menu ► Put Away Current Menu ► Save Changes.

ASSIGNING ACTIONS TO THE EXIT MENU

The Exit menu provides two options: Return to dBASE IV, which leaves the application and returns the user to the Control Center, and Exit to DOS, which returns the user to DOS. Make the Exit menu the current object by following the usual steps:

1. Choose Design ► Pop-Up Menu.
2. Select MEMEXIT from the submenu.

RETURN TO dBASE IV To assign the action to the Return to dBASE IV option, follow these steps:

1. Choose Item ► Change Action.
2. Select Quit.
3. Select Return to Calling Program.
4. Select OK.

EXIT TO DOS To assign the action to the Exit to DOS option, follow these steps:

1. Press or click PgDn to move to the next menu option.
2. Select Change Action.
3. Select Quit.
4. Select Quit to DOS.
5. Select OK.

Now you can choose Menu ► Put Away Current Menu ► Save Changes.

At this point, you have assigned an action to every menu option in the membership application. However, you still need to perform a few steps to complete the application.

BUILDING THE BATCH PROCESS

As you probably recall, you assigned the action Execute Batch Process to the Update This Month's Renewals menu option earlier and specified RENEW as the name of the batch process. Now you need to create that batch process. Two steps are involved: First you list the operations in the batch process, and then you assign an action to each operation. Let's create RENEW.BCH now.

LISTING THE OPERATIONS IN THE BATCH PROCESS

The first step is to list each operation (or step) in the batch process, in plain English. This procedure is similar to writing options into a pop-up menu frame. Here are the steps:

1. Choose Design ► Batch Process.
2. Select <create> from the submenu.
3. Enter **RENEW** as the batch-process name.
4. Enter **Automate monthly renewals** as the description.
5. Press or click Ctrl-End.
6. Press or click Size (Shift-F7) and widen the frame by at least two spaces. Then press ↵.
7. Type plain-English descriptions of each operation in the batch process, as shown in Figure 16.26.

ASSIGNING ACTIONS TO A BATCH PROCESS

Now you need to assign an action to each operation in the batch process, using a technique similar to that used to assign actions to menu options.

FLAG EXPIRED MEMBERSHIPS The Flag Expired Memberships operation in the batch process places F in the CURRENT field

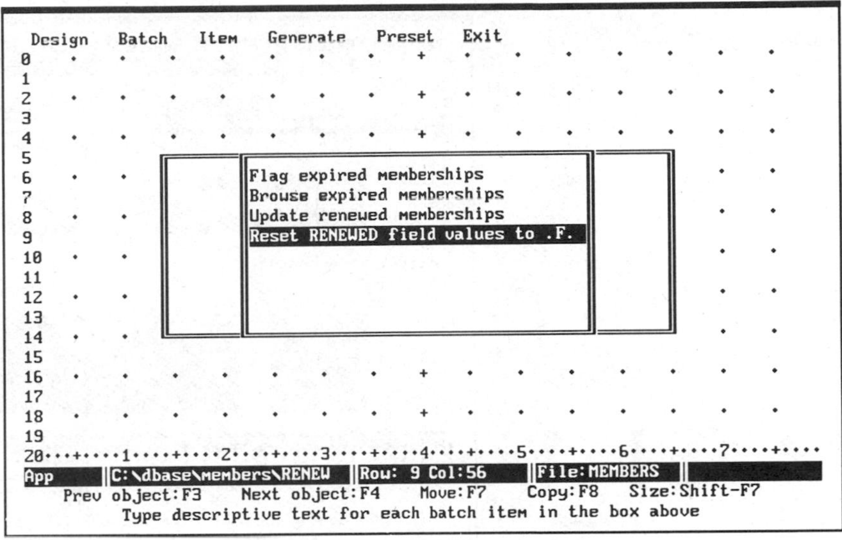

Figure 16.26: Descriptions of batch-process operations

for all memberships that have expired. Follow these steps to assign the appropriate action:

1. Press ↑ until the topmost item, Flag Expired Memberships, in the box is highlighted, or click on that item.
2. Choose Item ► Change Action.
3. Select Perform File Operation.
4. Select Substitute Field Values.
5. Fill in the Substitute Field Values dialog box as shown in Figure 16.27. Notice that you must specify the replacement value for the CURRENT field as .F. (with periods before and after the F) to prevent dBASE from confusing the logical value for False with a variable named F.
6. Press or click Ctrl-End when you are done.

BROWSE EXPIRED MEMBERSHIPS The second operation in the batch process displays all expired memberships on a browse

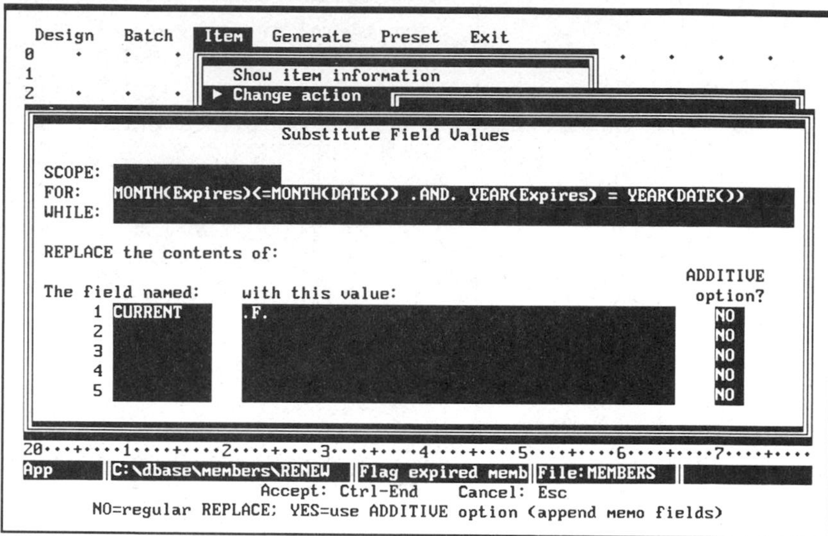

Figure 16.27: Dialog box for the first batch-process operation

screen so the user can quickly and easily identify renewed memberships. To simplify matters further, the cursor is locked into the RENEWED field, which is displayed in the leftmost column of the browse screen. Furthermore, the browse screen displays only selected, relevant fields (Figure 16.10 showed an example).

To assign the appropriate action to this second batch-process operation, follow these steps:

1. Press or click PgDn or click to move to the next step, Browse Expired Memberships.
2. Select Change Action.
3. Select Browse and fill in the form as in Figure 16.28.
4. Press or click Ctrl-End.

In Figure 16.28, the FIELDS box lists the fields that are to be displayed in the browse screen, in the order in which they are to be displayed. The FILTER box indicates that only records with F in the CURRENT field are to be displayed. The maximum column width

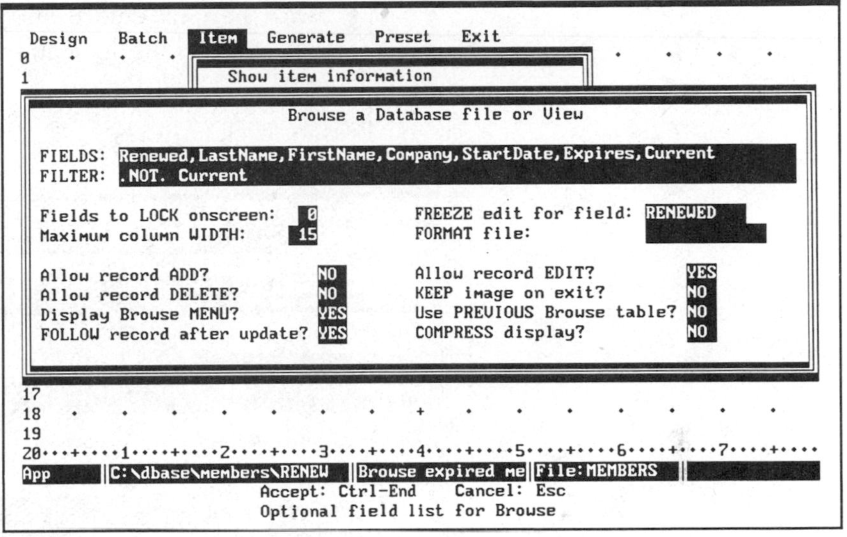

Figure 16.28: Dialog box for renewing memberships through a browse screen

of 15 allows all the fields to fit on the screen (only the first 15 letters of the COMPANY field will be visible on the screen; all other fields are less than 15 characters wide).

The FREEZE Edit for Field: RENEWED option locks the cursor into the RENEWED field, thereby making it easier to scroll up and down from record to record without scrolling left and right. (You'll see this feature in action later when we test the application.)

UPDATE RENEWED MEMBERSHIPS The third operation in the batch process changes the CURRENT field for all renewed memberships to T and increments their expiration dates by one year. Here are the steps to assign the appropriate action:

1. Press or click PgDn to move to the next batch operation.
2. Select Change Action.
3. Select Perform File Operation.
4. Select Substitute Field Values.
5. Fill in the dialog box as shown in Figure 16.29. Be sure to specify the replacement value for the CURRENT field as

.T. (with periods before and after the T) so that dBASE doesn't confuse the logical value for True with a variable named T.

6. Press or click Ctrl-End.

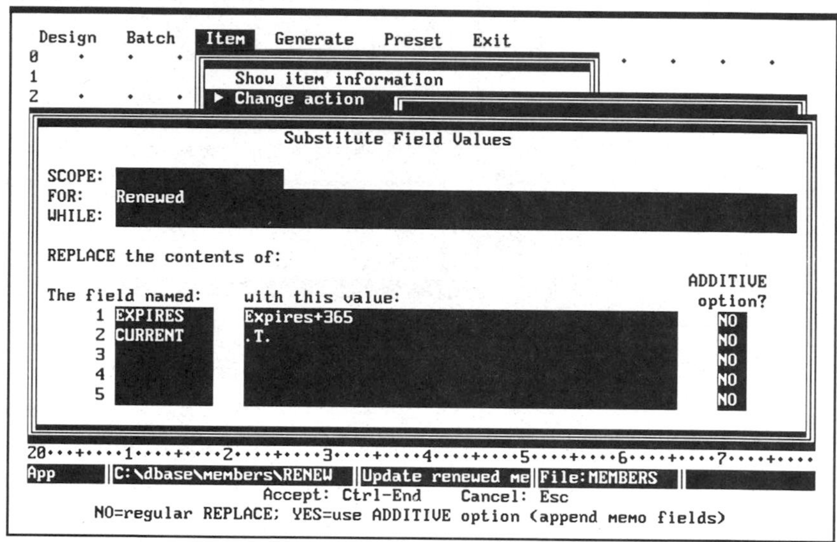

Figure 16.29: Dialog box for updating renewed memberships

In Figure 16.29, the FOR condition limits the operation to records that have T in the RENEWED field. For each of these renewed memberships, the date in the EXPIRED field is replaced with its current value plus 365 (thereby adding one year to the expiration date). The contents of the CURRENT field is replaced with T, indicating that the membership is now current.

RESET RENEWED FIELDS TO FALSE The fourth operation in the batch process resets the RENEWED field to false in all database records, so that no expiration dates are accidentally extended by another year the next time the user updates memberships. To assign the action to this operation, follow these steps:

1. Press or click PgDn to move to the next batch operation.
2. Select Change Action.

3. Select Perform File Operation.
4. Select Substitute Field Values.
5. Fill in the Substitute Field Values dialog box as shown in Figure 16.30. As for the Flag Expired Memberships option, the replacement value for the CURRENT field is specified as .F. (with periods before and after the F) to identify it as a logical value.
6. Press or click Ctrl-End.

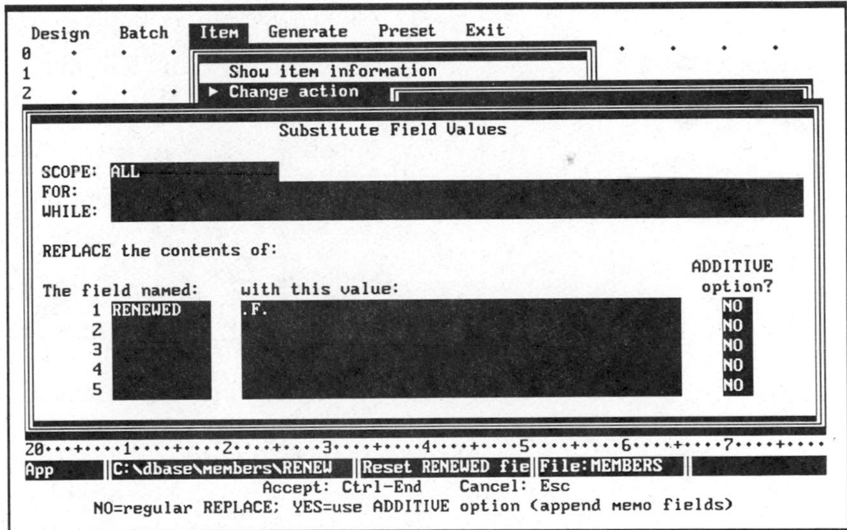

Figure 16.30: Dialog box for resetting all RENEWED fields to false

In Figure 16.30, the SCOPE option indicates that all records in the database should be included in the operation, and that the RENEWED field needs to be set to F. At this point, you have completed the RENEW.BCH batch process. Follow these steps to save it and put it away:

1. Choose Batch ► Put Away Current Batch Process.
2. When prompted, select Save Changes.

Now that the batch process is complete, there is only one more task to perform.

DEFINING SORT ORDERS

As you may recall, when you first started developing the application you defined MEMBERS as the default database and LASTNAME as the default index order. All options that display data (such as edit, browse, and the various reports) will use these default settings. However, we want letters and mailing labels to be printed in zip code order, so we need to override those settings for a few of the menu options.

1. Choose Design ► Pop-Up Menu.
2. Select MEMPRINT from the submenu.
3. Press ↓ to highlight All Mailing Labels, or click on that option.
4. Choose Item ► Reassign Index Order.
5. When the prompt "Set ORDER to:" appears, type **ZIP** and press ↵.
6. Press or click PgDn to move to the next menu option.

Repeat steps 4 through 6 six times to assign the ZIP index order to the remaining report and label options. When you are done, choose Menu ► Put Away Current Menu ► Save Changes.

GENERATING THE APPLICATION

The membership application is now complete, but before you can use it, you need to *generate* the application programs (or *code*). Unlike forms and reports, this step is not automatic when you develop an application. So follow these steps to generate the application programs:

1. Choose Generate ► Select Template, and then type in **MENU.GEN**.
2. Select Display During Generation and Yes.
3. Select Begin Generating.

You will see the code that the Applications Generator creates pass by in a window on the application design screen. When this operation is complete, you'll see the message "Generation is complete—press any key to continue." You can press any key (or click the mouse) to proceed.

GENERATING DOCUMENTATION

The Applications Generator can also create written documentation that can help you to refine your application later. Follow these steps to create this written documentation:

1. Choose Generate ► Select Template.
2. Enter **DOCUMENT.GEN** as the template to use.
3. Select Begin Generating.
4. Enter either **Y** or **N** when asked if you have an IBM graphics or compatible printer (enter **N** if you are not sure).

When the document is completed, you'll again be prompted to press any key. Press a key (or click the mouse), then choose Exit ► Save All Changes and Exit.

You'll be returned to the Control Center, where you can now test, and then use, the membership application.

TESTING THE COMPLETED APPLICATION

Before you give a completed application to the user (or before you use the application for serious work, if you are the user), you need to test it thoroughly. Use the application with some sample data and try every menu option. This section describes how to use the finished application and also provides a few examples for testing the application.

RUNNING THE MEMBERSHIP APPLICATION

To run the membership application, highlight MEMMGR in the Application panel and press ↵ (or double-click on MEMMGR), then select Run Application. Select Yes from the dialog box that appears. After a few seconds, you'll see the sign-on banner. Press ↵ or click the mouse to move on to the menus. You'll see the application horizontal menu bar and the Maintain pull-down menu on the screen.

You can click your mouse on the options along the menu bar to display the pull-down menus and to select menu options within a pull down menu. You can also use the arrow keys to scroll across the menu bar and up and down within a pull-down menu in the usual manner. Note, however, that the highlight will not land on text within a menu when you scroll with the arrow keys, nor will clicking the mouse on that text have any effect (the Print menu in your sample application contains text). Figure 16.31 shows the application menu bar and Print pull-down menu on the screen. Now let's test each option to make sure the application works as expected.

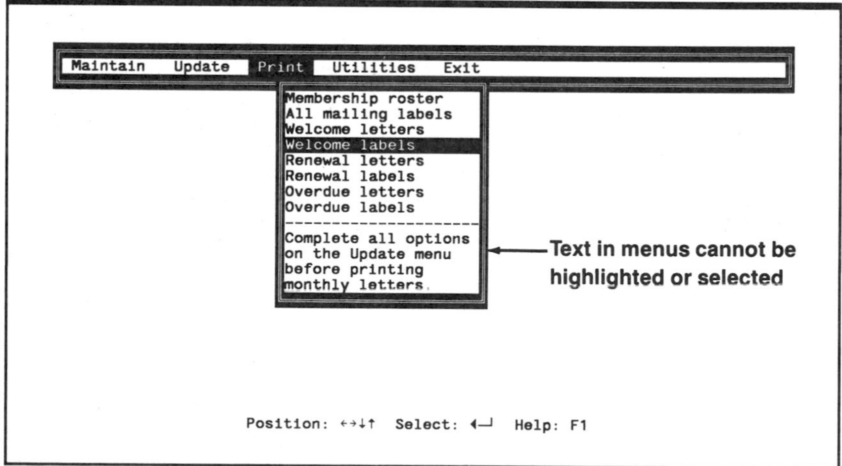

Figure 16.31: Print menu in the membership application

ADDING NEW MEMBERS

To add new members to the database, choose Maintain ► Add New Members. You'll be taken to a blank form for entering new records. The default starting date should match the current system date, and the default expiration date should be one year beyond the starting date.

For testing purposes, enter the following three records, using the dates specified in the samples rather than the default dates shown on your screen:

Mr. Bob B. Baker
Boeing International
Ballistics Dep't.
2744 Bering St.
El Monte, CA 91704
(818)555-1232 Ext. 999
Status: REGULAR
Start date: 02/01/93 Expiration date: 02/01/94
Dues Current?: Y

Miss Cara C. Carlson
Cookie Haven
Purchasing Dep't.
3211 Cantamar
Cucamonga, CA 91655
(818)555-9988
Status: OFFICER
Start date: 03/15/93 Expiration date: 03/15/94
Dues Current?: Y

Dr. Deedra D. Davis
Doctor's Hosptal
15th Floor
8843 Donga Dr.
Duarte, CA 91555
(818)555-9910 Extension 8851
Status: REGULAR
Start date: 04/30/93 Expiration date: 04/30/94
Dues current? Y

After entering the sample records, choose Exit ► Exit to return to the application menu.

CHANGING MEMBER DATA

The application offers two options for editing membership data: Browse All Members and Change/Delete a Member. Test each method now (but don't change any starting or expiration dates). Note that records should be displayed in alphabetical order by last name.

You should be able to perform an index search from either the custom form or the browse screen. To test this, choose Go To ► Index Key Search from the menu. Enter a valid last name, such as Carlson (with proper upper- and lowercase letters), and press ↵.

You can mark (and unmark) any record for deletion using the usual Ctrl-U keystroke. (The Del indicator appears in the status bar.) For the current test session, however, do not leave any records marked for deletion yet.

After testing each option, choose Exit ► Exit to return to the membership application main menu.

UPDATING THE MEMBERSHIP ROSTER

Suppose now that you are the user of the application, and you want to update the membership database to reflect renewed members and delete records where memberships have expired. The following sections present the steps you would take (they are the same steps you can use to test the application).

CHECK THE SYSTEM DATE First, make sure the current (system) date is accurate. For testing purposes, we'll assume that the current date is March 30, 1994. Choose Utilities ► Change System Date. The following DOS prompt appears on the screen (with the actual system date displayed in place of Mon 01-04-94):

```
Current date is Mon 01-04-1994
Enter new date (mm-dd-yy): _
```

Type the test date **3-31-94** and press ↵ to return to the menu.

UPDATE THIS MONTH'S RENEWALS Next, choose Update ► Update This Month's Renewals. You'll see a brief message as the application replaces the CURRENT field of expired memberships with F. Then a browse screen will appear showing the expired memberships, as in Figure 16.32.

RENEWED	LASTNAME	FIRSTNAME	COMPANY	STARTDATE	EXPIRES	CURRENT
F	Adams	Andy	ABC Technology	01/01/93	01/01/94	F
F	Baker	Bob	Boeing Internat	02/01/93	02/01/94	F
F	Carlson	Cara	Cookie Haven	03/15/93	03/15/94	F

Figure 16.32: Expired memberships ready for renewal

Mark the record for Carlson with a **T** (assume that hers is the only renewed membership). Note that the cursor stays locked into the RENEWED field, even if you press ← or → or try to click the mouse on any fields to the right.

After updating the one record, press F10 to display the pull-down menu, then choose Exit ► Exit. You'll see some brief messages as the application updates the records with renewed memberships. Then you'll be returned to the application main menu.

To verify that the update was accurate, choose Maintain ► Browse All Members or Maintain ► Change/Delete a Member. You should see Carlson's membership extended to 1994, and the CURRENT field for the record marked Y. If you're wondering why the CURRENT field is Y instead of T, recall that we used MEMFORM as the FORMAT file for the Browse All Members and Change/Delete a Member options. Because MEMFORM has a template of Y, the logical True value displays as Y instead of T (see Table 16.1).

DELETE EXPIRED MEMBERSHIPS Now it's time to delete memberships that expired 60 or more days ago and have not been renewed. Choose Update ► Mark Expired Memberships for Deletion. You'll see a brief message as the application marks one record for deletion (Andy Adams). Next, choose Update ► Purge Marked Records. Again, you'll see a message as the application packs the database.

To verify that the deletion was accurate, choose Maintain ► Browse All Members. You'll notice that Andy Adams' record has been permanently deleted.

PRINTING THE MEMBERSHIP ROSTER

Keep in mind that if you have a laser printer, you may need to eject a page when printing reports or mailing labels (including sample labels) that don't entirely fill a page.

At any time during the month, the user can print a list of all members by choosing Print ► Membership Roster. If you do so now, the application will print a list of all members currently in the Members database. These should be in alphabetical order.

PRINTING ALL MAILING LABELS

If you choose Print ► All Mailing Labels, the application should print a sample mailing label and display the message "Do you want more samples? (Y/N)." Type **Y** if you want to test the label alignment again or **N** to begin printing labels. The application should print three mailing labels in zip code order and then return you to the application menus.

PRINTING RENEWAL LETTERS AND LABELS

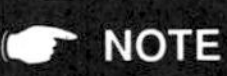

If you try to print Welcome, Renewal, or Overdue Letters, and none are pending, you'll see an End of File message. Just type I to select Ignore.

Each month the user can print letters and labels, reminding members whose memberships expire next month that it's time to renew. Choose Print ► Renewal Letters. The application should print a letter for Deedra Davis, whose membership expires next month (April 1994). Select Renewal Labels, and the application will print a label for this member.

PRINTING OVERDUE LETTERS AND LABELS

Each month the user can print Overdue letters and labels, reminding late payers that their memberships expired last month, and that they still have not renewed. Currently, Bob Baker is the only member who meets this description (his membership expired in February 1994, and he has not renewed yet).

Choose Print ► Overdue Letters. You should see a single letter printed for Bob Baker. Select Overdue Labels to print a mailing label for this letter.

PRINTING WELCOME LETTERS AND LABELS

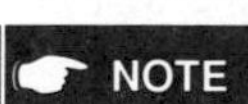

Changing the system date in this chapter is *only* for testing with a small database. In actual use with real data, you would never need to change the date to print a particular type of letter or mailing label.

Each month, the user can print a batch of welcome letters and matching mailing labels for all new members (those who joined in the current month and year). Currently, no records in the test database meet this description, so you'll need to alter the current date to test print at least one letter. Choose Utilities ► Change System Date and change the current date to **3-31-93**.

Choose Print ► Welcome Letters. You should see a welcome letter printed for Cara Carlson. Select Welcome Labels, and after printing samples, you should see a single label, again for Cara Carlson.

You may now want to reset the current date back to 3-31-94 or to the actual current date.

TESTING THE UTILITIES

You've already had a chance to test the Change System Date option on the Utilities menu. Now you can test the other three options on that menu. If you have a blank, formatted disk available, place it in drive A of your computer and choose Utilities ► Back Up Database to Drive A. You should hear the disk drive whir and see the file names MEMBERS.DBF and MEMBERS.MDX on the screen as the application makes the backup copy.

Next, choose Utilities ► Copy Application to Drive A. Once again, you should hear the disk drive and see the names of all files being copied on the screen as the application copies the entire \DBASE\MEMBERS subdirectory to the disk in drive A.

Finally, choose Utilities ► Repair Corrupted Index to test that option. (Even though the indexes are probably not corrupted at the moment, the option will still rebuild them.) You'll see several messages on the screen as the indexes are rebuilt.

EXITING THE APPLICATION

If you choose Exit ► Return to dBASE IV, you'll be returned to the Control Center. Choosing Exit ► Exit to DOS returns you all the way to the DOS prompt.

MODIFYING THE MEMBERSHIP APPLICATION

If you discovered an error during your testing phase, or if you wish to refine the application, use the Applications Generator to make changes. In this section, we'll discuss general techniques for modifying an existing application.

PRINTING THE DOCUMENTATION

As you may recall, you used the Applications Generator to generate some documentation earlier in this chapter. You might want to make a printed copy of this document now, as it can be handy when you are making changes. The document is always stored with the same name as the application, but with the extension .DOC (as MEMMGR.DOC in this example). To print this documentation, first exit dBASE IV and return to the DOS prompt. Be sure you have switched to the \DBASE\MEMBERS directory (if necessary, type **CD\DBASE\MEMBERS** and press ↵) and then type the command

```
TYPE MEMMGR.DOC >PRN
```

Press ↵ after typing the command. If you have a laser printer that won't eject the last printed page, enter the following command at the

DOS prompt (hold down the Ctrl key and press the letter L where you see <Ctrl-L>):

```
ECHO <Ctrl-L> >PRN
```

The command will appear on the screen as ECHO ^L >PRN. Press ⟵ after entering the command.

The documentation will provide pictures of all menus and descriptions of the actions and objects assigned to each menu option. For example, the tenth page of the MEMMGR application documentation displays this for the Welcome Letters option on the Print menu:

```
------------------------------------------------------------
Bar: 3
  Prompt: Welcome letters
  Action: Run Report Form WELCOME.frm
  Command Options:
  FOR MONTH(StartDate) = MONTH(DATE())
  .AND.YEAR(StartDate) = YEAR(DATE()) PLAIN

  Print mode: Send to default printer
  Set Order to:  ZIP
------------------------------------------------------------
```

If any options in your application are not working as expected, perhaps the first place you should check is the printed documentation to see what the action is doing. Then you can return to the Applications Generator and make changes if necessary.

RETURNING TO THE APPLICATIONS GENERATOR

When you are ready to modify your application, follow either of these steps to return to the Applications Generator:

- Highlight the application name in the Application panel of the Control Center and press ⟵ (or double-click the application name), then select Modify Application from the dialog box.

- Highlight or click on the application name in the Application panel of the Control Center and press or click Design (Shift-F2).

When you get back to the application design screen, you can select a particular menu to work with by selecting the type of object from the Design pull-down menu (for example, Horizontal Bar Menu or Pop-Up Menu) and then the name of the object you wish to work with from the submenu that appears (for example, MEMPRINT).

As discussed previously, you can resize or move the menu using Size (Shift-F7) and Move (F7), or your mouse. You can delete options by pressing Ctrl-Y and insert options pressing Ctrl-N. (If the frame is already tightened around the menu options, you'll need to expand it to make room for the insertion.)

To change all or any part of an action assigned to a menu option, highlight the menu option and choose Item ► Change Action. The action that is currently assigned to the menu option will be highlighted in all submenus. You can keep or change the current action at any level (that is, on any submenu).

SAVING YOUR CHANGES

It's important to remember that any changes you make to an application will *not* be reflected in the actual application until you save all those changes and regenerate the entire application. Therefore, any time that you make a change to an application, you should follow these exact steps before leaving the Applications Generator design screen:

1. Select Clear Work Surface from the Menu, Batch, or Application pull-down menu.
2. When prompted, select Save Changes.
3. Choose Generate ► Select Template and make sure MENU.GEN is in use.
4. Choose Generate ► Begin Generating.
5. Type **Y** and press ↵ when asked whether you want to overwrite the existing application. When the generation is complete, press a key or click the mouse.

6. If you want to regenerate the documentation, choose Generate ► Select Template and use DOCUMENT.GEN.
7. Choose Generate ► Begin Generating.
8. Type **Y** and press ↵ when asked if you want to overwrite the existing documentation.
9. When asked if you have an IBM-graphics compatible printer, type **Y** or **N** (as appropriate) and press ↵. When the generation is complete, press a key or click the mouse.
10. Choose Exit ► Save All Changes and Exit.

REFINING THE MEMBERSHIP APPLICATION

When we created the membership application, we did not add help screens or message line prompts. If you wish to add some of these now, highlight MEMMGR in the Application panel of the Control Center, press ↵, and select Modify Application.

ADDING MESSAGE LINE PROMPTS

Currently, the application always displays the message line prompt "Position: ← → ↓ ↑ Select: ↵ Help: F1." You can replace this default prompt with your own prompt. In fact, you can assign a different message line prompt to each menu option in your application to provide further instructions or information about each option to your user. (The message line prompt appears when the menu option is highlighted.)

To add message line prompts, follow these general steps (this example uses the Add New Members option from the Maintain menu):

1. Choose Design ► Pop-Up Menu.
2. Select MEMMAINT.
3. Highlight Add New Members.

4. Choose Item ► Assign Message Line Prompt.
5. Type the message line prompt **Add new members to the membership database** and press ↵.

You can press or click PgDn to scroll to the next item and then add a message line to that menu prompt. After assigning message lines to all items, choose Menu ► Put Away Current Menu ► Save Changes.

You may want to repeat the preceding steps for each menu and menu option in the application, substituting appropriate text. You can make up your own message line prompt for each menu option.

ADDING CUSTOM HELP SCREENS

You can also add a custom help screen to each menu option, which the user will see when he or she presses F1 when the option is highlighted. To add custom help screens to your application, use the same basic steps as for adding message line prompts, but rather than selecting Assign Message Line Prompt from the Item pull-down menu, select Write Help Text. You'll be given an entire screenful of space in which to enter up to 19 lines of help text. You can use the cursor movement keys or the mouse to move the cursor around on the screen, and can use many of the usual editing keystrokes to make changes—Del, Backspace, Ctrl-T, Ctrl-Y, and so forth. (For a list of valid editing keystrokes, press F1 while you're editing the help text; press Esc when you're done reading the list.) However, unlike memo fields or mail-merge reports, the help text doesn't automatically wrap when it reaches the right edge of the screen. Instead, you must press ↵ to start a new line of help text. Press or click Ctrl-End when you are finished. After editing the help text, remember to choose Menu ► Put Away Current Menu ► Save Changes.

Don't forget to regenerate the entire application after adding message line prompts and help screens.

DELETING APPLICATION MENUS

After refining an application, you may discover that you've created some menus that you no longer need. For example, suppose you added a "Test Reports" option to the print menu (MEMPRINT), which opens another menu named TESTMENU. Later you decide to delete TESTMENU because you no longer need to print test reports. Although dBASE doesn't offer any explicit options for deleting menus, you can still do so by following these steps:

1. Make the menu above the one you want to delete the current menu. In the example, MEMPRINT is the menu above the one you want to delete, so choose Design ► Pop-Up Menu and then select MEMPRINT.
2. Highlight the "Test Reports" option on MEMPRINT and press Ctrl-Y to delete the option. (If you still want to keep the Test Reports option but now want it to do something else, choose Item ► Change Action and assign it a different action.)
3. Choose Menu ► Put Away Current Menu ► Save Changes.
4. Generate the application again, as described earlier, then exit the Applications Generator and return to the Control Center by choosing Exit ► Save All Changes and Exit.
5. Now you're ready to delete the unneeded menu file. Choose Tools ► DOS Utilities.
6. Highlight the name of the menu you want to delete. For example, highlight TESTMENU.POP to delete the unwanted test reports menu.
7. Press the Del key, or choose Operations ► Delete ► Single File.
8. Select Proceed to delete the menu file.
9. Choose Exit ► Exit to Control Center.

NOTE

Pop-up menus have a .POP file name extension, whereas horizontal menus have a .BAR extension.

TIPS ON USING THE MEMBERSHIP APPLICATION

If you have actual data to store in the membership database, delete the example records by choosing Maintain ► Browse All

Members. Mark each record for deletion using Ctrl-U and exit from the browse screen. Then choose Update ► Purge Marked Records.

Next, type at least some portion of your real data. When you start using the membership system with real data, keep in mind a few points:

- When you first run the application, choose Utilities ► Change System Date and correct the current system date if necessary.
- Make a habit of always printing monthly letters on the same day each month (preferably the last day of the month).
- If for some reason you miss a month and want to print the previous month's letters in the current month, change the system date to the month that you are printing for. For example, if you don't get around to printing February's letters until March 2, change the system date to February 28, so that the application behaves as though it were still February. Be sure to restore the correct system date when you are done.
- Before printing any monthly letters, always perform all the operations on the Update menu in the order they are presented. That is, update the month's memberships, mark the expired memberships, and then purge the marked records. This will ensure that your mailing is based on current, accurate data.
- Make a habit of backing up the database to the disk in drive A at least once a month, using Utilities ► Back Up Database to Drive A. The best time to make this backup copy is after you print monthly letters, when the database is thoroughly up to date.
- You can designate renewed memberships by placing T in the RENEWED field when using Maintain ► Browse All Members. However, don't change the expiration date if you do so. The next time you choose Update ► Update This Month's Renewals, the expiration date will be extended by one year (so long as the RENEWED field still contains T).

If you were previously using a manual technique to manage your membership records, you may want to use both the manual technique and the membership application for a few months to make sure the application is performing the way you want it to. This is called running the application in parallel with the existing system and is one of the most common techniques used to test all types of applications.

CHAPTER 17

Adding Power with dBASE IV Commands

dBASE IV offers a complete programming language **606**
that consists of many commands and functions. You can use commands directly at the dot prompt or in *command files* (also called programs).

To get to the dot prompt from the Control Center, **608**
choose Exit ► Exit to Dot Prompt, or press Esc and select Yes from the dialog box.

To execute a command from the dot prompt, **608**
type it, using the correct syntax, and then press ↵.

To open a dBASE IV database file from the dot prompt, **608**
enter the command **USE** followed by the name of the database file that you want to open.

If you enter a command that dBASE IV cannot understand, **608**
dBASE displays an error message dialog box that briefly describes the error and presents options to cancel or edit (change) the command or to get some help.

To view the contents of the currently open database file, **609**
enter the command **LIST** at the dot prompt.

To perform a quick calculation at the dot prompt **611**
and see the results immediately, use the ? command followed by an expression. For example, the command ? 5*2 displays 10, the product of 5 times 2.

To store "scratchpad" data in temporary memory variables, 612
use the STORE command, or type a variable name followed by an equal (=) sign and a value to store in the memory variable. For example, both the commands STORE 10 TO Age and Age = 10 store the number 10 in a memory variable named Age.

To see the names, data types, and contents 614
of all current memory variables, enter the command **DISPLAY MEMORY** at the dot prompt.

To get quick help with the syntax and options of a command, 618
type the command **HELP** at the dot prompt, type the command you want help with, and press the ↵ key.

A dBASE IV command file, or program, 618
lets you store a series of commands in a file. Later, when you execute the command file, each command will be executed, one after the other, in the order you entered them.

To create a dBASE IV command file, 618
enter the command **MODIFY COMMAND <file name>** at the dot prompt (replacing <file name> with a valid DOS file name). When the editor appears, type the commands that you want the command file to perform.

To run a completed command file, 619
enter the command **DO <file name>**, replacing <file name> with the name of the command file that you want to run.

AT THIS POINT, YOU HAVE EXPERIENCE WITH ALL six panels in the Control Center and with each associated design screen: the reports design screen, the applications design screen, and so on. For many of you, the material covered in the preceding chapters will be sufficient to handle all of your database management tasks.

However, as you gain experience using thc Control Center, design screens, and Applications Generator, you may find that you need more power and flexibility to achieve some goal. This is particularly true if you want to develop large, complex business applications for big jobs like inventory management or accounts payable and receivable. When you need that added power and flexibility, it is available in the dBASE IV *programming language.*

THE dBASE IV PROGRAMMING LANGUAGE

The dBASE IV programming language is the program's most advanced and powerful feature. The programming language consists of *commands* that tell dBASE specific tasks to perform and functions (some of which you used in Chapter 12). Every action dBASE performs—including actions that you initiate from the Control Center, design screens, and pull-down menus—is actually handled by a dBASE command.

In most cases, the dBASE IV command used to perform an action is invisible to you. dBASE intentionally "hides" the command or commands involved in performing operations because many people don't really want, or need, to know what's going on "behind the scenes." In this respect, dBASE is no different from machines such as televisions and automobiles that we use every day. Almost everyone can use these machines, but very few people can explain exactly how they work, and even fewer can actually build a car or television from scratch.

When you are using dBASE IV, however, sometimes you can see what's going on behind the scenes. For example, in the previous chapter, after you designed the membership application and chose Generate ► Begin Generating, you saw a lot of code whiz by on the screen. You were watching dBASE IV convert your application design into a series of programming language commands. When you run your completed application, dBASE IV uses that series of commands to actually display the menus and perform the actions that you specified while designing the application.

We'll look at this relationship between the Control Center, the design screens, and the programming language more closely later in this chapter. For now, just keep in mind that the Control Center and design screens are an *alternative* to the programming language and are provided as a convenience. Everything you do at the Control Center or on a design screen is automatically converted into a dBASE IV command, usually without your realizing it.

Now let's get a little hands-on practice using dBASE IV commands directly at the dot prompt, outside of the Control Center. Some of the commands that you will enter will perform operations identical to those you can perform by making selections from the Control Center. Don't let this confuse you. There is no particular rule that says you must use the Control Center in one situation and a command in another. In many situations, the Control Center and programming commands are simply alternative ways to do the same thing. The only reason we use commands rather than the Control Center in this chapter is because commands are the topic at hand.

USING COMMANDS INTERACTIVELY

You can enter most dBASE IV commands directly at the dot prompt and get immediate results. (A few commands work only when used in dBASE IV programs, as discussed later. If you enter one of these commands at the dot prompt, dBASE IV will remind you of this.)

If you'd like to try some commands, log on to the \DBASE directory (the one you used in Chapters 1 through 15 in this book) before you start dBASE. If dBASE IV is already running and you are not logged on to the \DBASE directory, start at the Control Center and choose Tools ► DOS Utilities. Then choose DOS ► Set Default Drive/Directory. If necessary, type **C:\DBASE** as the drive and directory, press ↵, and choose Exit ► Exit to Control Center.

When you get to the \DBASE directory, you should see the LEARN catalog in the Control Center. To get to the dot prompt from the dBASE IV Control Center, you can use either of the following techniques:

- Choose Exit ▶ Exit to Dot Prompt.
- Press Esc and select Yes from the dialog box that appears.

When you get to the dot prompt, you'll see only the status bar at the bottom of the screen and a period (dot) with the cursor blinking to the right. You can type any valid dBASE IV command, followed by ↵, whenever you see the dot prompt. You can enter up to 254 characters at the dot prompt. However, if you need to type a very long command line, up to 1,024 characters, you can press Ctrl-Home to open up the full-screen editing window that works just like the memo fields editor. After editing your command, choose Exit ▶ Save Changes and Exit to exit the editor and execute the command.

OPENING A DATABASE FILE

Always press ↵ after typing a dBASE IV command at the dot prompt.

The dBASE IV USE command opens a database file. For example, to open the CUSTLIST database, you enter the command

```
USE CustList
```

You can use any combination of upper- and lowercase letters in a command. This book presents commands in uppercase letters and information that the command uses (such as the file name CustList in the preceding example) in lowercase or mixed-case letters.

After you enter the USE CustList command, you'll see the dot prompt again (not much appears to have happened, but the CUSTLIST database is indeed open, as you'll see momentarily). If you made an error while typing the command, something else will happen, as discussed next.

HANDLING ERRORS

If you make a mistake while typing a command, you can use the Backspace key to make changes (before you press ↵). If you enter a command that dBASE cannot process, you'll see a dialog box with an error message that briefly describes the problem and the command you entered and presents the options Cancel, Edit, and Help.

For example, if you enter the command **US CustList** (instead of USE CustList), dBASE displays an error dialog box with the error message "*** Unrecognized command verb:" (the first word in a dBASE IV command is the *verb,* and the error message is telling you that dBASE IV does not recognize US as a valid command verb). Figure 17.1 shows the error dialog box.

After the error dialog box appears, you can select Cancel to completely cancel the request and return to the dot prompt. If you select Edit, the cursor will return to the end of the faulty command, and you can use the ←, →, and other standard dBASE IV editing keys, or your mouse, to make changes. After making changes, press ↵ to reenter the command. If you aren't sure what an error message means or don't know how to correct an error, select Help and you'll be taken to the dBASE IV help system.

NOTE

You can also reenter or edit a previous dot-prompt command by pressing ↑ and ↓ at the dot prompt to scroll through the last ten commands entered. You can change any command with the Backspace and arrow keys (or the mouse) and reenter the command by pressing ↵.

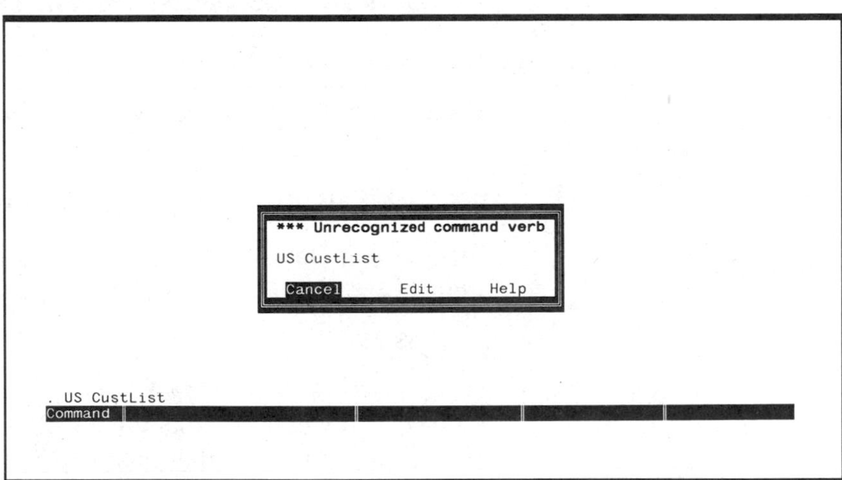

Figure 17.1: A sample error dialog box

THE LIST COMMAND

To verify that the CustList database is now open, you can use the LIST command to view the records in the file. You can limit the display to specific fields if you wish. For example, if you now enter the command

```
LIST LastName, FirstName, Company
```

and then press ↵, you'll see data from the CUSTLIST database on your screen, as in Figure 17.2.

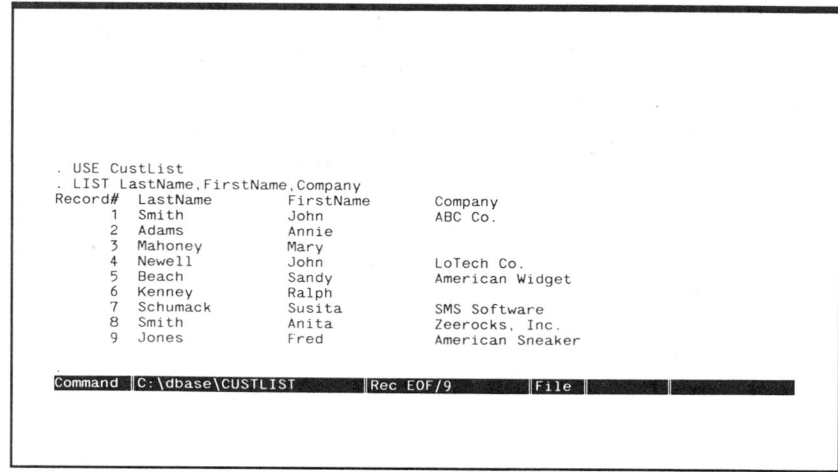

. USE CustList
. LIST LastName,FirstName,Company
Record# LastName FirstName Company
1 Smith John ABC Co.
2 Adams Annie
3 Mahoney Mary
4 Newell John LoTech Co.
5 Beach Sandy American Widget
6 Kenney Ralph
7 Schumack Susita SMS Software
8 Smith Anita Zeerocks, Inc.
9 Jones Fred American Sneaker
Command C:\dbase\CUSTLIST Rec EOF/9 File

Figure 17.2: Results of entering the LIST command

RETURNING TO THE CONTROL CENTER

To leave the dot prompt and return directly to DOS, type **QUIT** and press ↵.

You can leave the dot prompt and return to the Control Center at any time by using the ASSIST command. Enter the command

```
ASSIST
```

(remembering to press ↵), and you'll be returned to the Control Center. You will notice that CUSTLIST is above the line in the Data panel, indicating that that database is still open (because of the USE CustList command you entered at the dot prompt).

WHY TWO MODES?

Many dBASE IV commands perform exactly the same functions as options in the Control Center. You may be wondering why dBASE offers two modes—Control Center and dot prompt—to perform the same operations.

The answer to this question lies partly in dBASE IV's history. The first version of dBASE, dBASE II, offered only the dot-prompt mode for interacting with dBASE (there was no Control Center). The Control Center was added to dBASE IV simply because it is easier to select options from menus than it is to memorize and type commands. But the Control Center provides access to only the most essential dBASE IV capabilities.

Again, for the most common uses of dBASE, the essential capabilities are enough, and you may never need to use commands or the dot prompt. But if you do begin to develop large, complex business applications, the dot-prompt and programming language commands will let you take advantage of more advanced dBASE IV capabilities.

dBASE IV: THE CALCULATOR

One particularly handy feature of the dot prompt is that it allows you to get immediate answers to questions. You can use the ? command to display information or the results of a calculation. You can think of ? as a kind of PRINT command or WHAT IS? command.

For example, leave the Control Center now to get to the dot prompt. Then type the command

```
? 50*50
```

and press ↵. dBASE displays the results of 50 times 50, which is 2500.

Suppose you need to find the cube root of the number 127. You can ask dBASE for the result of raising 127 to the power (1/3) by entering the command

```
? 127 ^ (1/3)
```

dBASE responds with the answer: 5.03.

You can use any dBASE function with the ? command. For example, to find the square root of 81, you can enter the command

```
? SQRT(81)
```

and dBASE will respond with the answer: 9.

USING MEMORY VARIABLES

Up to this point, you've stored data in database files on disk. When programming, you will often want to store data temporarily in RAM (the computer's random-access memory). You can use RAM as a scratchpad for temporarily storing data that you want to use for only a short time. (Programming examples presented later demonstrate the power of storing data in RAM.)

You store temporary data in RAM through *memory variables* (also called *MemVars,* or *variables*). There are two ways to store data in memory variables: by using the STORE command or by using the equal (=) sign in an expression, with the variable name on the left and the value to store on the right. For example, if you enter the command

```
STORE 150000 TO Principal
```

a memory variable named Principal will be created containing the number 150,000. To verify that the variable exists, you can enter the command

```
? Principal
```

and dBASE will display 150000.

To try the other method for storing data in variables, enter the command

```
APR = 9.75
```

Again, if you then enter the command

```
? APR
```

you'll see that this variable now exists and contains the number 9.75.

Enter the command

```
Years = 30
```

and press ↵. Now suppose you want to know what the monthly payment on a loan with the principal, interest rate, and term (years) you've entered would be. You can use the PAYMENT( ) function with the ? command to find the result. Remember, though, that you must divide the annual interest rate by 1200 to convert it to the

NOTE

The annual interest rate must be divided by 1200 because the percentage value, 9.75, must be divided by 100 to produce the decimal value, 0.975, before the annual rate is divided by 12 to produce the monthly rate, 0.813.

monthly interest rate and multiply the years by 12 to determine the number of monthly payments. Hence, you enter the command

```
? PAYMENT(Principal,APR/1200,Years*12)
```

The result is 1288.73.

MEMORY VARIABLE DATA TYPES

Just like the data that you store in databases, memory variables store different data types. dBASE determines the data type by the delimiters you use in the command. For example, Principal, APR, and Years in the preceding examples are all Numeric data types because no delimiters were used when storing data.

To store Character data, surround the value being stored with quotation marks. For example, entering the commands

```
String1 = "Hello"
String2 = "there"
```

creates two Character memory variables, named String1 and String2. If you then enter the command

```
? String1,String2
```

dBASE displays the result: Hello there.

To enter variables of the Date data type, use curly braces as delimiters. For example, enter the following two commands:

```
StDate = {01/01/93}
EndDate = {06/15/93}
```

StDate and EndDate are now memory variables that contain dates.

To determine the number of days between StDate and EndDate, subtract the earlier date from the later date by entering the command

```
? EndDate-StDate
```

dBASE displays the result: 165.

The rules for memory variable names are the same as the rules for field names. A memory variable name can be up to 10 characters long, must begin with a letter, and may not contain spaces or punctuation. (But it may contain the underline (_) character.)

DISPLAYING MEMORY VARIABLES

To see a list of all memory variables currently stored in RAM, enter the command

```
DISPLAY MEMORY
```

at the dot prompt. You'll see all of the variables that you've created so far listed on the screen, as follows:

```
                                   User Memory Variables
ENDDATE      pub    D      06/15/93
STDATE       pub    D      01/01/93
STRING2      pub    C      "there"
STRING1      pub    C      "Hello"
YEARS        pub    N                       30      (30.000000000000000)
APR          pub    N                     9.75      (9.7500000000000000)
PRINCIPAL    pub    N                   150000      (150000.00000000000)
  7 out of 500 memvars defined (and 0 array elements)
```

The left column lists memory variable names. The second column lists *pub,* which stands for public. (We'll discuss public and private variables later.) The third column lists the data types (D for Date, C for Character, and N for Numeric). The fourth column lists the value stored in the variable. For the Numeric data type, the fourth column shows how the contents of the variable are displayed on the screen. The fifth column shows how dBASE actually stores the value (with up to 18 decimal places of accuracy).

You can press any key or click the mouse to scroll through other pages of information that DISPLAY MEMORY produces. (This additional information is not relevant to us at the moment.) When you get past the last page, you'll be returned to the dot prompt.

THE LIFE OF A VARIABLE

You learned earlier that variables are used for storing temporary, or scratchpad, data. As soon as you exit dBASE IV, all memory variables are erased. (Some variables, as you'll see later in the chapter, are erased even sooner than that.) Admittedly, the preceding examples with the ? commands did little more than turn your computer and dBASE IV into an overpriced pocket calculator. But as you'll see soon, memory variables are very powerful and important tools when you start developing dBASE IV programs.

GETTING HELP WITH COMMANDS

So far in this chapter, you've used a few dBASE IV commands, including USE (to open a database file), LIST (to display database records), and ? (to display results). dBASE actually offers about 200 commands (see Appendix F).

> NOTE
>
> Press or click Esc to exit the help screen and return to the dot prompt. Press Esc again to remove the help text from your computer screen.

To use a command properly, you need to use the correct *syntax*. To get some quick help with a command and to see its *syntax chart*, you can enter the command HELP at the dot prompt, followed by the name of the command in question. For example, if you enter the command

```
HELP LIST
```

dBASE will display a help screen for the LIST command, as in Figure 17.3. Note that the top portion of the help screen displays the *syntax chart*, the second paragraph describes the command, and the bottom portion of the screen describes the various options that the command supports.

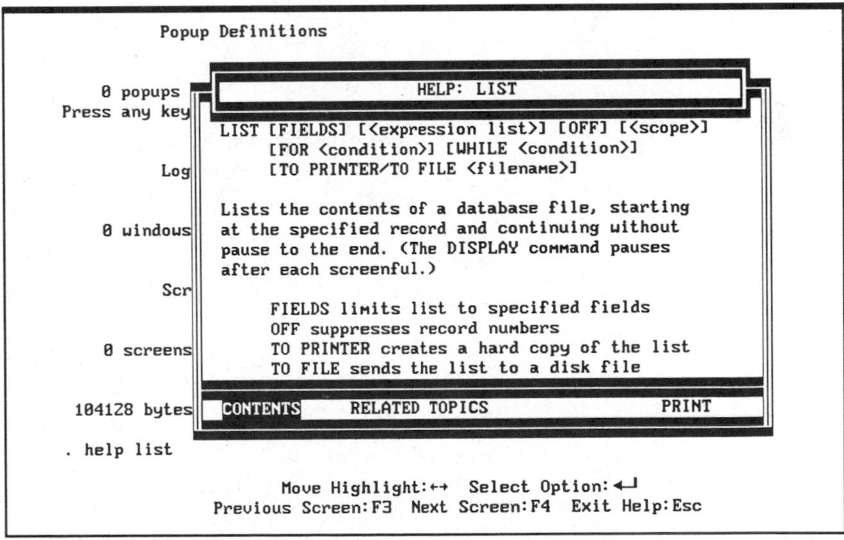

Figure 17.3: Help screen for the LIST command

At first, the command help screen may seem more confusing than helpful. However, after you understand how syntax charts work, you'll find it tells you a lot.

SYNTAX CHARTS

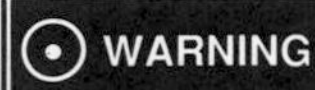

dBASE syntax charts use brackets and the slash to distinguish different types of command components, but you never type these brackets or the slash in your command.

The syntax chart for a command displays the components of a command and the order in which they are to be typed. dBASE uses the following symbols in a syntax chart:

[ ]	Items in square brackets are optional and can be omitted from the command.
/	One item or the other can be used, but not both.
<>	Items in angle brackets are to be replaced with specific information.
?	In some commands, the **?** can be used in place of specific information in angle brackets to see what objects are available in the current catalog (for example, **USE ?** displays a menu of database file names).

Following are some examples of the specific information that you provide in place of angle brackets and how it appears in a syntax chart.

<condition>	You must enter a valid filter condition, such as **State = "CA"** or **StartDate> = {01/01/93} .AND. StartDate< = {02/28/93}**.
<expression list>	You must enter an expression, or several expressions separated by commas. The expression might be a field name, variable name, or calculation (such as **Qty*UnitPrice**, where Qty and UnitPrice are field names from the currently open database).
<expC>	You must enter the name of a Character field, actual character data (enclosed in quotation marks), or an expression that results in the Character data type.
<expN>	You must enter the name of a Numeric (or Float) field, actual numeric data, or an expression that results in the Numeric or Float data type.

<expD>	You must enter the name of a Date field, an actual date enclosed in curly braces ({}), or an expression that results in the Date data type.

For example, any of the following LIST commands is valid (assuming that the CUSTLIST database is open at the moment). Note that even though the commands in the left column are broken into several lines, you must type each command as one long line next to the dot prompt.

LIST	Lists all fields and records from the current database.
LIST LastName,FirstName	Lists the LastName and FirstName fields from the current database (LastName,FirstName substitutes for <expression list>).
LIST FIELDS LastName,FirstName	Same as the preceding command, but includes the optional component FIELDS.
LIST StartDate, StartDate + 30 OFF	Lists the StartDate field and the start date with 30 days added. Omits record numbers because the OFF option is specified.
LIST RECORD 5	Displays the fifth record in the database (RECORD 5 is used in place of <scope>).
LIST City,State,Zip FOR State = "CA"	Lists the City, State, and Zip fields for records that have CA in the State field (State = "CA" substitutes for <condition>).
LIST LastName, FirstName, Company TO PRINTER	Lists the LastName, FirstName, and Company fields, sending output to the printer.

NOTE

If you are using a laser printer, enter the command **EJECT** at the dot prompt to eject the page.

As you can see from these examples, the LIST command offers quite a bit of flexibility, as do most dBASE IV commands. It takes some time and practice to fully master all of the commands in dBASE IV, but using the HELP command and understanding the syntax charts makes this learning experience much easier and more productive.

CREATING COMMAND FILES

A *command file,* or *program,* is a file that contains a list of commands that dBASE will execute in a series. The beauty of command files is that you can enter a few, or even hundreds of, commands into a single file and then have dBASE execute all of the commands in response to a single command by you.

You can create and edit command files using the dBASE IV editor. To get to the editor from the dot prompt, enter the command **MODIFY COMMAND <file name>** (where <file name> is a valid DOS file name, with no extension). For example, to create a program named Test, enter the command **MODIFY COMMAND Test** at the dot prompt.

When you get to the editor, you can type each command for your program, following each command with ↵ to ensure that each command is on a separate line. You can also use editing keys and your mouse to make changes and corrections. The keys used to create and edit command files are identical to those you use to manage memo field data (see Table 10.1 in Chapter 10 if you need a reminder). The options on the pull-down menus are also similar to those you use when editing memo fields.

To create a sample command file now, type the commands that follow. Be sure to press ↵ after you type each command. Note that the commands you enter will do nothing right now, because you are just storing them in a file. The commands will be executed later when you *run* the command file.

```
CLEAR
? "Here are the names in CustList..."
USE CustList
LIST LastName,FirstName
?
? "All done!"
```

When you are done, your screen should look like Figure 17.4.

To save the command file, choose Exit ► Save Changes and Exit. (You can also press Ctrl-End to save a command file and leave the editor.) You'll be returned to the dot prompt. dBASE will add the extension .PRG to the file name you provide, so the command file is actually stored as TEST.PRG.

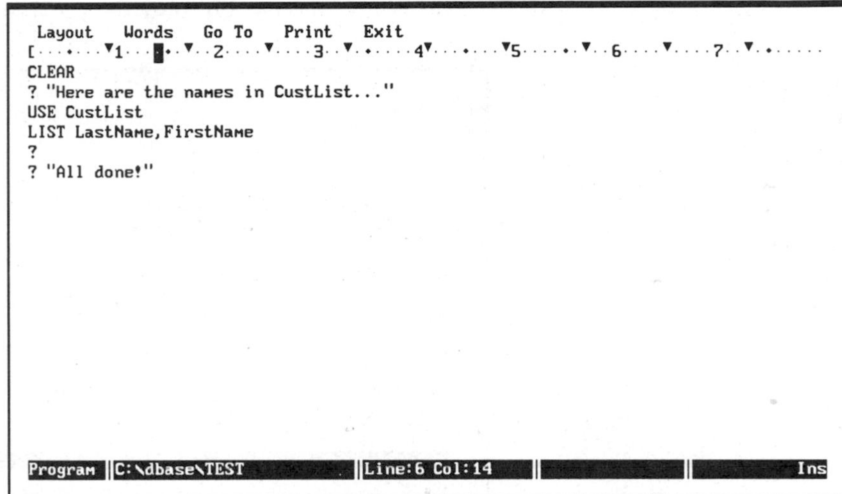
Layout Words Go To Print Exit
CLEAR
? "Here are the names in CustList..."
USE CustList
LIST LastName,FirstName
?
? "All done!"
Program
C:\dbase\TEST
Line:6 Col:14
Ins

Figure 17.4: The Test command file on the dBASE IV editor screen

RUNNING A COMMAND FILE

To run an existing command file, you use the DO command, followed by the name of the command file. For example, to run the Test command file that you just created, enter this command at the dot prompt:

```
DO Test
```

dBASE will take a moment to *compile* the program (more on this in the next section). When compilation is complete, you'll see the results of the command file. First, the CLEAR command clears the screen (except for the status bar). The command ? "Here are the names in CustList..." displays the message "Here are the names in CustList..." The command LIST LastName,FirstName displays the FirstName and LastName fields from the database. The command ? prints a blank line, and ? "All done!" displays the message "All done!"

Figure 17.5 shows how the screen looks after all the commands in the program have been executed. (The message at the top may scroll off on your screen.) Note that when dBASE finishes executing all the commands in CUSTLIST, it returns you to the dot prompt.

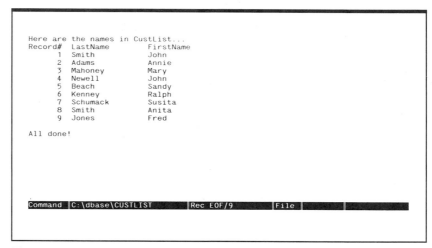

```
Here are the names in CustList...
Record#  LastName         FirstName
      1  Smith            John
      2  Adams            Annie
      3  Mahoney          Mary
      4  Newell           John
      5  Beach            Sandy
      6  Kenney           Ralph
      7  Schumack         Susita
      8  Smith            Anita
      9  Jones            Fred

All done!

Command ║C:\dbase\CUSTLIST        ║Rec EOF/9        ║File ║
```

Figure 17.5: Results of the TEST.PRG command file

You can run the program as many times as you wish by entering the **DO Test** command at the dot prompt (or press ↑ at the dot prompt to redisplay the command and then press ↵ to reenter it). On subsequent runs, dBASE will not need to recompile the program, because the compiled version already exists. Therefore, the program starts immediately after you enter the DO command.

If you need to make changes to the Test program, enter the command **MODIFY COMMAND Test** again at the dot prompt. You'll be returned to the editor, with the Test program displayed on the screen. If you make changes, save the program, and then rerun it, dBASE will automatically make a new compiled version of the program.

You can abbreviate any command to its first four letters. For example, MODI COMM is the same as MODIFY COMMAND.

LEVELS OF INTERACTING WITH THE COMPUTER

Now you know how to enter dBASE IV commands at the dot prompt, as well as how to store a group of commands in a command file and then execute the entire group serially using the dBASE DO command. You may be surprised to learn that the command file you created in this chapter is not the first one you've created in this book. In fact, you've created dozens of command files. Actually, dBASE has created them for you, but has done so behind the scenes or "under the hood," so to speak. Every time you design a query, a label format, a report format, or a custom form using one of the design screens, dBASE uses the information from the design screen to create a command file. The command file contains all the dBASE IV commands and functions (the code, or *source code,* that is) required to turn your design into a series of instructions the computer can interpret and execute.

Not only does dBASE automatically create a command file for each object you create, it also creates a compiled copy of the command file that the computer can read directly. Figure 17.6 shows this series of events from the "highest" level, the Control Center, to the "lowest," the actual computer hardware.

In the first 16 chapters of this book, you worked at the highest level, the Control Center. When you created the sample command file in this chapter, you worked directly at the second level from the top. That is, you personally created a command file rather than having the Control Center do it for you.

The third level down, the *object code*, is simply too technical and abstract for most people to deal with directly. But the computer can use it and execute its instructions very quickly. (You may be wondering where DOS fits into this scheme. Suffice it to say that the object code and DOS interact in a variety of ways. But this topic is very technical and need not concern you right now.)

PEEKING UNDER THE HOOD

By taking a peek at some of the files on your hard disk, you can see for yourself that dBASE creates all these files. Assuming that

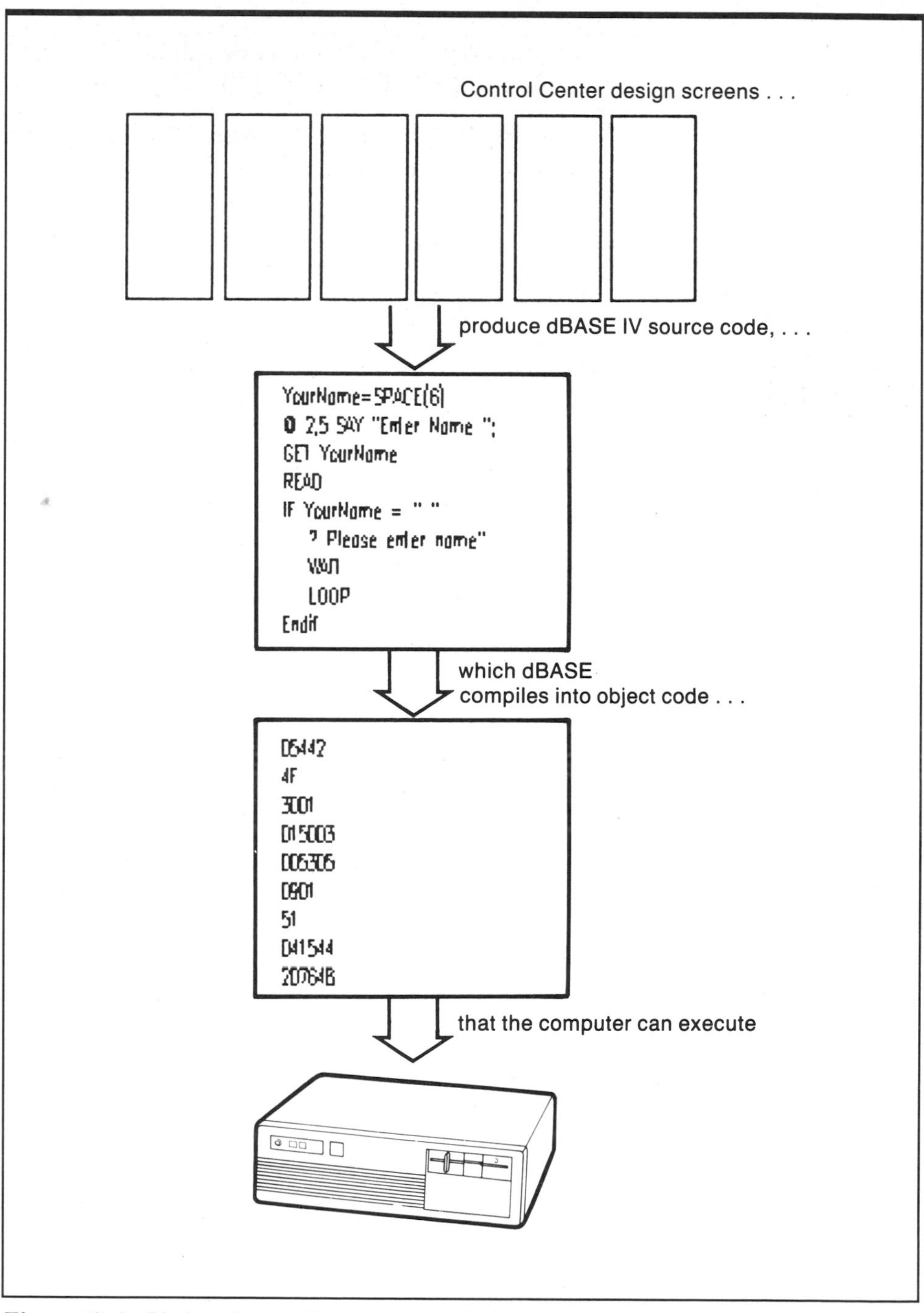

Figure 17.6: Various levels of interacting with the computer

dBASE IV is still running and you are still on the \DBASE directory, you can enter the command **DIR CUSTFORM.*** to see a list of all files with the file name CUSTFORM. (The command tells dBASE to display the names of all files on the current directory that have the first name CUSTFORM and any extension.) Assuming that you created the CUSTFORM custom form in Chapter 8, you should see the following list:

```
CUSTFORM.SCR
CUSTFORM.FMT
CUSTFORM.FMO
```

The file with the .SCR extension contains information pertaining to how you designed the form on the labels design screen. The .FMT file contains the source code for displaying the screen. The .FMO file displays the compiled object code.

You can look directly at the contents of the .FMT file (that is, the source code), but don't be alarmed if its contents do not mean anything to you now. To see the source code, enter this command at the dot prompt:

```
MODIFY COMMAND CustForm.FMT
```

When the source code appears, you can use the PgUp and PgDn keys to scroll through the entire file. When you are done, choose Exit ► Abandon Changes and Exit to return to the dot prompt. (The .SCR and .FMO files do *not* contain code that you can read directly, so don't try using the MODIFY COMMAND editor to view their contents.)

The file name extensions for the various files created for each object are listed in Table 17.1. If you wish, you can look at the source code file for any type of object. Note that database files (those with a .DBF extension) contain only data, not code, and so there is no compiled copy of those files.

> NOTE
> Appendix H contains a comprehensive list of the file name extensions that dBASE IV uses.

SO WHY PROGRAM?

If the dBASE IV design screens can create source code programs automatically, why should you bother creating your own dBASE IV programs? The only real reason for writing your own programs is to

Table 17.1: File Name Extensions for Various Objects

Type of Object	Design screen file	Source code	Object code
Queries	<None>	.QBE	.QBO
Labels	.LBL	.LBG	.LBO
Reports	.FRM	.FRG	.FRO
Forms	.SCR	.FMT	.FMO
Applications	.APP	.PRG	.DBO

create a program that the design screens cannot create for you. It is really a matter of personal choice and personal need.

Again, as discussed at the beginning of this chapter, you may find the Control Center, design screens, and Applications Generator sufficient for all your data processing needs. On the other hand, if you want to develop larger and more complex applications, you probably will need to learn the programming language. The next chapter discusses some general programming techniques that you can use to build powerful and efficient programs of your own.

CHAPTER 18

Programming Techniques

To have your custom program interact with the user 628

by asking questions and displaying messages, use the ACCEPT, INPUT, WAIT, @...SAY...GET READ, and ? commands.

To have your custom program make decisions 633

about what action to perform next, use the IF...ELSE...ENDIF or DO CASE...ENDCASE commands.

To make your programs more readable from a human standpoint, 642

follow the basic guidelines of structured programming: Use programmer comments and indent all commands that are nested within clauses.

To place a programmer comment in a dBASE IV program, 642

precede the text of the comment with the command NOTE, an asterisk (*), or two ampersands (&&).

To repeat a group of commands in a command file 644

as long as some condition is true, enclose the commands to be repeated between the DO WHILE and ENDDO commands in the command file.

To create a loop that operates on only certain records 650

in a database, use the SCAN...ENDSCAN looping commands instead of the DO WHILE...ENDDO commands.

To call (execute) a program from a command file, 652

use the DO command just as you would to run a program from the dot prompt.

THE PRECEDING CHAPTER INTRODUCED dBASE IV commands and showed you how to create your own command files (or programs) using the MODIFY COMMAND editor. In this chapter, you'll learn about programming *techniques* that give you precise control over what occurs when dBASE executes your command file, and thus over what happens to your data.

The tcchniques presented in this chapter are general and probably won't provide a quick fix for your accounts receivable, inventory management, and other data processing problems. But beginning in the next chapter, you will see these techniques used in some very practical applications that may well give you the solutions you need.

INTERACTING WITH THE USER

Command files are particularly useful for interacting with the user of a program (or application). They allow the program to ask the user questions and store the answers in memory variables. Later the program can use these answers to perform calculations, make decisions, or display information. The dBASE IV commands that you use to interact with a user are ACCEPT, INPUT, WAIT, and @.

THE ACCEPT COMMAND

This chapter describes basic command syntax using a format similar to dBASE IV's HELP screens, as discussed in Chapter 17.

The ACCEPT command displays a prompt on the screen and waits for the user to type an answer and press ↵. The user's answer is stored in a memory variable as the Character data type. The basic syntax for the ACCEPT command is

```
ACCEPT [<prompt>] TO <memvar>
```

To try out the ACCEPT command at the dot prompt, enter this command:

```
ACCEPT "What is your name? " TO Name
```

As soon as you press ↵ after entering the command, the screen displays the prompt "What is your name?" and waits for a response. Type your name and then press ↵. To verify that the command stored your name in a memory variable called Name, enter the command

```
? Name
```

or the command:

```
DISPLAY MEMORY
```

(Normally you would use user interface commands only in a command file, but here we'll test them at the dot prompt just for demonstration. Sample command files will follow.)

THE INPUT COMMAND

The INPUT command is similar to the ACCEPT command, except that it does not automatically create a Character data type memory variable. Instead it takes a best guess as to the data type based on what the user enters. The syntax is basically the same as the ACCEPT command:

```
INPUT [<prompt>] TO <memvar>
```

To try the INPUT command at the dot prompt, enter this command:

```
INPUT "How old are you? " TO Age
```

As soon as you press ↵ after entering the command, the screen displays its prompt and waits for an answer. Type your age and press the ↵ key. To verify that the command worked, enter the command

```
? Age
```

or the command

```
DISPLAY MEMORY
```

THE WAIT COMMAND

The WAIT command presents a prompt and waits for a single keypress. WAIT uses the syntax

```
WAIT [<prompt>] [TO <memvar>]
```

If no prompt is provided, WAIT displays the prompt "Press any key to continue...." If the [<TO memvar>] component is omitted, the user's keystroke is not saved in a memory variable (but the command still pauses and waits for a keystroke).

To try this command, enter the following command at the dot prompt:

```
WAIT "Are you ready to proceed? (Y/N) " TO Ready
```

As soon as you press ↵ after entering the command, the screen displays the prompt "Are you ready to proceed? (Y/N) " and waits for a keypress. You can press any key (preferably Y or N). You need not press ↵, because WAIT expects only a single keystroke.

To verify that the command worked, enter the command **? Ready** or **DISPLAY MEMORY** at the dot prompt. Note that if you press ↵ or the space bar in response to the WAIT command's prompt, the ? Ready command will not display a letter (but the DISPLAY MEMORY command will verify that the variable exists).

THE @...SAY...GET READ COMMANDS

The @ command is the most powerful and sophisticated of the user interface commands. It provides many optional features and can be used for entering and editing memory variables and database data. The basic syntax (excluding many options) for the @ command is

```
@ <row>,<col> [SAY <exp>] [GET <variable/field>]
```

NOTE

Beyond its basic syntax, the @ command offers options too numerous to list here.

The <row> and <col> variables must be valid row and column positions on the screen. The <exp> option can be any valid dBASE expression, including a prompt enclosed in quotation marks. The option <variable/field> must be the name of an *existing* memory variable or a field in the currently open database. If the variable or field already contains data, the @ command displays the existing value.

The @...SAY...GET commands only display information on the screen. To allow the contents of the GET field or variable to be entered or changed, you must use a separate READ command beneath the @...SAY...GET commands. Rather than demonstrate this at the dot prompt, let's create a command file that demonstrates all of the user-interface commands. We'll name this command file TestUser. To get started, enter the command

```
MODIFY COMMAND TestUser
```

at the dot prompt. When you get to the editor, type the command file exactly as shown in Figure 18.1.

After creating the command file, choose Exit ► Save Changes and Exit. To run the command file, enter the command

```
DO TestUser
```

at the dot prompt. The screen will clear, and you'll see the prompt "What is your name?" Type your name and press ↵. Next the prompt "What is your age?" appears. Type your age and press ↵. Now you'll see the prompt "Enter your birthdate [/ /]." Type your birthdate in MM/DD/YY format, but do not press ↵.

After filling in your birthdate, you'll see the following results (with your own name, age, and number of days displayed):

```
Hello Alan
How does it feel to be 35?
You were born 12999 days ago!
Press any key to view memory variables...
```

Press any key, and you'll see a list of all current memory variables, including those shown here:

```
BIRTHDATE   priv  D   03/31/55 TESTUSER (@ testuser.prg)
USERAGE     priv  N        35 (35.00000000) TESTUSER (@ testuser.prg)
USERNAME    priv  C   "Alan"   TESTUSER (@ testuser.prg)
```

```
 Layout   Words   Go To   Print   Exit
[·····▼1·····▼··2····▼····3··▼······4▼·······▼5······▼··6····▼····7··▼······
SET TALK OFF
CLEAR

ACCEPT "What is your name? " TO UserName
INPUT "What is your age? " TO UserAge

BirthDate = {  /  /  }
@ 10,1 SAY "Enter your birth date " GET BirthDate
READ

?
?
? "Hello",UserName
? "How does it feel to be "+STR(UserAge,2,0)+"?"
? "You were born "+STR(DATE()-BirthDate,5,0)+" days ago!"
?

WAIT "Press any key to view memory variables..."
DISPLAY MEMORY

Program |C:\dbase\TESTUSER |Line:20 Col:1 | | |  Ins
```

Figure 18.1: The TestUser command file

Note that the variables created in the TestUser file are defined as *priv,* for *private.* Unlike memory variables that you create at the dot prompt, variables that are created in a command file are *private* to that command file and disappear as soon as the command file is finished running. (TestUser is actually still running at this moment, so the variables have not yet disappeared.) The TESTUSER (@ testuser.prg) columns of the display show that the memory variable was created in a program named TestUser.PRG.

NOTE

dBASE IV offers the PUBLIC command, which can be used to create public memory variables that do not get erased.

You can press any key several times until DISPLAY MEMORY finishes its display. Then you'll be returned to the dot prompt. At this point, TestUser is finished running. To see that its memory variables have indeed been erased, enter the command **DISPLAY MEMORY** now. Only public memory variables (if any exist) will appear in the list of user memory variables.

Let's take a moment to discuss how this program worked. The SET TALK OFF command at the top of TestUser.PRG prevents dBASE IV extraneous messages (such as the immediate results of creating memory variables) from being displayed on the screen. Many command files use SET TALK OFF, because the extraneous messages can be distracting if they appear while a program is running. The CLEAR command clears the screen.

The ACCEPT and INPUT commands act exactly as they did at the dot prompt in earlier examples (except that these examples use different variable names). The command BirthDate = { / / } creates a Date memory variable that contains a blank date. (It is necessary to create this variable *before* using it in the @...SAY...GET command.) The command @ 10,1 SAY "Enter your birth date " GET BirthDate positions the cursor at the tenth row, first column of the screen. The SAY portion displays the prompt "Enter your birth date." The GET BirthDate part displays the current contents of the BirthDate variable in a highlighted box on the screen.

The READ command tells dBASE to put the cursor in the highlighted box on the screen, so that the user can enter or change information in that highlighted box. When the highlighted box is filled (or the user presses ↵), the READ command is done, and processing resumes with the next command.

The two ? commands each print a blank line on the screen. The command "Hello",UserName displays the word *Hello* followed by a space and the contents of the UserName variable. The command

"How does it feel to be " + STR(UserAge,2,0) + "?" displays the message "How does it feel to be" followed by a space, the user's age, and a question mark. The STR() function converts the numeric UserAge variable to a character string, so that it can be combined with the characters enclosed in quotation marks. This conversion is required when you use + in ? commands, just as it is when you use + in index expressions (as discussed in Chapter 12).

The next command, ? "You were born " + STR(DATE() − BirthDate,5,0) + " days ago!", calculates the number of days between the current date (DATE()) and the user's birthdate. The STR() function converts the result to a character string, so that it can be combined with the Character data enclosed in quotation marks in the command.

The command WAIT "Press any key to view memory variables ..." pauses execution, and waits for a keypress. As soon as the user presses a key to proceed, the DISPLAY MEMORY command displays all active (current) memory variables. After you scroll through the various pages of the DISPLAY MEMORY screens, the command file ends and returns control to the dot prompt.

DECISION MAKING IN COMMAND FILES

One of the most powerful capabilities of command files is their ability to make decisions "on the fly," based on user responses, data in database files, or current events. The following sample command files demonstrate this capability.

THE IF...ELSE...ENDIF COMMANDS

One of the most common set of commands for inserting a decision-making capability into a command file is IF...ELSE...ENDIF. The general syntax for this set of commands is

```
IF <condition>
   <do these commands>
```

```
[ELSE
    <do these commands>]
ENDIF
```

IF...ELSE...ENDIF can only be used in command files, not at the dot prompt. You can simulate IF...ELSE...ENDIF within a command by using the IIF function discussed in Chapter 12.

Every IF command must have exactly one ENDIF command associated with it. The ELSE portion of the command is optional. The <condition> portion of the command can be any expression that yields a true or false result (exactly like the filter conditions that you enter into Applications Generator dialog boxes to create FOR and FILTER conditions).

The <do these commands> portions within IF...ELSE...ENDIF commands can be any number of dBASE IV commands, each on a separate line. If the <condition> portion of the command is true, then all <commands> between the IF and ELSE commands are executed, and any commands between ELSE and ENDIF are ignored. If the <condition> proves false, all commands between the IF and ELSE commands are ignored, and only the commands between ELSE and ENDIF (if any exist) are executed.

To try a simple program with IF...ELSE...ENDIF commands in it, enter the command **MODIFY COMMAND TestIf1** at the dot prompt. When the editor appears, type the command file shown in Figure 18.2. When you've finished entering the program, choose Exit ► Save Changes and Exit to save it.

```
 Layout   Words   Go To   Print   Exit
SET TALK OFF
CLEAR

Answer = 0
@ 12,20 SAY "Enter any number " GET Answer
READ

IF Answer >= 100
   ? "That number is greater than or equal to 100"
ELSE
   ? "That number is less than 100"
ENDIF

Program  C:\dbase\TESTIF1     Line:13 Col:1                    Ins
```

Figure 18.2: Sample TestIf1 program

To test the program, enter the command **DO TestIf1** at the dot prompt. The screen will display a prompt asking you to enter any number. Type a number and then press ↵. If the number that you entered was greater than or equal to 100, the program displays the message "That number is greater than or equal to 100." If the number you entered was not greater than or equal to 100, the program displays the message, "That number is less than 100." The program ends after displaying its results and returns you to the dot prompt.

Let's see how the program works. The first commands, SET TALK OFF and CLEAR, turn off the TALK setting and clear the screen. The command Answer = 0 creates a Numeric memory variable named Answer, which contains the number zero. The command @ 12,20 SAY "Enter any number " GET Answer displays its message and the contents of the Answer variable in a highlighted box on the screen. The READ command moves the cursor into the highlighted box so the user can change the contents of the Answer variable.

After you enter a number, the command IF Answer > = 100 checks to see if the Answer variable contains a number that is greater than or equal to 100. If it does, then the command, ? "That number is greater than or equal to 100", is executed, and dBASE ignores the command between ELSE and ENDIF. If the number in the Answer variable is not greater than or equal to 100, then dBASE ignores the command between IF and ELSE and executes only the command between ELSE and ENDIF (that is, ? "That number is less than 100").

Note that the IF...ELSE...ENDIF commands must each be on a separate line in a command file. Yet, in a sense, they act like a single command because every IF must have an ENDIF command associated with it and you can only use an ELSE command between an IF and an ENDIF command. Commands with this type of structure can be thought of as programming *clauses*. For example, although there are five commands listed here, there is only one *IF clause*:

```
IF City = "San Diego"
   TaxRate = 7.75
ELSE
   TaxRate = 7.5
ENDIF
```

Let's look at a more practical example that includes two IF clauses that do not use the optional ELSE command. Figure 18.3 shows a sample command file named TestIf2.PRG that demonstrates the use of IF...ENDIF clauses in a program similar to the TestUser command file. To create the command file, enter **MODIFY COMMAND TestIf2** at the dot prompt. To save some typing, choose Words ► Write/Read Text File ► Read Text From File. When dBASE asks for the name of the file to insert, type TestUser.PRG and press ↵. You'll see a copy of the TestUser program that you created earlier.

```
SET TALK OFF
CLEAR

ACCEPT "What is your name " TO UserName
INPUT "What is your age " TO UserAge

BirthDate = {  /  /  }
@ 10,1 SAY "Enter your birth date " GET BirthDate
YesNo = "N"

@ 20,10 SAY "Send results to printer? (Y/N) " GET YesNo PICTURE "!"
READ

IF YesNo = "Y"
   SET PRINT ON
ENDIF

?
? "Hello",UserName
? "How does it feel to be "+STR(UserAge,2,0)+"?"
? "You were born "+STR(DATE()-BirthDate,5,0)+" days ago!"

IF UPPER(YesNo) = "Y"
   EJECT
   SET PRINT OFF
ENDIF
```

Figure 18.3: Sample command file with IF...ENDIF clauses

Modify the command file as shown in Figure 18.3. (To insert a blank line, position the cursor where you want the new line to appear and press Ctrl-N. To delete a line, position the cursor to the line and press Ctrl-Y.) Save the command file after modifying it. When you get to the dot prompt, enter the command

```
DO TestIf2
```

to run the command file.

The GET command is not activated until a READ command is executed.

At first, the modified program will run exactly as the TestUser program did, except that it will display the prompt "Send results to printer? (Y/N) [N]" near the bottom of the screen. After filling in all of the preceding prompts, type **Y** to send results to the printer or **N** to display them on the screen only. After printing or displaying the results, dBASE returns to the dot prompt.

Let's discuss the new commands in the TestIf2 program. First, the command YesNo = "N" creates a memory variable named YesNo that contains the character *N*. Then the command @ 20,10 SAY "Send results to printer? (Y/N)" GET YesNo PICTURE "!" displays the prompt "Send results to printer? (Y/N) " at row 20, column 10 of the screen. The PICTURE "!" component converts the entry in the YesNo variable to uppercase. (The PICTURE component is identical to the Template option in the forms design screen.)

After the user enters Y or N, the IF YesNo = "Y" command checks to see whether the user entered Y. If so, the SET PRINT ON command activates the printer. All subsequent display commands will send their results to the printer. If the user did not enter Y, dBASE ignores the SET PRINT ON command and does not send any output to the printer.

The ? commands that follow the first IF clause display their results normally (whether YesNo was entered as Y or N), because the ? commands are outside of the first IF...ENDIF clause and therefore are not affected by it. The second IF command once again checks to see if the YesNo variable contains a Y. If it does, the EJECT command ejects the page from the printer, and then the SET PRINT OFF command deactivates the printer (so that future displays are sent to the screen only).

When you test this program, be sure to try it both ways. That is, run the program once, entering **N** in response to the "Send results to printer" prompt. Then run the program again, entering **Y** in response to that prompt.

If your understanding of this command file is a little shaky, think of it this way: dBASE always executes the commands in a command file from left to right, top to bottom (in exactly the same progression that you read a page in a book). When dBASE encounters an IF command, it tests the condition to see if the result is true. If the result is true, dBASE continues executing commands until it encounters an ELSE command (if any exists). Once it encounters an ELSE command, it skims over all commands (not performing them) until it encounters ENDIF. Once it finds the ENDIF command, it forgets all about the IF condition and executes all remaining commands normally.

On the other hand, if dBASE encounters an IF command and its condition proves false, dBASE skims over all commands until it encounters an ELSE or ENDIF command. If it encounters an ELSE command, it resumes normal processing. When it encounters an ENDIF command, it forgets all about the IF condition and resumes normal processing.

THE DO CASE...ENDCASE COMMANDS

Like other "clause" commands discussed in this chapter, DO CASE...ENDCASE is valid only in command files; it cannot be used at the dot prompt.

The IF...ELSE...ENDIF clause is handy for simple either-or decisions, but some situations require that the program decide what to do based on several possibilities. In those situations, DO CASE...ENDCASE is preferable. The basic syntax for DO CASE is

```
DO CASE
   CASE <condition>
      <do these commands>
   [CASE <condition>
      <do these commands>]
   [additional CASE and commands allowed]
   [OTHERWISE
      <do these commands>]
ENDCASE
```

Every DO CASE command must have exactly one ENDCASE command associated with it. You can have any number of CASE <condition> commands between DO CASE and ENDCASE. The OTHERWISE command is optional. The <condition> portion must be an expression that results in a true or false result. The <do these commands> portion can be any number of commands, each on a separate line.

Like the IF...ELSE...ENDIF commands, the DO CASE, CASE, OTHERWISE, and ENDCASE commands must be on separate lines in a command file, and also form clauses, which are called *CASE clauses.* The DO CASE command must be the first command in a CASE clause. It can be followed by any number of CASE commands and an optional OTHERWISE command. The ENDCASE command is required to complete the clause.

To see how a DO CASE...ENDCASE clause works, use the MODIFY COMMAND editor to create a program named TestCase. Type the command file exactly as shown in Figure 18.4.

Save the command file after typing it and then run it by entering the command **DO TestCase** at the dot prompt. The screen will display the prompt, "Enter a number between 1 and 5 [0]." Type a number, and the program will display the appropriate message. For example, if you enter **1**, the program displays, "You entered a one." If you enter a number that is less than one or greater than five, the program displays the message, "I said from 1 to 5!" (You can run the program several times to try different numbers.)

Let's discuss how the program works. The Answer = 0 command creates a Numeric variable named Answer that contains a zero. The command @ 2,5 SAY "Enter a number between 1 and 5 " GET Answer PICTURE "9" displays the prompt that's in quotation marks and then displays the current contents of the Answer variable in a highlighted box. The PICTURE "9" component is a template (identical to the templates in the forms design screen) that displays

```
 Layout   Words   Go To   Print   Exit
[·····▼1·····▼··2····▼····3··▼······4▼·······▼5······▼··6····▼····7··▼······
SET TALK OFF
CLEAR
Answer = 0
@ 2,5 SAY "Enter a number between 1 and 5 " GET Answer PICTURE "9"
READ

DO CASE
   CASE Answer = 1
        ? "You entered a one"
   CASE Answer = 2
        ? "You entered a two"
   CASE Answer = 3
        ? "You entered a three"
   CASE Answer = 4
        ? "You entered a four"
   CASE Answer = 5
        ? "You entered a five"
    OTHERWISE
        ? "I said from 1 to 5!"
ENDCASE
Program ||C:\dbase\TESTCASE     ||Line:20 Col:9  ||        ||        Ins
```

Figure 18.4: Sample program to test DO CASE...ENDCASE

the number as a single digit and accepts only a single numeric digit. The READ command then moves the cursor into the highlighted box and waits for the user to enter a number.

The user's answer is stored in the variable named Answer. Once dBASE receives that number, it resumes processing at the next command after READ (DO CASE in this example). It tests each CASE condition to see if it is truc. If a CASE condition proves false, dBASE moves on to the next CASE condition. If a CASE condition proves true, dBASE executes all commands following that CASE condition, up to the next CASE condition. Then it completely ignores all remaining CASE conditions and the OTHERWISE command and resumes processing after the ENDCASE command. (In this example, there are no commands after ENDCASE, so the program just ends and returns control to the dot prompt.)

If none of the CASE conditions proves true (and *only* if none of the CASE conditions proves true), then the commands between OTHERWISE and ENDCASE are the only commands that dBASE executes. The optional OTHERWISE command must be listed beneath all preceding CASE commands.

You might think that the DO CASE...ENDCASE clause is similar to a series of stacked IF...ENDIF clauses, but it is not. There is a subtle difference, in that the DO CASE...ENDCASE clause executes only the *first* condition that proves true, whereas a series of IF...ELSE clauses executes all true conditions. To see this, note the series of commands in Figure 18.5.

In Figure 18.5, dBASE stores A-111 in the PartNumb variable and 100 in the Qty variable. The first IF command is true, as is the second, so the results of running this program are the following messages displayed on the screen:

```
Part number is A-111
Qty is greater than 10
```

Now observe the next series of commands in Figure 18.6. The result of that command file is

```
Part number is A-111
```

What happened to the second CASE statement? After all, it is true that Qty is greater than 10. But here is where the subtle difference in logic comes in. Once a CASE statement in a DO

```
******** Two stacked IF...ENDIF clauses.

*----- Assign values to memory variables.
PartNumb = "A-111"
Qty = 100

*----- Does PartNumb contain A-111?
IF PartNumb = "A-111"
   ? "Part number is A-111"
ENDIF

*----- Is Qty greater than 10?
IF Qty > 10
   ? "Qty is greater than 10"
ENDIF
```

Figure 18.5: Two stacked IF clauses

CASE...ENDCASE clause evaluates to true, all other CASE (and optional OTHERWISE) commands are completely ignored. Therefore, even though it is true the Qty is greater than 10 in Figure 18.6, dBASE never sees that CASE command, and hence it does not print any result.

Note that if none of the CASE options in a DO CASE...ENDCASE clause proves true and there is no OTHERWISE alternative, the entire clause does absolutely nothing. After all the CASE conditions prove false, processing resumes normally with the first command after the ENDCASE command.

```
******************* A DO CASE...ENDCASE clause.

*----- Assign values to memory variables.
PartNumb = "A-111"
Qty = 100

DO CASE
   *----- Does PartNumb contain A-111?
   CASE PartNumb = "A-111"
        ? "Part number is A-111"

   *----- Is Qty greater than 10?
   CASE Qty > 10
        ? "Qty is greater than 10"

ENDCASE
```

Figure 18.6: A DO CASE command

STRUCTURED PROGRAMMING

Before we begin to develop more complicated command files in this chapter, we should discuss structured programming. *Structured programming* is a technique for creating programs that are more readable from a human standpoint. The techniques do not affect the way a program runs; they only affect the way the program looks to you (and whoever else sees the program source code). The two main guidelines of structured programming are:

1. Use programmer comments to identify the meaning of commands.
2. Use indentations to align commands that are embedded in clauses.

PROGRAMMER COMMENTS

Programmer comments are notes to yourself that you embed in command files for future reference. They have no affect whatsoever on how the program runs and are, in fact, excluded from the compiled version of the program. There are two ways to enter comments into a command file:

- If the comment begins as the first character in a line, it must be preceded by at least one asterisk (*), the word NOTE, or two ampersands (&&).
- If the comment appears to the right of a command line, it must be preceded by two ampersands (&&).

Comments are useful for identifying the name and purpose of a program, the purpose of specific routines (or tasks) within the program, and the meaning of complex conditions. For example, Figure 18.7 shows TestIf2.PRG with comments added, as well as some blank lines to separate specific routines.

NOTE

You can use the Tab and Shift-Tab keys to indent and un-indent commands in a command file.

USING INDENTATIONS

You may have noticed that in all examples involving commands with multiple clauses, the commands within each clause are

```
************************************************** TestIf2.PRG
*---------------- Sample program with IF...ENDIF clauses.

SET TALK OFF
CLEAR

*----- Get information from the user.
ACCEPT "What is your name " TO UserName
INPUT "What is your age " TO UserAge

*------ Create birth date variable, and let user fill it in.
BirthDate = {  /  /  }
@ 10,1 SAY "Enter your birth date " GET BirthDate

*------ Create initial YesNo variable as N, then let user change it.
YesNo = "N"
@ 20,10 SAY "Send results to printer? (Y/N) " GET YesNo PICTURE "!"
READ

*------- If user wants results printed, set printer on.
IF YesNo = "Y"
   SET PRINT ON        && Send output to printer.
ENDIF

*------- Print the results.
?
? "Hello",UserName
? "How does it feel to be "+STR(UserAge,2,0)+"?"
? "You were born "+STR(DATE()-BirthDate,5,0)+" days ago!"

*------- If the results were printed, eject the page and
*------- deactivate the printer.
IF UPPER(YesNo) = "Y"
   EJECT               && Eject printed page.
   SET PRINT OFF       && Deactivate printer.
ENDIF
```

Figure 18.7: TestIf2.PRG with comments added

indented. A program will run fine if you do not indent commands within clauses. However, if you leave the indentations out, it is very difficult to see how the program is structured. For example, look at the version of the TestIf2.PRG program in Figure 18.8.

Some dBASE programmers believe that adding comments and indentations to a program slows it down, but this is not true.

Even though the program in Figure 18.8 does *exactly* the same thing as the TestIf2.PRG program in Figure 18.7, it is much more difficult to read and understand. The logical structure of the program is not apparent. Trying to modify or debug (remove the errors from) such a program would certainly be difficult.

Another technique you can use to add structure to your program is to use uppercase and lowercase letters consistently. For example, in

```
SET TALK OFF
CLEAR
ACCEPT "What is your name " TO UserName
INPUT "What is your age " TO UserAge
BirthDate = {  /  /  }
@ 10,1 SAY "Enter your birth date " GET BirthDate
YesNo = "N"
@ 20,10 SAY "Send results to printer? (Y/N) " GET YesNo PICTURE "!"
READ
IF YesNo = "Y"
SET PRINT ON
ENDIF
?
? "Hello",UserName
? "How does it feel to be "+STR(UserAge,2,0)+"?"
? "You were born "+STR(DATE()-BirthDate,5,0)+" days ago!"
IF UPPER(YesNo) = "Y"
EJECT
SET PRINT OFF
ENDIF
```

Figure 18.8: Unstructured version of TestIf 2.PRG

this book (and the dBASE IV manuals), all commands, functions, and command options are displayed in uppercase letters. Field names, variable names, and comments are displayed in mixed upper- and lowercase letters.

LOOPING

Looping allows a program to repeat a task as many times as necessary to complete a job. dBASE IV offers two looping commands: DO WHILE...ENDDO and SCAN...ENDSCAN.

THE DO WHILE...ENDDO COMMANDS

The DO WHILE...ENDDO clause repeats all commands between the DO WHILE and ENDDO commands, as long as the WHILE condition is true. The general syntax for DO WHILE...ENDDO is

```
DO WHILE <condition>
   <commands>
ENDDO
```

Every DO WHILE command must have exactly one ENDDO command associated with it. The <condition> component is an expression that results in a true or false result. The <commands> component is any number of commands, each on a separate line, that are all performed with each pass through the loop. If the <condition> statement is false when dBASE first encounters the DO WHILE loop, it ignores all commands between DO WHILE and ENDDO.

If <condition> is true to begin with, but never results in a false result, the loop attempts to run forever (such a structure is called an *infinite loop*). To escape from an infinite loop, you need to press the Esc key (perhaps several times) and select Cancel from the dialog box that appears.

Earlier we noted that dBASE always executes a program in the same way we read books, starting at the top and reading left to right from top to bottom. Loop commands are one exception to this top-to-bottom execution, because they can cause a series of commands to be repeated several times (as if you read to the end of this paragraph and then started at the top of the paragraph and read it again).

Figure 18.9 illustrates how a loop works. Note that the commands *between* the DO WHILE and ENDDO commands are executed, top-to-bottom, as long as the condition controlling the loop is true. As soon as the condition controlling the loop becomes false, execution resumes at the first command after the ENDDO command.

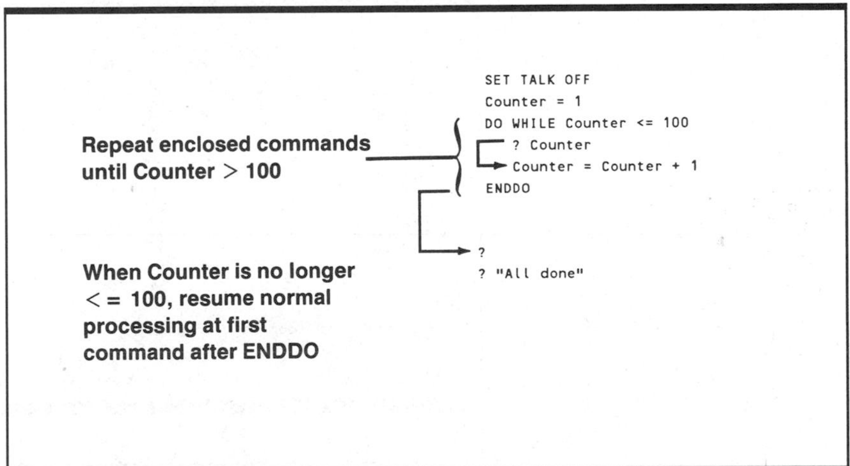

Figure 18.9: A loop causes enclosed commands to be executed several times

Figure 18.10 shows a sample loop that repeats two commands 15 times. To try this program, enter **MODIFY COMMAND Loop1** and type the command file exactly as shown in the figure.

After creating and saving the command file, you can run it by entering the command DO Loop1 at the dot prompt. After the program runs its course, your screen will look like Figure 18.11.

```
 Layout   Words   Go To   Print   Exit
[····▼1·····▼··2····▼····3··▼······4▼·······▼5······▼··6····▼····7··▼······
******************************** Loop1.PRG
*____ Test the DO WHILE...ENDDO commands.
SET TALK OFF
CLEAR

*____ Initialize Counter memory variable.
Counter = 1

*____ Begin loop.
DO WHILE Counter <= 15
   ? "Counter = ",Counter        && Display Counter
   Counter = Counter + 1         && Increment Counter by 1
ENDDO                         && Counter <= 15

?
? "All done with loop (and program)."


Program ||C:\dbase\LOOP1        ||Line:17 Col:1 ||           ||          Ins
```

Figure 18.10: Sample program with a loop

```
  Counter =              1
  Counter =              2
  Counter =              3
  Counter =              4
  Counter =              5
  Counter =              6
  Counter =              7
  Counter =              8
  Counter =              9
  Counter =             10
  Counter =             11
  Counter =             12
  Counter =             13
  Counter =             14
  Counter =             15

  All done with loop (and program).


  Command ||
```

Figure 18.11: Results of running the Loop1 program

Let's discuss each line in the sample program. The first two lines are comments (preceded by lots of asterisks, just to make them stand out). The SET TALK OFF and CLEAR commands turn TALK off and clear the screen.

The command Counter = 1 creates a numeric memory variable that contains the number 1. The command DO WHILE Counter<= 15 tells dBASE to repeat all commands between here and the ENDDO command as long as the Counter variable contains a number that is less than or equal to 15.

Within the loop, the command ? "Counter = ",Counter displays the message "Counter = " followed by the value that is currently stored in that variable. The command Counter = Counter + 1 increments the value of Counter by 1. For example, when the Counter variable contains the number 5, the command Counter = Counter + 1 adds 1 to that value and stores the result, 6, in the variable named Counter.

The ENDDO command marks the bottom of the loop. As soon as dBASE encounters the ENDDO command, it passes control back to the DO WHILE command, which checks to see whether the condition (Counter< = 15) is still true. If the condition is true, all commands between the DO WHILE and ENDDO are executed again. If the condition is not true, processing resumes at the first command after ENDDO. In this example, there are no commands after ENDDO, so the program ends and returns control to the dot prompt.

The text && Counter < = 15 next to the ENDDO command is a programmer comment and could be excluded. It is only a reminder to the programmer about the condition that is controlling the loop and has no effect whatsoever on the loop or the program. (The other comments preceded by && in the program also have no effect on the program.)

To get some extra practice with the DO WHILE command, you might want to try changing the number in the DO WHILE Counter<= 15 command. (Enter **MODIFY COMMAND Loop1** to edit the program.) For example, if you change the command to **DO WHILE Counter<= 100**, then the loop will be repeated 100 times. (If you enter a very large number and get tired of waiting for the loop to finish when you run the program, press the Esc key and select Cancel from the dialog box.)

You can set up a DO WHILE loop that repeats itself as many times as necessary to perform some operation on every record in the database. The general technique to do so is to make sure the appropriate database file is open, the record that you want to begin processing at is the current record, and the condition in the DO WHILE loop is .NOT. EOF(). EOF() is a dBASE function that returns .T. when the record pointer goes past the last record in the database.

NOTE

Type the command **SET HEADINGS OFF,** then enter **LIST TRIM (FirstName),LastName OFF** if you want to try some dot commands that are similar to the Loop2 program. Then turn the column headings back on by entering **SET HEADINGS ON.**

Figure 18.12 shows a sample program that uses such a loop. (The example does basically the same thing that a simple command such as LIST TRIM(FirstName),LastName OFF would do, but it demonstrates how the loop works nonetheless.) To create the command file, enter the command **MODIFY COMMAND Loop2** at the dot prompt, typing it exactly as shown in the figure.

After entering and saving the program, enter the command **DO Loop2** to test it. The results of running the program are shown in Figure 18.13 (but may be different on your screen if your CustList database has different records in it).

Let's discuss each command in the program. We've discussed the opening comments and SET TALK and CLEAR commands elsewhere. The command USE CustList ORDER LastName opens the CustList.DBF database (and, automatically, the CustList.MDX index file) and sets the sort order to the LastName index. (This command assumes that CustList.DBF and CustList.MDX exist on the current directory, and that an index named LastName has been created previously through the database design screen.)

The command GO TOP ensures that the record pointer starts at the top of the indexed sort order. (Actually, this command is somewhat redundant, because when you first open a database, the record pointer is automatically at the top of the database. But it's a good habit to remember to position the record pointer before you start a loop that processes records.)

The command DO WHILE .NOT. EOF() tells dBASE to process all commands between itself and the ENDDO command, until the EOF() function returns .T. The command ? TRIM(FirstName), LastName prints the FirstName from the current record, with trailing blanks removed, followed by a space and the LastName. (The , operator automatically places a blank space between two printed Character strings.)

```
Layout   Words   Go To   Print   Exit
[·······▼1······▼··2····▼····3··▼······4▼·······▼5······▼··6····▼····7··▼·······
******************************* Loop2.PRG
*- Program to demonstrate DO WHILE loop.
SET TALK OFF
CLEAR

*------ Open the database and use LastName index.
USE CustList ORDER LastName

*---- Begin loop.
GO TOP
DO WHILE .NOT. EOF()
   ? TRIM(FirstName),LastName
   SKIP
ENDDO

?
? "All done!"

Program |C:\dbase\LOOP2          |Line:1 Col:1 |          |          |     Ins
```

Figure 18.12: Sample program with DO WHILE .NOT. EOF() loop

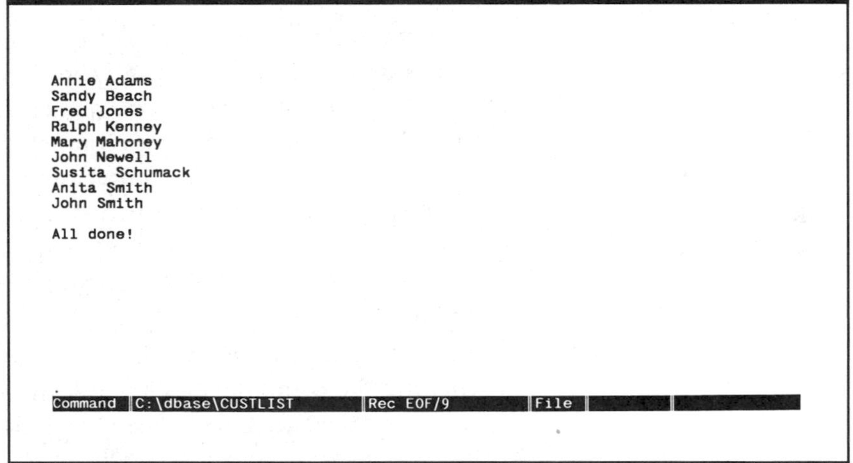

Figure 18.13: Results of the Loop2.PRG command file

The command SKIP tells dBASE to skip to the next record in the database (or, if an index order is in use, to the next record in the appropriate sort order). The SKIP command is vital to a DO WHILE .NOT. EOF() loop because, without it, the loop would print the same record over and over again. The only way to terminate the loop while the program was running would be to press Esc.

The ENDDO command marks the bottom of the loop. After the record pointer passes beyond the last record in the database, processing begins at the first command beneath the ENDDO command. In this case, ? prints a blank line and ? "All done!" prints the message "All done!" Then the program ends and returns control to the dot prompt.

THE SCAN...ENDSCAN COMMANDS

You can also use the SCAN...ENDSCAN commands to set up a loop that individually processes the records in a database. The SCAN...ENDSCAN loop, however, is generally used to process specific records (those that meet a filter condition) in a database. The general syntax for SCAN...ENDSCAN is

```
SCAN [<scope>] [FOR <condition>] [WHILE <condition>]
        <commands to perform>
ENDSCAN
```

The <condition> component must be a valid expression that results in a true or false result. The <commands to perform> component can be any number of commands, each on a separate line. Exactly one ENDSCAN command is required for every SCAN command.

Figure 18.14 shows a sample SCAN...ENDSCAN loop that acts upon every record in the CustList database that has .F. in the Logical field, Paid. To create the command file, enter the command **MODIFY COMMAND TestScan** at the dot prompt, typing it exactly as shown in the figure.

After creating and saving the command file, you can run it by entering the command **DO TestScan** at the dot prompt. The results will show the first name, last name, and paid status of records that have .F. in the Paid field, as follows:

```
Annie    Adams    .F.
Ralph    Kenney   .F.
All done.
```

The command file uses the command USE CustList to open the CustList database (which is presumably in the current directory).

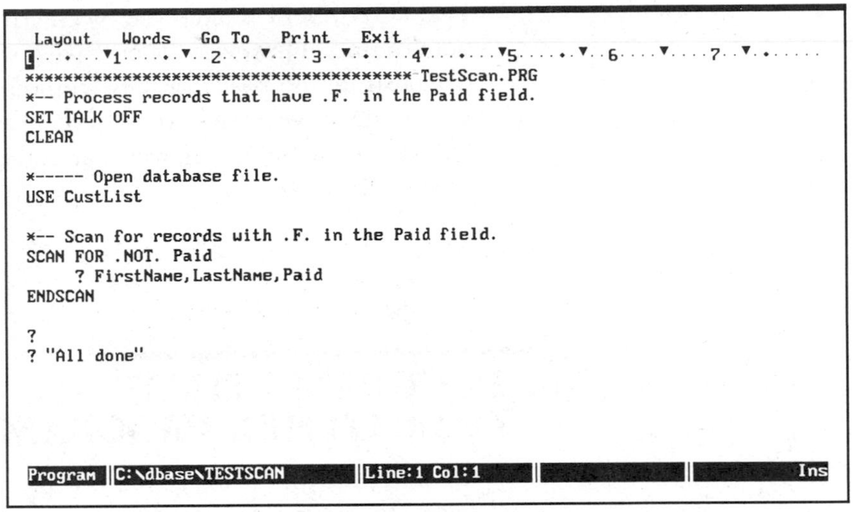

```
Layout   Words   Go To   Print   Exit
[····▼1····▼··2····▼····3··▼·····4▼······▼5·····▼··6····▼····7··▼······
************************************** TestScan.PRG
*-- Process records that have .F. in the Paid field.
SET TALK OFF
CLEAR

*----- Open database file.
USE CustList

*-- Scan for records with .F. in the Paid field.
SCAN FOR .NOT. Paid
     ? FirstName,LastName,Paid
ENDSCAN

?
? "All done"



Program ||C:\dbase\TESTSCAN        ||Line:1 Col:1 ||        ||         Ins
```

Figure 18.14: Sample program with SCAN...ENDSCAN commands

SCAN automatically starts processing from the first record in the database, so there is no need to use GO TOP to ensure that the record pointer is properly positioned. The command SCAN FOR .NOT. PAID tells dBASE to look at each record in the database, starting at the top and working downward (either in the natural order or in the order imposed by the current index, if one is in use).

In this example, dBASE automatically ignores every record that has .T. in the Paid field. As soon as dBASE encounters a record with .F. (that is, a record with .NOT. Paid), it processes all commands between the SCAN and ENDSCAN commands. In this case, it simply prints the contents of the FirstName, LastName, and Paid fields.

A SKIP command is not required in a SCAN...ENDSCAN clause, because the ENDSCAN command automatically skips records as it scans the database. When SCAN...ENDSCAN encounters the end of the file, it automatically passes control to the first command beneath the ENDSCAN command. In this example, the commands are ? (to print a blank line) and ? "All done." (to print the message "All done.").

Note that, again, this example is not very practical, because you could get the same results that the SCAN...ENDSCAN loop produces with the much simpler command LIST LastName, FirstName,

Paid FOR .NOT. Paid (even by entering the command directly at the dot prompt). However, for now we'll stick with simple programs that demonstrate the basics of these commands. In a real-life application, you might have many commands in a DO WHILE...ENDDO or SCAN...ENDSCAN clause that could not be duplicated with any single command.

PROGRAMS THAT CALL OTHER PROGRAMS

To run a program at the dot prompt, you enter the DO command followed by the name of a command file. Any command file that you create can also contain a DO command to run another program. As soon as dBASE encounters a DO command within a command file, it automatically executes the commands in the program that was *called by* (specified in) the DO command. When dBASE has executed all commands in the called program, processing resumes at the next command line in the calling program.

To see how programs that call other programs work, we'll create three files: Main.PRG, Sub1.PRG, and Sub2.PRG. Main.PRG will call Sub1.PRG, which will in turn call Sub2.PRG. Each command file will display some messages and create one memory variable. Sub2.PRG will return control to Sub1.PRG after it finishes its jobs, and Sub1.PRG will return control to Main.PRG after it finishes its jobs.

To try the command files, enter **MODIFY COMMAND Main** at the dot prompt and create the Main.PRG command file as shown in Figure 18.15. Save the command file after creating it, but don't run it yet.

After creating and saving Main.PRG, enter the command **MODIFY COMMAND Sub1** at the dot prompt and create the Sub1.PRG command file as shown in Figure 18.16. Then save the command file, but don't run it yet.

```
 Layout   Words   Go To   Print   Exit
[····•···▼1····█·▼··2····▼····3··▼·•·····4▼····•···▼5·····•·▼··6····▼····7··▼·•······
************************************** Main.PRG
*__ Calls separate Sub1 and Sub2 command files.
SET TALK OFF
CLEAR

? "Am currently running Main.PRG.  Here I will create"
? "a memory variable named MainVar."

MainVar = "Created in Main.PRG"
?
? "Now I will call Sub1.PRG"

*_________ Call the Sub1.PRG command file.
DO Sub1
?
? "Back to me, Main.PRG now.  Sub1 and Sub2 have finished their jobs."
?
WAIT "Now press any key to see remaining memory variables."

DISPLAY MEMORY
Program ||C:\dbase\MAIN          ||Line:20 Col:15 ||          ||          Ins
```

Figure 18.15: The Main.PRG command file

```
 Layout   Words   Go To   Print   Exit
[···•·█·▼1·····•·▼··2····▼····3··▼·•·····4▼····•···▼5·····•·▼··6····▼····7··▼·•······
************************************************* Sub1.PRG
*----------------- Sample command file called by Main.PRG.

?
? "        Hello.  Now I, Sub1.PRG, am running, and will"
? "        create a memory variable named Sub1Var"

Sub1Var = "I was created in Sub1.PRG"

?
? "        Now I will call Sub2.PRG."

*-------- Call Sub2.PRG
DO Sub2

?
? "        Back to me, Sub1.PRG now.  I'll just RETURN control to Main.PRG"

*-------- Return control to calling program.
RETURN
Program ||C:\dbase\SUB1          ||Line:20 Col:7  ||          ||
```

Figure 18.16: The Sub1.PRG command file

After creating and saving Sub1.PRG, enter the command **MODIFY COMMAND Sub2** at the dot prompt and type the Sub2.PRG command file exactly as shown in Figure 18.17. Save the command file after typing it, but don't run it yet.

```
 Layout   Words   Go To   Print   Exit
[····◆·█·▼1·····◆·▼··2····▼····3··▼·◆·····4▼·····◆····▼5·····◆·▼··6····▼····7··▼·◆·····
******************************** Sub2.PRG
* Sample command file called by Sub1.PRG

?
? "                   Howdy howdy.  It's me, Sub2.PRG running now."
? "                   I'll create a memory variable named Sub2Var."

Sub2Var = "I was created in Sub2.PRG"

?
? "                   Now I will RETURN to Sub2.PRG"

*--------- Return control to calling program.
RETURN




Program  C:\dbase\SUB2            Line:14 Col:7
```

Figure 18.17: The Sub2.PRG command file

After creating and saving all three files, run the Main.PRG command file by entering the command **DO Main** at the dot prompt. Your screen will show the results shown in Figure 18.18.

Note that each command file displayed its results on the screen. That's because each was called by a DO command in the preceding program. Also, Sub2.PRG and Sub1.PRG both used the RETURN

```
Am currently running Main.PRG. Here I will create
a memory variable named MainVar.

Now I will call Sub1.PRG

       Hello.  Now I, Sub1.PRG, am running, and will
       create a memory variable named Sub1Var

       Now I will call Sub2.PRG

             Howdy howdy.  It's me, Sub2.PRG running now.
             I'll create a memory variable named Sub2Var

             Now I will RETURN control to Sub1.PRG

       Back to me, Sub1.PRG now.  I'll just RETURN control to Main.PRG

Back to me, Main.PRG, now.  Sub1 and Sub2 have finished their jobs.

Now press any key to see remaining memory variables.
MAIN
```

Figure 18.18: Results of running Main.PRG

command to pass control back to the calling program. Study the results of running Main.PRG and refer to the original source code in Figures 18.15 through 18.17 to follow the exact steps that dBASE followed.

When you press any key to see all existing memory variables, you may be surprised to see that only one variable of the three created in Main.PRG, Sub1.PRG, and Sub2.PRG still exists, as shown here:

```
MAINVAR    priv    C    "Created in Main.PRG"    MAIN @ main.prg
```

What happened to the memory variables that were created in Sub1.PRG and Sub2.PRG?

As mentioned earlier, some variables have a shorter life than others. The rule of thumb is that any variable created in a command file is automatically erased when the program returns control to a calling program or to the dot prompt. Therefore, the Sub1Var and Sub2Var variables have been erased, because they were created in programs that eventually returned control to a calling program.

Press any key to scroll through the DISPLAY MEMORY screens until you get back to the dot prompt. If you then enter the command **DISPLAY MEMORY** at the dot prompt, you'll see that even the MainVar variable has been eliminated. That's because when Main.PRG ended and returned control to the dot prompt, the variable that it created, MainVar, was also erased.

NOTE

If you press the Esc key to interrupt the output of the DISPLAY MEMORY command, dBASE displays the message *** INTERRUPTED *** and returns you to the dot prompt.

PRIVATE AND PUBLIC MEMORY VARIABLES

In some situations, you may want to retain variables that were created in a called program after that program returns control to its calling program. To do so, you must declare the variables that you want to keep as public, using the PUBLIC command. A variable must be declared public before it is created.

To see how PUBLIC works, enter the command **MODIFY COMMAND Main** and add the command **PUBLIC MainVar, Sub1Var, Sub2Var** near the top of Main.PRG, as shown in Figure 18.19 (beneath the CLEAR command). This PUBLIC command declares all three memory variables created in the three separate programs as PUBLIC before any of them are created.

```
 Layout   Words   Go To   Print   Exit
[····•···▼1·····•·▼··2····▼····3··▼·•·····4▼·····•···▼5·····•·▼··6····▼····7··▼·•·····
************************************ Main.PRG
*__ Calls separate Sub1 and Sub2 command files.
SET TALK OFF
CLEAR
PUBLIC MainVar, Sub1Var, Sub2Var
? "Am currently running Main.PRG.  Here I will create"
? "a memory variable named MainVar."

MainVar = "Created in Main.PRG"
?
? "Now I will call Sub1.PRG"

*_________ Call the Sub1.PRG command file.
DO Sub1
?
? "Back to me, Main.PRG now.  Sub1 and Sub2 have finished their jobs."
?
WAIT "Now press any key to see remaining memory variables."

DISPLAY MEMORY
Program ||C:\dbase\MAIN          ||Line:5 Col:33 ||              ||
```

Figure 18.19: Main.PRG with PUBLIC command added

After making the change to Main.PRG and saving the modified command file, enter the command **DO Main** at the dot prompt to test the results. On the surface, the program will produce exactly the same results that it produced the first time you ran it. However, after you press any key to see remaining memory variables, you'll see that all three memory variables still exist, as follows:

```
SUB2VAR    pub   C   "I was created in Sub2.PRG"
SUB1VAR    pub   C   "I was created in Sub1.PRG"
MAINVAR    pub   C   "Created in Main.PRG"
```

In fact, if you press any key a few times to scroll through the remaining pages of the DISPLAY MEMORY display until you get to the dot prompt and then enter the command **DISPLAY MEMORY** again, you'll see that these same three memory variables still exist.

PROCEDURES AND PARAMETERS

As you know, dBASE IV offers many commands for building programs and managing your data. But dBASE IV's commands are very general, and you may need specialized commands for your own particular work that dBASE does not offer. Even though you cannot simply create your own commands, you can create procedures (also called *subroutines*) that are almost like custom commands.

For example, dBASE IV does not offer a command to center text on the screen; that is, you cannot enter the command **CENTER "Sales Summary Report"** to automatically have the title in quotation marks centered on the screen. However, you can create a procedure named CENTER that does indeed center any title on the screen. You could then access this procedure from any command file or application or even from the dot prompt with a command such as DO Center WITH "Sales Summary Report".

Procedures are generally stored in a *procedure file,* which is separate from any command files that you create. After you create a procedure file, you need to open it with SET PROCEDURE TO <file name>, where <file name> is the name of the procedure. Once the procedure file is open, you can access any of its procedures at any time.

You can also incorporate procedures directly into your command files, as discussed later in this chapter; in fact, doing so eliminates the need for many separate procedure files and can make your programs run more quickly. However, be sure that you do not assign the same name to a command file and to a procedure contained in that command file, because dBASE treats the compiled command file itself as a procedure. Also keep in mind that if you incorporate a procedure into a command file, you don't need to use the SET PROCEDURE TO command to open that procedure.

Within the procedure or command file, each procedure uses the general syntax

```
PROCEDURE <procedure name>
[PARAMETERS <parameter list>]
        <commands>
RETURN
```

No two procedures in the same procedure file or command file can have the same name, nor can they have the same name as the procedure file or command file itself.

where <procedure name> begins with a letter and can be any number of letters, numbers, and underscores (but no blank spaces or punctuation); however, only the first nine characters are used, and these must form a unique name. The PARAMETERS command assigns variable names to data that is passed to the procedure. In the <parameter list> component, you list these variable names, separating each with a comma. The <commands> component can be any number of dBASE IV commands, each on a separate line. Every procedure must end with a RETURN command.

CREATING A PROCEDURE FILE

To develop a procedure file, you use MODIFY COMMAND as usual. Let's create a procedure file that contains a procedure similar to the Center procedure discussed earlier. We'll name the procedure file ProcLib1 (for Procedure Library 1), so at the dot prompt enter the command **MODIFY COMMAND ProcLib1**. When the editor appears, type the CENTER procedure as shown in Figure 18.20.

Note that the procedure is named Center in the PROCEDURE command. We've told dBASE that we will be passing two PARAMETERS to this procedure file, which the procedure can store in memory variables named Titled and RMargin.

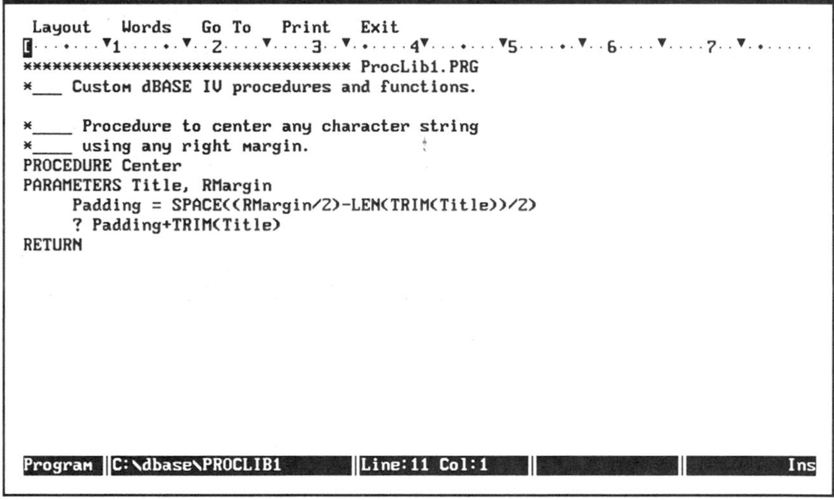

Layout Words Go To Print Exit
********************************** ProcLib1.PRG
*___ Custom dBASE IV procedures and functions.
*____ Procedure to center any character string
*____ using any right margin.
PROCEDURE Center
PARAMETERS Title, RMargin
Padding = SPACE((RMargin/2)-LEN(TRIM(Title))/2)
? Padding+TRIM(Title)
RETURN
Program
C:\dbase\PROCLIB1
Line:11 Col:1
Ins

Figure 18.20: The Center procedure in the ProcLib1 file

Within the body of the procedure, the first command Padding = SPACE((RMargin/2) – LEN(TRIM(Title))/2) calculates the number of blank spaces required to center the title and create the appropriate number of spaces. Let's see how dBASE does this. Suppose that the right margin (RMargin) is 80, and the Title to be centered is initially "Sales Summary Report." First, dBASE fills in the data in place of the variable named RMargin and Title, so the expression looks like this:

```
Padding = SPACE((80/2) – LEN(TRIM("Sales Summary Report"))/2)
```

Because dBASE works from the innermost parentheses out, it next trims off any trailing blanks from the title. (In this example, however, there are no trailing blanks.) Next, the LEN() function returns the length of the title, which is 20 characters in this example, so the expression now looks like this:

```
Padding = SPACE((80/2) – 20/2)
```

Next, dBASE does the division, so the expression looks like this:

```
Padding = SPACE(40 – 10)
```

The subtraction takes place, producing 30, so the Padding variable is assigned SPACE(30)—thirty blank spaces.

The command ? Padding + TRIM(Title) prints the leading blank spaces, followed by the title with any trailing blank spaces removed. Hence, the title is printed with exactly enough leading blank spaces to center it on an 80-character-wide screen.

After typing the entire procedure, choose Exit ► Save Changes and Exit to save it.

OPENING A PROCEDURE FILE

NOTE

dBASE also provides a SET LIBRARY TO command that's similar to SET PROCEDURE TO, as discussed later in this chapter. You only need to use these SET commands if your procedure is stored in a separate procedure or library file, but not if it's part of the command file that you're running from the dot prompt via DO <file name>.

You need to open a procedure file before you can use any of the procedures stored in it. To open a procedure file, you use the SET PROCEDURE command. In this example, you need to enter the following command to open the ProcLib1.PRG procedure file:

```
SET PROCEDURE TO ProcLib1
```

To test the procedure, enter the command

```
DO Center WITH "Sales Summary Report",80
```

You'll see the title perfectly centered on your screen (assuming that your screen is 80 characters wide).

You can also pass data stored in memory variables to the procedure. For example, if you enter the following commands at the dot prompt (making sure to follow each with a press on the ↵ key), you'll see the title "Accounts Receivable Aging Report" centered on the screen:

```
CenTitle = "Accounts Receivable Aging Report"
Right = 80

DO Center WITH CenTitle,Right
```

Note that in the preceding example, the DO Center command uses different variable names than were specified in the PARAMETERS statement of the procedure. This is perfectly okay, because the PARAMETERS statement assigns its own variable names to the data passed to it. You can use the same variable names as the PARAMETERS statement if you wish, but there is no need to do so. Just make certain that you pass the data in the same order that it is defined in the procedure. For example, the first variable passed in the WITH portion of the DO command must correspond to the first variable defined in the PARAMETERS command. Hence, the passed variable CenTitle corresponds to the Title variable in the procedure, and the passed variable Right corresponds to the RMargin variable in the procedure. If you pass the parameters to the procedure in a different order, the procedure will not work correctly.

Now suppose you are printing reports on paper that is 130 characters wide. To center a title on the wide paper, you pass 130 as the right margin to the parameter, as follows:

```
DO Center WITH "Customer List",130
```

As you can see, the procedure offers considerable flexibility, because you can pass any character string and any right margin to it.

Another feature that adds flexibility to procedures is dBASE's treatment of memory variables always as private (local) to the current command file or procedure. Therefore, you need never worry about what memory variables are being created or changed within a procedure. After a procedure finishes its job, it erases all its own memory variables and returns control to the calling program. Any memory variables that happened to have the same names as memory variables created and used in the procedure file will retain their original values.

Once you open a procedure file using the SET PROCEDURE command, the file stays open until you either exit dBASE IV or

The CLOSE ALL command closes all files of all types, including databases and libraries. CLOSE PROCEDURE only closes a procedure file.

enter the command **CLOSE PROCEDURE** or **CLOSE ALL**. If you attempt to access a procedure that is not in a currently open procedure file, dBASE responds with the error message, "File does not exist."

MODIFYING A PROCEDURE FILE

If you need to modify a procedure file, you should first enter the command **CLOSE PROCEDURE** to close the procedure file. Then use the MODIFY COMMAND editor to make your changes. After saving the modified procedure and returning to the dot prompt, enter the SET PROCEDURE TO <file name> command to open the new, modified procedure file.

USER-DEFINED FUNCTIONS

You've seen how to create procedures that act something like custom dBASE IV commands. You can also create your own custom dBASE IV functions, called *user-defined functions* (or UDFs). For example, suppose you often need to present dates in the format *January 15, 1993,* rather than in the MM/DD/YY format that dBASE offers.

NOTE

Actually, the dBASE MDY( ) function displays dates in the format *December 06, 1992,* but our function displays dates in *December 6, 1992* format.

dBASE does not offer any particular function to make this conversion for you automatically. But you can create your own function to make this conversion and use it in any command, report column, custom screen, or dBASE IV program, just as you use any other dBASE IV function.

Like procedures, user-defined functions can be stored in a procedure file or in a command file. The general syntax for creating a user-defined function is similar to that used to create a procedure, as shown here:

```
FUNCTION <name>
PARAMETERS <passed to function>
        <commands>
RETURN <result of function>
```

The name of the function, <name>, can be up to ten characters long, must begin with a letter, and cannot contain blank spaces or

WARNING

A UDF must not have the same name as an existing dBASE function (the UDF will be ignored in favor of the dBASE function). Furthermore, no two functions in a procedure file or command file can have the same name, nor can they have the same name as the procedure file or command file itself.

punctuation marks. The <passed to function> component assigns a memory variable name to whatever information is passed to the function. The assigned memory variable name is private to the current function and will not affect any previously defined variable that has the same name.

With some restrictions that don't concern us right now, the <commands> component can be any series of valid dBASE IV commands, but each one must be entered on a separate line. The <result of function> component specifies what should be returned to the calling command.

To see how user-defined functions work, we'll add such a function, named PropDate(), to the ProcLib1 procedure file. To do so, first enter the command **CLOSE PROCEDURE** (just to make sure that the procedure file is not still open from the previous exercise). Then enter the command **MODIFY COMMAND ProcLib1** at the dot prompt. When the procedure file appears on the screen, press the PgDn key to move the cursor to the bottom of the file. If you need to add some blank lines beneath the Center procedure, press the End key and then press ⟵ a couple of times. Type in the user-defined function as shown in Figure 18.21.

```
 Layout   Words   Go To   Print   Exit
[····▼1····▼·2····▼····3··▼·····4▼······▼5·····▼··6····▼····7··▼·····
********************************* ProcLib1.PRG
*__ Custom dBASE IV procedures and functions.

*___ Procedure to center any character string
*___ using any right margin.
PROCEDURE Center
PARAMETERS Title, RMargin
     Padding = SPACE((RMargin/2)-LEN(TRIM(Title))/2)
     ? Padding+TRIM(Title)
RETURN

*-- Function to convert MM/DD/YY dates to proper format.
FUNCTION PropDate
PARAMETERS ThisDate
     SET TALK OFF
     Month    = CMONTH(ThisDate)
     Day      = LTRIM(STR(DAY(ThisDate),2,0))
     Year     = STR(YEAR(ThisDate),4,0)
     ThisDate = Month+" "+Day+", "+Year
RETURN ThisDate
Program ||C:\dbase\PROCLIB1      ||Line:20 Col:16 ||          ||      Ins
```

Figure 18.21: Sample user-defined function

Let's discuss how the function works. The FUNCTION command assigns the name PropDate. The PARAMETERS command assigns the private variable name ThisDate to whatever date is passed to the function. The next command, Month = CMONTH (ThisDate), stores the month name (for example, June) in a variable named Month.

The command Day = LTRIM(STR(DAY(ThisDate),2,0)) converts the day of the month to a Character data type. For example, if the date being converted is 06/05/92, then DAY(ThisDate) returns the number 5, the STR() function converts that number to a Character string with two spaces and no decimal places (that is, " 5"), and LTRIM trims off any leading blanks (producing "5").

The command Year = STR(YEAR(ThisDate),4,0) converts the year (for example, 1992) to a four-digit Character string with no decimal places. Because all three components have been converted to Character data, they can be combined into a single character string; the ThisDate = Month + " " + Day + ", " + Year command takes care of that step.

Note that to insert a blank space between the month and the day, the command uses + " " +, rather than a comma. This entry is necessary because a comma is allowed only in commands that *display* data (such as ?). When combining character strings to *store* them in a memory variable or field, you must use + " "·+ to insert a blank space.

The last command, RETURN ThisDate, returns the value stored in the ThisDate variable to the calling command.

After creating the function, choose Exit ► Save Changes and Exit. When you get back to the dot prompt, enter the command **SET PROCEDURE TO ProcLib1** to open the procedure file.

There are several ways you can use the PropDate() function. To see the current date translated to the new format, enter the command **? PropDate(DATE())**. You will see the current date expressed in the format December 31, 1992.

If the CUSTLIST database is available on the current directory, you can enter this series of commands to list all dates in their original and converted formats (be sure to press ↵ after typing each command at the dot prompt):

```
USE CustList

LIST StartDate,PropDate(StartDate)
```

The resulting display should look something like this:

Record #	StartDate	PropDate(StartDate)
1	11/15/92	November 15, 1992
2	01/01/93	January 1, 1993
3	12/01/92	December 1, 1992
4	12/15/92	December 15, 1992
5	12/15/92	December 15, 1992
6	12/30/92	December 30, 1992
7	12/30/92	December 30, 1992
8	01/01/93	January 1, 1993
9	07/01/92	July 1, 1992
10	07/25/92	July 25, 1992

When the ProcLib1 procedure file is open, you can use the function PropDate( ) in any report format, label format, custom screen, or application. For example, you could add a calculated field that contains the expression PropDate(DATE()) to the top of a form letter to print the current date, in proper format, above the recipient's name and address. (The ProcLib1 procedure file must be open when you print the form letter that uses the PROPDATE() function, unless you've placed the function into a command file that prints the form letter.)

PROCEDURE FILE LIMITATIONS

A single procedure file can contain a maximum of 963 procedures and user-defined functions. However, an open procedure file is always stored in RAM (random-access memory). Therefore the real limitation on the number of procedures and user-defined functions that a procedure file can contain depends on the amount of RAM your computer has.

USING PROCEDURES AND FUNCTIONS IN A PROGRAM

We've already mentioned that you can place procedures and functions directly into a command file instead of creating a separate procedure file. Let's try a simple example that uses the Center procedure and PropDate function in a command file. To save some typing, you can copy the existing procedure file named ProcLib1.Prg to a new file named TestProg.Prg. Enter the following command at the dot prompt:

```
COPY FILE ProcLib1.Prg TO TestProg.Prg
```

If TestProg.Prg already exists, dBASE will display a warning message and give you a chance to Overwrite or Cancel the copy. If you choose to cancel the copy, you can re-enter the above command with a different file name in place of TestProg.Prg.

Now edit the new TestProg.Prg file by entering the command **MODIFY COMMAND TestProg,** and making the changes shown in the upper portion of Figure 18.22. When you finish making the changes, choose Exit ► Save Changes and Exit, then test the program by entering **DO TestProg** at the dot prompt.

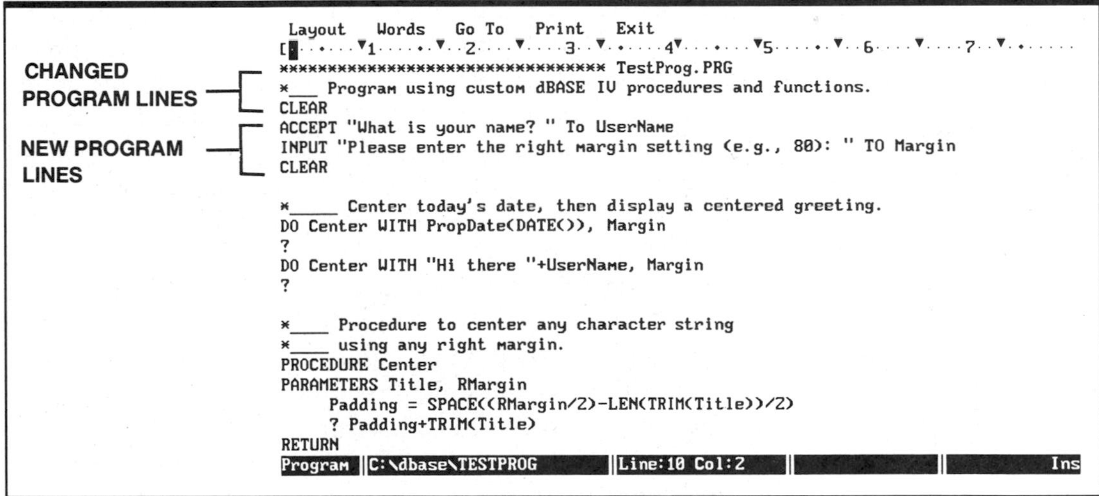

Figure 18.22: The TestProg.Prg program includes a procedure and function as well as program commands.

Let's see how this new program works. The first two lines are changed to reflect the new program name and purpose. The first CLEAR command clears the screen; the ACCEPT command prompts with "What is your name?" and stores the response in the UserName variable; then the INPUT command prompts for the right margin setting and stores the response in the Margin variable. Next, the program clears the screen again.

With the preliminaries out of the way, the command

```
DO Center WITH PropDate (DATE()), Margin
```

centers today's date on the screen. The first parameter of this command is PropDate(DATE()). As you already know, dBASE evaluates functions starting from the innermost set of parentheses and working outward. As always, the built-in dBASE function DATE () evaluates to today's date in MM/DD/YY format. So, if today is March 7, 1993, the DATE function returns "03/07/93", which is passed to the PropDate function as the parameter ThisDate. The function PropDate then returns the converted date as a character string (e.g., "March 7, 1993"), and the final result is March 7, 1993 centered on the screen using whatever margin setting you typed in response to the prompt. The ? following the first DO command displays a blank line. The second DO command centers the words "Hi there " combined with the name you entered earlier. Finally, the last ? displays another blank line on the screen. At this point the program is finished, so it returns you to the dBASE dot prompt.

The PROCEDURE ...RETURN and FUNCTION...RETURN clauses define procedures and functions, respectively, but they aren't executed unless a command calls them to action. Therefore, the program stops after the second question mark command.

The Center procedure and PropDate function are the same as in the ProcLibl.Prg procedure file discussed earlier (although the PropDate function has scrolled off the screen in Figure 18.22).

Now you may be wondering whether we could have created a small command file containing just the CLEAR, ACCEPT, INPUT, DO, and ? commands shown in Figure 18.22 *without* including the procedure and function. The answer is Yes, as long as we open the procedure file ProcLibl.Prg before executing our small program. In many ways, choosing to include procedures and functions along with the program that uses them, or deciding to place procedures and functions in a separate file, is a matter of personal preference. However, there are some reasons to choose one method over another, as we'll discuss in a moment. But before doing that, we must introduce two more wrinkles: procedure libraries and the SYSPROC configuration command.

PROCEDURE LIBRARIES

Procedure libraries are almost identical to the procedure files discussed earlier in that they can contain procedures, functions, or both. You create them the same way, with MODIFY COMMAND <filename>, and both have a .PRG file name extension. In fact, our procedure file ProcLibl can just as easily be used as a procedure library. The main differences between a procedure file and a procedure library are:

NOTE

The SET LIBRARY TO and SET PROCEDURE TO commands automatically close any library or procedure opened by a previous SET LIBRARY TO or SET PROCEDURE TO command.

- To open a procedure library, you use the SET LIBRARY TO <library name> command instead of the SET PROCEDURE TO command. For example, to open ProcLibl as a library, enter the command **SET LIBRARY TO ProcLibl.**
- To close a procedure library, you type SET LIBRARY TO without adding a library file name. (Typing SET PROCEDURE TO without adding a procedure file name is another way to close a procedure file.)
- dBASE searches procedure files before searching procedure libraries. For example, suppose you have a procedure file named ProcFile1.Prg and a procedure library named ProcLibl.Prg, both of which contain a procedure named Center. If you open both files using SET LIBRARY TO ProcLibl and SET PROCEDURE TO ProcFile1, dBASE will use the Center procedure from the ProcFile1 procedure file,and will ignore the Center procedure in the ProcLibl library file.

USING SYSPROC = TO ASSIGN A DEFAULT STARTUP LIBRARY

A special file named Config.Db defines certain startup information for dBASE, such as the type of monitor you use, the starting screen colors, whether you start up at the Control Center or the dot prompt, the type of printer you use, and so forth. Config.Db is maintained by the program named DBSETUP, which is described in Appendix B of this book.

NOTE

When you choose Files ► Sysproc and specify a pathname, DBSETUP adds the line *SYSPROC* = *<filename>* to your Config.Db file.

You can also use Config.Db to specify a library file that remains active throughout your dBASE session. For example, suppose you saved some general purpose procedures and functions in the file named MASTLIB.PRG in the \DBASE directory on drive C. After thoroughly testing those procedures and functions, you can run DBSETUP as explained in Appendix B. Choose Files ► Sysproc from the DBSETUP menu and enter **C:\DBASE\MASTLIB.PRG** as the Sysproc library. Save your changes and exit DBSETUP. The next time you run dBASE, those procedures and functions will be available, just as if they were built into dBASE.

HOW dBASE SEARCHES FOR PROCEDURES AND FUNCTIONS

With all these choices, how can you decide whether to use a default startup library, a command file containing procedures and functions, a procedure file, or a procedure library? The basic answer is this: Use a procedure file or procedure library if you want to share procedures and functions with other command files or if you want to use them at the dot prompt. Place procedures and functions directly in your command file if you want your program to run a bit faster, don't need to share those procedures and functions with other command files, and don't need to use them at the dot prompt.

Beyond that, it doesn't really matter unless the same procedure or function name exists in more than one place. If such duplicate names do exist, keep in mind that dBASE searches for a procedure or function in the following relative order:

> **NOTE**
> Remember that user-defined functions should never have the same name as a built-in dBASE IV function.

1. The filename specified in the SYSPROC = <filename> line in Config.Db, if this line exists.
2. The currently executing .DBO file (a .DBO file is the compiled version of a command file).
3. The SET PROCEDURE TO <filename>, if this command is active.
4. The SET LIBRARY TO <filename>, if this command is active.

OPENING MULTIPLE DATABASE FILES

Chapter 13 showed you how to open and manage multiple related database files through the queries design screen. You can also do so using dBASE IV commands. However, unlike the queries design screen, which protects data in multiple related database files through ReadOnly status, commands allow you to interact freely with these databases. This is particularly handy in complex business applications because it gives you the freedom to transfer data automatically from one database file to another. (You'll see examples of this in the chapters that follow.)

You use two primary commands to open and manage multiple database files: SELECT and USE. The SELECT command allows you to open up to forty work areas, each of which contains an open database file. These work areas are lettered A through J (for the first 10 work areas) or numbered 1 through 40. You select a work area, then use a database file in that work area.

You can experiment with these commands directly at the dot prompt. (In actual practice, you'll use them mostly in command files.) Assuming you are logged on to the \DBASE directory where the CUSTLIST.DBF and ORDERS.DBF databases are stored, enter the commands below at the dot prompt, pressing ↵ after each one (you won't see immediate results, but be patient):

```
SELECT A
USE Orders
SELECT B
USE CustList
```

Now that you have multiple databases open, you must use the SELECT command rather than the USE command to access a particular database. You can use either the work area number, the work area letter (for up to 10 work areas), or the database name with the SELECT command to access a particular work area.

As an example, try entering the command

```
LIST
```

When you enter this command, you'll see the contents of the *currently selected* database: CUSTLIST. To switch to the ORDERS database (making it the currently selected database), enter the command

```
SELECT Orders
```

To verify that the ORDERS database is now the currently selected database file, again enter the command

```
LIST
```

This time you'll see the contents of the ORDERS database. To switch back to the CUSTLIST database, making it the currently selected database, enter the command

```
SELECT CustList
```

To verify that the CUSTLIST database is now selected, enter **LIST** again.

Once you have opened multiple database files, you must avoid using the USE command to access a particular file. Let's try a brief experiment to demonstrate the reason. If you've followed along with all these steps and are currently in work area B with the CUSTLIST database opened, enter the command

```
USE Orders
```

dBASE will beep and display the error message "File already open." dBASE signals an error because it "thinks" you want to use the ORDERS database in the current work area (B), but "knows" that the ORDERS database is already open in work area A. (To remove the error message, select Cancel from the error message submenu.)

You are now ready to define a relationship between the two open database files; things are about to become much more interesting.

DEFINING RELATIONSHIPS AMONG FILES

When two or more open databases share a common field, you can use the SET RELATION command to define relationships between them. The general syntax for the SET RELATION command is SET RELATION TO <common field name> INTO <unselected database> where <common field name> is the name of the field that links the two files and <unselected database> is the name of the database that is being linked but is not currently selected. The unselected database must be indexed on the common field, and that index must be in use.

To demonstrate, let's assume that you want to see records from the ORDERS database along with customers' names, which are stored on the related CUSTLIST database. Let's start from scratch by closing all currently open databases. To do so, enter this command at the dot prompt:

```
CLOSE DATABASES
```

Now, to open the ORDERS and CUSTLIST databases and set up a relationship based on the common CUSTNO field, enter these commands:

```
SELECT A
USE Orders
SELECT B
USE CustList ORDER CustNo
SELECT Orders
SET RELATION TO CustNo INTO CustList
```

The first two commands open the ORDERS database in work area A. The next two open the CUSTLIST database and CUSTNO index in work area B. Because the relationship will be set from the ORDERS database into the CUSTLIST database, the CUSTNO index must be in use with the CUSTLIST database file.

The command SELECT Orders makes ORDERS the currently selected database. The SET RELATION command tells dBASE to set up a relationship from the currently selected ORDERS database INTO the CUSTLIST database based on the common field CUSTNO.

Note that ORDERS is the currently selected database because the last SELECT command in the preceding series was SELECT Orders. Assuming you have been following along through previous chapters and your ORDERS and CUSTLIST databases already contain some data, if you now enter the command

```
LIST
```

you should see whatever data you've entered into the Orders database up to this point. But suppose you want to see the customer name (that is, the COMPANY field from the CUSTLIST database) with each order as well.

Because you've opened both databases, and defined the relationship between them, you can list data from the unselected database by specifying an *alias* (the name, or work area, of the related database file), followed by a hyphen and a greater than sign (->), and then by the name of the field. For example, to see the CUSTNO and PARTNO fields from the ORDERS database and the appropriate last name and first name from the CUSTLIST database, enter the command

```
LIST CustNo,PartNo,B->FirstName,B->LastName
```

The screen will display each record from the ORDERS database, with the appropriate name from the CUSTLIST database, as shown here:

Record #	CustNo	PartNo	B->FirstName	B->LastName
1	1001	B-222	John	Smith
2	1002	B-222	Annie	Adams
3	1001	A-111	John	Smith
4	1001	C-333	John	Smith
5	1002	A-111	Annie	Adams
6	1003	A-111	Mary	Mahoney
7	1003	B-222	Mary	Mahoney
8	1004	C-333	John	Newell
9	1005	C-333	Sandy	Beach
10	1006	C-333	Ralph	Kenney

You can define relationships among up to forty databases at one time. Just remember that you can only add records to or change data in the currently selected database. In the next chapter, you will begin developing high-powered business data processing procedures and will see some practical applications of the SELECT, USE, and SET RELATION commands.

When you're finished experimenting with the LIST command, close the databases by typing **CLOSE DATABASES** and pressing ↵.

dBASE WINDOWS

Windows are a great technique for adding professional polish to your custom programs. A window pops up on the screen, temporarily overwriting any text behind it, to display information or options. After you select an option from the window, it disappears, revealing whatever was previously displayed in that position on the screen.

You've already seen many examples of windows in your work with dBASE IV. For example, error messages, prompt boxes, and messages

The Applications Generator also lets you create windows, as discussed in Chapter 21.

NOTE

Beyond the basic syntax discussed here, the DEFINE WINDOW command also provides options for creating custom borders and defining colors.

that present Yes/No options are all displayed in windows. In this section, you'll learn how to create, activate, and use windows. The chapters that follow will present some practical examples.

The command for defining a window is DEFINE WINDOW, which uses the basic syntax

```
DEFINE WINDOW <window name> FROM <row,column> TO <row,column>
[DOUBLE/PANEL/NONE]
```

where <window name> is a name you define, which can be up to ten characters long and may not contain spaces. The first <row, column> specifies the row and column position of the window's upper-left corner and the second <row,column> specifies the row and column position of the window's lower-right corner.

You can specify a border style with one of the last options in the command: DOUBLE (for a double-line border), PANEL (for a solid border with no lines), or NONE (no border).

Note that defining a window does not automatically display the window. To make the defined window appear on the screen, you must use the command ACTIVATE WINDOW <window name>. To remove a window from the screen, use the DEACTIVATE WINDOW <window name> command. Defined windows are stored in RAM and so take up a little memory space. To "un-define" a window, and free up the memory it uses, use the command RELEASE WINDOW <window name>. In all three commands, <window name> refers to the name used to define the window.

To try this command, we'll create a command file named TESTWIND.PRG. At the dot prompt, enter the command MODIFY COMMAND TestWind. When the blank editing screen appears, type the command file exactly as shown in Figure 18.23. After typing in the file, choose Exit ► Save Changes and Exit to return to the dot prompt.

To run the program, enter the command **DO TestWind** at the dot prompt and press ↵. You will see a message at the upper-left corner of the screen. Then, very quickly, you'll see the FirstName and LastName fields from the CUSTLIST database whiz by on the screen inside the window. Next, you'll see the messages "This LIST was displayed inside a window" and "Press any key to continue" displayed in the window, as shown in Figure 18.24.

```
 Layout   Words   Go To   Print   Exit
******************************************** TestWind.PRG
SET TALK OFF
CLEAR
@ 0,0 SAY "This is row 0, column 0, outside the window."

DEFINE WINDOW TestWind FROM 5,10 TO 15,70 DOUBLE
ACTIVATE WINDOW TestWind

USE CustList
LIST FirstName,LastName
? "This LIST was displayed inside a window"
WAIT

CLEAR
@ 0,0 SAY "This is row 0, column 0, inside the window"
WAIT "Press any key to remove the window..."

DEACTIVATE WINDOW TestWind
RELEASE WINDOW TestWind

Program ||C:\dbase\TESTWIND ||Line:1 Col:1 ||  ||  Ins
```

Figure 18.23: The TESTWIND.PRG command file

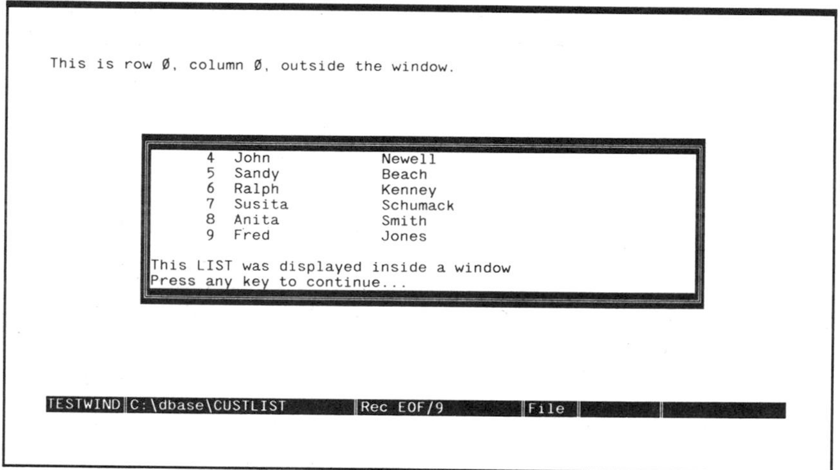

Figure 18.24: The TESTWIND window on the screen

After you press any key to continue, you'll see the messages "This is row zero, column 0, inside the window" and "Press any key to erase window" displayed in the window, as in Figure 18.25.

When you press any key, the window will be erased and you will be returned to the dot prompt. Let's discuss exactly why the TESTWIND program behaves the way it does.

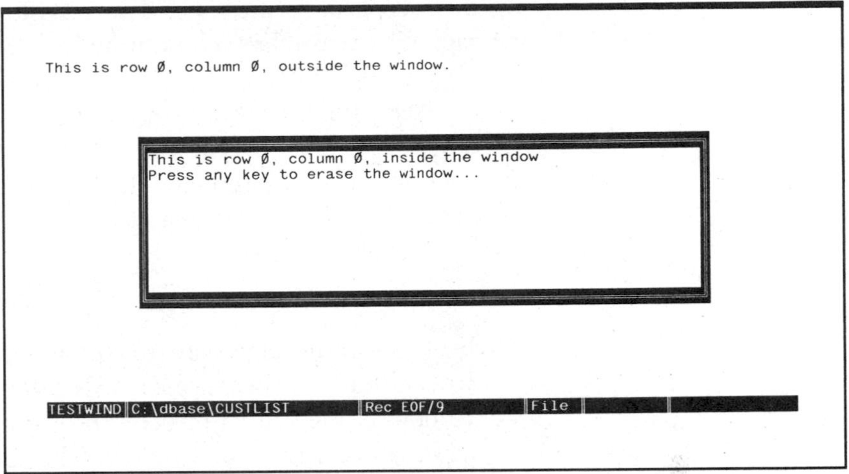
This is row Ø, column Ø, outside the window.
This is row Ø, column Ø, inside the window
Press any key to erase the window...
TESTWIND C:\dbase\CUSTLIST Rec EOF/9 File

Figure 18.25: Messages displayed inside the TESTWIND window

First, the opening commands SET TALK OFF and CLEAR turn the dBASE messages off and erase the entire screen (except for the status bar). Then the command

```
@ 0,0 SAY "This is row 0, column 0, outside the window."
```

displays the message in quotation marks at row zero, column zero, on the screen.

The next command,

```
DEFINE WINDOW TestWind FROM 5,10 TO 15,70 DOUBLE
```

defines a window named TestWind, that will extend from row 5, column 10 to row 15, column 70 on the screen. The command ACTIVATE WINDOW TestWind actually displays the window. When a window is activated, dBASE acts as though the area defined by the window is the entire screen and presents all displays within the window, as the remaining commands demonstrate.

The commands USE CustList and LIST FirstName,LastName open the CUSTLIST database and display the contents of the FirstName and LastName fields. Because the window is active, this display appears within the boundaries of the window. The command

```
? "This LIST was displayed inside a window"
```

then displays its message. The WAIT command produces the message "Press any key to continue" on the screen and waits for you to press a key.

Next, the CLEAR command clears just the contents of the window. Because the window is active, dBASE "thinks" that its boundaries are the entire screen. The message at the top of the screen, outside the window, is not erased.

The next command

```
@ 0,0 SAY "This is row 0, column 0, inside the window"
```

displays the message between quotation marks at row 0, column 0. But, once again, because dBASE "thinks" that the currently active window is the entire screen, the message actually appears at the upper-left corner of the window. The command

```
WAIT "Press any key to erase the window..."
```

displays its message and waits for you to press any key.

After you press a key, the command DEACTIVATE WINDOW TestWind removes the window from the screen. Then the command RELEASE WINDOW TestWind removes the window from memory. Finally, the command file ends and you are returned to the dot prompt with everything back to normal.

OTHER COMMANDS

Most of the commands in this chapter have focused on programming techniques, such as user-interfacing, decision making, looping, windows, and so on. These are the basic building blocks from which you create highly sophisticated and complex dBASE IV applications.

Other commands dBASE IV offers mimic actions that you can initiate from the Control Center. You can use these commands at the dot prompt, in command files, and even while developing applications using the Applications Generator (as you'll see in Chapter 21). They allow your applications and command files to perform operations automatically that would otherwise need to be selected from options on the pull-down menus. Hence, you can develop custom programs and applications that completely bypass the Control Center. Table 18.1 lists some of these commands.

Table 18.1: Some Useful dBASE IV Commands

Operation	Command
Activate custom form	SET FORMAT TO
Add new records	APPEND
Browse database records	BROWSE
Calculate results	CALCULATE
Copy from a database	APPEND FROM
Copy to a new database	COPY
Create a custom form	CREATE SCREEN
Create a label format	CREATE LABEL
Create a query	CREATE QUERY
Create a report format	CREATE REPORT
Edit a record	EDIT
Exit dBASE IV	QUIT
Forward search	LOCATE or LOOKUP()
Go to a record	GOTO
Index key search	SEEK or SEEK() function
Mark records for deletion	DELETE
Modify a custom form	MODIFY FORM
Modify a label format	MODIFY LABEL
Modify a query	MODIFY QUERY
Modify a report format	MODIFY REPORT
Open a database file	USE
Order records by index	SET ORDER or USE...ORDER
Print a report	REPORT FORM
Print labels	LABEL FORM
Remove marked records	PACK
Skip records	SKIP
Substitute field values	REPLACE

Remember, to get further information about any command, you can enter HELP <command> at the dot prompt; <command> represents a command that you want help with. In addition, the *dBASE IV Language Reference* manual that came with your dBASE IV package describes every command in detail. Rather than repeating all of that information here, the remainder of this book will demonstrate practical techniques for *using* dBASE IV commands and programming techniques for building applications.

CHAPTER 19

Business Data Processing

To automatically assign customer numbers 688
in a business application, use commands to locate the largest existing customer number and then use a SCAN...ENDSCAN loop with a REPLACE command to fill in new customer numbers.

To automatically assign invoice numbers 693
in a business application, use a SCAN...ENDSCAN loop with a REPLACE command that assigns invoice numbers to each group of orders for a customer.

To automatically update inventory in-stock quantities 701
from items received in a business application, use the UPDATE command.

To update in-stock quantities and handle backorders 706
simultaneously in a business application, open both the inventory and orders databases and use REPLACE commands to adjust in-stock and backorder quantities.

To prevent fulfilled orders from affecting in-stock quantities 708
in the future in a business application, move the fulfilled orders to a separate order-history file and convert backorders to outstanding orders.

To calculate order totals, 710
write an expression that subtracts the discount from the extended price and then add the tax and shipping amount.

To convert individual orders to invoices for accounts receivable, 711
use the TOTAL command to summarize individual orders and then copy the summarized data to a separate database file of invoices.

WHEN YOU BEGIN TO DEVELOP LARGER, MORE sophisticated applications, you will undoubtedly need to use a combination of all the tools that dBASE IV offers: the design screens, the Applications Generator, and programming commands and techniques. Programming is generally required to handle complex business *data processing* needs, such as managing accounts receivable, inventory, order processing, and so forth.

For example, the forms design screen lets you design custom forms for entering data into a database, as well as for making changes to existing data. The labels and reports design screens let you create formats for printing data. These screens allow you to enter data *into* the database and get information *out of* the database. This is sufficient if you use your application only for storing and retrieving information. But large, complex business applications usually need to do quite a bit of work after data is entered and before it's printed. For example, an inventory management and accounts receivable application might have to perform all of the following steps:

- Allow orders to be entered into a database.
- Check whether enough stock exists in inventory to fulfill the order.
- When an order is fulfilled, subtract the number of items shipped from the in-stock quantity to keep the inventory up to date.
- If an order cannot be fulfilled, subtract the stock that is in inventory and place the out-of-stock items on backorder.
- Prepare an invoice.
- Keep track of accounts receivable and print monthly statements.

These steps and decisions involved in fulfilling an order are all part of the data processing component of an application. Programming is usually required to achieve these steps because programming offers the precise control needed during each step in a data processing operation.

In this chapter, we'll look at some examples of business data processing programming techniques and begin building a sophisticated business management application. Be forewarned that building such a large and sophisticated application is going to take quite an investment of time on your part and a strong working knowledge of the information in all the chapters preceding this one.

Note that if you would prefer to use the sample application without investing all the time involved in creating it, you can purchase a ready-to-run copy of the application using the order form at the back of this book.

CREATING A DIRECTORY FOR THE APPLICATION

We'll store the business management application on a subdirectory named dBASE\Business. To create this subdirectory, you need to be at the DOS level. If you are currently using dBASE IV, choose Exit ► Quit to DOS from the menu above the Control Center. Then (assuming you are using hard disk drive C), follow these steps to create the new subdirectory:

1. Type **CD** and press ↵ to switch to the root directory.
2. Type **MD \dBASE\Business** and press ↵ to create the subdirectory.

SWITCHING TO THE NEW SUBDIRECTORY

Whenever you wish to work on or use the business management application, you must first switch to the \dBASE\Business subdirectory. To do so (before you run dBASE IV), enter the command **CD \dBASE\Business** at the DOS prompt (and press ↵, of course). If you are already in dBASE IV and the Control Center is displayed on your screen, you can switch to the \dBASE\Business directory by following these steps:

1. Choose Tools ► DOS Utilities.
2. Choose DOS ► Set Default Drive:Directory.

3. Specify **\dBASE\Business** as the new subdirectory (and press ↵).
4. Choose Exit ► Exit to Control Center.

RUNNING dBASE IV FROM THE SUBDIRECTORY

To run dBASE IV, enter the usual command **DBASE** at the DOS prompt. (If the error message "Bad command or file name" appears, refer to Appendix B for information about how to reconfigure your AutoExec.bat file.) When the dBASE IV Control Center appears, follow these steps to create a catalog named Business.cat:

1. Choose Catalog ► Use a Different Catalog.
2. Select <create> from the submenu that appears.
3. Type **Business** when prompted for the catalog name and press ↵.

In the future, whenever you run dBASE IV from the subdirectory \dBASE\Business, the Business catalog will appear in the Control Center automatically.

BUSINESS APPLICATION DATABASE FILES

NOTE

Remember: To create a database file, you select <create> from the Data panel of the Control Center.

In this chapter, we will develop some of the general data processing procedures for the sample business application. First, however, you need to create the database files for the application. After defining the structure of each database file, choose Exit ► Save Changes and Exit.

THE CUSTOMER DATABASE FILE

The first database file that you'll create will store customer information. We'll assume for this application that most customers are companies (though the application will also allow entries for individuals who have no company affiliation). Enter the structure of the database as shown in Figure 19.1. Note that the CustNo field is indexed (marked Y in the Index column). The descriptions in Figure 19.1 are for reference only; you cannot enter these on your screen.

When you save the database structure and are prompted for a name, assign the name **Customer**.

THE MASTER DATABASE FILE

The Master database file holds information about each item in the inventory, including current in-stock (on-hand) quantities. Figure 19.2 shows the structure of the Master database, which you can create now. Note that the PartNo field is marked Y for indexing.

After creating the structure, save it and specify **Master** as the file name.

Structure for database: C:\DBASE\BUSINESS\CUSTOMER.DBF

Num	Field Name	Type	Width	Dec	Index	Description
1	CUSTNO	Numeric	4		Y	Customer number
2	COMPANY	Character	25		N	Company name
3	CONTACT	Character	25		N	Contact person
4	ADDRESS	Character	25		N	Company address
5	CITY	Character	20		N	City
6	STATE	Character	2		N	State
7	ZIP	Character	10		N	Zip code
8	PHONE	Character	13		N	Phone numbers
9	STARTDATE	Date	8		N	Became customer
10	TAXRATE	Numeric	5	2	N	Tax rate, if any
11	DISCRATE	Numeric	5	2	N	Discount rate, if any
12	YTDCHRG	Numeric	8	2	N	Year-to-date charges
13	YTDPMT	Numeric	8	2	N	Year-to-date payments
14	TOTCHRG	Numeric	8	2	N	Year-to-date charges
15	TOTPMT	Numeric	8	2	N	Year-to-date payments
16	LASTDATE	Date	8		N	Last updated (ordered)

Figure 19.1: Structure of the Customer database file

THE ITEMSREC AND ITEMHIST DATABASE FILES

As the business receives new items from its vendors to replenish its stock, it will probably want to keep a record of these newly received items and update the in-stock quantity in the Master database file. The database file that keeps track of purchases (items received) is named **ItemsRec**.

The business application will initially store records of newly received items in the ItemsRec file. After it automatically updates the in-stock quantities (a procedure called *posting*), it will move the records to a separate database file named **ItemHist** (for item history). The ItemHist file has exactly the same structure as the ItemsRec file. The structure for both files is shown in Figure 19.3.

THE ORDERS AND ORDHIST DATABASE FILES

As the business sells items and accepts orders, it needs to keep track of all transactions, prepare invoices, and update the Master inventory

Structure for database: C:\DBASE\BUSINESS\MASTER.DBF

Num	Field Name	Type	Width	Dec	Index	Description
1	PARTNO	Character	5		Y	Part number
2	PARTNAME	Character	20		N	Part name
3	CATEGORY	Character	10		N	Category
4	INSTOCK	Numeric	4		N	In-stock (on-hand) quantity
5	REORDER	Numeric	4		N	Reorder point
6	PURCOST	Numeric	8	2	N	Purchase cost
7	SELPRICE	Numeric	8	2	N	Selling price
8	TAXABLE	Logical	1		N	Taxable?
9	VENDOR	Character	8		N	Vendor name or code
10	VENDITEMNO	Character	8		N	Vendor's reorder number
11	LOCATION	Character	10		N	Storage location
12	LASTUPDATE	Date	8		N	Date of most recent activity

Figure 19.2: Structure of the Master database file

Structure for database: C:\DBASE\BUSINESS\ITEMSREC.DBF

Num	Field Name	Type	Width	Dec	Index	Description
1	PARTNO	Character	5		Y	Part number
2	QTY_RECVD	Numeric	3		N	Quantity received
3	PRICE	Numeric	8	2	N	Purchase cost
4	DATERECVD	Date	8		N	Date received

Figure 19.3: Structure of the ItemsRec and ItemHist database files

database in-stock quantities. Initially, orders will be stored in a database named **Orders**. After an order is fulfilled, the application will move it to a file named **OrdHist** to prevent the Orders database from becoming excessively large and slowing down the whole process.

The Orders and OrdHist databases use exactly the same structures, shown in Figure 19.4. Note that the Invoice, CustNo, and PartNo fields are all indexed.

THE TRANSACT DATABASE FILE

The business application also keeps track of financial transactions to help manage accounts receivable. These are stored in a database file named **Transact**, which you should create with the structure shown in Figure 19.5. Notice that the Invoice and CustNo fields are indexed.

The application will also use a history file for old transactions, named TranHist. In addition, it will use some temporary databases to perform some aspects of the data processing. However, the application itself will create these files automatically, so you need not be concerned with them just now.

After you have created all the database files, the Data panel in the Control Center on your screen should show the names of all seven database files: Customer, ItemHist, ItemsRec, Master, Orders, OrdHist, and Transact.

```
Structure for database: C:\DBASE\BUSINESS\ORDERS.DBF

Num  Field Name   Type       Width  Dec  Index  Description
  1  INVOICE      Numeric      6          Y     Invoice number
  2  CUSTNO       Numeric      4          Y     Customer number
  3  PARTNO       Character    5          Y     Part number
  4  QTYORDERED   Numeric      3          N     Quantity ordered
  5  UNITPRICE    Numeric      8     2    N     Unit price
  6  DISCRATE     Numeric      5     2    N     Discount rate
  7  TAXRATE      Numeric      5     2    N     Tax rate
  8  SHIPPING     Numeric      8     2    N     Shipping cost
  9  ORDATE       Date         8          N     Date ordered
 10  QTYSHIPPED   Numeric      3          N     Quantity shipped
 11  BACKORDQTY   Numeric      3          N     Quantity backordered
 12  ORDTOTAL     Numeric      8     2    N     Total order
 13  CUSTPONUMB   Character   12          N     Customer P.O. number
 14  INVPOSTED    Logical      1          N     Posted to inventory yet?
 15  ARPOSTED     Logical      1          N     Posted to  A/R yet?
```

Figure 19.4: Structure of the Orders and OrdHist database files

```
Structure for database: C:\DBASE\BUSINESS\TRANSACT.DBF

Num Field Name  Type       Width  Dec  Index  Description
 1  INVOICE     Numeric      6           Y    Invoice number
 2  CUSTNO      Numeric      4           Y    Customer number
 3  ORDATE      Date         8           N    Order date
 4  ORDTOTAL    Numeric      9     2     N    Order total
 5  DATEPAID    Date         8           N    Date paid
 6  AMTPAID     Numeric      8     2     N    Amount paid
 7  REMARKS     Character   30           N    Remarks (reference)
 8  CUSTPOSTED  Logical      1           N    Posted to customer balance?
 9  PRINTED     Logical      1           N    Printed on statement?
```

Figure 19.5: Structure of the Transact database file

THE BUSINESS APPLICATION PROCEDURES

We will store all of the data processing components of the business application that we are building in a procedure file named BusProcs.prg. As you may recall, a procedure file is a collection of procedures and user-defined functions that you create yourself. We'll begin building the procedure file, named BusProcs.prg, now.

NUMBERING CUSTOMERS AUTOMATICALLY

In the business application that we are developing, each customer must have a unique customer number, so that orders and invoices in the Orders and Transact files can be related to a specific customer. Rather than leaving the responsibility of ensuring that each customer has a unique number to the user of the application, we will develop a procedure that automatically assigns customer numbers, starting with number 1001.

NOTE

In this chapter, dBASE IV commands and functions are presented in uppercase letters; and field names, variable names, and file names in mixed uppercase and lowercase letters. You can, however, use any combination of uppercase and lowercase letters that you choose.

Before we actually create the procedure, let's map out the steps using a technique called *pseudocode*. Pseudocode describes the steps, in plain English, that must be performed to accomplish a goal. Then you can use the pseudocode as a guide to developing the actual procedure. Here is the pseudocode for assigning customer numbers to records in the Customer database:

```
Open the Customer database
Find the largest existing customer number
If the largest current number is zero, use 1000 instead
Add 1 to largest existing customer number to
    calculate the next available customer number

Scan for records with customer number = 0
    Replace the zero with the next customer number
    Add one to increase next customer number
Continue scanning until no more customers have customer number = 0

Save all changes
```

To convert this logic into dBASE IV code, we will use several dBASE IV commands and functions. We'll use the USE command with the ORDER option to open the Customer database, with the CustNo index determining the sort order. We will also use the MAX( ) function, which returns the largest of two values. For example, MAX(10,2) returns 10 (because 10 is larger than 2).

We will also use the REPLACE command, which replaces the contents of a field in the current database file with a new value. For example, the command REPLACE CustNo WITH 1001 puts the number 1001 in the field named CustNo in the current database record.

CREATING THE AUTOCUST PROCEDURE

We will name the procedure AutoCust and store it in the BusProcs procedure file. Here are the steps to get started:

1. Get to the dot prompt by choosing Exit ► Exit to Dot Prompt from the menu above the Control Center.
2. Type the command **MODIFY COMMAND BusProcs** and press ↵.

NOTE

You need not be concerned about how many asterisks appear at the start of a program or comment so long as there is at least one.

3. Type the AutoCust procedure *exactly* as it is shown in Figure 19.6, remembering to press ↵ at the end of each line and wherever you want a blank line to appear. (The screen will scroll, when necessary, to give you room to type everything in the figure.)
4. After typing the entire procedure, being very careful not to make any mistakes, save the procedure file by choosing Exit ► Save Changes and Exit.

You'll now be back at the dot prompt.

Let's discuss how the procedure works. Recall that all of the lines that begin with an asterisk (*) or double ampersands (&&) are programmer comments, which are just notes for programmers such as yourself to read and for dBASE to ignore. The first actual command, PROCEDURE AutoCust, assigns the name AutoCust to the procedure.

The command USE Customer ORDER CustNo opens the Customer database file with the CustNo index controlling the sort order.

```
*********************************** BusProcs.PRG
*--- Procedures for order entry and editing.

**************************** Assign customer numbers.
PROCEDURE AutoCust

   *------------- Open Customer Database.
   USE Customer ORDER CustNo
   GOTO BOTTOM

   *-------- 1001 is smallest possible customer number.
   Largest = MAX(1000,CustNo)
   NextCust = Largest + 1

   *--------- Fill in customer numbers.
   USE Customer   && Deactivate index before using replace.
   SCAN FOR CustNo = 0
        REPLACE CustNo WITH NextCust
        NextCust = NextCust + 1
   ENDSCAN

   *---- Done.
   CLOSE DATABASES
RETURN
```

Figure 19.6: The AutoCust procedure

Note that you can only use the ORDER option in the USE command to activate an *existing* index, not to create a new index. Recall that when you initially created the Customer database, you created an index of the CustNo field by placing a Y in the Index column on the database design screen, so you can specify that order in the USE command.

As you might expect, if you open the database with the records in customer-number order, the smallest customer number will be at the top and the largest customer number will be at the bottom of the database. The command GOTO BOTTOM sends the record pointer to the last record in the Customer database, which contains the largest customer number. (If the database is empty, however, the customer number will be zero.)

The next command, Largest = MAX(1000,CustNo), stores a value in a memory variable named Largest; it stores either the number 1000 or the current customer number, whichever is larger. (That way, if the database is empty, the Largest variable contains the number 1000 rather than zero.)

The next command, NextCust = Largest + 1, calculates the next available customer number by adding 1 to the Largest memory variable and storing that result in a memory variable named NextCust. That is, the NextCust memory variable now contains the next available new customer number.

Never use the REPLACE command to replace values in a field included in the currently active index.

The next command, USE Customer, opens the Customer database *without* the CustNo index. In a moment, the procedure is going to use REPLACE to start filling in new customer numbers. If the CustNo index were still active during these replacements, dBASE would re-sort the database after each individual replacement, which would lead to most customer numbers not being replaced.

The next command begins a SCAN...ENDSCAN loop. The command SCAN FOR CustNo = 0 tells dBASE to look at each record in the database and stop scanning as soon as it finds a record with the customer number equal to zero. As soon as dBASE finds the first record with the customer number equal to zero, it stops scanning and processes all commands down to the ENDSCAN command.

Within the SCAN...ENDSCAN loop, the command REPLACE CustNo WITH NextCust replaces the customer number in one record with the value stored in the NextCust memory variable. Then the command NextCust = NextCust + 1 adds 1 to the NextCust variable. The

ENDSCAN command moves the record pointer to the next record in the database file and passes control back to the SCAN FOR CustNo = 0 command, which looks for the next record with zero as the customer number. The loop repeats until all records with zero customer numbers have been accessed and their customer numbers replaced with the new calculated customer numbers.

When the SCAN...ENDSCAN loop is done, processing resumes with the command CLOSE DATABASES, which closes the Customer database. This command is optional, but it's always a good idea to close a database after changing it to ensure that all changes are immediately stored on disk (portions of an open database are stored in RAM, which is susceptible to power failures and other maladies). The RETURN command marks the end of the procedure.

TESTING THE AUTOCUST PROCEDURE

To test the AutoCust procedure, you first need to add a couple of customers to the Customer database file. You do not need to return to the Control Center to do so. Instead, you can take a shortcut to the edit screen by typing the following commands at the dot prompt (press ↵ after typing each command):

```
USE Customer
APPEND
```

The first command opens the Customer database and the second command, APPEND, tells dBASE that you want to add (append) new records. Type two sample customers, assigning each the customer number zero. (You must actually type the zero, even though a zero already appears on the screen, because if you press ↵ without entering any data, dBASE will assume you are done entering records and return you to the dot prompt. The application we develop later will use a more elegant technique.)

For the time being, you can just fill in the CustNo and Company fields of two records, as follows:

CustNo	COMPANY
0	Adam Chandler Enterprises
0	Baker International

When you are done entering records, press Ctrl-End or choose Exit ► Exit.

NOTE

Whenever you type a command at the dot prompt, you must press ↵ to send the command to dBASE.

To verify that the Customer database has two new records, enter the command

```
LIST CustNo,Company
```

at the dot prompt. You should see the two company names you just added, preceded by the customer number 0.

To test the procedure, you first need to open the procedure file by entering the following command at the dot prompt:

```
SET PROCEDURE TO BusProcs
```

dBASE will take a moment to compile the procedure and then will return you to the dot prompt. To test the AutoCust procedure, enter this command at the dot prompt:

```
DO AutoCust
```

If all went well, and you did not make any mistakes along the way, you'll see some messages on the screen as dBASE replaces the customer numbers, then you'll be returned to the dot prompt. (If you did make a mistake, it's probably either a typographical error in the BusProcs procedure file or a misspelled field name in the Customer database file.)

To verify that the AutoCust procedure did its job, reopen the Customer database and look at the customer numbers by entering the following commands at the dot prompt:

```
USE Customer
LIST CustNo,Company
```

When we integrate this procedure into the business application later, the application user will be able to add customers to the database without entering any customer numbers. As soon as the user is finished entering new customers, the AutoCust procedure will number the customers automatically.

NUMBERING INVOICES AUTOMATICALLY

In some business applications, invoice forms are filled in on paper first, and then the information is typed into the computer from the paper form. If those paper invoices contain invoice numbers, then the invoice number can be typed directly at the screen. On the other hand, if clerks enter orders directly from phone calls or mailed order forms, then there is probably no way for the clerks to determine the next available invoice number. In this case, the application needs to number the invoices automatically.

Numbering invoices is a bit trickier than numbering customers, because several separate orders might actually belong on a single invoice. For example, suppose you receive orders from two customers, and each customer orders several items. In the Orders database, the orders might appear as follows (because initially the invoice number is not known, it is just left at zero at the time the order is entered):

Invoice	CustNo	PartNo	QtyOrdered
0	1001	A-111	10
0	1001	B-222	2
0	1002	A-111	1
0	1002	B-222	5
0	1002	C-333	20

If the last-used invoice number was 333330, then the preceding orders need to be assigned the invoice numbers shown here:

Invoice	CustNo	PartNo	QtyOrdered
333331	1001	A-111	10
333331	1001	B-222	2
333332	1002	A-111	1
333332	1002	B-222	5
333332	1002	C-333	20

As you can see, even though there are five separate orders, actually only two invoice numbers are involved. (The individual orders on an invoice are often called the invoice *detail*.)

A second problem to contend with concerns how and when you assign invoice numbers. As you'll see later, outstanding orders are stored in one database (Orders), and fulfilled orders are stored in another database (OrdHist). Depending on when the invoice numbers are assigned, the last-used invoice number will be in one database or the other.

The solutions to all these problems and the order in which they must be addressed are described in the following pseudocode (note that the smallest allowable invoice number is 100001):

```
Assume smallest invoice number is 100000

Use the Orders database in invoice number order
Find the largest invoice number
If greater than 100000, then use that
   value as the largest invoice number

Use the OrdHist database in invoice-number order
Find the largest invoice number
If greater than present largest value, use it
   as the largest-used invoice number

Close the databases
Calculate the next invoice number

Use the Orders database in customer-number order
Scan for records with invoice number = 0
   Note current customer number
   Replace invoice numbers for this customer
      with calculated invoice number
   Increment invoice number by 1
   Skip back to reposition record pointer
Stop scanning when no more invoice numbers equal zero

Save all new invoice numbers
```

CREATING THE AUTOINV PROCEDURE

To add the procedure, which we'll name AutoInv, to the BusProcs procedure file, first close the procedure file. Then go to the command-file editor by entering these commands at the dot prompt:

```
CLOSE PROCEDURE
MODIFY COMMAND BusProcs
```

You will see the AutoCust procedure on the screen. You want to place the new procedure beneath the existing one, so press Ctrl-PgDn to move the cursor to the bottom of the file. (After the cursor gets to the bottom of the procedure file, you can press ↵ to add new blank lines.) Then type the procedure exactly as shown in Figure 19.7. After typing the procedure, choose Exit ► Save Changes and Exit to return to the dot prompt.

In the command USE Orders ORDER Invoice, *Orders* is the name of the database file, and *ORDER* is part of the USE command.

Let's see how the procedure does its job. First, the command USE Orders ORDER Invoice opens the Orders database and selects Invoice sort order. Since this command opens the Orders database with the records in invoice-number order, the smallest invoice numbers are at the top and the largest invoice numbers are at the bottom of the database.

The command GOTO BOTTOM tells dBASE to send the record pointer to the bottom of the database file, making that record the

```
*----- Assign invoice numbers to current orders.
PROCEDURE AutoInv
   *- BusMgr application uses this procedure
   *- before printing invoices.

   *----- Find largest current invoice number.
   USE Orders ORDER Invoice
   GOTO BOTTOM
   Largest=MAX(100000,Invoice)

   USE OrdHist ORDER Invoice
   GOTO BOTTOM
   Largest=MAX(Largest,Invoice)

   CLOSE DATABASES
   NextInvNo=Largest + 1     && Next invoice number.

   *--------- Assign invoice numbers.
   USE Orders ORDER CustNo
   SCAN FOR Invoice=0
      ThisCust = CustNo
      REPLACE Invoice WITH NextInvNo ;
              WHILE CustNo = ThisCust ;
              FOR Invoice = 0
      NextInvNo = NextInvNo + 1
      SKIP -1   && Back up one record before resuming scan.
   ENDSCAN
   *------------ Done
   CLOSE DATABASES
RETURN
```

Figure 19.7: The AutoInv procedure

current record. (We know that the largest invoice in the database is there, because the records are in invoice-number order.) The command Largest = MAX(100000,Invoice) stores either the invoice number from the current record or the number 100000 in a memory variable named Largest. (If the Orders database is empty, the Invoice field will contain zero.)

The next two commands, USE OrdHist ORDER Invoice and GOTO BOTTOM, move the record pointer to the bottom of the OrdHist database file, which is also sorted into invoice-number order. Then the command Largest = MAX(Largest,Invoice) stores either the current invoice number or the current largest invoice number, whichever is larger, in the memory variable named Largest.

The CLOSE DATABASES command closes the OrdHist file, because we no longer need its records in this procedure. The command NextInvNo = Largest + 1 calculates the next invoice number by adding 1 to the largest invoice number and then stores that result in the memory variable named NextInvNo.

Now that the procedure has determined the next-available invoice number, it can start assigning invoice numbers to orders in the Orders database file. Let's see how it does this, using some sample data. Suppose that the Orders database contains the following data, and the NextInvNo memory variable now contains 333331.

Invoice	CustNo	PartNo	QtyOrdered
0	1001	A-111	10
0	1001	B-222	2
0	1002	A-111	1
0	1002	B-222	5
0	1002	C-333	20

NOTE

In this case, you can use an index even though a REPLACE command is operating on the database, because the index key is CustNo, but the field being replaced is Invoice.

The command USE Orders ORDER CustNo opens the Orders database file using the CustNo index (which you created when you initially structured the database). Thus, the orders are listed in customer-number order, as in the preceding sample records.

The command SCAN FOR Invoice = 0 tells dBASE to repeat all commands between this one and the ENDSCAN command until it finds no more records with zero as the invoice number. Here is what happens inside the loop.

First, the command ThisCust = CustNo stores the current customer number in a memory variable named ThisCust. For the preceding sample records, the pointer would initially start at the first record, and therefore ThisCust would contain 1001.

The next three lines actually compose only one command: REPLACE Invoice WITH NextInvNo WHILE CustNo = ThisCust FOR Invoice = 0. dBASE lets you break long commands like this one into separate lines with a semicolon (;) at the end of each line break. (It's a good idea to precede the semicolon with a blank space to ensure that blank spaces appear in the command where they should.)

In English, this long REPLACE command tells dBASE to replace the invoice number with the next available invoice number WHILE (as long as) the customer number does not change; FOR (but) within these customers, do not replace records that already have an invoice number. Hence, the first time through the SCAN...ENDSCAN loop, the REPLACE command replaces records with 1001 as the customer number and stops replacing as soon as it comes to a new customer number, producing the following results (the >> symbol shows where the record pointer is when the REPLACE command is finished):

	Invoice	CustNo	PartNo	QtyOrdered
	333331	1001	A-111	10
	333331	1001	B-222	2
>>	0	1002	A-111	1
	0	1002	B-222	5
	0	1002	C-333	20

The next command, NextInvNo = NextInvNo + 1, increments the value in the NextInvNo memory variable by 1, so now NextInvNo contains 333332. Now if we were not very careful in our planning here, we would have a problem on our hands. The ENDSCAN command automatically moves the record pointer to the next database record before resuming the scan operation, which can cause the current record to be skipped completely.

The procedure takes care of this potential problem by moving the record pointer back a record with the command SKIP -1, which puts the record pointer where the >> symbol appears:

	Invoice	CustNo	PartNo	QtyOrdered
	333331	1001	A-111	10
>>	333331	1001	B-222	2
	0	1002	A-111	1
	0	1002	B-222	2
	0	1002	C-333	20

Now the ENDSCAN command moves the record pointer ahead a record, and the scan operation resumes from the position marked by >>, as shown here:

	Invoice	CustNo	PartNo	QtyOrdered
	333331	1001	A-111	10
	333331	1001	B-222	2
>>	0	1002	A-111	1
	0	1002	B-222	5
	0	1002	C-333	20

On this second pass through the loop, the command ThisCust =CustNo stores the customer number 1002 in the variable named ThisCust. Then the REPLACE command replaces records with this customer number with the new invoice number, producing these results:

	Invoice	CustNo	PartNo	QtyOrdered
	333331	1001	A-111	10
	333331	1001	B-222	2
	333332	1002	A-111	1
	333332	1002	B-222	5
	333332	1002	C-333	20
>>				

TESTING THE AUTOINV PROCEDURE

To test the AutoInv procedure, you need first to put some test data in the Orders database. To do so, enter the following commands at the dot prompt:

```
USE Orders
APPEND
```

Now enter some sample orders to test the procedure. For testing purposes, you need not fill in all the fields. Instead, to mimic the examples discussed earlier in this section, you need only fill in the Invoice and CustNo fields for five records, using this data (you must actually type the zero into the Invoice field, even though a zero is already displayed):

Invoice	CustNo
0	1001
0	1001
0	1002
0	1002
0	1002

After you've filled in some sample records, press Ctrl-End to leave the edit screen and return to the dot prompt. To test the procedure, you need to open the BusProcs procedure file and run the AutoInv procedure by entering these commands at the dot prompt:

```
SET PROCEDURE TO BusProcs
DO AutoInv
```

When the procedure is complete and the dot prompt reappears, you can check the results by entering these commands:

```
USE Orders ORDER Invoice
LIST Invoice,CustNo
```

Because you have not previously entered any orders, the invoices should be numbered starting at 100001, as follows:

Invoice	CustNo
100001	1001
100001	1001
100002	1002
100002	1002
100002	1002

Of course, the actual results will depend on what you entered as sample records, but the general logic of the results should be as follows: Each group of records with identical customer numbers has the same invoice number.

The business application that we develop later will use the AutoInv procedure to automatically assign invoice numbers to all new orders. If you inadvertently added a blank record to your test data and it showed up in the results of your LIST command, don't worry about it now. The business application will automatically handle such blank records.

UPDATING THE MASTER DATABASE FROM ITEMS RECEIVED

As the business receives purchases from its vendors, it needs to record these and update the Master database in-stock quantities accordingly. To automate the updating task, you can use the dBASE IV UPDATE command. The command requires both the database file containing the information used in the update operation and the file being updated to be open simultaneously.

The general syntax for the UPDATE command is

```
UPDATE ON <common field> FROM <unselected database> REPLACE
<field name> WITH <new value>
```

where <common field> is the name of the field that relates the two databases, <unselected database> is the database that contains data used for updating, <field name> is the name of the field in the selected database that is being updated, and <new value> defines the new value for the field being updated. You can simultaneously update several fields, as you'll see in the procedure.

The only catch in performing the update operation is that dBASE has no way of knowing what records in a database have already been used in an updating procedure. Thus, you need to devise a scheme to prevent dBASE from using records in an update more than once. The business application handles this problem by moving all *posted* (that is, already updated) transactions to a file named ItemHist. Here is the pseudocode for the procedure:

```
Open the Master database in one work area
Open the ItemsRec database in another work area

Select the Master database for updating
Update by adding qty received to in-stock qty,
    replacing the last update date with the order date,
    replacing the original cost with the current cost
```

Close databases to save changes

Use the ItemHist database file
Add records from the ItemsRec file

Use the ItemsRec file
Delete all records
Save all changes

CREATING THE ADDITEMS PROCEDURE

The procedure for updating the Master database from items received will be named AddItems. To add this procedure to the BusProcs procedure file, follow these steps:

1. Enter the command **CLOSE PROCEDURE** to close the procedure file.
2. Enter the command **MODIFY COMMAND BusProcs** to edit the procedure file.
3. Press Ctrl-PgDn to move the cursor to the bottom of the procedure file.
4. If necessary, press ↵ to add a blank line or two.
5. Type the procedure exactly as shown in Figure 19.8. Note that to type the arrow, as in ItemsRec->QtyRecvd, you type a hyphen (-) followed by a greater-than sign (>).
6. After typing in the procedure, choose Exit ► Save Changes and Exit.

Let's take a moment to see how the procedure works. The first four commands open the Master database with the PartNo index in work area A and the ItemsRec and PartNo databases in work area B.

Now let's assume that the Master database contains the following records (though, of course, it may contain many more records):

PartNo	InStock	PurCost	LastUpdate
A-111	10	500.00	01/01/93
B-222	0	50.00	01/01/93

Let's also assume that the ItemsRec database contains the following records:

PartNo	QtyRecvd	Price	DateRecvd
A-111	5	0.00	01/15/93
B-222	25	75.00	01/15/93

```
*------------------ Update Master file from items received.
PROCEDURE AddItems

   *--- Close open files, then open Master and ItemsRec.
   CLOSE DATABASES
   SELECT A
   USE Master ORDER PartNo
   SELECT B
   USE ItemsRec ORDER PartNo

   *--- Perform the update.
   SELECT Master
   UPDATE ON PartNo FROM ItemsRec REPLACE ;
      InStock WITH InStock + ItemsRec->Qty_Recvd, ;
      LastUpdate WITH ItemsRec->DateRecvd, ;
      PurCost WITH ;
      IIF(ItemsRec->Price>0,ItemsRec->Price,PurCost)

   CLOSE DATABASES
   *------------- Move updated transactions to history file.
   SET SAFETY OFF
   USE ItemHist

   *-------------- Read in completed transactions.
   APPEND FROM ItemsRec

   USE ItemsRec
   ZAP
   CLOSE DATABASES
RETURN
```

Figure 19.8: The AddItems procedure

Note that each expression in the UPDATE command is separated by a comma. The semicolons are included to break the lengthy command into separate lines.

The command SELECT Master makes the Master database the currently selected database (the one that will be updated). Notice that in the command, field names from the unselected database, ItemsRec, are all preceded with the alias and the arrow.

The UPDATE command automatically processes every record in the unselected database (ItemsRec in this case). So for each record in ItemsRec, it adds the quantity received to the current in-stock quantity (InStock WITH InStock + ItemsRec->Qty_Recvd), replaces the

LastUpdate field with the date the item was received (LastUpdate WITH ItemsRec->DateRecvd), and replaces the purchase cost with the new purchase cost (PurCost WITH IIF(ItemsRec->Price>0, ItemsRec->Price, PurCost)).

In the last expression, the IIF() function makes a decision about exactly how to perform the replacement. In some situations, the person entering data into the ItemsRec file might not know the current purchase price and would therefore leave it as zero. The IIF function in effect says, "If the price in the ItemsRec file is greater than zero (IIF(ItemsRec->Price>0), *then* use the ItemsRec->Price value in the replacement; *otherwise*, use the PurCost field for the replacement." If the latter condition proves true, then the PurCost field is simply replaced with its own existing contents, which in essence leaves its contents unchanged.

Returning now to the sample data, after the update is complete, the Master database contains the following:

PartNo	InStock	PurCost	LastUpdate
A-111	15	500.00	01/15/93
B-222	25	75.00	01/15/93

The InStock quantity for part number A-111 was 10 but is now 15, because 5 of these parts were received. The purchase cost (PurCost) is still 500.00, because no new purchase cost was entered into the ItemsRec database. The LastUpdate field, which initially contained 01/01/93, now contains 01/15/93, the date that the items were received.

No parts with part number B-222 had been in stock, but now there are 25, because 25 were received. The PurCost field now contains the new purchase price, $75.00, and the LastUpdate field now contains the date 01/15/93.

Remember that the ItemsRec database still has the same records in it, so if you were to perform the update operation again, these same quantities would once again be updated to the Master file. But that would be an error. To prevent such an error, the routine moves the records from ItemsRec to the ItemHist file. Here's how.

First, the command CLOSE DATABASES closes all open databases. Then the command SET SAFETY OFF tells dBASE not to ask for permission to overwrite files or delete records while the next steps are carried out. The command USE ItemHist opens the

ItemHist database file. The command APPEND FROM ItemsRec tells dBASE to read all records from the ItemsRec file into the current ItemHist file, appending the new records to the end of the database (after any existing records).

The command USE ItemsRec then opens the ItemsRec database file, and the ZAP command deletes all records from that file. After ZAP does its job, the ItemsRec database is completely empty, but its structure still exists so that you can add new records again later.

The CLOSE DATABASES command closes all open databases, and the RETURN command marks the end of the procedure. The business application will automatically run the AddItems procedure whenever the user adds new records to the ItemsRec database file, so that updates are processed automatically, and immediately.

PROCESSING ORDERS

Order processing would be a simple task if businesses always had enough products in stock to immediately fulfill every order. Unfortunately, this is not always the case, and often items have to be backordered. However, you can develop powerful and efficient routines for updating the inventory in-stock quantities and handling backorders as orders are fulfilled.

In this section we'll develop a procedure to handle orders in the Orders database file. The logic that the procedure uses is described here in pseudocode:

```
Open the Orders database and PartNo index
Open the Master database and PartNo index

Select the Orders database for making changes
Define a relation, based on part number, in the Master database

Start at top of the Orders database
Scan for records that have not been posted
  If the qty ordered is less than or equal to in-stock qty
    Qty shipped equals qty ordered
  Otherwise
    Qty shipped equals in-stock qty
    Backorder qty equals qty ordered minus qty shipped
```

```
        Endif
        Select the Master database
        Subtract qty shipped from in-stock qty
        Select the Orders database
        Flag transaction as being posted
    End scanning (all records have been processed)

    Application can now print invoices
```

To add the new procedure to the BusProcs procedure file, use the same techniques that you used earlier. That is, at the dot prompt enter the command **CLOSE PROCEDURE**. Then enter the command **MODIFY COMMAND BusProcs** and position the cursor beneath the existing procedures. Then type the OrdUpdat procedure, exactly as shown in Figure 19.9. Remember to save your work after you type the entire procedure.

Now let's discuss how the order updating procedure works. First, the SELECT and USE commands open both the Orders and Master databases, each with its PartNo index in use. Then the SELECT Orders and SET RELATION TO PartNo INTO Master commands make the Orders database the current database and define a relationship, based on the common PartNo field, in the Master database file.

The GO TOP command moves the record pointer to the top (first record) in the Orders database file, and the command SCAN FOR .NOT. InvPosted sets up a loop that will process all records in the Orders database that have .F. in the InvPosted field. Within the SCAN...ENDSCAN loop, the following processes take place.

First, the command IF QtyOrdered<=Master->InStock checks whether the quantity ordered is less than or equal to the quantity in stock. If it is, REPLACE QtyShipped WITH QtyOrdered copies the contents of the QtyOrdered field to the QtyShipped field. If, on the other hand (ELSE), the quantity ordered is not less than or equal to the in-stock quantity, then these commands are executed:

```
REPLACE QtyShipped WITH MAX(0,Master->InStock)
REPLACE BackOrdQty WITH QtyOrdered-QtyShipped
```

The first command replaces the QtyShipped field in the Orders database with the quantity available in stock. However, if the ordering department gets ahead of the receiving department, or somebody

```
*------ Determine backorder requirements, and subtract
*------ fulfilled orders from in-stock quantities.
PROCEDURE OrdUpdat

   *-- Open Master and Orders database files.
   SELECT A
   USE Orders ORDER PartNo
   SELECT B
   USE Master ORDER PartNo

   *-- Must set up relationship if not using UPDATE command.
   SELECT Orders
   SET RELATION TO PartNo INTO Master

   *-- Update the Master in-stock quantities.
   GO TOP
   SCAN FOR .NOT. InvPosted
     *-- See if qty ordered exceeds in-stock qty.
     IF QtyOrdered <= Master->InStock
        REPLACE QtyShipped WITH QtyOrdered
     ELSE
        REPLACE QtyShipped WITH MAX(0,Master->InStock)
        REPLACE BackOrdQty WITH QtyOrdered-QtyShipped
     ENDIF
     *--- Update Master inventory database.
     SELECT Master
     REPLACE InStock WITH InStock-Orders->QtyShipped
     SELECT Orders
     REPLACE InvPosted WITH .T.
    ENDSCAN

    ********* Invoices can now be printed for posted records.
    ********* After printing invoices, must send fulfilled orders
    ********* to order history file, and convert backorders to
    ********* outstanding orders.  (The application will print
    ********* invoices as soon as this procedure is done).
    CLOSE DATABASES
RETURN
```

Figure 19.9: The OrdUpdat procedure

makes an error that causes the InStock quantity to be a negative number, the QtyShipped will be a negative number, a situation we want to avoid. Thus, the procedure takes this precaution: It sets the QtyShipped value to zero or to the InStock quantity, whichever is larger (MAX(0,Master->InStock)).

The following command, REPLACE BackOrdQty WITH QtyOrdered–QtyShipped, subtracts the quantity shipped from the quantity ordered and places that value in the BackOrdQty field. The ENDIF command marks the end of the IF...ENDIF clause.

Now the Master database in-stock quantity needs to be decremented to reflect the quantity of items shipped. However, the Master database file is not currently selected, so you cannot change any of its values. This problem is easily solved by temporarily making Master the selected database file. The command SELECT Master makes the Master database file the currently selected database.

The command REPLACE InStock WITH InStock-Orders ->QtyShipped subtracts the quantity shipped from the quantity in stock. The command SELECT Orders once again makes the Orders database the currently selected database, so that its contents can be changed once again. The command REPLACE InvPosted WITH .T. places .T. in the InvPosted field, which indicates that the current order has been posted (that is, its quantity has been subtracted from the in-stock quantity). The ENDSCAN command moves the record pointer to the next record in the Orders databases and passes control back to the SCAN command. The SCAN...ENDSCAN loop and the commands within it are repeated once for each record in the Orders database that has not yet been posted.

When the SCAN...ENDSCAN loop is complete, all current orders have been checked for backordering, and the Master database in-stock quantities have been updated accordingly. Now is the perfect time for the business application to print invoices. The RETURN command marks the end of the procedure and passes control back to the (currently nonexistent) application. The application will print invoices as soon as the OrdUpdat procedure is finished.

HANDLING FULFILLED ORDERS

When orders have been fulfilled and invoices have been printed, current orders can be moved to the order-history file, OrdHist. However, backorders need to stay in the current orders database and be converted to current (outstanding) orders. The MoveOrds procedure, which we'll develop next, will handle these tasks automatically.

The basic logic for the MoveOrds procedure is shown here in pseudocode:

```
Use the order-history file
Read in all fulfilled and posted orders
```

Use the Orders database
Delete all fulfilled orders

For remaining orders...
    Outstanding order qty is the backorder qty
    Qty shipped is zero
    Backorder qty is zero
    Posted flag is false
    Invoice number is zero

To add the procedure to the BusProcs procedure file, use the usual technique. That is, at the dot prompt, enter the command **MODIFY COMMAND BusProcs** and when the procedure file appears on the screen, use the Ctrl-PgDn and ↵ keys to scroll to the bottom of the procedure file and add some blank lines. Then type the MoveOrds procedure exactly as shown in Figure 19.10. Remember to choose Exit ► Save Changes and Exit to save your work. Let's take a moment to see how the procedure works.

First, the command USE OrdHist opens the OrdHist file, which contains records of fulfilled orders. The command APPEND FROM Orders FOR QtyShipped>0 .AND. InvPosted into the OrdHist database file copies records from the Orders database that have a quantity-shipped value greater than zero and .T. in the InvPosted field.

```
PROCEDURE MoveOrds
     *----------- Used in the BusMgr application after orders have
     *----------- been fulfilled and invoices have been printed.
     USE OrdHist
     APPEND FROM Orders FOR QtyShipped > 0 .AND. InvPosted
     USE Orders
     DELETE FOR BackOrdQty = 0 .AND. InvPosted
     PACK
     REPLACE ALL QtyOrdered WITH BackOrdQty, ;
                 QtyShipped WITH 0,  ;
                 BackOrdQty WITH 0,  ;
                 InvPosted WITH .F., ;
                 Invoice WITH 0
RETURN
```

Figure 19.10: The MoveOrds procedure

Next, the procedure works in the Orders database. First it opens the database, using the command USE Orders. Then it marks for deletion all orders that are not backordered and have been posted to the inventory database, using DELETE FOR BackOrdQty = 0 .AND. InvPosted. Then the command PACK permanently erases the records that are marked for deletion.

To convert backorders to current orders, the procedure then executes REPLACE ALL QtyOrdered WITH BackOrdQty, QtyShipped WITH 0, BackOrdQty WITH 0, InvPosted WITH .F., Invoice WITH 0, which converts the order quantity to the backorder quantity, the quantity shipped to zero, and the backorder quantity to zero. The command also marks the record as *not* having been posted to the master inventory yet and resets the invoice number to zero.

The backorder records now are no different from any other current order records, and they will be fulfilled and invoiced automatically when stock levels permit.

CALCULATING ORDER TOTALS

Each order in the Orders database includes a quantity, (QtyShipped), unit price (UnitPrice), discount rate, (DiscRate), tax rate (TaxRate), and shipping cost (Shipping). The DiscRate and TaxRate are stored as percentage values and hence need to be divided by 100 to convert them to decimal numbers before they are used in calculations (for example, 7.75 percent divided by 100 equals 0.0775).

To calculate the order total with a single expression, you need to use the calculation

```
(((QtyShipped*UnitPrice)–((DiscRate/100)*(QtyShipped*UnitPrice)))
*(1 + (TaxRate/100))) + Shipping
```

This is a complex expression, but if you test it manually, remembering that dBASE always works from the innermost parentheses outward, you'll see that it works.

For example, suppose a given order contains the following values:

QtyShipped = 2

UnitPrice = $100.00

DiscRate = 10%

TaxRate = 7.75%

Shipping = $5.00

Substituting the values into the expression results in the following formula:

```
(((2*100.00)-((10/100)*(2*100)))*(1+(7.75/100)))+5.00
```

Performing the innermost calculations first produces

```
((200.00-(.10*200))*(1+0.0775))+5.00
```

Performing the innermost remaining calculations produces

```
((200.00-20.00)*1.0775)+5.00
```

Performing the remaining innermost expressions produces

```
(180.00*1.0775)+5.00
```

This expression evaluates to

```
193.95+5.00
```

which yields the net result, 198.95.

This expression is used in the next business procedure and elsewhere in the business application.

UPDATING ACCOUNTS RECEIVABLE FROM FULFILLED ORDERS

The Transact file stores information about invoices, without the detail, for managing accounts receivable. The OrdHist database, rather than the Orders database, is used for updating the accounts receivable file because the OrdHist file contains records of fulfilled orders (those that have been invoiced).

Before dBASE copies information from the OrdHist database to the Transact database, individual orders need to be summarized into single invoices. The ARUpdate procedure handles this task with the help of the dBASE IV command TOTAL. The logic of the procedure is shown in pseudocode:

```
Use order-history file in invoice-number sort order.
Calculate total sale for each order

Create a summary database with invoice totals

Read the contents of the summary database
    into the AR transactions file

Use the orders-history file
Flag all records as being posted to accounts receivable
```

Figure 19.11 shows the ARUpdate procedure. Enter the command **MODIFY COMMAND BusProcs** at the dot prompt and then enter the procedure to the existing procedures exactly as it is shown in the figure. Be sure to choose Exit ► Save Changes and Exit to save the procedure file after you type the new procedure.

```
*-------- Moves fulfilled orders to the AR transactions file.
PROCEDURE ARUpdate
   *---------- Used in BusMgr application after moving
   *---------- fulfilled orders to OrdHist file.

   *---------- First calculate order totals.
   USE OrdHist ORDER Invoice
   REPLACE OrdTotal WITH (((QtyShipped*UnitPrice)- ;
           ((Discrate/100)*(QtyShipped*UnitPrice)))* ;
           (1+(TaxRate/100)))+Shipping ;
           FOR QtyShipped > 0

    *--------- Now create temporary database of totaled orders.
    GO TOP
    SET SAFETY OFF  && Prevents dBASE from asking for permission to overwrite
    TOTAL ON Invoice FIELDS OrdTotal TO OrdTemp FOR .NOT. ARPosted
    *--------- Copy summarized totals into AR transaction file.
    USE Transact
    APPEND FROM OrdTemp
    *---------- Mark orders as being posted to the AR transaction file.
    USE OrdHist
    REPLACE ALL ARPosted WITH .T.
    CLOSE DATABASES
RETURN
```

Figure 19.11: The ARUpdate procedure

Let's see how the procedure works. First the command USE OrdHist ORDER Invoice opens the OrdHist database with the Invoice index placing the records in sorted order from the smallest invoice number to the largest.

To examine the logic of the program, let's assume that the OrdHist database file currently contains the following records (the DiscRate, TaxRate, and some other fields are omitted here to save space, but you will include these values in calculations when you actually use the ARUpdate procedure):

Invoice	CustNo	PartNo	Qty Shipped	Unit Price	OrdTotal	OrDate
333333	1001	A-111	10	5.00		01/01/93
333333	1001	B-222	1	10.00		01/01/93
333333	1001	C-333	2	4.00		01/01/93
333334	1002	A-111	1	5.00		01/01/93
333334	1002	C-333	3	4.00		01/01/93

Next, the command

```
REPLACE OrdTotal WITH (((QtyShipped*UnitPrice)– ;
        ((DiscRate/100)*(QtyShipped*UnitPrice)))* ;
        (1+(TaxRate/100))) + Shipping ;
        FOR QtyShipped>0
```

calculates the total of each order that has a QtyShipped value greater than zero. So now the OrdHist database looks something like this:

Invoice	CustNo	PartNo	Qty Shipped	Unit Price	OrdTotal	OrDate
333333	1001	A-111	10	5.00	50.00	01/01/93
333333	1001	B-222	1	10.00	10.00	01/01/93
333333	1001	C-333	2	4.00	8.00	01/01/93
333334	1002	A-111	1	5.00	5.00	01/01/93
333334	1002	C-333	3	4.00	12.00	01/01/93

The GO TOP command positions the record pointer at the top of the OrdHist database, and SET SAFETY OFF makes sure that dBASE does not ask for permission to overwrite any old copy of the OrdTemp file when the next command creates that file.

The next command, TOTAL ON Invoice FIELDS OrdTotal TO OrdTemp FOR .NOT. ARPosted, performs all the totaling and summarizing. The TOTAL command always creates a new database containing the totaled and summarized results. The first part of the command, TOTAL ON Invoice, tells dBASE that records are to be grouped by invoice number in the totaled results. The database being totaled must be indexed on the field used for grouping, as the Orders database is in this procedure.

The portion of the command that reads FIELDS OrdTotal tells dBASE which fields are to be totaled: OrdTotal in this example. The portion of the command that reads TO OrdTemp tells dBASE where to store summarized and totaled results. In this case, the results are stored in a database file named OrdTemp.dbf. If OrdTemp.dbf does not already exist, the TOTAL command creates it. If OrdTemp.dbf does exist, the TOTAL command attempts to overwrite it.

In this particular application, the OrdTemp.dbf database is used as a temporary database file—a holding area for summarized transactions coming out of the OrdHist database before they go into the Transact file—so it's okay for dBASE to overwrite the OrdTemp.dbf database if it already exists. dBASE would normally ask for permission before overwriting an existing file, but because the preceding command set the SAFETY feature off, dBASE will not ask for permission before overwriting the file.

The portion of the TOTAL command that reads FOR .NOT. ARPosted limits the totaling to records that have not already been posted to the Transact file. (As you'll see in a moment, posted orders are flagged with a .T. in the ARPosted field after they have been posted.)

The results of the TOTAL command are a database named OrdTemp.dbf that contains the following information, using the sample orders listed previously:

Invoice	CustNo	PartNo	Qty Shipped	Unit Price	OrdTotal	OrDate
333333	1001	A-111			68.00	01/01/93
333334	1002	C-333			17.00	01/01/93

Next, the command USE Transact opens the Transact database file, and the command APPEND FROM OrdTemp copies records from the OrdTemp.dbf database to the bottom of the Transact database. The APPEND FROM command copies only fields that have identical names in both databases. Hence, after the APPEND

FROM command, Transact contains the following records (plus any other records that were already in it):

Invoice	CustNo	Ordate	OrdTotal
333333	1001	01/01/93	68.00
333334	1002	01/01/93	17.00

Next, the commands USE OrdHist and REPLACE ALL ARPosted WITH .T. place .T. in the ARPosted field of all records in the OrdHist database to indicate that the orders have been posted to the transaction file. The CLOSE DATABASES command closes open database files, and RETURN marks the end of the procedure.

DETERMINING ACCOUNT BALANCES

To determine the current account balances for each customer, the application needs to keep track of total accumulated charges and balances. The Customer database provides four fields for this: TotChrg and TotPmt, which accumulate all charges and payments, and YtdChrg and YtdPmt, which also accumulate charges and payments, but can be reset to zero at the end of the accounting year to track year-to-date charges and balances. The balance at any given time is simply the accumulated charges minus the accumulated payments.

To keep customer charges and payments current, you need a procedure that can summarize all transactions and then update the appropriate fields in the Customer database. The logic for the procedure is shown in the following pseudocode:

```
Open the Customer file with CustNo index
Open Transaction file with CustNo index

Hide posted records in the Transaction file

Select the Customer database for updating

Update Customer database by...
    adding current charges to accumulated charges
    adding current payments to accumulated payments
    replacing the last update date with today's date
```

Save all updates
Use the Transaction file
Mark all transactions as posted to the Customer file

We'll name the procedure that performs the accounts receivable posting ARPost. To add it to the BusProcs procedure, first enter the command **MODIFY COMMAND BusProcs** at the dot prompt; then position the cursor at the end of the procedure file by pressing Ctrl-PgDn. Type the procedure exactly as shown in Figure 19.12. Be sure to save the procedure file after typing the ARPost procedure.

```
*---- Update customer balances.
PROCEDURE ARPost

   SELECT A
   USE Customer ORDER CustNo
   SELECT B
   USE Transact ORDER CustNo
   *---- Exclude records that have been posted.
   SET FILTER TO .NOT. CustPosted
   GO TOP  && Always move the record pointer after SET FILTER.

   SELECT Customer
   UPDATE ON CustNo FROM Transact REPLACE ;
     TotChrg WITH TotChrg + Transact->OrdTotal, ;
     YtdChrg WITH YtdChrg + Transact->OrdTotal, ;
     TotPmt WITH TotPmt + Transact->AmtPaid, ;
     YtdPmt WITH YtdPmt + Transact->AmtPaid, ;
     LastDate WITH DATE()

   *---- Customer balances now updated, flag transactions.
   CLOSE DATABASES
   USE Transact
   REPLACE ALL CustPosted WITH .T.
   CLOSE DATABASES
RETURN
```

Figure 19.12: The ARPost procedure

Let's see how the ARPost procedure does its job. Let's assume that the Customer database includes (at least) the following two records, each of which was last updated on January 31, 1993:

CustNo	TotChrg	TotPmt	YtdChrg	YtdPmt	LastDate
1001	0.00	0.00	0.00	0.00	01/31/93
1002	100.00	10.00	100.00	10.00	01/31/93

Let's also assume that the Transact database contains the following records (note that the first record has already been posted, as indicated by .T. in the CUSTPOSTED field):

CustNo	OrdTotal	AmtPaid	CustPosted
1002	10.00		.T.
1001	500.00	0.00	.F.
1001		400.00	.F.
1002	200.00		.F.

(Note that both databases contain other fields as well, but these are irrelevant to the present example.)

The first four commands after the PROCEDURE command in the ARPost procedure open the Customer and Transact databases, both with the CustNo index controlling the sort order. (Later the procedure will use the UPDATE command, so both of these databases must be indexed on the field that relates the two files.)

Then the command SET FILTER TO .NOT. CustPosted tells dBASE to include only records that have .F. in the CustPosted field (that is, records that have not already been posted to the Customer database). The SET FILTER command requires you to take some action to move the record pointer immediately after the filter is set, which the ARPost procedure does through the command GO TOP. When these two commands finish their jobs, the transactions already posted are hidden, and the record pointer (indicated by >>) is at the beginning of the visible records, like this:

CustNo	OrdTotal	AmtPaid	CustPosted
>>1001	500.00	0.00	.F.
1001		400.00	.F.
1002	200.00		.F.

Next, the command SELECT Customer makes the Customer database the currently selected database, whose values will be updated. Then the long UPDATE command, broken into six separate lines with semicolons, performs the actual update operation. The databases are related using the common CustNo field, so dBASE automatically knows which charge and payment belongs to which customer.

The portion of the UPDATE command that reads TotChrg WITH TotChrg + Transact->OrdTotal adds the value in the OrdTotal field of the Transact database to the value currently in the TotChrg field of the Customer database. Similar expressions are used to update the YtdChrg, TotPmt, and YtdPmt fields, with payments updated from the Transact file AmtPaid field (that is, the field named Transact->AmtPaid).

The last expression, LastDate WITH DATE(), replaces the contents of the LastDate field in the Customer database with the current date. Assuming that the updating took place on February 28, 1993, when the UPDATE command is done, the two sample records in the Customer database will contain the following new values:

CustNo	TotChrg	TotPmt	YtdChrg	YtdPmt	LastDate
1001	500.00	400.00	500.00	400.00	02/28/93
1002	300.00	10.00	300.00	10.00	02/28/93

Note that customer 1001 has now accumulated $500.00 in charges and $400.00 in payments. Customer number 1002 now has accumulated $300.00 in charges (the customer originally had $100.00 in charges, but another $200.00 was added during the update operation). The LastDate field in both records reflects the current date.

The CLOSE DATABASES command closes both open database files, ensuring that the updates are saved on disk. Then, to ensure that none of these transactions is posted again in the future, the procedure opens the Transact database with the USE Transact command and then uses the command REPLACE ALL CustPosted WITH .T. to replace the CustPosted field with .T. in all records. This marks the records as posted, so they will not be posted again in the future.

RESETTING YEAR-TO-DATE TOTALS

Most business applications store at least some numbers that keep track of accumulated year-to-date totals. At the end of the accounting year, these year-to-date values need to be reset to zero. A REPLACE command can handle the job easily enough, but there are some factors to take into account.

First of all, application users occasionally do not pay much attention to what is happening on their screens and therefore might unwittingly select an option to reset all year-to-date totals to zero prematurely. To prevent such accidental resetting, you can make the procedure pause and double-check whether the user really wants to reset the values.

Once the accounting year is closed, there is no need to keep all of the transactions for that entire year in the database of current transactions. Thus, the business application that we are developing will move the old transactions to a history file named TranHist. The application will create this database automatically, which is why you need not create a structure for the TranHist database.

Let's look at the pseudocode for the entire procedure, which we'll name YearEnd:

```
Ask if it is Ok to proceed

If Ok to proceed
    Replace all year-to-date totals with zero
    Copy completed transactions to the transaction history file
    Mark completed transactions for deletion
    Remove deleted transactions
End of If clause
```

As usual, to add the procedure to the end of the procedure file, first enter the command **MODIFY COMMAND BusProcs** at the dot prompt. Then use the Ctrl-PgDn and ↵ keys as necessary to scroll to the end of the file and add blank lines. Type the YearEnd procedure exactly as shown in Figure 19.13. After typing the procedure, choose Exit ► Save Changes and Exit to save the completed procedure file and return to the dot prompt.

Now let's examine each command in the procedure. First, the command GoAhead = .F. stores *false* in a memory variable named GoAhead. Then the commands @ 4,5 SAY "Are you sure you want to reset year-to-date" and @ 5,5 SAY "totals to zero now? (Y/N) " GET GoAhead PICTURE "Y" display a two-line prompt on the screen along with the current contents of the GoAhead variable, using a template that displays .F. as N and .T. as Y, as shown here:

```
Are you sure you want to reset year-to-date
totals to zero now? (Y/N)  [N]
```

The next command, READ, moves the cursor into the highlighted area where the contents of the GoAhead variable are displayed, allowing the user to change its value.

```
*------------------ Resets year-to-date values to zero
*------------------ in the customer database, and moves
*------------------ old transactions to history file.
PROCEDURE YearEnd

   *-------- Double-check for permission.
   GoAhead = .F.
   @ 4,5 SAY "Are you sure you want to reset year-to-date"
   @ 5,5 SAY "totals to zero now?  (Y/N) " GET GoAhead PICTURE "Y"
   READ

   *------ If ok to proceed, do so.
   IF GoAhead
      SET TALK ON
      SET SAFETY OFF
      USE Customer
      REPLACE ALL YtdChrg WITH 0, YtdPmt WITH 0
      USE Transact
      COPY TO TranHist FOR CustPosted .AND. Printed
      DELETE FOR CustPosted .AND. Printed
      PACK
      SET TALK OFF
   ENDIF

   CLOSE DATABASES
RETURN
```

Figure 19.13: The YearEnd procedure

If the user does change the contents of the GoAhead variable to Y (.T.), then the IF GoAhead command is true, and dBASE executes all commands down to the ENDIF command. (If the GoAhead variable is false, then dBASE ignores all commands down to the ENDIF command.)

Within the IF...ENDIF clause, the command SET TALK ON turns on the dBASE TALK setting, which shows command progress on the screen as events take place. The command SET SAFETY OFF prevents dBASE from asking for permission later when the COPY command creates the TranHist database file. The USE Customer command opens the Customer database.

The command REPLACE ALL YtdChrg WITH 0, YtdPmt WITH 0 replaces the contents of the YtdChrg and YtdPmt fields with zero in every database record. Then the command USE Transact opens the Transact database. The command COPY TO TranHist FOR CustPosted .AND. Printed copies all records that have .T. in the CustPosted and Printed fields to a database file named TranHist. (If the TranHist file already exists because a previous year's totals were reset to zero, the COPY command completely overwrites the existing TranHist file.)

The command DELETE FOR CustPosted .AND. Printed marks for deletion all records with .T. in the CustPosted and Printed fields, and the command PACK permanently removes those records. Then SET TALK OFF turns off the dBASE progress display, and ENDIF marks the end of the IF...ENDIF block.

Finally, the command CLOSE DATABASES closes the open database file, thereby ensuring that all changes are saved, and RETURN marks the end of the procedure.

REBUILDING INDEX FILES

As mentioned earlier, every application should include an option to rebuild index files in case these become corrupted by a power failure or some other malady. The Applications Generator includes an option for indexing a single database file, but the business application that we are developing uses many database files. Therefore, let's now write a procedure that can reindex all database files.

The command to rebuild all the indexes associated with a particular database is REINDEX. All you need to do is issue the USE command for the database of interest and then execute the REINDEX command. For this application, we'll name the procedure to rebuild all indexes BusRendx. Figure 19.14 shows the complete procedure.

To add this procedure to the BusProcs procedure file, enter the command **MODIFY COMMAND BusProcs**, as usual, at the dot prompt. Then move the cursor to the end of the procedure file and type the entire procedure exactly as shown in Figure 19.14. When you are done, choose Exit ► Save Changes and Exit to save your work and return to the dot prompt.

At this point, you have finished developing all the basic data processing procedures for the business application. But before you start actually building the application, the next chapter presents still more programming techniques that you can use to refine your business applications.

```
*------------------- Rebuild index files for all databases.
PROCEDURE BusRendx

   SET TALK ON    && Show progress
   USE Customer
   REINDEX
   USE Master
   REINDEX
   USE Orders
   REINDEX
   USE OrdHist
   REINDEX
   USE ItemsRec
   REINDEX
   USE ItemHist
   REINDEX
   USE Transact
   REINDEX
   SET TALK OFF   && Suppress progress messages.

RETURN
```

Figure 19.14: The BusRendx procedure

CHAPTER 20

Intelligent Custom Forms for Business Applications

Fast Track

THE PROCEDURES THAT YOU DEVELOPED IN THE preceding chapter will certainly help you build a powerful, integrated business management application. However, even the best business application is only as good as the data it uses. When meaningless or faulty information is entered, stored, and processed, then meaningless or faulty information appears in the various reports, such as invoices, inventory status, and so forth, printed from the database.

DATA VALIDATION

The best way to avoid erroneous or meaningless information in a business application is to try to prevent it from being stored in a database in the first place. There are two basic techniques that you can use to prevent errors: You can have your application reject obviously invalid data, and you can have the application provide feedback that allows users to quickly check their entries.

The first method of error prevention, having the application reject invalid information, prevents meaningless data from being entered into a database. For example, suppose the user enters a customer number and a part number for an order. A good application will check whether the customer number and part number entered for the order actually exist in the Customer and Master databases and if either entry is invalid, will reject the entry. The user then must reenter the order with a new value.

The second method of error prevention, having the application provide feedback, is not as foolproof as the first method, but can at least help reduce the number of errors. For example, suppose the user is entering an order for customer number 1001, but accidentally enters customer number 1010. Let's also assume that some other customer has the number 1010. The user might not catch the error unless, when the customer number is entered, the customer's name appears on the screen, as in Figure 20.1.

A quick glance at the screen tells the user the name of the customer assigned to the customer number entered. Assuming that the user knows the name of the customer for whom the order was

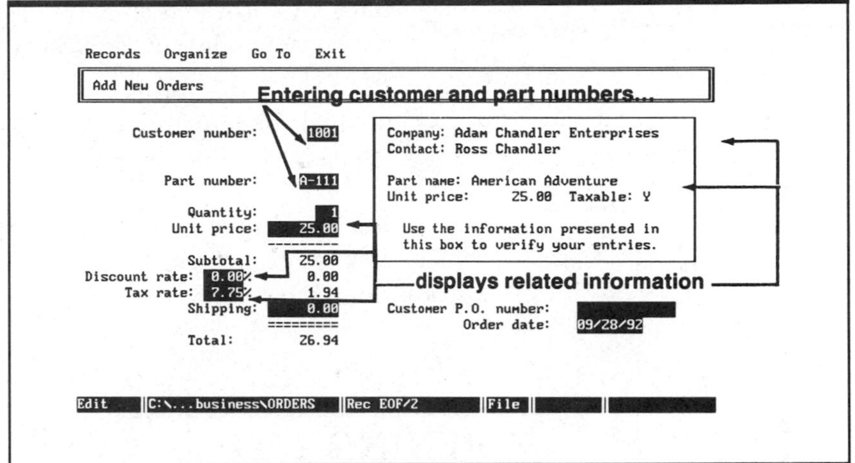

Figure 20.1: Customer information on the screen

entered, a quick glance at the screen tells the user whether the customer number is correct. As a convenience, the screen also displays that customer's standard discount and tax rates.

When the user enters a part number for the order, the screen displays the name and selling price of the part. A quick glance at the screen lets the user verify the entry, once again reducing the likelihood of an error.

Developing "intelligent" custom forms that can trap errors and supply feedback requires some advanced programming techniques. But if you are considering developing sophisticated applications, the techniques are well worth learning, because a sophisticated *user interface* (that is, the screens for entering and editing data) is one of the hallmarks of a professional-quality application.

The basic steps involved in developing such forms are

1. Open all the necessary databases needed to enter orders and verify entries.
2. Use the forms design screen to create custom forms for entering and editing data.
3. Note the exact row and column positions of all calculated fields (including fields from related database files).

4. Save the form and create user-defined functions for validating entries and displaying calculated information.
5. Return to the forms design screen and attach the user-defined functions to specific fields using the Accept Value When edit option.

You'll see examples of how to perform each step as you develop sophisticated screens for entering and editing orders in the business application in the sections that follow.

OPENING THE DATABASES FOR ORDER ENTRY

The Orders database stores order information, including the customer number and part number for each order. To allow the application to verify customer numbers and part numbers and provide information from these databases on the screen, the Orders, Customer, and Master databases must be open simultaneously and related through the fields that link them together.

You can store the appropriate commands for opening and relating the database files in the same procedure file, BusProcs, that you developed in the preceding chapter. To do so, follow these steps:

1. At the dot prompt, enter **MODIFY COMMAND BusProcs**.
2. Use the Ctrl-PgDn and ↵ keys to position the cursor at the end of the procedure file and add some blank lines.
3. Type the procedure, which we'll name OrdOpen, exactly as shown in Figure 20.2.
4. After typing the entire procedure, choose Exit ► Save Changes and Exit to save the modified procedure file.

Let's take a moment to see what the procedure does when executed. The SELECT and USE commands open the Orders, Customer, and Master databases. Notice that the Customer and Master databases are opened with indexes of the CustNo and PartNo, fields

```
*------------------- Opens database files and sets relations
*------------------- for order entry and editing.
PROCEDURE OrdOpen
   SELECT A
   USE Orders
   SELECT B
   USE Customer ORDER CustNo
   SELECT C
   USE Master ORDER PartNo

   *-------- Set up relationship based on key fields.
   SELECT Orders
   SET RELATION TO CustNo INTO Customer, PartNo INTO Master
   GO TOP
RETURN
```

Figure 20.2: The OrdOpen procedure

> **NOTE**
> When you create a query from the Queries panel at the Control Center, you're actually creating a file of commands similar to those in Figure 20.2. For example, in Chapter 13 you created a query file named CRSLINK.QBE. To take a quick look at the commands in that file, type **MODIFY COMMAND C:\DBASE\CRSLINK.QBE** at the dot prompt. Choose Exit ► Abandon Changes and Exit when you're finished, so that you don't actually change the query file.

which relate them to the Orders database. The command SELECT Orders then makes the Orders database the currently selected database. Orders must be the currently selected database in this situation, because the main purpose of the form you will be developing is entering and editing orders.

The command SET RELATION TO CustNo INTO Customer, PartNo INTO Master tells dBASE to set up a relationship between Orders and Customer based on the common CustNo field, and between Orders and Master based on the common PartNo field. Figure 20.3 illustrates this relationship, assuming that all three databases contain some data.

The GO TOP command simply moves the record pointer to the beginning of the Orders database, and RETURN marks the end of the procedure.

CREATING THE ORDER-ENTRY CUSTOM FORM

Now you need to create a custom form for editing orders (later you'll use this form as the basis for creating some other forms). Before you can create the form, however, you must run the OrdOpen

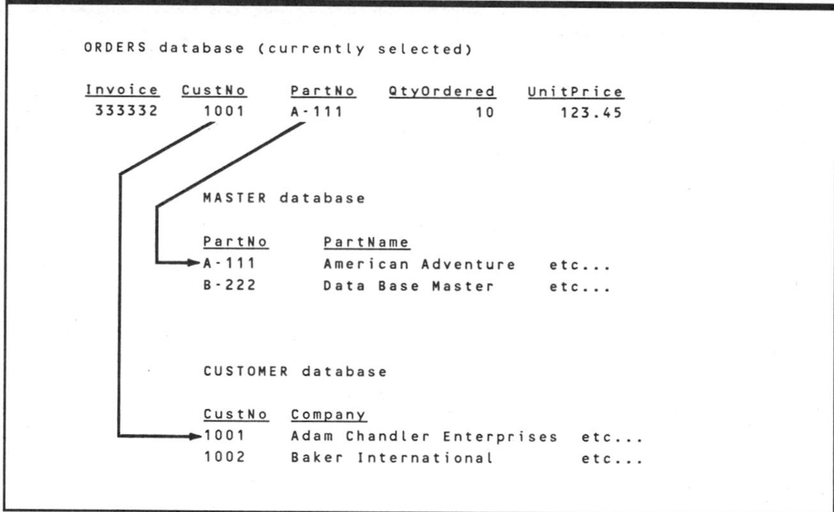

```
ORDERS database (currently selected)

Invoice  CustNo   PartNo   QtyOrdered   UnitPrice
 333332   1001    A-111          10       123.45

           MASTER database

           PartNo     PartName
           A-111      American Adventure    etc...
           B-222      Data Base Master      etc...

           CUSTOMER database

           CustNo  Company
           1001    Adam Chandler Enterprises   etc...
           1002    Baker International         etc...
```

Figure 20.3: Relationships defined among three databases

procedure to open the appropriate databases and set up the relationships so that dBASE can verify that fields coming from related database files do indeed exist as you design the form.

To open the database files and set up the relationship, run the OrdOpen procedure by entering these commands at the dot prompt:

```
SET PROCEDURE TO BusProcs
DO OrdOpen
```

You can enter DISPLAY STATUS at the dot prompt to see the names of all open database files, as well as the current status of various settings and keys.

When the dot prompt reappears, rest assured that the three databases are open and related (assuming you typed the OrdOpen procedure correctly). Now go to the forms design screen to create a custom form, which we'll name EDITORD. You can bypass the Control Center and simply enter the following command at the dot prompt:

```
MODIFY SCREEN EditOrd
```

If you need to review basic form design techniques, refer to Chapter 8.

You'll see the familiar forms design screen, where you can now use the usual techniques and keys to design your customer form.

Figure 20.4 shows the completed form on the screen.

Table 20.1 lists the row and column positions of field templates on the form. To place the templates, position the cursor at the row

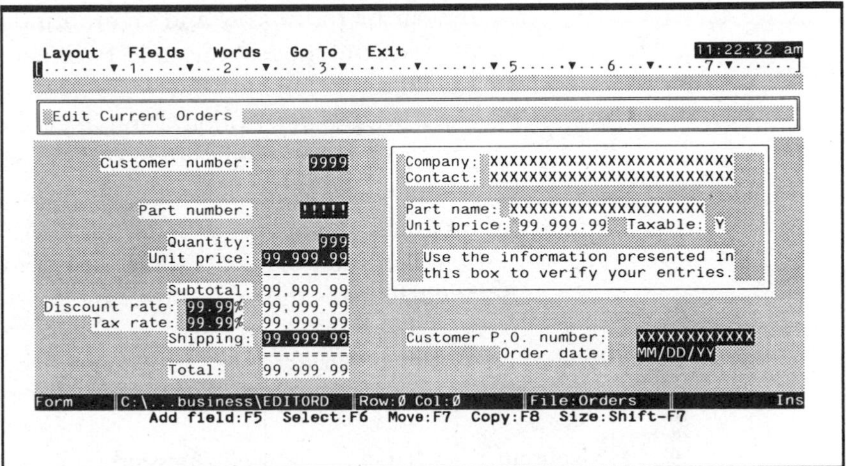

Figure 20.4: EditOrd custom form on the forms design screen

Table 20.1: Fields on the EditOrd Form

Row, column	Name
5,29	CUSTNO
8,28	PARTNO
10,30	QTYORDERED
11,24	UNITPRICE
14,16	DISCRATE
15,16	TAXRATE
16,24	SHIPPING
16,63	CUSTPONUMB
17,63	ORDATE

and column indicated, then press F5 (or double-click the mouse at that position) and select the field name from the left column of the submenu that appears.

Table 20.2 lists the row and column positions of the calculated fields on the EditOrd form. To place the calculated fields, position the cursor to the row and column indicated; then press F5 (or double-click the mouse) and select <create> from the right (calculated) side of the submenu. Enter the name and expression indicated (you can leave the description blank in each calculated field).

Use Figure 20.4 to guide you in specifying template characters as you place fields on the form. For example, as you can see in the figure, the PartNo field uses the template !!!!!.

After entering the text and field templates onto the form, you can add the boxes shown by choosing Layout ► Box from the menu.

Table 20.2: Calculated Fields on the EditOrd Form

Row, column	Name	Expression
5,48	CustComp	Customer->Company
6,48	CustCont	Customer->Contact
8,50	PtName	Master->PartName
9,51	MPrice	Master->SelPrice
9,71	MTax	Master->Taxable
13,24	ExtPrice	QtyOrdered*UnitPrice
14,24	DiscAmt	–(DiscRate/100)*(QtyOrdered*UnitPrice)
15,24	TaxAmt	(TaxRate/100)*(QtyOrdered*UnitPrice)
18,24	TotSale	Enter as a single long expression (hint—use the F9 key or double-click in the Expression box to zoom): (((QtyOrdered*UnitPrice) – ((DiscRate/100)* (QtyOrdered*UnitPrice)))* (1 + (TaxRate/100))) + Shipping

NOTING CALCULATED-FIELD LOCATIONS

If you were designing your own form rather than copying this one from the book, you would want to jot down on paper the exact location of each calculated (Calc'd) field on the form. You would also want to note the locations of regular fields that might accept new values automatically from related databases. For example, the TaxRate and DiscRate fields in the Orders database in the EditOrd form will be assigned values from the Customer database during data entry, so these should be included in your list.

You would also want to note the templates used for Numeric and Logical fields, as shown in Table 20.3. (It will become clear to you why this information is necessary when you develop user-defined functions in the next section.)

When your form looks exactly like the one in Figure 20.4, choose Exit ► Save Changes and Exit to save the form and return to the dot prompt.

Table 20.3: Fields used in Recalculations on the EditOrd Form

Row, column	Expression	Template
5,48	Customer->Company	
6,48	Customer->Contact	
8,50	Master->PartName	
9,51	Master->SelPrice	99,999.99
9,71	Master->Taxable	Y
13,24	QtyOrdered*UnitPrice	99,999.99
14,24	–(DiscRate/100)* (QtyOrdered*UnitPrice)	99,999.99
15,24	(TaxRate/100)* (QtyOrdered*UnitPrice)	99,999.99
18,24	(((QtyOrdered*UnitPrice) –((DiscRate/100)* (QtyOrdered*UnitPrice))) * (1 +(TaxRate/100))) +Shipping	99,999.99
11,24	UNITPRICE	99,999.99
14,16	DISCRATE	99.99
15,16	TAXRATE	99.99

At this point, you have a form that includes calculated fields for displaying information from the related Customer and Master databases and for calculating the extended price, tax amount, discount amount, and total sale. However, your job is not complete yet, because the form will not reject invalid entries during data entry. Instead, it will only show the results of the calculated field while you are editing *existing* data.

You need to add some *user-defined functions* to your BusProcs procedure to handle the data validation. As discussed in Chapter 18, a user-defined function is similar to a procedure and can be stored in a procedure file with existing procedures.

CREATING USER-DEFINED FUNCTIONS

Before we actually develop the user-defined functions for the business application, let's take a moment to clarify exactly when these functions will be used. First, as you've seen throughout most of the preceding chapters, whenever you enter or edit database data, the screen displays a highlighted area with the cursor in it, where you can enter or change information, as shown here (where [ ] represents the highlighted area on the screen and the underline represents the cursor):

```
Customer number: [ _  ]
```

The cursor blinks and waits for you to enter new data or change any existing data or to press some other key to move out of the field.

Regardless of which key you use to leave the field, it is at that precise moment, when the cursor leaves the field and before it moves into the next field, that your user-defined functions will be executed. These functions can perform any number of operations, including validating the entry, displaying data from related database files, and displaying calculations on the screen.

When a user-defined function is done with its task, it must return some value (as discussed in Chapter 18). Typically, in a custom screen a user-defined function returns either .T. or .F. If the function returns .T., the cursor moves to the next field on the screen as it normally would. If your function returns .F., then the cursor *does not* move to the next field on the screen. Instead, the computer beeps, the bottom line of the screen displays an error message (which you design), and the cursor stays in the current field. In other words, the entry is rejected and must be corrected.

Because you are the person who defines what is and what is not a valid entry in a user-defined function, you have enormous control over what the user can and cannot enter into the database. And because user-defined functions can perform many tasks, you also have enormous power in determining what takes place on the screen (and even in the databases) at the moment the cursor leaves a particular field on the screen.

Unfortunately, with enormous power also comes responsibility. You must be aware of one particular problem with such powerful data entry and editing screens so you can deal with it effectively. Consider the following situation.

Suppose the user is adding orders to the Orders database. Initially, the customer number, tax rate, and discount rate fields are blank, as shown here:

```
Customer number:  [_   ]
    Part number:  [    ]
       Tax rate:  [  . ]
  Discount rate:  [  . ]
```

As soon as the user types a customer number, your user-defined function conveniently fills in the standard discount rate and tax rate for that customer on the order form (screen), as follows:

```
Customer number:  [1001]
    Part number:  [_   ]
       Tax rate:  [ 7.75]
  Discount rate:  [10.00]
```

The user then enters the part number for the order:

```
Customer number:  [1001]
    Part number:  [A-111]
       Tax rate:  [ 7.75]
  Discount rate:  [10.00]
```

Now suppose that the standard 10 percent discount rate does not apply to this particular order, so the user changes the discount rate to

0 when the cursor reaches that field, as follows:

```
Customer number:  [1001]
    Part number:  [A-111]
       Tax rate:  [ 7.75]
  Discount rate:  [ 0.  ]
```

The user fills in any other fields on the screen, checks the entries, verifies that everything looks okay, and then moves on and enters several more orders. When the user is done entering orders, he or she exits the application or moves on to some other task.

Now suppose that later the user returns to the orders and decides to check them by using the edit mode and scrolling through existing orders using the PgUp and PgDn keys. It's at this moment that a real problem could arise.

As the user is scrolling through the orders, the order entered in the example reappears on the screen, as follows:

```
Customer number:  [1001]
    Part number:  [A-111]
       Tax rate:  [ 7.75]
  Discount rate:  [ 0.  ]
```

The user sees that it's okay and then presses the PgDn key to check the next record. At that precise moment, dBASE executes your user-defined function (because the cursor has left the field, as well as the entire record), and your user-defined function quickly puts the customer's standard discount rate, 10 percent, back into the discount rate field, as shown here:

```
Customer number:  [1001]
    Part number:  [A-111]
       Tax rate:  [ 7.75]
  Discount rate:  [10.00]
```

This happens so quickly—in the fraction of a second that dBASE takes to scroll from one record to the next—that chances are good that the user will not even know the change took place. But now the order is wrong, because the original discount rate of zero was the correct entry for that particular record.

NOTE

Appendix G lists all ASCII characters and their code numbers.

How do you solve this problem? The solution is a dBASE IV built-in function named LASTKEY(). The LASTKEY() function *always* contains the ASCII code number of the most recent keypress.

You can decide for yourself which keystrokes activate your user-defined function. If the user completely filled the field highlight on the screen, then the LASTKEY() function will return a number in the range 32 to 122 (all characters from a blank to a lowercase *z*). If the user presses ↵ to leave the field, then LASTKEY() will contain 13. Other special keystrokes used to manage the cursor on the screen are listed here.

NOTE

No keypress is recorded when you click the mouse in a field.

Keystroke	LASTKEY()
PgUp	18
PgDn	3
↑	5
↓	24
Tab	9
Shift-Tab	–400
Esc	27
Ctrl-End	23

For the user-defined functions in this chapter, we'll assume that if the user presses any letter or number (a key in the range 32 to 122) or presses ↵ (number 13), the user-defined function will be executed. If the user presses any other key (such as PgUp, PgDn, Tab, or an arrow key), the function will assume the user is just scrolling and will not modify existing entries. To make this decision, we'll use an IF clause that starts with the command IF LASTKEY() = 13 .OR. (LASTKEY()> = 32 .AND. LASTKEY()< = 122) in our user-defined function, as you'll see in a moment.

VALIDATING CUSTOMER NUMBERS

The first user-defined function that you will develop will perform the tasks shown here in pseudocode:

```
In case user leaves customer number blank to exit
    Skip validation
    Return "Ok"
In case a valid customer number was entered
    Display the company name
```

```
    Display the contact
    If user not just scrolling
        Replace order discount rate with customer discount rate
        Allow discount rate to be changed for this order
        If item is taxable
            Replace order tax rate with customer tax rate
        Else
            Replace order tax rate with zero
        End "taxable" IF clause
        Allow tax rate to be changed for this order
        Recalculate screen
        Return Ok

In case invalid customer number ordered
        Reject entry and display "No such customer!"
        Return "not Ok"
```

To add the user-defined function to the BusProcs procedure file, use the same basic technique you used to add new procedures. That is, first enter the command **CLOSE PROCEDURE** at the dot prompt. Then enter the command **MODIFY COMMAND BusProcs**, and position the cursor beneath the existing procedures. Then enter the complete user-defined function, as shown in Figure 20.5. Be sure to save the BusProcs procedure after adding the IsCust function by choosing Exit ► Save Changes and Exit.

Now let's examine this user-defined function and its commands. The first command, FUNCTION IsCust, defines the name of the user-defined function as IsCust. The command PARAMETERS MCustNo assigns the temporary name MCustNo to the value passed to the function. (As you'll see later, this function is called from the custom screen using the syntax IsCust(CustNo), where CustNo is the customer number that the user entered and is also the value passed to the user-defined function.)

The command DO CASE (discussed in Chapter 18) sets up a clause in which the first true condition will be the only one executed between the DO CASE and ENDCASE commands. The first CASE statement, CASE MCustNo = 0, checks whether the user just pressed ↵ without entering a customer number, which implies that he or she has finished entering orders. If this is the case, then the command Ok = .T. stores .T. in the memory variable named Ok, and dBASE

```
*______________________________ Validate customer number.
FUNCTION IsCust
PARAMETERS MCustNo
   DO CASE

      *_ If user is exiting, do nothing.
      CASE McustNo = 0
           Ok=.T.

      *__________ Customer number was entered.
      CASE SEEK(MCustNo,"Customer")
           @ 5,48 SAY Customer->Company
           @ 6,48 SAY Customer->Contact
           *___ Recalculate (depending on last keypress).
           IF LASTKEY()=13 .OR. (LASTKEY()>=32.AND.LASTKEY()<=122)
              REPLACE Orders->DiscRate WITH Customer->DiscRate
              @ 14,16 GET DiscRate PICTURE "99.99"
              IF Master->Taxable
                 REPLACE Orders->TaxRate WITH Customer->TaxRate
              ELSE
                 REPLACE Orders->TaxRate WITH 0
              ENDIF &&taxable
              @ 15,16 GET TaxRate PICTURE "99.99"
              Ok=Recalc(QtyOrdered)
           ENDIF  && last keypress
           Ok=.T.
      OTHERWISE
         @ 5,48 SAY "No such customer!          "
         @ 6,48 SAY SPACE(25)
         Ok=.F.
   ENDCASE
RETURN (Ok)
```

Figure 20.5: The IsCust user-defined function

ignores all other CASE conditions. (The Ok memory variable plays an important role in this user-defined function, as you'll see.)

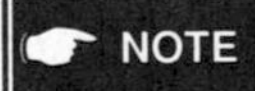

dBASE IV includes both a command called SEEK and a built-in function named SEEK(). Both the command and the function search the currently active index file only.

If the user did indeed enter a new customer number for the current order, then the next CASE statement, CASE SEEK(MCustNo,"Customer"), is evaluated. The SEEK() function very quickly searches for its first argument in the current index of the database specified in its second argument. Let us see how this operation works.

The OrdOpen procedure, which you created earlier in this chapter, opens the Customer database with the CustNo index controlling the sort order. The memory variable MCustNo currently contains the customer number that the user entered on the screen. Therefore, the expression SEEK(MCustNo,"Customer") searches the CustNo index of the Customer database for a customer number that matches the one the user entered on the screen.

If the SEEK() function does *not* find a matching customer number, it returns .F., and dBASE then ignores all commands up to the OTHERWISE command in the DO CASE clause. If, on the other

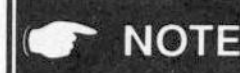

Even though it takes quite a while to *explain* some of the operations performed in these user-defined functions, dBASE IV actually executes them in a fraction of a second.

hand, the SEEK() function *does* find a matching customer number, it returns .T., in which case dBASE executes all commands between the CASE SEEK(MCustNo,"Customer") and OTHERWISE commands and ignores the commands between OTHERWISE and ENDCASE.

Assuming that the SEEK() function did indeed find a matching customer number in the Customer database, dBASE executes the following commands. First, the @ 5,48 SAY Customer->Company command displays on the form the company name from the related record on the Customer database. That is, if the user entered **1001** as the customer for the current order and customer number 1001 identifies Adam Chandler Enterprises in the Customer database, then Adam Chandler Enterprises is the company name displayed on the screen. If you are wondering why the company name needs to be displayed specifically at row 5, column 48, refer back to Figure 20.4 or Table 20.2; you'll see that this is precisely where the company name is displayed on the custom form you developed earlier.

The next command processed, if the customer number was valid, is @ 6,48 SAY Customer->Contact, which displays the Contact field from the Customer database directly beneath the company name.

The phrase "&& last keypress" after the ENDIF command is just a programmer comment to remind you which ENDIF statement belongs to which IF statement. It does not affect the actual processing.

The command IF LASTKEY() = 13 .OR. (LASTKEY()> = 32 .AND. LASTKEY()< = 122) checks whether the user last typed a letter or character or pressed ↵. If the user did so, dBASE processes all commands between this command and the ENDIF && last keypress command. If the user presses any other key (such as PgUp, PgDn, or some other scrolling key), the IF statement evaluates to false, and dBASE ignores all commands between this command and the ENDIF && last keypress command.

The next command, REPLACE Orders->DiscRate WITH Customer->DiscRate copies the customer's standard discount rate into the current record on the Orders database. But this value may need to be changed for a particular order, so the next command, @ 14,16 GET DiscRate PICTURE "99.99", places the field, with its new contents, back on the screen so that it can be changed if necessary. (If the user changes the discount rate, it is changed for the current order only in the Orders database, *not* in the Customer database.)

Note that the command @ 14,16 GET DiscRate PICTURE "99.99" exactly matches the row and column position, field name, and template (99.99) specified back in Table 20.2. This command displays the new discount rate at exactly the same position, using exactly the same template, that the EditOrd custom screen does.

Next, an IF...ENDIF clause, nested within the IF...ENDIF clause that determined the last key that the user pressed, determines how to present the tax rate. If the user is editing an existing record, then the part number is already on the screen and in the database record. The first command, IF Master->Taxable, determines whether the related item from the Master database is taxable. If the item is taxable, then TaxRate in the current record of the orders database is replaced with the customer's standard tax rate. The command REPLACE Orders->TaxRate WITH Customer->TaxRate effects the replacement.

If the item ordered is *not* taxable (ELSE), then the command REPLACE Orders->TaxRate WITH 0 puts a zero in the TaxRate field of the order currently being entered or edited. The ENDIF &&taxable command marks the end of the IF...ENDIF decision clause for determining the tax rate for the current order.

In case the default tax rate assigned to the order needs to be changed for the current order, the command @ 15,16 GET TaxRate PICTURE "99.99" displays the customer's tax rate on the screen and makes it available for editing. Again, the command uses exactly the same row and column positions and template that was specified in the EditOrd custom form.

The command Ok = Recalc(QtyOrdered) activates another user-defined function, named *Recalc*, which we'll develop later. The Recalc function will recalculate all the subtotals and totals on the screen and then return .T. dBASE stores this .T. in the memory variable named Ok. Later, this .T. will be returned to the custom form, indicating that a valid part number was entered and the user can proceed with the order.

The next command, ENDIF &&last keypress, marks the end of the IF...ENDIF clause that was used to determine the last key that the user pressed. The next command, Ok = .T., stores the value .T. in the memory variable named Ok, which this user-defined function will return to the field that called it (as you'll see later).

The commands beneath the OTHERWISE command are executed only if neither of the preceding CASE conditions is true (that is, the user is not exiting, and the user did not enter a valid customer number). If the OTHERWISE condition is executed, then the

IsCust user-defined function displays the message "No such customer!" at exactly the position where a valid customer name would appear (row 5, column 48). The next command, @ 6,48 SAY SPACE(25), displays 25 blank spaces where the customer contact name would appear, thereby overwriting any previous contact name at that screen position.

Next, the command Ok = .F. stores .F. in the memory variable named Ok, because if the entire OTHERWISE clause is executed, then the customer number that the user entered is not valid (that is, it does not exist in the Customer database). When this .F. is returned to the custom form, the cursor will not move to the next field on the form, but instead will wait for a new, valid customer number to be entered (as you'll see later). The ENDCASE command marks the end of the DO CASE...ENDCASE decision clause.

The last command in the IsCust user-defined function, RETURN (Ok), returns the value currently stored in the memory variable named Ok to the custom form that initially called the procedure. You'll see how to attach the IsCust user-defined function to the customer field in the EditOrd custom screen soon.

For now, suffice it to say that if the user entered a valid number, or if the user was just scrolling or exiting, then the Ok value returned will allow the user to proceed. However, if the Ok value returned is .F. (that is, the customer number for the current order is invalid), then the user will need to enter a different, valid customer number before moving to the next field in the custom screen.

VALIDATING PART NUMBERS

The user-defined function for validating part numbers, named IsPart, validates part numbers as they are entered or edited in the current Orders database. The IsPart procedure uses the same basic logic and the same programming techniques as the IsCust user-defined function. The main difference is that the IsPart function validates part numbers rather than customer numbers as they are entered or changed on the screen, and it displays related data from the Master, rather than the Customer, database file.

Also, the IsPart user-defined function does not need to check whether the user is just exiting, because dBASE exits a custom screen only if the first field on the custom form (CustNo in this example) is left blank. So the IsPart function uses a simple IF...END-IF clause to determine whether the part number that the user entered was valid: IF SEEK(MPartNo,"Master"), or not (ELSE).

The basic logic of the IsPart user-defined function is shown here in pseudocode:

```
*-------------------------------- Validate part number
FUNCTION IsPart
PARAMETERS MPartNo
If a valid part number was entered
   Display part name
   Display selling price
   Display taxable status
   If the user is not just scrolling
      Replace the order unit price with the selling price
         REPLACE Orders->UnitPrice WITH Master->SelPrice
         Allow suggested selling price to be changed for this order
         If the item is taxable
            Replace order tax rate with customer's tax rate
         Else
            Replace order tax rate with zero
         End IF (for taxable status)
         Allow order tax rate to be changed
         Recalculate screen
      Endif (for last keypress)
      Entry is Ok
   Else
      Display error message "No such part number!"
      Reject entry
   End If (part number validation)
```

To add the IsPart user-defined function to the BusProcs procedure file, follow these steps:

1. At the dot prompt, enter **MODIFY COMMAND BusProcs** to edit the BusProcs procedure file.
2. Position the cursor at the end of the file (beneath the IsCust user-defined function) by pressing Ctrl-PgDn.
3. Enter the IsPart user-defined function exactly as shown in Figure 20.6.

```
*--------------------------------- Validate part number
FUNCTION IsPart
PARAMETERS MPartNo
   IF SEEK(MPartNo,"MASTER")
      @ 8,50 SAY Master->PartName
      @ 9,51 SAY Master->SelPrice PICTURE "99,999.99"
      @ 9,71 SAY Master->Taxable PICTURE "Y"

      IF LASTKEY()=13 .OR. (LASTKEY()>=32.AND.LASTKEY()<=122)
         REPLACE Orders->UnitPrice WITH Master->SelPrice
         @ 11,24 GET UnitPrice PICTURE "99,999.99"
         *---- If item not taxable, replace tax rate with 0
         IF Master->Taxable
            REPLACE Orders->TaxRate WITH Customer->TaxRate
         ELSE
            REPLACE Orders->TaxRate WITH 0
         ENDIF
         @ 15,16 GET TaxRate PICTURE "99.99"
         Ok = Recalc(QtyOrdered)
      ENDIF &&lastkey
      Ok=.T.

   *--- Invalid part number.
   ELSE
         @ 8,50 SAY "No such part number!     "
         Ok=.F.
   ENDIF && seek() true or false.

RETURN (Ok)
```

Figure 20.6: The IsPart user-defined function

4. After typing the new user-defined function, choose Exit ► Save Changes and Exit to save the modified BusProcs procedure file.

RECALCULATING TOTALS

As mentioned previously, dBASE will automatically recalculate subtotals and totals as you scroll through existing records in the database, because of the various calculated fields that you placed on the form. But these fields will not recalculate while the user is entering new data. Therefore, you need a user-defined function to force recalculation to take place whenever you want it to.

The name of the recalculation user-defined function is Recalc(). To add this function to the BusProcs procedure, enter the command

MODIFY COMMAND BusProcs at the dot prompt and then position the cursor at the bottom of the procedure file. Type the procedure as shown in Figure 20.7. Be sure to save the procedure file after adding the new function.

```
*______________________________ Recalculate totals for screen display.
FUNCTION Recalc
PARAMETERS MQty
   @ 13,24 SAY QtyOrdered*UnitPrice PICTURE "99,999.99"
   @ 14,24 SAY -(DiscRate/100)*(QtyOrdered*UnitPrice) PICTURE "99,999.99"
   @ 15,24 SAY (TaxRate/100)*((1-DiscRate/100)*(QtyOrdered*UnitPrice)) ;
     PICTURE "99,999.99"
   @ 18,24 SAY ((QtyOrdered*UnitPrice)- ;
     ((DiscRate/100)*(QtyOrdered*UnitPrice)))* ;
     (1+(TaxRate/100)) + Shipping;
      PICTURE "99,999.99"
   Ok=.T.
RETURN (Ok)
```

Figure 20.7: The Recalc user-defined function

If you compare the contents of the Recalc function to the row and column positions of calculated fields listed previously in Table 20.2, you'll see that it basically performs the same calculations as the calculated fields in the form. But again, because we can control when the Recalc function does its job, we gain control over when recalculations occur on the screen.

All user-defined functions must return some value, so the Recalc function always returns .T. (in a variable named Ok). Unlike the previous user-defined functions, which return .F. when invalid data is entered into a field, the Recalc function never rejects data. Its job is simply to recalculate, not to validate.

You may recall that both the IsCust and IsPart user-defined functions included the command Ok = Recalc(QtyOrdered). This command forces the Recalc function to recalculate all the subtotals and totals on the screen and then stores .T. in the variable named Ok.

ATTACHING USER-DEFINED FUNCTIONS TO FIELDS

Now that you have created all of your user-defined functions for order entry, you need to go back to your custom screen and determine when each user-defined function is executed. As you do so, dBASE will check to make sure each user-defined function is available, so the procedure file must be open. Assuming that the dot prompt is showing on your screen, open the BusProcs procedure file now by entering the command

```
SET PROCEDURE TO BusProcs
```

To work with the EditOrd screen, the Orders, Customer, and Master databases must be open simultaneously as well. To open all three files, enter the command

```
DO OrdOpen
```

to execute the OrdOpen procedure.

To get back to the forms design screen with the EditOrd form displayed, enter the command

```
MODIFY SCREEN EditOrd
```

ATTACHING THE ISCUST FUNCTION

To attach a particular user-defined function to a particular field on the form, you need to move the cursor to the appropriate field template, press or click Add Field (F5), or double-click on that template, and then use the appropriate syntax for the user-defined function as the Accept Value When edit option. Let's work through the exact steps involved in attaching the IsCust user-defined function to the Customer field template.

1. Position the cursor on the CustNo field template (row 5, column 29).
2. Press or click Add Field (F5), or double-click on the CustNo field template.
3. Select Edit Options.
4. Select Accept Value When.
5. Type the expression **IsCust(CustNo)** and press ↵.
6. Select Unaccepted Message, type the message **Please reenter a valid customer number**, and press ↵.

When you are done, your screen should look like Figure 20.8 (dBASE adds the curly braces automatically; you do not type them).

Let's take a moment to review what this step has done. As soon as the user adds or changes a customer number, the Accept Value When option executes the custom IsCust function, passing it the customer number (CustNo) that the user entered. The IsCust user-defined function will do the jobs you specified and return either .T. (if the entry is valid) or .F. (if the entry is invalid).

If the IsCust function returns .T., the Accept Value When option accepts the entry and moves the cursor to the next field on the form. If the IsCust function returns .F., then the Accept Value When option rejects the entry, displays the Unaccepted Message, and waits for a new entry. The cursor remains in the CustNo field on the form until the user enters a valid customer number (that is, the IsCust function returns .T.).

After defining the Accept Value When and Unaccepted Message fields, press or click Ctrl-End twice to return to the form.

ATTACHING THE ISPART FUNCTION

Next, to validate part numbers, attach the IsPart user-defined function to the PartNo field template on the form. Use the same

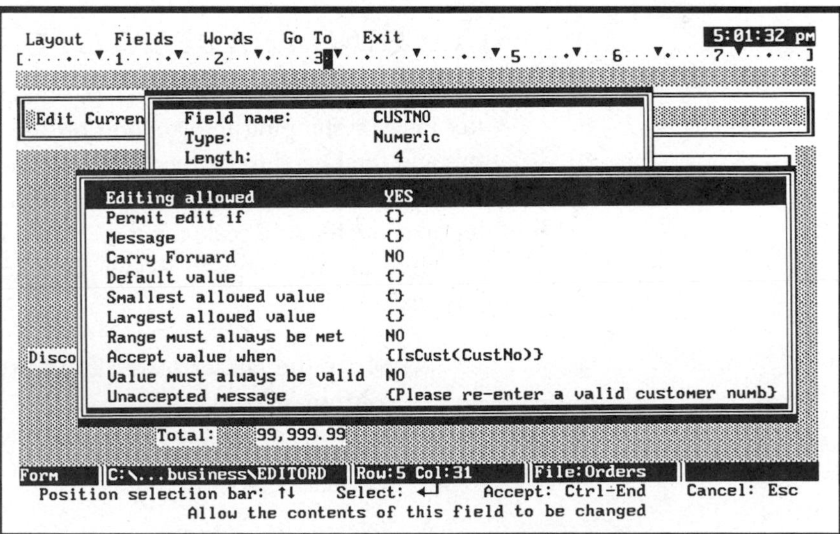

Figure 20.8: IsCust function attached to the CustNo field

basic steps that you used before:

1. Move the cursor to the PartNo field template (located at row 8, column 28).
2. Press or click Add Field (F5), or double-click on the PartNo field template.
3. Select Edit Options.
4. Select Accept Value When.
5. Type the expression **IsPart(PartNo)** and press ↵.
6. Select Unaccepted Message.
7. Type the message **Please re-enter a valid part number** and then press ↵.

Figure 20.9 shows how your screen should look when you've properly entered the expressions. Note that the Accept Value When option for this field activates the IsPart user-defined function and passes to it the part number that the user entered. The IsPart user-defined function will return .T. if the part number is valid. Otherwise, it will return .F., and the form will not accept the entry. Press or click Ctrl-End twice to return to the forms design screen.

ATTACHING THE RECALC FUNCTION

Whenever the user changes the quantity, unit price, discount rate, tax rate, or shipping information on the order-entry screen, the subtotals and total need to be recalculated. Therefore, you need to attach the Recalc user-defined function to each of these fields. The expression you use to activate the Recalc function is Recalc(QtyOrdered).

Here are the steps to follow to attach the Recalc function to the QtyOrdered field:

1. Move the cursor to the QtyOrdered field template (row 10, column 30).
2. Press or click Add Field (F5), or double-click on the field template QtyOrdered.
3. Select Edit Options.

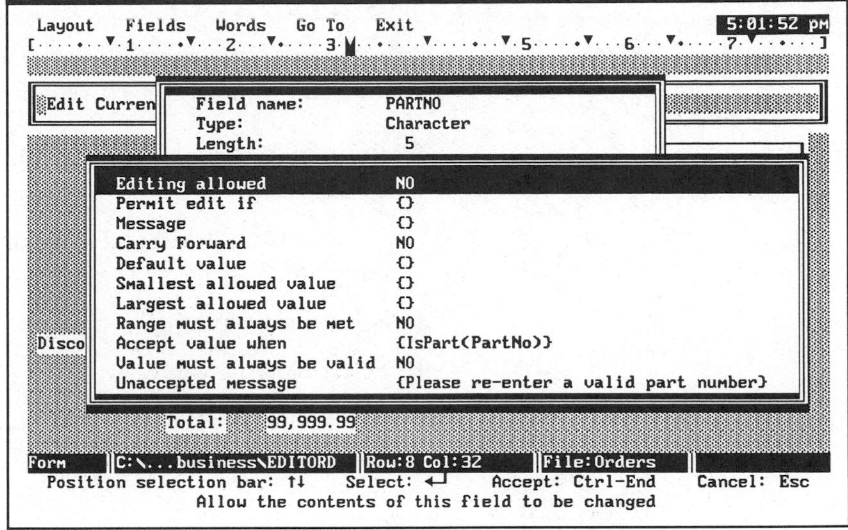
Layout Fields Words Go To Exit 5:01:52 pm
Edit Curren
Field name: PARTNO
Type: Character
Length: 5
Editing allowed NO
Permit edit if {}
Message {}
Carry Forward NO
Default value {}
Smallest allowed value {}
Largest allowed value {}
Range must always be met NO
Disco
Accept value when {IsPart(PartNo)}
Value must always be valid NO
Unaccepted message {Please re-enter a valid part number}
Total: 99,999.99
Form C:\...business\EDITORD Row:8 Col:32 File:Orders
Position selection bar: ↑↓ Select: ←┘ Accept: Ctrl-End Cancel: Esc
Allow the contents of this field to be changed

Figure 20.9: IsPart function attached to the PartNo field

4. Select Accept Value When.
5. Type **Recalc(QtyOrdered)** and press ←┘.
6. Press or click Ctrl-End twice to return to the forms design screen.

You did not define an Unaccepted Message in the preceding steps because the Recalc function always returns .T. Again, its job is not to validate data, but rather to recalculate. Nonetheless, as soon as the cursor leaves the QtyOrdered field on the form, the Accept Value When option will force the Recalc function to do its job.

Now repeat steps 2 through 6 for each of the field templates listed here (in place of step 1, first position the cursor on the field template at the row and column positions indicated):

Field template	**Position**
UnitPrice	Row 11, column 24
DiscRate	Row 14, column 16
TaxRate	Row 15, column 16
Shipping	Row 16, column 24

SETTING A DEFAULT DATE

Before you save the current form, you might first want to make the default order date equal to the current date. To do so, follow these steps:

1. Position the cursor on the Ordate field template (row 17, column 63).
2. Press or click Add Field (F5), or double-click the Ordate field template.
3. Select Edit Options.
4. Select Default Value.
5. Type the expression **DATE( )** and press ↵.
6. Press or click Ctrl-End twice.

SAVING THE FORM FOR ORDER EDITING

You actually need two forms for managing orders: one for editing orders and one for adding orders. The form for editing orders is done, so follow these steps to save the forms yet stay on the forms design screen:

1. Choose Layout ► Save This Form.
2. Press ↵ to accept the suggested name EditOrd.

SAVING THE FORM FOR ORDER ENTRY

The form for entering new orders is basically the same as the editing form, but there is no need to display the calculated field templates that appear on the form. (These would be accurate only while scrolling through existing records.) Thus, you can delete these for the order entry form.

First move the cursor to the title Edit Current Orders and change it to Add New Orders. Then delete each of the calculated field templates by moving the cursor to the field template and pressing the Del key. Be careful to delete *only* the following calculated fields:

Field name	Position
ExtPrice	Row 13, column 24
DiscAmt	Row 14, column 24
TaxAmt	Row 15, column 24
TotSale	Row 18, column 24
CustName	Row 5, column 48
CustCont	Row 6, column 48
PtName	Row 8, column 50
Price	Row 9, column 51
Taxable	Row 9, column 71

When you are done, your screen should look like Figure 20.10.

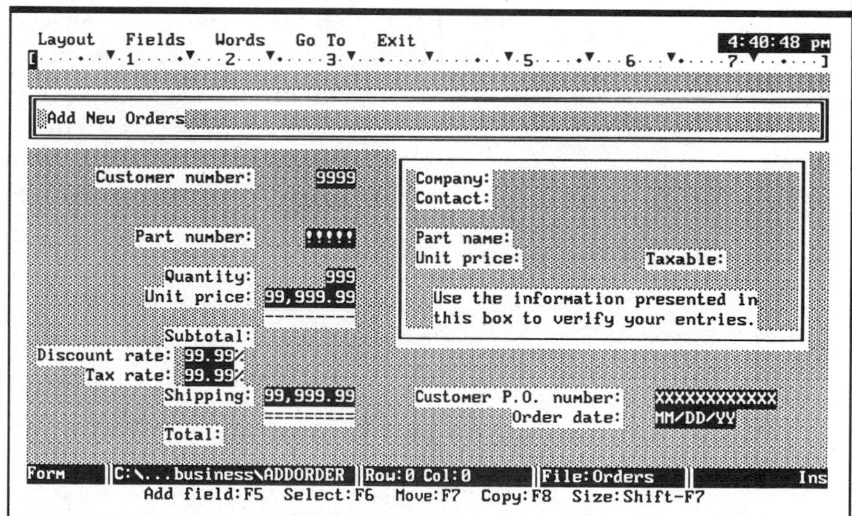

Figure 20.10: Form for entering new orders

To save this form with the file name AddOrder, follow these steps:

1. Choose Layout ► Save This Form.

2. Press Backspace 11 times to erase EditOrd.scr and then type the new form name **ADDORDER**.
3. Press ↵.

Now choose Exit ► Abandon Changes and Exit. You'll be returned to the dot prompt.

TESTING THE FORMS

NOTE

In this section, you'll use dot-prompt commands to test your forms, but after you build the business application, you'll be able to access the forms through simpler menu selection.

Both the Customer and Master databases need to have some information in them before you can enter orders into the Orders database. Let's check the status of the databases now and, if necessary, add some data. At the dot prompt enter the command **CLOSE DATABASES** to close all currently open databases. Enter the command **USE Customer** to open the Customer database and then enter the command **EDIT**. If you get an error message indicating that the end-of-file was encountered immediately, the file is empty; enter the command **APPEND** instead to add new records.

Add some sample records (or edit existing ones) so that the database contains at least the two records shown here (you can press F2 to switch to the browse screen if you prefer):

CustNo:	1001
Company:	Adam Chandler Enterprises
Contact:	Ross Chandler
Address:	1221 West Gaines
City:	Pine Valley
State:	NY
Zip:	12345
Phone:	(123)555-0123
StartDate:	12/01/93
TaxRate:	7.75
DiscRate	10.00
YtdChrg:	0.00
YtdPmt:	0.00
TotChrg:	0.00
TotPmt:	0.00
LastDate:	/ /

CustNo:	1002
Company:	Baker International
Contact:	Linda Grey
Address:	456 Ocean St.
City:	San Diego
State:	CA
Zip:	92067
Phone:	(619)555-0912
StartDate:	12/01/93
TaxRate:	0.00
DiscRate	0.00
YtdChrg:	0.00
YtdPmt:	0.00
TotChrg:	0.00
TotPmt:	0.00
LastDate:	/ /

Press Ctrl-End after adding or editing records to save them and return to the dot prompt. Note that the first customer, 1001, has a discount rate of 10 percent, and a tax rate of 7.75 percent. The second customer has zero as both these rates.

Now add or edit some Master database file records. First enter the command **USE Master** to open the Master database. Then enter the command **EDIT** (or **APPEND**, if you get an error message). Enter at least two records with the following characteristics:

PartNo:	A-111
PartName:	American Adventure
Category:	BOOK
InStock:	10
Reorder:	20
PurCost:	10.00
SelPrice:	25.00
Taxable:	T
Vendor:	HBJ
VendItemNo:	HBJ-101
Location:	WH-A10
LastUpdate:	/ /

PartNo:	B-222
PartName:	Data Base Master
Category:	MAGAZINE

```
InStock:        30
Reorder:        5
PurCost:        3.50
SelPrice:       5.00
Taxable:        F
Vendor:         ZD
VendItemNo:     Z-444-01
Location:       WH-001
LastUpdate:     / /
```

Note that the first item, A-111, is taxable, and the second is not. Press Ctrl-End when you are done to return to the dot prompt.

Now you are ready to start testing. First make sure the BusProcs procedure file is open by entering **SET PROCEDURE TO BusProcs**. Then open the required databases by entering the command **DO OrdOpen**.

The dot prompt command for activating a custom form is SET FORMAT. To activate the AddOrder form, enter the command **SET FORMAT TO AddOrder** (initially, only the dot prompt will appear). Then, to start adding new records, enter the command **APPEND**. You should see the AddOrder custom form on the screen, ready to accept data, as in Figure 20.11.

First try entering an invalid customer number such as 4444. You should see the message "No such customer!" in the single-line box and the message "Please re-enter a valid customer number (press SPACE)." Press the space bar and then enter a valid customer number, such as **1001**.

The screen should immediately display the customer information, as shown in Figure 20.12. (The tax rate is initially set to zero, however, because you have not yet entered a part number.)

Now try entering an invalid part number, such as W-333. You should see an error message indicating that no such part number exists and asking you to press the space bar. Enter a valid part number, such as **A-111**, and you should see the name, unit price, and taxable status (Y or N) of the part on the screen.

Next enter a quantity, such as **10**. Immediately, the screen calculates the subtotal, discount, tax, and total, as shown in Figure 20.13. At this point, you can change any of the other fields (if necessary) to finish entering the order, or just press PgDn to enter the next order.

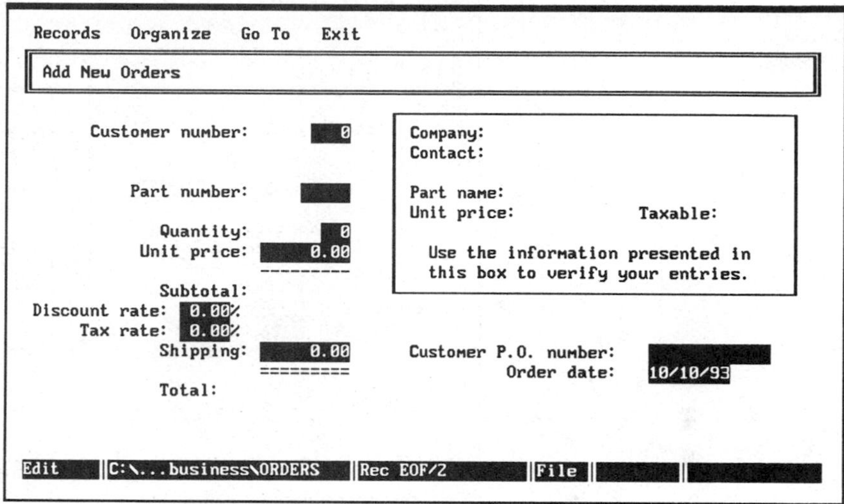

Figure 20.11: The AddOrder form, ready to accept data

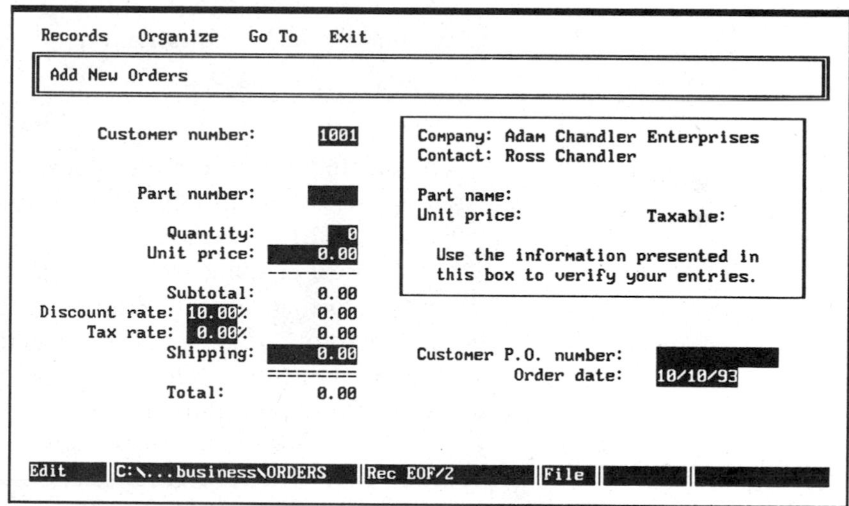

Figure 20.12: Valid customer number entered on the screen

Feel free to experiment with the form for as long as you wish. After you enter at least two sample orders, you can leave the customer number as zero on a new, blank record or press Ctrl-End to save your work and return to the dot prompt.

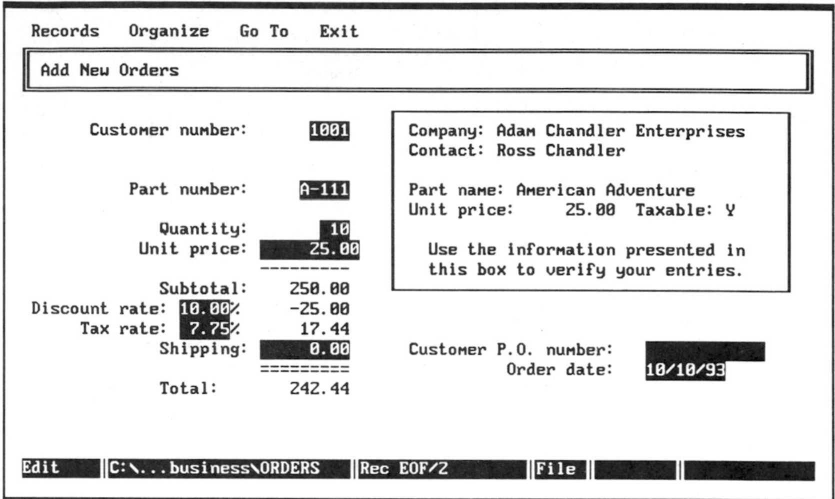

Figure 20.13: A valid order entered on the screen

To review or change the orders you've entered, use the EditOrd screen and the EDIT command. At the dot prompt, enter

```
SET FORMAT TO EditOrd
EDIT 1
```

When the editing screen appears, you can use the PgUp and PgDn keys to scroll through the records. Again, feel free to experiment. Press Ctrl-End when you are done experimenting.

In the next chapter, we'll develop some additional custom forms and report formats for the business application and use the Applications Generator to tie everything together into a single, integrated application. For future reference, Figure 20.14 shows the entire completcd BusProcs procedure file.

```
****************************************** BusProcs.PRG
*---- Procedures for order entry and editing.

***************************** Assign customer numbers.
PROCEDURE AutoCust

   *---------- Open Customer database.
   USE Customer ORDER CustNo
   GOTO BOTTOM
```

Figure 20.14: The complete BusProcs.PRG procedure file (continued)

```
    *---------- 1001 is lowest possible customer number.
    Largest = MAX(1000,CustNo)
    NextCust = Largest + 1

    *---------- Fill in customer numbers.
    USE Customer  && Deactivate index before using REPLACE.
    SCAN FOR CustNo = 0
      REPLACE CustNo WITH NextCust
      NextCust = NextCust + 1
    ENDSCAN

    *--- Done
    CLOSE DATABASES
RETURN

*--------- Assign invoice numbers to current orders.
PROCEDURE AutoInv

    * BusMgr application uses this procedure
    * before printing the invoices.

    *---- Find largest current invoice number
    USE Orders ORDER Invoice
    GOTO BOTTOM
    Largest = MAX(100000,Invoice)

    USE OrdHist ORDER Invoice
    GOTO Bottom
    Largest=MAX(Largest,Invoice)

    CLOSE DATABASES
    NextInvNo = Largest + 1  && Next invoice number.

    *------ Assign invoice numbers.
    USE Orders ORDER CustNo
    SCAN FOR Invoice = 0
      ThisCust = CustNo
      REPLACE Invoice WITH NextInvNo ;
           WHILE CustNo = ThisCust ;
           FOR Invoice = 0
      NextInvNo = NextInvNo + 1
      SKIP -1
    ENDSCAN
    *--- Done
    CLOSE DATABASES
RETURN

*----------------- Update Master file from items received.
PROCEDURE AddItems

    *--- Close open files, then open Master and ItemsRec.
    CLOSE DATABASES
    SELECT A
    USE Master ORDER PartNo
    SELECT B
    USE ItemsRec ORDER PartNo
```

Figure 20.14: The complete BusProcs.PRG procedure file (continued)

```
    *-------- Perform the update.
    SELECT Master
    UPDATE ON PartNo FROM ItemsRec REPLACE ;
       InStock WITH InStock + ItemsRec->Qty_Recvd, ;
       LastUpdate WITH ItemsRec->DateRecvd, ;
       PurCost WITH ;
       IIF(ItemsRec->Price > 0,ItemsRec->Price,PurCost)

    CLOSE DATABASES

    *------------- Move updated transactions to history file.
    SET SAFETY OFF  && So dBASE does not ask for permission.
    USE ItemHist    && History file for ItemsRec database.

    *-------------- Read in completed transactions.
    APPEND FROM ItemsRec

    *---------- Remove completed transactions from ItemsRec file.
    USE ItemsRec
    ZAP
    CLOSE DATABASES
RETURN

*------ Determine backorder requirements, and subtract
*------ orders from in-stock quantities.
PROCEDURE OrdUpdat

    *-- Open Master and Orders database files.
    SELECT A
    USE Orders ORDER PartNo
    SELECT B
    USE Master ORDER PartNo

    *-- Must set up relationship if not using UPDATE command.
    SELECT Orders
    SET RELATION TO PartNo INTO Master

    *-- Update the Master in-stock quantities.
    GO TOP
    SCAN FOR .NOT. InvPosted
      *-- See whether or not qty ordered exceeds in stock qty.
    IF QtyOrdered <= Master->InStock
         REPLACE QtyShipped WITH QtyOrdered
      ELSE
         REPLACE QtyShipped WITH MAX(0,Master->InStock)
         REPLACE BackOrdQty WITH QtyOrdered-QtyShipped
      ENDIF
      *---------- Update Master inventory database.
      SELECT Master
      REPLACE InStock WITH InStock-Orders->QtyShipped
      SELECT Orders
      REPLACE InvPosted WITH .T.
     ENDSCAN

     ********* Invoices can now be printed for posted records.
     ********* After printing invoices, must send fulfilled orders
     ********* to order history file, and convert backorders to
     ********* outstanding orders.  (The application will print
     ********* invoices as soon as this procedure is done).
     CLOSE DATABASES
RETURN
```

Figure 20.14: The complete BusProcs.PRG procedure file (continued)

```
PROCEDURE MoveOrds
   *---- Used in the BusMgr application after orders have
   *---- been fulfilled and invoices have been printed.
   USE OrdHist
   APPEND FROM Orders FOR QtyShipped > 0 .AND. InvPosted
   USE Orders
   DELETE FOR BackOrdQty = 0 .AND. InvPosted
   PACK
   REPLACE ALL QtyOrdered WITH BackOrdQty, ;
            QtyShipped WITH 0, ;
            BackOrdQty WITH 0, ;
            InvPosted WITH .F., ;
            Invoice WITH 0
RETURN

*--------- Moves fulfilled orders to the AR transaction file.
PROCEDURE ARUpdate
   *--- Used in BusMgr application after moving
   *--- fulfilled orders to OrdHist file.

   *--- First calculate order totals.
   USE OrdHist ORDER Invoice
   REPLACE OrdTotal WITH (((QtyShipped*UnitPrice)- ;
        ((DiscRate/100)*(QtyShipped*UnitPrice)))* ;
        (1+(TaxRate/100)))+Shipping ;
        FOR QtyShipped > 0

    *--- Now create temporary database of totaled orders.
    GO TOP
    SET SAFETY OFF
    TOTAL ON Invoice FIELDS OrdTotal TO OrdTemp FOR .NOT. ARPosted
    *---- Copy summarized totals into the AR transaction file.
    USE Transact
    APPEND FROM OrdTemp
    *--- Mark orders as being posted to the AR transaction file.
    USE OrdHist
    REPLACE ALL ARPosted WITH .T.
    CLOSE DATABASES
RETURN

*--- Update customer balances
PROCEDURE ARPost

   SELECT A
   USE Customer ORDER CustNo
   SELECT B
   USE Transact ORDER CustNo
   *-- Exclude records that have been posted.
   SET FILTER TO .NOT. CustPosted
   GO TOP  && Always move the record pointer after a SET FILTER.

   SELECT Customer
   UPDATE ON CustNo FROM Transact REPLACE ;
     TotChrg WITH TotChrg + Transact->OrdTotal, ;
     YtdChrg WITH YtdChrg + Transact->OrdTotal, ;
     TotPmt WITH TotPmt + Transact->AmtPaid, ;
     YtdPmt WITH YtdPmt + Transact->AmtPaid, ;
     LastDate WITH DATE()
```

Figure 20.14: The complete BusProcs.PRG procedure file (continued)

```
    *----- Customer balances now updated, flag transactions.
    CLOSE DATABASES
    USE Transact
    REPLACE ALL CustPosted WITH .T.
    CLOSE DATABASES
RETURN

*---- Resets year-to-date values to zero
*---- in the customer database, and moves
*---- old transactions to history file.
PROCEDURE YearEnd

    *--- Double-check for permission.
    GoAhead = .F.
    @ 4,5 SAY " Are you sure you want to reset year-to-date"
    @ 5,5 SAY "totals to zero now? (Y/N) " GET GoAhead PICTURE "Y"
    READ

    *-- If Ok to proceed, do so.
    IF GoAhead
       SET TALK ON
       SET SAFETY OFF
       USE Customer
       REPLACE ALL YtdChrg WITH 0, YtdPmt WITH 0
       USE Transact
       COPY TO TranHist FOR CustPosted .AND. Printed
       DELETE FOR CustPosted .AND. Printed
       PACK
       SET TALK OFF
    ENDIF

    CLOSE DATABASES
RETURN

*---- Rebuild index files for all databases.
PROCEDURE BusRendx

     SET TALK ON   && Show progress
     USE Customer
     REINDEX
     USE Master
     REINDEX
     USE Orders
     REINDEX
     USE OrdHist
     REINDEX
     USE ItemsRec
     REINDEX
     USE ItemHist
     REINDEX
     USE Transact
     REINDEX
     SET TALK OFF && Suppress progress messages.
RETURN
```

Figure 20.14: The complete BusProcs.PRG procedure file (continued)

```
*------------------ Opens database files and sets relations
*------------------ for order entry and editing.
PROCEDURE OrdOpen
   SELECT A
   USE Orders
   SELECT B
   USE Customer ORDER CustNo
   SELECT C
   USE Master ORDER PartNo

   *--- Set up relationship based on key fields.
   SELECT Orders
   SET RELATION TO CustNo INTO Customer, PartNo INTO Master
   GO TOP
RETURN

*--------- Validate customer number.
FUNCTION IsCust
PARAMETERS MCustNo
   DO CASE
       *-- Is user is exiting, do nothing.
       CASE MCustNo = 0
         Ok=.T.

     *-- Customer number was entered.
     CASE SEEK(MCustNo,"Customer")
          @ 5,48 SAY Customer->Company
          @ 6,48 SAY Customer->Contact
          *-- Recalculate (depending on last keypress)
          IF LASTKEY()=13 .OR. (LASTKEY()>=32.AND LASTKEY()<=122)
          REPLACE Orders->DiscRate WITH Customer->DiscRate
          @ 14,16 GET DiscRate PICTURE "99.99"
          IF Master->Taxable
             REPLACE Orders->TaxRate WITH Customer->TaxRate
          ELSE
             REPLACE Orders->TaxRate WITH 0
          ENDIF  && taxable
          @ 15,16 GET TaxRate PICTURE "99.99"
          Ok=Recalc(QtyOrdered)
          ENDIF && last keypress
          Ok=.T.
     OTHERWISE
          @ 5,48 SAY "No such customer!"
          @ 6,48 SAY SPACE(25)
          Ok=.F.
   ENDCASE
RETURN (Ok)

*------------------------- Validate part number.
FUNCTION IsPart
PARAMETERS MPartNo
   IF SEEK(MPartNo,"Master")
      @ 8,50 SAY Master->PartName
      @ 9,51 SAY Master->SelPrice PICTURE "99,999.99"
      @ 9,71 SAY Master->Taxable PICTURE "Y"
```

Figure 20.14: The complete BusProcs.PRG procedure file (continued)

```
        IF LASTKEY()=13 .OR. (LASTKEY()>=32.AND.LASTKEY()<=122)
           REPLACE Orders->UnitPrice WITH Master->SelPrice
           @ 11,24 GET UnitPrice PICTURE "99,999.99"
           *--- If item not taxable, replace tax rate with zero.
           IF Master->Taxable
              REPLACE Orders->TaxRate WITH Customer->TaxRate
           ELSE
              REPLACE Orders->TaxRate WITH 0
           ENDIF
           @ 15,16 GET TaxRate PICTURE "99.99"
           Ok = Recalc(QtyOrdered)
        ENDIF &&lastkey
        Ok=.T.

     *--- Invalid entry.
     ELSE
        @ 8,50 SAY "No such part number!     "
        Ok=.F.
     ENDIF  && seek() true or false

RETURN (Ok)

*---------------- Recalculate totals for screen display.
FUNCTION Recalc
PARAMETERS MQty
   @ 13,24 SAY QtyOrdered*UnitPrice PICTURE "99,999.99"
   @ 14,24 SAY -(DiscRate/100)*(QtyOrdered*UnitPrice) PICTURE "99,999.99"
   @ 15,24 SAY (TaxRate/100)*((1-DiscRate/100)*(QtyOrdered*UnitPrice)) ;

       PICTURE "99,999.99"
   @ 18,24 SAY ((QtyOrdered*UnitPrice)- ;
            ((DiscRate/100)*(QtyOrdered*UnitPrice)))* ;
            (1+(TaxRate/100)) + Shipping;
            PICTURE "99,999.99"
   Ok=.T.
RETURN (Ok)
```

Figure 20.14: The complete BusProcs.PRG procedure file

CHAPTER 21

The Business Management Application

To prevent posted records from being edited, 772
use the Permit Edit If edit option.

When developing applications that manage multiple files, 791
you can use IN EFFECT AT RUN TIME as the default database for each menu and then use embedded code to open and close databases as needed.

To have an application automatically open a procedure file, 795
embed a SET PROCEDURE TO <filename> command before the main application menu (highlight the main menu on the application) design screen, and then choose Menu ► Embed Code ► Before to open the embedded code editing screen.

To embed dBASE code (commands) to be executed 799
before or after an application menu option performs its action, choose Item ► Embed Code and then select Before or After from the submenu that appears.

To access custom procedures from within an application, 799
use embedded code.

To define a window for an application menu action, 801
choose Item ► Define logical Window and specify a name and the upper-left and lower-right corners of the window.

IN CHAPTERS 19 AND 20, WE BUILT THE DATABASE structures, procedure file, and two custom forms for the business application. In this chapter, we'll complete the application by designing the remaining screens and report formats and then use the Applications Generator to pull all the pieces together into an integrated system with pull-down menus.

DESIGNING THE CUSTOM FORMS

In Chapter 20, you created the AddOrder and EditOrd screens for entering and editing orders in the Orders database. Now you need to develop forms for entering and editing data in the Customer, Master, ItemsRec, and Transact files. This section will present examples of various forms, though you can design the forms in any way you wish.

You can create each form using the forms design screen from the Control Center. If the dot prompt is displayed on your screen right now, enter the command **ASSIST** to return to the Control Center. You should see the names of the various files you created in Chapter 19 listed in the panels. (Don't forget that you must be on the \dBASE\Business subdirectory and the Business.cat catalog must be displayed on the screen when you use the business application.)

DESIGNING THE FORMS FOR THE CUSTOMER DATABASE

If you need reminders about techniques or special keys that you use to create and edit custom forms, refer to Chapter 8.

To create forms for the Customer database, open the Customer database and select <create> from the Forms pull-down menu. Figure 21.1 shows a suggested format for the form. Table 21.1 lists the exact locations of field templates on the form. Special display attributes assigned to the fields, such as picture functions or default values, are listed to the right of the field name. The template that each field uses on the form is visible in the figure.

Note that Balance is a calculated field. Remember: To place a calculated field on the screen, you position the cursor at the field's location, press F5 (or double-click at that location), and select <create> from the Calculated column. Then type a name for the calculated

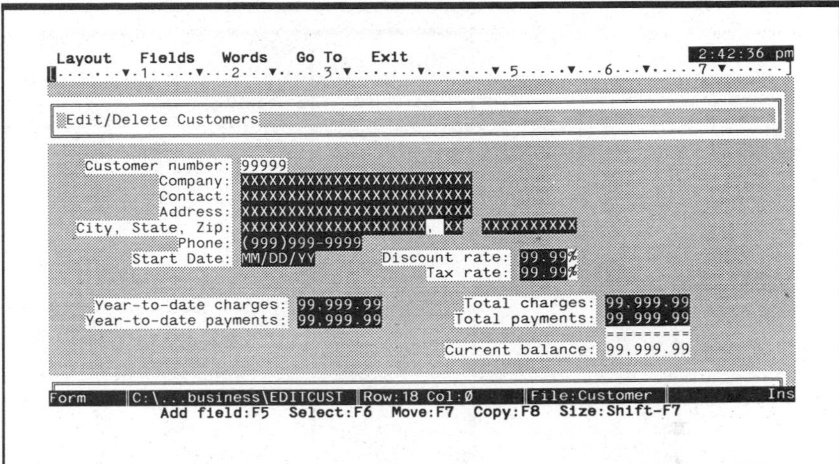

Figure 21.1: The EditCust custom form on the forms design screen

Table 21.1: Fields and Options on the EditCust Form

Row, Column	Field Name	Options
5, 21	CUSTNO	Edit option: Editing Allowed: NO
6, 21	COMPANY	
7, 21	CONTACT	
8, 21	ADDRESS	
9, 21	CITY	
9, 43	STATE	
9, 47	ZIP	
10, 21	PHONE	
11, 21	STARTDATE	Edit option: Default Value: DATE()
11, 51	DISCRATE	
12, 51	TAXRATE	

Table 21.1: Fields and Options on the EditCust Form (continued)

Row, Column	Field Name	Options
14, 27	YTDCHRG	
14, 60	TOTCHRG	
15, 27	YTDPMT	
15, 60	TOTPMT	
17, 60	(Calculated field) Name: BALANCE Expression: TOTCHRG – TOTPMT	

NOTE

Remember: To add a field template or change a field template, picture functions, or edit options, use the F5 key, or double-click at the location of the new or existing field template.

field (**Balance** in this example) and the expression (**TotChrg – TotPmt** in this example).

After you create the form, choose Layout ► Save This Form and save the form using the name **EditCust**. Then remove the Customer number: prompt and the CustNo field template and change the form title as shown in Figure 21.2. After making the changes, again choose Layout ► Save This Form and then save the modified form with the name **AddCust**. After saving the forms, you can choose Exit ► Abandon Changes and Exit to return to the Control Center.

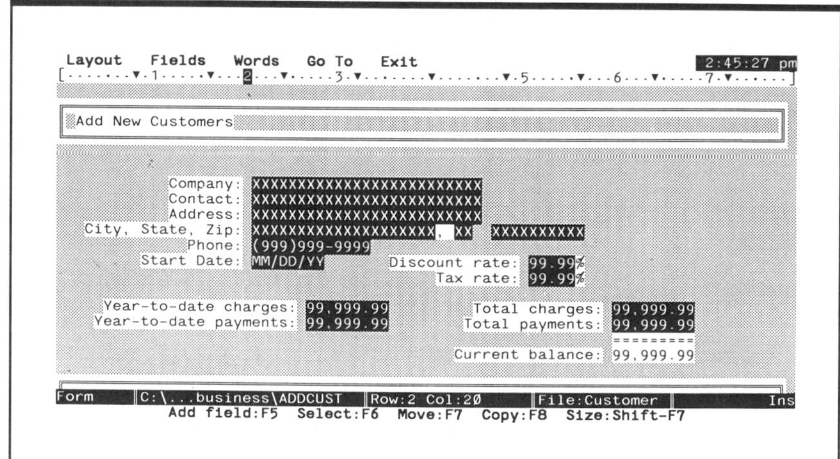

Figure 21.2: The AddCust custom form

DESIGNING THE FORMS FOR THE MASTER INVENTORY

The forms for the Master database are named AddParts and EditPart. To create these forms, first open the Master database and then use the PartNo index by pressing or clicking Data (F2) and choosing Organize ► Order Records by Index. Then press Ctrl-End to return to the Control Center.

Next, select <create> from the Forms panel. Design the form to your own liking or use the suggested format shown in Figure 21.3. The row and column locations and picture functions associated with each field are listed in Table 21.2.

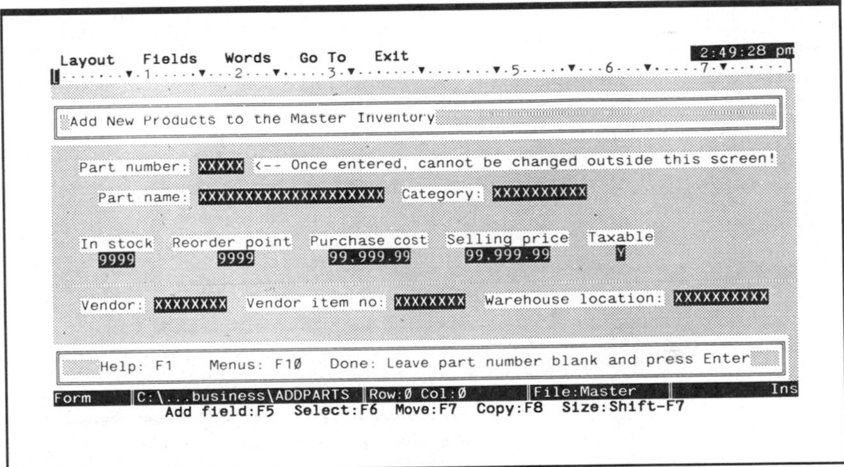

Figure 21.3: Suggested format for the AddParts custom form

Table 21.2: Fields and Options on the AddParts Form

Row, Column	Field Name	Options
5, 16	PARTNO	Picture Function: !
7, 16	PARTNAME	
7, 48	CATEGORY	
11, 5	INSTOCK	

Table 21.2: Fields and Options on the AddParts Form (continued)

Row, Column	Field Name	Options
11, 18	REORDER	
11, 30	PURCOST	
11, 45	SELPRICE	
11, 61	TAXABLE	
14, 11	VENDOR	
14, 37	VENDITEMNO	
14, 67	LOCATION	

After creating the AddParts custom form, choose Layout ► Save This Form and save the form with the file name **AddParts**.

To create the form for editing the part information, leave the AddParts custom form on the screen and change the Editing Allowed option for the PartNo field from Yes to No. Modify the form to look like Figure 21.4. Save the modified version of the form with the file name **EditPart**. Then you can choose Exit ► Abandon Changes and Exit to return to the Control Center.

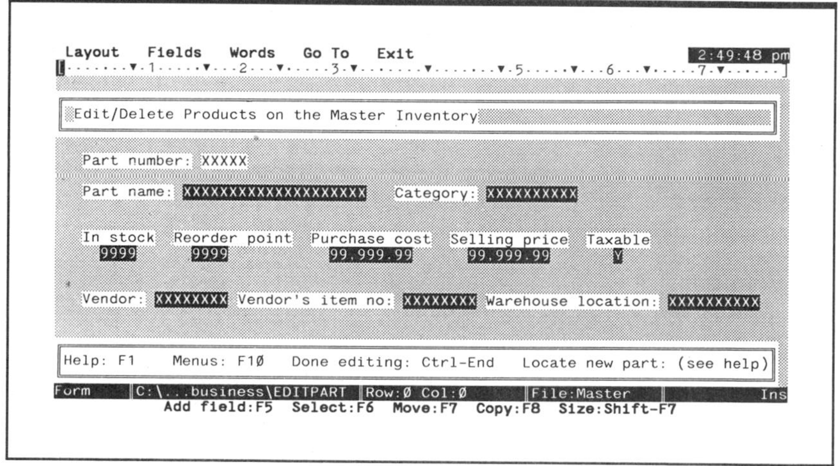

Figure 21.4: Suggested format for the EditPart custom form

DESIGNING THE FORM FOR THE ITEMSREC DATABASE

The ItemsRec database file holds information about newly received purchases (items that the business received to replenish its stock). To create the form, first open the ItemsRec database file and then select <create> from the Forms panel. Figure 21.5 shows a suggested format for the custom form.

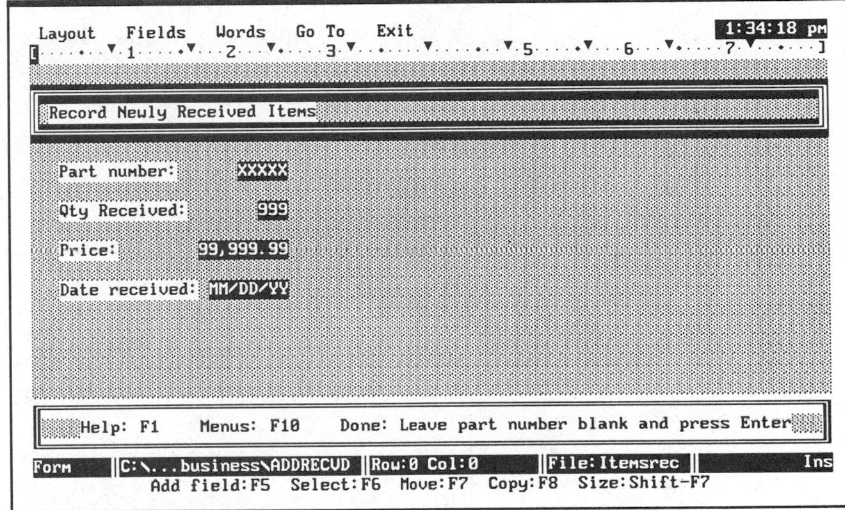

Figure 21.5: AddRecvd custom form for recording purchases

The locations of field templates and the display attribute assigned to the DateRecvd field are listed in Table 21.3.

Table 21.3: Fields on the AddRecvd Custom Form

Row, Column	Field Name	Options
5, 21	PARTNO	
7, 23	QTY_RECVD	
9, 17	PRICE	
11, 18	DATERECVD	Edit option: Default Value: DATE()

After creating the form, choose Exit ► Save Changes and Exit and assign the name **AddRecvd** when prompted.

DESIGNING THE FORMS FOR THE TRANSACTION DATABASE

Most of the information on the Transact (transactions) database comes from the Orders database automatically. However, you do need a couple of forms to view and change existing data, as well as to record customers' payments. To create these forms, first open the Transact database, then select <create> from the Forms panel.

VIEWING AND EDITING TRANSACTIONS Figure 21.6 shows a suggested screen format for editing transactions. Field template positions and display attributes are listed in Table 21.4. Note that most fields use the Permit Edit If edit option with the expression .NOT. (Printed .OR. CustPosted). This edit option prevents the user from editing transactions that have already been billed and updated and are reflected in the Customer balances. (As you'll see later, to change transactions that have already been printed and

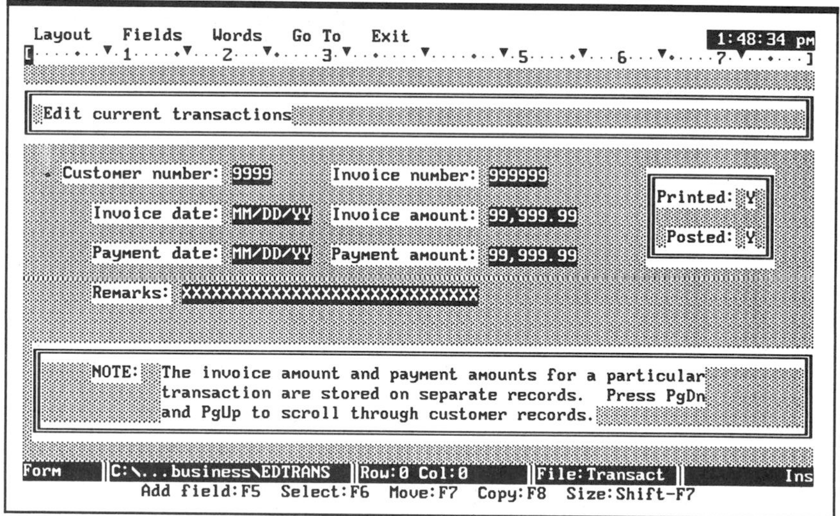

Figure 21.6: The EdTrans custom form for the Transact database

posted, the user can enter adjustment transactions, which provide an audit trail.) Name the form **EdTrans** when saving it.

ENTERING PAYMENTS The form for entering payments displays only a few fields from the Transact database. The form requires no special display attributes, except that you might want to use DATE() as the Default Value edit option for the DatePaid field so that the current date is filled in automatically. Figure 21.7 shows a suggested format for the custom form on the forms design screen. Create the form in the usual manner and save it using the file name **AddPmts**.

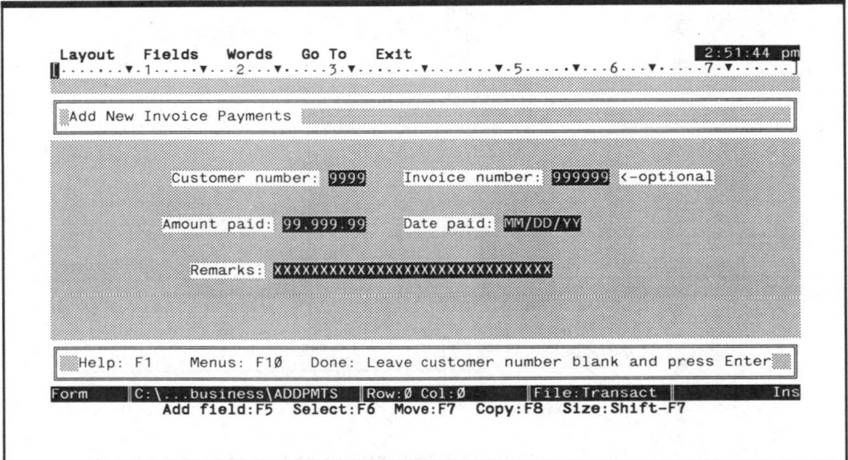

Figure 21.7: The AddPmts custom form on the forms design screen

Table 21.4: Fields on the EdTrans Custom Form

Row, Column	Field Name	Options
5, 21	CUSTNO	Edit option: Permit Edit If: .NOT. (Printed .OR. CustPosted)
5, 47	INVOICE	Edit option: Permit Edit If: .NOT. (Printed .OR. CustPosted)

Table 21.4: Fields on the EdTrans Custom Form (continued)

Row, Column	Field Name	Options
6, 73	PRINTED	Edit option: Editing Allowed: No
7, 21	ORDATE	Edit option: Permit Edit If: .NOT. (Printed .OR. CustPosted)
7, 47	ORDTOTAL	Edit option: Permit Edit If: .NOT. (Printed .OR. CustPosted)
8, 73	CUSTPOSTED	Edit option: Editing Allowed: No
9, 21	DATEPAID	Edit option: Permit Edit If: .NOT. (Printed .OR. CustPosted)
9, 47	AMTPAID	Edit option: Permit Edit If: .NOT. (Printed .OR. CustPosted)
11, 16	REMARKS	

DESIGNING THE REPORT FORMATS

NOTE

If you need additional reminders about how to use the reports design screen, refer to Chapters 7 and 9.

Next, you need to develop some report formats for the business application. Remember: To create a report format, you must first open the database that contains the data that the report is to print. Then select <create> from the Reports panel in the Control Center.

DESIGNING THE CUSTOMER LIST REPORT

The Customer List report displays names and addresses, charges, payments, and the current balance for each customer. Figure 21.8 shows a suggested format for the report on the reports design screen. Figure 21.9 shows two records from the Customer database printed with the suggested format.

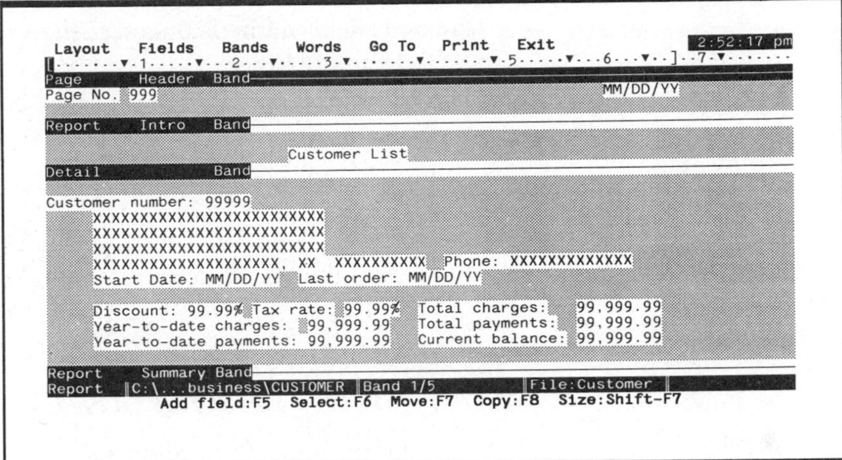

Figure 21.8: Suggested format for the Customer report

The dates shown in sample reports are for the example only.

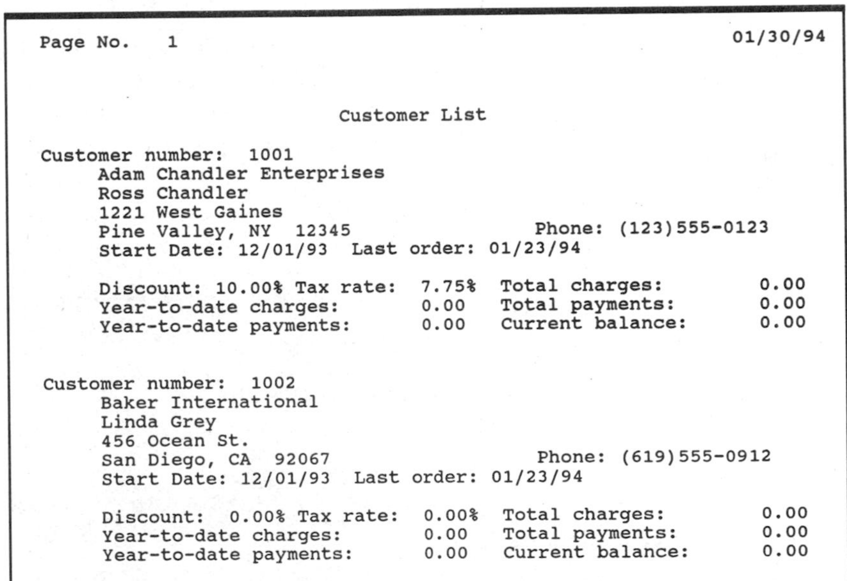

```
Page No.   1                                                01/30/94

                         Customer List

Customer number:  1001
     Adam Chandler Enterprises
     Ross Chandler
     1221 West Gaines
     Pine Valley, NY  12345                 Phone: (123)555-0123
     Start Date: 12/01/93  Last order: 01/23/94

     Discount: 10.00% Tax rate:  7.75%  Total charges:        0.00
     Year-to-date charges:       0.00   Total payments:       0.00
     Year-to-date payments:      0.00   Current balance:      0.00

Customer number:  1002
     Baker International
     Linda Grey
     456 Ocean St.
     San Diego, CA  92067                   Phone: (619)555-0912
     Start Date: 12/01/93  Last order: 01/23/94

     Discount:  0.00% Tax rate:  0.00%  Total charges:        0.00
     Year-to-date charges:       0.00   Total payments:       0.00
     Year-to-date payments:      0.00   Current balance:      0.00
```

Figure 21.9: Customer records printed using the Customer format

Note that in the suggested format, the current balance is a calculated field named Balance that uses the expression TotChrg – TotPmt. All other fields are taken directly from the database. The large field templates beneath the customer number are the Company, Contact, Address, City, State, and Zip fields, in that order from top to bottom.

After you create the report format, save it using the file name **Customer**. When you return to the Control Center, you'll be ready to develop the report formats for the Master inventory database.

DESIGNING THE MASTER INVENTORY REPORTS

The business application uses two report formats for displaying data from the Master inventory: One shows the entire current inventory, and the other lists items that need to be reordered.

MASTER INVENTORY REPORT The Master Inventory report displays the current status of all items in stock. Figure 21.10 shows a suggested format for the report. Figure 21.11 shows some sample records from the Master database printed with the suggested format. To create the Master Inventory report, first make sure that the Master

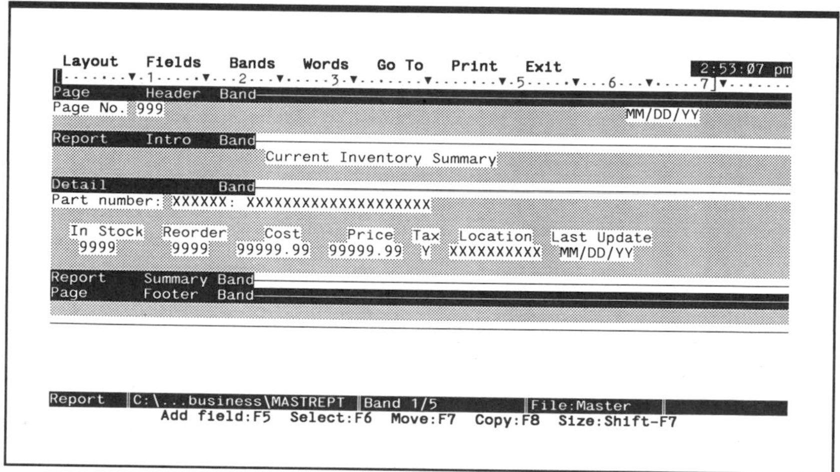

Figure 21.10: Suggested format for the Master Inventory report

```
Page No.    1                                                        02/28/93
                              Current Inventory Summary

Part number: A-111: American Adventure

  In Stock   Reorder      Cost       Price    Tax   Location    Last Update
     10         20        10.00      25.00     Y   WH-A10        01/01/93

Part number: B-222: Data Base Master

  In Stock   Reorder      Cost       Price    Tax   Location    Last Update
     30          5         3.50       5.00     N   WH-001        01/05/93
```

Figure 21.11: Sample records printed using the MastRept format

database file is open and then select <create> from the Reports panel.

Note that in the suggested format, the templates displayed as XXXXXX : XXXXXXXXXXXXXXXXXXXX are the field templates for the PartNo and PartName fields, respectively, separated by a colon. The field template beneath the Cost heading is for the PurCost field, and the field template beneath the Price heading is for the SelPrice field. After creating the report format, save it with the file name **MastRept**.

REORDER REPORT To create the Reorder report, once again be sure that the Master database file is open and then select <create> from the Reports panel. Figure 21.12 shows a suggested format for

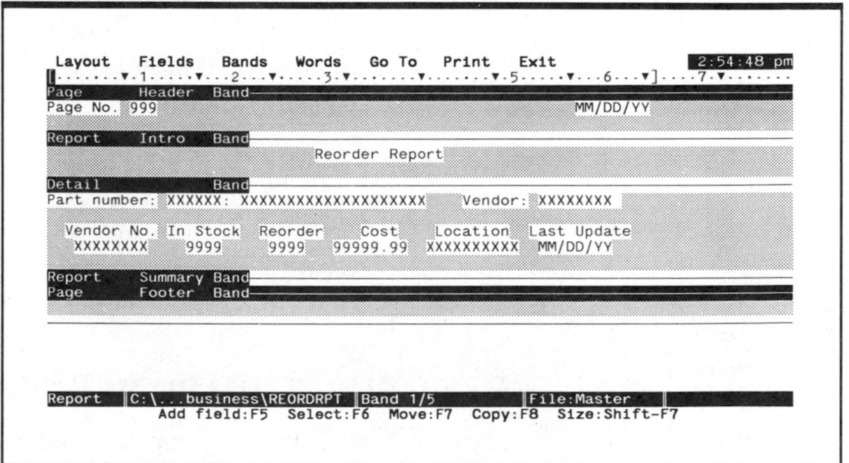

Figure 21.12: Suggested format for the ReordRpt report

the report. Figure 21.13 shows some sample data printed using the format. After you create the report format, save it using the file name **ReordRpt**.

```
Page No.    1                                                02/28/93

                              Reorder Report

Part number: A-111: American Adventure         Vendor: HBJ

  Vendor No. In Stock  Reorder     Cost     Location  LastUpdate
   HBJ-101        10        20     10.00   WH-A10       01/15/93
```

Figure 21.13: Sample record printed using the ReordRpt format

PRINTING INVOICES AND AN INVOICE SUMMARY

To print invoices and an invoice summary (or invoice register, as it is often called), you need data from three separate databases: the Customer database, for customers' names and addresses; the Orders database, for current orders; and the Master database, for part names. Recall that in Chapter 20 you created a procedure named OrdOpen to open and relate these three database files. So rather than go through all the steps again, you can just run the OrdOpen procedure by following these steps:

1. From the Control Center, choose Exit ► Exit to Dot Prompt.
2. At the dot prompt, open the procedure file by entering the command **SET PROCEDURE TO BusProcs**.
3. When the dot prompt reappears, enter the command **DO OrdOpen**. When the dot prompt reappears again, you can be sure that the three databases are open and related.

DESIGNING THE INVOICE FORMAT

Now that the three required database files are open, you can create the invoice report format, which we'll name Invoices. You can go directly to the reports design screen, bypassing the Control Center, by entering the command **MODIFY REPORT Invoices.**

Figure 21.14 shows a suggested format for the report. Figure 21.15 shows a sample invoice for one customer.

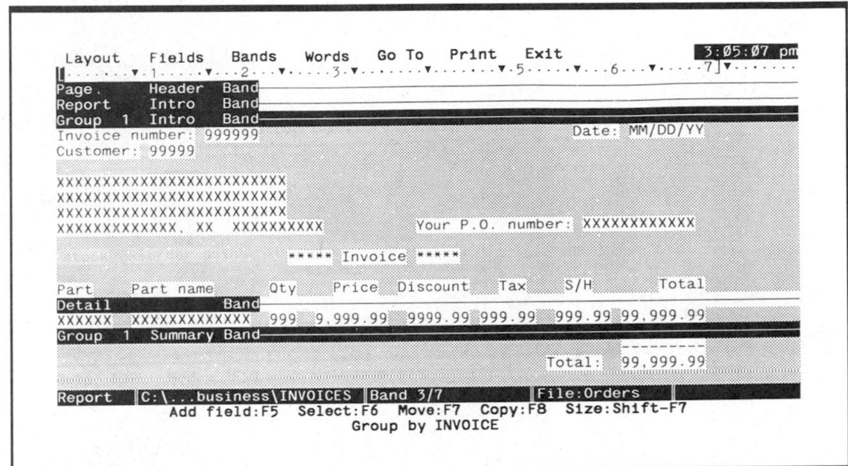

Figure 21.14: Suggested format for the invoices

```
Invoice number: 100003                                   Date: 02/28/93
Customer:   1001

Adam Chandler Enterprises
Ross Chandler
1221 West Gaines
Pine Valley, NY  12345                      Your P.O. number: 123-45-6789

                          ***** Invoice *****

Part     Part name        Qty    Price  Discount   Tax     S/H        Total
---------------------------------------------------------------------------
A-111    American Adve     2     25.00     -5.00   3.49    0.00       48.49
B-222    Data Base Mas     1      3.50     -0.35   0.00    0.00        3.15
                                                                  ---------
                                                                      51.64
```

Figure 21.15: Sample printed invoice

The Invoices report format uses many of the techniques discussed in Chapter 13 for printing invoices. To get started (assuming that you are already at the reports design screen), follow these steps:

1. Move the cursor into the Report Intro band border (so that "Band 2/5" appears in the status bar).
2. Choose Bands ► Add a Group Band.
3. Select Field Value from the submenu.
4. Select Invoice as the grouping field (because you want each invoice to print all orders for a specific invoice number).
5. Move the the Page Header band border (band 1/7) and press ↵ (or click the mouse on that band border) to close the band.
6. Move to the Report Intro band border (band 2/7) and press ↵ (or click the mouse on that band border) to close that band.
7. Use the same basic techniques to close the Report Summary band (band 6/7) and Page Footer band (band 7/7) near the bottom of the report format.
8. Move the cursor to the Group 1 Intro band border (band 3/7), choose Bands ► Begin Band on New Page, and press the space bar or click the mouse on that option until the setting reads "Yes." This ensures that each invoice is printed on a separate page.

Remember: To add a blank line to a report band, move the cursor inside the band and press Ctrl-N.

Next, you need to place field templates in the Group 1 Summary Band. The date in the upper-right corner of the band (line 0, column 62) is the Date from the Predefined column that appears when you press F5 or double-click on that part of the screen. The following table lists the row and column positions of fields from the Orders database. To place these on the report format, position the cursor at the row and column position shown, press F5 (or double-click at that position), and select the field name from the Orders column of the submenu that appears.

Line, Column	Name
0, 16	Invoice
1, 10	CustNo
6, 57	CustPONumb

The rest of the fields in the Group 1 Summary band are calculated fields. To place these, position the cursor at the line and column position shown, press F5 (or double-click at that position), and select <create> from the Calculated column. Leave the Name entry blank, and enter the Expression shown here:

When using a calculated field to display data from separate databases, it's best not to assign a name to that calculated field.

Line, Column	Expression
3, 0	Customer->Company
4, 0	Customer->Contact
5, 0	Customer->Address
6, 0	Customer->City
6, 15	Customer->State
6, 19	Customer->Zip

Next you can enter the field templates in the Detail band. Note that fitting all of the information into the Detail band of the invoice is a tight squeeze. Therefore, you need to reduce most of the field templates to the smallest acceptable size. Here, the part-name template is reduced to only 13 spaces wide. If your printer is capable of compressed print, you could widen the margins and thereby make more room for the part name. You could also use the Vertical Stretch picture function to word-wrap the part name onto two separate lines if you prefer.

Detail band fields, taken directly from the Orders database, are listed here:

Line, Column	Name
0, 0	PartNo

Line, Column	Name
0, 23	QtyShipped
0, 28	UnitPrice
0, 54	Shipping

The following table lists the position, name, and expression for each calculated field in the Detail band. The ROUND() function, described in Chapter 12, is used to prevent rounding errors in sums. Note that most of the expressions are broken into several lines only to fit within the book. When entering an expression into the report format, however, you must enter it on one line.

Line, Column	Name	Expression
0, 8		Master->PartName
0, 38	DISCAMT	ROUND(–(DiscRate/100) *(QtyShipped*UnitPrice) , 2)
0, 46	TAXAMT	ROUND((TaxRate/100) *((QtyShipped*UnitPrice) –((DiscRate/100) *(QtyShipped*UnitPrice))) , 2)
0, 61	TOTSALE	ROUND((((QtyShipped*UnitPrice) –((DiscRate/100) *(QtyShipped*UnitPrice))) *(1 +(TaxRate/100))) + Shipping, 2)

The total for each invoice appears in the Group 1 Summary band at line 1, column 61. To place this field, position the cursor, press F5 (or double-click at that position), and assign SumTotSal as the name. Select SUM as the Operation and TotSale as the field to summarize on and set Reset Every to Invoice (so the total is reset to zero before each invoice is printed).

When you have finished designing the report, choose Layout ► Save This Report and press ↵ to accept Invoices as the file name.

DESIGNING THE INVOICE SUMMARY FORMAT

The invoice summary report allows the application user to preview printed invoices before they are printed to check for errors. It uses a format similar to the invoices report, but more compressed. Figure 21.16 shows a suggested format on the reports design screen, and Figure 21.17 shows some sample data printed using the format.

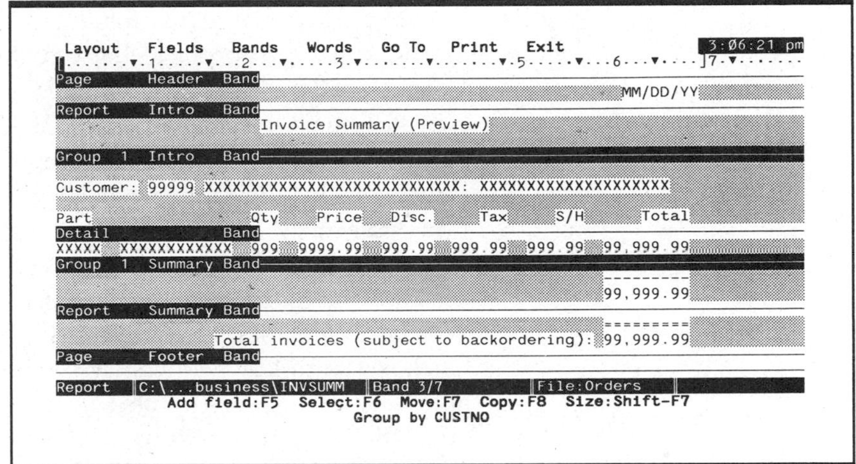

Figure 21.16: Suggested format for the InvSumm report

```
                                                          01/30/93
                    Invoice Summary (Preview)

Customer:  1001 Adam Chandler Enterprises: Ross Chandler

Part                  Qty    Price   Disc.      Tax     S/H       Total
------------------------------------------------------------------------
A-111  American Adve   2     25.00   -5.00     3.49    0.00       48.49
B-222  Data Base Ma    1      3.50   -0.35     0.00    0.00        3.15
                                                               ---------
                                                      Total:      51.64

Customer:  1002 Baker International: Linda Gray

Part                  Qty    Price   Disc.      Tax     S/H       Total
------------------------------------------------------------------------
B-222  Data Base Ma    1      3.50    0.00     0.00    0.00        3.50
                                                               ---------
                                                      Total:       3.50
                                                               =========
                 Total invoices (subject to backordering):        55.14
```

Figure 21.17: Sample data printed using the InvSumm format

To modify the Invoices report format to create the invoice summary report format, move the cursor to the Group 1 Intro band border (band 3/7), choose Bands ► Begin Band on New Page and change the setting to No. Then choose Bands ► Modify Group, select Field Value, and specify CustNo as the field to group on.

Invoice numbers are not assigned until invoices are printed, so you can also delete the Invoice Number field template in row 0 of the Group 1 Intro band. Also, because the invoice summary report is printed prior to the actual fulfillment (and possible backordering) of orders, you need to delete the QtyShipped field template from the Detail band (near line 0, column 21) and replace it with a field template for the QtyOrdered field. You'll also need to replace QtyShipped with QtyOrdered wherever QtyShipped appears in the expressions for the DiscAmt field (near line 0, column 35), TaxAmt field (near line 0, column 43), and TotSale field (near line 0, column 59); of course, calculations for those fields on the preview report are accurate only if the company later ships the full order.

The grand total of invoices, displayed in the Report Summary band, is a summary field named GrandTot that uses SUM as its operation and TotSale as the field to summarize on and is Reset Every REPORT. You may also want to remove the customer's address and add the report title, as shown in the suggested format.

After creating the report format, choose Layout ► Save This Report and assign the file name **InvSumm** to the report format. Then you can choose Exit ► Abandon Changes and Exit to return to the dot prompt.

PRINTING CUSTOMER STATEMENTS

Customer statements are printed once a month to display current charges, payments, and balances. To create this report, you need to open and relate the Transact and Customer databases. From the dot prompt, enter this series of commands:

```
CLOSE DATABASES

SELECT A
USE Transact ORDER Custno
```

```
SELECT B
USE Customer ORDER CustNo

SELECT A
SET RELATION TO CustNo INTO Customer
```

Then, to get to the reports design screen to create the report format, named Statmnts, enter this command:

```
MODIFY REPORT Statmnts
```

Figure 21.18 shows a suggested format for the Statmnts report on the reports design screen. In the suggested format, the Page Header, Report Intro, Report Summary, and Page Footer bands are closed (though several of these bands have scrolled off the screen in Figure 21.18). Figure 21.19 shows a sample printed statement. The Group band is based on the field value CustNo. After adding the Group band, choose Bands ► Begin Band on New Page and change the setting to Yes to print each statement on a separate page.

The Group 1 Intro Band contains Regular, Predefined, and Calculated fields. The location, type, and expression of each is listed

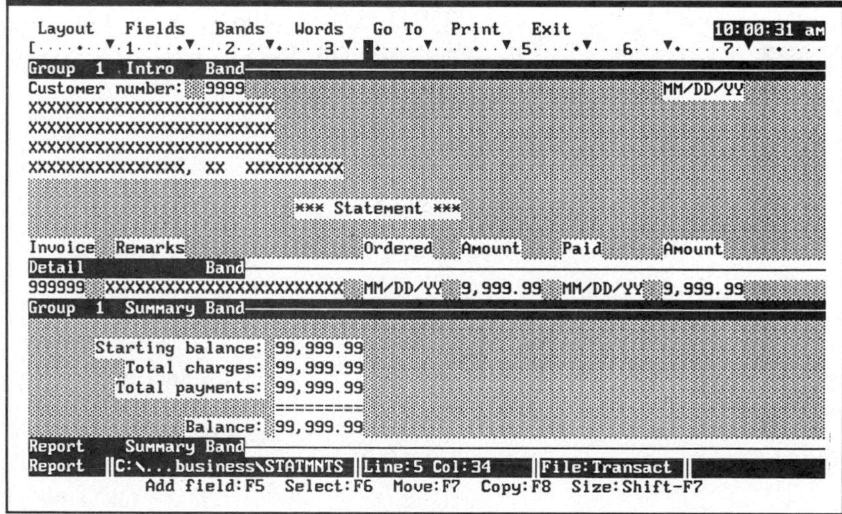

Figure 21.18: Format of the Statmnts report

```
Customer number:  1001                                                   02/28/93
Adam Chandler Enterprises
Ross Chandler
1221 West Gaines
Pine Valley, NY  12345

                              *** Statement ***

Invoice  Remarks                      Ordered    Amount     Paid        Amount
100003                                01/30/93    27.11     /  /          0.00
100005                                02/08/93   100.00     /  /          0.00
100003   Check # 552                   /  /        0.00   02/05/93       27.11

       Starting balance:      0.00
          Total charges:    127.11
         Total payments:     27.11
                          =========
                Balance:    100.00
```

Figure 21.19: Sample data printed using the Statmnts report format

below. For example, to place the first field template, move the cursor into the Group 1 Intro band, press F5 (or double-click at line 0, column 18 on the screen), then select CUSTNO from the first column of the menu that appears, and press or click Ctrl-End to leave the submenu. When adding calculated fields, move the cursor to the line/column position shown, press F5 (or double-click at that position), select <create> from the Calculated column, then select Expression and type in the expression that is shown (for example, CUSTOMER->Company). Then press ↵ and press or click Ctrl-End. As with the Invoices report, you don't want to use names with these calculated fields:

Line,Column	Type	Expression
0,18	Regular	CUSTNO
0,64	Predefined	DATE
1,0	Calculated	Customer->Company
2,0	Calculated	Customer->Contact
3,0	Calculated	Customer->Address
4,0	Calculated	Customer->City
4,18	Calculated	Customer->State
4,22	Calculated	Customer->Zip

The Detail band contains templates for fields from the Transact database. From left to right, the fields are Invoice, Remarks, Ordate, Ordtotal, Datepaid, and Amtpaid.

The Group 1 Summary band contains two calculated fields and two summary fields. The first calculated field, called StartBal, appears at line 0, column 26 and uses the expression Customer->TotChrg – Customer->TotPmt. At line 1, column 26, the summary field named CurrChrg sums the OrdTotal field and is Reset Every CustNo. At line 2, column 26, a summary field named CurrPmts sums the AmtPaid field, and it, too, is Reset Every CustNo. Line 4, column 26 contains a calculated field that is named CurrBal and uses the expression STARTBAL + CURRCHRG – CURRPMTS.

After creating the report format, choose Exit ► Save Changes and Exit to return to the dot prompt. When you get back to the dot prompt, enter the following command to close the database files and return to the Control Center:

```
CLOSE DATABASES
ASSIST
```

BUILDING THE APPLICATION

We have now created all the objects needed for the business management application, including the database structures, custom procedures and functions, screens, and report formats. Now we need to pull these together into an integrated application with easy-to-use pull-down menus. Of course, we'll use the dBASE IV Applications Generator for this phase of the operation.

Before designing your application, you may wish to add the reports you created at the dot prompt to the Business.Cat catalog, although this isn't strictly necessary. The new reports are Invoices, InvSumm, and Statmnts. Recall that the steps for adding a report to the catalog are to highlight the Reports panel of the Control Center, then choose Catalog ► Add File to Catalog. Select a name from the submenu that appears, and then enter a description for the report (or press ↵ to leave the description blank). For example, to add the Invoices report to the catalog, move the highlight to the Reports panel, choose Catalog ► Add File to Catalog, select Invoices.Frm from the submenu, then press ↵. Repeat this procedure to add the InvSumm.Frm and Statmnts.Frm names to the catalog.

Figure 21.20 shows the menu tree for the business management application, including the names of the various menus. You'll use the

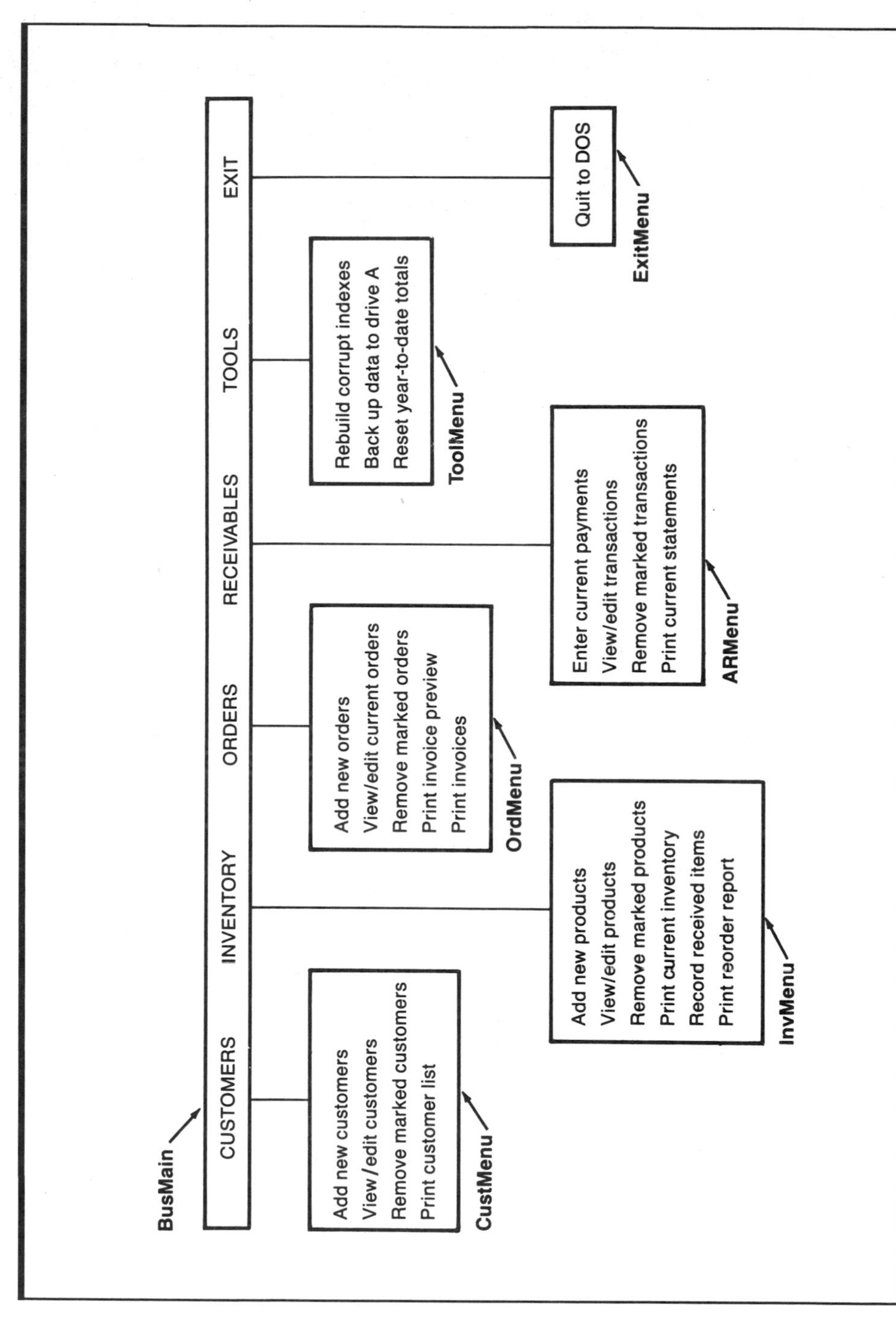

Figure 21.20: Menu tree for the business application

Applications Generator to design the menus and assign an action to each menu item.

DEFINING THE APPLICATION

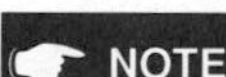

If you need to take a break during the design of the application, mark the place in the book where you left off and choose Exit ► Save Changes and Exit.

To begin, select <create> from the Applications panel of the Control Center. From the submenu that appears, select Applications Generator. Then, when you get to the Application Definition dialog box, fill it in as shown in Figure 21.21.

We've defined the main menu type as (horizontal) BAR, and given it the name BUSMAIN. Later, we'll actually create a menu with that name. The Applications Generator also requires that a database be opened right away, even if the application will manage many databases. In this example, it's not particularly important which database is opened when the application is first run, so we've somewhat arbitrarily selected CUSTOMER as the database and the CUSTNO tag as the index that controls the sort order. (The Set INDEX To option is required only if you want the application to use dBASE III PLUS .NDX files.)

The business application uses many database files. But dBASE requires that a default database and index be defined with the appli-

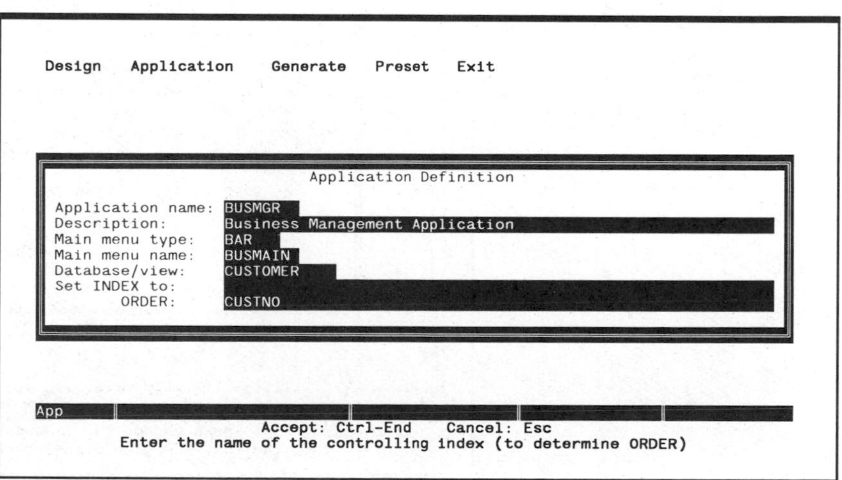

Figure 21.21: The Application Definition dialog box

cation definition. Thus, this application specifies the Customer database with the CustNo index, though you could specify any database and order that the application uses.

CREATING THE SIGN-ON BANNER

After defining the application, press or click Ctrl-End to get to the Applications Generator design screen. You can modify the sign-on banner to match that shown in Figure 21.22. If you want the application to display the sign-on banner, remember to choose Application ► Display Sign-On Banner and change the setting to Yes.

CREATING THE MAIN MENU

To create the main menu, choose Design ► Horizontal Bar Menu and select <create> from the submenu. When the dialog box appears, enter **BusMain** as the menu name. You can then press or click Ctrl-End to leave the other options blank. When the blank menu bar appears at the top of the screen, enter the **Customers**,

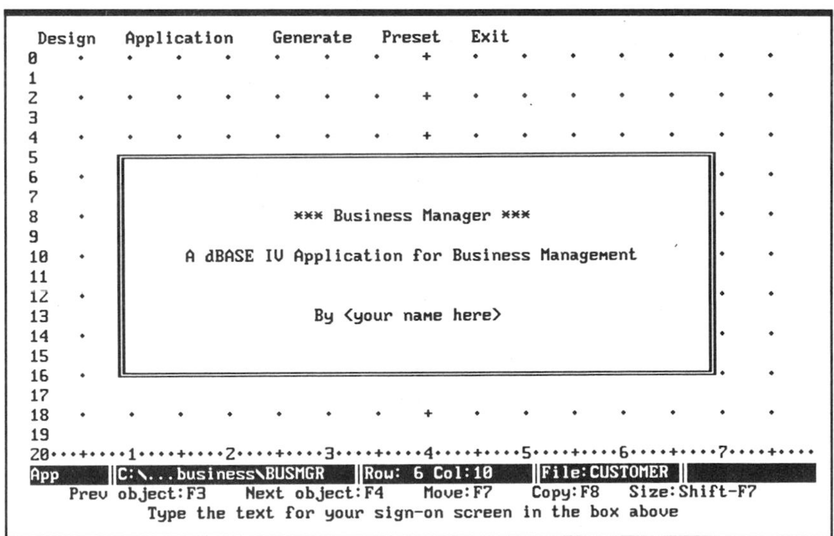

Figure 21.22: The BusMgr sign-on banner

Inventory, **Orders**, **Receivables**, **Tools**, and **Exit** options, each separated by three spaces. (Remember to press the F5 key before and after typing each item.) Figure 21.23 shows the horizontal bar menu with the six options entered.

CREATING THE PULL-DOWN MENUS

The business application uses six pull-down menus, which you can begin designing now. Note that for this application, each pull-down menu will use the IN EFFECT AT RUN TIME option as the default database. This setting is used because the application uses many different databases. Any particular option might use one or several database files. So rather than assigning a particular database to each individual pull-down menu, the application tells dBASE just to use whatever database is open at the moment.

Each of the six pull-down menus that you will create will require you to follow these eight general steps (but don't do them now):

1. Choose Design ► Pop-Up Menu.
2. Select <create> from the submenu that appears.

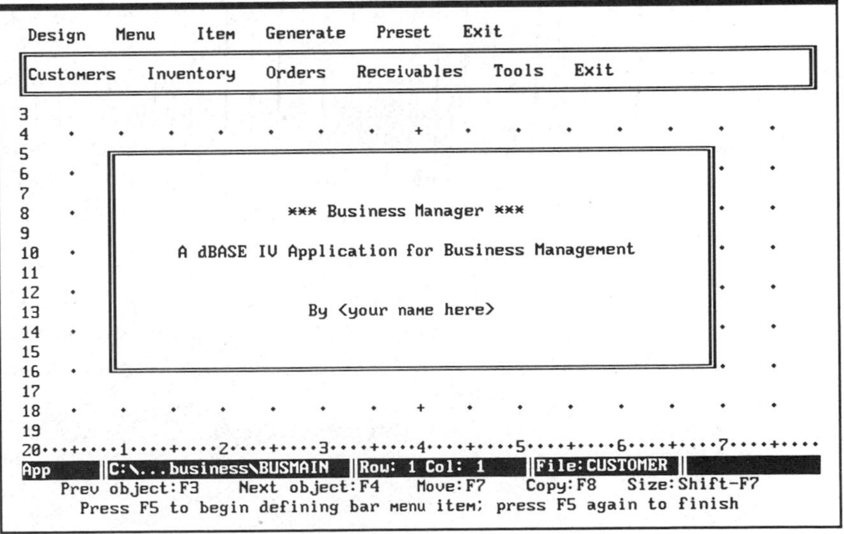

Figure 21.23: The business application horizontal bar menu

3. Enter the menu name, an optional description, and an optional message line prompt in the dialog box that appears, and then press or click Ctrl-End (specific information for each menu will be provided).

If you accidentally click the mouse outside of the menu you're working on, the menu may seem to disappear. If this happens, press or click F4 until the hidden menu frame reappears and is highlighted, then continue working with the menu as usual.

4. Press or click Size (Shift-F7) to enlarge the menu frame as necessary and press ↵ when done sizing; or size the menu frame with the mouse by dragging the bottom or right border, or the lower right-hand corner (as described in Chapter 16.)
5. Type the menu options, sizing the menu frame as necessary (specific information will be provided).
6. After creating the menu, choose Menu ► Override Assigned Database or View, and press the space bar or click the mouse until the IN EFFECT AT RUN TIME option appears. Then press or click Ctrl-End and press Esc to accept the change and return to the design screen.

Do not choose Item ► Override Assigned Database or View in this next step.

7. Press or click Move (F7), select Entire Frame, and move the completed menu to beneath the main menu option it is associated with, or use the mouse to drag the frame by its top or left border to the appropriate location (the exact location will be provided).
8. Choose Menu ► Put Away Current Menu ► Save Changes.

In the descriptions that follow, use the preceding general steps to create each pull-down menu, but fill in the specific information provided for each menu. The descriptions list just this particular information, with the step number to which the information applies indicated in parentheses.

CUSTMENU PULL-DOWN MENU The CustMenu pull-down menu provides options for managing the Customer database. Here is the specific information for the menu:

(Step 3) Name: CUSTMENU
Message line prompt: Manage the Customer database

(Step 5) Specific menu options:
Add new customers
View/edit customers
Remove marked customers
Print customer list

(Step 6) Menu database file/view: IN EFFECT AT RUN TIME

(Step 7) Upper-left corner of menu frame aligned beneath the first *s* in Customers on the main menu

INVMENU PULL-DOWN MENU The menu for managing the Master inventory database is named InvMenu. Repeat the general steps for creating a pull-down menu, using the specific information listed here:

(Step 3) Name: INVMENU
Message line prompt: Manage the Master inventory database

(Step 5) Specific menu options:
Add new products
View/edit products
Remove marked products
Print current inventory
Record received items
Print reorder report

(Step 6) Menu database file/view: IN EFFECT AT RUN TIME

(Step 7) Upper-left corner of menu frame aligned beneath the *v* in Inventory on the main menu

ORDMENU PULL-DOWN MENU The menu for managing orders is named OrdMenu. Follow the preceding general steps, using the specific information presented here, to create the menu:

(Step 3) Name: ORDMENU
Message line prompt: Manage current orders and invoices

(Step 5) Specific menu options:
Add new orders
View/edit current orders
Remove marked orders
Print invoice preview
Print invoices

(Step 6) Menu database file/view: IN EFFECT AT RUN TIME

(Step 7) Upper-left corner of menu frame aligned beneath the *d* in Orders on the main menu

ARMENU PULL-DOWN MENU The ARMenu pull-down menu provides options for managing accounts receivable. Use the preceding general steps to create the menu, filling in the specific information listed here:

(Step 3) Name: ARMENU
Message line prompt: Manage accounts receivable and customer statements

(Step 5) Specific menu options:
Enter current payments
View/edit transactions
Remove marked transactions
Print current statements

Print all current invoices before
printing customer statements

(Step 6) Menu database file/view: IN EFFECT AT RUN TIME

(Step 7) Upper-left corner of menu frame aligned beneath the *c* in Receivables on the main menu

TOOLMENU PULL-DOWN MENU The ToolMenu pull-down menu provides general tools for the business application. To create the menu, follow the general steps listed previously, filling in the specific information provided here:

(Step 3)	Name: TOOLMENU Message line prompt: General purpose file management tools
(Step 5)	Specific menu options: Rebuild corrupted indexes Backup data to drive A Reset year-to-date totals
(Step 6)	Menu database file/view: IN EFFECT AT RUN TIME
(Step 7)	Upper-left corner of menu frame aligned beneath the second *o* in Tools on the main menu

EXITMENU PULL-DOWN MENU The ExitMenu pull-down menu provides a single option to exit the application. Follow the eight general steps, filling in the specific information provided here:

(Step 3)	Name: EXITMENU Message line prompt: Exit the application and return to DOS
(Step 5)	Specific menu options: Quit to DOS
(Step 6)	Menu database file/view: IN EFFECT AT RUN TIME
(Step 7)	Upper-left corner of menu frame aligned beneath the *i* in Exit on the main menu

OPENING THE PROCEDURE FILE

At this point, you've designed all of the menus for your application. Remember too that earlier you developed many custom procedures for the application, and you want to make sure the application can use them. Therefore, you need the application to execute a SET PROCEDURE TO BusProcs command as one of its first steps. To do so, embed the SET PROCEDURE TO command above (before) the application main menu. Here are the steps to follow:

1. Press the F4 key until the frame on the BUSMAIN horizontal bar menu (the one containing the options Customer, Inventory, Receivables, and so forth) is highlighted, or click that menu with the mouse.
2. Choose Menu ► Embed Code (*do not* choose Item ► Embed Code—I'll explain the difference between those options in a moment).
3. Select Before.
4. Type the following two lines (pressing ↵ after typing each line) as shown in Figure 21.24:

```
*--- Open the procedure file.
SET PROCEDURE TO BusProcs
```

5. Press Ctrl-End three times to save your changes and return to the application design screen.

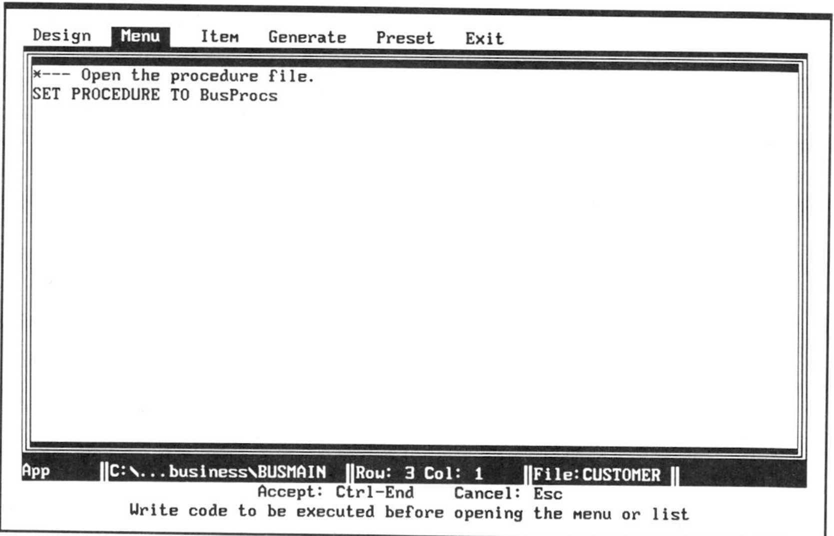

Figure 21.24: Command to open the BusProcs procedure file

If you need to take a break, now would be a good time to do so. Choose Menu ► Clear Work Surface ► Save Changes. Then choose Exit ► Save All Changes and Exit to return to the Control Center. When time permits, you can resume your work by switching to the C:\dBASE\Business subdirectory and running dBASE IV. Then proceed with the next section.

ASSIGNING ACTIONS TO MENU OPTIONS

The next step in building the business application is to assign actions to each menu option and batch-process operation. To begin, we will assign actions to the main menu options.

ASSIGNING ACTIONS TO THE MAIN MENU

If you have taken a break and exited dBASE IV, you'll need to get back to the applications design screen. To do so, highlight BusMgr in the Applications panel of the Control Center and press ↵, or double-click on BusMgr. Then select Modify Application. To bring the application's horizontal bar menu back onto the applications design screen, choose Design ► Horizontal Bar Menu and select BUSMAIN from the submenu that appears.

If you did not take a break, make sure that the horizontal bar menu is the current object by pressing the F4 key until the horizontal bar menu frame is highlighted, or by clicking on that menu.

Before assigning actions, make sure the first menu option, Customers, is highlighted (if necessary, move the cursor to that option using the ← and → keys, or by clicking the mouse on that option). Then choose Item ► Change Action. For each menu option, follow these five general steps, using the specific information provided later:

1. Select Open a Menu.
2. Specify POP-UP as the menu type and press ↵.

3. Press Shift-F1 to view menu names and select the appropriate name for the current option, or type the menu name (as specified later).
4. Press or click Ctrl-End.
5. Press or click PgDn to move to the next menu option (its name is centered in the status bar near the bottom of the screen).

The following list shows the name of each menu assigned to each action in the application main menu. Select the name shown when you perform Step 3:

Option	**Opens this menu**
Customers	CUSTMENU
Inventory	INVMENU
Orders	ORDMENU
Receivables	ARMENU
Tools	TOOLMENU
Exit	EXITMENU

ATTACHING THE PULL-DOWN MENUS

After you have assigned the Open a Menu action to each of the six main menu options, choose Menu ► Attach Pull-Down Menus and then select the Yes option.

ASSIGNING ACTIONS TO PULL-DOWN MENUS

In the sections that follow, you will assign actions to each option in each pull-down menu. In addition, most options will use *embedded code* to perform custom operations, and some will use windows to display progress. Let's take a moment to discuss these topics in general before you start working on the pull-down menu actions, so that you can better understand why they are used and how to use them.

USING EMBEDDED CODE

NOTE

Use the usual dBASE IV editing techniques to enter and change text while writing embedded code.

Both the Menu and the Item pull-down menus on the application design screen provide an option called Embed Code. When you select this option, you'll be provided with two options: Before and After. The Before option lets you enter up to 19 lines of dBASE commands to be executed before the action assigned to a menu option is executed. The After option lets you enter up to 19 lines of dBASE code to be executed after the menu action takes place.

Embedded code lets you call your custom procedures when they are required for a specific task. You can also use embedded code to open and close databases and to define relationships among databases as necessary while the application is running. This feature gives you a great deal of control over exactly when various operations take place and also lets you manage the many multiple databases in the application with great efficiency.

NOTE

From this point on, in this particular application, you should never choose Menu ► Embed Code. Always choose Item ► Embed Code instead.

There is one area of potential confusion in using embedded code that you must watch out for very carefully when developing an application: Even though both the Menu and the Item pull-down menus provide the Embed Code option, there is a big difference between the two. When you select Embed Code from the *Menu* pull-down menu, any commands that you enter will be executed before or after the *menu* is displayed when the user runs the application. When you select Embed Code from the *Items* pull-down menu, any commands that you embed will be executed before or after the current menu *option* performs its action.

USING CUSTOM PRINT FORMS

NOTE

Custom print forms are especially handy with laser printers, which typically need a page length of 60 lines instead of the dBASE default of 66 lines. To change the page length for a print form, choose Print ► Page Dimensions ► Length of Page from the reports design screen.

In Chapter 7, you learned how to customize the print forms for a report. Custom print forms are stored on disk in files with the extension .PRF when you choose Save Settings to Print Form from the Print menu.

When you print a report from the Control Panel, dBASE automatically uses either the default print form, named Report.Prf, or whatever print form you assigned by choosing Use Print Form or Save Settings to Print Form from the Print menu. However, this is not the case when you print a report from a menu created by the

Applications Generator, or when you use the REPORT FORM command to print a report at the dot prompt. In these situations, *no* print form is used automatically, unless you first assign a value to the system variable named _pform. Luckily, this is quite easy to do. For example, to assign the default C:\dBASE\Report.prf print form at the dot prompt in a command file or in embedded code, enter this command:

```
_pform = "c:\dBASE\Report"
```

To assign a print form named "Customer.prf" (in the current directory) to the _pform variable, enter this command:

```
_pform  =  "Customer"
```

If you want to use a custom print form with reports you designed for the BusMgr application, save any changes made to the application so far and return to the Control Panel by choosing Exit ► Save All Changes and Exit from the Applications Generator design screen.

NOTE

You can also change reports and add the appropriate embedded code later on, as a refinement to your application.

Modify your report layouts by highlighting the report you want to change in the Reports panel and pressing ↵ (or by double-clicking the report name) and choosing Modify Layout from the submenu that appears. Next, open the print menu and change the Destination, Control of Printer, Output Options, and Page Dimensions as necessary. Then choose Save Settings to Print Form to record new settings for the print form (and, optionally, to change the name of the print form used for this report). Save the changes to your report and return to the Control Panel by choosing Exit ► Save Changes and Exit. Repeat this process for all the reports you want to change. When you're finished, return to the Applications Generator design screen, as explained in the earlier section on "Assigning Actions to the Main Menu."

NOTE

Margin notes later in this chapter will remind you about assigning a value to _pform when you're defining various report options for the BusMgr application.

When you're ready to define the Item ► Embed Code Before for a report option on a menu, simply add the appropriate _pform = "*filename*" command at the end of the embedded code. Because you're defining the embedded code before the report option is performed, the custom print form settings will be in effect when the report is printed.

USING LOGICAL WINDOWS

Some operations will use windows, discussed in Chapter 18, to show command progress as the business application is performing a lengthy task. The Applications Generator allows you to set up logical windows via a dialog box, as shown in Figure 21.25.

All of the logical windows in this application will use DOUBLE as the border. You need not be concerned with colors or custom borders in this application. When windows are used, you'll be given the name to assign to the window as well as the upper-left and lower-right row and column coordinates for each window.

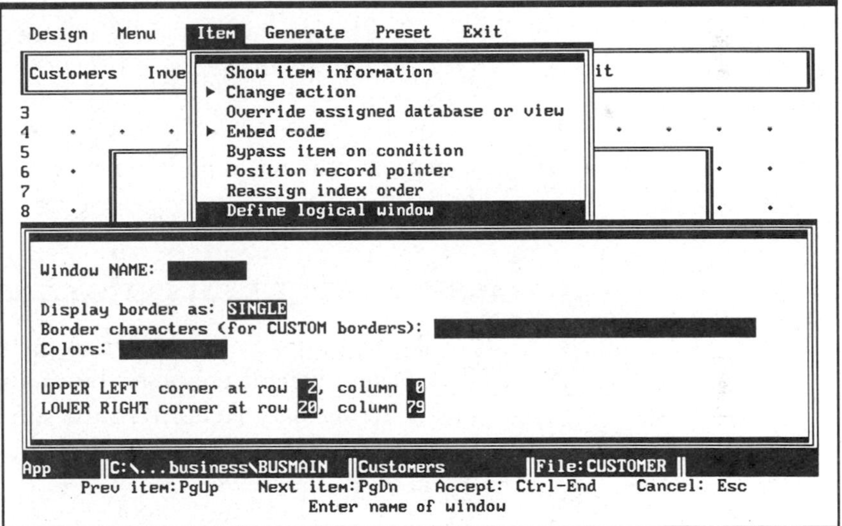

Figure 21.25: The Define Logical Window dialog box

GENERAL STEPS FOR ASSIGNING ACTIONS

To assign actions to pull-down menus, you first need to make the pull-down menu the current object. Then you need to perform the five general steps listed here for each option on your pull-down menu (you'll be provided with specific information for each step in the sections that follow):

1. Open the Item pull-down menu.

2. Select Change Action and assign the appropriate action for the item (specific information will be provided later). Press Ctrl-End to return to the Item menu.
3. If the option requires embedded code, select Embed Code and Before or After (as indicated by the specific information provided later). Press Ctrl-End twice to save the code and leave the Before or After submenu.
4. If the option requires a logical window, select Define Logical Window and enter the window name and coordinates (as specified later). Press Ctrl-End to return to the Item pull-down menu.
5. Press or click PgDn to move to the next menu item (it appears in the status bar).

Follow these steps for each option in each pull-down menu (note that some options do not require embedded code or logical windows, and you can skip these steps for those options).

ASSIGNING CUSTMENU ACTIONS

To begin assigning actions to the CustMenu pull-down menu, first make it the current object by choosing Design ► Pop-Up Menu and selecting CustMenu from the submenu that appears. Then use the five general steps to assign actions and embedded code to each menu option as specified.

ADD NEW CUSTOMERS The Add New Customers option lets the user add new customers to the Customer database and then automatically numbers them. To ensure that the Customer database is open when the user selects this option, you need to specify Embed Code Before to open the Customer database. To have the application automatically number customers, you need to specify Embed Code After to have the application execute the AutoCust procedure.

Using the five general steps, assign the actions and enter the embedded code specified here (Figure 21.26 shows how the "before" embedded code should look on your screen after you enter it.)

(Step 2) Action: Edit form (add, delete, edit)
Format file: ADDCUST
Mode: APPEND

(Step 3) Item ► Embed Code Before:

```
*--- Open Customer database to add new customers.
USE Customer
```

Item ► Embed Code After:

```
*--- After adding new customers, number them.
DO AutoCust
```

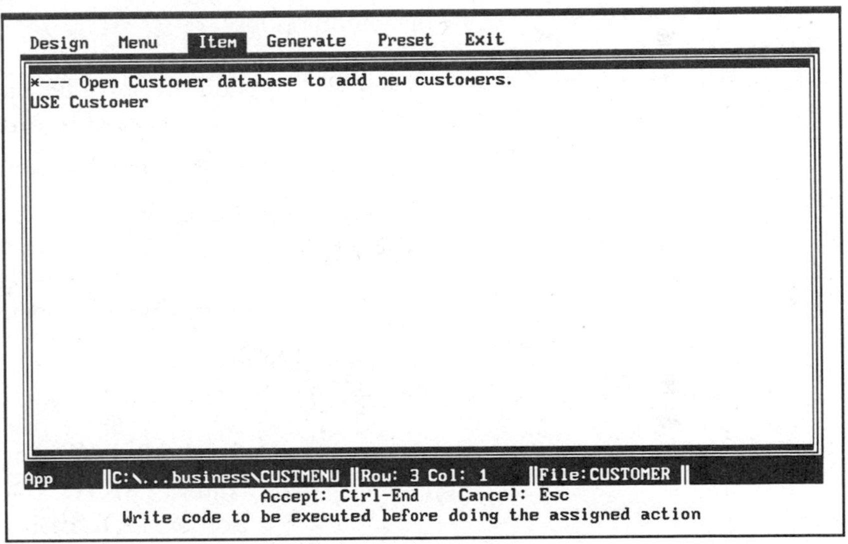

Figure 21.26: Sample embedded code typed on the screen

VIEW/EDIT CUSTOMERS The View/Edit Customers menu option uses the Customer database with the CustNo index to allow the user to search for, view, and if necessary, modify customer information using the EditCust form that you created earlier. The specific embedded code and actions are listed here:

(Step 2) Action: Edit form (add, delete, edit)
Format file: EDITCUST
Mode: EDIT
Options: Allow Record Add?: NO

(Step 3) Item ► Embed Code Before:

```
*--- View/edit customers with CustNo index in control.
USE Customer ORDER CustNo
```

Item ► Embed Code After:

```
*--- Save changes and close database.
CLOSE DATABASES
```

REMOVE MARKED CUSTOMERS The Remove Marked Customers menu option packs the Customer database and displays its progress through a window named PakWindo. Here are the specifics for this menu option:

(Step 2) Action: Perform file operation
Discard marked records

(Step 3) Item ► Embed Code Before:

```
*--- Pack Customer database.
USE Customer
```

Item ► Embed Code After:

```
*--- Save changes and close database.
CLOSE DATABASES
```

(Step 4) Define Logical Window:
Name: PAKWINDO
Border: DOUBLE
Upper-left corner: 10, 10
Lower-right corner: 20, 60

> NOTE
>
> If you customize the print form for the Customer report, enter a command that assigns a value to _pform after the last line of embedded code shown for Step 3 (for example, **_pform = "Customer"**).

PRINT CUSTOMER LIST The Print Customer List prints all customer information using the Customer report format that you developed earlier. Specifics for this option are as follows:

(Step 2) Action: Display or print report
Form name: Customer

(Step 3) Item ► Embed Code Before:

```
*--- Print customer list.
USE Customer ORDER CustNo
```

Item ► Embed Code After:

```
*--- Close database
CLOSE DATABASES
```

After you have assigned actions to all of the options on the Customer pull-down menu, choose Menu ► Put Away Current Menu ► Save Changes.

ASSIGNING INVMENU ACTIONS

To assign actions to the InvMenu options, first make InvMenu the current object by choosing Design ► Pop-Up Menu and selecting InvMenu from the submenu. Then assign actions, define windows, and embed codes using the five general steps listed previously and the specific information provided.

ADD NEW PRODUCTS The Add New products option lets the user add new products to the master inventory file. Specific actions and embedded code for this menu option are listed here:

(Step 2) Action: Edit form (add, delete, edit)
Format file: ADDPARTS
Mode: APPEND

(Step 3) Item ► Embed Code Before:

```
*--- Use Master database to add new items to the inventory.
USE Master ORDER PartNo
```

Item ► Embed Code After:

```
*--- Save changes and close.
CLOSE DATABASES
```

VIEW/EDIT PRODUCTS The View/Edit Products option lets the user search for and, optionally, change or delete products in the inventory. The specific actions and embedded code for this menu option are as follows:

(Step 2) Action: Edit form (add delete, edit)
Format file: EDITPART
Mode: EDIT
Allow Record Add?: No

(Step 3) Item ► Embed Code Before:

```
*--- Use Master database with PartNo index.
USE Master ORDER PartNo
```

Item ► Embed Code After:

```
*--- Save changes and close file.
CLOSE DATABASES
```

REMOVE MARKED PRODUCTS The Remove Marked Products option packs the database, thereby removing any records that were marked for deletion during editing. Specific actions, windows, and embedded code for this option are listed here:

(Step 2) Action: Perform file operation
Discard marked records

(Step 3) Item ► Embed Code Before:

```
*--- Use Master database for packing.
USE Master
```

Item ► Embed Code After:

```
*--- Save changes and close database.
CLOSE DATABASES
```

(Step 4) Define Logical Window:
Name: WINDOW2
Border: DOUBLE
Upper-left corner: 10, 10
Lower-right corner: 20, 60

PRINT CURRENT INVENTORY The Print Current Inventory option prints the current inventory. Specific actions and embedded

If you customized the print form for the MastRept report, enter a command that assigns a value to _pform after the last line of embedded code shown for Step 3 (for example, **_pform = "MastRept"**).

code for this option are listed here:

(Step 2) Action: Display or print: report
Form Name: MASTREPT

(Step 3) Item ► Embed Code Before:

```
*--- Use Master database to print current inventory.
USE Master ORDER PartNo
```

Item ► Embed Code After:

```
*--- Close the database.
CLOSE DATABASES
```

RECORD RECEIVED ITEMS The Record Received Items option lets the user record received purchases in the ItemsRec database. This option uses the AddItems procedure that you developed earlier to update the Master database in-stock quantities and move the updated records to a history file named ItemHist.

Note that the "after" embedded code for this option defines, activates, and closes a window to display progress during the update operation. We use embedded code, rather than the Define Logical Window option, in this instance, because we want the application to display the window only during the updating process, not while the user is entering records.

The specific actions, embedded code and windows for this menu option are listed here:

(Step 2) Action: Edit form (add delete, edit)
Format file: ADDRECVD
Mode: APPEND

(Step 3) Item ► Embed Code Before:

```
*--- Use ItemsRec for recording received purchases.
USE ItemsRec
```

Item ► Embed Code After:

```
DEFINE WINDOW UpdatWIn FROM 10,5 TO 20,65 DOUBLE
ACTIVATE WINDOW UpdatWin
```

```
SET TALK ON   && Show progress on screen.

*--- In case records were marked for deletion
*--- during entry, pack the database.
USE ItemsRec
PACK
*--- Now update the MASTER inventory.
DO AddItems

SET TALK OFF

*--- Get rid of window.
DEACTIVATE WINDOW UpdatWin
RELEASE WINDOW UpdatWin
```

NOTE

If you customized the print form for the ReordRpt report, enter a command that assigns a value to _pform after the last line of embedded code shown for Step 3 (for example, **_pform = "ReordRpt"**).

PRINT REORDER REPORT The Print Reorder Report option displays items in the inventory whose in-stock quantities are at or below the level specified in the reorder report. This option uses the ReordRpt report format with the condition FOR INSTOCK < = REORDER to display the appropriate records. Here are the specific embedded code and actions for this option:

(Step 2) Action: Display or print: report
Form name: REORDRPT
For: InStock < = Reorder

(Step 3) Item ► Embed Code Before:

```
*--- Print reorder report in part number order.
USE Master ORDER PartNo
```

Item ► Embed Code After:

```
*--- Close database.
CLOSE DATABASES
```

Now that you have assigned actions to each option on the InvMenu pull-down menu, choose Menu ► Put Away Current Menu ► Save Changes.

ASSIGNING ORDMENU ACTIONS

The OrdMenu lets the user enter new orders, preview and change current orders, and print the invoices. Options on this menu use many of the custom procedures that you developed earlier to manage information.

To start assigning actions and embedded code to the options on this menu, first make this menu the current object by choosing Design ► Pop-Up Menu and then selecting OrdMenu from the submenu that appears.

ADD NEW ORDERS The Add New Orders option needs to open all the databases required to enter orders through the AddOrder custom screen. It uses the OrdOpen procedure that you developed earlier to accomplish this task. The specific embedded code and actions assigned to this option are listed here:

(Step 2) Action: Edit form (add, delete, edit)
Format file: ADDORDER
Mode: APPEND

(Step 3) Item ► Embed Code Before:

```
*--- Open databases for entering orders.
DO OrdOpen
```

Item ► Embed Code After:

```
*--- Closes the databases.
CLOSE DATABASES
```

VIEW/EDIT CURRENT ORDERS The option View/Edit Current Orders allows the user to scroll through current orders (that is, those that have not been fulfilled) and make changes or corrections if necessary. The specific actions and embedded code for this option are listed here:

(Step 2) Action: Edit form (add, delete, edit)
Format file: EDITORD
Mode: EDIT
Allow Record Add?: No

(Step 3) Item ► Embed Code Before:

```
*--- Open related database files.
DO OrdOpen
```

```
SELECT Orders
SET ORDER TO CustNo
GO TOP
```

Item ► Embed Code After:

```
*--- Close databases after action is complete.
CLOSE DATABASES
```

REMOVE MARKED ORDERS The Remove Marked Orders option packs the Orders database to remove any records that may have been marked for deletion during editing. This option uses a window named PakWindo to display progress. The specific actions and embedded code for this menu option are listed here:

(Step 2) Action: Perform file operation
Discard marked records

(Step 3) Item ► Embed Code Before:

```
*--- Pack the Orders database only.
USE Orders
```

Item ► Embed Code After:

```
*--- Close after action complete.
CLOSE DATABASES
```

(Step 4) Define Logical Window:
Name: PAKWINDO
Border: DOUBLE
Upper-left corner: 10, 10
Lower-right corner: 20, 60

NOTE

If you customized the print form for the InvSumm report, enter a command that assigns a value to _pform after the last line of embedded code shown for Step 3 (for example, **_pform = "InvSumm"**).

PRINT INVOICE PREVIEW The Print Invoice Preview option displays current orders using the format InvSumm report format that you created earlier. The specific embedded code and actions for this menu option are listed here:

(Step 2) Action: Display or print: report
Form name: INVSUMM

(Step 3) Item ► Embed Code Before:

```
*--- Open related database files.
DO OrdOpen

*--- Specify sort order.
SELECT Orders
SET ORDER TO Invoice
```

Item ► Embed Code After:

```
*--- Close databases.
CLOSE DATABASES
```

NOTE

If you customized the print form for the Invoices report, enter a command that assigns a value to _pform after the last line of embedded code shown for Step 3 (for example, **_pform = "Invoices"**).

PRINT INVOICES The Print Invoices option performs several operations. First, it checks all current orders for backordering and adjusts the Orders database accordingly (it uses the OrdUpdat procedure you developed earlier to perform this job). Then it uses the AutoInv procedure to automatically assign invoice numbers to outstanding orders.

The menu option then prints the invoices. After printing the invoices, it moves fulfilled orders to the OrdHist database using the MoveOrds procedure that you developed earlier. This option also adds outstanding orders to the accounts receivable transaction file, Transact, using the ARUpdate procedure that you developed earlier.

Specific embedded code and actions assigned to this menu option are listed here:

(Step 2) Action: Display or Print: report
Form Name: INVOICES
For: QtyShipped >0

(Step 3) Item ► Embed Code Before:

```
*--- Update master inventory before printing invoices.
CLOSE DATABASES
DO OrdUpdat

*--- Automatically assign invoice numbers.
DO AutoInv
```

```
*--- Open databases for printing invoices.
DO OrdOpen

*--- Specify sort order.
SELECT Orders
SET ORDER TO Invoice
```

Item ► Embed Code After:

```
*--- Move invoiced transactions to history file.
DO MoveOrds

*--- Summarize orders and move to transaction file.
DO ARUpdate

*(ARUpdate procedure closes databases when done).
```

Now that you have assigned actions to all the options on the OrdMenu menu, you can choose Menu ► Put Away Current Menu ► Save Changes.

ASSIGNING ARMENU ACTIONS

The ARMenu pull-down menu provides options for managing the accounts receivable database, Transact. To begin assigning actions to this menu, first make it the current object by choosing Design ► Pop-Up Menu and selecting ARMenu from the submenu that appears.

ENTER CURRENT PAYMENTS The Enter Current Payments option lets the user record invoice payments as they are received. The actions and embedded code for this option are listed here:

(Step 2) Action: Edit form (add, delete, edit)
Format file: ADDPMTS
Mode: APPEND

(Step 3) Item ► Embed Code Before:

```
*--- Store payments in transaction file.
USE Transact
```

Item ► Embed Code After:

```
*--- Save changes and close.
CLOSE DATABASES
```

VIEW/EDIT TRANSACTIONS The View/Edit Transactions option lets the user view all transactions, but allows him or her to edit only those that have not been printed and posted. (Adjustment transactions, discussed later, allow corrections to printed and posted transactions.) The specific actions and embedded code required for this menu option are listed here:

(Step 2) Action: Edit form (add, delete, edit)
Format file: EDTRANS
Mode: EDIT

(Step 3) Item ► Embed Code Before:

```
*--- Open transaction database in customer order for editing.
USE Transact ORDER CustNo
```

Item ► Embed Code After:

```
*--- Save changes and close database.
CLOSE DATABASES
```

REMOVE MARKED TRANSACTIONS The Remove Marked Transactions option erases any records that may have been marked for deletion while the user was editing. The specific action, embedded code, and window requirements for this option are listed here:

(Step 2) Action: Perform file operation: Discard marked records

(Step 3) Item ► Embed Code Before:

```
*--- Open the transaction database.
USE Transact
```

Item ► Embed Code After:

```
*--- Save changes and close database file.
CLOSE DATABASES
```

(Step 4) Define Logical Window:
Name: PAKWINDO
Border: DOUBLE
Upper-left corner: 10, 10
Lower-right corner: 20, 60

NOTE

If you customized the print form for the Statmnts report, enter a command that assigns a value to _pform after the last line of embedded code shown for Step 3 (for example, **_pform = "Statmnts"**).

PRINT CURRENT STATEMENTS The Print Current Statements option prints the customer statements, updates the balances in the Customer database, and marks all records as printed and posted. This option uses the Statmnts report format to print the statements. The specific actions and embedded code for this option are listed here:

(Step 2) Action: Display or print: report
Format File: STATMNTS
For: .NOT. Printed

(Step 3) Item ► Embed Code Before:

```
*--- Open files needed to print statements.
SELECT A
USE Transact ORDER CustNo
SELECT B
USE Customer ORDER CustNo

*--- Set up relationship.
SELECT A
SET RELATION TO CustNo INTO Customer

********* (Application will now print statements)
```

Item ► Embed Code After:

```
*--- After printing statements, flag transactions.
SELECT Transact
REPLACE ALL Printed WITH .T.
CLOSE DATABASES

*--- Next, update Customer database charges and payments.
DO ARPost

*---(ARPost procedure closes databases when done)
```

At this point, you can choose Menu ► Put Away Current Menu ► Save Changes.

ASSIGNING TOOLMENU OPTIONS

The ToolMenu menu provides general-purpose options for managing the business application database files. To assign actions to this menu, first make it the current object by choosing Design ► Pop-Up Menu and selecting ToolMenu from the submenu that appears.

REBUILD CORRUPTED INDEXES The Rebuild Corrupted Indexes option rebuilds all indexes using the BusRendx procedure that you developed earlier. This option does not require embedded code. Specific requirements for this option are listed here:

(Step 2) Action: Run program
Do dBASE program: BUSRENDX

(Step 4) Define Logical Window:
Name: RNDXWIND
Border: DOUBLE
Upper-left corner: 10, 5
Lower-right corner: 20, 75

BACK UP DATA TO DRIVE A The Back Up Data to Drive A option copies all database (.dbf) files from the current directory to a floppy disk in drive A. This option requires only that you assign an action to it, as listed here:

(Step 2) Action: Run program
Run DOS program
Program: COPY
Parameters: *.DBF A:

RESET YEAR-TO-DATE TOTALS The Reset Year-to-Date Totals option resets all customer year-to-date charges and payments to zero and moves old transactions to the TranHist history file. It uses the YearEnd procedure that you developed earlier to accomplish this task. The specific window settings and action required for this option are listed here:

(Step 2) Action: Run program
Do dBASE Program
Program: YEAREND

(Step 4) Define Logical Window:
Name: YEARWIND
Border: DOUBLE
Upper-left corner: 10, 5
Lower-right corner: 20, 70

At this point, you have finished assigning actions to the ToolMenu menu options. Choose Menu ► Put Away Current Menu ► Save Changes.

ASSIGNING EXITMENU OPTIONS

To assign an action to the ExitMenu pull-down menu, first make it the current object by choosing Design ► Pop-Up Menu and then selecting ExitMenu from the submenu that appears.

QUIT TO DOS The action for the Quit to DOS menu option is described here:

(Step 2) Action: Quit
Quit to DOS

After assigning the action, choose Menu ► Put Away Current Menu ► Save Changes.

GENERATING THE APPLICATION

When you have finished assigning actions to each option in every menu and batch process for the application, you can have the Applications Generator write all of the code for the completed application.

Here are the steps:

1. Choose Application (or Menu) ► Clear Work Surface.
2. If prompted, select Save Changes.
3. Choose Generate ► Select Template.
4. If necessary, change the template name to Menu.gen.
5. Press ↵.
6. Select Display during Generation and change the setting to Yes.
7. Select Begin Generating.
8. When generation is complete, press any key to continue, as prompted on the screen.
9. Choose Exit ► Save All Changes and Exit to return to the Control Center.

At this point, you have (finally) completed the entire business management application. You should be at the Control Center, and the BusMgr application name should appear in the Applications panel.

USING THE COMPLETED APPLICATION

The remainder of this chapter discusses general techniques for using the completed application. If you plan to use the application in an actual business setting, be sure to use it in parallel with any existing manual or automated system for a while to make sure that it is adequate for your needs.

STARTING THE APPLICATION

To start the application directly from the DOS prompt (before starting dBASE IV), follow these steps:

1. Enter the command **CD\dBASE\Business** at the DOS prompt to switch to the application directory.

2. At the DOS prompt, enter the command **dBASE BusMgr**.
3. Press ↵ when prompted to leave the copyright screen.

If dBASE IV is already up and running on your computer, you can run the business application by following these steps:

1. Choose Tools ► DOS Utilities.
2. Choose DOS ► Select Default Drive:Directory.
3. Specify **C:\dBASE\Business** as the default drive and directory.
4. Choose Exit ► Exit to Control Center.
5. If the Business catalog does not appear on your screen, choose Catalog ► Use a Different Catalog.
6. Select BUSINESS.CAT from the submenu that appears.
7. Highlight BUSMGR in the Applications panel and press ↵, or double-click on BUSMGR. Select Run Application and select Yes if prompted.

In a moment, you will see the application sign-on banner appear on the screen along with the message "Press ↵ to continue." Do so to access the pull-down menus.

Use the ← and → keys to open a pull-down menu on the application's menu bar, or click the mouse on the name of the menu you want to open. Then use the ↑ or ↓ keys, type the first letter of an option, or click the mouse on an option to select an option from an open pull-down menu. If you type the first letter of an option, and more than one option starts with the same letter, the next matching option below the highlight is selected.

MANAGING CUSTOMER RECORDS

The pull-down menu under the Customer option allows you to manage customer data. Note that you must enter customer information into the Customer database before you can place orders for the customer.

ADDING NEW CUSTOMER RECORDS You can add new customers to the customer database at any time by choosing Customer ► Add New Customers. You will not be prompted to enter a customer number, as the application numbers customers automatically. When you are done entering new customers, leave the Company field blank on a new record and press ↵.

VIEWING AND EDITING CUSTOMER RECORDS To view or edit customer data, choose Customers ► View/Edit Customers. To locate a particular customer by number, follow these steps:

1. Choose Go To ► Index Key Search.
2. Enter the customer number you want to find and press ↵.

To locate a customer by company, contact, or some other field, choose Go To ► Forward Search, as discussed in Chapter 6.

Charges and payments for all customers are maintained automatically by the application, so you will rarely, if ever, want to modify these fields. Note, however, that these values are updated only after customer statements are printed, and so the values you see on the screen are accurate only to the last printing. (Do not change these values to make them more current, because when the system updates them automatically in the future, it will not be aware that you have already made changes.)

To delete a customer, press Ctrl-U while the customer record appears on the screen (the word "Del" appears in the lower-right corner of the screen when a customer is marked for deletion). When you are done editing, press Ctrl-End to save your changes and return to the application menus.

REMOVING MARKED CUSTOMER RECORDS If you marked any records for deletion while editing customer records, you can permanently remove these records by choosing Customers ► Remove Marked Customers. The application displays some messages in a window indicating that the deletion is in progress and then returns you to the application menus.

PRINTING CUSTOMER DATA To print a list of all customers, choose Customers ► Print Customer List. Note that the charges and payments in the report are current only to the date of the last printing of customer statements. For this reason, it might be a good idea to print the customer list immediately after printing customer statements.

MANAGING THE INVENTORY

The Inventory pull-down menu lets you manage the current inventory. Note that you must store information about a product in the master inventory database before you can process orders for that product.

ADDING NEW PRODUCTS Whenever you add a new product to your product line, you need to assign a unique part number to that product and then add a record for that product to the master inventory database. Choose Inventory ► Add New Products to do so. If you enter a part number that already exists, dBASE will only use the *first* part number's information when performing operations that combine data from the Master database with the Customer and Orders databases. Therefore, you should take care to make each part number unique. Because the database is kept in part number order, spotting duplicate parts is relatively easy, especially if you press F2 to switch to the Browse screen (press F2 again to return to the data entry form). If you detect a duplicate part number, mark it for deletion by pressing Ctrl-U, and remove the marked product records later using Inventory ► Remove Marked Products.

When you have finished entering new products, leave the PartNo field blank and press ↵ or Esc. (Alternatively, you can choose Exit ► Exit.)

VIEWING OR EDITING PRODUCT INFORMATION To view or change product information, choose Inventory ► View/Edit Products. To search for a particular product by part number, follow these steps:

1. Choose Go To ► Index Key Search.
2. Enter the part number to search for (using uppercase letters if part numbers include letters) and press ↵.

Note that in-stock quantities are updated immediately after invoices are printed, and therefore are accurate only to that date. Do not change the in-stock quantity to reflect the actual in-stock quantity, unless you are sure that invoices have been printed recently and in-stock quantities in the Master database are therefore truly up to date.

To delete a product from the master inventory database, display the product name on the edit screen and press Ctrl-U. Then press Ctrl-End or choose Exit ► Exit.

REMOVING MARKED PRODUCT RECORDS If you marked any records for deletion while editing the database, choose Inventory ► Remove Marked Products to permanently remove those marked records from the database.

PRINTING THE CURRENT INVENTORY To print a list of the current inventory, choose Inventory ► Print Current Inventory. Once again note that in-stock quantities are updated after invoices are printed and therefore are most accurate immediately after you print a batch of invoices.

RECORDING PURCHASES As you place orders and receive new items to replenish your stock, you can record these purchases by choosing Inventory ► Record Received Items. For each shipment received, include the part number and quantity received. If possible, record the purchase price as well (if you leave this value at zero, it remains unchanged on the Master database.)

After recording all shipments received, leave the Part Number field blank on a new record and press ↵. The master inventory in-stock quantities will be updated immediately to reflect these newly received shipments.

PRINTING THE REORDER REPORT To print a list of items that need to be reordered, choose Inventory ► Print Reorder Report. After the report is printed, you'll be returned to the application menus.

MANAGING ORDERS

The Orders pull-down menu provides options for entering and editing orders and for printing invoices.

ENTERING NEW ORDERS To enter new orders, choose Orders ► Add New Orders. You can fill in as many orders as necessary. Note that an invalid customer number or part number will be rejected. Also note that the customer's standard discount rate and tax rate (if the item being ordered is taxable) are automatically displayed on the screen and used in calculations, but either of these two standard values can be changed directly on the current screen.

If the customer used a purchase order to place an order, you can record that number in the Customer P.O. Number field, and it will be printed on the invoice.

When you are done entering orders, press ↵ while a blank record appears on the screen and a zero still appears in the Customer Number field.

VIEWING AND EDITING CURRENT ORDERS Current orders are those that have not yet been invoiced. You can change any current orders by choosing Orders ► View/Edit Current Orders. To search for a particular order by customer number, choose Go To ► Index Key Search, enter the customer number, and press ↵. Use the PgDn and PgUp keys to scroll through multiple orders for that customer.

To delete a particular order, bring that order onto the edit screen and press Ctrl-U. The Del indicator will appear in the status bar.

After viewing and, optionally, changing current orders, press Ctrl-End or choose Exit ► Exit to return to the application menus.

REMOVING MARKED ORDERS If during editing, you marked some orders for deletion, you can choose Orders ► Remove Marked Orders to permanently erase the marked orders.

PREVIEWING INVOICES Before printing invoices, you can print an invoice summary by choosing Orders ► Print Invoice Preview. Check the printout for errors. If you find any errors, you can still correct them at this point, using the View/Edit Current Orders option discussed previously.

PRINTING INVOICES When you are ready to print the invoices and fulfill the orders, choose Orders ► Print Invoices. The application will quickly check whether backordering is required and will make adjustments accordingly. In addition, the option will calculate the invoice numbers. (This process may take a while, so don't be alarmed if invoices don't start printing immediately.)

The option then will print invoices that bill only for the quantity shipped, not the quantity backordered. Later, when in-stock quantities permit, backorders will automatically be fulfilled and invoiced.

After invoices have been printed, you may not make changes through the View/Edit Current Orders option. However, you can make corrections by entering adjustment transactions, as discussed later in this chapter.

MANAGING RECEIVABLES

Most of the data used to manage accounts receivable comes directly from fulfilled orders. However, you do need to keep track of payments and print monthly customer statements. The options to do so are on the Receivables pull-down menu.

RECORDING CURRENT PAYMENTS As customers send in payments, record these by choosing Receivables ► Enter Current Payments. You must enter a customer number for each payment, though entering an invoice number is optional. Use the Remarks field to reference the payments (for example, enter "Check no. 555" or "Credit for Returned Items").

After recording all current payments, leave the customer number on a new blank record as zero and press ↵.

EDITING TRANSACTIONS Any time during the month, you can view all financial transactions. However, you can edit only transactions that have not yet been posted to the customer's balances or printed on a customer statement (you'll need to use adjustment transactions to make such changes).

To locate transactions for a particular customer, choose Go To ► Index Key Search, enter the customer number, and press ↵. Use the PgDn and PgUp keys to scroll through that customer's transactions. To delete a transaction, bring the transaction to the screen and press Ctrl-U. When you are done editing current transactions, press Ctrl-End or choose Exit ► Exit.

REMOVING MARKED TRANSACTIONS If you mark any records for deletion while editing the transactions database, you can choose Receivables ► Remove Marked Transactions to permanently erase those records.

PRINTING CUSTOMER STATEMENTS You can print customer statements by choosing Receivables ► Print Current Statements at any time during the month, but note that individual payments and invoices are printed only once (not on every statement). For that reason, you may want to print customer statements only once, perhaps at the end of the month. Printing customer statements automatically updates all current charges, payments, and balances in the Customer database.

USING THE GENERAL-PURPOSE TOOLS

The Tools pull-down menu provides general-purpose tools for managing the overall application.

If your databases become very large, they probably won't fit onto a single backup diskette. In this case, you must assign the BACKUP action (instead of COPY) when specifying the DOS program to run. Unlike COPY, the BACKUP command prompts you to insert a new disk when the current backup disk is full. Your DOS manual provides information on using the BACKUP command and its companion command, RESTORE.

REBUILDING CORRUPTED INDEXES A sudden power outage or other mishap might cause database indexes to become corrupted. Then the application will tend to fail regularly and display an error message specifying a problem with an index. If this problem occurs, choose Tools ► Rebuild Corrupted Indexes. The option will rebuild all indexes and return you to the application menu, where you can resume your work.

BACKING UP DATA From time to time, you should make copies of all the application database files. To do so, put a formatted disk in drive A (either a blank one or one you use only for making backup copies), and then choose Tools ► Backup Data to Drive A. When copying is done, you'll be returned to the application menus.

RESETTING YEAR-TO-DATE TOTALS At the end of each accounting year, you can reset customer year-to-date charges and payments to zero by choosing Tools ► Reset Year-to-Date Totals. To verify that you did not select this option in error, a window will appear asking for verification. If you are sure you want to reset year-to-date totals, type **Y**. Otherwise, press ↵ to select the default answer, no.

ENTERING ADJUSTMENT TRANSACTIONS

When an error or some other problem occurs that disrupts the normal flow of information through the business application, you can respond in any of several ways. Let's look at an example.

Suppose that customer number 1001 pays for an invoice, and the payment goes through and is posted to the customer's current payments. Later you discover that the check bounced. You cannot alter the original payment record, because it has already been posted. You *could* simply edit the customer's balance in the customer database (for example, subtract $100 from the customer's total payments), but doing so leaves no audit trail.

A better method would be to enter an *adjustment transaction*, which corrects the balances and leaves a record of when and why the change occurred. In the example of the bounced check for customer number 1001, you could choose Receivables ► Enter Current Payments to add a new payment to the transaction database that specifies a negative payment amount equal to the check (plus your charges, if any). Figure 21.27 shows an example.

Note that the entry specifies –110.00 as the payment amount (assuming that the check that bounced was for $100.00, and you've charged $10.00 as a returned check fee). The remark for the entry explains the negative payment value.

Later, when you print customer statements, the adjustment will appear on the customer's bill, and the negative value will indeed be subtracted from the customer's total payments. The customer's balance will still be correct, and the adjustment will be recorded in the transaction database for future reference.

Let's look at another example. Suppose a customer returns two of part number B-222 because he or she hadn't actually ordered these items (someone made a mistake while entering orders). To put the items back into the in-stock inventory quantities, you choose Inventory ► Record Received Items and enter the two received items as though they were received from a vendor. Automatically, the application will add the two returned products to the in-stock quantity, and you will have a record of the transaction on the ItemHist database.

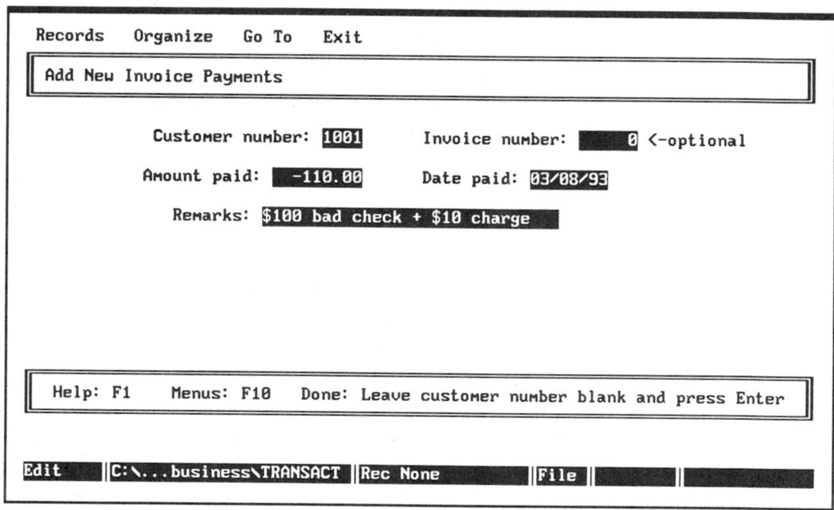

Figure 21.27: An adjustment transaction for a bounced check

Then choose Receivables ► Enter Current Payments and enter a payment equal to whatever the customer was charged for the two items. In the remarks field, enter a description such as "Credit for returned items." The transaction is logged as a payment, therefore keeping the customer's balance correct. In addition, the customer's statement will reflect the adjustment, to show that he or she received credit for the mistake.

Note that you cannot make adjustments through Orders ► Add New Orders, because a negative quantity will not be calculated correctly (because of all the computation involved in backordering). However, you should be able to make any adjustments through the Inventory ► Record Received Items and Receivables ► Enter Current Payments menu options.

LEAVING THE APPLICATION

You can leave the application and return to dBASE IV by pressing Esc or clicking the mouse outside the application's menu bar rather than selecting Quit to DOS.

When you have finished a session with the business manager application and want to stop using dBASE, choose Exit ► Quit to DOS. All your work will be saved, and you will be returned to the DOS prompt, at which time you can turn off your computer or run another program.

WHERE DO YOU GO FROM HERE?

At this point you've seen examples of practically every feature that the dBASE IV Control Center and its various design screens have to offer, had a lot of hands-on experience in creating database objects, and have also learned a little bit about the dBASE IV programming language.

Where you go from here depends largely on what you want to do with dBASE IV. If you are still feeling a bit overwhelmed by all these capabilities, you might want to stay in the Control Center and design screens, and practice creating databases, queries, forms, and report and label formats on your own, and perhaps even some applications.

If you want to focus on creating applications, you'd be better off "graduating" to a more advanced book that focuses on the dBASE IV programming language and/or applications development. For example, you might try the *dBASE IV 1.5 Developer's Handbook* also published by SYBEX, which offers a set of programs for developing a model application.

APPENDIX A

A DOS Primer

IF YOU'VE NEVER USED A COMPUTER BEFORE, YOU'D be wise to invest a little time in learning a few things about your computer's *operating system.* Even though you are probably ready to start putting dBASE IV to work now, the time you spend learning about your computer's operating system will be well spent. The more you know about the operating system, the more easily you will get along with your computer, and with dBASE IV as well.

The operating system acts as a sort of a middleman between the *hardware* of the computer and the *software* that you are using. The fact that you are reading this book indicates that your hardware is probably an IBM or compatible microcomputer. The operating system that you are using is probably DOS. The specific software package (or program) that you will be using in this book is dBASE IV.

DISKS AND DISK DRIVES

Information that you store in the computer, whether it be a sales report, customer list, graph, or letter, is *written* in a *file.* Programs, such as dBASE IV, are also stored in files. Each file is stored on a disk, similar to the way that a song is stored on a compact disk or cassette tape. Your tape or disk player lets you hear your cassette tapes and compact disks; your computer lets you *read* the contents of a file on your computer disk.

Most computers can use at least two types of disks for storing files. One type is removable and is called a *floppy disk* or *diskette.* The other type of disk is a *hard* or *fixed disk.* A hard disk cannot be removed.

FLOPPY DISKS

Removable disks come in two sizes: 5¹/₄-inch minifloppy disks and 3¹/₂-inch microfloppy disks. Your computer might accept one size or both. Figure A.1 shows the 5¹/₄-inch and 3¹/₂-inch diskettes.

To access the files stored on a disk, you first have to put the disk into the *disk drive* of your computer. Always insert the disk with the label facing upward and toward you. Most 5¹/₄-inch disk drives have

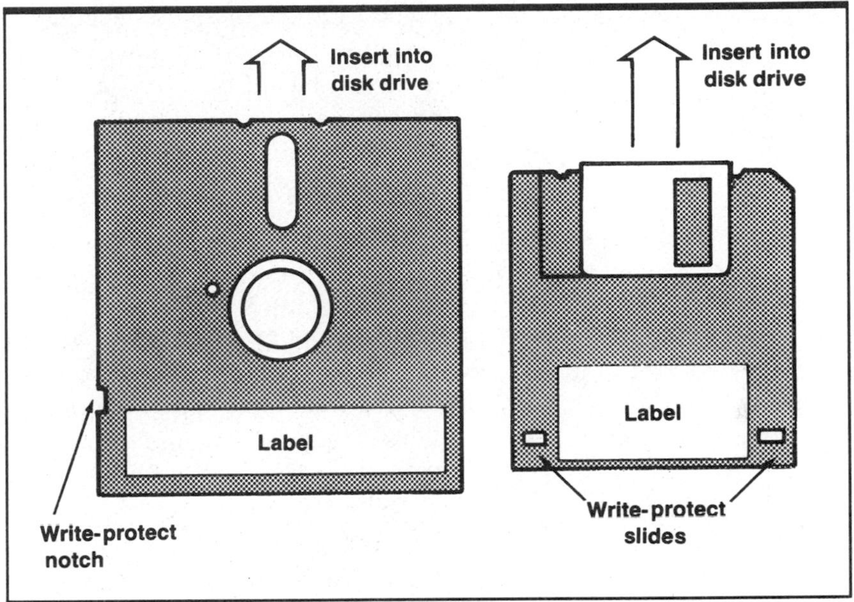

Figure A.1: A 5¼-inch and a 3½-inch disk

a latch or door that you must close after inserting the disk. To remove the disk, open the drive door or latch. The disk will pop out slightly. Gently pull the disk out of the drive to remove it.

The 3½-inch disk drives do not have a door or latch. Instead, you push the disk in until it clicks and pops into the drive. To remove a 3½-inch disk, you press the eject button, which is usually slightly below and to the right of the slot where you insert the disk. The disk will pop out slightly. Gently pull the disk the rest of the way out of the slot.

The write-protect notch on a 5¼-inch disk lets you protect the files stored on the disk. When the notch is uncovered, you have full access to the files on that disk. That is, you can read and copy information from the disk, change files on the disk, copy new files to the disk, and erase files from the disk.

If you cover the notch with one of the tabs that comes with a box of 5¼-inch disks, you can only read or copy files from the disk; you cannot add, erase, or change any of the files that are already stored on the disk.

The $3^1/_2$-inch disks use a sliding tab to protect files. (Some have two sliding tabs, others have only one.) When the sliding tab is closed, you have full access to the files on the disk. You can read, copy, change, erase, and add new files to the disk. When the sliding tab is open, you can only read or copy files from the disk; you cannot add new files or erase or change existing ones.

HARD DISKS

Your computer is probably equipped with at least one hard disk (or fixed disk) drive as well as a floppy disk drive. You can't see the hard disk because it's inside the main unit of the computer. The hard disk has certain advantages over a floppy disk. For instance, a single hard disk can hold much more information than a floppy disk; it can hold perhaps as much information as 100 disks. A hard disk is also much faster than a floppy disk, which makes all your work on the computer faster.

The reason the computer has both hard and floppy disk drives is that you need some way to transport files from one computer to another. The removable floppy disks provide that capability. For example, when you buy dBASE IV, it comes to you on floppy disks. Before using the program, you *install* it, which includes copying dBASE IV from the disks on which it was delivered to the hard disk in your computer.

Floppy disks are also useful for making backup copies of important information. For example, if you store all your accounting data on a hard disk, you might also want to make an extra copy and store it on a floppy disk. You can store that extra copy in a safe place. If someone accidentally erases the accounting data from your hard disk, you can then recopy it from the backup disk onto your hard disk.

You might also want to copy information from your hard disk to a floppy disk for use on another computer. For example, you might want to give a copy of the accounting data to someone else for use elsewhere. Or if you have computers both at home and in your office, you might want to copy data from the hard disk on one computer for use on the other.

DISK DRIVE NAMES

DOS identifies each disk drive on your computer with a single letter. Typically, if your computer has one floppy disk drive and one hard disk, the floppy disk drive is named A and the hard disk is named C. If you have two floppy disk drives and one hard disk, the floppy drives are named A and B, with A usually being the one on the top or at the left. The hard disk is still named C.

Your computer might have additional hard disks named D, E, F, and so on. For example, if you share a computer with other users in a network, you might work on a hard disk named E or F. The network administrator (that is, the person in charge of the computer) can tell you the letter assigned to the drive that you are using.

DIRECTORIES AND FILES

A single hard disk can store many thousands of files. To help keep all of these files organized, you can create separate work areas, called *directories* (or *subdirectories*). Each directory holds its own set of files, just like each department in a company has its own set of files.

DIRECTORY NAMES

Each directory on a disk has a name, which you assign. The name can be up to eight characters long, but it cannot contain any blank spaces or punctuation. You can use numbers, the underline character (_), and the hyphen or minus sign (-) in a directory name. Table A.1 lists examples of valid and invalid directory names.

DOS often precedes a directory name with a backslash (\) to distinguish it from a file name. For example, the DBASE directory might be identified as \DBASE. To pinpoint the *exact* location of a particular directory, DOS often precedes the directory name with the drive name, followed by a colon (:) and a backslash. For example, C:\DBASE identifies a directory named DBASE on disk drive C.

Table A.1: Valid and Invalid Directory Names

Directory name	Status
DBASE	Valid
ACCOUNTS	Valid
JAN1991	Valid
GL	Valid
ACCT_REC	Valid
FIRST QTR	Invalid (contains a blank space)
RECEIVABLES	Invalid (too long)
ACCT:REC	Invalid (colon is a punctuation mark)

SUBDIRECTORIES

You can also create subdirectories on your disk. The name of a subdirectory can also be up to eight characters long. A subdirectory name is always preceded by the names of higher-level directories and a backslash. For example, suppose you create a directory named SALES to store information for the sales department of your company. Also suppose you want to keep the accounting data and personnel data for the sales department on separate subdirectories. To do so, you could create one subdirectory named SALES\ACCTNG and another subdirectory named SALES\PERSONNL. Note that the directory and subdirectory names are separated by a backslash.

DIRECTORY TREES

You can envision the directory structure (or directory *tree,* as it's sometimes called), on a disk as a hierarchy. The *root* directory (which every floppy or hard disk has) is the highest level directory. The root directory is always named simply \. There can be any number of directories and subdirectories beneath the root directory. Figure A.2 shows a sample directory tree (the directory on your disk is probably much different).

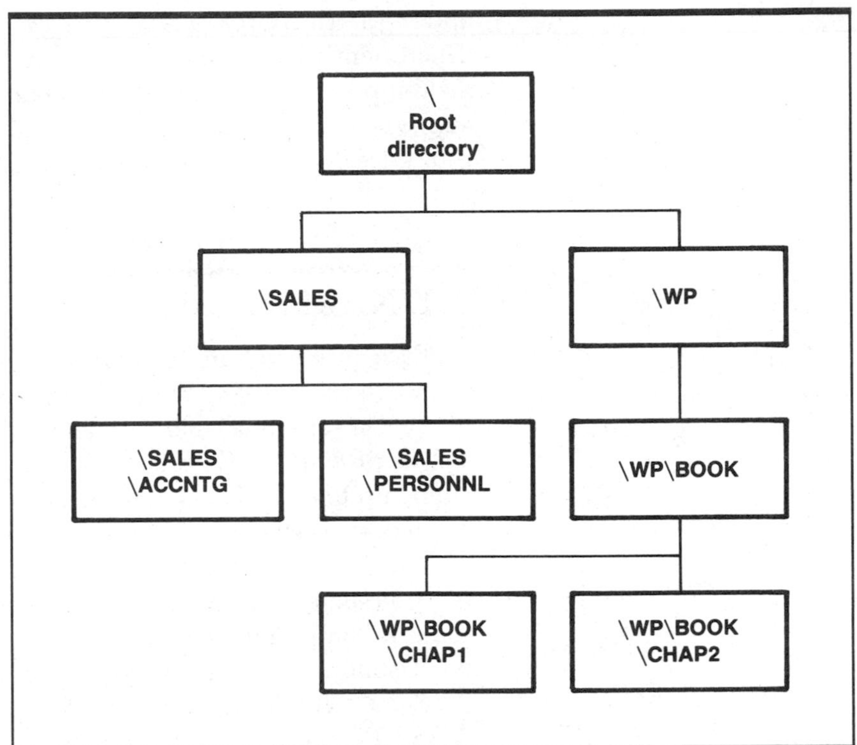

Figure A.2: Sample directory structure

The terms *parent* and *child* are often used to describe the hierarchical relationships between directories and subdirectories. For example, in Figure A.2 the SALES (or \SALES) directory is the *parent* to both \SALES\ACCTNG and \SALES\PERSONNL. The \SALES \ACCTNG subdirectory is a *child* to the \SALES directory, as is \SALES\PERSONNL.

Be aware that the terms *directory* and *subdirectory* are used interchangeably in most computer literature. For example, it is not unusual to see a phrase such as "switch to the \SALES\ACCTNG directory" or even "the \SALES subdirectory."

The reason for this loose terminology stems from the fact that, from the computer's standpoint, directories and subdirectories are pretty much the same thing: each is just a place on the disk where files are stored. Subdirectory names, such as \SALES\ACCTNG, are for human convenience. That is, when you see the subdirectory name \SALES\ACCTNG, you can quickly recall that the sales department's accounting information is stored in that work area. But the computer just sees a work area named \SALES\ACCTNG (and has no idea that the information stored there has anything to do with your sales department or with accounting).

FILE NAMES

Each directory (and subdirectory) on a disk may contain many files, such as a file containing a customer list; another file containing a parts list; and other files containing letters, graphs, and programs such as dBASE IV. Each file has a name that, like a directory name, can be up to eight letters long and cannot contain spaces. Numbers, the underline character (_), and the hyphen or minus sign (-) are allowed.

A file name can also have an *extension* (or last name). The extension can be up to three letters long and is always preceded by a period. Usually, the file name identifies the contents of a file and the extension identifies the type of information in the file. (When using dBASE IV, you usually provide the file name, and dBASE automatically adds the extension.)

Table A.2 lists examples of valid and invalid file names. Table A.3 lists examples of file name extensions and indicates the type of data stored in the files. (Appendix H lists all file name extensions that dBASE IV automatically assigns to different types of files.)

The exact location of specific information filed on a disk is often displayed by DOS (and dBASE IV) as a combination of the disk drive, directory (and subdirectory) names, and the file name preceded by a backslash. For example, the complete name C:\DBASE \MYDATA.DBF identifies a database file named MYDATA.DBF stored on the \DBASE directory on disk drive C. The complete name C:\SALES\PERSONNL\NAMELIST.TXT identifies a text file named NAMELIST.TXT on the \SALES\PERSONNL subdirectory on disk drive C.

Now suppose that, while using dBASE IV, you create a database containing customer names and addresses. You assign the name

Table A.2: Valid and Invalid File Names

File name	Status
MYREPORT.TXT	Valid
ACCTREC.DAT	Valid
QRT1.91	Valid
1991TAX.FRM	Valid
JAN_1991.DBF	Valid
MAIL LIST.DAT	Invalid (contains a space)
1991SUMMARY.REP	Invalid (file name too long)
MAILIST.DATA	Invalid (extension too long)

Table A.3: Examples of File Name Extensions

Extension	Type of information
.TXT	Text (such as a letter, report, or document)
.BAK	Backup copy of another file
.DBF	dBASE database file
.COM	Program
.EXE	Another extension used for programs

CUSTLIST to this database and store it on a directory named \DBASE on drive C. Because dBASE automatically adds the extension .DBF, the customer names and addresses will actually be stored in a file named CUSTLIST.DBF. To completely identify the location and name of the customer list, DOS (and dBASE) use C:\DBASE \CUSTLIST.DBF. Figure A.3 illustrates how the CUSTLIST database is stored on a disk.

Another term that you may encounter while using DOS or dBASE IV is *path.* The path refers to the disk drive, directory, and subdirectory name (if any) that describes the location of a file. Figure A.4 shows a sample of a path, using a file named FORMLET.TXT stored on the \WP\LETTERS subdirectory of drive C.

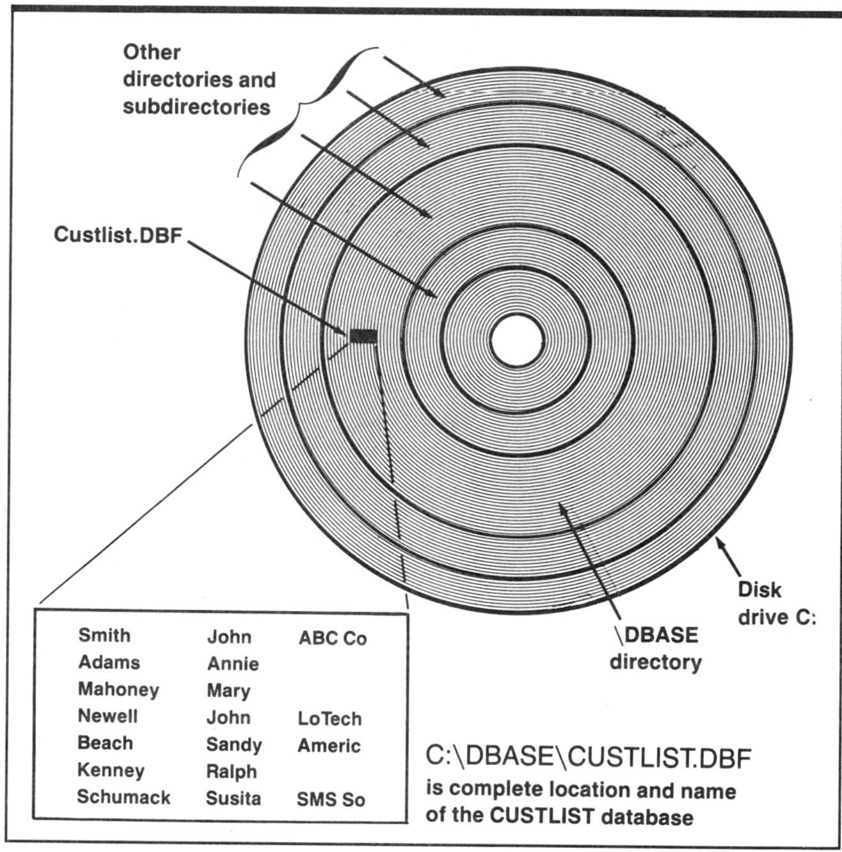

Figure A.3: CUSTLIST.DBF database stored on a disk

NOTE

If your computer automatically displays a menu or "DOS Shell" at startup, you'll need to find an option for exiting or for accessing the DOS Command Prompt to get to the DOS prompt.

THE DOS PROMPT

When you first turn on your computer, DOS automatically *boots* the system and takes control. Your screen shows the *DOS prompt,* which consists of the name of the current disk drive, followed by the > sign. The DOS prompt will probably be C> on your computer (if you boot from a hard disk) or A> (if you boot from a floppy disk).

When the DOS prompt is showing, the computer is ready to accept certain *DOS commands*. The following sections discuss some basic DOS commands that can help you use your computer more effectively. For a more complete discussion of DOS commands, refer to the manual that came with your copy of DOS.

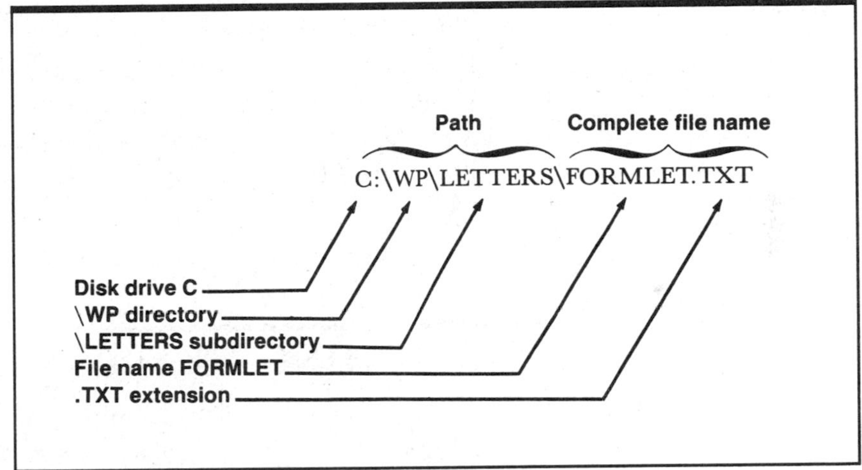

Figure A.4: A file name, preceded by its path

SETTING THE DATE AND TIME

Your computer stores the current date (sometimes called the *system date*) in its memory, and dBASE IV can access that date. To see if the date is correct, type the command **DATE** next to the DOS prompt. (If you make a mistake, you can back up by pressing the Backspace key.) After typing the DATE command, press ↵ (called the Enter or Return key on some keyboards).

Your screen will display a prompt such as this one:

```
Current date is Sat 03/14/1992
Enter new date (mm-dd-yy):
```

If the date shown on your screen is not correct, type a new date in *mm-dd-yy* format (for example, 11/15/93 for November 15, 1993). Press ↵ after typing the new date, and you'll be returned to the DOS prompt.

To check and correct the system time, type the command **TIME** and press ⏎. The screen will display the current time and a prompt for entering the correct time, as follows:

```
Current time is 12:26:15.92a
Enter new time:
```

☞ NOTE

Versions of DOS prior to DOS 4.0 do not have the "a" and "p" options; for those versions, you must use 24-hour clock format. To find out which version of DOS you are using, type **VER** and press ⏎.

If the current time shown is not correct, type the new time using a 24-hour clock format, or by adding the letter "a" (for A.M.) or the letter "p" (for P.M.) after the time. (You need not enter seconds or hundredths of seconds.) For example, if the current time is 8:30 A.M., type **8:30** or **8:30a** and press ⏎. If the current time is 2:15 P.M., type **14:15** or **2:15p** and press ⏎. You'll be returned to the DOS prompt.

SWITCHING TO A DISK DRIVE

To switch to a particular disk drive, type the letter of that drive followed by a colon and press the ⏎ key. (You can only switch to a floppy disk drive if there is a disk in the drive and the drive door, if any, is closed.) For example, if you are currently on disk drive A and want to switch to hard disk drive C, you would enter the command **C:** and then press ⏎. (This command works, of course, only if your computer has a hard disk named C.)

SWITCHING TO A DIRECTORY

☞ NOTE

Be sure to use the backslash (\) rather than the forward slash (/) when specifying directory names.

To switch to a directory or subdirectory, use the DOS CHDIR (for Change Directory) command or the abbreviation CD. For example, after you have installed dBASE on your computer, you can switch to the \DBASE directory by typing the command **CD \DBASE** and pressing ⏎. To switch to a subdirectory, enter both the parent and child directory names. For example, if your computer has a directory named \DBASE\SAMPLES, you switch to that subdirectory by typing **CD \DBASE\SAMPLES** and pressing ⏎.

VIEWING THE CURRENT DIRECTORY NAME

> **NOTE**
> Whatever directory you happen to be on at the moment is the *current* directory.

If you switch to a new directory and its name does not appear next to the DOS prompt, you can see the directory name by typing the command **PROMPT PG** and pressing ↵. The current disk drive and directory will appear at the DOS prompt. For example, if you are currently on the \DBASE directory on drive C, the DOS prompt will be followed by C:\DBASE>. This technique is very handy for keeping track of which directory you are currently on.

VIEWING FILE NAMES

> **NOTE**
> All DOS commands require you to press ↵ after typing the command. Hence, the phrase "enter the command" means "type the command and then press ↵."

To view the names of files stored on the current directory, you can enter the DIR command at the DOS prompt. If the directory contains many files, you can enter the command **DIR /W** to display the file names in a wide (columnar) format, or you can enter the command **DIR /P** to have DOS pause after it presents each screenful of file names. (Press any key after each pause to view the next screenful.)

When DIR displays file names, it does not show a period between the file name and the extension. Instead, it displays the name and extension in separate columns. If you do not use the /W option for a wide display, DIR also shows the size of each file and the date and time that the file was created or was last changed. DIR also shows the names of directories that are children to the current directory. These have <DIR>, rather than a file size, in the third column of the list.

Here is a sample DIR display (your computer will show something completely different):

```
Directory of  C:\

ASSIGN      COM      6399     04-09-91    5:00a
DBASE       <DIR>             03-31-92    8:00a
DISKCOPY    COM      11793    04-09-91    5:00a
FIND        EXE      6770     04-09-91    5:00a
PRINT       EXE      15656    04-09-91    5:00a
```

The first row shows that there is a file named ASSIGN.COM on the current directory and that this file occupies 6399 *bytes* of disk space. (A byte is the same as a character; for example, the word *CAT* contains three bytes.) ASSIGN.COM was created (or last changed) at 5:00 A.M. on 4/9/91 in this example.

The second row shows that a directory named \DBASE exists on the disk. That directory was created on 3-31-92 at 8:00 A.M.

VIEWING THE DIRECTORY TREE

To view the names of all directories and subdirectories on the current disk drive, switch to the root directory and enter the TREE command. For example, to see the names of directories on disk drive C, you would enter these commands (press ↵ after typing each command):

```
C:      ↵
CD\     ↵
TREE    ↵
```

The C: command brings you to drive C. The CD\ command switches you to the root directory, which is always named \. The TREE command runs a DOS program named TREE, which displays the directory tree. Note that if the TREE.COM program is not accessible from the root directory, DOS displays only the message "Bad command or file name." Don't worry about this; you can still use the other commands discussed in this chapter.

NOTE

On DOS Version 4.0 and higher, the tree appears in a graphical format, with directories and subdirectories connected by lines, and child subdirectories indented below their parent directory.

If a particular directory has child directories beneath it, these are listed separately. For example, suppose your TREE display includes

```
Path: \DBASE

Sub-directories: SQLHOME
                 DBTUTOR
                 SAMPLES
```

This display informs you that the hard disk includes a directory named \DBASE, with subdirectories \DBASE\SQLHOME, \DBASE\DBTUTOR, and \DBASE\SAMPLES.

To switch to the \DBASE directory, you would enter the command **CD \DBASE**. To switch to the \DBASE\SAMPLES subdirectory, you would enter the command **CD \DBASE\SAMPLES**. Then you could enter the DIR command to see the names of files on the directory (or subdirectory).

CREATING DIRECTORIES

To create a new directory (or subdirectory) on your hard disk, you use the DOS MKDIR command (or the abbreviation MD). Include the full directory name and a preceding backslash. For example, to create a directory named \DBASE, you enter **MD \DBASE** at the DOS prompt. (You need not create any new directories right now.) To switch to that new directory, you would then enter the command **CD \DBASE ↵**.

RUNNING PROGRAMS FROM THE DOS PROMPT

All programs are stored in files that have the extension .COM, .EXE, or .BAT. To run a program, you usually need to switch to the appropriate directory and type the program name (without the extension).

For example, after you install dBASE IV (according to the instructions in Appendix B), the dBASE IV program and its associated files will be stored in a directory named \DBASE. The main dBASE IV program is named DBASE.EXE. Therefore, to run dBASE IV, you will first need to switch to the \DBASE directory on drive C and then to enter the command DBASE at the DOS prompt. The exact commands you enter at the DOS prompt are

```
C:          ↵
CD\DBASE    ↵
DBASE       ↵
```

If you attempt to run a program that is not on thc current disk drive and directory, DOS will respond with the message "Bad command or file name" (or something equivalent, depending on the version of DOS that you are using).

There is an exception to the rule of having to be on a particular directory before running a program. The next section discusses this exception.

FILE SEARCH PATHS

Normally, when you ask DOS to run a program (such as dBASE IV), you must be on the directory that the program or file is stored in. However, DOS offers a command, PATH, that tells the computer to search other directories if it cannot find a particular program on the current directory.

When you install dBASE IV on your computer (as discussed in Appendix B), it will ask if you want to be able to start dBASE IV from any directory. If you answer Yes to this question (by pressing ↵ when prompted), the installation automatically creates the appropriate PATH so that you can run dBASE IV from any directory.

You can check the current PATH at any time by entering the command **PATH** at the DOS prompt. After you have installed dBASE IV, you should see C:\DBASE as one of the paths displayed on the screen. For example, you might see PATH = C:\DBASE. If other files are included in the path, you'll see these as well, each separated by a semicolon. For example, if the root directory, a directory named \WP, and the \DBASE directory are included in the search path, you'll see PATH =C:\;C:\WP;C:\DBASE.

If for some reason, you find that you cannot start dBASE from directories other than the \DBASE directory, you can alter the DOS path as discussed in Appendix B.

GETTING HELP AT THE COMMAND PROMPT

If you're using DOS Version 5, you can get help on any DOS command at the command prompt. To display a list of all DOS commands and a brief description of what each one does, type **HELP** and press ↵. To display information about a specific DOS command and how to use it, type **HELP** *command* where *command* is the name of the command you're interested in. For example, to find out more about the PATH command, type **HELP PATH** and then press ↵.

APPENDIX B

Installing dBASE IV

BEFORE YOU CAN USE dBASE IV ON YOUR COMPUTER, it needs to be installed. You need only go through the installation process once. This appendix discusses general techniques for installing dBASE IV on a single-user computer. If you wish to install dBASE IV on a network, refer to the network installation instructions that came with your dBASE IV package.

HARDWARE REQUIREMENTS

The minimum hardware requirements for running dBASE IV are:

- An IBM PC, AT, PC/XT, or PS/2 model 30, 50, 60, or 80; a Compaq Deskpro 286 or 386; or any 100 percent compatible microcomputer.
- IBM DOS or MS-DOS version 2.1 or higher for the DOS version of dBASE IV, or OS/2 for the OS/2 version.
- At least 640K total RAM, with 450K available when starting dBASE IV.
- A hard disk with at least 5 megabytes (Mb) of available disk space.

LOCATING YOUR SERIAL NUMBER

If this is the first time you are installing this copy of dBASE IV, you should jot down your Borland serial number. The serial number is printed on the Warranty Registration Card Sticker that you attached to System Disk 2.

PREVIOUS VERSIONS OF dBASE

If you have an earlier version of dBASE, such as dBASE IV version 1.0 or dBASE III PLUS, on your computer, you might want to "uninstall" those, or move them to another directory. You can use the install program that came with that earlier version of program to uninstall it.

If you want to keep an earlier version of dBASE on your hard disk, make sure that you do not install dBASE IV on the same directory as that earlier version. Either move the earlier version to another directory, or use a new directory name when installing dBASE IV.

DISK CACHING

Do not install caching if you plan to run dBASE IV under Windows 3. If you intend to run dBASE IV under Windows, answer No when asked if you want to install disk caching. See Appendix D for more information.

Disk caching (pronounced "cashing") is a technique used by dBASE IV 1.5 to speed processing. It stores heavily used data in extended (EMS) or expanded (LIM) memory to reduce the slower hard disk activity. If you answer Yes when asked if you want to install disk caching, the dBASE IV installation program automatically makes a guess about whether your computer has extended or expanded memory. Therefore, you normally won't need to worry about the exact type of memory you have. However, if you decide to change the setting later, you will need to know which type of memory your computer has. Here are some guidelines to help you determine this:

- If you have an 8088 or 8086 computer (such as an IBM PC or XT), you don't have extended memory. You may, however, have expanded memory if you've purchased and installed an expanded memory board.
- If you have an AT-type (80286) computer, chances are you have extended memory.
- An 80386 computer generally has extended memory, which can easily be converted to expanded memory using the device driver in the CONFIG.SYS file.
- If you have DOS version 4 or higher, you can enter the command **MEM** (and press ↵) to see what memory is available. You might also have some other utility that can provide this information.

If you need to uninstall or change the disk caching setting, refer to the section "Reinstalling Disk Caching" later in this chapter.

INSTALLING dBASE IV

In this appendix, we'll cover the basic single-user installation of dBASE IV. Installing dBASE IV on a network is trickier and varies with the type of network in use. Please refer to the documentation that came with your dBASE IV package if you will be installing it on a network.

To begin the actual single-user installation, follow these steps:

1. Start your computer in the usual manner and get to the DOS command prompt.
2. Insert the dBASE IV Install Disk in disk drive A, and close the drive door (if any).
3. Type **A:** and press ↵ to switch to drive A.
4. Type **INSTALL** and press ↵.
5. After a few moments, you'll see a dBASE IV screen followed by a Copyright screen. When instructed at the bottom of the screen, press ↵ to proceed with the installation.
6. Select QUICK when you see the dBASE IV Installation screen by pressing ↵, or by typing the letter Q.
7. On the next screen, dBASE suggests C:\DBASE as the installation drive and directory. Press ↵ to accept this suggestion, or change it using the arrow keys, then press ↵. (If you wish to cancel the installation, press Esc, then select Yes when prompted.)
8. If dBASE already exists in the directory specified in the previous step, you'll see a message indicating this. Select Proceed to overwrite the previous version, or select Change Drive:Directory to repeat step 7 and assign a different drive and directory. (If you proceed, it may take a few minutes for the program to uninstall the previous version.)
9. If this is the first time you're installing dBASE IV, or if you've uninstalled and are reinstalling the program, you'll see a screen for registering your copy of dBASE IV. As prompted on the screen, type your name, company, and serial number, pressing ↵ after each entry. When done, press Ctrl-End.

NOTE

If the arrow keys don't work on your keyboard, press NumLock, then try again.

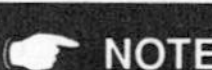

The Quick installation procedure copies all the dBASE program and support files to the \DBASE, \DBASE\SQLHOME, \DBASE\DBTUTOR, and \DBASE\SAMPLES subdirectories on your hard disk. If the \DBASE \SAMPLES subdirectory already exists, you'll be prompted to choose Proceed to overwrite the existing sample files, Skip to leave the existing files unchanged, or Change Drive:Directory to install the sample files in a different directory. In most cases it's safe to choose Proceed.

10. Next, you'll be asked if you want to install caching for extended/expanded memory. Answer Yes if your computer has either extended or expanded memory. Answer No if your computer doesn't have either type of memory, or if you plan to use dBASE IV with Windows.
11. Follow the instructions on the screen for replacing the disk in drive A. After replacing a disk in drive A, press ↵ so the dBASE IV Install program can continue copying files to your hard disk. As installation proceeds, you'll be prompted to insert System Disk 1, System Disk 2, and the Tutorial disk, which contains sample files, SQL files, tutorial files, and the dBASE template language toolkit. Note that the Runtime and Access disks 5 and 6 aren't needed for the Quick installation that you're doing now.
12. When copying is complete, you'll see a screen asking for permission to modify your AUTOEXEC.BAT file in order to place the dBASE IV directory in the PATH statement. Press ↵ to proceed; if you prefer to modify AUTOEXEC.BAT later, press Esc instead, though it's better to let dBASE do the modification for you.
13. Next, you'll see a screen asking for permission to modify your CONFIG.SYS file so that FILES is set to at least 99 and BUFFERS is set to at least 15. Press ↵ to proceed; if you prefer to modify the CONFIG.SYS file later, press Esc instead (again, it's better to let dBASE do this for you).
14. Finally, you'll see a message indicating that installation is complete. Press ↵ to end the installation.

The basic installation of dBASE is now complete, and you should be at the drive and directory where dBASE IV was installed (typically, C:\DBASE).

USING DBASE IV WITH MICROSOFT WINDOWS

You can run dBASE IV directly from Windows 3. When you install dBASE, the program searches for the word WINDOW in your PATH statement. If it finds the word, it automatically changes the Windows Program Initialization file named ProgMan.Ini to allow you to run dBASE IV from Windows.

If you have installed Windows in a directory that doesn't include the word WINDOW (for example, \WIN386), or if you install Windows after installing dBASE, you'll need to modify ProgMan.Ini yourself. Please see the section titled "Using dBASE IV with Windows 3" in Appendix D for more information about installing and using dBASE IV with Windows.

INSTALLING PRINTERS

You can use DBSETUP at any time to install a new printer for use with dBASE IV.

To install one or more printers with dBASE IV, follow these steps:

1. Assuming you are at the DOS command prompt on the dBASE IV (C:\DBASE) directory, type **DBSETUP** and press ↵.
2. Select Modify Existing CONFIG.DB by pressing ↵ when that option is highlighted.

You cannot use your mouse with the DBSETUP program.

3. If the drive and directory shown is where you've stored dBASE IV, press ↵. Otherwise, enter the correct drive and directory, then press ↵.
4. Select Drivers from the Printer pull-down menu (by pressing ↵).
5. For each of up to four printers, press Shift-F1 while the cursor is in the Printer Name column. Use the ↑, ↓, PgUp, and PgDn keys to move the highlighter to the name of the company that made your printer, then press ↵.

To quickly move the highlight to the name you want to use, simply begin typing that name. For example, type the letter P to move quickly to the PostScript printer name.

6. Use the same techniques to highlight the printer model on the next menu to appear, and press ↵ to select it.
7. When the cursor is in the Device column, press Shift-F1 to see a list of printer ports, then highlight the appropriate port for that printer and press ↵.
8. You can repeat steps 5–7 for up to four printers, or four "versions" of the same printer (for example, the Hewlett-Packard LaserJet IID offers 6.5 lpi (lines per inch), 6 lpi,

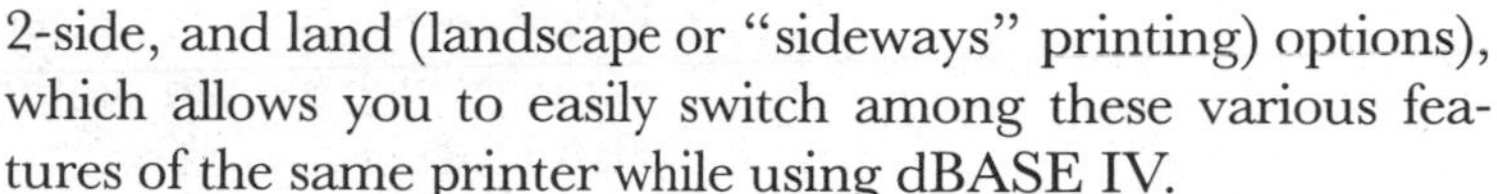

2-side, and land (landscape or "sideways" printing) options), which allows you to easily switch among these various features of the same printer while using dBASE IV.

9. Press Ctrl-End after selecting your printers.
10. Next, select Default Printer by highlighting that option and pressing ↵.
11. Choose the printer driver you want to use for general-purpose printing. (If you forgot the name of the driver, press Esc, then select Drivers again to review the driver names. Then press Ctrl-End and repeat step 10.)

TIP

You can use the LJII printer drivers for the HP LaserJet IIP and Laserjet III printers.

If your printer offers a variety of built-in fonts, and you know the codes for starting and ending those fonts, you can install those fonts now. Or, you can install them later after you've had a chance to check your printer manual. Either way, you can refer to the section "Installing Printer Fonts" later in this appendix for information.

OPTIMIZING THE DISPLAY

Some CGA monitors produce "snow" (interference) when used with dBASE IV. You can check for snow now (while you're still in DBSETUP) by following these steps:

1. Press → until the Display pull-down menu appears.
2. Select Optimize Color Display by typing **O** or highlighting the option and pressing ↵.
3. Press ↵ to select Proceed.
4. Type **Y** if you see interference (snow), otherwise type **N**.
5. Press ↵ to return to the menu.

This completes the basic installation of dBASE IV. To save all changes and exit, follow these steps:

1. Press → until the Exit pull-down menu is displayed.
2. Press ↵ to select Save and Exit.

3. Press ↵ again to accept the suggested drive\directory name (which should be the same as the drive\directory that dBASE IV is stored on).
4. Select Ok when asked for permission to overwrite.
5. Press → until the Exit pull-down menu is displayed, then press ↵ to select Exit to DOS.

Now you've installed dBASE, one or more printers, your monitor, and perhaps disk caching. The next section describes how to test the installation.

STARTING dBASE IV

To check your installation, follow these steps to start dBASE IV:

If you chose not to have the installation program automatically update AUTOEXEC.BAT and CONFIG.SYS, be sure to make those updates yourself before rebooting the computer (see "Installing dBASE IV" earlier in this appendix).

1. If you changed the AUTOEXEC.BAT or CONFIG.SYS files during installation (or are not sure whether you did or not), reboot by removing any floppy disks from their drives and simultaneously pressing the Ctrl, Alt, and Del keys momentarily.
2. When the DOS command prompt appears, switch to the directory that you installed dBASE on. For example, if you stored dBASE on C:\DBASE, type **C:** and press ↵, then type **CD\DBASE** and press ↵.
3. Type **DBASE** and press ↵.

If you opted to install disk caching, and did so properly, you should see a brief message indicating that the Hyperdisk disk caching software is being loaded. If instead you see a message indicating the Hyperdisk was *not* installed, refer to the following section titled "Reinstalling Disk Caching."

After the dBASE IV copyright screen displays for a moment, you'll see the dBASE IV Control Center (which is discussed in Chapter 2).

To exit dBASE, press Alt-E (hold down the Alt key while typing the letter E), then type the letter Q to select Quit to DOS. You will be reminded of these steps when you actually start putting dBASE to work in Chapter 2.

REINSTALLING DISK CACHING

If you attempted to install disk caching, but received a message indicating that Hyperdisk was not installed when you ran dBASE, then one of the following things is wrong:

- The automatic installation process selected the wrong type of memory (extended rather than expanded, or vice versa).
- Your computer has neither expanded nor extended memory.
- An incompatible TSR (terminate stay resident) program is already in memory.
- An incompatible memory manager is already in place and will not relinquish control to the dBASE disk cache.

NOTE

You can also install or uninstall caching through the Reconfigure menu of the DBSETUP program.

If either of the first two is the problem, the solution is fairly simple. Follow these steps:

1. Make sure you are still at the drive\directory where dBASE is stored.
2. Type **CACHEDB <type>** where <type> is either EXT (for extended memory), LIM (for expanded memory), or OFF (for no disk caching). For example, the command **CACHEDB EXT** sets up disk caching to use extended memory.
3. Press ↵.
4. Run dBASE again to see if the current memory type is acceptable.

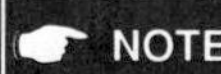

NOTE

If you are unfamiliar with DOS, TSR programs, and other topics discussed here, skip to the section titled "Customizing dBASE IV with DBSETUP" later in this section until you learn more about DOS.

If neither the EXT nor LIM options work, then either your computer does not have extended or expanded memory, or some other memory manager is in control. In this case, turn caching off by entering the command **CACHEDB OFF**.

If the problem concerns other TSR programs that are already loaded, add the command **DEVICE = C:\DBASE\DBCINIT** to your AUTOEXEC.BAT file. Place this command above any other commands in the AUTOEXEC.BAT file that load TSR programs, so that DBCINIT is loaded first.

If the problem is an incompatible memory manager, such as HIMEM.SYS (used with Windows 3.0), you simply have to choose between one or the other. For example, while Windows 3.0 is running, HIMEM.SYS is in control of memory, and if you run dBASE IV from within Windows, you'll see a message indicating that disk caching cannot be loaded because of incompatibility with HIMEM's XMS extended memory. (dBASE will still run, but without the cache.)

However, if you exit Windows before running dBASE (and have installed DBCACHE for extended memory), dBASE IV caching will be installed when you run dBASE IV.

Also, if a disk cache is already in operation on the computer when you start dBASE IV, the dBASE cache may still be installed, creating a sort of "cache within a cache." This could actually impede performance, so you may want to disable the dBASE caching in that case.

FINE TUNING dBASE IV PERFORMANCE

When you use dBASE, it creates many temporary files that are later erased when you exit dBASE normally. Two DOS environmental variables, TMP and DBTMP, define where dBASE IV temporary files will be created. TMP is a general area that programs other than dBASE IV will use, while DBTMP is used by dBASE IV only.

dBASE IV will check the DOS environment for a directory defined by DBTMP first to determine where to store temporary files. If DBTMP is not defined in the environment, dBASE will then check for a directory defined by the TMP variable in the environment, and use that directory for storing temporary files. If neither DBTMP nor TMP is defined in the environment, dBASE will store temporary files on the same directory that dBASE IV (dBASE.EXE) is stored on.

NOTE

DBCACHE uses whatever extended or expanded memory is available, but anything over 1.6Mb does not increase performance significantly.

One way to speed up the execution of dBASE IV (a little bit) is to use a RAM disk to store the temporary files, but only if you have over 2Mb of extended or expanded memory, and only if you are well enough versed in DOS already to know how to set up a RAM disk in extended or expanded memory. (This is a DOS topic, and space does not allows us to teach advanced DOS topics right here and now.) Leave at least 1.6Mb of memory free for DBCACHE.

The RAM disk must be created before you can use it for storing temporary files. Typically, you create a RAM disk by using the VDISK or RAMDISK device driver (which are part of DOS, not dBASE) in your DOS CONFIG.SYS file.

For example, suppose your system has 4Mb of extended memory. Depending on your version of DOS, you could include a command like the one below to use 1Mb of that memory as a RAM disk:

```
DEVICE = C:\DOS\VDISK.SYS 1024 /E
```

Assuming that your computer already has drives named C:, D:, and E:, the RAM disk will be drive F:.

Your AUTOEXEC.BAT file could then contain the command

```
SET TMP = F:\
```

or

```
SET DBTMP = F:\
```

dBASE would then use the fast RAM disk (drive F:) to store temporary files.

CUSTOMIZING dBASE IV WITH DBSETUP

This section describes additional features of the DBSETUP program which you can use to refine and customize dBASE IV to your liking.

RUNNING DBSETUP

To run the DBSETUP program, follow these steps:

1. Assuming you are at the DOS command prompt on the dBASE IV (C:\DBASE) directory, type **DBSETUP** and press ↵.
2. Select Modify Existing CONFIG.DB by pressing ↵ when that option is highlighted.

3. If the drive and directory shown is where you've stored dBASE IV, press ↵. Otherwise, enter the correct drive and directory, then press ↵.

This brings you to the DBSETUP main menu. The sections that follow assume that you are starting your selections from this point. As usual, you can select any menu option by moving the highlighter to it with the arrow keys and pressing ↵.

CHANGING THE SCREEN COLORS

If you find that the screen colors used by dBASE IV are not adequate for your needs, and want to change them for all future sessions with dBASE, select the Display option on the DBSETUP main menu. There, you can experiment with different color combinations using the color palette. (See Chapter 14 for information on using the color palette.)

INSTALLING FONTS

dBASE IV can access only built-in (resident) fonts, not downloadable soft fonts stored on disk.

You can use up to five additional fonts (beyond the default font) for printing with dBASE IV, provided your printer offers additional fonts. (That is, dBASE IV can't *create* a font; it can only *use* a font that's built into your printer.) You can check your printer manual to see what, if any, additional fonts are available to you.

To get access to additional fonts, you need to install them for use with dBASE IV via the DBSETUP program. If you are using a PostScript printer, please skip to the section titled "PostScript Printing" below for information on using PostScript fonts. Otherwise, continue reading in this section.

The first step to using printer fonts is to determine the codes used to activate and deactivate that font. These codes are usually available in your printer manual or, in some cases, by printing a Font List directly from the printer.

You may also need to know which is the normal default font for your printer, and the code for activating that font, so you can use that as the ending code to terminate another font. (Courier 10pt is the default font on most laser printers.)

When choosing your fonts, keep in mind that there is no need to select the Italic, Bold, and other styles of a single typeface, as these can be activated in the reports design screen within dBASE. Also, you have three choices of sizes within dBASE, Condensed, Pica, Elite (16.67, 10, and 12 lpi), so you need not select more than one of these sizes for a particular typeface.

When you locate the codes for using fonts in your printer manual, keep in mind the following points:

- dBASE requires that you represent the Escape character as {Esc}, though your printer manual might represent this character as <Esc>, Escape, \027, CHR(27), CHR$(27), or some other character.
- Ctrl-*key* characters must be represented as {Ctrl-A}, {Ctrl-B}, and so forth, in dBASE, where {Ctrl-A} is ASCII character 1, {Ctrl-B} is ASCII character 2, and so forth, up to {Ctrl-Z}, which is ASCII character 26.
- A null character (ASCII character 0) is represented as {Null} in dBASE.

NOTE

You need not define the printer's default font as one of your "extra" fonts, as dBASE always has access to the default font.

As an example of setting up fonts for use with dBASE IV, suppose you have a Hewlett-Packard Laserjet III Printer. In going through the printer documentation, you find that you can get a listing of all the available fonts and their start codes by taking the printer off line and pressing the Print Fonts key. (Don't forget to put the printer back on line after printing the fonts.)

You also discover that the default font is Courier 10 pitch, and the startup code for that font is:

```
{Esc}(8U{Esc}(s0p10.00h12.0v0s0b3T
```

so you know that is the ending code for each optional font you choose.

Suppose you decide to create the following fonts, and determine the startup codes as below:

NOTE

Your printer manual may represent the Escape key as <Esc> or <027> or \027, but you want to use {Esc} to represent the Esc key with dBASE.

Font	Start Code
Huge Univers-24pt	{Esc}(8U{Esc}(s1p24.00v0s0b4148T
Large CG Times-16pt	{Esc}(8U{Esc}(s1p16.00v0s0b4101T
Large Unvers-16pt	{Esc}(8U{Esc}(s1p16.00v0s0b4148T

CG Times-12pt	{Esc}(8U{Esc}(s1p12.00v0s0b4101T
Line Printer-8.5pt	{Esc}(8U{Esc}(s0p16.67h8.5v0s0b0T

The end code for each font would be the code used for specifying the default Courier 10 pitch font.

The steps to installing the fonts for use with dBASE IV are as follows:

1. If you are not already at the DBSETUP main menu, follow the instructions under "Running DBSETUP" earlier in this section to get to that menu.
2. Press ← until the Print pull-down menu appears, then move the highlight to the Fonts option and press ↵ (or type the letter **F**).
3. Press PgDn (Page Down) until the description of the printer that you want to install fonts for is displayed at the top of the window (next to Printer Number).
4. Type in a name (of your choosing) to describe the font, then press ↵.
5. Type in the exact start code for activating the font, then press ↵.
6. Type in the code for ending the font, or for activating the default font, then press ↵.
7. Repeat steps 4 through 6 for up to five fonts.
8. Press Ctrl-End when done.

Keep in mind that this series of steps assigns fonts for only one printer driver. If you have more than one driver for a printer, for example, both Portrait and Landscape drivers for a Laserjet, you'll need to set up fonts for each driver separately. When you've finished installing fonts for your printers, either proceed with the next section or proceed to Saving CONFIG.DB Settings later in this section.

INTERNATIONALIZING dBASE IV

dBASE IV initially comes configured to display dates and currencies in American formats. You can change the formats of currencies and dates using the DBSETUP program.

CHANGING THE DATE FORMAT By default, dBASE displays dates in the format MM/DD/YY. To use a different date format in all future sessions of dBASE IV, run DBSETUP as described earlier and then move the highlight to the General option on the menu bar. Then move the highlight to the Date option (or type the letter D) and press the space bar to scroll through the various options. Table B.1 displays the date format that each option uses.

Table B.1: International Date Formats for dBASE VI

Option	Format	Example
American	MM/DD/YY	12/31/92
Ansi	YY.MM.DD	92.12.31
British	DD/MM/YY	31/12/92
French	DD/MM/YY	31/12/92
German	DD.MM.YY	31.12.92
Italian	DD-MM-YY	31-12-92
Japanese	YY/MM/DD	92/12/31
USA	MM-DD-YY	12-31-92
MDY	MM/DD/YY	12/31/92
DMY	DD/MM/YY	31/12/92
YMD	YY/MM/DD	92/12/31

You can convert any date format so that it accepts and displays the year as a four-digit number (for example, 1993) rather than a two-digit number (for example, 93). To do so, highlight the Century option on the General pull-down menu and press the space bar to change the setting to On.

CHANGING THE CURRENCY FORMAT By default, dBASE IV prints currency amounts that use currency templates or picture functions with a leading dollar sign (for example, $123.45). You can modify the display of these currency amounts by changing the currency symbol, the position of the currency symbol, and the character used as the decimal place. To change the currency symbol, run DBSETUP as described earlier, move the highlight to the General pull-down menu, then highlight Currency and press ↵. Highlight Symbol and press ↵, then enter a symbol (or several characters) to use for the currency sign. The symbol that you enter can be up to ten characters long. However, to prevent the symbol from being repeated in displays (that is, to display $123.45 rather than $$$$123.45), you should make the first character a blank space (by pressing the space bar).

To use currency symbols that are not available from the keyboard, hold down the Alt key and type the three-digit ASCII code for the symbol on the numeric keypad. (You must use the numeric keypad, not the numbers at the top of the keyboard.) The symbol appears on the screen after you type all three digits and then release the Alt key. Table B.2 shows currency symbols and their ASCII codes.

Table B.2: International Currency Symbols

Code	Symbol	Meaning
155	¢	Cent
156	£	Pound
157	¥	Yen
158	Pt	Peseta
159	*f*	Franc

To display the currency sign to the right of a number rather than to the left, select Justification from the Currency pull-down menu and press the space bar to change the setting from Left to Right.

To use a character other than a period as the decimal point, select Point from the General pull-down menu. When prompted, type the character to use (for example, a comma) and press ↵. To use a character other than a comma to separate thousands, select Separator from the General pull-down menu. Then type the character you wish to use as the separator, and press ↵.

Note that regardless of the format you define while in DBSETUP, you still must enter numeric values in the usual manner later when storing data, (for example, **12345.67**) in the database. However, when you design a custom form or report format to print the data, the number will be formatted according to the template or picture function you define at that time.

For example, suppose you define *f* as the currency symbol, Right as the currency justification, the comma (,) as the point, and the period (.) as the separator. If you design a report or custom form and use the Financial Format picture function and the template 999,999.99 to display the field, the number 12345.67 will be displayed as 12.345,67*f*.

CHANGING THE CLOCK FORMAT The Control Center always displays a clock in the upper-right corner of the screen. You can use DBSETUP to remove the clock, change its position, or change its format. Run DBSETUP as described earlier and then move the highlight to the General pull-down menu.

To turn the clock off, first select Clock. On the submenu that appears, highlight the Clock option and press ↵ to change the setting to Off. To change the position of the clock, leave the Clock setting at On and select Screen Row and then Screen Column, specifying a location for each setting. The upper-left corner of the screen is row 0, column 0.

To change the clock display from a 12-hour clock (for example, 1:00 P.M.) to a 24-hour-clock (for example, 1300), highlight the Hours option on the General pull-down menu, and press the space bar to change the setting to 24.

SAVING CONFIG.DB SETTINGS

After customizing any options from the CONFIG.DB pull-down menu, open the Exit pull-down menu and select Save and Exit. When prompted for the drive and directory of the CONFIG.DB file, press ↵ to reuse the original drive and directory. To exit the DBSETUP program, open the Exit pull-down menu and select Exit to DOS.

POSTSCRIPT PRINTING

Chapter 7 discusses creating and printing reports, in general, with dBASE IV. This section talks about features that are unique to printing on PostScript printers, and overlaps with the material in Chapter 7.

PostScript is a *page description language* used by certain types of laser printers such as the Apple LaserWriter. If you have a PostScript printer (even if it is not an Apple LaserWriter), you should install the Apple LaserWriter as one of your printers, and use it as the driver when printing on your PostScript printer.

INSTALLING POSTSCRIPT FONTS

You can use three typefaces from your PostScript printer, Courier, Times, and Helvetica. To install these three fonts for use with dBASE IV, follow the steps for installing fonts as described in the section "Installing Fonts" earlier in this appendix. When you get to step 3, be sure to press PgUp or PgDn until the Apple LaserWriter is the selected printer.

In steps 4–6, set up the screen using *exactly* the font names, begin codes, and end codes shown below:

Font name	*Begin code*	*End code*
1FONT	1FONT{32}	1FONT{32}
2FONT	2FONT{32}	1FONT{32}
3FONT	3FONT{32}	1FONT{32}

Then resume with the remaining steps in that section to save your changes.

Later, when selecting fonts at the reports design screen (Chapter 7), remember that 1FONT is Courier, 2FONT is Helvetica, and 3FONT is Times Roman. If you are printing a columnar report, you should use only the Courier (a monospaced font) for the Detail band to ensure that the printed data aligns properly in each column.

SENDING SPECIAL CODES TO POSTSCRIPT PRINTERS

This section describes techniques for activating special features of a PostScript printer for a particular report. That is, while defining a report design (as described in Chapter 7), you can initiate the codes described here on the Print pull-down menu so they affect the current report only. If you want to change the default value for any of these features, so that all future reports use that feature, see the section "Changing PostScript Defaults" later in this appendix.

LANDSCAPE PRINTING WITH POSTSCRIPT If you want a particular report to be printed in landscape mode (sideways on the page) on your PostScript printer, follow these steps while designing your report at the reports design screen:

1. Press Alt-P to pull down the Print menu.
2. Select Control of Printer.
3. Select Starting Control Codes.
4. Type **LAND** then press the space bar.
5. Press ←┘.
6. Select Ending Control Codes.
7. Type PORT and press the space bar.
8. Press ←┘.
9. Press → to leave the menu.
10. Select Page Dimensions.
11. Select Length of Page.
12. Type **45** and press ←┘.
13. Press → to leave the menu.

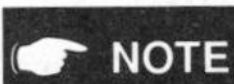
NOTE

Use all uppercase, or all lowercase letters when typing commands such as LAND and PORT for your PostScript printer.

Save your report format and the new print form settings in the usual manner. It's important to press the space bar after typing LAND and PORT so that the options appear as

```
{LAND }
{PORT }
```

rather than

```
{LAND}
{PORT}
```

on the menu, otherwise the codes will be ignored.

CHOOSING LEGAL PAPER SIZE WITH A POSTSCRIPT PRINTER If your PostScript printer supports legal size (8.5 × 14 inch) paper, you can select the legal paper size as the page length for the report you are currently designing by following these steps:

1. At the reports design screen for the report, press Alt-P to access the Print pull-down menu.
2. Select Control of Printer.
3. Select Starting Control Codes.
4. Type **LEGAL** and press the space bar.
5. Press ↵.
6. Select Ending Control Codes.
7. Type **LETTER** and press the space bar.
8. Press ↵.
9. Press → to leave the submenu.
10. Select Page Dimensions.
11. Select Length of Page.
12. Type **78** and press ↵.
13. Press → to leave the submenu.

Save your report format and print form settings in the usual manner.

COMBINING POSTSCRIPT COMMANDS If you want to print in Landscape mode on legal size paper, you can combine the LAND and LEGAL command in the Starting Control Codes option of the Print menu. Be sure to press the space bar after each command so that the Starting Control Codes appear as

```
{LAND LEGAL  }
```

in the menu, and the Ending Control Codes appear as

```
{PORT LETTER  }
```

on the menu.

SETTING THE LINES PER INCH WITH POSTSCRIPT PRINTERS If you are printing in Portrait rather than Landscape mode on your PostScript printer, you can adjust the number of lines per inch to be printed by following these steps:

1. At the reports design screen for the report, press Alt-P to access the Print pull-down menu.
2. Select Control of Printer.
3. Select Starting Control Codes.
4. Type **60LPP** and press the space bar if you want 60 lines per page, or type **66LPP** and press the space bar if you want 66 lines per page.
5. Press ↵.
6. Press → to leave the submenu.
7. Select Page Dimensions.
8. Select Length of Page.
9. Type either **60** or **66** to match your selection in step 4, then press ↵.
10. Press → to leave the submenu.

Save your report format and print form settings in the usual manner.

CHANGING POSTSCRIPT PRINTER DEFAULTS

The EDIT command in DOS 5.0 provides a full-screen ASCII editor that is easy to use. To edit the PostScri.dld file, type **EDIT PostScri.dld** and press ↵ at the DOS prompt. For help while using the editor, press the F1 key.

dBASE uses an ASCII text file named PostScri.dld to send information to your PostScript printer. This file contains the PostScript printer defaults, and also accepts changes to those defaults, such as LAND, LEGAL, fonts changes, and so forth, that an individual report may use.

The PostScri.dld file is actually a "PostScript program" which you can modify. But be forewarned—you must be well versed in editing ASCII text files and aware that if your text editor adds a Ctrl-Z file to the end of the PostScript.dld file (as most do), chances are all future reports will "time out" before they're printed (that is, printing appears to be going along normally, the printer light blinks as though its going to print, but the printed report never appears).

If you encounter this particular problem after editing your PostScript.dld file, you can remove the Ctrl-Z from the end of the file using the DOS COPY command. For example, if you suspect that your current PostScript.dld file has a Ctrl-Z at the end of it, the following DOS commands will remove that Ctrl-Z:

```
COPY PostScri.dld PostScri.tmp            ↵
COPY PostScri.tmp /A PostScript.dld /B    ↵
```

To play it doubly safe, you should first make a copy of your original, unmodified PostScri.dld file, perhaps with the name Postscri.org (for "PostScript Original") and never make changes to that particular file. That way, if you make a mistake and your modified PostScri.dld file does not work, you can just copy the Postscri.org file to the PostScri.dld file (using the DOS COPY command) to "undo" any changes. (You can also obtain a copy of the original PostScri.dld file from the dBASE DRIVERS.EXE file by entering the command **DRIVERS PostScri.dld** at the DOS command prompt on the dBASE IV directory.)

I'd also recommend that you get a book about the PostScript language as well (such as SYBEX's *Understanding PostScript*, Third Edition, by David A. Holzgang) if you plan on utilizing your PostScript printer to its utmost capacity.

CHANGING THE DEFAULT ORIENTATION AND PAGE LENGTH The PostScri.dld file assumes that you will be using letter (8.5 × 11 inch) paper. If you want to use legal (8.5 × 14 inch) paper, change the line

```
/paper 1 def        %(1 = letter, 2 = legal, 3 = A4)
```

to

```
/paper 2 def        %(1 = letter, 2 = legal, 3 = A4)
```

in the PostScri.dld file.

dBASE also assumes that you will normally print in portrait (normal) mode rather than in landscape (sideways) mode. If you prefer to change the default orientation for your PostScript printer to Landscape, change the command

```
/orient 1 def          %(1 = portrait,2 = landscape)
```

to

```
/orient 2 def          %(1 = portrait,2 = landscape)
```

The line

```
/nLPP 66 def           % lines per page (60, 66, 78, or 88 for portrait;
                       %                 45 for landscape)
```

in the PostScri.dld file specifies the default number of lines to print per page. You should adjust this setting to match your default page size (for example, change the 66 to 60 if your default page size is 60 lines), as below:

```
/nLPP 60 def           % (letter portrait, 6 lines per inch)
/nLPP 66 def           % (letter portrait, 6.48 lines per inch)
/nLPP 78 def           % (legal portrait)
/nLPP 88 def           % (legal portrait, 6.48 lines per inch)
/nLPP 45 def           % (landscape)
```

If you do change the number of lines per page, you should make the corresponding change to the Length of Page option on the Print pull-down menu, and save that change in Reports.prf, as described in Chapter 7.

NOTE

A *point* is approximately 1/72 inch.

CHANGING THE DEFAULT POSTSCRIPT OFFSET If text is not properly aligned on your printed PostScript pages, you can modify the printer offsets in the PostScri.dld file. There are four pairs of offsets, each measured in points, as shown below:

```
% printer-dependent portrait offsets
/tpxoff 18 def         % x (letter)
/tpyoff 28 def         % y (letter)
/gpxoff 22 def         % x (legal)
/gpyoff 26 def         % y (legal)
/apxoff 16 def         % x (A4)
/apyoff 18 def         % y (A4)
% printer-dependent landscape offsets
/tlxoff 18 def         % x (letter)
/tlyoff 44 def         % y (letter)
```

```
/glxoff 18 def        % x (legal)
/glyoff 80 def        % y (legal)
/alxoff  0 def        % x (A4)
/alyoff 29 def        % y (A4)
```

Notice that one pair of offsets, tpxoff and tpyoff, is for portrait mode, letter-size paper. The other pairs are for portrait legal, portrait A4, landscape letter, landscape legal, and landscape A4 modes. These are entirely independent of one another.

Each pair has an x value and a y value. To move the printing to the right on a page, increase the x-offset number. To move text to the left on the page, decrease the x-offset value.

To move printing up (higher) on the page, increase the y-offset value. To move printing down in the page, decrease the y-offset value.

For example, suppose that you want to increase the left margin on your printed letter portrait paper by 1/2 inch (36 points). In the PostScri.dld file, you would want to change

```
% printer-dependent portrait offsets
/tpxoff 18 def %                x (letter)
```

to

```
% printer-dependent portrait offsets
/tpxoff 54 def %                x (letter)
```

CHANGING THE DEFAULT POINT SIZES When designing reports, dBASE gives you three point sizes to choose from for each report band (as discussed in Chapter 7):

Pica	12pt
Elite	10pt
Compressed	8pt

You may prefer to use Pica and Compressed for printing your data (in the Detail band) and a larger font for report titles and such. For example, you might want to change the definition of Elite to 20 points for printing very large titles.

The point definitions are in the section of the PostScri.dld file shown below:

```
% point sizes to use
/PicaPoint 12 def                % Pica
```

```
/ElitePoint 10 def                  % Elite
/CompressedPoint 8 def              % compressed
```

To convert Elite to a 20-point size, simply change its definition as below:

```
/ElitePoint 20 def                  % Elite
```

When designing your reports later (in the dBASE IV reports design screen), remember that any band that you assign the ELITE text pitch to will actually be printed in the large 20-point size.

When designing reports, you have the option of selecting the default font, which is Pica on PostScript printers. If you want to change the default size to Elite or Compressed, change the line that reads

```
/CurPoint     PicaPoint def  % initial pointsize
```

to either

```
/CurPoint     ElitePoint def % initial pointsize
```

to make Elite the default, or

```
/CurPoint     CompressedPoint def % initial pointsize
```

to use compressed print as the default.

CHANGING THE DEFAULT POSTSCRIPT FONTS There are three fonts offered in dBASE for use with PostScript printers: 1FONT (Courier), 2FONT (Helvetica), and 3FONT (Times Roman). These are defined in the PostScri.dld file in Figure B.1.

You can assign a different font to either 1FONT, 2FONT, or 3FONT, provided that you know the correct name of the font (as defined in your printer manual). For example, if your printer has a resident Palatino font, and you want to use that instead of Times-Roman as the 3FONT, you would change the CurFSet 3 portion of the file to

```
CurFSet 3 eq
  {
  /n        /Palatino-Foreign def
  /b        /Palatino-Bold-Foreign def
  /i        /Palatino-Italic-Foreign def
  /bi       /Palatino-BoldItalic-Foreign def
  } if
```

```
/CurFSet 1 def                                  % default font set
/FSet {
        /CurFSet exch def
        % Font Set 1 (default)
        /n      /Courier-Foreign def                    % normal
        /b      /Courier-Bold-Foreign def               % bold
        /i      /Courier-Oblique-Foreign def            % italic
        /bi     /Courier-BoldOblique-Foreign def        % bold+italic
        CurFSet 2 eq
                {
                /n      /Helvetica-Foreign def
                /b      /Helvetica-Bold-Foreign def
                /i      /Helvetica-Oblique-Foreign def
                /bi     /Helvetica-BoldOblique-Foreign def
                } if
        CurFSet 3 eq
                {
                /n      /Times-Roman-Foreign def
                /b      /Times-Bold-Foreign def
                /i      /Times-Italic-Foreign def
                /bi     /Times-BoldItalic-Foreign def
                } if
        /FontNorm n def
        /FontBold b def
        /FontItal i def
        /FontBoldItal bi def
        Norm
   } def
% --------- End User-adjustable parameters -------
```

Figure B.1: Three fonts defined in PostScri.dld

You must also change the commands near the bottom of the Postscri.dld file used to re-encode the font, so that the font can use the extended character set. So in this example, you would need to change the commands

```
/Times-Roman /Times-Roman-Foreign ReEncode
/Times-Bold /Times-Bold-Foreign ReEncode
/Times-Italic /Times-Italic-Foreign ReEncode
/Times-BoldItalic /Times-BoldItalic-Foreign ReEncode
```

to

```
/Palatino /Palatino-Foreign ReEncode
/Palatino-Bold /Palatino-Bold-Foreign ReEncode
/Palatino-Italic /Palatino-Italic-Foreign ReEncode
/Palatino-BoldItalic /Palatino-BoldItalic-Foreign ReEncode
```

ADDING A POSTSCRIPT FONT You can also add up to two new fonts to your PostScri.dld file, for a total of five fonts. You need to know the proper name of the additional fonts (as defined in your printer manual), and make additions to the PostScri.dld file in three places. Name the additional fonts 4FONT and 5FONT.

As an example, the section of the modified PostScri.dld file below shows the addition of ITC Bookman as a fourth font beneath the existing 3FONT in the PostScri.dld file:

```
CurFSet 3 eq
  {
  /n            /Times-Roman-Foreign def
  /b            /Times-Bold-Foreign def
  /i            /Times-Italic-Foreign def
  /bi           /Times-BoldItalic-Foreign def
  } if
CurFSet 4 eq
  {
  /             /Bookman-Light-Foreign def
  /b            /Bookman-Demi-Foreign def
  /i            /Bookman-LightItalic-Foreign def
  /bi           /Bookman-DemiItalic-Foreign def
  } if

/FontNorm n def
```

Next, the 4FONT and synonyms need to be defined a little lower in the PostScri.dld file in this section:

```
/1Font   {1 FSet} def
/2Font   {2 FSet} def
/3Font   {3 FSet} def
/4Font   {4 FSet} def
```

and in this section:

```
/1FONT {1Font} def /1font {1Font} def
/2FONT {2Font} def /2font {2Font} def
/3FONT {3Font} def /3font {3Font} def
/4FONT {4Font} def /4font {4Font} def
```

Finally, near the bottom of the Postscri.dld file, you need to add four commands to re-encode the new font to use the foreign characters in the extended ASCII set. The four commands you would need to add for the Bookman font are shown below (above the PSet and % --- commands that mark the end of the file):

```
/Bookman-Light /Bookman-Light-Foreign ReEncode
/Bookman-Demi /Bookman-Demi-Foreign ReEncode
/Bookman-LightItalic /Bookman-LightItalic-Foreign ReEncode
```

```
/Bookman-DemiItalic /Bookman-DemiItalic-Foreign ReEncode
PSet
%----- end of Postscri.dld ----
```

At this point, you can save the Postcri.dld file.

Any new fonts that you add to the PostScri.dld file must also be installed for use with dBASE, using DBSETUP as described under "Installing PostScript Fonts" previously in this appendix. Otherwise, the font will not even appear as an option on the reports design screen when you design reports later (see Chapter 7).

APPENDIX C

Summary of Changes in dBASE

dBASE IV 1.5 OFFERS SEVERAL IMPROVEMENTS OVER dBASE IV 1.1. Perhaps the most obvious is dBASE's entry into the world of point-and-click simplicity, where you can use the mouse to make selections from menus and lists, and to edit text. In addition, the program now offers more powerful query by example (QBE) features, is generally snappier and more responsive, sports an improved Control Center, and includes a number of enhancements that apply mostly to dBASE developers. The most important revisions in dBASE IV 1.5 are summarized in the sections that follow.

MOUSE SUPPORT

As mentioned already, mouse support is included throughout the Control Center, the menu system, and at the dot prompt (only the installation and DBSETUP procedures do not include mouse support). The standard mouse techniques of click, double-click, and drag are used throughout the program, although the exact effect of these operations often depends on what you're doing at the moment.

For example, you can click the mouse on a menu name or option to pull down that menu or select the option. And instead of pressing arrow keys to move the highlight to a field or a specific place on the screen, you can simply click the mouse wherever you want to position the cursor. In addition, you can click the mouse on any navigation line option (near the bottom of the screen) to select that option, which is often more convenient than pressing the corresponding key or key combination.

Mouse operations are covered throughout this book (see especially Chapters 2, 4, and 7).

EXPANDED QUERY BY EXAMPLE

dBASE IV's powerful query by example (QBE) is considerably enhanced, with the biggest news being updatable multifile views. The following sections highlight the major new features in QBE.

UPDATABLE MULTIFILE VIEWS

In the past, if you related (linked) two or more databases by using the SET RELATION TO dot command or the queries design screen on the Control Panel, the resulting view was read-only and field values couldn't be changed. Now, you can usually update the data in the multifile view and have that change carry over into the source database (see Chapter 13).

DELETING INDIVIDUAL CALCULATED FIELDS

dBASE IV now lets you delete an individual calculated field from a query. In the past, your only option was to delete all calculated fields by deleting the field skeleton, or by overwriting one calculated field with another. In version 1.5, you can highlight the calculated field you want to delete, and then choose Fields ► Delete Calculated Field to delete just that field (see Chapter 9).

SPEEDING UP SUBSEQUENT QUERIES

dBASE often creates temporary indexes during a query to make processing more efficient. Normally, these indexes are deleted automatically when the query is finished, but you can now save them on disk to speed up subsequent executions of the same or similar queries. To do so, choose Fields ► Keep Speedup Indexes from the queries design menu, then change the setting to Yes. If you prefer to conserve disk space, rather than save some time, change the setting back to No (which is the default).

NEW EXPRESSION BUILDER COLUMN

When you open the Expression Builder by pressing Shift-F1 in the queries design screen, you'll see a new QBE Operator column, which includes QBE operators such as Count, Every, Find, Group By, Like, Mark, and so forth. You can select an item from the QBE Operator column in the same way you select an item from the Fieldname, Operator, or Function column of the Expression Builder: by highlighting the item you want and pressing ↵, or by double-clicking on that item (see Chapter 6).

SUMMARY OPERATORS IN CALCULATED FIELDS

dBASE IV now lets you use summary operators (Sum, Average, Min, Max, Count) and Group By in calculated fields. For example, the query in Figure C.1 provides summary information about orders, grouped by part name (PartName). For each unique part name, the query shows how many of those parts were ordered (sum in the Qty field), the average price of those parts (average in the UnitPrice field), and the extended price (sum in the Amount field). Amount is a calculated field that multiplies the quantity by the unit price. The result of this query appears in Figure C.2. These results show 9 orders for Astro Buddies (at $55.00 apiece), for a total of $495.00; 6 orders for Cosmic Critters (at $500.00 apiece), for a total of $3000.00; and 4 orders for Mondo Man (at $100.00 apiece), for a total of $400.00.

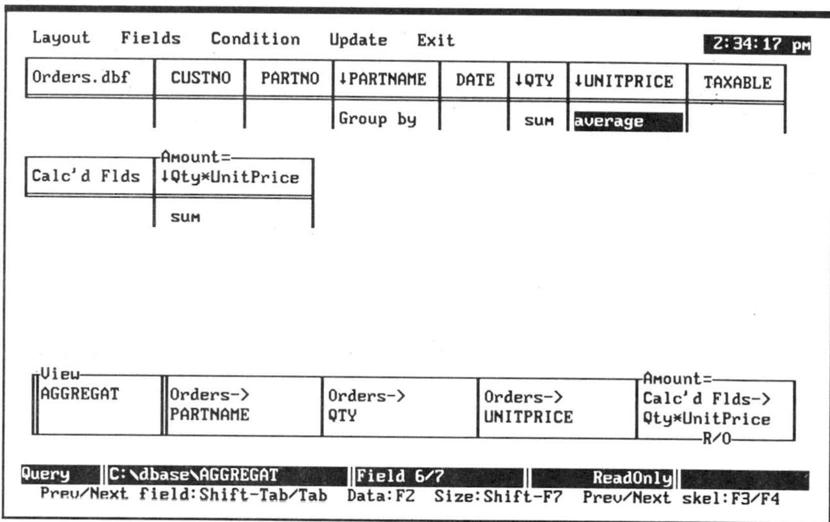

Figure C.1: A sample query using a summary operator (Sum) with a calculated field (Amount)

ABILITY TO OPEN FORTY WORK AREAS

dBASE IV now allows you to open up to 40 work areas (the previous limit was 10), which are numbered from 1 to 40 or from A to J (for the first 10 work areas). These work areas are only placed

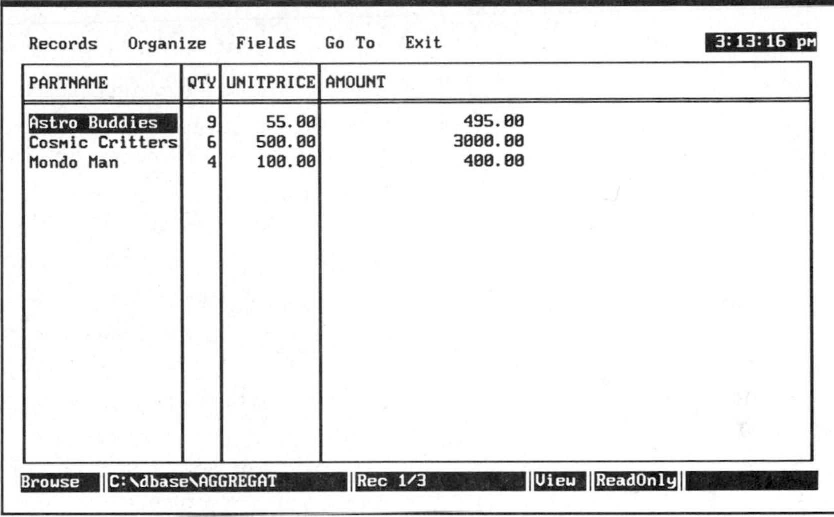

Figure C.2: The results of the sample query shown in Figure C.1

in memory when you define them with the SELECT command, so memory isn't taken up by undefined work areas. You can find out which work areas are active by typing DISPLAY STATUS at the dot prompt (see Chapter 18).

IMPORTING AND EXPORTING FILES

You can import and export the following new file formats using the IMPORT and EXPORT commands at the dot prompt, or the Tools ► Import and Tools ► Export menu options at the Control Center:

- Lotus 1-2-3 Release 1.0 (.WKS file format)
- Lotus 1-2-3 Release 1A and Release 2.X (.WK1 file format)
- Framework III (.FW3 file format)
- Framework IV (.FW4 file format)

See Appendix D for more information about interfacing with other programs.

CHANGES FOR DEVELOPERS

dBASE IV version 1.5 includes a number of changes that apply primarily to programmers who develop dBASE applications. Briefly, these changes are:

- The DBSETUP program includes many new options for customizing the dBASE startup configuration. Each of these new options adds a command to the Config.db file. In addition, the menus for every design surface include new options for calling programs defined in the Config.db file. These options—which are on the Catalog, Layout, Field, and Field Define menus—include Open Custom Utility, Invoke Layout Program, and Load Field Program (depending on which surface is being used).
- dBASE IV includes new functions for obtaining information about indexes. These functions are DESCENDING(), FOR(), TAGCOUNT(), TAGNO(), and UNIQUE().
- The REINDEX keyword for the APPEND FROM, REPLACE, BLANK, and UPDATE commands allows programmers to update a database index either as records are being updated or when all updates are complete.
- The /c parameter allows users to specify a file other than Config.db as the configuration file when they start dBASE.
- The WITH keyword is available for the QUIT command to let a calling program know whether dBASE IV ran successfully and quit normally.
- dBASE IV includes eleven new functions dealing with low-level file input and output, and three new functions for determining the size, last modification date, and last modification time of a file (see Appendix E).
- Three new functions, DGEN(), ARGUMENT(), and TOKEN(), were added for use with template language programs.

- Miscellaneous language improvements include management of blank fields or records; conditional compilation; procedure library support (see Chapter 18); an enhanced KEYBOARD command; a NOORGANIZE keyword for APPEND, BROWSE, CHANGE, EDIT, and INSERT to prevent users from changing indexes or sorting the database during an application; faster filters; a @...SCROLL option to scroll the contents of a specified region of the screen; and several new options for the SET() function.
- The transaction log file format has changed, so dBASE IV version 1.5 cannot use an old transaction log file.

APPENDIX D

Interfacing with Other Programs

dBASE IV OFFERS SEVERAL OPTIONS FOR DIRECTLY importing and exporting data in a variety of formats. These are discussed at the beginning of this appendix and illustrated in an example of importing and exporting data from a Lotus 1-2-3 spreadsheet.

In some cases, you may want to transfer data to software products that dBASE IV does not support. In those situations, you will need to use one of the following alternative methods to complete the transfer.

If the foreign software product has the ability to transfer dBASE IV, dBASE III, or dBASE III PLUS database files, use the foreign software's transfer capabilities (dBASE IV can read dBASE III and dBASE III PLUS database files directly). If the foreign software product does not support dBASE file transfers, but does allow exporting of ASCII text files, then use the ASCII text files as intermediary files to complete the transfer.

The examples presented later in this appendix demonstrate numerous general techniques for importing and exporting dBASE IV data.

BUILT-IN IMPORT AND EXPORT OPTIONS

To import data from a format used by another program to dBASE, start at the Control Center and choose Tools ► Import. You will see the submenu of importing formats shown in Figure D.1.

To export data from a dBASE IV database to a format used by another program, start at the Control Center and choose Tools ► Export. You will see the submenu of exporting formats shown in Figure D.2.

Each of the import and export formats is summarized in Table D.1, along with file name extensions and relevant notes. Notice that you can both export and import RapidFile, dBASE II, Framework, Lotus 1-2-3, and PFS:File file formats, but can only export VisiCalc, SYLK-Multiplan, Text Fixed-Length Fields, Blank Delimited, and Character Delimited file formats.

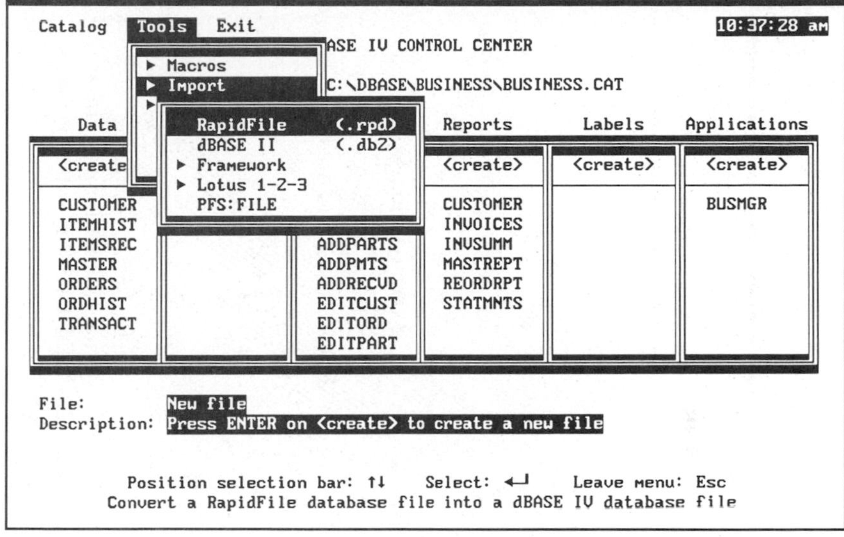

Figure D.1: The Tools ► Import submenu

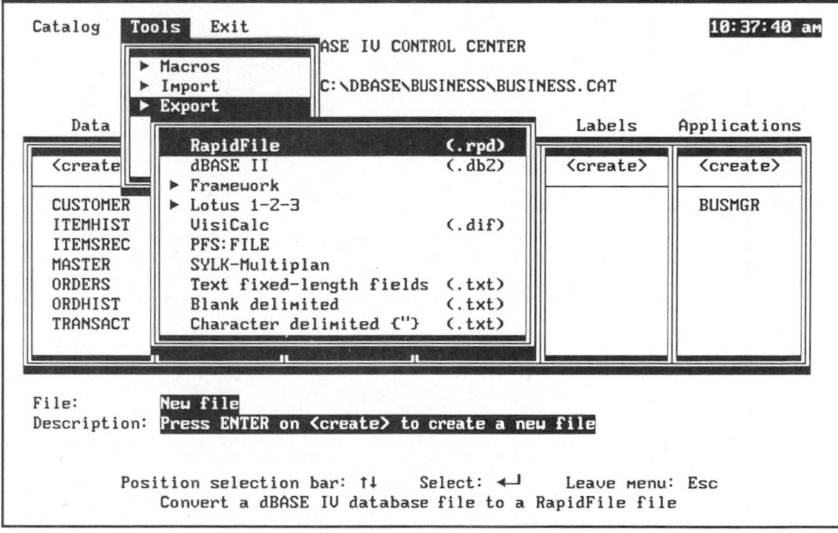

Figure D.2: The Tools ► Export submenu

Table D.1: Import and Export File Formats for dBASE IV

Format	Import	Export	File Name Extension	Notes
RapidFile	Yes	Yes	.RPD	
dBASE II	Yes	Yes	.DB2	
FrameWork II	Yes	Yes	.FW2	
FrameWork III	Yes	Yes	.FW3	
FrameWork IV	Yes	Yes	.FW4	
Lotus 1-2-3 Release 1A	Yes	Yes	.WKS	.WKS files can also be created and used by Symphony and Quattro.
Lotus 1-2-3 Release 2 and higher	Yes	Yes	.WK1	.WK1 files can also be created and used by Symphony and Quattro.
VisiCalc	No*	Yes	.DIF	
PFS:File	Yes	Yes	None (blank)	
SYLK-Multiplan	No*	Yes	None (blank)	
Text Fixed-Length Fields	No*	Yes	.TXT	Data fields are in equal-width columns. This format was called SDF format in earlier versions of dBASE.
Blank Delimited	No*	Yes	.TXT	Each data field is separated by a single blank space, and individual fields contain no blank spaces.
Character Delimited {''}	No*	Yes	.TXT	Each data field is surrounded by a delimiter character of your choosing (the default quotation mark is most commonly used), and separated by a comma. Most software packages can import this format.

*Although you cannot import these file formats through the Tools ► Import options, you can import them by choosing Append ► Copy Records from Non-dBASE File from the database design menu (see Example 4, Example 5, and Example 7 later in this chapter).

EXAMPLE 1: IMPORTING DATA FROM LOTUS 1-2-3

> ⊙ WARNING
>
> The first part of the file name you're importing (that is, the part to the left of the extension) should not match that of any existing database in the directory; otherwise you will overwrite the existing database when you import the file (for example, TRANSFER.DBF and TRANSFER.WK1 have the same first name). If necessary, rename the file before importing it using options on the Tools ► DOS Utilities menu (see Chapter 14 and Appendix A for details on file management and file naming).

Database files store data in even rows and columns, whereas spreadsheets allow data to be stored in any format. If you want to import data from a spreadsheet to a dBASE IV database, you should import only that portion of the spreadsheet that stores data in even rows and columns, as the example that follows demonstrates.

Suppose you have a Lotus 1-2-3 spreadsheet in which you've stored data for invoices, and you wish to switch to dBASE IV to manage the database. For this example, let's assume that the invoices are stored in a Lotus 1-2-3 Release 2.x spreadsheet file named INVOICES.WK1, which is stored on a directory named C:\123. Let's go through the steps required to import the spreadsheet data to a dBASE IV database named INVOICES.DBF on the C:\DBASE directory.

ISOLATING DATA TO IMPORT

The first phase of the import process is to isolate the data to be imported to a dBASE IV database. Assuming that both Lotus 1-2-3 and the file to import are on the C:\123 directory, and that you are currently at the DOS prompt (not in dBASE), you would follow these steps:

1. At the DOS prompt, enter the command **CD\123** to switch to the 123 directory.
2. Enter the command **123** to start Lotus 1-2-3.
3. Type **/FR** (File Retrieve) and select the name of the file that you want to copy to dBASE IV (INVOICES in this example).
4. Move the cell pointer to the upper-left corner of the range that you want to export to dBASE IV.
5. Type **/FXV** (File Xtract Values) to begin extracting data.
6. Enter a drive, directory, and file name for the exported file. To simplify matters, be sure to specify the drive and directory on which you want the imported database file to be

stored. For example, in this case you want to store the imported data on the C:\DBASE directory, so press Esc twice to erase the suggested drive and directory and then enter as the file name **C:\DBASE\TRANSFER**. (Versions 2 and higher of 1-2-3 will automatically add the .WK1 extension. If you are using some earlier version, include the .WK1 extension; that is, enter the file name **C:\DBASE \TRANSFER.WK1**.)

7. Highlight the data to copy to dBASE IV, excluding column titles, underscores, totals, or any other spreadsheet embellishments. Figure D.3 shows an example. Press ↵ after specifying the range to export.
8. Type **/QY** (Quit Yes) to leave 1-2-3 and return to DOS.

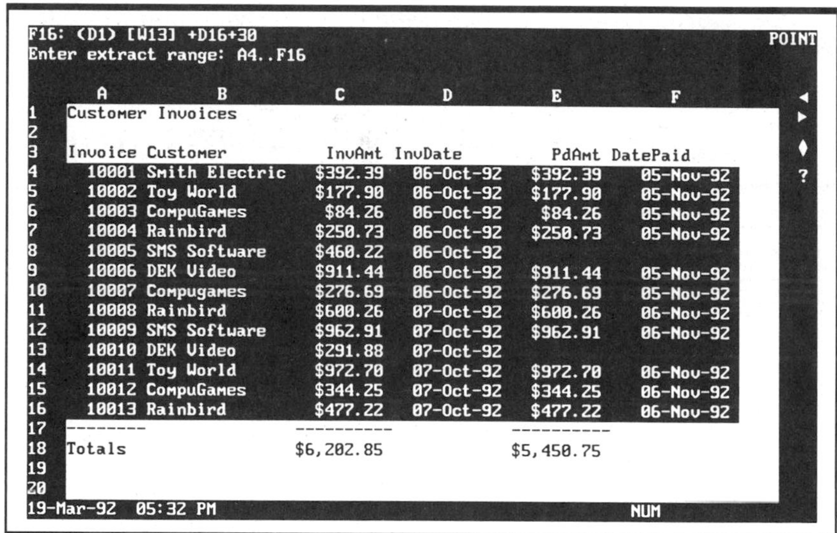

F16: (D1) [W13] +D16+30
POINT
Enter extract range: A4..F16
A B C D E F
1 Customer Invoices
2
3 Invoice Customer InvAmt InvDate PdAmt DatePaid
4 10001 Smith Electric $392.39 06-Oct-92 $392.39 05-Nov-92
5 10002 Toy World $177.90 06-Oct-92 $177.90 05-Nov-92
6 10003 CompuGames $84.26 06-Oct-92 $84.26 05-Nov-92
7 10004 Rainbird $250.73 06-Oct-92 $250.73 05-Nov-92
8 10005 SMS Software $460.22 06-Oct-92
9 10006 DEK Video $911.44 06-Oct-92 $911.44 05-Nov-92
10 10007 Compugames $276.69 06-Oct-92 $276.69 05-Nov-92
11 10008 Rainbird $600.26 07-Oct-92 $600.26 06-Nov-92
12 10009 SMS Software $962.91 07-Oct-92 $962.91 06-Nov-92
13 10010 DEK Video $291.88 07-Oct-92
14 10011 Toy World $972.70 07-Oct-92 $972.70 06-Nov-92
15 10012 CompuGames $344.25 07-Oct-92 $344.25 06-Nov-92
16 10013 Rainbird $477.22 07-Oct-92 $477.22 06-Nov-92
17 -------- ---------- ----------
18 Totals $6,202.85 $5,450.75
19
20
19-Mar-92 05:32 PM
NUM

Figure D.3: Export range highlighted

IMPORTING THE SPREADSHEET DATA

To import the spreadsheet data to dBASE IV, you first need to get dBASE up and running, then choose Tools ► Import. Here are the steps:

1. Enter the command **CD\DBASE** to switch to the dBASE directory.
2. Enter the command **DBASE** to run dBASE IV.
3. Choose Tools ► Import.
4. Select Lotus 1-2-3.
5. Select Release 2 (.wk1).
6. Select the name of the extracted spreadsheet file (TRANSFER.WK1 in this example).
7. Type in a description for your imported database and press ↵. dBASE will create the database and return to the Control Center.
8. Highlight TRANSFER in the Data panel of the Control Center and press or click Data (F2) to see the database's contents. (Use the F2 and PgUp keys to switch back and forth between the browse and edit screens and to scroll through records.)

If a database named TRANSFER.DBF already exists, dBASE will overwrite that database without asking permission. If you don't want to overwrite that database, press Esc until you return to the Control Center. Then rename the extracted spreadsheet file using the Tools ► DOS Utilities menu options, return to the Control Center, then restart the import procedure from Step 3.

Figure D.4 shows how the file appears on the browse screen after importing. dBASE has assigned the simple field names A, B, C, D, and so on to the fields (you will probably want to change these names).

REFINING THE DATA TYPES

Next you'll want to see what data types dBASE has assigned to the imported fields. Follow these steps:

1. If the browse or edit screen appears, press Esc to return to the Control Center.
2. With the highlight still on TRANSFER, press or click Design (Shift-F2) to switch to the database design screen.
3. Press Esc to remove the Organize pull-down menu.

Records Organize Fields Go To Exit

A	B	C	D	E	F
10001.00	Smith Electric	392.39	10/06/92	392.39	11/05/92
10002.00	Toy World	177.90	10/06/92	177.90	11/05/92
10003.00	CompuGames	84.26	10/06/92	84.26	11/05/92
10004.00	Rainbird	250.73	10/06/92	250.73	11/05/92
10005.00	SMS Software	460.22	10/06/92	.	
10006.00	DEK Video	911.44	10/06/92	911.44	11/05/92
10007.00	Compugames	276.69	10/06/92	276.69	11/05/92
10008.00	Rainbird	600.26	10/07/92	600.26	11/06/92
10009.00	SMS Software	962.91	10/07/92	962.91	11/06/92
10010.00	DEK Video	291.88	10/07/92	.	
10011.00	Toy World	972.70	10/07/92	972.70	11/06/92
10012.00	CompuGames	344.25	10/07/92	344.25	11/06/92
10013.00	Rainbird	477.22	10/07/92	477.22	11/06/92

Browse | C:\dbase\TRANSFER | Rec 1/13 | File

Figure D.4: Sample data imported from Lotus 1-2-3

Figure D.5 shows the structure of the imported file. Note that dBASE automatically assigned two decimal places to Numeric fields and specified the Character fields as Date fields.

Layout Organize Append Go To Exit 5:37:39 pm

Bytes remaining: 3931

Num	Field Name	Field Type	Width	Dec	Index
1	A	Numeric	9	2	N
2	B	Character	16		N
3	C	Numeric	11	2	N
4	D	Character	10		N
5	E	Numeric	12	2	N
6	F	Character	11		N

Database | C:\dbase\TRANSFER | Field 1/6 | Num

Enter the field name. Insert/Delete field:Ctrl-N/Ctrl-U

Field names begin with a letter and may contain letters, digits and underscores

Figure D.5: Initial structure of the imported file

You can change the data types of any fields and also mark fields for indexing. However, during this phase you should not perform any other operations, such as renaming, adding, or deleting fields. (dBASE may become confused when copying backup data back into the database and probably will lose some of your data.)

Figure D.6 shows a suggested structure for the imported database. After making appropriate changes, choose Exit ► Save Changes and Exit, then select Yes from the prompt box that appears.

When you get back to the Control Center, you can press or click F2 and press PgUp to view the data and verify that the changes are correct. Then press Esc to return to the Control Center.

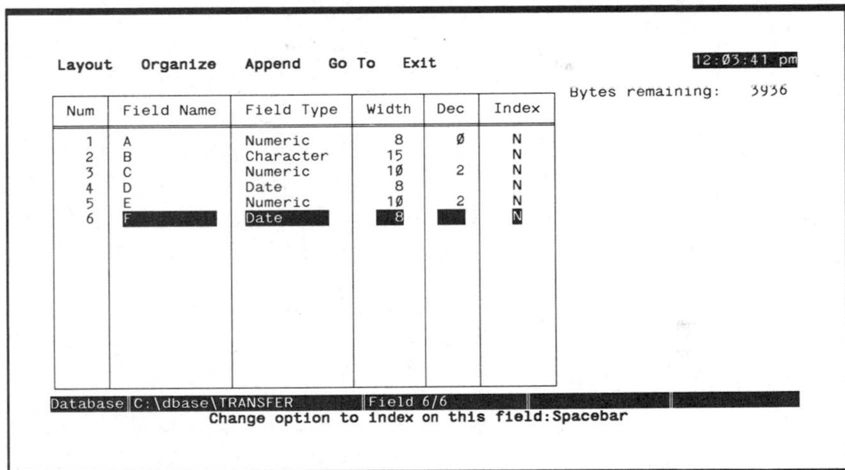

Figure D.6: More accurate data types for the imported database

RENAMING FIELDS

You probably want to use field names that are more descriptive than the single-letter names that dBASE assigned. To do so, follow these steps:

1. With the highlight on TRANSFER in the Control Center, press or click Design (Shift-F2) to get to the database design screen.
2. Press Esc to leave the Organize pull-down menu.

3. Enter new field names, but do not make any other changes to the database structure. (Figure D.7 shows some suggested field names for this example.)
4. Choose Exit ► Save Changes and Exit.
5. Answer Yes to the prompts that appear until you get back to the Control Center.
6. To view the database and verify your changes, press or click Data (F2) and press PgUp.

The database will appear on the edit or browse screen with the new field names. To return to the Control Center after viewing your data, press Esc. At this point, importing is complete, and you can use the imported data just as you would any dBASE IV database file. If you wish to change the name of the imported database, choose Tools ► DOS Utilities and highlight the TRANSFER.DBF file. Then choose Operations ► Rename ► Single File, and enter a new file name (see Chapter 14). Choose Exit ► Exit to Control Center and then add the renamed database to the catalog by choosing Catalog ► Add File to Catalog.

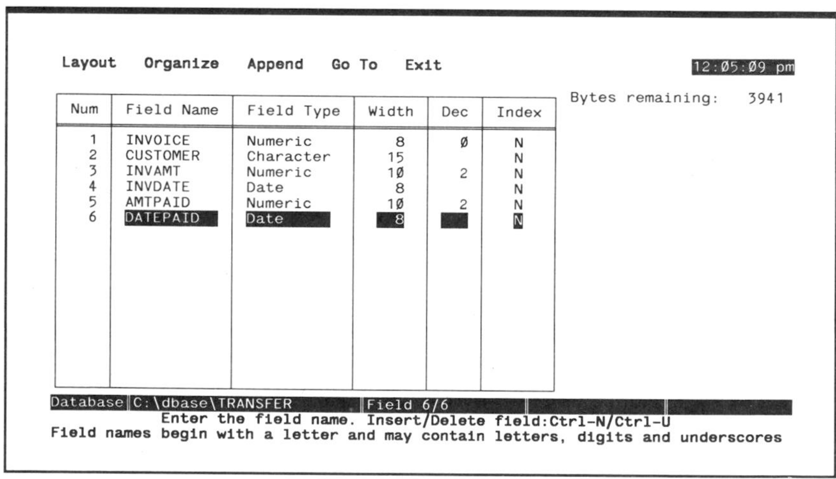

Figure D.7: New field names assigned to the imported database

EXAMPLE 2: EXPORTING DATA TO LOTUS 1-2-3

Suppose you have a dBASE IV database named ORDERS.DBF on the C:\DBASE directory, and you want to use Lotus 1-2-3 to print a graph of total orders for each part number stored in the database. Assume that the ORDERS.DBF has the structure shown in Figure D.8. Figure D.9 shows a small portion of the sample database (additional records are scrolled off the bottom of the screen).

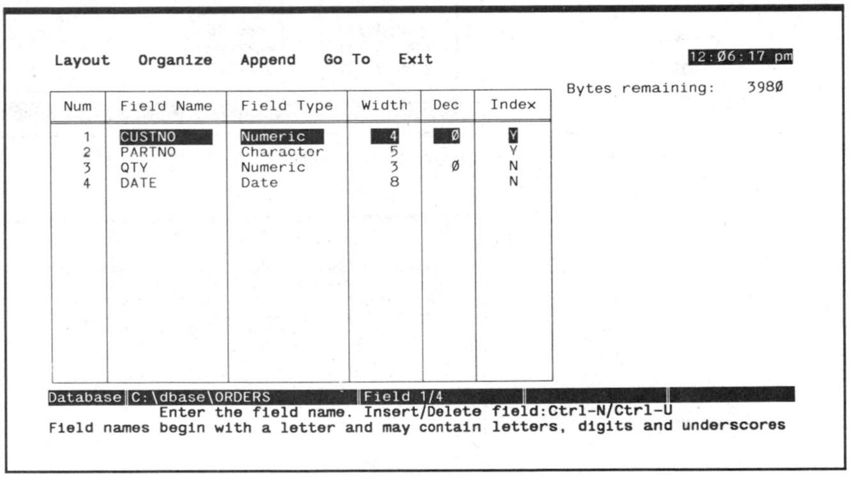

```
Layout   Organize   Append   Go To   Exit                          12:06:17 pm

                                                        Bytes remaining:   3980
 Num | Field Name | Field Type | Width | Dec | Index
   1 | CUSTNO     | Numeric    |   4   |  0  |   Y
   2 | PARTNO     | Character  |   5   |     |   Y
   3 | QTY        | Numeric    |   3   |  0  |   N
   4 | DATE       | Date       |   8   |     |   N

Database C:\dbase\ORDERS          Field 1/4
        Enter the field name. Insert/Delete field:Ctrl-N/Ctrl-U
Field names begin with a letter and may contain letters, digits and underscores
```

Figure D.8: Structure of the sample ORDERS database

Before you actually export the database to Lotus 1-2-3 in this example, you need to generate total sales for each part number, because that is the information that you want to graph. To do so, you follow these steps:

1. Open the ORDERS database by highlighting its name in the data panel and pressing ↵ (or by double-clicking the name). Then select Use File.
2. Select <create> from the Queries panel.
3. Choose Fields ► Include Indexes.
4. Set up a query to total the Qty field for each part number, as in Figure D.10.

Records Organize Fields Go To Exit

CUSTNO	PARTNO	QTY	DATE
7991	B-222	2	07/01/93
8833	B-222	1	07/01/93
4077	A-111	2	07/01/93
9584	C-333	1	07/01/93
7986	A-111	3	06/02/93
8270	A-111	4	06/05/93
3780	B-222	1	06/15/93
2556	C-333	2	06/15/93
9556	C-333	1	06/15/93
4458	C-333	2	07/01/93
7215	B-222	2	07/01/93
1819	B-222	1	07/01/93
7346	A-111	2	07/01/93
1516	C-333	1	07/01/93
4462	A-111	3	06/02/93
7746	A-111	4	06/05/93
8259	B-222	1	06/15/93

Browse | C:\dbase\ORDERS | Rec 1/160 | File

Figure D.9: Some sample data in the ORDERS database

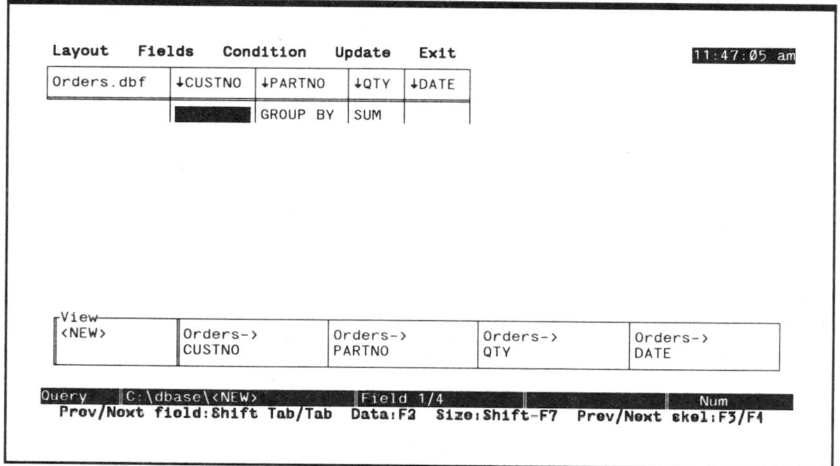

Figure D.10: Query to total orders by part number

5. Press or click F2 to test the query and view the results; then choose Exit ► Transfer to Query Design.
6. Create a database file from the results of the query by choosing Layout ► Write View as Database File.

7. When prompted, enter a file name for the new database file (such as **ORDTOTS** in this example). You can leave the description blank by pressing ↵.
8. Choose Exit ► Abandon Changes and Exit and answer Yes when prompted for verification.

When you get back to the Control Center, you are ready to export the totaled data in ORDTOTS.DBF to Lotus 1-2-3 (in this example, we assume you're using Release 2.0 or higher of Lotus 1-2-3). To do so, you follow these steps:

1. Choose Tools ► Export.
2. Select Lotus 1-2-3.
3. Choose Release 2 (.wk1).
4. Select ORDTOTS.DBF from the submenu that appears.
5. To move the exported ORDTOTS.WK1 file to the C:\123 directory (where Lotus 1-2-3 is presumably stored), choose Tools ► DOS Utilities.
6. Choose Files ► Display Only and change the setting to *.wk1, then press ↵.
7. Use the PgDn and arrow keys (or your mouse) to locate and highlight ORDTOTS.WK1 in the files list.
8. Choose Operations ► Move ► Single File.
9. Press Ctrl-Y to erase the suggested destination and type **C:\123** as the new destination.
10. Press Ctrl-End.
11. Choose Exit ► Exit to Control Center.
12. To leave dBASE IV, choose Exit ► Quit to DOS.

Now you want to load the exported data into Lotus 1-2-3 and build the graph. First you need to switch to the appropriate directory (C:\123 in this example), run 1-2-3, and retrieve the file. Here are the steps:

1. Enter the command **CD\123** at the DOS prompt.

2. Enter the command **123** at the DOS prompt to run 1-2-3.
3. When the blank spreadsheet appears, type **/FR** (File Retrieve) and select the name of the exported dBASE IV file (ORDTOTS.WKS in this example).
4. You'll see the exported totals on the spreadsheet. As necessary, use the /WCS (Worksheet, Column, Set-Width) options to alter column widths in the spreadsheet.
5. Type **/GTB** (Graph Type Bar) to select a graph type.
6. Select **X** and highlight X-axis titles (part numbers in the range B2..B7 in this example) as shown in Figure D.11.
7. Select **A** and specify the values to plot on the graph (C2..C7 in this example).
8. Select **V** for View.

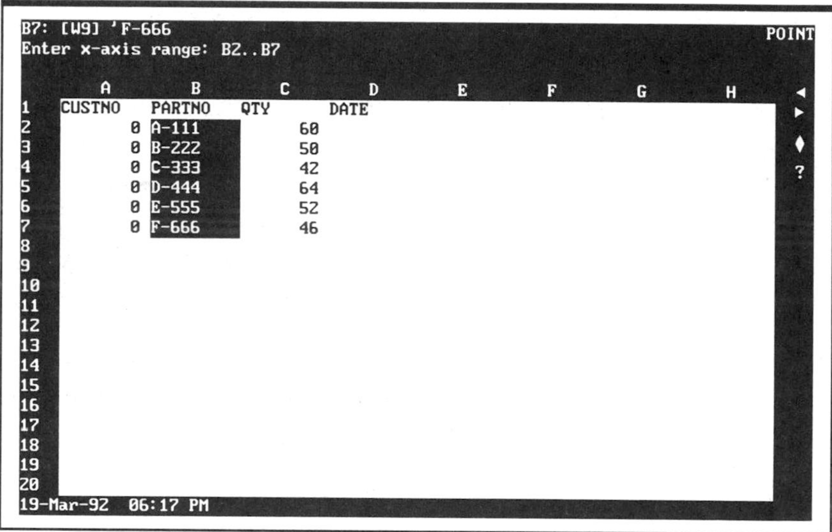

Figure D.11: Part names selected as the X-axis titles in 1-2-3

The graph will appear on the screen. You can use other 1-2-3 graph options to add titles or other features, as in the example shown in Figure D.12. After viewing the graph, press any key, then type **Q** (Quit) to return to the spreadsheet. You can treat the imported data as you would any other spreadsheet data. Remember: If you wish to

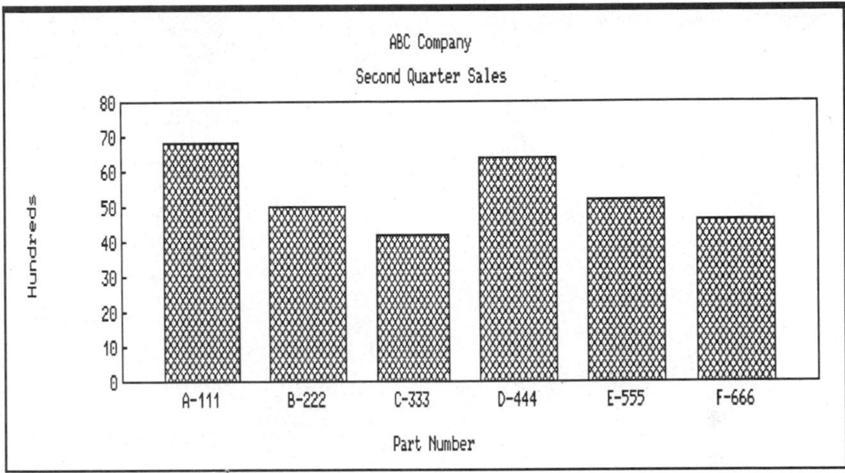

Figure D.12: Sample graph printed from the ORDERS database file

save any changes to the spreadsheet, use the 1-2-3 **/FS** (File Save) options. To leave 1-2-3, type **/QY** (Quit Yes).

EXAMPLE 3: EXPORTING PRINTED REPORTS

In some situations, you may want to export printed, formatted data rather than raw data from a database file. For example, suppose you create a report format to display totals and subtotals and wish to embed a copy of the report in a document you created with WordStar, WordPerfect, or some other word processing program. To do so, you only need to send the printed report to a disk file and then read that file into the appropriate word processing document (or into a new word processing document).

CREATING THE TEXT FILE

In this section, we'll discuss the general steps for creating a text file from a report or label format. We'll use the CUSTLIST.DBF database and the LIST report format in the LEARN catalog as examples.

1. Open the database (CUSTLIST in this example) by highlighting its name in the Data panel of the Control Center and pressing ↵, or by double-clicking on the database name. Then select Use File.
2. To export only certain records or to sort the database, create a query or use an existing query to display the appropriate records (as discussed in Chapter 6). Press or click F2 to verify the query, then return to the Control Center.
3. Highlight the name of the report format in the Reports panel (LIST in this example) and press ↵, or double-click on the name of the report format. Then select Print Report.
4. Select Destination and press the space bar or click the mouse to change the Write To setting to DOS FILE.
5. Select Name of DOS File and note the suggested file name (LIST.PRT in this example) or change the drive, directory, or suggested file name.
6. To view the report on the screen as it is stored on disk, select Echo to Screen and press the space bar or click the mouse until the setting changes to Yes.
7. Press Ctrl-End.
8. Select Begin Printing.
9. When you get back to the Control Center, choose Exit ► Quit to DOS to leave dBASE IV.

You can use the DOS TYPE command to verify that the file exists. In this example, you would enter the command **TYPE LIST.PRT** (and press ↵) at the DOS prompt. You should see the entire formatted report.

READING THE REPORT INTO WORDSTAR

If you use WordStar as your word processor, you can follow these general steps to read the printed report into a word processing document:

1. Enter the DOS command **CD** to switch to the directory that contains WordStar or the WordStar document into which you want to insert the report.
2. Run WordStar in the usual manner (that is, type **WS** at the dot prompt and press ↵).
3. Type **D** to select Document and then enter the name of a new or existing document file.
4. If you are inserting the report into an existing document, move the cursor to exactly the place that you want the incoming report to be inserted.
5. Press Ctrl-KR and, when prompted, type the full path and file name of the file to insert (**C:\DBASE\LIST.PRT** in this example). Press ↵.

You will see the formatted report appear in your document. Use the PgUp and PgDn keys to scroll and make changes if necessary. Save the document after inserting the report using the usual Ctrl-KD, Ctrl-KS, or Ctrl-KX keystrokes.

READING THE REPORT INTO WORDPERFECT

To read the formatted report into a WordPerfect document, follow these general steps:

1. Enter the DOS **CD** command to switch to the directory that contains WordPerfect or the document into which you want to insert the formatted report.
2. If you want to read the formatted report into a new document, run WordPerfect by entering the command **WP** at the DOS prompt. If you want to read the report into an existing Word-Perfect document, start WordPerfect by entering the command **WP <filename>**, where <filename> is the name of the existing WordPerfect document.

3. If you are inserting the formatted report into an existing document, move the cursor to the location where you want the inserted report to appear.
4. Press Text In/Out (Ctrl-F5).
5. Select DOS Text, and then Retrieve (CR/LF to [HRt]).
6. Enter the full path and file name of the formatted report (**C:\DBASE\LIST.PRT** in this example) and press ↵.

You'll see the formatted report embedded in the document. Use the usual scrolling keys to verify that the entire file was inserted and to make any changes, if necessary. Save the document using the usual Exit (F7) key.

EXAMPLE 4: EXPORTING TO WORDSTAR MAILMERGE FILES

Suppose you wish to use dBASE IV to manage names and addresses and to use WordStar to print form letters. To do so, you need to export records from the DBASE IV database to an ASCII text file that delimits (separates) each field with a comma. Then you need to use the WordStar MailMerge dot commands in a form letter to read in the exported data.

Let's look at an example where we will export data from the CUSTLIST database to a WordStar MailMerge file named CUSTLIST.MRG on a directory named C:\WS4. Here are the steps to get started:

1. Choose Tools ► Export.
2. Highlight Character Delimited, and press ↵ to accept the quotation mark (ASCII character number 34) as the delimiter.
3. Select CUSTLIST.DBF.
4. When the export is done, choose Exit ► Quit to DOS.

At the DOS prompt, you can verify that the export was successful by entering the command **TYPE CustList.TXT**. You should see the CUSTLIST database records, with Character data surrounded by quotation marks and commas between each field. A sample record is shown here:

```
1001,"Smith","John","ABC Co.","123 A St.","San Diego",
"CA","92067","(619)555-1234",19921115,Y
```

Now suppose you want to store a copy of this exported file on a directory named WS4 (where WordStar is stored) and to change its name to CUSTLIST.MRG. To do so, enter this command at the DOS prompt:

```
COPY CustList.TXT C:\WS4\CustList.MRG
```

After you press ↵ and the copy operation is complete, you can switch to the C:\WS4 directory by entering the command **CD\WS4**. Now you need to create a form letter, following these steps:

1. At the DOS prompt, enter the usual command for running WordStar (usually **WS**).
2. Select D and enter a name for the form letter (for example, **FORMLET.TXT**).
3. Press Ctrl-O and then S1 to set line spacing to 1.

Figure D.13 shows a sample form letter that is capable of printing letters using exported data in the CUSTLIST.MRG file. Note that the .DF dot command specifies the name of the file containing the data to merge. The .RV command assigns a variable name to each field in the merge file. Note that you must include a variable name for each field in the merge file, whether or not you plan to actually use it in the letter, and you must use the same left-to-right order as the fields in the merge file.

To place data from the merge file onto the printed letter, use the variable name assigned in the .RV command surrounded by ampersands. If you think that a particular field may be blank in some records (such as COMPANY in the CUSTLIST database), add /o to the right of the variable name, as in the example &Company/o&. Doing so ensures that WordStar will close the gap left by this empty variable, rather than printing a blank line.

```
 C:FORMLET.TXT        P01 L16 C23 Insert Align
L----!----!----!----!----!----!----!----!----!----!----!--------R
.MT 8                                                                1
.DF CustList.MRG                                                     :
.RV CustNo,Last,First,Company,Address,City,State,Zip,Phone,Start,Paid :
.OP                                                                  :
.LS1                                                                 .
                                                                     <
June 11, 1991                                                        <
                                                                     <
&First& &Last&                                                       <
&Company/o&                                                          <
&Address&                                                            <
&City&, &State&  &Zip&                                               <
                                                                     <
Dear &First&:                                                        <
                                                                     <
This is a sample WordStar form letter.  The name and address
above were exported from a dBASE IV database to a delimited text
file, which in turn was used as a mailmerge file to print these
letters.                                                             <
                                                                     <
(etc... etc... etc...)                                               <
                                                                     <
.PA                                                                  .
```

Figure D.13: Sample WordStar form letter

After creating the form letter, save it using the usual Ctrl-KD command. Then select M (for Merge Print) and specify the name of the form letter file (FORMLET.TXT in this example). Press Esc to bypass other options and begin printing.

IMPORTING ASCII TEXT FILES

If neither dBASE IV nor a foreign software product provides built-in options for interfacing, you'll usually need to use an ASCII text file as an intermediary file for the transfer operation. Most software products, even those with very limited interfacing capability, have some means of storing data in ASCII text files.

If you can use that foreign software product to produce the ASCII text file, then chances are that you can import that text file into a dBASE IV database. There are several general steps involved, listed in the next sections. (The general steps are illustrated in an example that follows.)

STEP 1: CREATE THE ASCII TEXT FILE

Suppose that you are using a product, which we'll name FlashBase, to store data and you want to transfer copies of that data to a dBASE IV database. You need to look in the FlashBase manual for information about creating ASCII text files, either through a file exporting option or by storing printed reports or data on disk files. Use whatever means are available to create the file and note the disk drive, directory, and complete file name of the exported ASCII text file.

STEP 2: NOTE THE STRUCTURE OF THE ASCII TEXT FILE

The next step is to look at the ASCII text file and ascertain its structure. To do so, starting from the DOS prompt, switch to the directory where the file is stored and use the DOS TYPE command to look at the contents of the file. For example, if the ASCII text file is stored in C:\FBASE\EXPORTED.DAT, you enter the following commands at the DOS prompt to view the contents of the file:

```
CD\FBASE
TYPE Exported.DAT
```

Most likely, the file will be in one of three formats: delimited, blank delimited, or fixed field length (also called structured data format, or SDF). Delimited ASCII files generally place a comma between each field and surround character strings with quotation marks or some other character. Blank-delimited files separate each field with a single blank space, and individual fields contain no blank spaces. Fixed field-length storage places each field in evenly spaced columns. Figure D.14 shows examples of these three formats.

Note that in the example in the figure, the delimited file uses double quotation marks as delimiters. If, while viewing the file, you notice that some other character is used to delimit character strings, make a note of this character to remind yourself later. For example, the following text file uses apostrophes (') to delimit character strings:

```
1001,'Smith','John','ABC Co.','123 A St.','San Diego'
1002,'Adams','Annie','','3456 Ocean St.','Santa Monica'
```

Note that you may find that the file uses none of the formats discussed in this section, in which case you might need to write a program to perform the conversion. WordPerfect secondary (mail-merge) files are an example of files that use a very unusual format

Delimited (with ") format:

```
1001,"Smith","John",19921115,T
1002,"Adams","Annie",19930101,F
```

Blank-delimited format:

```
1001 Smith John 19921115 T
1002 Adams Annie 19930101 F
```

Fixed field-length (SDF) format:

```
1001Smith          John           19921115T
1002Adams          Annie          19930101F
```

Figure D.14: Examples of ASCII file formats

which cannot be easily imported into or exported from dBASE IV database files.

STEP 3: PLAN A dBASE IV DATABASE STRUCTURE

While viewing the contents of the ASCII text file on your screen, you need to plan a structure for the dBASE IV database. Assign a name, data type, width, and number of decimal places (for numbers) to each field. Be sure to list file names in the same order that they are listed, from left to right, in the text file.

If the fields in the file are separated by commas or single blank spaces, then you can assign any width that you wish to each field. If, however, the file has the fixed field-length (SDF) structure, the width you assign to your dBASE IV database must exactly match the widths of the fields in the ASCII text file.

STEP 4: COPY AND RENAME THE TEXT FILE

Next, you copy the file to the C:\DBASE directory and change the extension to .TXT. (If you have a DOS redirect or move utility, you can move the file instead.) For example, to copy the C:\FBASE

\EXPORTED.DAT file to C:\DBASE\EXPORTED.TXT, you enter this command below at the DOS prompt:

```
COPY C:\DBASE\Exported.DAT C:\DBASE\Exported.TXT
```

STEP 5: CREATE THE DATABASE STRUCTURE

Now you can switch to the DBASE directory and run dBASE, by entering the commands

```
CD\DBASE
DBASE
```

When the Control Center appears, select <create> from the Data panel and design a database with the field names and data types that you noted earlier. Save the database structure by choosing Layout ► Save This Database File Structure from the menu on the database design screen. Then choose Append ► Copy Records from Non-dBASE File, and select the appropriate option from the submenu that appears (shown in Figure D.15).

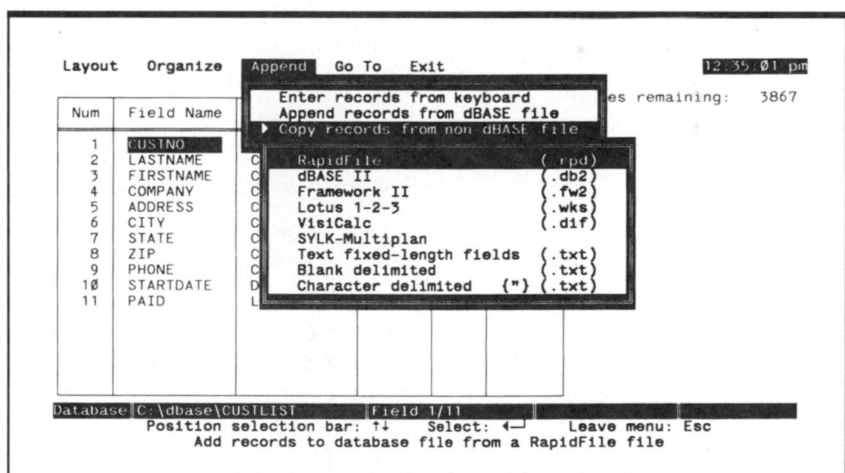

Figure D.15: Menu for importing data into a database file

The next section demonstrates some of these steps, showing you how to import data from a WordStar mailmerge file into a dBASE database.

EXAMPLE 5: IMPORTING WORDSTAR MAILMERGE DATA

Suppose you have already created a fairly large list of names and addresses for WordStar MailMerge operations, simply by typing them using WordStar. Now that you have dBASE IV, you want to import those names and addresses to a database file and use dBASE to manage them. You can easily import this list to a dBASE IV database. (Because WordStar MailMerge files are already in ASCII delimited format, you need not take any action to export them to a different format.)

For example, suppose you have stored the names and addresses in a file named C:\WS4\NAMES.MRG. Here is how you import them to a dBASE IV database:

1. From the DOS prompt, enter the command **CD\WS4** to switch to the WS4 directory.
2. To view the contents of the file, enter the command **TYPE NAMES.MRG** at the DOS prompt.
3. Suppose now that the screen displays the contents of the NAMES.MRG file, as shown in Figure D.16. Jot down notes about the file and define field names and data types, as follows (because commas separate fields in this example, you can assign any widths that you wish to each field):

   Format: Delimited (with ")

LastName	Character	15
FirstName	Character	15
Company	Character	20
Address	Character	30
City	Character	20
State	Character	2
Zip	Character	10

4. Copy the text file to the \DBASE directory and change its extension to .TXT by entering the command **COPY C:\WS4\NAMES.MRG C:\DBASE\NAMES.TXT** at the DOS prompt.

```
C:\WS4>TYPE Names.MRG
"Smith","John","ABC Co.","123 A St.","San Diego","CA",92Ø67
"Adams","Annie","","3456 Ocean St.","Santa Monica","CA",92ØØ1
"Mahoney","Mary","","211 Seahawk St.","Seattle","WA",88977
"Newell","John","LoTech Co.","734 Rainbow Dr.","Butte","MT",54321
"Beach","Sandy","American Widget","11 Elm St.","Portland","OR",76543
"Kenney","Ralph","","11Ø1 Rainbow Ct.","Los Angeles","CA",966Ø7
"Schumack","Susita","SMS Software","47 Broad St.","Philadelphia","PA",45543
"Smith","Anita","Zeerocks, Inc.","2ØØ1 Engine Dr.","Hideaway","CA",9222Ø
"Jones","Fred","American Sneaker","P.O. Box 3381","Newark","NJ",Ø1234


C:\WS4>
```

Figure D.16: Contents of a WordStar MailMerge file

5. Log on to the dBASE directory by entering the command **CD\DBASE** at the DOS prompt.
6. Run dBASE in the usual manner (enter the command **DBASE** at the DOS prompt).
7. Select <create> from the Data panel in the Control Center.
8. Design the database according to your earlier notes, as in Figure D.17.
9. Choose Layout ► Save This Database File Structure and assign a valid file name (such as **NAMES**).
10. Choose Append ► Copy Records from Non-dBASE File.
11. Select Character Delimited from the submenu.
12. Because the text file uses quotation marks as delimiters, and the submenu that appears suggests this character, just press ↵.
13. Select the name of the text file (NAMES.TXT in this example) from the submenu that appears.
14. Choose Exit ► Save Changes and Exit.

The import is now complete. You can press F2 to switch to the edit and browse screens and use the PgUp, PgDn, and arrow keys or

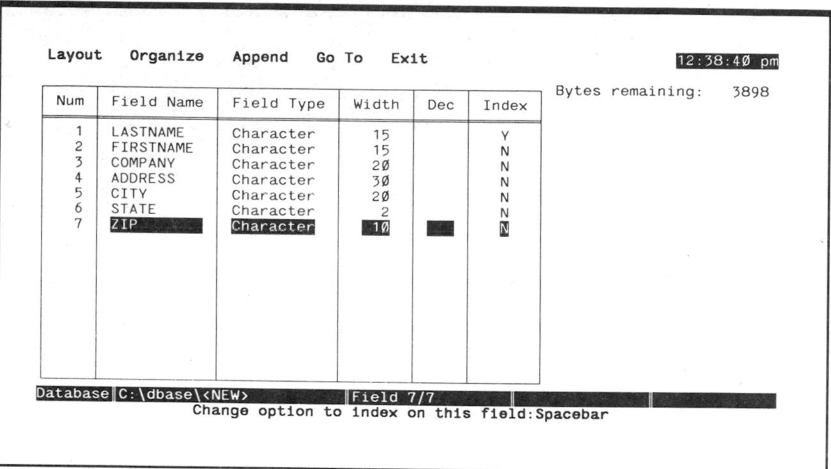

Figure D.17: Structure of the database to receive MailMerge records

your mouse to scroll through the database and verify that all appropriate records were imported.

EXAMPLE 6: EXPORTING TO WORDPERFECT SECONDARY MERGE FILES

In some cases you need to use a little ingenuity to get your files transferred. WordPerfect secondary merge files (used for printing form letters and such) are a good example, because dBASE does not have an option for exporting directly to such files.

However, if you were to check the menu on the WordPerfect Convert program (the one that comes with WordPerfect 5.1), you'd see that it has an option to import DIF (Data Interchange Format) files into Secondary Merge Files. dBASE IV, in turn, can export to DIF. Hence, you need to export from dBASE to DIF, then import from DIF to WordPerfect. Here are the steps using CUSTLIST.DBF as the sample database being exported to WordPerfect 5.1. These steps assume that dBASE IV is stored on C:\DBASE and WordPerfect 5.1 is stored on C:\WP51 (you would need to change the drive\directory names accordingly if your copies are stored elsewhere):

1. Run dBASE IV in the usual manner so that the Control Center appears.
2. If the catalog containing the database file that you want to export does not appear, choose Catalog ► Use a Different Catalog to go to the appropriate catalog.
3. Choose Tools ► Export.
4. Select VisiCalc (.dif) from the submenu.
5. Select the name of the file you want to export from the submenu of database names (the exported file will have the same first name, but the extension .DIF rather than .DBF).
6. Choose Exit ► Quit to DOS to leave dBASE IV.
7. Switch to the WordPerfect directory (**CD \WP51** < if you are using WordPerfect 5.1, and if it's stored on C:\WP51).
8. Enter the CONVERT command followed by the location and name of the exported DIF file, a blank space, and the location and name of the new WordPerfect secondary merge file you'll be creating. For example, if you were exporting CUSTLIST.DBF, you would type

   ```
   CONVERT C:\DBASE\CUSTLIST.DIF CUSTLIST.SCD
   ```

   and press ↵.
9. Select A Spreadsheet DIF to WordPerfect Secondary Merge.

That completes the export. You can now run WordPerfect and retrieve the exported file (CUSTLIST.SCD in this example) using the Retrieve (Shift-F10) key or List Files (F5). There will, however, be a couple of problems you need to repair.

First, the new secondary merge file will have the dBASE IV field names as the first record. These can help you determine the number of each imported field because as you scroll up and down in this file, the number of each field appears in the lower-left corner of the screen. However, you probably don't want to print these field names either. So, at your leisure you can delete them by highlighting everything from the top of the file to the first {END RECORD} (or ^E) merge command and pressing Delete (Del).

The second problem is that any dates that were exported will be in the generic format yyyymmdd (such as 19921231 for 12/31/92). To display dates in the more familiar mm/dd/yy (12/31/92) format, you would need to use a merge expression with the {MID} macro command to isolate each component of the date and display it in the format you want. Assuming that the date is stored in field 9, the exact expression is

```
{MID}{FIELD}9~~4~2~/{MID}
    {FIELD}9~~6~2~/{MID}{FIELD}9~~2~2~
```

To create each {MID} expression on your WordPerfect primary merge file, you need to follow these general steps (assuming your WordPerfect primary file is on your WordPerfect Edit screen ready for editing):

1. Place the cursor to where you want the imported date to appear in your primary merge file.
2. Press Merge Codes (Shift-F9) and select More.
3. Select {MID}expr~offset~count~.
4. Press ↵ when prompted to enter an expression.
5. When prompted for an Offset, type **4** and press ↵.
6. When prompted for a count, type **2** and press ↵.
7. Press ← enough times to move the cursor to beneath the first tilde (~), to the right of the }.
8. Press Merge Codes (Shift-F9).
9. Select More.
10. Select {FIELD}field~.
11. Type the number of the field to display and press ↵ (**9** in this example because the imported date is in Field 9).
12. Press Home → to move to the end of the expression.
13. Type / (because you want the expression to type a / here).

At this point you will have typed **{MID}{FIELD}9~~4~2~/** (assuming the date is in Field 9), which tells WordPerfect to print the month followed by a slash—the 4 refers to the fourth character in the string where the first character is number 0, and the 2 refers to the length. Hence, if the imported date is 19921231, then the expression **{MID}{FIELD}9~~4~2~/** will display 12/ after the merge.

You need to repeat the general steps above to complete the entire expression, displaying the portion {MID}{FIELD}9~~6~2~ (the day of the month) the second time, followed by a slash, and then displaying the portion {MID}{FIELD9~~2~2~ on the third time through (the two characters representing the year).

NOTE

See your WordPerfect manual or a WordPerfect book for additional information on merging with WordPerfect.

Figure D.18 shows a sample WordPerfect 5.1 primary merge file that can print letters using data that was exported to dBASE IV, both on the normal Edit screen and on the Reveal Codes screen. All of the merge codes shown in curly braces ({ }) were placed using the Merge Codes key (Shift-F9). Once you've completed your primary merge file, you can use the Merge key (Ctrl-F9) to merge the primary and secondary files in the usual manner.

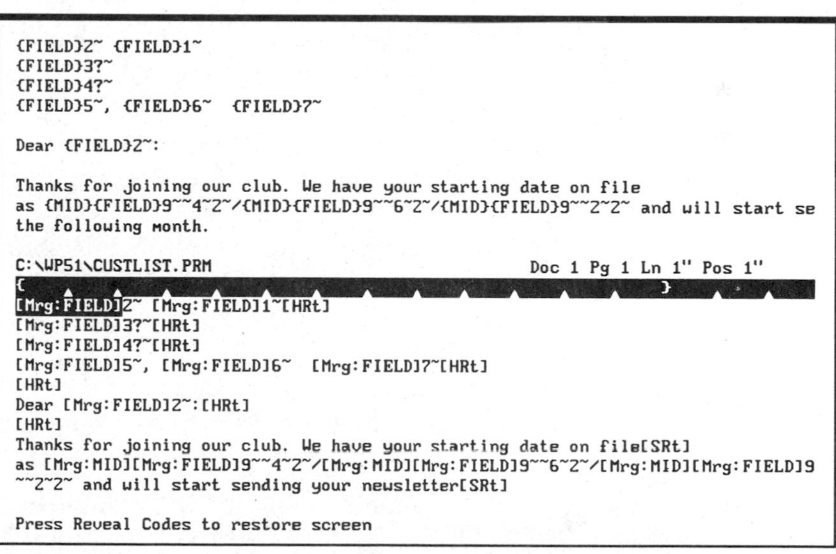

```
{FIELD}2~ {FIELD}1~
{FIELD}3?~
{FIELD}4?~
{FIELD}5~, {FIELD}6~  {FIELD}7~

Dear {FIELD}2~:

Thanks for joining our club. We have your starting date on file
as {MID}{FIELD}9~~4~2~/{MID}{FIELD}9~~6~2~/{MID}{FIELD}9~~2~2~ and will start se
the following month.

C:\WP51\CUSTLIST.PRM                                  Doc 1 Pg 1 Ln 1" Pos 1"
[Mrg:FIELD]2~ [Mrg:FIELD]1~[HRt]
[Mrg:FIELD]3?~[HRt]
[Mrg:FIELD]4?~[HRt]
[Mrg:FIELD]5~, [Mrg:FIELD]6~  [Mrg:FIELD]7~[HRt]
[HRt]
Dear [Mrg:FIELD]2~:[HRt]
[HRt]
Thanks for joining our club. We have your starting date on file[SRt]
as [Mrg:MID][Mrg:FIELD]9~~4~2~/[Mrg:MID][Mrg:FIELD]9~~6~2~/[Mrg:MID][Mrg:FIELD]9
~~2~2~ and will start sending your newsletter[SRt]

Press Reveal Codes to restore screen
```

Figure D.18: Sample WordPerfect 5.1 primary merge file

EXAMPLE 7: IMPORTING FROM WORDPERFECT SECONDARY MERGE FILES

WARNING

I have found one flaw with the technique described here: The first record from the WordPerfect secondary merge file is not appended from the DIF file, because this is where field names are usually stored. To ensure that all of your WordPerfect secondary merge records are exported, place a blank record at the top of that file before exporting to DIF format.

Importing data from a WordPerfect secondary merge file into a dBASE database also takes a little ingenuity, primarily because Tools ► Import has nothing that's compatible with WordPerfect's Convert program. However, you can add records from a DIF file to an existing database file. That is, you first need to create a dBASE database with the appropriate structure. For each field in the WordPerfect secondary merge file, there must be a corresponding field in the dBASE database.

If you will be importing any dates from the WordPerfect file (typed or entered with the WordPerfect Date Text key in 12/31/92 format), define the dBASE fields that will store those as the Character data type with a length of 8. You might want to use a temporary name for this field. For example, if the third field in the WordPerfect secondary file contains a date, then you might want the third field in your dBASE database structure to be named IMPDATE, have a Character data type, and a length of 8.

Similarly, even though WordPerfect does not support the Logical data type per se, you might have used some sort of Yes/No or Y/N field in your secondary merge file. If that is the case, make the dBASE field that will be receiving that field the Character data type as well, with a length of 1.

After creating that dBASE database, which in this example we'll assume is named FROMWP.DBF, you need to switch to the directory where the WordPerfect secondary file is stored, and use the WordPerfect Convert program to make a copy of that file converted to DIF format. For example, if the WordPerfect secondary merge file is named MEMBERS.SCD, you could enter this command to initiate the export:

```
CONVERT C:\WP51\MEMBERS.SCD
        C:\DBASE\MEMBERS.DIF
```

When the Convert menu appears, select option **1** WordPerfect to Another Format. Then select **8** WordPerfect Secondary Merge File to Spreadsheet DIF. The DIF version of the file will be stored on the C:\DBASE drive and directory in this example.

Next, go back to the dBASE directory and run dBASE. At the Control Center, highlight the name of the database file that you want to import records to (FROMWP in this example). Press or click Design (Shift-F2), then choose Append ► Copy Records from Non-dBASE File and select VisiCalc (.dif). Highlight the name of the DIF file (MEMBERS.DIF in this example) and press ↵.

When the import is complete you can return to the Control Center by pressing Ctrl-End.

If the imported data contained any dates, you may want to convert them to the dBASE Date data type now. For example, if you imported dates into a Character field named IMPDATE, you might want to go back to the database design screen and add a new field to the database named STARTDATE, giving the Date data type. Save the database structure and get to the dot prompt. At the dot prompt, enter the command:

```
REPLACE ALL STARTDATE WITH CTOD(IMPDATE)
```

The STARTDATE field will then have "real" dBASE dates. You can then return to the dBASE database design screen, remove the IMPDATE field, and (immediately) save the new database structure.

If you imported Logical data into a Character field, named IMPLOGIC for example, you can use a similar technique to convert that to a Logical field. After the importing, add a new field to the database with whatever name you want (we'll use PAIDYET in this example), and make it the Logical data type. Save the new structure, and get to the dot prompt.

Assuming the IMPLOGIC field contains either Y (for true) or N (for false), you could use the following command to convert those values to Logical values in the PAIDYET field:

```
REPLACE ALL PAIDYET WITH IIF(IMPLOGIC = "Y",.T.,.F.)
```

When the replacement is finished, you can go back to the database design screen and remove the IMPLOGIC field. Then save the database structure immediately.

CONVERTING FROM dBASE III PLUS TO dBASE IV

If you want to use your dBASE III PLUS databases, reports, and so forth with dBASE IV, you should go through the following steps to bring all the files up to date:

1. Copy all the dBASE III PLUS database (.DBF and .DBT), index (.NDX), screen (.SCR), report (.FRM), label (.LBL), and program (.PRG) files to a separate directory where they can be converted to dBASE IV format. You can use the DOS COPY command, or the dBASE IV DOS Utilities options covered in Chapter 14.
2. Start dBASE IV from the new directory, and create a catalog for the old dBASE III PLUS files (see Chapter 14).
3. After creating the catalog, add the various files from dBASE III PLUS to it (Chapter 14).
4. Open a database in the Data panel.
5. Update each Form, Report, and Label format for that database by first highlighting its name in the Control Center and pressing or clicking Design (Shift-F2). This will bring the object to the appropriate design screen.
6. Make any changes you want to the object then save it by pressing Ctrl-End or by choosing Exit ► Save Changes and Exit.
7. Repeat steps 5 and 6 for each Form, Report, and Label format in each database so that a dBASE IV version of the file is generated.

You can also update any dBASE III PLUS view (.VUE) files by bringing a copy to the Queries panel of the Control Center and pressing or clicking Design (Shift-F2) to modify the view. However, not all dBASE III PLUS views are easily translated to dBASE IV, so you may have to re-create a portion of each view before saving them as dBASE IV query (view) files.

CONVERTING INDEX FILES

You will probably want to combine any dBASE III PLUS index (.NDX) files into dBASE IV multiple index (.MDX) files, since this is by far a more convenient way to manage indexes. You can use the COPY INDEX command (from the dBASE dot prompt) to do this.

To see how you would convert dBASE III PLUS index files to dBASE IV indexes, suppose you have a dBASE III PLUS database named PRODUCTS.DBF that uses two index files named PROD-NO.NDX and PRODDATE.NDX. First, run dBASE IV in the usual manner and then, from the Control Center, choose Exit ► Exit to Dot Prompt. At the dot prompt, open the database file and both indexes by entering the command

```
USE Products INDEX ProdNo,ProdDate
```

To copy both indexes to a production index file named PROD-UCTS.MDX, enter the command

```
COPY INDEX ProdNo,ProdDate
```

(The default production index name, Products.MDX in this example, is assumed by the COPY INDEX command.) When the dot prompt reappears, the conversion is complete.

To avoid confusion between the new and old indexes, you can delete the dBASE III PLUS .NDX files now by entering the following series of commands at the dot prompt:

```
CLOSE ALL
ERASE ProdNo.NDX
ERASE ProdDate.NDX
```

To open the Products database and both indexes, you simply need to enter the command

```
USE Products
```

When the dot prompt reappears, enter the command

```
DISPLAY STATUS
```

You'll notice that the status report displays the following (with the directory, file name, and index names for your converted files substituted):

```
Currently selected database:
Select area: 1, Database in Use: C:\DBASE\PRODUCTS.DBF
```

```
Production   MDX file:   C:\DBASE\PRODUCTS.MDX
             Index TAG:  PRODNO    Key: Partno
             Index TAG:  PRODDATE  Key: Date
```

At the moment, the database file and both indexes are open. However, no particular index is controlling the sort order, nor can any of the indexes currently be searched with a SEEK or FIND command. But if you add, change, or delete data, both indexes will be updated automatically.

Note that each index within a production index file includes a *tag*. A tag is simply the name of the individual index within the larger production index file.

To select one of the indexes for ordering records or searching with a SEEK or FIND command, use the SET ORDER command:

```
SET ORDER TO ProdNo
```

The ProdNo index will control the sort order and can be searched. Other indexes within the production index file are still updated automatically whenever data is added, changed, or deleted.

Note that if you now attempt to use the dBASE III PLUS command SET INDEX TO ProdNo, dBASE IV will still attempt to find an index file named ProdNo.NDX. However, you've erased that index file, so dBASE displays the error message "File not found."

To open the database with one of the indexes controlling the sort order, use the syntax USE <database> ORDER <index tag>. For example, the command

```
USE Products ORDER ProdDate
```

opens the Products database with the ProdDate index controlling the sort order. (Of course, all other indexes in the production index file are open and will be updated to include any new, changed, or deleted data.)

Note that if you attempted to use the dBASE III PLUS command USE Products INDEX ProdDate, dBASE IV would attempt to find the ProdDate.NDX index file, which you've erased. The error message "File not found" would appear.

The dBASE IV INDEX ON command will still create an .NDX index file unless you specify the TAG option in place of the TO option. For example, the following command creates an index named PartName, which is stored in the production index file with other indexes:

```
INDEX ON PartName TAG PartName
```

The following dBASE IV command creates a dBASE III .NDX index file, which is stored outside the production index file:

```
INDEX ON PartName TO PartName
```

COMPILER WARNINGS

dBASE IV will automatically compile a dBASE III PLUS program the first time it is executed and whenever it is modified in the future. If the dBASE III PLUS program includes remarks to the right of ENDDO, ENDIF, ENDCASE, or other commands that terminate program clauses, dBASE will present a warning, such as the one shown here, when compiling the line:

```
ENDDO (while not eof)
Warning on line XXX: Extra characters ignored at end of command
```

The warning will not prevent the program from compiling or running properly. However, if you want to prevent future compilations from displaying the warning message, precede all such comments with double ampersands, as follows:

```
ENDDO  &&(while not eof)
```

COPYING CATALOGS AND APPLICATIONS ACROSS PCs

In this section we'll talk about interacting with multiple (licensed) copies of dBASE IV on several PCs in terms of copying and moving catalogs and applications between these PCs. In this situation there is no need to actually translate data, since you are just going from dBASE IV on one machine to dBASE IV on another machine. However, there is some potential confusion about how to go about copying entire applications and catalogs, which we'll discuss here.

COPYING APPLICATIONS

As mentioned in the chapters on creating applications, it's always a good idea to create each new application on its own, unique directory. If you do so, it's simple to copy an application from one computer to another. When describing how to do this, we'll refer to the computer that currently has the application stored on it as the *source* computer, and the computer that you want to copy the application to as the *target* computer.

NOTE

See the MKDIR, CHDIR, and COPY commands in your DOS manual for additional information on directories and copying files. The more comfortable you are with these commands, the better.

Basically you need to create a directory on the target computer (using the DOS MKDIR or MD command) with the same name as the directory used to store the application on the source computer.

Then, you simply need to copy every file from the application's directory on the source computer to the directory with the same name on the target directory. You can use the DOS COPY command (COPY *.*) or the dBASE IV DOS Utilities screen to do so. If you are using floppy disks as an intermediary (that is, copying from the source to a floppy, then from the floppy to the target), you may need to use more than one disk, or erase files from the floppy after they've been copied to the target directory to make room for more files.

As an alternative to using floppies, you can use a linking program such as LapLink or Brooklyn Bridge (available at most computer or software stores) to simply send the file through a wire (if the computers are close enough to each other). Optionally, you can use a modem if the two computers are far apart. Whichever technique you use to copy the application, just make sure to copy every file from the application's directory on the source computer to the corresponding directory on the target computer.

After copying the files to the target computer, run dBASE IV from the application's directory on the target computer (which, of course, assumes that the dBASE IV directory is already in the PATH statement on the target computer). If the application's catalog does not appear in the Control Center when you first start dBASE on the target computer, choose Catalog ► Use a Different Catalog, then select the catalog name (if it appears) from the submenu, or select <create> from that submenu, type in the catalog's name, and press ↵. You should then see the entire application's catalog with all its file names appear on your screen.

COPYING CATALOGS

I've often been asked how one goes about copying a catalog (meaning the catalog itself, and all the files within it) from one computer to another. Intuitively, it seems as though this should be a simple process—simply copy the catalog.

However, intuition is not correct in this case, mainly because a catalog is only a collection of file *names,* not a collection of the actual files. As a matter of fact, a catalog is actually a dBASE database file with a predefined structure and the extension .CAT. You can see this for yourself by experimenting at the dot prompt. For example, if you've created all (or some) of the files in the LEARN catalog used throughout the first few chapters of this book, you can follow the steps below to view the contents of the LEARN.CAT file:

1. Start dBASE IV from its usual directory (typically C:\DBASE) in the normal manner.
2. At the Control Center, choose Exit ► Exit to Dot Prompt.
3. Type the command **SET CATALOG TO** and press ↵ to close any open catalogs.
4. Type **USE LEARN.CAT** and press ↵ (you can substitute any catalog name on the current directory for LEARN.CAT).
5. Type **BROWSE** and press ↵.

If you browse through this database with the Tab, Shift-Tab, ↑ and ↓ keys (or your mouse), you'll see the names of files, their types, descriptions, and so forth stored within this database.

If you were to copy this catalog (that is, the .CAT file) to another computer, disk, or directory, the only thing you would be copying is this list of names. The actual files that the catalog refers to would *not* be copied, hence the catalog is useless in whatever location you've moved it to.

Before we proceed, let me mention that to leave this browse screen and get back to the Control Center, you first need to close all files. Here are the steps to return to the Control Center from this browse screen:

1. Press Esc to leave the browse screen.

2. Type **CLOSE ALL** and press ↵ to close all open files.
3. Type **ASSIST** and press ↵ to return to the Control Center.

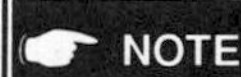

See Appendix H for a complete list of dBASE IV file extensions.

A second problem with catalogs concerns the fact that they are actually incomplete. For example, every database (.DBF) file may also have a multiple index (.MDX) file and memo field (.DBT) file associated with it, but these files are not included in the catalog. Similarly, an application (.APP) file also may have several other files associated with it, such as a bar (.BAR) menu, pop-up (.POP) menus, program (.PRG) files, and so forth. These additional files are also excluded from the catalog. Why? Because dBASE is designed to search for these additional files automatically and "behind the scenes."

Unfortunately, neither the DOS COPY command, nor the Operations ► Copy on the dBASE Tools ► DOS Utilities menu is quite so smart. Which leaves us with the conclusion that, while catalogs are useful for keeping families of files together within the Control Center, they are of virtually no use outside of dBASE, and therefore there is no easy way to copy a catalog and its contents from one drive\directory to another unless that catalog is stored in its own directory (in which case you can simply copy all the files on the directory as described under copying applications above). You must copy each file in the catalog individually (more on this in a moment).

With some dBASE IV programming, you *could* write a command file that will copy every file that's listed in a .CAT file to another drive or directory, and even catch all the .MDX, .DBT, and other files in the process. But there would be no easy way to write a program that could also copy all the unlisted files that belong in the Applications panel of that catalog. Therefore, my best recommendation at the moment to those of you who will need to copy catalogs and their associated files to other computers is to be sure to create each catalog on its own directory, and to create only one catalog on each directory.

If it's too late for that, and you need to copy a catalog that's on a directory with other catalogs, you can copy each file individually by following these general steps:

- At the dBASE IV Control Center, choose Catalog ► Use a Different Catalog, then select the name of the catalog that

Instead of writing down the names of all the objects and the catalog, you can press the Print Screen key on your keyboard while you're at the Control Center to print a copy of that screen (don't be concerned that the graphic characters from the screen look rather strange on the printout; this is normal). Remember that you may need to eject the page containing your screen printout if you're using a laser printer.

you want to copy, so that catalog appears on your screen.

- Jot down a list of all the names of objects that you want to copy from the various panels of the Control Center.
- Jot down the name of the catalog itself.
- Exit dBASE IV to get to the DOS command prompt.
- Use the DOS COPY command to copy the catalog (using .CAT as the extension), and use a * to represent the extension on other object names.

For example, suppose you want to copy a catalog named RESEARCH that contains a database file named MYDATA and a report named MYREPORT to a disk in drive A. At the DOS command prompt, the following commands would do the trick:

```
COPY RESEARCH.CAT A:
COPY MYDATA.* A:
COPY MYREPORT.* A:
```

To copy the catalog and its files from that floppy to another PC, switch to the directory on the other PC (where you want to store the catalog and its objects) and use the DOS command COPY A:*.* to copy all the files from disk drive A to the current directory.

Finally, run dBASE IV and choose Catalog ► Use a Different Catalog when the Control Center appears. If the name of the catalog you just copied appears in the list, select that name. If that name does not appear in the list, select <create>, type in the name of the catalog you just copied, and press ↵.

USING DBASE IV WITH WINDOWS 3

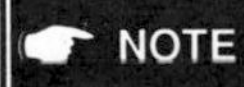

These sections assume you already know the basics of using Windows 3. Refer to your Windows 3 manual for more detailed information.

You can run dBASE IV directly from Windows 3, and if you have a 386 or 486 machine, you can run other programs while dBASE is running (perhaps play a little Reversi while dBASE prints your invoices). Of course, dBASE is not a true Windows application, although it does support a mouse. The following sections show you how to create the dBASE IV icon so that you can run dBASE from Windows, and explain the interaction between Windows and the dBASE cache.

INSTALLING THE DBASE GROUP WINDOW AND ICONS

NOTE

The three dBASE IV icons are stored in the dBASE directory (for example, C:\dBASE) and are named DBASEIV.ICO, DBSETUP.ICO, and DBINFO.ICO. The corresponding PIF files are DBASEIV.PIF, DBSETUP.PIF, and DBINFO.PIF. (A PIF is a special file containing settings that tell Windows how to run a non-Windows application.)

NOTE

Do not use the Windows Setup application from the Main group window to install the dBASE IV icons. Instead, use the method described here, which takes advantage of the Borland authorized .PIF files and icons, rather than the original Windows dBASE IV .PIF files and icons.

The dBASE IV Install program checks for a directory in your PATH statement that contains the word WINDOWS. If it finds that directory, the program automatically adds a dBASE IV group window containing three icons: dBASE IV (the dBASE IV program), dBSETUP (the dBASE setup program described in Appendix B), and dBINFO (a handy utility that provides information about your system configuration). In this case, you'll only need to open the dBASE IV group window (if it's not already open) by double-clicking its icon, and then double-click the dBASE IV application icon to start the program. Most likely, dBASE IV will take over the entire screen until you exit. When you exit dBASE, you'll actually be returned to Windows instead of DOS.

If Windows is installed in a directory that doesn't have WINDOWS as part of its name (for example, WIN386), or if you install Windows after installing dBASE IV, you'll need to carefully edit the Program Manager initialization file named PROGMAN.INI. This file is located in the same directory as Windows (for example, C:\WINDOWS\PROGMAN.INI). To make the changes, exit Windows if you're currently using it, then edit PROGMAN.INI with any ASCII (text-only) editor such as the DOS EDIT or EDLIN command, or the dBASE editor.

For example, to use the dBASE editor for this job, start dBASE from the DOS prompt in the usual way, then choose Exit ► Exit to Dot Prompt from the Control Center menu. Type the command **MODIFY FILE C:\WINDOWS\PROGMAN.INI** and press ↵ (assuming PROGMAN.INI is in the \WINDOWS subdirectory on drive C).

Regardless of which editor you use, add a line to the end of PROGMAN.INI as follows:

```
Group<n>=<dBASE directory>\DBASEIV.GRP
```

Replace <n> with the next available group number, and replace <dBASE directory> with the name of your dBASE IV directory. For example, assuming Group8 is the highest group number in your PROGMAN.INI file at the moment, you could add the following line to the end of the file to set up the dBASE IV group window and icons:

```
Group9 = C:\DBASE\DBASEIV.GRP
```

After making your changes, save PROGMAN.INI as an unformatted ASCII file, exit the editor, then start Windows (typically by entering the command **WIN** at the DOS prompt).

At this point, you should see the dBASE IV group icon or opened group window. If the group window isn't open, double-click its icon. Then open dBASE itself by double-clicking the dBASE IV icon inside the group window.

DBASE CACHING AND WINDOWS

You should be aware that the DBCACHE program is incompatible with Windows' XMS (SMARTDRIVE) memory manager. You'll still be able to run dBASE, even if you installed it with the caching on (as described in Appendix B). However, you may see an error message indicating that HyperDisk has not been installed. dBASE will still work fine, but may be a little slower without its own cache.

If you start dBASE IV from within Windows, the XMS memory management system will be active, and therefore the dBASE caching system will not be installed. However, if you've previously installed dBASE caching and exit Windows before starting dBASE IV, dBASE caching may be activated automatically when you start dBASE IV from the DOS command prompt.

If you want to see whether or not caching is in use during a dBASE session, and how much memory is dedicated to it, go to the dBASE dot prompt, type **!DBCACHE**, and press ↵. You'll get the complete lowdown on the current status of dBASE caching on your screen, or the message *HyperDisk is not installed* if dBASE caching is not installed at the moment.

APPENDIX

E

dBASE IV Functions

THIS APPENDIX CATEGORIZES AND SUMMARIZES ALL dBASE IV functions. Functions can be used in any dBASE IV expression and with any command. Each function must use the appropriate syntax and operate on the appropriate data type.

For the syntax, data type, and further information about a particular function, type the command **HELP <function name>**, where <function name> is the function for which you want help. For example, typing **HELP PAYMENT( )** displays helpful information about the PAYMENT function.

Chapter 12 presents practical examples of using functions to sort, group, and manipulate data. For additional information, refer to the language reference manual that came with your dBASE IV package or to a dBASE IV programmer's reference guide.

DATE FUNCTIONS

The date functions operate upon the Data data type and return numeric, date, or character results.

CDOW( )	Returns the day for the week as a character string (for example, Monday).
CMONTH( )	Returns the month as a character string (for example, April).
DATE( )	Returns the current system date.
DAY( )	Returns the day of the month as a number.
DMY( )	Returns a date converted to date, month, year format (for example, 31 December 93).
DOW( )	Returns the day of the week as a number.
DTOS( )	Converts a date to a character string in the format "19931231".
MDY( )	Returns a date converted to month, date, year format (for example, December 31, 92).
MONTH( )	Returns the month as a number (1 to 12).
TIME( )	Returns the current system time.
YEAR( )	Returns the year of a date.

STRING FUNCTIONS

The string functions allow you to manipulate data stored as the Character data type. The term *string* refers to any Character data. For example, "XYZ" is a string of 3 characters, and "Hello there" is a string of 11 characters (spaces always count as characters).

Many functions manipulate *substrings*. A substring is any string embedded in a larger string. For example, the letters "ABC" are a substring of the sentence "Now I know my ABC's..." because ABC appears in the larger sentence.

&	Indicates macro substitution.
ASC( )	Returns the numeric ASCII code for a character.
AT( )	Returns the position of a substring within a string.
CHR( )	Returns the ASCII character for a number.
DIFFERENCE( )	Returns the difference between two SOUNDEX codes.
FOR( )	Returns the FOR condition, if any, of an index tag.
LEFT( )	Returns a substring of the leftmost characters.
LEN( )	Returns the length of a character string.
LOWER( )	Returns the lowercase equivalent of string.
LTRIM( )	Trims leading blanks.
REPLICATE( )	Repeats a character string.
RIGHT( )	Returns a substring of the rightmost characters.
RTRIM( )	Removes trailing blanks.
SOUNDEX( )	Returns the SOUNDEX code of a character string.
SPACE( )	Generates blank spaces.

STUFF( )	Replaces or inserts a substring in a character string.
SUBSTR( )	Returns a substring from a larger character string.
TAG( )	Returns the tag name of an index.
TRANSFORM( )	Displays data in a predefined format.
TRIM( )	Removes leading and trailing blanks.
UPPER( )	Returns the uppercase equivalent of a string.

MEMO FIELD FUNCTIONS

The Memo field functions return information about Memo fields.

MEMLINES( )	Returns the number of lines required to print a Memo field.
MLINE( )	Returns a specified line from a Memo field.

NUMERIC FUNCTIONS

The numeric functions return the results of calculations on Numeric and Float data types.

ABS( )	Returns the absolute (positive) value.
CEILING( )	Returns the smallest integer that is greater than or equal to the specified number.
EXP( )	Returns the exponential (value of e^x).
FLOOR( )	Returns the largest integer that is less than or equal to the specified number.
INT( )	Returns the integer value with any decimal value truncated.

LOG( )	Returns the natural logarithm.
LOG10( )	Returns the common log to the base 10.
MAX( )	Returns the larger of two numbers.
MIN( )	Returns the smaller of two numbers.
MOD( )	Returns the modulus (remainder) of dividing two numbers.
PI( )	Returns π (approximately 3.14159265).
RAND( )	Returns a random number between 0 and 1.
ROUND( )	Rounds a number to the specified decimal place.
SIGN( )	Returns 1 for a positive number, – 1 for a negative number, and 0 for zero.
SQRT( )	Returns the square root of the specified number.

FINANCIAL FUNCTIONS

The financial functions perform common financial calculations. When using the financial functions PAYMENT( ), FV( ), and PV( ), you must make sure that all parameters refer to the same time period. For example, if you want to determine the *monthly* payment on a loan given the *annual* percentage rate and a term expressed in *years*, then you must divide the annual interest rate by 12 to obtain the monthly rate and multiply the term of the loan by 12 to determine the number of months.

For example, suppose you want to calculate the *monthly* payment on a loan given an *annual* interest rate of 6.75 percent and a term of 30 *years*. First you need to convert the percentage rate, 6.75 percent, to the decimal value 0.0675 by dividing by 100. Then you need to divide the resulting annual decimal rate by 12 to obtain the monthly percentage rate. Finally, you need to convert the *years* for the loan to months by multiplying by 12.

You can perform all of the appropriate conversions directly in the expression used to calculate the payment. If the loan principal is stored in a field or variable named PRINCIPAL, the annual interest is stored in a field or variable named APR, and the term is stored in a field or variable named YEARS, then the expression to calculate the monthly payment is PAYMENT(Principal,APR/1200,YEARS*12).

FV( )	Returns the future value of equal, regular deposits into an investment.
NPV( )	Returns the net present value of a series of future cash flows (used only with the CALCULATE command).
PAYMENT( )	Returns the periodic payment on a loan.
PV( )	Returns the present value of equal, regular deposits into an investment.

TRIGONOMETRIC FUNCTIONS

The trigonometric functions assume that their arguments are expressed in radians. You can use the DTOR( ) function to convert degrees to radians. For example, COS(DTOR(45)) returns the cosine, in radians, of a 45-degree angle. The RTOD( ) function converts radians to degrees. The expression RTOD(COS(DTOR(45))) returns the cosine, in degrees, of a 45-degree angle.

ACOS( )	Returns the arccosine, in radians, of a cosine expressed in radians.
ASIN( )	Returns the arcsine, in radians, of a sine expressed in radians.
ATAN( )	Returns the arctangent, in radians, of any tangent.
ATN2( )	Returns the two-quadrant arctangent of a sine.
COS( )	Returns the cosine, expressed in radians, of an angle expressed in radians.
DTOR( )	Converts degrees to radians.
RTOD( )	Converts radians to degrees.
SIN( )	Returns the sine, in radians, of an angle expressed in radians.
TAN( )	Returns the trigonometric tangent of an angle expressed in radians.

DATA TYPE CONVERSION FUNCTIONS

The functions described in this section all convert values from one data type to another.

CTOD( )	Converts Character data to Date data.
DTOC( )	Converts Date data to Character data in MM/DD/YY format.
DTOS( )	Converts Date data to Character data in YYYYMMDD format.
FIXED( )	Converts Float data to Numeric data.
FLOAT( )	Converts Numeric data to Float data.
STR( )	Converts Numeric data to Character data.
VAL( )	Converts Character data to Numeric data.

KEYPRESS FUNCTIONS

The keypress functions return information regarding the most recent keypress.

INKEY( )	Returns the numeric code of keypress without interrupting program execution.
LASTKEY( )	Returns the ASCII numeric value of the most recent keypress.
READKEY( )	Returns the ASCII code used to exit a full-screen editing session.

MENU FUNCTIONS

The menu functions return information about horizontal bar, pop-up, and pull-down menus used in applications.

BAR( )	Returns the number of the last-selected option from a pop-up or pull-down menu.

MENU( )	Returns the name of the currently active menu.
PAD( )	Returns the name of the currently selected horizontal bar menu option.
POPUP( )	Returns the name of the currently active pop-up menu.
PROMPT( )	Returns the prompt of the most recently selected menu option.

IDENTIFICATION AND TESTING FUNCTIONS

The identification and testing functions return information about the current environment.

ALIAS( )	Returns the alias assigned to a work area.
BOF( )	Returns .T. when the record pointer is at the beginning of a database file.
CATALOG( )	Returns the name of the active catalog file or the null string, if there is no active catalog.
CERROR( )	Returns the number associated with the last error during compilation.
COL( )	Returns the current column position of the cursor on the screen.
COMPLETED( )	Returns .T. if a transaction has been completed.
DBF( )	Returns the name of the database file currently in use.
DELETED( )	Returns .T. if the current record is marked for deletion.
DESCENDING( )	Returns .T. for a descending index tag number and .F. for an ascending index tag number.

DGEN( )	Runs the Template Language interpreter and generates template programs from screen, report, label, and menu design objects.
DISKSPACE( )	Returns the amount of available disk space in bytes.
EOF( )	Returns .T. when the record pointer is past the last record in a database file.
ERROR( )	Returns the number generated by an ON ERROR command.
FDATE( )	Returns the date a specified file was last modified.
FSIZE( )	Returns the size of a specified file, in bytes.
FTIME( )	Returns the time a specified file was last modified.
FIELD( )	Returns the name of a field in database file.
FILE( )	Returns .T. if the specified file exists.
FKLABEL( )	Returns the name of a function key.
FKMAX( )	Returns the number of function keys on the keyboard.
FLDCOUNT( )	Returns the number of fields in the specified database file, or 0 if no file is active.
FOR( )	Returns the FOR condition, if any, used for an index tag number.
FOUND( )	Returns .T. if the record being searched for was found.
GETENV( )	Returns information about the operating system environment.
HOME( )	Returns the path from which the current dBASE session was invoked.

IIF( )	Immediate IF, embedded inside command lines or report columns; selects one of two alternatives.
ISALPHA( )	Returns .T. if the first character is a letter.
ISBLANK( )	Returns .T. if the expression is blank, or .F. otherwise.
ISCOLOR( )	Returns .T. if a color monitor is in use.
ISLOWER( )	Returns .T. if the first character is a lowercase letter.
ISMARKED( )	Returns .T. if a database is in a state of change.
ISUPPER( )	Returns .T. if the first character is an uppercase letter.
KEY( )	Returns the index expression associated with an index file or tag.
LIKE( )	Compares a value to a wildcard string and returns .T. if they match.
LINENO( )	Returns the line number of the next command to be executed in a command file.
LUPDATE( )	Returns the date of most recent change to a database file.
MDX( )	Returns the name of the currently open production index file.
MEMORY( )	Returns the amount of available RAM in kilobytes.
MESSAGE( )	Returns the error message that triggered an ON ERROR condition.
NDX( )	Returns the name of the active index (.NDX) file.
ORDER( )	Returns the name of the index currently controlling the sort order.

OS( )	Returns the name of the operating system in use.
PCOL( )	Returns the current printer column position.
PCOUNT( )	Returns the number of parameters passed to a procedure or user-defined function.
PRINTSTATUS( )	Returns .T. if the printer is ready to accept data.
PROGRAM( )	Returns the name of the program or procedure in which an error occurred.
PROW( )	Returns the current printer row position.
RECCOUNT( )	Returns the number of rccords in a database file.
RECNO( )	Returns the number (position) of the current record.
RECSIZE( )	Returns the size of each record in a database file.
ROLLBACK( )	Returns .T. if the most recent transaction rollback was successful.
ROW( )	Returns the current row position of the cursor on the screen.
RUN( )	Sends a command to DOS and returns a code between 0 and 255.
SELECT( )	Returns the number of the highest unused work area (between 0 and 40).
SET( )	Returns the current status of a SET command.
TAGCOUNT( )	Returns the number of active tags in a specified .MDX file or work area.
TAGNO( )	Returns the index number of an index.
TYPE( )	Returns the data type of current field or variable.

UNIQUE( )	Returns .T. if the specified index tag number is unique, or .F. otherwise.
VARREAD( )	Returns the name of the highlighted field or memory variable being edited.
VERSION( )	Returns the version number of the dBASE program in use.
WINDOW( )	Returns the name of the currently active window.

FUNCTIONS THAT MIMIC COMMANDS

The following functions operate similarly to the CALL, SEEK, and LOCATE commands:

CALL( )	Executes a loaded binary program.
LOOKUP( )	Searches any field for a value and returns .T. if the value is located.
SEEK( )	Searches an index for a value and returns .T. if the value is located.

NETWORK FUNCTIONS

The network functions can be used when developing applications that run on a network. (Note that the Applications Generator always develops applications that are ready for use on either a single-user system or a network.)

ACCESS( )	Returns the level of access for the last logged-in user.
CHANGE( )	Returns .T. if a value has been changed by a network user.
FLOCK( )	Locks a database file.

ID( )	Returns the name of the current user on a multiuser system, or a null string if no user name is registered.
LKSYS( )	Returns the time, date, and user name of a locked file.
LOCK( )	Locks a database record.
NETWORK( )	Returns .T. if dBASE is currently installed on a network.
RLOCK( )	Same as LOCK.
USER( )	Returns the log-in name of a network user.

LOW-LEVEL FILE I/O

The low-level file input/output (I/O) functions provide full access to sequential file operations.

FCLOSE( )	Closes a low-level file, returning .T. if successful and .F. if unsuccessful.
FCREATE( )	Creates and opens a low-level file, returning a file handle if successful or a null string if unsuccessful.
FEOF( )	Returns .T. if the file pointer is at the end of the file, or .F. otherwise.
FERROR( )	Returns the operating system error number of the last low-level file I/O operation, or 0 if the operation was successful, never executed, or intercepted by dBASE.
FFLUSH( )	Writes the contents of the buffer to a disk file, returning .T. if successful and .F. otherwise.
FGETS( )	Reads and returns the specified number of characters from a low-level file (does not include end-of-line indicators).
FOPEN( )	Opens an existing low-level file and returns its file handle number.

FPUTS( )	Writes a string of characters to a low-level file and inserts an end-of-line indicator.
FREAD( )	Reads and returns the specified number of characters, including end-of-line indicators, from a low-level file.
FSEEK( )	Moves the file pointer in an open low-level file a specified number of bytes, returning the final location of the file pointer relative to the beginning of the file.
FWRITE( )	Writes a string of characters to a low-level file without adding end-of-line indicators.

APPENDIX F

dBASE IV Commands

THIS APPENDIX CATEGORIZES AND SUMMARIZES ALL dBASE IV commands. Remember that you need be concerned with these commands only if you want to go beyond the capabilities of the Control Center and Applications Generator to develop highly sophisticated custom programs and applications.

You can use any of the commands in a command file or as Applications Generator embedded codes. You can also enter most commands directly at the dot prompt (exceptions are programming clause commands such as DO WHILE...ENDDO, DO CASE...ENDCASE, IF...ENDIF, SCAN...ENDSCAN, and TEXT...ENDTEXT).

Each command must be entered on a single line and must use proper syntax. For the exact syntax of a command, refer to the dBASE IV language reference manual that came with your dBASE IV package or type the command **HELP** followed by the command at the dot prompt. For example, to get help regarding the BROWSE command, you type **HELP BROWSE** at the dot prompt and press ↵.

Chapter 17 provides additional information about entering commands, creating command files, and interpreting syntax charts, and the sample application in Chapter 21 demonstrates Applications Generator embedded codes. However, an in-depth discussion of all programming commands and techniques is beyond the scope of this book.

COMMANDS TO CREATE AND USE DATABASE FILES

CLOSE DATABASES	Closes all open database files, saving their contents to disk.
CREATE	Enters the database design screen to create a new database file.
SELECT	Specifies a work area, from A to J or 1 to 40, in which to open a database file. Also used to switch among currently open database files.

SET RELATION	Defines the relationship between two or more open database files based on a common field, which must be indexed in the nonselected database file.
USE	Opens a database file for use.

COMMANDS TO ENTER AND EDIT DATABASE DATA

APPEND	Adds new records to the bottom of the current database through the edit or browse screen. If a custom form has been activated through the SET FORMAT command, that form is used instead of the edit screen.
APPEND BLANK	Adds a new blank record to the end of a database file.
APPEND FROM	Copies records from a separate or foreign database file or an array to the currently open database file.
BEGIN TRANSACTION	Records changes to a database file, permitting ROLLBACK to undo those changes.
BLANK	Fills fields and records according to the data type of the specified field.
BROWSE	Enters the browse screen for entering or editing database data.
CHANGE	Same as EDIT.
DELETE	Marks records for deletion.
EDIT	Allows data in the currently open database to be edited, using either the default edit screen or a custom form opened with the SET FORMAT command.

END TRANSACTION	Marks the bottom of a BEGIN TRANSACTION block and commits any changes to the database.
INSERT	Inserts a new record into a database.
PACK	Permanently removes from a database records that have been marked for deletion with the DELETE, CHANGE, EDIT, or BROWSE command.
RECALL	Reclaims records that have been marked for deletion.
REPLACE	Replaces the data in a database field with a new value.
RESET	Removes the integrity tag from a database involved in a transaction begun by a BEGIN TRANSACTION command. This is sometimes necessary when you do not want to ROLLBACK a database file, or when a successful ROLLBACK isn't possible. Use only at the dot prompt, not in an application program.
ROLLBACK	Undoes all changes to a database file since the last BEGIN TRANSACTION command.
ZAP	Erases all records from a database file, but leaves the structure intact.

COMMANDS TO SORT AND INDEX

COPY TAG	Converts production indexes to individual index (.NDX) files.
DELETE TAG	Removes an index from a production (.MDX) index file.

INDEX	Creates an index if TAG is specified or an index file with the .NDX extension if TO is specified.
REINDEX	Rebuilds all indexes in the current production index file.
SET ORDER	Selects an index from the production index file to determine the sort order and the field that can be used for SEEK and FIND searches.
SORT	Creates a new, sorted database file from the currently open database file.
USE...ORDER	Through the ORDER option, specifies a controlling index for the database being opened.

COMMANDS TO LOCATE A RECORD

CONTINUE	Used in conjunction with the LOCATE command to find the next record matching the search criterion.
FIND	Locates a value in the controlling index file.
GO or GOTO	Moves the record to a specific record according to its record number or position (that is, TOP or BOTTOM, or a specified record number).
LOCATE	Positions the record pointer at the first record in the database that matches a search criterion.
SEEK	Locates a value in the current index (the one controlling the sort order).
SKIP	Moves the record pointer forward or backward relative to its current position.

COMMANDS TO DISPLAY DATA

@...SAY	Specifies a row and column position on the screen or printer and displays data.
@...TO	Draws a line or box.
?	Prints information starting on a new line or prints a blank line when used alone.
??	Prints information at the current cursor or printer position.
???	Sends special characters to the printer without changing the printing position.
DISPLAY	Displays the contents of a database record or of several records.
LABEL FORM	Prints mailing labels in the format specified by the CREATE LABEL command.
LIST	Displays database records.
REPORT FORM	Prints a report with the format specified by the CREATE REPORT command.

COMMANDS TO CALCULATE DATA

AVERAGE	Calculates and displays the average of a numeric field in a database.
CALCULATE	Calculates the sum, average, count, highest value, lowest value, net present value, standard deviation, or variance using numeric fields.
COUNT	Counts the number of records in a database that meet some criterion.
REPLACE	Replaces the contents of specified database records with a new value.

SUM	Calculates and displays the sum of a numeric field in a database.
TOTAL	Creates a summary of an existing file containing totals of specified numeric fields.
UPDATE	Changes the values of fields in one database based upon the fields in a separate, related database.

COMMANDS TO COPY AND MOVE DATABASE DATA

APPEND FROM	Adds records from a separate or foreign database file to the end of the currently open database file.
COPY	Copies the currently open database to another database or to a foreign file format.
JOIN	Combines the fields from two related databases into a new database.

COMMANDS TO MANAGE MEMO FIELDS

APPEND MEMO	Copies external data to a Memo field.
COPY MEMO	Copies a Memo field to another file.
SET WINDOW OF MEMO	Uses a defined window for editing a Memo field during browse and edit operations.

COMMANDS TO CREATE NEW OBJECTS

COPY STRUCTURE	Copies a database structure to a new database file.
COPY STRUCTURE EXTENDED	Creates a new database file that has the same field names, data types, field widths, number of decimal places (numeric fields), and index flags as the currently active database file. Primarily used with CREATE FROM in application programs to bypass interactive processes for creating or modifying a database structure.
CREATE	Enters the database design screen to create a new database file.
CREATE APPLICATION	Enters the Applications Generator to create a new application.
CREATE FROM	Creates and activates a new database file using the structure of a file previously created with the COPY STRUCTURE EXTENDED command.
CREATE LABEL	Calls up the labels design screen to create a new label format for the currently open database.
CREATE QUERY	Calls up the queries design screen to create a new query for the currently open database.
CREATE REPORT	Calls up the reports design screen to create a new report format for the currently open database.
CREATE SCREEN	Calls up the forms design screen to create a new custom form for the currently open database.

CREATE VIEW FROM ENVIRONMENT	For compatibility purposes, creates a dBASE III PLUS view (.VUE) file from the currently selected database files and relationships. CREATE VIEW is the same as CREATE QUERY if used without FROM ENVIRONMENT.
MODIFY COMMAND	Creates or modifies a command file (or program) with the file extension .PRG.

COMMANDS TO MODIFY EXISTING OBJECTS

MODIFY APPLICATION	Enters the Applications Generator to modify an existing application.
MODIFY COMMAND	Enters the editor to create or modify a command file or procedure file.
MODIFY LABEL	Enters the labels design screen to modify a label format.
MODIFY QUERY	Enters the query design screen to modify an existing query.
MODIFY REPORT	Enters the reports design screen to modify an existing report format.
MODIFY SCREEN	Enters the forms design screen to modify an existing custom form.
MODIFY STRUCTURE	Enters the database design screen to modify the current database file.

COMMANDS TO MANAGE DISK FILES

COPY FILE	Copies any file to another file name, drive, or directory.

DELETE FILE	Erases a disk file.
ERASE	Erases a file from the directory (same as DELETE FILE).
RENAME	Changes the name of any file.
SET ALTERNATE	Activates the screen-capture file defined by the SET ALTERNATE TO command.
SET ALTERNATE TO	Creates a file to capture all screen activity.

COMMANDS TO MANAGE KEYSTROKE MACROS

KEYBOARD	Stores keystrokes in the buffer as though they had been typed.
PLAY MACRO	Executes a keystroke macro.
RESTORE MACROS	Copies recorded keystroke macros from a disk file into memory.
SAVE MACROS	Saves recorded keystroke macros to a disk file.

COMMANDS TO IMPORT OR EXPORT DATA

APPEND FROM	Appends data from foreign software to the currently open database file.
COPY	Copies data from the currently open database file to a foreign file format.
COPY INDEXES	Copies dBASE III PLUS .NDX index files to dBASE IV production (.MDX) index files.

DEXPORT	Creates a binary named list (BNL) file from a screen, report, or label design file. This command is used in Template Language programming.
EXPORT	Exports dBASE data to a new foreign file.
IMPORT	Imports data from a foreign file format to a new dBASE IV database file.

COMMANDS TO GET ASSISTANCE

ASSIST	Switches from the interactive dot-prompt mode to the Control Center.
DIR	Displays the names of files in a directory.
DISPLAY/LIST FILES	Displays information about files in a directory and, optionally, sends the output to a printer or a file.
DISPLAY/LIST STATUS	Displays information about the database files currently in use and other dBASE environmental parameters.
DISPLAY/LIST STRUCTURE	Displays the structure of the currently open database file.
HELP	Provides on-line assistance for specific dBASE commands as well as other information.
TYPE	Displays the contents of an ASCII text file.

COMMANDS TO CREATE AND CONTROL COMMAND FILES

CANCEL	Terminates command-file processing and returns control to the dot prompt.

CASE	Begins an option within a DO CASE clause (must be placed between DO CASE and ENDCASE commands).
COMPILE	Converts a command (.PRG) file to an executable object-code (.DBO) file.
DO	Executes a command file or procedure.
DO CASE	Begins a block of several mutually exclusive routines (must be terminated with an ENDCASE command).
DO WHILE	Begins a loop in a command file (must be terminated with an ENDDO command).
ELSE	Used within an IF clause as the alternate path when the IF expression is false (must be enclosed between IF and ENDIF commands).
ENDCASE	Marks the end of a DO CASE clause.
ENDDO	Marks the end of a DO WHILE loop.
ENDIF	Marks the end of an IF clause.
ENDSCAN	Marks the end of a SCAN...ENDSCAN loop.
ENDTEXT	Marks the end of a TEXT block.
EXIT	Passes control outside of a loop.
IF	Makes a decision based on a single expression (must be terminated with an ENDIF command).
LOOP	Passes control to the beginning of a DO WHILE loop.
ON ERROR	Executes a specified command when an error occurs.
ON ESCAPE	Executes a specified command when the Esc key is pressed (SET ESCAPE parameter must be on).
ON KEY	Executes a specified command when the user presses any key.

ON PAGE	Executes a specified command when dBASE has printed a specified line number. Typically used to handle page breaks with headers and footers while printing reports.
ON READERROR	Executes a specified command when the user enters an invalid date, or when RANGE or VALID criteria aren't met. Specifying ON READERROR without a command prevents a program from trapping errors.
OTHERWISE	Used as an alternative path in a DO CASE clause when no CASE statement evaluates to true (must be enclosed between DO CASE and ENDCASE commands).
QUIT	Terminates command file processing, closes all open files, and leaves dBASE IV.
RETURN TO MASTER	Returns control to the first calling program in a series of DO commands.
SCAN	Marks the beginning of a loop to process database records.
TEXT	Begins a block of text in the command file to be displayed on the screen or printer.

COMMANDS FOR PROCEDURES AND USER-DEFINED FUNCTIONS

CLOSE PROCEDURE	Closes a procedure file.
DO...WITH	Calls a command file or procedure and passes parameters to it.
FUNCTION	Marks the beginning and defines the name of a user-defined function.
PARAMETERS	Specifies internal names for values passed to a procedure, user-defined function, or command file.

PROCEDURE	Marks the beginning of and assigns a name to a procedure.
RETURN	Marks the end of a procedure or user-defined function, passes control back to a calling command file or procedure, and resumes processing at the next line.
SET LIBRARY	Opens a library file containing procedures and user-defined functions. If a SET PROCEDURE command already opened a procedure file, dBASE will search the procedure file before searching the library file for procedures and functions.
SET PROCEDURE	Opens a procedure file.

COMMANDS TO ADD COMMENTS TO COMMAND FILES

*	Specifies a programmer comment when used as the first character in a line.
&&	Specifies a programmer comment to the right of a command line in a program.
NOTE	Marks a programmer comment in a command file (same as *).

COMMANDS TO MANAGE MEMORY VARIABLES AND ARRAYS

APPEND FROM ARRAY	Copies data from an array to a database file.
CLEAR ALL	Closes all open database files and removes all windows, menus, and memory variables from memory.

CLEAR MEMORY	Erases all current memory variables.
COPY TO ARRAY	Fills an existing array structure with records from the active database file.
DECLARE	Defines the name and dimensions of an array.
DISPLAY MEMORY	Displays the names, data types, and contents of all currently active memory variables and arrays.
PRIVATE	Specifies that a memory variable is local to a given command file or procedure.
PUBLIC	Makes a memory variable global to all levels of command files and procedures.
RELEASE	Erases memory variables.
REPLACE FROM ARRAY	Updates one or more records with the contents of an array.
RESTORE	Brings memory variables that have been stored on disk in a memory (.MEM) file back into memory.
SAVE	Saves memory variables and arrays in a memory (.MEM) file on disk.
STORE	Creates a memory variable and assigns a value to it.

COMMANDS FOR INTERFACING WITH USERS

@...SAY...GET	Displays a message and the current contents of a field or memory variable for editing.
ACCEPT	Stores user input in a Character memory variable.
INPUT	Waits for user entry and stores input in a Numeric memory variable.

READ	Allows data to be entered via the @...SAY...GET command.
WAIT	Waits for the user to press a single key and optionally stores that keypress in a Character memory variable.

COMMANDS TO CONTROL THE SCREEN AND WINDOWS

@...CLEAR	Clears an isolated portion of the screen.
@...FILL	Colors an isolated portion of the screen.
@...SCROLL	Shifts the contents of an isolated portion of the screen up, down, left, or right by a specified amount.
ACTIVATE SCREEN	Sends all output to the entire screen, covering but not removing active windows.
ACTIVATE WINDOW	Activates and displays an existing window.
CLEAR	Clears any windows, menus, custom forms, or pending GETs on the screen.
DEACTIVATE WINDOW	Removes a window from the screen, but leaves its definition intact for future use.
DEFINE BOX	Defines the border and location of a box.
DEFINE WINDOW	Defines the name, border type, and screen position of a window.
MOVE WINDOW	Moves a window to a new screen location.
READ	Allows data to be entered through a custom form if one has been activated by SET FORMAT.

RELEASE SCREENS	Removes saved screen images from memory.
RELEASE WINDOWS	Erases windows from the screen and removes them from memory.
RESTORE SCREEN	Redisplays a screen that was previously saved by a SAVE SCREEN command.
RESTORE WINDOW	Restores windows from a .WIN file that was previously saved by a SAVE WINDOW command.
SAVE SCREEN	Saves the current screen image in memory, which can be redisplayed with RESTORE SCREEN.
SAVE WINDOW	Saves a window definition to a disk file.
SET COLOR	Determines colors used on screen displays.
SET FORMAT TO	Determines the format file to be used with APPEND, EDIT, and READ commands.
SET WINDOW OF MEMO	Uses a defined window for editing a Memo field during browse and edit operations.

COMMANDS TO MANAGE MENUS

ACTIVATE MENU	Activates an existing horizontal bar menu.
ACTIVATE POPUP	Activates an existing pop-up menu.
DEACTIVATE MENU	Deactivates a bar menu and erases it from the screen.
DEACTIVATE POPUP	Deactivates a pop-up menu and removes it from the screen.
DEFINE BAR	Defines an option in a pop-up menu.

DEFINE MENU	Defines a horizontal bar menu.
DEFINE PAD	Defines an option in a horizontal bar menu.
DEFINE POPUP	Defines a pop-up menu.
ON PAD	Defines which pop-up menu is activated when the user positions the selection bar or clicks the mouse on the prompt pad (menu bar option) of the specified menu.
ON SELECTION	Assigns an action to a horizontal bar menu option (PAD) or pop-up menu option (POPUP), to be executed when the option is selected.
RELEASE MENUS	Removes defined horizontal bar menus from memory.
RELEASE POPUPS	Removes defined pop-up menus from memory.
SHOW MENU	Displays a horizontal bar menu without activating it.
SHOW POPUP	Displays a pop-up menu without activating it.

COMMANDS TO CONTROL THE PRINTER

EJECT	Ejects the page in the printer.
EJECT PAGE	Similar to the EJECT command, but can be sent to any device, such as a disk file or the screen.
ENDPRINTJOB	Marks the end of a print operation.
PRINTJOB	Marks the beginning of a print operation.
SET DEVICE	When DEVICE is set to PRINT, @...SAY, output is directed to the printer rather than to the screen.

SET PRINTER	Sets printing on or off for commands that display data.

COMMANDS TO INTERFACE WITH EXTERNAL PROGRAMS

CALL	Runs an assembly language (binary) subroutine that has already been loaded into memory.
LOAD	Copies an assembly language subroutine into memory.
RELEASE MODULE	Removes a loaded assembly language subroutine from memory.
RUN	Runs an external DOS program and automatically returns control to the dot prompt.
!	Same as RUN.

COMMANDS TO AID DEBUGGING

DEBUG	Activates the dBASE IV debugger.
DISPLAY HISTORY	Displays commands stored in the history file.
LIST HISTORY	Same as DISPLAY HISTORY, but does not pause each after each screenful of information.
RESUME	Resumes command-file processing after temporary suspension.
SET DEBUG	Sends the results of the SET ECHO command to the printer rather than the screen.
SET ECHO	Displays command lines from command files on the screen before executing them.

SET HISTORY	Specifies the number of lines to be recorded in the history file.
SET STEP	Pauses execution after every line in a command file.
SUSPEND	Temporarily suspends processing of a command file and returns control to the dot prompt.

COMMANDS TO CONTROL THE dBASE ENVIRONMENT

SET	Displays a menu for interactively changing dBASE environmental settings.
SET AUTOSAVE	Determines whether database changes are saved immediately.
SET BELL	Determines whether the bell sounds during data entry and editing.
SET BELL TO	Determines the pitch and duration of the bell tone.
SET BLOCKSIZE	Defines the block size for storing memory variables.
SET BORDER	Defines the border for menus and windows.
SET CARRY	Determines whether data from the previous record is carried over to the next record during data entry.
SET CARRY TO	Determines which fields are carried to new records when SET CARRY is on.
SET CATALOG	Determines whether new files are added to an active catalog.
SET CATALOG TO	Creates, opens, or closes a catalog file.

SET CENTURY	Determines whether the century appears in dates.
SET CLOCK	Determines whether the clock appears on the screen.
SET CLOCK TO	Determines the position of the clock on the screen.
SET COLOR	Automatically set at startup, depending on whether a monochrome or color monitor is in use.
SET COLOR TO	Determines colors (or shading) for the screen.
SET CONFIRM	Determines whether a carriage return is required after a data entry field is filled in.
SET CONSOLE	Turns the screen on or off.
SET CURRENCY	Determines whether currency symbols are displayed to the left or right of numbers.
SET CURRENCY TO	Defines the currency sign.
SET CURSOR	Lets you hide (OFF) or display (ON) the cursor.
SET DATE	Sets a format for displaying dates.
SET DBTRAP	Protects against errors caused during complex event processing.
SET DECIMALS	Determines the number of decimal places displayed in the results of mathematical calculations.
SET DEFAULT	Specifies the disk drive used to store and retrieve files.
SET DELETED	When set to ON, does not display records that are marked for deletion.
SET DELIMITERS	Determines whether delimiters appear around fields on screen displays.

SET DELIMITERS TO	Specifies the characters to use as delimiters around fields on screen displays.
SET DESIGN	Determines whether design screens can be accessed from the dot prompt or Control Center.
SET DEVELOPMENT	Turns automatic compilation and recompilation on or off.
SET DIRECTORY	Lets you define the current drive and directory from within dBASE IV.
SET DISPLAY	Sets the screen display mode to monochrome, color, EGA, or VGA.
SET DOHISTORY	Retained in dBASE IV for compatibility with dBASE III PLUS, but performs no action (the DEBUG command is used for debugging).
SET ECHO	Determines whether lines from command files are displayed on the screen before execution.
SET ESCAPE	Determines whether pressing the Esc key interrupts command file processing.
SET EXACT	Determines whether exact matches are required in character-string searches.
SET FIELDS	Activates or deactivates the most recent SET FIELDS command.
SET FIELDS TO	Determines which fields from a database or from multiple related databases are displayed and edited.
SET FILTER	Hides database records that do not match a specified search criterion.
SET FIXED	Retained in dBASE IV for compatibility with dBASE III PLUS, but performs no action (replaced by SET DECIMALS in dBASE IV).

SET FULLPATH	When on, mimics dBASE III PLUS by including the pathname in file names returned by functions such as DBF( ).
SET FUNCTION	Assigns tasks to function keys.
SET HEADINGS	Determines whether field names appear at the beginning of the output from LIST and DISPLAY commands.
SET HELP	Determines whether the "Do you want some help?" message appears on the screen after an error occurs.
SET HISTORY	Determines whether commands are recorded in the history file.
SET HISTORY TO	Determines the number of lines to be recorded in the history file.
SET HOURS	Determines whether the clock display uses 12-hour or 24-hour format.
SET KEY	Displays only those records whose ordering index key meets specified conditions. SET KEY has priority over SET FILTER.
SET INDEX	Opens index files for the database currently in use.
SET INSTRUCT	Determines whether Control Center prompt boxes appear on the screen.
SET INTENSITY	Determines whether enhanced display with reverse video is used for full-screen operations.
SET MARGIN	Adjusts the left margin setting on the printer.
SET MARK	Changes the separator used in dates.
SET MEMOWIDTH	Determines the display width of Memo fields.
SET MENU	Retained in dBASE IV to maintain compatibility with dBASE III PLUS, but performs no function (replaced by SET INSTRUCT).

SET MESSAGE	Displays a message centered at the bottom of the screen (if SET STATUS is on).
SET NEAR	Determines whether or not FIND, SEEK, and SEEK( ) go to the nearest record when an exact match can't be found.
SET ODOMETER	Determines the frequency of updating on the odometer displayed with COPY and other commands (when SET TALK is on).
SET ORDER	Determines which index in a production index file is used for the sort order and for SEEK searches.
SET PATH	Specifies a path of directories to search for files.
SET PAUSE	When on, the SQL SELECT command pauses for a key press like the DISPLAY ALL command.
SET POINT	Determines the character used as the decimal point in numeric values.
SET PRECISION	Determines the decimal accuracy used in fixed-point arithmetic.
SET PRINTER	Determines whether or not output is directed to the printer.
SET PRINTER TO	Directs printing to a specified device or file.
SET SAFETY	Determines whether the overwrite warnings appear on the screen.
SET SCOREBOARD	Determines whether dBASE messages appear in the status bar (or in row zero on the screen if SET STATUS is off).
SET SEPARATOR	Determines the character used to separate thousands in numeric displays.

SET SKIP	Determines the order in which multiple related database files are changed during update operations.
SET SPACE	When on, prints a blank space between fields displayed with ? and ?? commands.
SET SQL	When on, dBASE IV accepts SQL commands.
SET STATUS	Determines whether the status bar appears near the bottom of the screen.
SET STEP	Determines whether dBASE pauses before processing each line in a command file.
SET TALK	Determines whether the results of commands and calculations are displayed on the screen.
SET TITLE	Determines whether the SET CATALOG command prompts for file names as new files are added to the catalog.
SET TRAP	When on, the dBASE IV debugger is activated whenever an error occurs during program execution.
SET TYPEAHEAD	Specifies the number of keystrokes stored in the typeahead buffer.
SET UNIQUE	Determines whether only unique records are included in an index.
SET VIEW	Opens multiple database files and sets up their relationships based upon a previous CREATE QUERY or MODIFY QUERY command.

COMMANDS FOR NETWORKING

CONVERT	Adds a field to a database for multiuser lock detection.
DISPLAY/LIST STATUS	Displays information about the current status of dBASE IV in the network.
DISPLAY/LIST USERS	Displays the names of all currently logged dBASE network users.
LOGOUT	Logs a user out of the network, allowing a new user to log in.
PROTECT	Activates the dBASE IV file security system.
RETRY	Returns to a calling program and executes the same line.
SET ENCRYPTION	Determines whether protected files are encrypted when copied.
SET EXCLUSIVE	Sets a file open attribute to either exclusive or shared mode.
SET LOCK	Determines whether automatic record locking is activated.
SET PRINTER	Selects a printer on the network.
SET REFRESH	Determines the interval for checking multiuser database changes and updating user screens.
SET REPROCESS	Sets the number of times dBASE tries to access a network file or data lock before quitting.
UNLOCK	Removes record and file locks.

APPENDIX G

ASCII Chart

ASCII CHART

ASCII Value	Character	ASCII Value	Character
000	(null)	037	%
001	☺	038	&
002	☻	039	'
003	♥	040	(
004	♦	041	)
005	♣	042	*
006	♠	043	+
007	(beep)	044	,
008	◘	045	-
009	(tab)	046	.
010	(line feed)	047	/
011	(home)	048	0
012	(form feed)	049	1
013	(carriage return)	050	2
014	♫	051	3
015	☼	052	4
016	►	053	5
017	◄	054	6
018	↕	055	7
019	!!	056	8
020	¶	057	9
021	§	058	:
022	▬	059	;
023	↨	060	<
024	↑	061	=
025	↓	062	>
026	→	063	?
027	←	064	@
028	(cursor right)	065	A
029	(cursor left)	066	B
030	(cursor up)	067	C
031	(cursor down)	068	D
032	(space)	069	E
033	!	070	F
034	"	071	G
035	#	072	H
036	$	073	I

ASCII Value	Character	ASCII Value	Character
074	J	113	q
075	K	114	r
076	L	115	s
077	M	116	t
078	N	117	u
079	O	118	v
080	P	119	w
081	Q	120	x
082	R	121	y
083	S	122	z
084	T	123	{
085	U	124	¦
086	V	125	}
087	W	126	~
088	X	127	⌂
089	Y	128	Ç
090	Z	129	ü
091	[	130	é
092	\	131	â
093	]	132	ä
094	^	133	à
095	_	134	å
096	`	135	ç
097	a	136	ê
098	b	137	ë
099	c	138	è
100	d	139	ï
101	e	140	î
102	f	141	ì
103	g	142	Ä
104	h	143	Å
105	i	144	É
106	j	145	æ
107	k	146	Æ
108	l	147	ô
109	m	148	ö
110	n	149	ò
111	o	150	û
112	p	151	ù

ASCII Value	Character	ASCII Value	Character
152	ÿ	191	┐
153	Ö	192	└
154	Ü	193	┴
155	¢	194	┬
156	£	195	├
157	¥	196	─
158	Pt	197	┼
159	ƒ	198	╞
160	á	199	╟
161	í	200	╚
162	ó	201	╔
163	ú	202	╩
164	ñ	203	╦
165	Ñ	204	╠
166	ª	205	═
167	º	206	╬
168	¿	207	╧
169	⌐	208	╨
170	¬	209	╤
171	½	210	╥
172	¼	211	╙
173	¡	212	╘
174	«	213	╒
175	»	214	╓
176	░	215	╫
177	▒	216	╪
178	▓	217	┘
179	│	218	┌
180	┤	219	█
181	╡	220	▄
182	╢	221	▌
183	╖	222	▐
184	╕	223	▀
185	╣	224	α
186	║	225	β
187	╗	226	Γ
188	╝	227	π
189	╜	228	Σ
190	╛	229	σ

ASCII Value	Character	ASCII Value	Character
230	μ	243	≤
231	τ	244	⌠
232	Φ	245	⌡
233	θ	246	÷
234	Ω	247	≈
235	δ	248	°
236	∞	249	•
237	Ø	250	·
238	ϵ	251	√
239	∩	252	ⁿ
240	≡	253	²
241	±	254	■
242	≥	255	(blank 'FF')

APPENDIX

H

dBASE IV File Extensions

See Appendix A for a discussion of DOS file names.

The two- or three-character extension following the period in a file name tells dBASE a lot about the contents of that file and, to a great extent, determines how dBASE will process the file. For example, when you create a file, such as a database, an index, or a file to be exported to another program, dBASE IV automatically adds an extension that reflects the contents of that file. Likewise, when you open a database, dBASE IV automatically knows to open a file with the name you specified and a .DBF extension. This appendix summarizes all dBASE IV file name extensions that you're likely to encounter as you work with the program.

Extension	Meaning
.$$$	Temporary file where the action was not complete
.$AB	Temporary file; virtual memory
.ACC	Multiuser access control file
.APP	Applications design object file created by the Applications Generator
.BAK	Command, procedure, or database backup file
.BAR	Horizontal bar design object file created by the Applications Generator
.BCH	Batch process design object file created by the Applications Generator
.BIN	Binary file
.CAC	Cache file on install disks (renamed to .EXE)
.CAT	Catalog file
.CHT	Chart-master file
.COD	Template source file
.CPT	Encrypted memo file, which is used with a password information (.CRP) file
.CRP	Password information file, which is created with PROTECT
.CVT	Database file with a change detection field
.DB2	dBASE II file used for import and export
.DB	Configuration file used for dBASE IV startup settings

.DBF	dBASE IV database file
.DBK	Database backup file
.DBO	Command or procedure object file generated from .PRG or .PRS file
.DBT	Database memo field file
.DEF	Selector definition file
.DIF	Data Interchange Format or VisiCalc file used for import and export
.DOC	Documentation file created by the Applications Generator
.ERR	Error file created if forms generation fails
.EXE	Executable file
.FIL	Files list design object file created by the Applications Generator
.FMO	Compiled format file (from .FMT file)
.FMT	Generated format file (from .SCR file)
.FNL	Report binary name list file (Template Language)
.FR3	dBASE III report form file (renamed from .FRM file)
.FRG	Generated report form file (from .FRM file)
.FRM	Report form file
.FRO	Compiled report form file (from .FRG file)
.FW2, .FW3, .FW4	Framework spreadsheet or database file used for import and export
.GEN	Template file
.GRP	Windows group file for dBASE IV
.HLP	Help file for dBASE IV
.ICO	Windows icon file for dBASE IV
.KEY	Keyboard macro library file
.LB3	dBASE III label form file (renamed from .LBL file)
.LBG	Generated label form file (from .LBL file)
.LBL	Label form file

.LBO	Compiled label form file (from .LBG file)
.LNL	Label binary name list file (Template Language)
.LOG	Transaction log file
.MBK	Multiple index backup file
.MDX	Multiple index file
.MEM	Memory file
.NDX	Single index file
.OVL	dBASE IV overlay file
.PIF	Settings file for running dBASE IV under Windows 3
.POP	Pop-up menu design file created by the Applications Generator
.PR2	Printer driver file
.PRF	Print form file
.PRG	dBASE command or procedure file
.PRS	dBASE SQL command or procedure file
.PRT	Printer output file
.QBE	QBE query file
.QBO	Compiled QBE query file (from .QBE file)
.QRY	Query filter file
.RES	Resource file
.RPD	RapidFile file used for import and export
.SC3	dBASE III screen file (renamed from .SCR file)
.SCR	Screen file
.SNL	Screen binary name list file (Template Language)
.STR	Structure list design object file created by the Applications Generator
.T44, .W44	Intermediate work files used by SORT and INDEX
.TBK	Database memo backup file
.TXT	Text output file (ASCII format)
.UPD	QBE update query file

.UPO	Compiled QBE update query file (from .UPD file)
.VAL	Values list design object file created by the Applications Generator
.VUE	dBASE III PLUS view file
.WIN	Logical window save file
.WK1, .WKS	Lotus 1-2-3 files used for import and export

INDEX

A

B

C

D

E

F

G

H

J

K

L

M

N

O

P

Q

S

T

U

V

Selections from The SYBEX Library

DATABASES

The ABC's of dBASE III PLUS

Robert Cowart

264pp. Ref. 379-1

The most efficient way to get beginners up and running with dBASE. Every 'how' and 'why' of database management is demonstrated through tutorials and practical dBASE III PLUS applications.

The ABC's of dBASE IV 1.1

Robert Cowart

350pp, Ref. 632-4

The latest version of dBASE IV is featured in this hands-on introduction. It assumes no previous experience with computers or database management, and uses easy-to-follow lessons to introduce the concepts, build basic skills, and set up some practical applications. Includes report writing and Query by Example.

The ABC's of FoxPro 2 (Second Edition)

Scott D. Palmer

308pp; Ref. 877-7

This fast, friendly introduction to database management is now in a new edition for version 2. Concise tutorials show you how to use essential FoxPro features and commands, while hot tips give you special pointers for avoiding pitfalls. Covers everything from simple customer files to multi file databases.

The ABC's of Paradox 3.5 (Second Edition)

Charles Siegel

334pp, Ref. 785-1

This easy-to-follow, hands-on tutorial is a must for beginning users of Paradox 3.0 and 3.5. Even if you've never used a computer before, you'll be doing useful work in just a few short lessons. A clear introduction to database management and valuable business examples make this a "right-to-work" guide for the practical-minded.

The ABC's of Q & A 4

Trudi Reisner

232pp; Ref. 824-6

A popular introduction to Q & A 4, packed with step-by-step tutorials for beginners. Learn to create databases, use the word processor, print out reports, and more. Easy instructions incorporate practical business applications. With special coverage of the Intelligent Assistant.

Advanced Techniques in dBASE III PLUS

Alan Simpson

454pp. Ref. 369-4

A full course in database design and structured programming, with routines for inventory control, accounts receivable, system management, and integrated databases.

dBASE Instant Reference SYBEX Prompter Series

Alan Simpson

471pp. Ref. 484-4

Comprehensive information at a glance: a brief explanation of syntax and usage for every dBASE command, with step-by-step instructions and exact keystroke sequences. Commands are grouped by function in twenty precise categories.

dBASE III PLUS Programmer's Reference Guide SYBEX Ready Reference Series

Alan Simpson

1056pp. Ref. 508-5

Programmers will save untold hours and effort using this comprehensive, well-organized dBASE encyclopedia. Complete technical details on commands and functions, plus scores of often-needed algorithms.

dBASE IV 1.1 Programmer's Desktop Reference

Alan Simpson

1050pp. Ref. 539-5

This comprehensive seven-part reference is a must for dBASE programmers. It offers full details on every command and function, as well as practical techniques and algorithms for achieving specific programming goals. Fully cross-referenced and indexed by command, function, and topic.

dBASE IV 1.1 Programmer's Instant Reference (Second Edition)

Alan Simpson

555pp, Ref. 764-9

Enjoy fast, easy access to information often hidden in cumbersome documentation. This handy pocket-sized reference presents information on each command and function in the dBASE IV programming language. Commands are grouped according to their purpose, so readers can locate the correct command for any task—quickly and easily.

dBASE IV User's Instant Reference (Second Edition)

Alan Simpson

356pp, Ref. 786-X

Completely revised to cover the new 1.1 version of dBASE IV, this handy reference guide presents information on every dBASE operation a user can perform. Exact keystroke sequences are presented, and complex tasks are explained step-by-step. It's a great way for newer users to look up the basics, while more experienced users will find it a fast way to locate information on specialized tasks.

Mastering DataEase

Susan Harmon

531pp. Ref. 689-8

A thorough, hands-on introduction to database management with DataEase, stressing skills for on-the-job productivity. Build a sample inventory management system, while mastering quick reporting, custom form design, multi-file applications, using Data Query Language, and system maintenance.

Mastering dBASE III PLUS: A Structured Approach

Carl Townsend

342pp. Ref. 372-4

In-depth treatment of structured programming for custom dBASE solutions. An ideal study and reference guide for applications developers, new and experienced users with an interest in efficient programming.

Mastering dBASE IV 1.1 Programming

Carl Townsend

546pp. Ref. 782-9

An in-depth introduction especially for applications developers, and for experienced dBASE users seeking programming skills. This up-to-date new edition covers 1.1 basics, structured programming and database design, and specific techniques for business application programming—with examples for general ledger and invoicing.

Mastering FoxPro 2 (Second Edition)

Charles Siegel

650pp; Ref. 808-4

This highly readable hands-on guide now covers FoxPro version 2.0, with its graphical interface and other powerful new features. Part I is a practical introduction to business database management. Part II adds macros, custom menus, and other special features. Part III is a concise introduction to structured programming with FoxPro 2.0 development language.

Mastering Paradox 3.5

Alan Simpson

650pp, Ref. 677-4

This indispensable, in-depth guide has again been updated for the latest Paradox release, offering the same comprehensive, hands-on treatment featured in highly praised previous editions. It covers everything from database basics to PAL programming—including complex queries and reports, and multi-table applications.

Mastering Q&A 4

Alan R. Neibauer

500pp. Ref. 735-5

This hands-on guide is now covering the latest Q&A release. Tutorials and sample applications illustrate every aspect of using Q&A: treating and manipulating data bases, printing reports, multi-file applications and look-up tables, and integrating Q&A with Lotus 1-2-3; plus networking, macros, and programming the IA. Special sections for word processing and generating form letters and labels.

Paradox 3.5 User's Instant Reference

Loy Anderson
Cary Jensen

186pp. Ref. 766-5

Quick access to concise information on every feature of Paradox 3.0 and 3.5. Entries are organized by function, and provide exact keystrokes, command options, instructions for common tasks, and thorough cross-references. Topics include creating and working with tables; forms; reports; queries; crosstabs; graphs; tools; scripts and PAL; networking; and SQL.

Understanding dBASE III

Alan Simpson

300pp. Ref. 267-1

dBASE commands and concepts are illustrated throughout with practical, business oriented examples—for mailing list handling, accounts receivable, and inventory design. Contains scores of tips and techniques for maximizing efficiency and meeting special needs.

Understanding dBASE III PLUS

Alan Simpson

415pp. Ref. 349-X

A solid sourcebook of training and ongoing support. Everything from creating a first database to command file programming is presented in working examples, with tips and techniques you won't find anywhere else.

Understanding dBASE IV 1.1

Alan Simpson

900pp, Ref. 633-2

Simpson's outstanding introduction to dBASE—brought up to date for version 1.1—uses tutorials and practical examples to build effective, and increasingly sophisticated, database management skills. Advanced topics include custom reporting, managing multiple databases, and designing custom applications.

Understanding Oracle

James T. Perry
Joseph G. Lateer

634pp. Ref. 534-4

A comprehensive guide to the Oracle database management system for administrators, users, and applications developers. Covers everything in Version 5 from database basics to multi-user systems, performance, and development tools including SQL*Forms, SQL*Report, and SQL*Calc. Includes Fast Track speed notes.

Understanding Professional File

Gerry Litton

463pp. Re. 669-3

Build practical data management skills in an orderly fashion with this complete step-by-step tutorial—from creating a simple database to building customized business applications.

Understanding R:BASE 3.1

Alan Simpson
Ron Dragushan

656pp. Ref. 727-4

The definitive introduction to database management with R:BASE—now in an up-to-date new edition for release 3.1. Easy-to-follow tutorials for everything from designing a first table to editing data, searching, sorting, reporting, multi-table applications, macros, and programming. With a complete sample application for accounts receivable.

Understanding SQL

Martin Gruber

400pp. Ref. 644-8

This comprehensive tutorial in Structured Query Language (SQL) is suitable for beginners, and for SQL users wishing to increase their skills. From basic principles to complex SQL applications, the text builds fluency and confidence using concise hands-on lessons and easy-to-follow examples.

Up & Running with Clipper 5.01

Richard Frankel

158pp; Ref. 693-6

Start programming your own database applications in just 20 time-coded steps. No step takes longer than an hour to complete, and most take just 15 or 30 minutes. Learn to create and modify source code, customize reports, debug your programs, run database applications on local networks, and more. Covers versions 5.0 and 5.01.

Up & Running with dBASE III PLUS

Robert Cowart

140pp; Ref. 886-6

Now you can learn dBASE III PLUS in just 20 easy steps. This streamlined tutorial is designed for the reader who may be new to databases or to dBASE, but who does have fundamental computer skills. Each step covers an essential dBASE III PLUS function, and is designed to take less than an hour to complete; many take no more than 15 minutes.

Up & Running with Q&A 4

Alan Simpson

140pp. Ref. 719-3

A concise tutorial and software overview in 20 "steps" (lessons of 15 to 60 minutes each). Perfect for evaluating the software, or getting a basic grasp of its features. Learn to create databases, use the word processor, print out reports, and more. Includes coverage of the Intelligent Assistant.

UTILITIES

The Computer Virus Protection Handbook

Colin Haynes

192pp. Ref. 696-0

This book is the equivalent of an intensive emergency preparedness seminar on computer viruses. Readers learn what viruses are, how they are created, and how they infect systems. Step-by-step procedures help computer users to identify vulnerabilities, and to assess the consequences of a virus infection. Strategies on coping with viruses, as well as methods of data recovery, make this book well worth the investment.

Mastering the Norton Utilities 5

Peter Dyson

400pp, Ref. 725-8

This complete guide to installing and using the Norton Utilities 5 is a must for beginning and experienced users alike. It offers a clear, detailed description of each utility, with options, uses and examples—so users can quickly identify the programs they need and put Norton right to work. Includes valuable coverage of the newest Norton enhancements.

Mastering PC Tools Deluxe 6
For Versions 5.5 and 6.0

425pp, Ref. 700-2

An up-to-date guide to the lifesaving utilities in PC Tools Deluxe version 6.0 from installation, to high-speed back-ups, data recovery, file encryption, desktop applications, and more. Includes detailed background on DOS and hardware such as floppies, hard disks, modems and fax cards.

Norton Desktop for Windows Instant Reference

Sharon Crawford
Charlie Russell

200pp; Ref. 894-7

For anyone using Norton's version of the Windows desktop, here's a compact, fast-access guide to every feature of the package—from file management functions, to disaster prevention tools, configuration commands, batch language extensions, and more. Concise, quick-reference entries are alphabetized by topic, and include practical tips and examples.

Norton Utilities 5 Instant Reference

Michael Gross

162pp. Ref. 737-1

Organized alphabetically by program name, this pocket-sized reference offers complete information on each utility in the Norton 5 package—including a descriptive summary, exact syntax, command line options, brief explanation, and examples. Gives proficient users a quick reminder, and helps with unfamiliar options.

Norton Utilities 6 Instant Reference

Michael Gross

175pp; Ref. 865-3

This pocket-size guide to Norton Utilities 6 provides fast answers when and where they're needed. Reference entries are organized alphabetically by program name, and provide a descriptive summary, exact syntax, command line options, brief explanations, and examples. For a quick reminder, or help with unfamiliar options.

PC Tools Deluxe 6 Instant Reference

Gordon McComb

194pp. Ref. 728-2

Keep this one handy for fast access to quick reminders and essential information on the latest PC Tools Utilities. Alphabetical entries cover all the Tools of Version 6—from data recovery to desktop applications—with concise summaries, syntax, options, brief explanations, and examples.

Understanding Norton Desktop for Windows

Peter Dyson

500pp; Ref. 888-2

This detailed, hands-on guide shows how to make the most of Norton's powerful Windows Desktop—to make Windows easier to use, customize and optimize the environment, take advantage of shortcuts, improve disk management, simplify disaster recovery, and more. Each program in the Norton Desktop gets thorough treatment, with plenty of practical examples.

Understanding the Norton Utilities 6 (Second Edition)

Peter Dyson

500pp; Ref. 855-6

Here is a detailed, practical sourcebook for PC users seeking to streamline their computing and extend the power of DOS with Norton 6. Features hands-on examples and up-to-date coverage of such topics as file management and security, hard disk maintenance, disaster recovery, and batch programming. Includes a complete command guide.

Understanding PC Tools 7

Peter Dyson

500pp; Ref. 850-5

Turn here for a complete guide to taking advantage of the new version of PC Tools for DOS 5 and Windows—with hands-on coverage of everything from installation to telecommunications. Special topics include networking; data security and encryption; virus detection; remote computing; and many new options for disk maintenance, disaster prevention, and data recovery.

Up & Running with Carbon Copy Plus

Marvin Bryan

124pp. Ref. 709-6

A speedy, thorough introduction to Carbon Copy Plus, for controlling remote computers from a PC. Coverage is in twenty time-coded "steps"—lessons that take 15 minutes to an hour to complete. Topics include program set-up, making and receiving calls, file transfer, security, terminal emulation, and using Scripts.

Up & Running with Norton Desktop for Windows

Michael Gross
David Clark

140pp; Ref. 885-8

Norton's new desktop utility package lets you customize Windows to your heart's content. Don't miss out! Learn to use this versatile program in just 20 basic lessons. Each lesson takes less than an hour to complete, and wastes no time on unnecessary detail.

Alan Simpson's

Understanding dBASE IV 1.5 for DOS

Optional Companion Disk

If you want to use the sample databases, reports, custom forms, and the membership and business management applications presented in this book without keying them in yourself, you can send for an optional companion disk containing all the files (excluding the files that already came with your dBASE package). You can use these files to speed your learning (less typing), or as modifiable applications that you can refine to better suit your needs. You must already have access to dBASE IV to use these files.

To purchase the optional companion disk, please complete the order form below and return it with a check, international money order, or purchase order for $30.00 U.S. currency (plus sales tax for California residents) to the address shown on the coupon. Or, we can bill you later. Sorry, we cannot accept credit cards.

If you prefer, you can return the coupon without making a purchase to receive free periodic newsletters and updates about Alan Simpson's latest books.

Alan Simpson Computing
P.O. Box 945
Cardiff-by-the-Sea, CA 92007
Phone (619) 943-7715 FAX (619) 943-7750

☐ Please send the companion disks for *Understanding dBASE IV 1.5 for DOS.*

☐ No disk thanks, but please send free newsletters from Alan Simpson Computing.

Name ______________________________
Company ______________________________
Address ______________________________
City, State, Zip ______________________________
Country ______________ P.O. Number (if applicable) ______________

Check one:

☐ Payment enclosed ($30.00 + sales tax for CA residents) made payable to Alan Simpson Computing.

☐ Bill me later. ☐ No charge (newsletters only).

Check one disk size:

☐ 5¼-inch disk ☐ 3½-inch disk

SYBEX is not affiliated with Alan Simpson Computing and assumes no responsibility for any defect in the disk or files.

FREE BROCHURE!

Complete this form today, and we'll send you a full-color brochure of Sybex bestsellers.

Please supply the name of the Sybex book purchased.

____

How would you rate it?

____ Excellent ____ Very Good ____ Average ____ Poor

Why did you select this particular book?

____ Recommended to me by a friend
____ Recommended to me by store personnel
____ Saw an advertisement in ______________________
____ Author's reputation
____ Saw in Sybex catalog
____ Required textbook
____ Sybex reputation
____ Read book review in ______________________
____ In-store display
____ Other ______________________

Where did you buy it?

____ Bookstore
____ Computer Store or Software Store
____ Catalog (name: ______________________)
____ Direct from Sybex
____ Other: ______________________

Did you buy this book with your personal funds?

____Yes ____No

About how many computer books do you buy each year?

____ 1-3 ____ 3-5 ____ 5-7 ____ 7-9 ____ 10+

About how many Sybex books do you own?

____ 1-3 ____ 3-5 ____ 5-7 ____ 7-9 ____ 10+

Please indicate your level of experience with the software covered in this book:

____ Beginner ____ Intermediate ____ Advanced

Which types of software packages do you use regularly?

____ Accounting ____ Databases ____ Networks
____ Amiga ____ Desktop Publishing ____ Operating Systems
____ Apple/Mac ____ File Utilities ____ Spreadsheets
____ CAD ____ Money Management ____ Word Processing
____ Communications ____ Languages ____ Other ______________________ (please specify)

Which of the following best describes your job title?

____ Administrative/Secretarial
____ Director
____ Engineer/Technician
____ President/CEO
____ Manager/Supervisor
____ Other ______________________
(please specify)

Comments on the weaknesses/strengths of this book: ______________________

Name ______________________
Street ______________________
City/State/Zip ______________________
Phone ______________________

PLEASE FOLD, SEAL, AND MAIL TO SYBEX

SYBEX, INC.
Department M
2021 CHALLENGER DR.
ALAMEDA, CALIFORNIA USA
94501

SEAL

The Labels, Reports, and Forms Design Screens

You use the labels, reports, and forms design screens to design custom formats for displaying data. All three use the same keys to perform tasks. The forms design screen shown here presents a custom format for displaying data from the CUSTLIST database.

(CHAPTERS 7 AND 8)

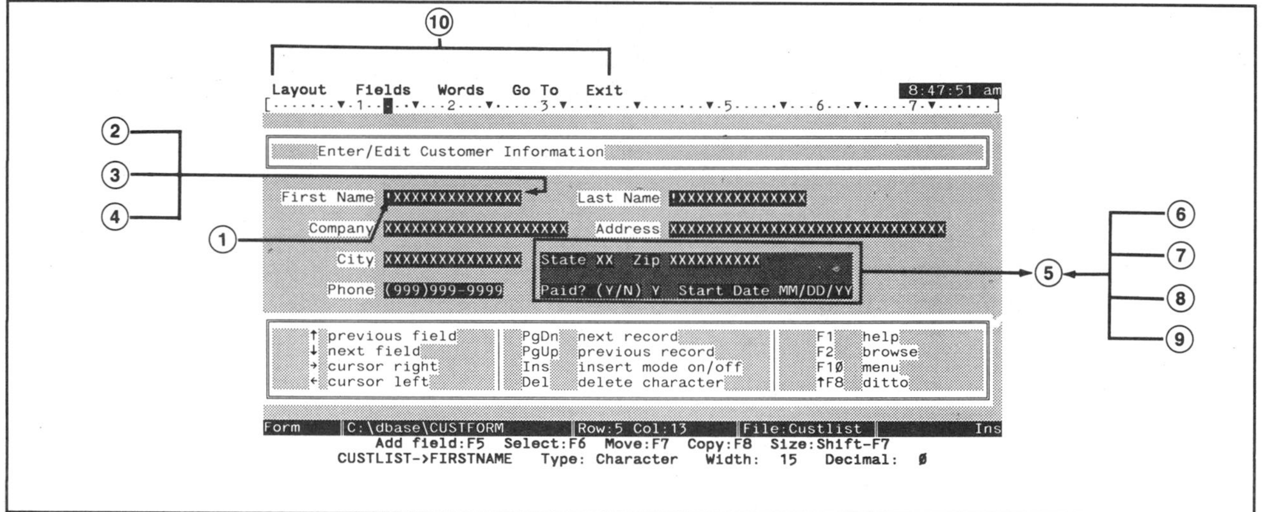

If you want to:	Here's how:
① Position the cursor	Use the arrow keys, Home, End, PgUp, and PgDn; or click the mouse.
② Add or modify a field template	Position the cursor and press or click Add Field (F5), or double-click on the template.
③ Delete a field template	Position the cursor and press Del.
④ Size a field template	Position the cursor and press or click Size (Shift-F7).
⑤ Select a field or area for the next operation	Position the cursor and press or click Select (F6), or drag the mouse to highlight.
⑥ Move a selected field or area	Press or click Move (F7) after making your selection.
⑦ Copy a selected field or area	Press or click Copy (F8) after making your selection.
⑧ Delete a selected field or area	Press Del after making your selection.
⑨ Unselect a selected area	Press Escape.
⑩ Access pull-down menus	Press Menus (F10) and use ← and →; press Alt, plus the first letter of a menu bar option; or click on a menu bar option.